Lovable Crooks
and Loathsome Jews

Lovable Crooks and Loathsome Jews

Antisemitism in German and Austrian Crime Writing Before the World Wars

T. S. KORD

McFarland & Company, Inc., Publishers

Jefferson, North Carolina

ISBN (print) 978-1-4766-7012-6
ISBN (ebook) 978-1-4766-3396-1

LIBRARY OF CONGRESS CATALOGUING DATA ARE AVAILABLE

BRITISH LIBRARY CATALOGUING DATA ARE AVAILABLE

Front cover illustration from the cover of the 1937 publication
The Eternal Jew (United States Holocaust Memorial Museum)

Printed in the United States of America

McFarland & Company, Inc., Publishers
Box 611, Jefferson, North Carolina 28640
www.mcfarlandpub.com

Table of Contents

Resolutions?

Acknowledgments

I am grateful to a number of people and institutions for their support of the research and writing of this book. Dr. Lars Fischer pointed me to valuable materials on the history of antisemitism. Franz Preitler, Gerhard Lindenstruth and Dr. Robert Engele kindly helped in clarifying unsolved mysteries; Franz Preitler and Gerhard Lindenstruth were also extremely generous in sharing their materials with me. The staff at the British Library, UCL's Special Collections, the Wiener Library in London, the Deutsche Nationalbibliothek Frankfurt, the Deutsches Exilarchiv Frankfurt, the Landesarchiv Berlin, the Akademie der Künste in Berlin, the Bundesarchiv Koblenz, the Gedenkstätte Grafeneck, the Österreichische Nationalbibliothek, the Stadtarchiv Wiener Neustadt, the Landesgericht für Strafsachen in Vienna, the Yale University Library, the New York Public Library, and the National Széchényi Library in Budapest were unfailingly helpful and cordial. For their willingness to grant me access to some documents and photographs in their possession, thanks are also due to three private collectors of NS-era materials in Salt Lake City, Utah and San Luis Obispo, California respectively, whose names I am withholding at their request. And finally, I'd like to thank the many colleagues and friends who patiently listened to my ideas, cheered me on when the writing was going well and commiserated when it wasn't. You are too numerous to be individually named here, but you know who you are.

The research and writing of this book were generously funded by a Major Research Fellowship from the Leverhulme Trust from 2015 to 2018.

Finally, I'd like to thank John Landau, my wonderful husband and the most patient man alive. I say this whenever I finish a book, and it is always true: without you, I'd never get anything written.

Settings

Criminals and Mass Men
in Pre-Totalitarian
Peace Time

Preliminaries[1]

In October 2002, John Allen Muhammad and Lee Boyd Malvo went on a shooting spree in the Washington, D.C., area, killing ten people and wounding three others in the space of three weeks.[2] A year later, the search for their motive became one of the most central aspects of their trial. Since Malvo was 17 years old at the time of the shootings and assumed to be under his older partner's influence, motive theories focused largely on Muhammad. They included his "deranged" condition, family trouble, his perceived ostracization as a Muslim after the 9/11 attacks, latent trauma dating back to his military career,[3] even the suggestion that he was a "government 'hit man' operating under psychological programming."[4] Eventually, Muhammad's estranged wife weighed in with a twist on Agatha Christie's *The ABC Murders*, claiming that Muhammad's shooting of thirteen people was merely a cover-up "because he was trying to hide his efforts to murder me."[5]

One motive not on offer was Muhammad's and Malvo's repeated self-description as Muslim jihadists. In fact, investigators, the prosecution and the press did everything they could to *avoid* linking the events of October 2002 with those of September 2001. In the face of some evidence presented at the trial, this cannot have been easy. A Virginia court eventually found Muhammad guilty of killing "pursuant to the direction or order" of terrorism.[6] Nine exhibits at their trial associated the shooting spree with jihadism, including a father-and-son portrait of Muhammad and Malvo with the legend "We will kill them all. Jihad." The most direct link to the 9/11 attacks (which, according to a statement attributed to Muhammad by a friend, "should have happened a long time ago") was Exhibit 65–117: a picture of the White House drawn in crosshairs, embellished with the comment "Sep. 11 we will ensure will look like a picnic to you."[7] Barely two years after what is now commonly considered "the deadliest terrorist attacks on American soil in U.S. history,"[8] one might have expected such colorful statements to be endlessly expounded, scrupulously scrutinized, and comprehensively commented on. Instead, they were barely mentioned. The idea of Muhammad and Malvo as jihadist fighters received no more than sporadic attention, neither at the time of the trial nor in the years to follow, and what little there was tended to be limited to publication venues whose breadth of distribution or degree of impartiality might be called into question.[9] The mainstream press, on the other hand, did not even engage with the theory sufficiently to bother refuting it.

The question "why not?" seems hardly worth asking, or at least not in the biographical sense. Maybe the courts and the press downplayed the jihadist link in an effort to protect America's Muslim community. Maybe there was no jihadist link and the killers simply tried to endow deeds committed for contemptible motives with a political purpose they perceived as lofty. Or maybe both. The question worth asking is not what motivated two killers in 2002, but why America as a nation, when presented with two possible explanations for their crimes—terrorism on the one hand and, on the other, a plethora of contradictory and unconvincing motives—opted for the latter. Commentators both at the time and later noted that the demotion of Muhammad and Malvo from jihadists to garden-variety American serial killers was greeted with palpable relief, even with a sense that things had returned to "normal."[10] To be sure, serial killing is an odd signifier of normality, but on the heels of the trauma of 9/11, it seemed an idea whose time had come. Serial killer movies were released at a noticeably accelerated clip in the years immediately following the 9/11 attacks.[11] As Schmid has noted, "the figure of the serial killer plays an even more central role in post–9/11 America than it did before the attacks," conceivably because "The serial killer provided a way to present the figure of the terrorist to the American public in a way that was [...] familiar enough to keep public fear and paranoia at manageable levels."[12] In an America plunged into chaos by terrorism, cinema and the news media attempted to re-establish a semblance of order by focusing on the devil they knew, on an evil that—unlike terrorism—could be defeated. In a world of Us Against Them, Serial Killers 'R Us.

The basic premise of this book is that something very similar was going on in Germany and Austria in the years leading up to both World Wars. These years saw not only an escalation of hate literature directed at Jews (the "Them" of the time), but also an unprecedented increase in the study and depiction of the criminal (by the contemporary "Us," as I will show in this book). Trial coverage in the press, crime fiction, and criminological studies in the wake of Lombroso's *Criminal Man* (1876) and *Criminal Woman* (1893) increasingly conceptualized the criminal as a human being who could be analyzed, explained, understood, and predicted, even sympathized with. Works in early criminology were split into two camps: those who subscribed to Lombroso's notions of criminal predisposition or "character" on the one hand, and, on the other, those who attributed criminality to a more complex mix of hereditary and environmental factors. While this debate went on in academic circles, the criminal became a major character in German literature, which offered a hypothesis that criminologists never even considered: that crime is attributable to environmental factors *alone*. In fact, criminals in literature of the time rank among German culture's most lovable, sympathetic, and abjectly pitiable characters. Pre–World War I literature gave us the heartbreaking stories of Gerhart Hauptmann's "Signalman Thiel" ("Bahnwärter Thiel," 1888) and *The Weavers* (*Die Weber*, 1892), that of the bank teller in Georg Kaiser's *From Morning to Midnight* (*Von Morgens bis Mitternachts*, 1912) and Kafka's helpless accused or condemned characters in *The Trial* (*Der Prozeß*, 1914) and *The Penal Colony* (*In der Strafkolonie*, 1914).

Pre–World War II literature depicted both the tragic criminal, like the son in Arnolt Bronnen's *Parricide* (*Vatermord*, 1922) or Biberkopf in Alfred Döblin's *Berlin Alexanderplatz* (1929), and the criminal as a wit, dunce or schlemiel, for instance Jaroslav Hašek's *Good Soldier Švejk* (1923) or the characters in Brecht and Weill's *The Threepenny Opera* (*Die Dreigroschenoper*, 1928). An undisputed darling of the German nation was (and remains) Friedrich Wilhelm Voigt, an East Prussian shoemaker who, with the help of a troupe of gullible soldiers, occupied Köpenick's city hall in 1906, arrested the mayor, and made off with the money in the city treasury. His miniature coup d'état was much fêted in literature and film, including three films made in 1906 (the year of Voigt's feat and arrest) and another in 1908 (the year of Voigt's release from prison), followed by a substantial body of texts and films spanning the entire twentieth century and the beginning of the twenty-first.

This book focuses on writing, fictional and otherwise, about criminals, Jewish and otherwise, in an effort to determine whether reading these texts in the context of each other shows an inverse relationship between the "foreign" (Jewish) and the "familiar" ("German") criminal. It attempts, in other words, to link two developments that are already—separately—well documented: the more dangerous, contemptible, and incomprehensible Jews appear in antisemitic[13] texts, the safer and more understandable (predictable, sympathetic, pitiable, helpless, harmless, tragically misunderstood, "driven" to crime, farcical, or funny) the non–Jewish criminal appears in criminology, fiction, even crime reporting on court cases. Implicitly juxtaposed with Jewish criminals, perceived as the "foreign element" within German and Viennese society, the "ordinary" (non–Jewish) criminal became familiar, the devil one knows. We might read the exceptional attention lavished on understanding the criminal in the years immediately preceding both World Wars as a simultaneous and paradoxical act of both conflict resolution (in this case, crime prevention and the rehabilitation of the criminal) and conflict fabrication. This fabrication can be broken down into four distinct steps: first, the definition of the German "national character" in direct juxtaposition with Jews as the antithesis of Germanness and the "foreign" element within German society; second, the creation of the perception of a conflict between the two groups; third, the presentation, in antisemitic literature, of the "conflict" between Germans and Jews as intractable; and finally a distinct refusal to engage with this intractable conflict and the "foreign" element within society, coupled with a focus on the "homegrown," familiar, and fixable problem of crime.

Precursors

Among the many who deserve to have their work gratefully acknowledged,[14] two historians have written particularly eloquently (and, apparently, concurrently, since both books appeared in the same year) on how the tale of Jewish criminality was spun in times and places relevant to this book. Together, Daniel Vyleta's *Crime, Jews and News: Vienna, 1895–1914* (2007) and Michael Berkowitz's *The Crime of My Very Existence: Nazism and the Myth of Jewish Criminality* (2007) provide us with a roadmap tracing the intersection of crime and antisemitism in texts written during the years before both world wars. Vyleta's point of departure is the fact that both criminology and antisemitism created narratives of biological difference, and that both did so with the aim of "othering" and excluding, that is: separating the criminal, or the Jew, from "regular" (law-abiding/gentile) society. However, Vyleta's findings, based on an examination of contemporary criminology and his extensive analysis of press coverage of court trials involving Jewish defendants, complicate the easy parallel between the criminologist's born criminal and the antisemite's racially predestined Jewish crook. For one thing, even though Lombroso's themes "were absolutely central to contemporary antisemitic constructions of the criminal Jew," rather surprisingly "no clear example of the construction of a specifically Jewish 'born criminal' exists in the contemporary criminological literature in any language."[15] In fifteen years of writing in the two most important criminological journals of the time,[16] Vyleta found only twenty articles on any aspect of "Jewish" crime. Early warners against antisemitic misrepresentations of the theme—which included Lombroso himself—pointed out, often buttressed by impressive statistics, that Jewish criminality was typically lower than that of the overall population, and markedly lower in terms of violent crime. Yet even these well-meaning works established a precedent that would later stand arguers in favor of a racial understanding of crime in good stead: suddenly "it made sense to contemporary commentators to break down criminal patterns according to racial allegiance, and specifically in terms of Jews versus non–Jews."[17]

While Vyleta's findings document a general reluctance among criminologists to treat Jewish criminality as a function of "race,"[18] press coverage of Jews on trial was similarly inclined. Even where it portrayed crimes committed by individual Jews as implicating "Jewry," it was far likelier to invoke fears of modernity than racial panic. Jewish criminality as portrayed in the press of the day was rational and cunning, competent and organized, and volitional rather than "driven"—a considerable distance, in other words, from the degenerate race arguments that marked NS discourse a generation later. Even racially inclined antisemitic venues like the *Deutsches Volksblatt* emphasized the Jewish crook's rationality and cunning over biological characteristics.[19] Thus Vyleta concludes that Jewish criminals in the Viennese *fin-de-siècle* were not seen as biologically propelled but merely as the winners of modernity, in brief: "symbols of all those modern institutions and phenomena despised by many antisemites, including capitalism, materialism, secularisation, and scientific progress."[20] Criminals were not defined physiognomically and psychologically, as Lombroso had suggested, but intellectually and socially: "those who were pushed into crime because of economic hardship, but were badly equipped for it intellectually, and those who prospered in this modern world of criminality that so resembled the capitalist world of production at large."[21] It is a generalizing, dehumanizing and deindividualizing argument, as Vyleta recognizes in his paraphrase of Herz's 1908 book *Criminals and Criminality in Austria*: "Jews successfully 'judaised' crime, even as they 'capitalised' the economy; they effectively brought into being a whole new criminal scene."[22] But it is not yet, Vyleta argues, a racial argument.

This, as Berkowitz explores at length and as Vyleta also points out in his conclusion, would change drastically in the following generation, which apparently saw no reason to abandon one antisemitic argument in favor of another merely because the two directly contradict each other. Thus "[w]hile notions of Jews as malign financial and criminal geniuses, as manipulators of public opinion and so on, remained a mainstay of anti-semitic discourse, they were joined by a much more racially reductive vision of Jewish crime."[23] Berkowitz's book, whose title *The Crime of My Very Existence* already alludes to the idea of Jews as "born criminals," is dedicated to exploring how this played out during the NS era in Germany. The Nazis, Berkowitz shows, established and popularized the principle of a racially predetermined and hence fundamental Jewish criminality: "'Judentum', Jewry and Judaism, proclaimed a prominent Nazi billboard, 'ist Verbrechertum'—is criminality."[24] The NS State, touting itself as a bastion of "law and order," set about the systematic creation and promotion of this racial under-standing of Jewish criminality. It did this by—to cite a few of Berkowitz's examples—converting leading criminologists to teach racially inherent ("Jewish") crime at universities[25]; by implicating the German police in the mass murder of Jewish civilians ("criminals")[26]; by identifying all Jews as criminals—for instance by establishing mug shots as the default manner of photographing Jews[27]; and by conversely, and falsely, identifying notable criminals such as Al Capone and "Legs" Diamond as Jews.[28] Ghettos, which could not be anything but hotbeds of crime since the Nazis made living there within the law impossible, became self-fulfilling prophecies[29]; more generally, Jews in the Nazi era were pushed into "criminality" because the laws governing their lives changed constantly and changes were usually not announced.[30] German news media were exhorted to leave readers in no doubt "that every single Jew, wherever he is and whatever he does, is an accessory to crime."[31] A directive to the German press from April 2, 1943, curtly sums it all up: "Jews are criminals."[32] In effect, the now explicitly racial criminalization of Jews created a dehumanized and deindividualized collective "Jewry," and it was this, in Berkowitz's argument, that enabled Nazis not only to "rob and kill them with impunity" but also "helped a huge number of Germans and their fellow perpetrators, as well as bystanders, to accept what the Nazis were doing to the Jews."[33]

The map jointly drawn by Vyleta's and Berkowitz's books indicates that despite the suggestive biological aspects of criminological writing of earlier times, Jewish crimi-nality as a racial category did not, or not fully, come into vogue until Nazi Germany. In pre–World War I Austria, the antisemitic view of Jewish criminality still entertained a variety of explanations that took into account the radical transformation of the West-ern world into the increasingly internationalized, mercantilized, urbanized, industri-alized, bureaucratized, democratized, secularized and commodified space in which all Europeans, Jewish or not, were beginning to live. A generation later, the Nazis' inter-pretation of Jewish criminality exploited these external contexts further but transferred them from the realm of the *causal* to that of the *incidental*. To them, all of modernity's ills were "caused" by Jews, but modernity, in turn, could not serve as an explanation for Jewish criminality. There could only be one explanation for that: a racial predilection for crime. We should ask at this point whether this reduction and simplification of the "motive," from global contexts describing an entire epoch to the inner workings of a specific ostracized group, describes not only crime writing, but more generally the pro-gression of Austrian and German antisemitism from the years preceding the First World War to those preceding the Second.

Theories

One problem with the "eternal hatred" theory—the idea that the Holocaust was "simply the culmination of a long unbroken line of anti–Semitism, from pharaoh and Nebuchadnezzar to Hitler and Arafat"[34]—is that it muddles the view of specifics. Broad strokes writers who have viewed the entire history of antisemitism as a dress rehearsal for the Holocaust have possibly attracted the most attention and inspired the loudest debates.[35] Yet much of our concrete knowledge has actually come from scholars who have focused on the details: how antisemitism debates tied in with ideas of the nation state and liberalism[36]; why "progressive" people like Imperial Germany's Social Democrats did not rise in defense of the Jews[37]; how liberalism linked with antisemitism in literature[38]; how antisemitism was staged—literally as well as figuratively[39]; how Austrian antisemitism differed from the German version[40]; what the conceptual differences are—if any—between antisemitism and racism[41]; how and why Nazi propaganda focused on Jews,[42] and how antisemitism manifested itself in Imperial Germany and the Weimar Republic[43] as opposed to the Nazi era.[44] From writers like Levy and Pulzer we know that antisemitic parties in Imperial Germany were losing, not gaining, power,[45] and we owe Jochmann, Mosse and other historians for another significant insight: that the decline of antisemitic political parties did not mean the decline of antisemitism.[46] Too much has been written about the history of antisemitism to attempt a representative overview here. I will instead focus on the two historians and philosophers whose ideas have had the most significant impact on my thinking about the specific link between antisemitism and crime: Shulamit Volkov's understanding of antisemitism as a "cultural code" and Hannah Arendt's exposé on the human condition in totalitarian States.

In *Germans, Jews, and Antisemites* (2006),[47] Volkov explains that antisemitism in pre–Nazi Germany most particularly functioned as a "cultural code" that created a larger semantic vessel for desired contents. As an "-ism," it could be unproblematically placed on a par with other "-isms" such as "liberalism" or "conservatism," "thus entering respectable linguistic company, no doubt"[48]; it "pretended to connote an entire corpus of social and political opinions, a cohesive worldview, an ideology."[49] In the late 19th century, the evolution of the crass Jew-hating perpetrated by loonies on the fringe to an antisemitism that could be espoused by the intellectual or moneyed élites was achieved by what Volkov calls "wrong metaphors" and, using a term coined by Kenneth Burke, "associative mergers."[50] Both established a link between social ills and the "Jewish question" that had not existed before, as did, for example, an 1879 pamphlet by Otto Glagau that called upon working men to unite against their exploitation by "a foreign race" and culminated in an associative merger: "The social question *is* the Jewish question."[51] By far the richest harvest of wrong metaphors and associative mergers, according to Volkov, can be found in the works of Heinrich von Treitschke, where the "Jewish Question" becomes the problem that stands for all others:

> The "Jewish Question" was not one problem among others, but the essence of all evil. A quick turn of the pen made a single problem stand for all others. The Jews were equated with every negative aspect of German life, everything that Treitschke and his readers detested. Their equation with an entire syndrome of ills—social, political, and cultural—was a stroke of genius. By using a simple rhetorical technique, an unsatisfactory situation was suddenly made comprehensible. A

strong opposition to government policies could now be coupled with an idolizing of the state. The responsibility for weakness of character, for folly and failure, was placed where it hurt the least—at the margin, on the outcast, on the Jews.[52]

Volkov's view of antisemitism in turn-of-the-century Germany goes a good bit further than Rürup's definition of antisemitism as a "world view,"[53] or Mosse's view of it as a "German ideology,"[54] or Jochmann's idea of it as part of German "cultural pessimism."[55] Volkov opts for the broader term "culture" to express her understanding of antisemitism as "operating, in society as well as in individuals, both on the intellectual-rational level and on that of implicit values, norms, lifestyle and thought, common ambitions, and emotions."[56] Neither "ideology" nor "world view" quite capture this "cluster of ideas, sentiments, and public behavior patterns," she claims; only "culture" articulates "the total interconnected ways of thinking, feeling, and acting," subsumes both *Weltanschauung* and ideology, does not exclude philosophy, science, and the arts, and "includes traditions that consciously and subconsciously affect such a collectivity, habits of mind, a variety of automatic reactions, and a plethora of accepted norms."[57]

Volkov's term "culture" has much to recommend it. It allows us to view anti-semitism as culturally specific (in this case: pertaining to Germany and Austria during the twenty years preceding both World Wars) rather than eternal and ubiquitous (from Pharaoh to Hitler). Yet it also militates for an understanding of antisemitism as a gradual, insidiously subtle, and encompassing process—the creeping encroachment of culture, not the big bang of political incident. Much historical writing does not see it that way. In *fin-de-siècle* Vienna, Vyleta claims, most readers were aware that antisemitic language was used by a specific camp and that to use it was to ally oneself with it: "One might go so far as to say that antisemitism remained somewhat of a 'forbidden' language used only by those who prided themselves on their defiance of good social manners."[58] Yet by the 1930s, he continues, the well-mannered classes had become ardent antisemites: "the electoral success of the Nazi party was to a good part due to voters with middle-class, even intellectual, backgrounds: civil servants, architects and business men. The *Anschluss*-movement and the Great Depression further fostered antisemitic sentiments."[59] The change, within a mere generation, from a society that squirmed at anti-semitic language to one that embarked on the road to extermination policies, is described as sudden, radical, and tied to specific political events (the Nazis' electoral triumph, the Great Depression, the *Anschluss*). Volkov, who is more interested in sliding scales and slippery slopes than in contrasts, and more concerned with language, writing, and conceptualization than with events, would demur: "Antisemitism was not a direct response to real events. Indeed, human beings do not react directly to events. They construct their own interpretation of world-events in a process of conceptualization and verbalization, and they can only respond to this home-made concept of reality."[60] Vyleta's idea of a "forbidden" antisemitism in the *fin de siècle* versus its general acceptance a generation later is beholden to the idea of antisemitism as an ideology, inspired by concrete incidents or propaganda, each of which might be individually accepted or rejected. But within a culture of antisemitism, Volkov claims, "such a separation of issues was no longer possible."[61] Cultural codes, wrong metaphors and associative mergers—in other words, *writing*—had assigned to Jews a far more encompassing value than that of people, or even a people, under attack; they had become "a symbol of the time,"[62] not only to their persecutors, but also to their defenders. Treitschke, in claiming that the "Jewish Question" was not one problem among others but the essence of all evil, and Theodor Mommsen interpreting antisemitism as hatred not of Jews alone but of "*Bildung*, freedom and humanity"[63] invoked the same symbolic view of Jews and the same cultural code of antisemitism. Both lived in a world in which it is "impossible to separate one's attitude toward Jews and Judaism from the rest of one's ideological and cultural 'package deal.'"[64]

Forty years before Volkov first outlined these ideas, Hannah Arendt's *The Origins of Totalitarianism* (1951) anticipated some of her most significant historical points. "The simultaneous rise of antisemitism as a serious political factor in Germany, Austria, and France" occurred, according to Arendt, at the same time during which Volkov diagnoses the rise of a "cultural code" of antisemitism, namely "in the last twenty years of the nineteenth century."[65] Similar to Volkov, who describes the rise of antisemitic culture as a protracted, subtle and all-encompassing process that ultimately resulted in a broad consensus on the "Jewish Question," Arendt viewed antisemitism as "slowly and gradually" infiltrating society until it emerged "as the one issue upon which an almost unified opinion could be achieved."[66] In Arendt's view, totalitarianism—her focus, although closely tied in with antisemitism—vanquishes by similar means: by creeping up on you. One of its most distinguishing features, she claims, is that you normally don't notice it because it appears both normal and familiar. "The only rule of which everybody in a totalitarian state may be sure is that the more visible government agencies are, the less

Mural of Hannah Arendt in Hanover on the wall of the house in which she was born ("Nobody has the right to obey"). Graffiti art by Patrik Wolters and Kevin Lasner, based on a photograph by Käthe Fürst (photograph by Bernd Schwabe, Hannover. Wikimedia Commons).

power they carry, and the less is known of the existence of an institution, the more powerful it will ultimately turn out to be."[67]

Arendt's main point is that totalitarian societies engage in "a gigantic massing of individuals," ultimately replacing individuals with what she terms "mass men," or, alternately, "inanimate men," "atomized individuals," or "One Man" ("In a perfect totalitarian government [...] all men have become One Man.")[68] Mass Man is characterized by "the radical loss of self-interest, the cynical or bored indifference in the face of death or other personal catastrophes, the passionate inclination toward the most abstract notions as guides for life, and the general contempt for even the most obvious rules of common sense."[69] Unlike the individual, Mass Man is both expendable and aware of it, as illustrated by Arendt's citation of Himmler's description of his SS men: "they were not interested in 'everyday problems' but only 'in ideological questions of importance for decades and centuries, so that the man ... knows he is working for a great task which occurs but once in 2,000 years.'" Thus the massing of individuals, Arendt concludes, "produced a mentality which [...] thought in continents and felt in centuries."[70] Her citation and analysis of Hitler's announcement to the German Reichstag in January 1939 is another case in point:

> "I want today once again to make a prophecy: In case the Jewish financiers ... succeed once more in hurling the peoples into a world war, the result will be ... the annihilation of the Jewish race in Europe." Translated into nonutilitarian language, this meant: I intend to make war and I intend to kill the Jews of Europe. [...] the liquidation is fitted into a historical process in which man only does or suffers what, according to immutable laws, is bound to happen anyway.[71]

In other words: in a totalitarian State, there are no individual pronouncements, intentions, or personal responsibility, just as there are no individual citizens—only continents, centuries, and the processes of history.

According to Arendt, totalitarian societies, unused as they have become to thinking in terms of the individual, have difficulty imagining crime, criminality or the criminal. One passage in Arendt's book over which readers might well puzzle is her somewhat obscure assessment of what she calls a moment of "social glory" for Jews in *fin-de-siècle* Europe, namely, the Dreyfus affair. His alleged crime of treason, she claims, raised all Jews temporarily from "insignificance," but as soon as the traitor was discovered to be the innocent victim of an ordinary frame-up, "Jews were again looked upon as ordinary mortals."[72] The Dreyfus passage, murky in itself, makes sense only in the context of Arendt's larger assessment of how totalitarianism works: its main job is to deny and eradicate the individual. Dreyfus, a Jew, was marked as an individual by his perception as a traitor, a criminal. Criminals are individuals. Crime is an individual act. Far from establishing a universal discourse in which all Jews were labeled as criminals (see Berkowitz), totalitarian societies, at least in Arendt's thinking, would be compelled to *remove* this label, and all other distinguishing characteristics of individuality, particularly from hated groups. For this reason, Arendt claims, totalitarianism finds a deindividualizing means of expressing the idea of Jewish criminality. The brush with which the Nazis tarred the Jews is not that of crime but that of vice. Crime is something one commits (and, by implication, can stop doing); "vice" describes what one is (and, by implication, cannot stop being). Thus vice

> is but the corresponding reflection of crime in society. Human wickedness, if accepted by society, is changed from an act of will into an inherent, psychological quality which man cannot choose or

reject but which is imposed upon him from without, and which rules him as compulsively as the drug rules the addict. In assimilating crime and transforming it into vice, society denies all responsibility and establishes a world of fatalities in which men find themselves entangled.[73]

Such thinking in grand categories, in terms of history, continents, centuries, and Fate ("fatalities"), is the extermination of individuals in a speech act and a precursor to the real thing. According to Arendt, this is precisely what happened to the Jews. Their subsumption under the category of "Jewishness," which "from then on could be considered only in the categories of virtue or vice,"[74] already implies both racial antisemitism and the Final Solution: "the transformation of the 'crime' of Judaism into the fashionable 'vice' of Jewishness was dangerous in the extreme. Jews had been able to escape from Judaism into conversion; from Jewishness there was no escape. A crime, moreover, is met with punishment; a vice can only be exterminated."[75]

The Nazis' refusal to treat Jews as criminals (that is: to acknowledge them as individuals), Arendt holds, was not merely expressed philosophically but resulted in concrete policy decisions. She takes care to differentiate between the internment of "criminals" and that of "Mass Men," claiming that Jews who actually happened to be criminals were safer throughout the NS regime than innocent Jews. Just as the concentration camp system was placed outside the normal penal system, law-abiding Jews were placed outside the law. Jews in their millions were imprisoned in concentration camps for no reason; criminals were not ordinarily sent there until after they had completed their prison sentence and were entitled to their freedom. Total erasure of the individual implies the elimination of the "juridical person in man"[76] and therefore also the elimination of all recognizable and comprehensible links between crime and punishment. "Under no circumstances must the concentration camp become a calculable punishment for definite offenses."[77] The world of crime and punishment is anathema to the totalitarian regime, simply because crime leaves traces. "The murderer leaves behind him a corpse, and although he tries to efface the traces of his own identity, he has no power to erase the identity of his victim from the memory of the surviving world."[78] Totalitarian States, conversely, erase their victims to the point where they never existed; they create "veritable holes of oblivion into which people stumble by accident and without leaving behind them such ordinary traces of former existence as a body and a grave."[79]

Throughout *The Origins of Totalitarianism*, Arendt's focus is on Mass Man as an encapsulation of what happens to human beings under totalitarianism, and thus she has little time for the ordinary criminal. And yet, more often than not, the last vestiges of individuality and humanity in her book tend to be linked directly with crime, criminality and the criminal. Crimes leave clues, thus denying the total erasure of the individual. Crimes may result in "calculable punishments," thus resurrecting the principle of action and consequence and breathing new life into the "juridical man," who finds paradoxical embodiment particularly in those who do not obey the law. Criminals— and here I am, of course, speaking of the criminal type as established in criminology, press coverage and fiction of the time—do not think in terms of history, centuries or Fate. They do not consider themselves expendable. Potentially at least, they are the very antithetis of Mass Man, with his "radical loss of self-interest, the cynical or bored indifference in the face of death or other personal catastrophes, the passionate inclination toward the most abstract notions as guides for life."[80] On the contrary, criminals tend to be direct rather than abstract, ruled by self-interest, and anything but indifferent to their fate.

In the Age of Mass Man, Arendt claims, "the masses are obsessed by a desire to escape from reality because in their essential homelessness they can no longer bear its accidental, incomprehensible aspects." This manifests itself, above all, in "their longing for fiction."[81] Arendt is speaking here of Mass Man's response to propaganda, but there is really no reason not to take the passage literally. Mass Man's longing for fiction would certainly go some way toward explaining the extraordinary success of the lovable, laughable or pitiable criminal in writing before the World Wars. In a society headed for totalitarianism, fiction provided a much-needed reminder of a comprehensible world and of a not-atomized, not-inanimate individual. The criminal analyzed in criminological treatises, the criminal celebrated or condemned in the press, the criminal adored or pitied in fiction held considerable potential to serve as an antidote to what Germans were becoming: Mass Men. Criminals, by their very existence, imply a legal system that still works. Send a criminal to prison and he knows why he's there. The same does not apply to innocents interned in a camp. Punishment is meted out to the individual; extermination, as Arendt has shown, is not. Criminals can be read as symbols for a non-totalitarian order in two contradictory ways. By breaking society's rules, they assert a defiant individuality—they're in business for themselves. Yet they also represent legality—their punishment makes sense and in making sense contrasts starkly with the senseless slaughter of innocents. Criminals thus both defy and represent a comprehensible order.

And yet, the very fact that it is the criminal who symbolizes individuality clearly implies a sense that the individual can only exist *outside* of ordinary society, or, at best, on its fringes. It is perhaps no accident that the lovable, hapless, tragic or funny criminal came into vogue at the precise historical juncture when German society became more consolidated and more rigidly defined: during the later years of the Second Reich, which had unified Germany after a thousand years of particularism, and during the early years of the Third. Defining the individual as a societal outsider already implies a clear understanding that the individual is on his last gasp, that the Age of Mass Man is arriving. No matter how funny or lighthearted they may appear, these are nostalgic tales (it is also no accident that most crime fiction written during the NS era is set in earlier periods).

At the same time that criminology individualized the criminal and fiction and the press showered him with love, admiration, tears of compassion, or gales of laughter, Jews came to be viewed as the antithesis of individuality. Neither the mass of anonymous Jewish victims nor the anonymous Jewish crime organizations of Nazi propaganda could answer the yearning for the imagined whole individual. Witness the description of rats in *The Eternal Jew*, one of the Nazi era's most notorious antisemitic films: "They mostly emerge as a great mass[...], no different from the way Jews emerge among humans."[82] Rarely do Jewish criminals in the writing of the time, either during or preceding the NS era, appear as individuals harming other individuals; they appear as a group or as a great conspiracy out to destroy entire nations. Any ritual murder of a single victim involves at least three Jewish monsters standing over the corpse. Any rape of a German maiden is perpetrated not for the culprit's own satisfaction but to pollute the blood of the entire Aryan race. Stories of German criminals usually stress not only individuality but a hyper-charged individuality, an individuality beyond the norm. Stories of Jewish criminality tend to invoke the paranoid fear of a mass: world conspiracy, international Jewry, Jewish Bolshevism, the Jewish "race," or the "Jewish financiers" of Hitler's Reichstag speech. What Arendt said about pronouncements in totalitarian societies holds true in this context as well. Tales of German criminality are told as *stories*; tales of Jewish criminality masquerade as *history*. The lovable, understandable, funny or tragic criminal—in brief: the criminal capable of embodying individuality—is a German criminal.

Structures

Criminals appear most regularly in three text types: criminological treatises, press reporting on actual court cases, and crime fiction. My main interest is to ask to what extent criminals in these texts, written in Germany and Austria during the twenty years immediately preceding each World War, are individualized or portrayed as part of a "mass," what mechanisms are used to humanize or dehumanize them, and to what extent writing turns them into symbols standing in for something else entirely (assuming, with Vyleta, that "reporting on crime was always also a means of reporting on the state of society"[83]). Specifically: did the individualized (lovable, tragic, funny, etc.) criminal evolve as a German self-image that explicitly excluded Jews? And if so, what might this new German self-image, with its implications of a subversiveness that stops short of actual criticism or opposition, indicate about the self-perception of citizens transitioning from a chaotic to an organized and vastly more powerful and centralized State (initially from particularism to the Second German Reich, later from a fragmented Republic to the Third)?

My choice of time frame has been influenced by Arendt's and Volkov's view of antisemitism as a gradual development that remained imperceptible to many but that eventually gained sufficient universality to be called a "culture." Cultures flourish not in periods of upheaval but in periods of transition. For this reason, this book focuses on pre-totalitarian peacetime, specifically the twenty years before each World War: ca. 1894–1914 and 1919–39. In this, I am swayed by Arendt's argument that Germany was not on an irreversible path to totalitarianism until the outbreak of the war; certainly, war enabled Hitler to embark on measures that, as Arendt asserts, "would have been unthinkable in peacetime."[84] My purpose here is not to examine explicit propaganda but texts that had a chance to be perceived by contemporaries as neutrally scientific, informative or entertaining. Few works written during wartime would have achieved this, regardless of the degree to which they presented themselves as apolitical, non-propagandistic, or non-militaristic. War, whether waged by totalitarian societies or others, is by definition a national emergency and often results in a consolidation of power and a narrowing of permitted viewpoints. As Arendt has argued elsewhere, in a non-criminal State, the criminal is an exception, whereas in a criminal (that is: in a totalitarian) State the opposite applies; "the relationship of exception and rule [...] was reversed."[85] If we assume, with Arendt, that Germany did not fully become a totalitarian regime until the outbreak of the Second World War, and if we further understand war, like totalitarianism, as an emergency situation and thus a departure from the status quo, then wartime texts written about crime and the criminal would be significantly affected because these are the texts that define both perceived normality and deviations from it. A focus on pre-totalitarian peacetime documents, in other words, will be more likely to yield a text base whose understanding of "criminality" is closer to ours today.

Conversely, as Volkov has shown, some form of antisemitism was already at the turn of the century a universal "culture" that seemed, to most contemporaries, neither extreme nor unreasonable, in other words: one that was entirely compatible with the status quo. My search for texts about crime and/or Jewishness will therefore focus on the two places where antisemitism had become uncontroversial enough to be accepted as the "new normal," namely Germany and Austria. Austria's capital Vienna, as Vyleta has pointed out, was at the time marked by "disturbing levels of antisemitism" and moreover the only European capital with a democratically elected mayor who had run on an explicitly antisemitic platform. The city also plays a significant part in *Mein Kampf*, where Hitler identifies Vienna as the place where he first learned to "recognize" Jews as quintessentially non–German, thus creating the antisemitic legend "that turned into something like the nursery of the 'Final Solution.'"[86] Beyond their particular vulnerability to antisemitism, Vienna and Berlin or, more broadly speaking, Prussia (with its capital Berlin) and Austria (with its capital Vienna) are also linked by a much longer and not always affable history. For long centuries, Prussia and Austria were the largest and most powerful German States, each struggling, in a fraught process now dubbed "German Dualism," to emerge as the predominant political force in Germany. Under Prussia's King Frederick II and Austria's Empress Maria Theresia, they spent a considerable portion of the eighteenth century at war with each other, a conflict that was reprised briefly in the form of the Austro-Prussian War of 1866. In the years preceding the World Wars, these old enmities were anything but forgotten; they flare up, time and again, in press coverage on famous crime cases across the border. For example, while many Austrian newspapers took the Köpenick coup of 1906 as occasion to poke fun at Prussian nationalism and militarism, others argued more seriously that the "typical" Prussian gullibility and submissiveness towards a uniform essentially amounted to an abrogation of a citizen's right and duty to think for himself.

To the significant insights about crime and antisemitism that we already owe to Daniel Vyleta, Michael Berkowitz, Shulamit Volkov and Hannah Arendt, I hope to add some new aspects. Among these are a consideration of the German criminal (all four writers focus on antisemitism), the inclusion of crime fiction (all four deal exclusively with nonfictional texts such as State-sponsored propaganda, criminology or press coverage), and a comparative and contrastive approach to both prewar periods and both places (all four concentrate either on the *fin de siècle* or the Nazi period, and either on Vienna specifically or Germany). My focus on both prewar periods provides a means of asking to what extent key aspects of totalitarianism already appear at earlier historical junctures. Hannah Arendt, for example, saw the "massing" of individuals as an aspect of totalitarian societies and its culmination in mass extermination. But perhaps we can observe the inception of the idea of the expendable mass much earlier, for instance in that defining moment in August 1914, when the German Emperor looked down from his balcony upon a crowd cheering another war and saw no parties, no classes, no confessions, and no Thuringians, Hessians, Saxons or Bavarians, but only "Germans."[87]

Throughout, I favor cases, texts and contexts that have rarely been examined and that thus have the potential to provide us with fresh insights over others that have previously received a lot of attention (such as the writings of senior propagandists like Joseph Goebbels or the writers of *Der Stürmer*).[88] For the same reason, I largely exclude canonical texts on the criminal (by Hauptmann, Döblin, Kafka and many others) to which entire libraries are already devoted. As Vyleta has noted, historians tend to bother only with the talent and ignore the gutter press and the popular.[89] Yet an argument can be made, and has been made in other contexts, that "Popular culture does not make the political parties, the legislation, the armies that fight to sustain and defend racism, but it has always been their best recruiting agent."[90] The crime fiction avidly devoured by fans all over Germany, the popular films that drew huge crowds after the First World War have much to teach us on contemporary ideas on "German" versus "Jewish" criminality, and their universal availability and popularity make them at least as indicative of contemporary thinking on these subjects as academic treatises and newspaper articles.

My discussion of fictional texts alongside those that lay claim to factuality, such as criminological works or press reporting, is not meant to reduce the discussion to the dissatisfying divide between "literature" and "real life." Nor do I intend to make the undoubtedly true but profoundly uninteresting claim that "real life" is described in literature or that literature shapes "real life." Instead, I assume the "literariness" of all texts, whether or not they would normally be understood as fictional, and question any text's ability to describe "reality." In this, I have been influenced by both Volkov's understanding of antisemitism as a "cultural code," that is: as a reality initiated in and through *writing*, and by Vyleta's treatment of all text types—scientific journals, true crime accounts and reporting—"as narratives, i.e. stories that order and construct knowledge about criminals and Jews." Citing Miri Rubin, Vyleta advocates thinking

> of narrative as a mode of organising events, unified by plot[...]. Whole cultural systems are carried in myths, and myth is carried in rituals and through narratives. People act through narratives and they remember through narrative.
>   This vision of narrative takes seriously Alasdair MacIntyre's claim that human kind is a storytelling animal, a creature that can only exist and impose meaning upon his or her world through constant narration.[91]

Focusing on narrative means to shine a light on *how* a story presents its truth claims, which may lead us to recognize the fragility of such claims. Stories may or may not advance truth claims per se, but they can—as Volkov has shown—combine and develop to form a culture that is universally or nearly universally accepted as "history." We might think of the relationship between literary and non-literary, or less literary, genres in terms of Turner's concept of "modes of symbolic action," which he defines as "the peculiar relationship between the mundane, everyday sociocultural processes (domestic, economic, political, legal and the like) found in societies [...] and what may be called [...] their dominant genres of 'cultural performance.'"[92] He sees this relationship not as "unidirectional and 'positive'—in the sense that the performative genre merely 'reflects' or 'expresses' the social system or the cultural configuration," but as "reciprocal and reflexive—in the sense that the performance is often a critique, direct or veiled, of the social life it grows out of, an evaluation (with lively possibilities of rejection) of the way society handles history."[93] If authors, as he puts it,

> "hold the mirror up to nature," they do this with "magic mirrors"[...]. The mirrors themselves are not mechanical, but consist of reflecting consciousnesses and the products of such consciousnesses formed into vocabularies and rules, into metalinguistic grammars, by means of which new unprecedented performances may be generated. [...] The result is something like a hall of mirrors—magic mirrors, each interpreting as well as reflecting the images beamed to it, and flashed from one to the others.[94]

Throughout this book, I read texts describing the "German" versus the "Jewish" criminal—regardless of their genre or their degree of fictionality—as "magic mirrors," in the sense that I assume them to "interpret as well as reflect the images beamed into them." Tales of lovable criminals, hapless dunces, and Jewish conspiracies told in academic works, court records, press articles, and crime fiction are examined for their potential to generate new "unprecedented performances." Turner's hall of mirrors allows us to think of stories rooted in real life and in fiction not in terms of origin and influence, cause and effect, but as drawing water from the same well, the well in this case being the "culture" (Volkov) of thinking about Jews and crime. In the hall of mirrors, all tales are more or less fictional, and in the act of interpretation, reflection and beaming back, they all participate in a cultural performance. My primary interest in these tales lies not in the chicken-and-egg question, but in the persistency of these tales and the perniciousness of their meanings: how they reflect and interpret common beliefs about crime and Jews, or about individuals and mass men, and what they add to this store of ideas when they are "beamed back." I further presume that the cultural performers who add to the lore of crime and antisemitism incorporate both "rehearsed" and "spontaneous" elements[95] into their performance. Rehearsed elements describe the cultural heritage of ideas, passed down in tales and traditions until they become the things "we have always known" about Jews: that they are usurers and swindlers, for example, or that their "congenital" cruelty, immorality, dishonesty, etc., predestine them for crime. Spontaneous elements would describe what cultural performers then do with this knowledge. Like Vyleta, I focus throughout on narrative elements; like Volkov, I concentrate on the creation of a culture; like Turner, I am interested in showing that culture is created through repeated "cultural performances." For the purposes of this project, I define such performances as the telling of tales whose relationship with each other may be causal, contrastive, or simply analogical, all of them creating and recreating the same interrelated thought system on Germans, Jews, and crime.

If we accept Arendt's claim that discourse in totalitarian States masquerades as *history*, it becomes more important than ever to retain a sense that discourse is, in fact, composed of *stories*, of tales that, their fragility and dubious truth-claims notwithstanding, have the power to create myths and new meanings.[96] This sense guides my readings throughout this book, not only of fiction but also of artifacts that lay claim to factual accuracy, such as press articles, court records and criminological treatises. Arendt's mandate to recognize that which impersonates *history* as a *story* has also stood godmother to the titles of the book's sections, which are named after the five essential elements of a story: *Setting* (what others might term an "Introduction"); *Characters*, *Plot*, and *Conflict* (comprising the three main parts of the book and containing, between them, eight chapters), and *Resolutions?* (what might elsewhere be called a "Conclusion"). *Characters* focuses on the criminal "character" described in criminology before the World Wars, texts on Jewish criminality in both prewar periods, and the victory of criminal biology over criminal sociology during the Weimar Republic and the early Nazi era. *Conflicts* contrasts two pairs of trials, one pair in each prewar period, each featuring Jewish v. non–Jewish accused, chosen for compatibility both of time periods (the trials in each pairing took place within five years) and similarity of crime (all defendants were accused of nonviolent crimes and thus theoretically eligible for sympathetic or humorous treatment in the press). This part of the book focuses on the myth of the lovable "rogue" criminal, outlines how and why he was conceptualized as a *German* criminal in courts and in press coverage, and shows that criminals who had committed similar crimes but were coded as "Jewish" were considered ineligible for the role. *Plots* showcases the criminals, Jewish and otherwise, of crime fiction, and asks whether and how the Jewish v. German "coding" of criminals familiar from criminology and press reporting on real-life trials was reflected in fiction. *Resolutions?*, with an emphatic question mark, asks whether the lovable criminal's ability to represent "Germanness" and the implications of this model ended with the Second World War or if it reached into a past much closer to our present.

The inverse trajectory I'm proposing between literature celebrating the lovable German criminal and antisemitic texts demonizing the Jewish crook, between the individuation of the one and the "massing" of the other, is, on the one hand, specific to German and Viennese history. Yet it also entails broader implications about conflict resolution and conflict avoidance strategies in times of national crisis. Clearly, the decision to define conflicts as either solvable or intractable is predicated upon definitions of others as either comprehensible or unfathomable. Ultimately, this book aims to increase our understanding of *historical mechanisms* of conflict resolution and conflict avoidance: which problems (or people) we choose to understand at specific historical junctures, which ones we relegate to the realms of the incomprehensible, which mechanisms we rely on to either promote or preclude understanding, and why we make these choices. As modern depictions of "terrorists" versus "criminals" since the beginning of the global War on Terror shows, the gulf between the incomprehensibly foreign and the homegrown and familiar, between lovable individuals and hateful mass conspiracies, between solvable and intractable conflicts, is still with us. Taking another good, hard look at mechanisms that paved the way for totalitarianism in Germany and Austria can perhaps help us recognize the ways in which we reproduce these patterns today. As Koepnick once put it: "The point of any reconstruction lies in the present."[97]

Characters:
Crime Theories

Compulsion v. Conspiracy: German and Jewish Criminals in Criminology (1890s–1914)

A Criminal Is Born

The criminal rose to prominence in the late 19th century on the back of Cesare Lombroso (1835–1909). His work *L'uomo delinquente* (*Criminal Man*, 1876, first available in Germany in 1887 and then followed by endless re-editions) was the first to proclaim that the determining aspect of crime was not the deed, its circumstances or its punishment, but its perpetrator. Walter Gerteis has likened the appearance of Lombroso's book to a rock thrown into the placid pond of then nonexistent German criminology. Barely twenty years after the pond was thus disturbed, Germany boasted two new and flourishing disciplines: criminal anthropology and criminal psychology. Both spent years discussing, adapting and responding to Lombroso's ideas.[1] Under Lombroso's formidable influence, the focus shifted from penal reform in the mid–19th century to the causes of crime at century's end,[2] and the undisputed star of the new debate, the criminal, underwent a radical change of character. The mid–19th-century crook, viewed as individually accountable for his evil deeds and as the primary responsibility of the courts and the police, had gone into hiding by the end of the century. He was supplanted at first by the atavistic and later by the degenerate criminal, compulsively driven by inborn and hereditary physical and psychological factors that became the object of medical study.[3] It was not only a new characterization of the criminal, but also a radical shift in the personnel primarily entrusted to deal with him: from practitioners to theorists and from law to medicine.[4]

Lombroso, a physician himself, collected, studied, measured, weighed, and looked inside bodies on the slab and at cells under the microscope. A committed Darwinist, he saw humans as the result of a long development reaching across the animal world and the world of primitive Man to the present day, and he was convinced that setbacks in this development, which he called "atavisms," could manifest themselves physically. His eureka moment, an autopsy of a particularly objectionable criminal during which he found evidence of such atavism in the form of a cranial abnormality, set him on a decades-long course of trying to convince the world that there was such a thing as the "born" criminal, a throwback to an earlier form of humanity who could be recognized by physiognomic and psychological traits. Lombroso aimed to create for criminals what

Linné had achieved for plants and Brehm for animals: a fundamental classification, a "Natural History of the Criminal" in which he would add to *homo sapiens* and *homo oeconomicus* a third type: *homo delinquens*. And he foresaw his work resulting in significant changes in the practice of not only medicine but also law, among them the abolition of jury courts, an expansion of the death penalty, and the life-long internment of "incurable" criminals.

Lombroso was probably the first to distinguish between habitual and occasional offenders. All of his interest was invested in the former. Over the course of thirty years he studied 27,000 criminals and, in control studies, nearly as many law-abiding citizens,[5] creating a vast database of physical and psychological traits in an attempt to prove that the born criminal was "an atavistic being who reproduces in his person the ferocious instincts of primitive humanity and the inferior animals."[6] In subsequent editions of *Criminal Man* he changed his mind on the numbers: initially convinced that all

Cesare Lombroso, Father of the "Born Criminal" (*Galerie hervorragender Ärzte und Naturforscher* (1890). **Wikimedia Commons**).

lawbreakers were "born" criminals, he later amended this to about one third.[7] He did not, however, amend the defining characteristics of habitual criminals, which saddled them with smaller skulls, larger lower jaws and abnormal wisdom teeth, flat back skulls, low foreheads, protruding eyebrows, attached earlobes, thick head hair coupled with sparse beard growth, and various cranial and genital abnormalities. Born criminals had disproportionately long arms—"ape arms," as Lombroso called them. They did not go bald but grey. They were predominantly left-handed since they were steered by the right and less developed side of the brain, whereas the opposite was true of law-abiding citizens. In psychological terms, the born criminal was defined by moodiness, vengefulness, laziness, profligacy, remorselessness, impulsiveness, insensitivity to pain, a tendency to brag about his own misdeeds, and an inability to imagine getting caught. Lombroso considered it his main task to distinguish *homo delinquens* from *homo sapiens*, but his passion for classification led him also to make some inroads into sub-cataloguing by criminal profession. Some of Lombroso's links between criminal traits and professions were indebted to his belief that offenders committed the crimes for which they were physically predestined. Thus murder, manslaughter, and robbery required a strong body, whereas fraudsters could get away with a weak stature but needed more smarts. Other pairings seemed random, unrelated to the crime at hand. Forgers were slender and arsonists fat. Robbers, forgers and fraudsters had the biggest heads. Killers sported the largest and pickpockets the smallest jaws. Thieves and rapists were of slight build. The greatest number of hunchbacks could be found among rapists, arsonists and forgers. And so on.[8]

Criminal Character

Lombroso's idea of the "born" criminal was immediately opposed by German psychiatrists, some of whom, like Emil Kraepelin (1856–1926), Eugen Bleuler (1857–1939) and Richard Krafft-Ebing (1840–1902) accepted psychological abnormality as a trait of the habitual criminal while denying that he was a physical type.[9] Still others, like Gustav Aschaffenburg (1866–1944), denied the existence of the "born" criminal altogether. Although Lombroso's theory was apparently inspiring enough to launch entire criminological disciplines, he managed to acquire only one true disciple: the neurologist and electrotherapist Hans Kurella (1858–1916). Kurella took it upon himself to distribute and defend Lombroso's theories to Germany's scientific community, translated Lombroso's work, wrote a book about him (*Cesare Lombroso as a Man and Scientist*, 1910) and published almost exclusively on him between 1892 and 1913.

In his *Natural History of the Criminal* (*Naturgeschichte des Verbrechers*, 1893), Kurella translates Lombroso's ideas as follows:

> all true criminals possess a distinct and causally connected series of physical characteristics, which can be anthropologically substantiated, and mental characteristics, which can be psychologically and physiologically substantiated. These attributes turn their owner inevitably and necessarily into a criminal—albeit, perhaps, an undiscovered one—completely independent of all social and individual life circumstances. Such a person is born to be a criminal; he is, as Lombroso says, "delinquente nato."[10]

It is a passage in which Kurella not only paraphrases Lombroso but trumps him. Nine years before Kurella wrote this, in the third edition of *Criminal Man* (1884), Lombroso had already modified his own theory of the "delinquente nato," claiming that the type represented about 40 percent of all criminals (rather than Kurella's "all"); later, Lombroso would reduce this percentage further to one third of the criminal population. The link between physical and psychological traits and criminality that Kurella confidently pronounced "inevitable and necessary" was already, to Lombroso himself, no more than "likely."[11] Kurella moreover conjures the disturbing image of the undiscovered criminal, driven inexorably to crime but running around free until he commits one. Kurella's little aside—"perhaps, an undiscovered one"—opens the door to an idea that would later preoccupy penal reformers considerably: that the safety of the populace might demand the decoupling of punishment from deed and the linking of penalty and "character." A mere three years later, the psychiatrist and eugenicist Eugen Bleuler considered it "self-evident that psychological and anthropological investigation would define as 'criminals' neither exclusively those nor all of those who have been caught committing an illegal act."[12]

In his many comparisons of criminals to apes throughout his book,[13] Kurella seems to signal his allegiance to Lombroso's atavism theory. And yet, some passages in his book throw doubt on both this and his passionate denial of the link between crime and social circumstance:

the most miserable wages, a lifelong diet of potatoes and sauerkraut, deep humiliation in hopeless dependence, contempt and squalor are not sufficient to make a criminal out of a human being with a normal predisposition. These conditions do, however, affect the crime rate in another way. As the effects of bad nutrition accumulate over generations, they cause a degeneration of the descendants of this wretched population, and it is from the degenerate children of these malnourished parents that criminals are recruited.[14]

Poverty, in other words, is an indirect rather than a direct cause of crime: it does not occasion it, but it does set in motion a process of degeneration which, in individuals born generations later, creates a predilection for crime. Degeneration, which came to dominate thinking about the "born" criminal in Germany and Austria, is, like atavism, a biological process, but it is nevertheless a significant departure from Lombroso's thinking. Atavism is unexplained: Lombroso offered no speculation as to *why* some humans revert to subhumanity and criminality and others do not. Degeneration, conversely, points at social circumstance as the root cause of a biological consequence. Atavism, in its universality, is disturbingly unpredictable; degeneration envisions criminals safely contained in the slums. And unlike atavism, degeneration is not static but progressive; thought to be hereditary, it spells ever-greater deterioration from one generation to the next.[15] Endowed with a concrete origin that is moreover linked with modernity, "degeneration" drags "atavism" kicking and screaming into the modern age.

Degeneration marks the historical moment when social conditions, although weirdly assigned a biological role rather than a political one, enter the debate. Yet this did not lead to a more progressive, or modern, attitude toward crime and punishment, let alone toward the criminal. Many writers on the subject saw no contradiction in pointing to social circumstance as a driver of crime without dethroning biological imperative as its main cause. Bleuler, for example, held that the inborn drive toward criminality would remain a mere predisposition unless accompanied by circumstances leading to the crime.[16] And Emil Kraepelin, despite his lifelong belief in the "born criminal," wrote a suggestively titled essay "Crime as a Social Disease" (1906) in which he attributed crime to a combination of personal and communal aspects.[17] Yet neither writer indicated anywhere that the link between social background and crime might merit a social or political response.

Character, Classification, Categorization

While these and other writers merely modified the "born" criminal's environment, others took issue with the concept itself. At a conference in Amsterdam in 1901, Adolf Baer, a prison doctor from Berlin, announced to the scientific community that years of studying deformities on the heads, faces and skeletons of convicted offenders had convinced him that these abnormalities were no more than sporadically occurring and moreover equally present in non-criminals of the same age.[18] Of even greater import was the intervention of Gustav Aschaffenburg, initially Kraepelin's assistant and later professor of psychiatric medicine in Cologne. Together with Franz von Liszt (1851–1919), he founded and coedited the *Monthly Journal for Criminal Psychology and Penal Reform (Monatsschrift für Kriminalpsychologie und Strafrechtsreform*, from 1904), which became Germany's premier criminological journal and published predominantly the work of German psychiatrists responding to Lombroso's theories. The foundational idea of the journal was simple: "criminology ought to provide the basis of penal policy."[19]

Aschaffenburg's seminal work *Crime and Its Repression* (*Das Verbrechen und seine Bekämpfung*, 1903) likewise understands, as its title already announces,[20] criminology not as an independent science but as one in the service of penal reform. *Crime and Its Repression* defines the criminal as a degenerate and crime as born of social circumstance, concluding that only the presence of both paves the way to crime. Degeneration, Aschaffenburg claims, is not necessarily the result of heredity and does not necessarily express itself in physical characteristics (he reiterates Baer's claim that the physical deformities Lombroso had attributed to "born" criminals also afflicted, in equal numbers, the law-abiding). Predestination for crime in the individual exists; but for an actual crime to occur, it needs to be partnered with an external factor: economic conditions, geography (urban v. rural areas), industrialization, nationality, race, occupation, or acquired habits such as alcoholism. Even research seemingly pointing at heredity, such as studies showing that nearly half of all criminals descended from criminal parents, is interpreted as an indication of environment affecting, not heredity determining, behavior.[21]

Aschaffenburg's book is a clear-eyed and balanced account of crime and its causes. Where it falls back into the Lombrosian trap is in its discussion of the criminal and—this the avowed purpose of his study—in its mission to offer concrete recommendations for adequate punishment. Punishment, Aschaffenburg claimed, should be determined not by the nature of the crime but by the specific character of the criminal. Determining this character mandated classification. His catalogue includes seven categories: coincidental, impulse-driven, opportunistic, premeditated, recidivist, habitual, and professional criminals. This, in turn, enabled a more principal distinction between offenders whose actions were occasioned by circumstance (Aschaffenburg's categories 1–3) and those whose criminal tendencies would be more difficult to eradicate since they were born either of inclination, hereditary conditioning, or a combination of internal and external factors. Punishment, Aschaffenburg concluded, should no longer address a crime but a criminal character: mere "indemnification" ("Schadloshaltung") for Types 1–3 versus integration of Types 4–7 in a penal system that allowed for the continual adjustment of the State's response to the individual criminal.[22]

This brings us to one of the most problematic consequences of the Lombroso debate in Germany: the uncoupling of punishment from crime and its linking with criminal "character." Aschaffenburg's coeditor Franz von Liszt sat on the fence when it came to Lombroso's theories: he focused on the social causes of crime and discounted anatomical criteria, but he nevertheless accepted Lombroso's category of the "born" criminal for the most serious offenders. His comparatively simple categorization of criminal characters comprised relatively harmless occasional offenders, actual criminals (sub divided into corrigible and incorrigible types), and professional criminals (by definition incorrigible). His suggestions for adequate punishment included the reformation of corrigible criminals; the deterrence of incorrigibles, and, for professional criminals, *Unschädlichmachung* (an unspecific term that, depending on context, might mean anything from "neutralization" to "extermination"; Liszt, as it turns out, meant permanent imprisonment[23]). A central task of crime fighting thus became distinguishing between these criminal types. With regard to corrigible criminals, Liszt held, the primary purpose of punishment should be behavior modification; with regard to incorrigibles it should be the safeguarding of society. This latter category comprised, according to Liszt, not only fully half of the prison population, but also people who had been released from prison, had never been imprisoned or had not even committed a crime. In a draft bill he wrote in 1904, he confidently claimed that people could be classified as criminally dangerous even if "favorable external factors have thus far prevented the commission of a crime."[24] Liszt went on to become one of Germany's most prominent voices advocating preventive imprisonment.[25]

Many criminologists of the time adopted Liszt's three-part categorization, which unbalanced previous legal thinking particularly about culpability and diminished responsibility. Under the classic 19th-century model, diminished responsibility due to mental illness meant a lessening of the penalty. Now Liszt and other definers of the criminal character argued that mentally deficient offenders should not be treated differently from others, that penalties should be assigned based on the criminal's dangerousness rather than his degree of guilt, and that in effect, the mentally deficient should be preemptively and indefinitely imprisoned because they were sure either to offend or to reoffend. Under the suggested new model, the punishment no longer fit the crime but the offender: suspended sentences for first-time offenders for the purpose of deterrence; jail sentences for recidivists for the purpose of rehabilitation, and indefinite detention for incorrigible repeat offenders—and those likely to become so, like the mentally ill—for the sake of incapacitation.[26] Most criminologists weighing in on penal reform, an ongoing project in the Wilhelminian age, were in favor of the permanent imprisonment of so-called "incorrigibles." Some even went so far as to propose the idea of "correctional post-penalty internment" (*korrektionelle Nachhaft*) for beggars, prostitutes, vagrants, recidivists and the mentally ill.[27]

Biological Character and Preemptive Punishment

In the course of the debate surrounding Lombroso's "born" criminal, criminologists had by now taken two major steps: uncoupling punishment from crime while linking it with "criminal character," and shifting the focus in penal reform thinking from rehabilitation or punishment of the individual toward the protection of society and the prevention of crime. In so doing, they offered the State scientific legitimation for two unparalleled measures: the option to fight crime preemptively on the one hand, and, on the other, the inclusion of people who had never committed a crime in such preemptive punishment. To be sure, there was a debate about crime prevention, but Aschaffenburg's pleas for State support for the poor and the rare—very rare—proposals for the reintegration and resocialization of criminals[28] were overwhelmed by calls for the constant surveillance or preemptive internment of the mentally ill or relatives of criminals, even if they did not appear dangerous and had committed no crimes. The German association of *Hilfsschulen* (schools for students with learning disabilities) launched a petition for surveillance of their students on the assumption that they were "likely to come into conflict with the law."[29] Castration of and a marriage ban for so-called "degenerates" and the poor were suggested as early as 1899, by, among others, Paul Näcke (1851–1913) and Hans Groß (1847–1915)—people who were not, as Wetzell has emphasized, considered crackpots but well-respected and influential voices on the subject of criminal psychology and penal reform.[30]

Racial hygiene became a frequent topic of discussion in the early years of the 20th century, some 30 years before Hitler ever came to power, and tended to address not the "whether" but the "how" and the "where," not moral but practical questions, such as which strata of society might benefit the most from sterilization or castration measures.[31] Hans von Hentig (1887–1974), a criminal psychologist who believed that the criminal psyche was more important than the actual crime, raised the question whether the penal system should address not only actual but also attempted crimes. Writing on the eve of the First World War, he redefined penal law as a means for the Darwinesque "selection" of individuals, proposing that the social traits of individuals could be improved upon by what he called a "cull effected with the help of penal law" ("strafrechtliche Selektion"):

> If humans have succeeded in breeding hornless cattle (Suffolkcattle) and pitless plums by selecting and retaining the favorable variants while excluding pitted plums and horned cattle from the process of procreation, then I don't know why it should not be possible to cultivate systematically a moral breed of Man. So long as we do not yet possess a very exacting knowledge of the laws of heredity, the great means of selection will have to bring us closer to this goal.[32]

What this meant on the ground he clarified elsewhere in the book: "We are talking about the elimination of the individual by subjecting the individual to an artificial environment to which he cannot adapt without perishing, generally immediately, or else after some time."[33] This is also why Hentig opposed short-term imprisonment: "The great peril would be that these nonviable individuals allow themselves to be hosted in prisons for a few short months or weeks and then emerge into freedom freshly invigorated, continuing their vermin's existence there and possibly even bequeathing their tainted germplasm to the future."[34]

Richard Wetzell has drawn a clear dividing line between such discourse and that of the concentration camps: "efforts to provide both a biological explanation and solution to the crime problem dated back to the origins of criminology in the late nineteenth century and were not intrinsically connected with Nazi ideology."[35] Yet three of the cornerstones of Nazi antisemitic discourse—the degrading of Jews to "vermin," the idea of their "tainting" the pure Aryan race through co-mingling and marriage, and the practical solution of working them to death in prison camps and ghettoes—are all rather clearly prefigured in Hentig's penal recommendations for inmates, including for those innocent of all crime. Whether "intrinsically" connected or not, Hentig and other criminologists of his age established a public discourse that was already familiar, even normalized, by the time the Nazis came to power. All that was required to revive it was a bit of repackaging and application to other segments of the population, just like the discussion of the "born" criminal had ultimately ended up yielding suggestions for penal law reform that targeted not only criminals, but anyone the State perceived as potentially "deviant" or harmful to the community.

Biological ideas about the criminal character were most ardently debated in criminological journals of the time, but also familiar to the educated reading public. Articles on the subject appeared regularly throughout the 1890s in Maximilian Harden's (1861–1927) popular social-democratic weekly *The Future* (*Die Zukunft*).[36] Popularizers such as Erich Wulffen (1862–1936), a court judge and highly prolific author, sought to make the latest insights on criminal "types" available to a broad audience of medical and legal professionals as well as the general public. Wulffen was familiar with both Lombroso's work and that of his principal critics, both of which he summarized for his readers, and generally attributed crime to a combination of prior disposition and external variables. Yet much of Lombroso's thinking reappears, in a fairly undiluted fashion, in Wulffen's description of the criminal. In his seminal *Types of Crooks and Criminals* (*Gauner- und Verbrechertypen*, 1910), he claimed confidently that "all criminal psychologists are agreed that the criminal is characterized by a certain mental inferiority, which manifests itself, among others, in crime."[37] Criminals, he goes on to explain, start out as weak school pupils, demonstrating early a lifelong incapacity for concentration and intellectual achievement of any kind. To Wulffen, there was thus no such thing as a clever crook or criminal genius. All criminal activity, no matter how cunning it may appear, is indebted to mere practice (all criminals, according to Wulffen, start early), repetition, and imitation. "In general," he elaborates, "the criminal shows little originality. Often he merely follows the simple urge to imitate. He always repeats what he's done from childhood on, what he has heard and seen from comrades of his ilk, what he's read in the newspaper etc. Even great criminals never leave their childhood behind."[38]

Wulffen does not go so far as to compare criminals to apes, as both Lombroso and Kurella had, but he does adopt their definition of crime as resulting not from a conscious decision but from an inescapable psychic state: "The state of somnambulism, of night walking, augments this constitution [criminal predilections, TSK] into the realm of the pathological, of disease. The instinctual criminal commits his deeds with the same confidence with which a somnambulist sure-footedly climbs over roofs."[39] Planning, decision-making, and intellect have no part in any criminal career, a claim Wulffen documents in many amusing anecdotes of criminal carelessness and stupidity that inevitably lead to capture. All of this, Wulffen concludes, should reassure us that criminals are actually not to be feared. None of the hundreds of hapless villains listed in his book escape justice; all fall victim to non-criminal Man's greater intellectual, moral and forensic acumen. "At the conclusion of this book," Wulffen intones, "a comforting feeling of safety encircles us [...]. We are beset by thoughts of the inevitable fate towards which the criminal steers in his fragile craft."[40]

Jewish Criminality and Racial Character

While at least some contemporaries were thus comforted by the dependable superiority of *homo sapiens* over *homo delinquens*, the spectre of Jewish criminality appeared a great deal more troubling. Fuelled in part by the 1899 murder of Anežka Hrůzová in Bohemia[41] (named the "Hilsner affair" after her purported killer) and the 1900 murder of Ernst Winter in West Prussia[42] (dubbed the "Konitz affair" after the scene of the crime), the ritual murder charge, which had lain dormant throughout the nineteenth

century, staged an astounding comeback in the early years of the twentieth.[43] There
was certainly no shortage of claims that Jewish crime was virtually universal: in his
German History (1909), the nationalist writer Heinrich Claß (1868–1953) blamed "Jewish poison" for a general decline of the understanding of Right and Wrong during the
foundational years of the Second German Reich,[44] and the Austrian daily *Deutsches
Volksblatt* had a regular column dedicated specifically to Jewish criminals, simply titled
"Yet Another" ("Wieder einer").[45]

Given the increasing tendency among criminologists to discuss the criminal in
biological rather than social terms, you would think that the stage was now set for racial
profiling of the Jewish criminal. Whether or not this actually happened is a matter of
scholarly debate. Sander Gilman has claimed that in contemporary writing, "the signs
of criminality and of Jewishness merge,"[46] based partly on the works of Hans Kurella,
Lombroso's single German disciple, and on similarities between Yiddish and the German
criminal argot alleged by writers going all the way back to Martin Luther.[47] Daniel
Vyleta, on the other hand, maintains that criminological writing between 1895 and 1914
shows a general reluctance among writers to treat Jewish criminality as a function of
race and does not yield "any example where criminological literature would directly
and immediately collapse 'the criminal' and 'the Jew' into a single figure."[48] Physical and
psychological parallels between Lombroso's "born" criminal and the Jewish stereotype
that should have been so tempting to antisemitic crime writers—things like dark com-
plexions, large noses, abnormally strong sexual appetites, mental disease, and a separate
argot—functioned, as Vyleta has claimed, "solely on the level of analogy"[49] and were
not, by and large, exploited by criminologists. At a time when heredity and degeneracy,
physical or psychological stigmata were increasingly motivated by criminologists as
the basis for criminal character and as at least part of the explanation for crime, these
aspects "did not play an important role in the construction of Jewish crimes [...]. Only
extremely rarely was the claim made that Jews were criminal because it was 'in their
blood.'"[50] The debate about Jewish crime in the Wilhelminian age, Vyleta concludes,
was not dominated by biological characteristics, but linked with aspects of modernity,
a context in which Jewish crooks appeared routinely as "modern, rational and predatory
upon victims less adjusted to modernity than they themselves."[51] Untroubled by com-
pulsions beyond his control, the Jewish criminal of contemporary writing committed
his crimes deliberately and purposefully, his "co-operation in criminal acts [...] not one
of mechanical solidarity but of wilful conspiracy."[52]

Girls, Girls, Girls (and Jewish Greed)

The conspiracy theory can perhaps best be tested by looking at texts that accuse
Jews particularly of crimes that cannot be committed individually but necessitate the
participation of a group (or perhaps an entire race). The three "typically Jewish" crimes
that recur most insistently are aspirations to world domination (particularly economic),
ritual murder, and white slavery. White slavery, or, to use the German term, "trade in
girls" (*Mädchenhandel*), became one of the hottest topics in writing about Jewish crime.
One of the most radical among the mass of treatises that appeared on this throughout

the 1880s and 1890s was Alexander Berg's *Jewish Brothels: Revelations from Dark Houses* (*Juden-Bordelle: Enthüllungen aus dunklen Häusern*), whose publication in 1892 coincided with the sensational trial of twenty-seven human traffickers in Lemberg, all Jewish.[53] Berg's rabid treatise portrays white slavery as a process in which "predators" (always Jewish) peddle the "purest" (mostly German) girls to "the lowest races and the dregs of humanity—the negroes, the Chinese, slaves and mulattoes, the Hottentots, the Turks and the Samojeds [Siberian tradesmen who were held to be particularly filthy and savage]."[54] Despite such racy passages, sex and even the profit motive are not cited as the primary motivation for white slavery. White slavery is defined as a race war waged on the world's Aryan peoples by an inferior race; its means is racial pollution, its goal is world domination. Dividing the entire world into "brothel States" and "non-brothel States,"[55] Berg claims not only that all white slavers are Jews but also that all Jews are white slavers: "the entire gang participates in this, regardless of rank or education, social standing or profession."[56] Jews are predestined for white slavery owing to "their universally base racial character" defined by "the most insidious perfidy, the most cruel inhumanity, the most unscrupulous treachery and breach of faith, which are the essential prerequisites of the soul required for such trade./No other people is capable of producing such monsters."[57]

On the surface, Berg's claim that Jews, whom he frequently terms "throwbacks,"[58] are predestined by inferior racial "character" to become white slavers sounds analogous to Lombroso's argument that "atavistic throwbacks" are predestined for crime. But whatever our objections to Lombroso's prejudiced theories, we should at least acknowledge that Lombroso based his prejudice on years of painstaking research. Berg's evidence base, conversely, runs the gamut from the generally obtuse to the deliberately mendacious to the hopelessly bizarre. His stories of dirty Jews doing a roaring trade with German girls in South America come from the Swiss writer Otto Henne am Rhyn, who makes no mention of Jewish traders and in fact does not comment in any way about the identity of the enslavers: as usual, when Berg cites his sources, he adds this significant element.[59] His support for claims about the tragic fate of English innocents who fall victim to Jewish slavers comes from the novel *Clarissa*,[60] glossing over the patent absurdity of basing declarations he presents as factual on fiction. And his claim that at least half of all forced prostitutes are German is buttressed by no better evidence than another unsupported assertion: that port cities in English colonies call their red-light districts "little Germany."[61] Berg's suggestions for crime prevention echo calls among German criminologists for preemptive imprisonment, but not on the basis of research but on that of mere appearance: anyone with a Jewish "physiognomy" accompanied by a girl or a woman, he recommends, should be arrested immediately.[62] In a world where there are no longer individuals but only races at war with one another, there can also be no individual rights. Ninety-nine wrongful arrests, Berg states, are an acceptable price to pay for a single capture of a true trader.[63] Ultimately, Berg's hellish vision of racial war can only result in the extermination of one race by the other. "Let us hope," he concludes,

> that despite the decades-long attempts of the Jewish press to unnerve and benumb us, despite Jewish advocates defending members of their race who peddle human flesh, the German nation has retained sufficient vengeful energy to tackle That which national honor and true humanity has

long demanded, and which should have happened a long time ago, namely: to begin a merciless war of extermination against this semitic criminal vermin who so disgracefully debase the entire German nation, both internally, to itself, and to the nations of the world.[64]

Twelve years later, Josef Schrank (1838–1907), president of the Austrian League to Combat Trafficking in Women, took up the theme again in *White Slavery and Its Repression* (*Der Mädchenhandel und seine Bekämpfung*, 1904). Schrank is to Berg what late Lombroso, the 40 percent–Lombroso, is to the early all-in Lombroso. He tones down Berg's inflammatory rhetoric, claiming to have "avoided everything that smacks of political, religious or national bias,"[65] and amends Berg's incendiary "all" to a hardly more reasonable-sounding "nearly all." The "export" of girls, he maintains, targets "only, with few exceptions, European States," and in a halfhearted move away from Berg's claim that all slavers are Jews and all Jews are slavers, Schrank asserts that "they are nearly uniformly Jews."[66] His protestations of impartiality notwithstanding, nearly all of his culprits are identified as Jewish; their special language is likened to Yiddish[67] and statements that white slavery is "almost exclusively" perpetrated by Jews are thick on the ground.[68] Where he deviates from Berg is in his presentation of evidence, in his identification of the victims, and in his interpretation of motive.

First, Schrank does his best to present his work as based on extensive research, citing, among others, police statistics, press reports, trial records, the white slavery laws of various nations in Europe, Asia, the Near East and the Americas, and conference reports on the subject in various European countries since 1901.[69] Secondly, Schrank throws a wrench into Berg's simple juxtaposition of Jewish culprit and German victim by stating that many victims of white slavery are themselves Jewish. On this subject, in fact, he seems strangely conflicted. Twice he wavers in his antisemitic tale, seemingly moved by the plight of the Jews in Russia and Eastern Europe who were forced to sell their own girls due to the "ruthless exploitation" of their economic distress.[70] Elsewhere he claims that Jewish girls are not pure like Aryan girls but prostitutes "from childhood on" and thus undeserving of pity.[71] Yet when he encounters a similar attitude in a Viennese daily newspaper, which claims that Christians and Aryans had no reason to be perturbed, given that nine tenths of girls "exported" from Austria were Jews, he castigates their indifference and calls on everyone to fight white slavery "no matter to which religion, nation or race the victims belong."[72] Among the heroes in this fight he reserves special praise for Jewish organizations, such as the Hamburg Jewish Sub-Committee of the German National Committee for the Repression of White Slavery and the London Jewish Association for the Protection of Girls and Women, which has "worked tirelessly and achieved great things."[73]

Finally, Schrank moves the motive of Jewish traders away from the racial predisposition assumed by Berg and towards another antisemitic cliché, describing "Jewish white slavery as the most devilish outgrowth of Jewish greed."[74] Jewish traders were, in Vyleta's formulation, "motivated by boundless greed: it lay in their ability to trade in human beings as though they were any other type of commodity." In luring girls with promises or presents, "Jews were depicted as master criminals who were marked, above all, by their callous criminal competence."[75] Even Jewish victims were compromised by greed, this most Jewish of all racial traits: while Hungarian girls are frivolous and German girls deceived, many Jewish girls "willingly passed themselves over to the traders,

Poster published by the German National Committee, warning young girls traveling alone not to go off with strangers, ca. 1910.

to make so much money through prostitution abroad that they could return home and marry or set up a business."[76] In this way, as Vyleta sums up, "Schrank was able to implicate Jews at both ends of the trade, and differentiate between worthy victims and Jewish ones, whose sense of profit, just like the traders', overrode any moral objections."[77]

Conspiracy Theories (and Jewish Greed)

On the heels of Schrank's book, Carl Mommert (1840–ca. 1910), introduced on the book's title page as "Knight of the Holy Grave and Pastor of Schweinitz," published *Ritual Murder Among Talmud Jews (Der Ritualmord bei den Talmud-Juden*, 1905). Mommert claims from the outset that ritual murder is not linked to race but to a specific sub set of Jewry, "Talmudic" Jewry, which is, he claims, often wrongly conflated with Mosaic Jewry.[78] Since the horrid practice is kept a strict secret from all non–Jews and even most Jews, most regular ("Mosaic") Jews, he claims, have no idea that the practice even exists. Mommert's book presents itself as a historical study going back all the way to the ancient Hebrews, providing an extensive overview of ritual murder cases since the 12th century for which Jews were blamed and discussing at length two specific cases from the fifteenth and nineteenth centuries respectively. His appendix includes a list of 159 murder cases between 1071 and 1892, based on a single source: an 1892 pamphlet entitled "Jews and Christian blood."[79]

Mommert's book must certainly be counted among those that move the motivation for Jewish crime away from racial predilection and onto the next big theme: a vast but secret Jewish conspiracy that, while not including all Jews, encompasses all of history and the entire world. Talmudism, he explains, came into being after the Jews had rejected the Messiah that they had so ardently awaited and that the Christians had accepted. Talmudic law is a body of Jewish secret laws against the property and life of non–Jews and regulates all interaction between Jews and non–Jews. No Jew can bear witness against another Jew on behalf of a non–Jew, on pain of excommunication; non–Jews, by this law, are declared subject to confiscation of their property, fines, or any other punishment up to and including the death penalty, even in the absence of any evidence for a crime. Talmudic law entitles Jews to cheat non–Jews or refuse them payment, and obliges Jews to support each other in this activity; Jews are not permitted to accept the laws of the State in which they live; Jews are obliged to protect each other when faced with secular law and not to betray a fellow Jewish criminal; Jews are obliged to kill anyone who has indicted another Jew of a crime or denied Jewish law; Jews are allowed to obtain the property of non–Jews by any and all means. Non-Jews are formally deprived of human status by Talmudic law, which refers to non–Jewish humans as "two-legged animals" ("Zweifüßler").

By far most horrendous crime of which Talmudic Jews in Mommert's text stand accused is the ritual murder of "two-legged animals," preferably children, for the purpose of obtaining Christian blood used in ritual cleansing ceremonies and at Jewish festivities ranging from Passover to weddings. Christian blood is only efficacious if obtained under torture (the description of the 1475 murder of Simon of Trient, a boy of three, leaves nothing at all to the fevered imagination; it includes the tearing of pieces of flesh from the body, crucifixion, the elaborate cursing of the Christian religion, and toasting each other with the boy's blood[80]). Women's blood, as is clearly stated, is no good[81] (presumably, later writers endlessly banging on about the Jewish murder of innocent Christian girls in *Der Stürmer* were not quite up to snuff in their study of Talmudic law). While the history of ritual murder according to Mommert shows that some Talmudic Jews content themselves with "inferior" blood like that of Christian virgins or priests, the torture requirement remains non-negotiable in all cases.[82] Whenever such a crime leaks out and leads to the prosecution of the criminals, the Jewish world community rises as one, demanding the release of the prisoners, denying everything and causing an almighty ruckus and diplomatic incidents, and in this concerted perversion of justice, Mommert states, they are usually successful.[83]

Mommert attributes ritual murder to two apparently contradictory motives, one a religious motivation to cleanse the soul through Christian blood, the other the by now familiar profit motive. To the first, Mommert the Pastor and Knight of the Holy Grave offers a simple remedy: clearly, drinking Christian blood is no good at all for the salvation of souls; "it would be so much simpler and more appropriate if all Jews agreed

The ritual slaughter of Simon of Trient. Woodcut by Wohlgemuth from the Latin edition of *Schedelsche Weltchronik*, 1493 (Reprinted in: Liebe, *Das Judentum*, 1923. Wikimedia Commons).

to be baptized and become Christians."[84] On the second motive, greed, Mommert elaborates in a chapter dedicated entirely to the worldwide trade in human blood. Even as far as world conspiracies go, this is scary stuff. To supply the planet's seven million Jews with Christian blood, Jews have developed a roaring, if secret, worldwide trade. Quotations from court records dating all the way back to the fifteenth century "document" the existence of Jewish blood merchants whose wares command high prices among *"those members of the faith who have not themselves had the opportunity to slaughter Christian boys."*[85] Kosher wares, Mommert asserts, are really nothing but foodstuffs and wine "fortified" with Christian blood.[86] Given the sheer scale of this trade, Mommert concludes, the two or three cases that come to light every year can constitute no more than a minuscule percentage of the number of ritual murders actually taking place.[87]

Ritual murder, in Mommert's account, has in abundance what every good conspiracy theory needs: secrecy. Talmudic law exists nowhere in writing; it is passed down exclusively in oral tradition, from child-killing father to child-killing son. Jewish ritual murderers blessed with several sons are moreover charged to pass the secret on to only a single son, who is then entrusted with keeping the tradition alive. Thus the practice remains a secret to most Jews and certainly to all non–Jews, and death awaits all non–Jews studying the Talmud for this reason.[88] Convincing readers of the existence of a worldwide conspiracy thousands of years old but so secret that evidence for it is virtually nonexistent is certainly one of Mommert's greatest difficulties. He skirts it by wrapping his feverish fantasies in the mantle of scholarship, citing extensively from the works of Jewish converts and ex-rabbis, from court records, from Professors of Hebrew and, of course, from the Talmud itself. His bibliography includes 269 sources plus a list of works published since first printing. Ultimately, he claims, the secret is no longer all that secret. Jewish ritual murderers are now becoming careless, "as if trying to *demonstrate their strength* and show us how much power they have due to their money, their solidarity, and the friends they have pushed into high places, and how helpless the 'two-legged animals' (non–Jews) of all countries are when faced with them."[89] The Jewish world conspiracy, he concludes ominously, is moving from the secret underground out into the open, testing their strength against that of Aryans in the final struggle for world domination.

According to Hans Rost (1877–1970), writing two years after Mommert, this struggle is already well along, and it does not look good for the Aryan race. In his *Thoughts and Truths About the Jewish Question* (*Gedanken und Wahrheiten zur Judenfrage*, 1907),[90] he laments the "tremendous dominance of Jews in all areas of economic life." While in the "fervently fought struggle against the moloch of capitalism, the struggle for the preservation of Christianity is inextricably bound up with the struggle against Judaism," his tract claims that acknowledging Jews as veritable role models is the first step towards supplanting them at the top.[91]

Chief among the three evils of modernity (the other two being urbanization and alcoholism) is Jewry, described by Rost as a "splinter-people breathing down the necks of nations, like inescapable doom."[92] Jews, he continues, own the financial rights to all lands in Germany, thus having placed themselves in a perfect position to squeeze German peasants or squeeze them out. Until Christians began to trade after the Crusades, organizing themselves in trade organizations from which Jews were excluded, Jews dominated world trade; thereafter, they focused on moneylending and usury, enriching themselves by ruining others. Jewish emancipation in the 19th century passed the baton of trade back to the Jews, turning them into "a terrible and now predominant power in the economic life of nations."[93] The rest, Rost elaborates, is Modern History: Jews live predominantly in cities and are disproportionately represented at German universities—both as students and as professors; they dominate high-level professions like doctors, lawyers, chemists and engineers; twice as many Jews as Christians are self-employed; they earn, on average, three times the salary of non–Jews; they own most high-priced houses in Berlin as well as the stock market, railways, coal mines, and all trade in grain, hops and leather. Private Germans and the German State are utterly dependent on Jewish money and credit; when Jews refuse to lend, wars are canceled.[94]

Yet Jews not only dominate the legal economy, they are also, as Rost avers in his chapter on Jewish crime, the undisputed kings of the economic underworld. Crime statistics from various European countries reveal that Jews, while under-represented in violent crime, top the list in all material crimes (Rost's ledger includes fraudulent bankruptcy, usury, theft of intellectual property, violation of laws "regulating the Sunday rest and closing times," production of harmful foods, the dissemination of obscene materials, draft evasion, religious crimes, fraud and perjury, pimping and procuration[95]). The lower participation of Jews in violent crime cannot count in their favor, Rost asserts, because Jews, on average rich, highly educated and abstemious, are neither driven to theft by economic necessity nor driven to violence by excessive drinking.[96] While this seems to indicate that Jews commit their crimes untroubled by compulsion, in cold blood and in full possession of their faculties, Rost takes it all back in rather spectacular fashion when he blames Jewish criminality on race. Jews, he explains, are plagued by a predilection for greed that goes well beyond volition or decision-making. He describes it as an addiction that is racially determined and hence inescapable, all-encompassing and not subject to individual control. "This addiction to make capitalist speculation your life's work is an indisputable racial characteristic of Jewry. The drive to enrich yourself through trade and financial transactions weighs upon Jewry like an irresistible compulsion."[97] Thus even country Jews trade in cattle rather than tilling the land, and when Joseph II tried to turn them into farmers, the Jews would have none of it.[98] In the end, Rost defines "the Jewish race [as] the incarnation of the capitalist-mercantilistic spirit."[99] Combatting this "spirit" means, in the short run, both limitation and imitation of the Jewish traits of success: a ban on Jewish immigration, a boycott of Jewish business and trade, the establishment of an antisemitic press, increasing the number of Christians at universities, and abstinence from alcohol.[100] And yet, since the root problem, the cause of Jewish crime, is a racial one, an ultimate solution must similarly focus on the entire race. Thus there can be only one answer to the "Jewish Question" of Rost's title: "Racial antisemitism must result, in its final consequence, in the expulsion of Jews from the State."[101]

Debunking Jewish Criminality

That the ideas expressed by Berg, Schrank, Mommert and Rost were not considered outlandish emerges from the frequency with which they are recycled in the work of other writers. Among the many that could be cited here are Erich Wulffen's popular *The Sexual Criminal* (*Der Sexualverbrecher*, 6th ed. 1910), in which he claimed that although the "Semitic races" were very highly sexualized, white slavery was merely an expression of the famous "Jewish entrepreneurial spirit,"[102] and Willy Hellpach (1877–1955), who in 1906 defined the increase of economic crimes among Jews as an "occupational psychosis" that provided evidence of "something foreign in their souls."[103] Yet such ideas, common as they were, did not remain uncontested. Around the turn of the century, there still existed an actual debate on Jewish criminality featuring some critical voices that became increasingly timid as time went on, until they were extinguished altogether in the NS regime. Among them was Hermann Strack (1848–1922), a Christian theologian, Talmudic scholar and author of a Hebrew grammar, who repudiated the ritual murder accusation as a "malicious untruth."[104]

Others used crime statistics to debunk this and other malicious untruths circulating about Jewish criminality.[105] As early as 1885, Ludwig Fuld presented his book *Jewish Criminality* (*Das jüdische Verbrecherthum*) as a treatise on the question to what extent religious confession (he states at the outset that he does not consider Jews a "race") can be linked with crime. Based on an extensive analysis of the nationwide crime statistics of 1881 broken down by three religious confessions (Protestants, Catholics and Jews), he found that expressed in percentages, Protestant participation in crime was the highest and Jewish the lowest.[106] A far cry from the bloodthirsty monsters or the wily crooks of antisemitic tracts, Jews in his book appear as boringly sober and unwaveringly law-abiding. His explanation for this amounts to an indictment of the society in which they live. Members of any religious minority in a hostile environment, he explains, tend to keep their heads down to avoid persecution, and their hesitancy to run afoul of the law will increase with the degree to which they feel threatened as a group:

> Commonly individual offenders belonging to a religious minority are not held *individually* accountable for their dastardly deed. On the contrary, every crime committed by adherents of a religious minority is used to cast stones on the entire community, to portray them as a "gang of crooks," a conglomerate of criminal and depraved people from whom only force and emergency rule can protect us.[107]

Emancipation, he claims, has accordingly wrought its effect on the Jewish crime rate: the more assimilated Jews become in German society, the more their crime statistics approach that of the non–Jewish German population.[108] Fuld cites regional differences between Jews in Poland, Silesia and East Prussia, where there was a higher degree of Jewish poverty and a correspondingly higher Jewish crime rate than in the rest of Germany, as evidence that crime is closely linked with social circumstance and that religious factors should be discounted (unless, he adds laconically, readers feel moved to presume a higher degree of faith among Eastern Jews).[109] As many statisticians in his wake would also do, Fuld explained the rare property crimes where Jewish participation was higher than average—among them fraud and bankruptcy—with the overrepresentation of Jews in the merchant class. Jews also perjured themselves more often than non–Jews simply because they found themselves dragged into court far more often and thus had an elevated opportunity for this particular crime.[110]

Eleven years later, the Berlin Committee for the Defense Against Antisemitic Attacks (Comite zur Abwehr antisemitischer Angriffe in Berlin) edited a substantial conglomerate of crime statistics comparing the criminality of Jews and non–Jews over ten years (1882–1892). Against the undocumented antisemitic claim that Jews are predestined for crime, a claim that, as the editors state, has assumed the appearance of truth through sheer repetition, the book pits "plain statistics with brief explanations written not for fanatics but for people seeking the objective truth."[111] Statistical evidence comprises not only German and Austrian Jewish and non–Jewish crime rates but also statistics of acquittals, presumably in an effort to counteract the common allegation that Jews in court routinely lied their way out of trouble.[112] The Committee's analysis showed that Jews, compared with non–Jews, were vastly under-represented in all crime categories but one; they committed far fewer offenses in the categories "Professional Crimes" ("Verbrechen und Vergehen im Amte begangen"), Property Crime ("Verbrechen und Vergehen gegen das Vermögen begangen") and Crimes Against People ("Verbrechen und Vergehen gegen die Person begangen"). The sole category in which Jewish criminality, percentage-wise, outstripped that of non–Jews is "Crimes Against the State, Public Order and Religion" ("Verbrechen und Vergehen gegen Staat, öffentliche Ordnung und Religion").[113] This alone is, of course, revealing, because a "crime against the State" or "public order" may simply describe the infraction of a mandate written specifically for that group. Crimes "against the State" may not be crimes in any other State or in any other context; the term may not express anything beyond a measure of how that State, at that historical moment, defines itself or, indeed, the concept of "crime."

The Committee's findings based on crime statistics from 1882 to 1892 echo Ludwig Fuld's analysis of the 1881 statistics in every detail. Like Fuld, the Committee found Jews guilty of a higher percentage of some specific crimes like fraud. Like Fuld, they linked this to the statistical over-representation of Jews in the merchant class, adding, however, that since the percentage of Jews working in trade was four times higher than the percentage of Jews in the population overall, non–Jews on average actually out-perpetrated Jews in the fraud category as well.[114] Similarly, the percentage of Jewish acquittals turned out to be no more than average when the statistical control group was merchants, whereas it was significantly higher when the control group was the population at large.[115]

Above all, the Comittee's findings reveal the virtual absence of Jews among violent criminals.[116] Particularly interesting is the extremely low Jewish participation in crimes that antisemitic literature had by now labelled as typically Jewish. In ten years, the Committee found the following numbers of convictions for the following crimes: incest: 7 Jews, 3667 non–Jews; rape, including of children: 354 Jews, 33,748 non–Jews; murder: 2 Jews, 1411 non–Jews; manslaughter: 4 Jews, 1646 non–Jews; infanticide: 5 Jews, 1945 non–Jews.[117] For white slavery and abduction, a very popular "Jewish" crime in anti-semitic tracts, two Jews were convicted between 1882 and 1892, compared to 168 non–Jews.[118] In every single category of "public violence," Jews scored far lower than the non–Jewish population. If criminal parity between Jews and non–Jews can be expressed by a ratio of 1:1 (adjusted for relative percentage of the population), Jews scored low for murder (0.54), infanticide (0.54), manslaughter (0.17), grievous bodily harm (0.25), rape (0.38), arson (0.37), theft (0.67), and robbery (0.30). On average, Jewish crime "ravaged" Germany to the tune of 0.84 to the non–Jewish score of 1. During these same ten years, not a single Jew was convicted of rioting, insurrection, inciting public violence, enslavement, or use of explosives.[119] The statistics are clear: Jews living in Germany between 1882 and 1892 did not make trouble.

They didn't later, either. Rudolf Wassermann (1884–1965), in his *Profession, Confession and Crime* (*Beruf, Konfession und Verbrechen*, 1907) shows the same disparity between the Jewish over-representation in "merchants' crimes" like fraud and their under-representation in violent crimes, based on crime statistics for the years up to 1900 in both Germany and Austria. The Jewish criminal in his book is mostly guilty of profoundly unsexy misdemeanors like "indictable self-interest" ("strafbarer Eigennutz") and "infringing the law regulating the Sunday rest and shop closing times" ("Zuwiderhandlung gegen das Gesetz über die Sonntagsruhe und den Ladenschluss").[120] Wassermann concludes that criminality has nothing at all to do with race or religion—therefore also nothing at all to do with Judaism or Jewishness, however conceived—and everything to do with profession and social circumstance.[121] This conclusion is taken up in the same year by Franz von Liszt—whom we have encountered earlier as one of Germany's earliest proponents of preemptive and permanent imprisonment—in his essay "The Problem of Jewish Criminality" ("Das Problem der Kriminalität der Juden," 1907). Based on crime statistics from 1882 to 1901, he notes regional differences in the Jewish crime rate, which he uses to repudiate the link between Jewish crime and "Jewishness" conceived either as race or religion. Using the same methodology as the Berlin Comittee and Wassermann (the expression of parity between Jewish and non–Jewish crime as 1:1, adjusted for population percentage), his statistics bear out the same results for the later period that Fuld had arrived at for 1881 and the Comittee for the following ten years: a higher Jewish participation in "merchants' crimes" like fraud, usury and perjury, and a lower Jewish participation in every other crime category.[122]

Principal Incompatibilities: From "Crime" to "Vice"

Taken as a whole, this debate among antisemites and statistical defenders of unjustly maligned Jews lends some credence to the theory that talk of Jewish criminality was not part of the general criminological debate in the wake of Lombroso but went its own way. Criminological treatises focus on the individual whereas Jews are routinely portrayed as a group or a race acting in concert. Even Jews not directly party to the crime are often implicated as accessories—as in Mommert's stories of World Jewry rising up as one to protect ritual murderers from prosecution and punishment. Whereas criminology frequently portrays non–Jewish criminals as "driven" and predetermined, Jews appear as cold and unemotional planners, motivated purely by greed and self-interest. This applies even, or perhaps particularly, to crimes with considerable potential for emotiveness and passion, such as ritual murder and white slavery. The extreme torture of ritual murder victims, supposedly necessary to render their blood efficacious for religious ceremonies, is committed by unfeeling Jewish traders who keep their dry eyes firmly on the profit margin; just as white slavery has nothing to do with sex and everything to do with money: it is merely, as Rost puts it, a "specifically Jewish branch of business."[123] The Jewish criminal's emotional coldness is elsewhere expressed in the long list of rather boring property crimes committed purely for financial gain. Crimes of passion that might define the criminal as a human being compelled by impulse, need or stress, from robbery to rape and from manslaughter to murder, are the exclusive province of non–Jews.

Daniel Vyleta is right in claiming that Jews are nearly universally cast as modern and rational criminals, but wrong in claiming that this precludes racial stereotyping. True, anatomical criteria like Lombroso's low foreheads or Kurella's ape-arms were not part of the Jewish criminal's racial profile. But race raised its ugly head in the discussion in other ways. Some writers, as we have seen, saw no contradiction in describing the Jewish criminal as the calculating predator of modernity *while* claiming that this expressed a racially determined predilection. Such a balancing act between the ills of modernity and ancient racial stereotyping was performed with perfect ease by Alexander Berg, who claimed that "their universally base racial character" predestined Jews for careers as white slavers, and by Hans Rost, who blamed the Jewish propensity for financial crimes on a compulsive greed that is addictive in nature and besets the entire Jewish race.

This narrative of Jewish criminality mirrors the post–Lombroso debate about criminal character in one way: it establishes the idea of *principal* incompatibility between the criminal and the non-criminal, and between Jews and non–Jews. The "born" (or, in the terms of some writers, "habitual" or "professional") criminal of German criminology is a "throwback" and therefore ineligible for reintegration into normal society. The idea of a "natural" Jewish predilection for crime, either by way of race or religion, equally precludes integration or assimilation as a solution to crime. Thus the only remedy on offer is the permanent separation of the populations: preemptive and indefinite imprisonment of the "habitual" or "professional" criminal; expulsion from the country of the "Jewish" criminal; even, as Berg advocated, "a merciless war of extermination." Writers like Fuld, Wassermann, Strack and the Berlin Committee not only tried to inject some reason into the Jewish criminality debate, but also tried to steer it in a different direction. More than one of them pointed out that Jewish criminality, whether the statistics revealed it to be comparatively low or comparatively high, was inextricably bound up by the way in which Jews were forced to live in their host societies, and that thus, to quote Wassermann, every country got the Jewish criminality it deserved.[124] And more than one of them pointed out that compared to the rage-driven, alcohol-fueled, poverty-inspired, violent and *scary* criminality of non–Jews, Jewish crimes tended to be a bit humdrum. Real Jewish crime, as it existed inside German society and outside of antisemitic tracts, was boring and bureaucratic stuff, certainly not up to emotional par with a good ritual torture murder, drinking the blood of Christian babies or selling blonde pigtailed girls into the brothels of Brazil. Could pogroms have been started by Christians outraged because Jews infringed the Sunday rest or closed up shop an hour late?

There are, of course, significant thematic intersections between such voices of reason and the ravings of antisemites. If sensible voices offered statistics-heavy and coherently argued evidence that Jews committed far fewer violent crimes than property crimes, antisemites could answer that *all* Jewish crimes are, in a way, property crimes. When we talk about Jewish criminality, we are always talking about buying, selling, and owning things—selling girls into slavery; trading in Christian blood; overcharging on interest; cheating good German peasants out of their land; buying up the stock markets of the world, and so, interminably, on. Ultimately, what specific crimes Jews could be shown to have committed mattered less than how the discourse of Jewish criminality was made relevant to Germans. The "job" of antisemitic writing on Jewish criminality was to dehumanize Jews by denying that they were individuals and treating them exclusively as a group. Statistics, which also necessarily talk about population groups, were powerless to counterbalance this narrative. In an antisemitic tract screaming at its readers that Jewish criminality is all about organized crime and world domination, even the lackluster nature of Jewish crime as described in a statistically informed and level-headed academic treatise lends itself to reinterpretation as underhanded and scheming, a crafty way of hiding in plain sight.

The debate about Jewish criminality was, in effect, entirely segregated from the post–Lombroso debate taking place in criminology about criminal "character," both thematically and in terms of method. Research on non–Jewish criminals was generally *inductive.* It tested the specific individual for cranial and psychological abnormalities, repeated the experiment a number of times, and drew from this collection of individual experiments conclusions about the criminal community, or a large part of it (one-third, 40 percent, all). Conversely, arguments about Jewish criminality tended to be *deductive:* a general theory about the community served as the basis for conclusions about all individuals belonging to that group. The point of departure in criminological treatises about non–Jewish criminals was usually the individual; the point of departure of writers on Jewish criminality was usually the group. Non-Jewish criminals were further individualized and differentiated by profession (murderers have bigger jaws, thieves longer arms, etc.), whereas Jews were further "massed" by being accused predominantly, and *collectively*—as a race or religious community—of three crimes: white slavery, ritual murder, and nefarious aspirations to world domination. It hardly needs pointing out that none of these crimes can effectively be committed by an individual or even a "group" of individuals: it takes a worldwide conspiracy. And it also hardly needs pointing out that many crimes of which Jews routinely stood accused were not, in fact, crimes at all. Being highly educated, successful, cultured or wealthy, dominating professions like medicine and law, even buying and selling stocks were all perfectly legal, even if these traits were constantly motivated as a sign that the Jewish "mass" or "race" was eating up the entire civilized world. Even around the turn of the century, when there was still a debate about it, "Jewish" criminality already inhabited two spheres—the literal limited to its surface meaning and the implied where it could be made to stand in for something else entirely. And it was moving, slowly but surely, from the literal to the implied, from "Judaism" to "Jewishness," and from "crime" to "vice."

Incorrigibles v. Inferiors:
German and Jewish Criminals
in Criminal Biology
(1919–1939)

The Rise of Criminal Biology

Before the First World War, scholars had considered three possible causes of crime: character (the individual propelled by his body, his psyche, or both), circumstance, or a combination of the two. During the Weimar Republic, the balance began to tip towards character, and the question whether a criminal was "born" or "made" began to be decided in favor of heredity. When the Nazis stepped in with their narrative of biological determination and gave it teeth by passing legislation mere months after assuming power, there wasn't all that much debate left to stifle.

The scientific discipline that rose to preeminence during the Weimar years was criminal biology. Originally christened in 1888 by Franz von Liszt to distinguish its reasoning from that of criminal sociology, and defined by one of its adherents as "*the science of the personality and its causal relation to crime*,"[1] criminal biology dominated criminological writing from 1920 to 1945.[2] Its path was smoothed by the failure of its rival disciplines. Sociologists were never particularly interested in the study of crime and its causes, leaving the entire discussion in the hands of medical men whose search for such causes was far more likely to focus on the individual.[3] And psychology, already under suspicion as a "Jewish" science and as a spurious discipline dedicated to getting off the guilty with phony insanity pleas, endured further attacks from within its own ranks. Notable psychologists like Theodor Reik (1888–1969), one of Freud's first students, were busily dismantling the relevance of psychological expertise in criminal investigation and in the courtroom. In his *The Unknown Murderer* (*Der unbekannte Mörder*, 1925), Reik stated that psychologists in court were often misled by the nervousness of the innocently accused and the certainty of the guilty, and pronounced psychology "useless" as a means of determining guilt.[4] "No, I do not wish for psychoanalysis to be 'admitted' to the courtroom," he concluded, holding out no hope for the future: "Will psychology offer no help in the foreseeable future with solving crime? I believe that it will not."[5]

Judges often agreed. The presiding judge in Fritz Haarmann's 1925 trial rejected a request by the defence to introduce the expert testimony of psychiatrists and psychologists on the defendant's behalf, ruling that "Psychology has no place in the courtroom."[6] The solutions to crime that might have been suggested by psychology—probing the criminal's mind for motive and ultimately treating it—or sociology—investigating society's role in crime and ultimately changing it—were cumbersome and difficult. Biological classification, on the other hand, offered an easy diagnostic tool, just as eugenics came to be seen as a quick fix for crime. This may explain why "by the mid–1920s at the latest, the vast majority of German physicians and psychiatrists were enthusiastic supporters of eugenics."[7] The NS State made it its business to support criminal biology and suppress all other directions of research, expelling criminal sociologists from the country[8] and denouncing criminal psychology as part of the Jewish world conspiracy that aimed at the pollution of Aryan races by permitting dangerous criminals to run free in Aryan societies.[9] But even before the final descent into NS-style madness, criminal biology had already left its rival disciplines in the dust. In the 1920s, the most prominent German institution conducting criminological research was Theodor Viernstein's Criminal-Biological Service (Kriminalbiologischer Dienst), founded in 1924 in Bavaria and dedicated to gathering biological data on prison inmates. From 1921 on, as one observer noted with approval in 1938, criminal biological institutes were sprouting like mushrooms all over Germany.[10] Other than that, there was nothing: no institutes, no organizations, no academic chairs in other areas of criminology.[11]

Corrigibles v. Incorrigibles

Paradoxically, criminal biology rose to prominence within a "progressive" penal system ("Stufensystem") originally intended to give inmates the incentive for rehabilitation. To uphold this system, the Bavarian Ministry of Justice sought to distinguish between corrigible and incorrigible prisoners by means of testing them for "incorrigibility" right at arrival. These new arrivals became the research base for the prison doctor Theodor Viernstein (1878–1949), who launched his massive data collection of "offender personalities" ("Täterpersönlichkeiten") in 1922.[12] Viernstein's investigation took the form of a ten-page questionnaire filled in by prison doctors in the course of a four-hour interview per questionnaire, during which they collected physical, biographical, familial, and social information on each prisoner, with a heavy emphasis on heredity and a corresponding sidelining of social contexts. Most significantly, the questionnaire narrowed Liszt's category of the criminal's social "environment" to mean his family background.[13] The questionnaire consisted of four main sections: Section 1, aiming at documenting a hereditary predilection for crime, contained questions about the inmate's parents and relatives; Section 2 collected information about the prisoner's relationship with his parents and about his schooling, occupation, military service and earlier criminal offenses as well as his description of his current crime; Section 3 contained a psychological assessment of temperament, intelligence, facial expression, handwriting, possible mental conditions, IQ and psychological tests as well as an assessment of the subject's attitudes toward himself, family, work, superiors, religion and politics, and Section 4 contained the examiner's "provisional social prognosis," that is, the prisoner's classification as either corrigible or incorrigible. The test concluded with anthropometric measurements, a detailed physical description of the inmate, and two photographs. In addition to all this, test subjects were asked to write an account of their lives, and questionnaires about the inmate and his family were sent to police, school and church authorities in the inmate's home town.[14]

In 1924, these questionnaires were made mandatory for all Bavarian prisons. By the early 1930s, there were over 20,000 criminal-biological reports from Bavarian prisons based on this questionnaire, and other German states and some prisons in Austria had begun to introduce Viernstein's system in the mid- to late 1920s.[15] The purpose of the questionnaires was to divide the criminal population into those who were deemed "educable" ("erziehbar") and able to benefit from a four-step system of privileges ("stufenweise Vergünstigungen") which could, in some cases, include early release, and those who, conversely, were deemed incorrigible and thus automatically excluded from such perks. Since Viernstein's three-category distinction into impulse criminals ("Affektverbrecher"), occasional criminals ("Gelegenheitsverbrecher") and habitual criminals ("Gewohnheitsverbrecher") was made largely based on hereditary factors, no one who had been downgraded from corrigible to incorrigible could ever rise into the "educable" class again.[16] The system thus resulted in the radical shrinking of the prison population deemed eligible for privileges or capable of rehabilitation. Of the 800 inmates of Straubing prison, Viernstein considered 61 percent incorrigible[17]; Hans Trunk, a prison doctor working with Viernstein on his classification system, reported similar numbers in 1931 when he claimed that the percentage of "incorrigibles" had risen from 37 percent to 62 percent following the introduction of the questionnaire and was expected to rise further.[18]

This strict division into hopeful and desperate cases already indicates that the main objective was not resocialization but selection. Viernstein himself pointed this out in 1924, when he enigmatically stated that criminal biology could have its uses for the "elimination of national comrades who had been recognized as undesirable for the preservation of our *Volk* and race."[19] This, of course, might include people both within and outside of prison. Thus Viernstein, not content with advocating the permanent detention or sterilization of incorrigible inmates, took the logical next step: he advocated the expansion of his system beyond prison walls, arguing that its broad application to the general population could diminish crime by identifying potential offenders before they had the chance to commit a crime.[20]

Racial Hygiene

Viernstein's ideas hardly seemed out of place in the context of pre–Nazi thinking on racial hygiene. Already a mainstay in criminological writing throughout the 1920s,[21] racial hygiene became a "scientific" discipline in 1923, with the foundation of the Kaiser Wilhelm Institute for Anthropology, Human Heredity and Eugenics in Berlin (Kaiser-Wilhelm-Institut für Anthropologie, menschliche Erblehre und Eugenik).[22] That same year, the University of Munich endowed an Extraordinary Professorship in Racial Hygiene; Gustav Emil Boeters, a public health official, sent the Saxon government a call for a sterilization law, helpfully providing a draft,[23] and the Prussian Ministry of Welfare convened a meeting of its Racial Hygiene committee to discuss the voluntary sterilization of people afflicted with hereditary diseases and extending such measures to criminals and those deemed "anti-social."[24] The year 1927 saw the foundation of the Criminal-Biological Society with Theodor Viernstein as its vice president. Its statutes defined it as both a research society and as a pressure group trying to influence penal law reform; its central demand, as formulated in the inaugural speech of the Society's president, was to "consider all crime, if it is to be fought successfully, as deducible from the offender's personality."[25]

Lawyers and psychiatrists sometimes formed unholy alliances in their joint defense of eugenic measures, as is shown by the 1920 appearance of the tellingly titled call for *The Liberalization of the Destruction of Life Not Worth Living* (*Die Freigabe der Vernichtung lebensunwerten Lebens*), jointly authored by the lawyer Karl Binding and the psychiatrist Alfred Hoche.[26] Since only a firm link between biology and criminality could justify eugenic measures from sterilization to euthanasia, academic books attempting to establish it began to appear in great numbers. One strange outgrowth of this literature are twin studies, for example Johannes Lange's (1891–1938) *Crime as Destiny* (*Verbrechen als Schicksal*, 1929) and Friedrich Stumpfl's (1902–97) *Origins of Crime as Shown in the Lives of Twins* (*Die Ursprünge des Verbrechens dargestellt am Lebenslauf von Zwillingen*, 1936). Johannes Lange's twin study compared the criminal histories of 13 pairs of identical twins and 17 pairs of fraternal twins and found a much higher correlation of criminal histories among the identicals (77 percent versus 12 percent among fraternals). He saw this as proof of a genetic criminal trait and concluded that society had a duty to prevent people with an active criminal gene from being born.[27] Seven years later, Friedrich Stumpfl's investigation of 32 pairs of criminal twins found an 89 percent "concordance" among identicals, as opposed to a high divergence among fraternals, in five areas: degree of penalty, severity of the offense, modus operandi, day-to-day social behavior, and psychopathic character. In consequence, he reiterated the conclusion he had arrived at a year earlier in *Heredity and Crime* (*Erbanlage und Verbrechen*, 1935), namely that "the inescapable conclusion must be that racial hygiene-measures are absolutely imperative particularly with respect to serious criminals."[28] In the earlier study, he had tested the families of 195 recidivists and 166 one-time offenders and found that "the criminal behavior of habitual, recidivist criminals had genetic origins, whereas that of occasional, one-time offenders did not."[29] Stumpfl's books, which Wetzell has called "the most important and influential books published in the field of criminal biology in the 1930s,"[30] concluded with a simple recommendation: the sterilization of all recidivist criminals.

Richard Wetzell has fair-mindedly pointed out that some criminologists of the age insisted that criminality as such was not hereditary; rather, they believed that many criminals were characterized by hereditary psychopathic abnormalities that contributed to criminal behavior.[31] But such niceties seemed to make little difference to the increasing willingness to embrace eugenic remedies to the problem of crime. What enabled contemporaries to rush to this solution was the disappearance of "environment" as the cause or partial cause of crime, summed up belatedly by Franz Exner (1881–1947) in his *Fundamentals of Criminal Biology* (*Kriminalbiologie in ihren Grundzügen*, 1939) and surely the most significant difference between prewar and inter-war criminological thinking.[32] It is also the disappearance of this factor that moved the discussion away from the criminal as an individual "character" and redefined him as both "offspring and progenitor of a tribe," his crime no longer an individual act but "the act of a member of that tribe."[33] Advocacy of eugenics centrally relied on such tribal thinking, both with regard to the group to be exterminated, or at least prevented from procreating (the criminal "tribe"), and with regard to the group to be protected (the law-abiding "Volk"). And this, along with the disappearance of "environment" as a factor and the supplanting of the criminal "character" by the criminal "tribe," is the third significant change in criminological thinking during the Weimar Republic and the early Nazi years: its self-professed purpose was no longer finding a remedy for crime, but protecting the populace from it.

By now, we have left Lombroso's meticulous measurements long behind and entered the murky realm of broad strokes categorization that could, in theory, apply to anyone. To cite a habitual criminal in a popular text by a (perhaps not coincidentally, Jewish) crime writer of the age: "Who can even distinguish between a professional and an occasional criminal? Well? We're the only ones who know, and we're not about to tell you."[34] The three new words in criminal biology that enabled the large-scale application of eugenic measures, not only to criminals but to anyone deemed undesirable by the State, were *incorrigible* ("unverbesserlich") on the one hand, a term that continued to be applied to criminals in particular, and, on the other, *feeble-minded* ("schwachsinnig") and *inferior* ("minderwertig"), both terms that could easily be linked to criminality but just as easily applied to the non-criminal population, particularly in racial contexts.[35] The task of criminal biology, as per Edmund Mezger (1883–1962), one of Germany's most renowned professors of penal law, was not to combat crime but to further the "racial enhancement of the German people" and the "elimination of elements harmful to the Volk and race"[36]; he saw the entire penal system as a "martial law for the protection and evolution of the people."[37] Building on research done in the 1920s,[38] Mezger introduced the idea of *hereditary* incorrigibility, which categorized recidivist criminals as a principally different class of humans who could neither be cured nor resocialized, but only permanently separated from society. Criminal biology, already convinced that most criminals were "congenital degenerates" ("erblich Entartete") based on hereditary factors, ancestry studies and racial theories,[39] quickly expanded this category to include not only law-abiding individuals but also entire population groups, peoples and nations. Calls for eugenic measures for the protection and "purification" of the German race, ranging from the sterilization and euthanasia of the racially "inferior" to the preemptive death penalty for would-be murderers, abounded during the later years of the Republic and the early NS years.[40] And criminal biology provided the "scientific" basis for it all. Its main proponents, Friedrich Stumpfl, Johannes Lange, Edmund Mezger and Franz Exner all became part of the inner circle in the Nazi regime. Theodor Viernstein, too, flourished in the Reich, obtaining a professorship at the University of Munich and all sorts of academic honors in addition to his elevated position as Head of the Center for Criminal Biology (Kriminalbiologische Sammelstelle). His criminal-biological evaluation system, which had, during the Weimar Republic, been introduced widely but not systematically, was adopted nationwide by 1935, followed by the establishment of a Reichs-wide Criminal-Biological Service (Kriminalbiologischer Dienst) in 1937.[41]

Penal Law Reform

Penal law reform, a perennial project since the early years of the Second Reich,[42] was attempted again in the Third. Here, too, the Nazis were able to draw on groundwork that had been laid during the Weimar Republic by reviving bills that had been seriously considered then but in the end had failed to pass Parliament.[43] Over fifty new laws and codicils were enacted during the NS era, many taking up reform suggestions of the Weimar Republic, such as the 1928–9 proposal for the indefinite detention of "habitual" criminals, with an option of release for those who agreed to sterilization.[44] Both indefinite detention uncoupled from a specific crime and eugenic measures became regular features of penal law after 1933. The 1933 Law for the Prevention of Genetically Diseased Offspring (Gesetz zur Verhütung erbkranken Nachwuchses) and the 1935 Law for the Protection of German Blood and German Honor (Gesetz zum Schutze des deutschen Blutes und der deutschen Ehre), both of which enacted eugenic measures, drew heavily on research in criminal biology.[45] November of the same year saw the passage of the Law against Dangerous Habitual Criminals (Gesetz gegen gefährliche Gewohnheitsverbrecher), which provided for the indefinite "security detention" ("Sicherheitsverwahrung," meaning the potentially lifelong imprisonment of criminals who had already completed prison sentences for specific crimes), and for the "preventive police custody" ("vorbeugende Polizeihaft") permitting the indefinite internment of "professional criminals" without a crime, trial, sentence or court order. The *National Socialist Guidelines for a New German Penal Law* ("Nationalsozialistische Leitsätze für ein neues deutsches Strafrecht"), issued in 1935, mandated the "protection of German blood, the preservation of loyalty to the people and the community as the foremost aim of penal law" and formally uncoupled punishment from crime: "Culpability begins as soon as criminal intent is perceptible." Work on the reformed Penal Code began in autumn of 1933, resulting, after about 100 sessions, in a 1936 draft; a complete draft emphasizing the "Protection of State Order, Race and the People" ("Schutz der Staatsordnung, der Rasse und des Volkstums") was submitted to Cabinet in 1939.[46]

In his *Penal Law of the Will: Attempt and Completion* (*Willensstrafrecht, Versuch und Vollendung*, 1935), Roland Freisler (1893–1945), who went on to become one of the Reich's most notorious judges, summed up the difference between NS law and that of the Republic: "Penal Law is no longer the Magna Carta protecting the individual in his transgressive attacks against the State Order but dedicated to the protection of all interests of *Volk* and State."[47] Four years later, the guidelines for SS judges contained the following instruction: "The SS judge serves justice. The only just decision is that expressing the will of the *Volk*. The will of the *Volk*, however, is the will of its best man: that of the Führer."[48] It was the final step on the path that had begun with the punishment of people rather than crimes: crime had already, during the Empire and the Weimar Republic, suffered severe blows to its legal supremacy as the determinator of punishment. Now there was no longer even a concrete definition of what constituted a "crime";

"You carry this burden too: A congenitally diseased person will cost on average 50,000 marks by the time he reaches the age of 60" (*Volk und Rasse. Illustrierte Monatsschrift für deutsches Volkstum* 10 [1936]. Courtesy Archiv Gedenkstätte Grafeneck).

like its punishment, this could be decided ad hoc. If the purpose of punishment is the protection of the law-abiding community, punishment requires neither crime nor criminal. A legal bill submitted by Freisler in 1939 called for the sterilization, permanent internment in camps, or death penalty for all who could not be integrated into the *Volk*.[49]

Nazi Crime-Fighters

The murkiness of what even constituted a "crime" or a "criminal" contrasts starkly with the confidence with which writers throughout the Weimar Republic and the early NS period held forth on both. Robert Heindl (1883–1958), Head of the CID Dresden and the man who had introduced fingerprinting into German police procedures, wrote his seminal work on *The Habitual Criminal* as *A Contribution to Penal Reform* (*Der Berufsverbrecher: Ein Beitrag zur Strafrechtsreform*) in 1926.[50] For those who, like Lombroso, tried to distinguish by criminal types, or who, like Aschaffenburg, racked their brains in search of motive, or who, like Liszt, tried to match criminal character to adequate penalties, Heindl simplified matters considerably. Based on statistics showing a marked rise in crime and soaring recidivism between 1882 and 1912,[51] Heindl tapers all previous differentiations down to one single criminal type, motive, method and penalty. The habitual criminal according to Heindl is motivated exclusively by greed (even the most infamous serial killers of the age, Karl Denke and Fritz Haarmann, had only committed their multiple murders in order to sell the flesh or clothes of their victims).[52] Intellectual limitations constrain the habitual criminal to a single modus operandi, a "stupid routine" that is endlessly repeated in a process Heindl termed "perseverance."[53] Whereas occasional criminals first deny and then confess, habituals confess either immediately, if they see an advantage to this, or never.[54] And of course, all habituals are inevitable recidivists who benefit from the current system of release and rearrest for the same crime, making permanent imprisonment for all recidivists irrespective of offense the only sensible option. The fact that Heindl's crime statistics are off in several instances[55] did not deter him from stating confidently that the habitual criminal "has both deserved this treatment and made it necessary through his *general* behavior" and that, in fact, "between 1885 and the World War *not a single* inmate has shown himself worthy of release."[56]

Heindl's book was a considerable success; it saw seven editions in as many years and was widely considered the authoritative work on the habitual criminal. Its main points—the principal hopelessness of rehabilitation, the justified and necessary sacrifice of individual rights to the cause of protecting the populace, the decoupling of crime and punishment, the criminalization of "thought" or "attitude" ("Gesinnung"[57]), and the call for permanent imprisonment or sterilization of large swathes of the criminal (and eventually the non-criminal) population—were reiterated endlessly throughout the Nazi period. Some writers, like CID Detective Arthur Nebe (1894–1945), held that 90 percent of inmates were professional criminals and recommended "security imprisonment" following the completion of their regular sentences for all of them.[58] Others, like SS-Obergruppenführer and Colonel General of the German Police Kurt Daluege

(1897–1946), praised the effectiveness of new crime-fighting methods like the surveillance and preemptive imprisonment of people suspected of *intending* to commit a crime (based on, for example, possession of suspicious utensils like drills or screwdrivers that might be used in the commission of a burglary).[59] Still others, like Iwan Antonow in his 1938 *Criminal Biology in the Service of Crime Fighting and Crime Prevention in Germany* (*Die Kriminalbiologie im Dienste der Verbrechensbekämpfung und -verhütung in Deutschland*), rehashed the argument that "congenital" criminality was inheritable like any other disease and could, in fact, originate in any illness, no matter how unrelated it seemed. He helpfully demonstrated the link between crime and disease in genealogical tables, one of which traced a killer's murderous predilection back to his grandfather's rheumatoid arthritis.[60]

The Nazis were forever claiming, and massaging statistics, to show that the Weimar Republic had stood idly by as its crime rate rose into the stratosphere and that only the new state had finally turned the corner. Philipp Greiner, presiding chair of the NS Council of the Berlin CID since August 1932, claimed that there had been an incessant rise in crime between 1919 and 1932 (the actual statistics for those years show a relatively stable crime rate and a decline in 1927).[61] Part of the Nazi myth of crime-fighting was that criminals in the new State were not only outgunned and outwitted but also more cooperative than ever before; cons who had stubbornly denied everything during the Republic, costing the state millions in investigation and court expenses, sang like birds for their Nazi captors.[62]

As the crime rate supposedly plummeted, both the prison population and the number of inmates deemed incorrigible rose immeasurably[63]—not necessarily because these people were guilty of actual crimes but because they had their part to play in the construction of the Nazi state. In March 1937, 2000 "professional" criminals were imprisoned in concentration camps by order of Heinrich Himmler (1900–45), who happened to require just that number of laborers for the rapid construction and expansion of concentration camps. He accordingly plucked the number 2000 out of thin air and ordered the Prussian CID to supply them (the CID had previously considered 525 prisoners the absolute maximum achievable).[64] Himmler's authorization of the Gestapo to arrest the "work-shy" ("Arbeitsscheue") in 1937 swelled the prison and concentration camp population by another 1,500 people. From 1937, the CID were issued quotas for minimal arrest numbers, which they usually fulfilled by rounding up the homeless. One homeless shelter in Hamburg, the "Pik As" (the "Ace of Spades," named after the unluckiest card in the deck) reported 10,246 overnight guests for April 1938; a year later, in April 1939, they were down to 2,378.[65] By New Year's Day of 1939, 12,921 people were in preemptive custody, a further 3,231 under constant surveillance and another 13,000 had been deported to concentration camps as either professional criminals or as "socially maladjusted" ("sozial Unangepaßte").[66] Heindl's thought that crime could be prevented through the preemptive imprisonment of likely, future or suspected criminals had become a firm credo among criminalists in the NS era and led to the constant identification of new population groups as eligible for such treatment.[67] Like the number of people imprisoned preemptively, the number of convicts or ex-cons subject to imprisonment after serving their time rose steadily. "Security imprisonment" was added to the original crime-related prison sentence and applied retroactively to prisoners already serving time; it required neither sentencing nor a court order and could last a lifetime. All told, 14,351 people endured this form of imprisonment throughout the NS years.[68] And like "preemptive custody" and "security imprisonment," the Nazis' use of the death penalty encompassed, over the years, an ever-widening circle of people and an ever-multiplying number of crimes.[69]

Between the end of the First World War and the beginning of the Second, ideas about crime moved from debate to consensus. A single explanation for crime, heredity, began to dominate. Disciplines likely to advance other explanations, like criminal sociology and criminal psychology, withered. Perhaps it is indeed unfair to claim that these developments were "intrinsically connected with Nazi ideology."[70] Certainly, however, the Nazis inherited a ready-made discourse. Two regular features of criminal-biological thinking throughout the Weimar Republic proved extremely useful for the construction of the Nazis' story of Jewish criminality: the idea that crime was genetically determined and the absence of other explanations. Where consensus is so overwhelming and so untroubled by alternative views, "synchronization" ("Gleichschaltung") seems hardly worth the trouble.[71]

Jews as "Born" Criminals

The Nazi consensus that Jews were "born" criminals relied centrally on a combination of two ideas, one dating back to the Weimar Republic and the other developed during the Nazi period: that crime was congenital and that Jews were a race. Hitler himself laid the foundation for this view in *Mein Kampf* (1925–6), where he declared Jewish criminality to be a racial and congenital factor and linked it with Jewish survival instincts honed during millennia of persecution. Whereas Aryans are fundamentally motivated by idealism and self-sacrifice, he explains, Jews are propelled exclusively by a "self-preservation without consideration of the well-being of others" that manifests itself inevitably as crime, particularly property crime like "theft, usury, robbery, burglary, etc."[72] The link between Jewishness and crime, particularly property crime, is also a constant in the works of NS criminologists, including its two leading lights, Edmund Mezger and Franz Exner. Exner's *Fundamentals of Criminal Biology* (*Kriminalbiologie in ihren Grundzügen*, 1939) mused that the disproportionately high number of property crimes committed by Jews showed a "remarkable congruence with the essential features of Jewish nature" since Jews are "driven by the strongest acquisitive drive and often heedlessly and ruthlessly pursue their material interests."[73] Similarly, Edmund Mezger claimed, in the first edition of his *Penal Policy on a Criminological Basis* (*Kriminalpolitik auf kriminologischer Grundlage*, 1934), that there was a distinct link between Jewish "nature" and Jewish criminality, but seemed uncertain whether Jews were "natural" criminals because of their race or their religion. In the second edition of 1942, he had made up his mind: it was race, after all.[74] The long history of racially motivated Jewish crimes were regular subjects at criminological conferences,[75] and there is considerable evidence that police officials from the 1930s onward considered recidivism genetically produced and Jews racially predisposed toward crime.[76]

Propaganda saw to it that the idea of a "natural" and racially predetermined Jewish criminality spread beyond the specialist circles of criminologists, lawyers and police-men.[77] A contemporary foreign observer noted that reports on crimes supposedly com-mitted by Jews all over the world flooded the German airwaves from July 1935 onward.[78] Jewish criminality became a regular feature of the *People's Observer* (*Völkischer Beobachter*), the most prominent daily of the NS era.[79] *The Stormtrooper* (*Der Stürmer*) ran dozens of Jewish criminality issues from 1925 onward, including a special issue on ritual murder (no. 14, April 1937), another on white slavery (no. 32, August 1937) and a third defining Jews as a "Criminal People" and proclaiming Judaism the "origin of all crime" (no. 7, September 1937).[80] *Der Stürmer* had an index of its own articles on Jewish criminality for the years 1926–1938; its fifteen sub sections by crime document impres-sively not only which crimes were considered most "typically" Jewish but also the sheer scale of the obsession (the list of crimes under the heading "race defilement" alone spans 12 pages for a time period of ten years).[81] That propaganda on Jewish criminality was effective, in the sense that it reached a broad general readership and created a high degree of consensus on the theme, is well documented. Showalter has shown, for exam-ple, that few of the tens of thousands of letters addressed to *Der Stürmer* were hoaxes: they were not written by the editorial team but "by everyone from prosperous busi-nessmen to unemployed day laborers."[82] Similarly, Dennis's analysis of articles published in the *Völkischer Beobachter* reveals that only 11 percent were written by editors-in-chief, editors or staff writers; the remaining 89 percent were authored by "occasional contributors," giving us some idea of the degree to which normal Germans participated in the process of their own indoctrination.[83]

Academic writing on Jewish criminality during the NS era, no matter what the discipline, is consensus writing, "synchronized" to hit the same four or five points. Johann von Leers (1902–65) presented his long essay "Jewish Criminality" ("Die Krim-inalität des Judentums," 1936) as a historical work. His list of Jewish criminals goes all the way back to the Biblical Abraham, whom he accuses of incest, and from there embarks on a whistle-stop tour of Jewish crime in the ancient Roman period, the Holy Roman Empire, the Peasants' Revolt, the medieval Crusades, the Thirty Years' War, the eighteenth century and the Wars of Liberation all the way up to his present day. Accord-ing to Leers, no Jew had ever lived, in- or outside of the Bible, "who would not be justly thrown into jail and stripped of his civil rights if modern Penal Law were applied to them."[84] In the place of documentation, Leers points vaguely at "laments in contempo-rary literature about Jewish criminality"[85] or the similarity between Yiddish or Hebrew and what he calls "thieves' language" ("Gaunersprache").[86] In the modern age, he rehashes the already familiar arguments about the inseparable link between Marxism and Judaism, symptomatically indicated by the high Jewish participation in property crime and aiming at world domination through the financial and racial ruination of all non–Jews. Ultimately, he claims, the issue is not merely that Jews harbor a greater num-ber of criminals in their midst than other peoples; the issue is that they are "criminal by nature" ("wesenhaft kriminell") because they are operating under a divine law that both authorizes and commands them to commit crimes against non–Jews. A criminal race led by a criminal God who has promised them all the wealth of non–Jews, Jews are not merely criminals and not even merely a criminal "race"; they are, in his words, the "'Ahrimanic animal,' the Warrior of Darkness against Light."[87] His casting of the

"A Heinous Crime Discovered in the torture chamber on Bauerngasse. German girls and women whipped and raped. The Jew Schloß arrested" (*Der Stürmer* 52 [December 1925], front cover).

battle against Jews as an apocalyptic End-of-Days struggle echoes—undoubtedly intentionally—Hitler's own view of the matter in *Mein Kampf*: "By fighting off the Jew I am fighting for the work of the Lord."[88]

A year later, J. Keller and Hanns Andersen replicated Leers's list of laments in *The Jew as a Criminal* (*Der Jude als Verbrecher*, 1937). Adorned with a laudatory foreword by *Stürmer* editor Julius Streicher (1885–1946), the book rehashes the link between Judaism and Bolshevism and that between Yiddish and thieves' language, the ontologically criminal nature of Jews, the objective of Jewish criminality, which masquerades as acquisition of goods but really is world domination, and the missionary/apocalyptic casting of the war on Jews as the struggle against the Antichrist.[89] Amid these ravings, Keller and Andersen also offer a seemingly academic discussion of crime rates based on statistics, which, however, diverge radically from all earlier criminological studies on Jewish criminality by assigning to Jews a far higher crime rate, expressed in percentages, than to non–Jews. The authors rationalize this divergence by proceeding on the assumption that Jewish crime is vastly under-reported. For one thing, they explain, crime statistics available to them are confessional rather than racial, so that crimes committed by baptized or assimilated Jews (about one third of all crimes, the authors assume) aren't even counted.[90] For another, a "noteworthy and specifically Jewish" trait of Jewish criminals is their attempt to hide their crimes or, if discovered, escape their just punishment by lying or defending themselves in court[91] (whereas German criminals, we must conclude from this, immediately turn themselves in after committing their crimes, a full written confession in hand). Keller and Andersen's use of statistics is clearly designed not only to uphold the pretense of academic respectability, but also to scare the bejesus out of readers. Although the authors readily admit that boring and petty property crimes top the list of crimes committed by Jews, their chapter on murderers—a category in which Jews, according to every single statistic published between 1880 and 1933, are vastly underrepresented—is by far the longest in the book. In all, the authors devote 13 pages to thieves, 27 to confidence tricksters, 19 to fraudsters and racketeers, 22 to gamblers, 20 each to pimps, white slavers and sexual criminals, and 53 to murderers.

Keller and Andersen's tome is a strange concoction of sweeping and uncorroborated statements and a throwback to earlier days when academic work still adhered to some minimal standards of substantiation. *The Jew as Criminal* treats evidence as a formality rather than a necessity; the extensive footnotes offer no discernible relationship to statements made in the text and crime statistics are massaged heavily to indicate what the authors need them to mean. Their sample stories of Jewish crime inevitably begin with a sweeping statement, such as the following: "It is not within the Jewish nature to murder someone out of jealousy or anger. [...] Jewish murderers are cold and calculating killers."[92] Corroboration for this amounts to a single example (in this case, the story of Fritz Saffran, who committed murder planning to pass the corpse off as his own and cash in on a large insurance payout).[93] The example is then assigned the status of a parable that stands for a much larger context: all Jews murder for the same reasons; no differentiation of motive, context or circumstance can possibly exist. Taking a single instance as parabolic evidence for worldwide developments enables some truly spectacular claims. All gangsters in the U.S., for example, are Jews engaged in an organized battle against American Law and Order, and the Tsar and his entire family were murdered by Jews (who were also, naturally, behind the Russian Revolution).[94] Money is no object since Jewish crimes, while appearing to be motivated by greed, are actually committed in pursuit of world domination.[95] Motive is also beside the point since Jews commit crime because they are Jews (the confession of David Frankfurter is quoted as simply stating: "I shot him because I am a Jew."[96]) A Jew, the authors conclude, is not only sub-human or inhumane but antihuman: "His 'religion' is antithetical to God, his law to justice, his ethics to morality. His nature is anti-natural, his patriotism anti-*völkisch*, his nationalism international and his politics crime. Thus the Jew is the true *anti-human*, the decayed member of an inferior racial mix. He is the born leader of subhumanity."[97]

Most of these points are reworked with little change by Herwig Hartner-Hnizdo, who expressed the strength of his feelings on Jewish criminality by publishing no fewer than two books about it in the same year: *Jewish Criminality* (*Das jüdische Gaunertum*) and *A People of Crooks: An Investigation of Jewish Criminality* (*Volk der Gauner: Eine Untersuchung des jüdischen Gaunertums*, both 1939). Like his predecessors, he claims that all words in the thieves' argot are Yiddish or Hebrew (he does not, in fact, find it necessary to distinguish between the two).[98] He, too, points out, offering no evidence whatsoever, that most Jewish criminals are never caught or prosecuted, so that the extent of their criminal activity is vastly underestimated.[99] Like earlier writers, Hartner-Hnizdo claims that Jewish crime rates were constant and unvarying since the Dawn of Time, showing that the criminality of Jews could not be attributed to individual destitution, social or political circumstance, or historical change, but only to the one constant spanning the millennia: their race.[100] And like his predecessors, Hartner-Hnizdo was no stranger to mind-bogglingly bizarre illogic. His "proof" that white slavery was a specifically Jewish business, for example, is the existence of Jewish organizations *fighting* white slavery since—he concludes—we must presume that if the victims of white slavery are predominantly Jewish, their abductors and traders must also be Jews.[101]

Where Hartner-Hnizdo enters territory not often trodden by Nazi writers on the theme is in his attempt to apply Lombroso's ideas about stigmata to race, and this is also where he parts company with the propagandistic physical description of Jews as filthy, hook-nosed, hump-backed and so forth. Lombroso's work on stigmata, that is: recognizable physiological traits indicating a criminal predilection, had been inductive; his autopsies and measurements of individuals had furnished corroboration for his conclusions regarding the group to which they belonged. Hartner-Hnizdo's application of Lombroso's work, conversely, relied on deductive reasoning and skipped the research and corroboration entirely. In his chapter on physical racial characteristics in *Jewish Criminality*, he states that it is basically impossible to recognize a Jewish criminal by physical characteristics, whereas one would immediately recognize a lower class (and thus, more likely than not, a criminally inclined) German just by looking at him. The reason is simply that there is a considerable distance, physically and in all other ways, between a German criminal and a law-abiding German citizen, whereas there isn't much of a difference, if any, between a Jewish criminal and a law-abiding Jew. German criminality, he claims, is caused by hereditary factors like disease and "inferior" genes, whereas Jewish criminality is simply an expression of the normal predilections of the Jewish race as a whole.[102] In one stroke, Hartner-Hnizdo thus managed to validate the heredity theory for Aryan criminals *only*, while claiming that Jewish criminality was racially inherent and thus, for Jews, not abnormal in any way. Types that would be the dregs of humanity among Aryans and thus easily recognizable as such, he elaborates in *A People of Crooks*, are ordinary Jewish citizens and thus indistinguishable from every other Jew.[103]

Thus the problem of Jewish crime, Hartner-Hnizdo argues, is identical with the problem of the existence of the Jewish race and its parasitical presence among its host nations; it is a global disease. "The Jewish Question is a fever that attacks, again and again, Aryan cultures. Diseases, however, should be cured,"[104] and not only for the good of the infected Aryan culture: "Jews themselves are sick with Jewishness; apart from the artificial unity created by intense antisemitism, they are only protected from self-destruction to the extent that an Aryan sense of Order prevails among them."[105] In the end, Hartner-Hnizdo actually managed to sound magnanimous in advocating the universal expulsion of Jews—for their own good—as the ideal solution to the problem of Jewish crime.[106] Elsewhere, though, he ominously denies the workability of this solution, *"for it is now clear that the 'Vengeful God' is the Jewish unscrupulousness that permits every kind of immorality and criminality to grow and operate to the extent that it will ultimately scourge its own people and, at the same time, cause all the Aryan world to rise up against Israel."*[107] The final solution, as Hartner-Hnizdo screams in boldface and italics at his readers, is nothing less than the utter annihilation of all Jews. He leaves it conveniently open whether this outcome will be effected through extermination from the outside (by Aryans "rising up" against Jews) or through a kind of self-annihilation in which Jews are smitten by their own Vengeful God or drown in the morass of their own immorality and crime. Either way, the conclusion must be that Jews will only have themselves to blame for their own demise, just as they are also at fault for their own persecution.

These texts, which are paradigmatic for a vast landscape of antisemitic writing on Jewish criminality, are characterized by similar traits: an argumentation that is at best associative and at worst bizarre, the misuse and decontextualization of the crime statistics and research of earlier ages, and the replacement of debate with consensus ("synchronization"). All of them make the same points: criminality is inherently Jewish (as shown, for example, by the similarity between Yiddish and the common argot of criminals). Its aim is world domination by virtue of the dispossession and subjugation of non–Jewish peoples (cite here the link with Marxism and Bolshevism). Jewishness *is* criminality (insert here copious and meaningless Jewish crime anecdotes from the Bible to the present). Both Jewishness and criminality are a disease attacking the clean Aryan body; the "healing" of the body (by way of exterminating the virus) is no more than self-preservation. Criminal traits and activities that had been viewed, before the First World War, as specific to a subset of Jewry (the ritual murder accusation launched at "Talmudic" Jews, for example) are now generalized to apply to all Jews, whether Talmudic or Mosaic, baptized or assimilated, pious or agnostic. And although Jews are not considered a religious community but a race, the fight against them is, more often than not, cast as a *religious war*, a war that does the Lord's work by exterminating the Antichrist (Leers; Keller and Andersen), by cleansing the Earth with fire and sword from a terrible virus (Hartner-Hnizdo), or—the option that must have appealed most to practical minds—leaving all of this cleansing work to the Jews' own "Vengeful God."

Berkowitz is absolutely right in his assertion that the Nazis' conflation of Jews with criminals furnished the moral justification for their annihilation.[108] But that does not quite describe the duplicity at work here. Just as many of these writers felt entirely free to use previous research even as they ignored it, or to assign the cause of crime *simultaneously* to heredity (in the case of Germans) and race (in the case of Jews), their arguments moved seamlessly back and forth between an ethical universe (in which the destruction of the Antichrist could only be considered a moral duty) and an amoral one (in which the expulsion of a virus from the body is a simple act of self-preservation, bare of any ethical dimension). When it came to Jewish criminality, Nazi writers had truly mastered the art of having their cake and eating it, too.

Social Pathologies

Before the Nazis, and certainly before the First World War, criminology behaved like an academic discipline; it conducted conscientious research, insisted on some standards of evidence, and fostered and debated different approaches, methods and models in publications and at conferences. But it was never a disinterested science. From its very inception, it was an *applied* science in an "unholy alliance"[109] with the State. Its stated goal—to provide the empirical basis for penal law reform—was antithetical to the freedom of inquiry that is the basis of all academic work. It is difficult to question your approaches, test your methods or allow the evidence to detonate your most cherished theories when you have to produce results within a certain timeframe.

The second aspect that hampered criminological efforts at disinterested research was the consensus culture established early on by the elimination of criminal sociology and criminal psychology. The constriction of criminology to criminal biology and the resulting streamlining of thinking about crime was still some distance from the "synchronization" of ideas under the Nazis. And yet, while synchronization itself originated in the NS era, many ideas that seem firmly at home there did not. Some writers, like Hans von Hentig, were perfectly happy to advocate working congenital undesirables to death as early as 1914. What we can say with certainty is that the ascendancy of criminal biology resulted in three significant developments. First: the suggested solutions to crime, like its perceived causes, focused on the individual and ignored society. Secondly: crime began to be defined as a disease attacking the healthy body politic, an idea that directly parallels antisemitic discourse under the NS regime. And finally: society's right to be safe from crime began to be rated more highly than the individual's rights to personal freedom, a fair trial, or legal safety (in the sense of the calculability of punishment).

The first dilemma—that honest research into the causes of crime could not result in solutions addressing those causes—was already apparent before the First World War. Even then,

> although most criminal biologists acknowledged the role of social factors in crime, they were generally pessimistic about being able to change the social conditions that pushed so many people into a life of crime. Time and time again major criminal biologists, including Aschaffenburg, Näcke, and Viernstein, and even the hard-line eugenicist Rüdin, explicitly admitted that in many cases changes in the social milieu of a recidivist could, in principle, prevent that person from offending again. But such acknowledgments were always followed by the qualification that this environment could not, in practice, be changed, so that the criminal in question would have to be considered "incorrigible." In other words—and this is crucial—the prognosis of incorrigibility was

not based on the conviction that the individual's criminal behavior resulted from unalterable genetic factors but on the belief that it was simply too difficult to change the social factors involved.[110]

Where institutions—the police, penal law reformers, the State—take the path of least resistance (it is, of course, easier to blame the individual than to change the world), research in the service of these institutions has to adjust accordingly. The practical applications of the research both predetermine and invalidate its findings. At this point, research no longer expresses what we think, but what we think we can fix.

The third development—the privileging of societal safety over individual rights— was a direct result of the second, the medicalization of criminals and crime.[111] Given that the entire discussion had been left in the hands of medical men, this was, perhaps, inevitable. Already before the First World War, psychiatrists routinely described not only individual criminals as physically or psychologically ill, but also crime itself as a "social disease." For Kraepelin, for instance, psychiatry did not address the individual; his goal was to implement a "mass psychiatry" based on an extensive data collection comprising medical, criminal and population statistics in order to determine the degree of "public mental health." Fighting crime meant fighting the "degradation of the race."[112] Criminals in his writing are "carriers of a dangerous infection" that weakens the "social organism" and endangers the "moral health of the entire structure."[113] Kraepelin's cure-all was permanent imprisonment, or, in his medical vocabulary, a "permanent quarantine" to effect the "elimination of infectious elements from the community of those able to recover."[114]

Kraepelin wrote this in 1880, fifty-three years before the Nazis came to power, and reiterated it in his essay "Crime as a Social Disease" in 1906. The point here is not, or not only, that he anticipated Nazi talk of the Jewish bacillus infecting the body of the *Volk*, creating a discourse that the Nazis merely had to adapt to their own purposes. The larger point is that the medicalization of crime eliminates the moral dimension from the discussion. Medicine, biology and psychiatry, the disciplines "in charge" of the "born" criminal, left no room for the most essential axiom of moral law: free will and personal responsibility. If eliminating crime (and the criminal) restores the body politic to health like a body is restored to health by ousting a viral infection, this is an act that takes place in a state of nature and thus in an amoral universe. Or, to speak with Kant for a moment, it amounts to the subordination of moral law (for instance, the individual's rights within society) to natural law (for instance, society's right to self-preservation and survival).[115] The Nazis honed the thought to perfection and exploited it for their treatment particularly of Jews, but the idea had already emerged in the context of the crime discussion decades earlier: that crime-fighting is an act of social self-defense without ethical implications.

Whether the relationship between the two is causal, analogical, coincidental or something else entirely has been a matter of long debate. Forty years after the end of the Second World War, Martin Broszat, one of the clearest thinkers about perversions of justice under the NS regime, raised the question whether these perversions had been prefigured in earlier periods. Was the criminal biology of the Empire and the Weimar Republic a precursor of the Nazis' racial crime politics? Did the uncoupling of punishment from crime, the preemptive and "security" imprisonment recommended by countless criminologists of earlier ages, pave the way to the "selection" and annihilation of innocents in NS camps? Broszat suspected that a "Historicization of National Socialism" would reveal the "social pathologies" of earlier societies in a way that would inform our view of the NS regime.[116] Conversely, and equally persuasively, both Wetzell and Vyleta have warned against over-concluding, against establishing causal links and direct successions where there are none. Vyleta has argued that criminologists before the First World War did not promote a racial definition of crime or postulate the identity of the criminal with the Jew.[117] Wetzell has similarly maintained that "it is wrong to assume that criminal biology and racism (including anti–Semitism) were intrinsically connected" and clarified that while "some criminologists did indeed hold racist prejudices against Jews and other groups, the criminal-biological project focused primarily on individual, as opposed to racial, characteristics of biological abnormality."[118] Perhaps this is the point at which we need to start thinking differently about the link between the two "social pathologies," between the Nazis' extermination policies and the criminological discussion of earlier periods: not as cause and consequence but as drawing water from the same well.

In *Depravity and Degeneracy* (*Verderbnis und Entartung*, 2002), a history of 19th-century criminology, Peter Becker begins not with the new definition of the criminal but with that of Modern Man. Earlier Man, who had been subject to constant trials and tribulations, was superseded by Modern Man, who saw himself as *homo sapiens* at the apex of his physical, intellectual and cultural development. At the same time, criminology removed Criminal Man from his legal and moral context and placed him into a medical one.[119] The naturalization of criminality resulted in a view of the criminal as sick and degenerate, a significant departure from the previous understanding of the criminal as an (im)moral being exercising his free will. The criminal's new status as principally inferior relieved him of the moral responsibility for his crime, but it also meant that his integration into society was no longer an option. The diagnosis of inferiority furnished not only the justification to exclude the offender from civic rights, but also "de-tribunalized" individuals and society by defining delinquents as beings who were fundamentally and forever incapable of undergoing the "inner development" that would allow them to function as citizens. Delinquents are thus by definition "non-citizens."[120]

The idea of the criminal (or Jew) as belonging to an inferior species (*homo delinquens*, not *homo sapiens*) was already common criminological coin around the turn of the century. Inferiority thinking entered the crime discussion around the same time that the German nation reconstituted itself for the first time in a thousand years; in the NS era, it furnished the excuse for stripping people of their citizenship. Yet distinctions by race or heredity both comprise and transcend national boundaries. Lombroso himself had worked heavily with physiognomic characteristics that distinguished the criminal class of humans from the law-abiding; he was less interested in psychic deviations (which might have involved either psychological or sociological explanations), simply assuming them to be present as soon as he had found physiological traits "typical" of criminals in a subject. Based largely on physiology, he claimed that there was a great similarity between criminals of all nations, so that an Italian criminal was basically indistinguishable from a German one.[121]

Along very similar lines, the Nazis forever claimed that the Jews were a distinct "race" fundamentally different from and utterly incompatible with the community of nations comprising the Aryan "race." From 1926 on, the *Völkischer Beobachter* ran dozens of articles "proving" that cultural geniuses of all nations, from Saint Thomas Aquinas and Shakespeare to Goethe, Schopenhauer and Wagner, had had an abhorrence for "the Jew," whom they had identified by physiognomy. As Wagner put it in *Judaism in Music:* "The Jew—who, as everyone knows, has a God all to himself—in ordinary life strikes us primarily by his outward appeareance, which, no matter to what European nationality we belong, has something disagreeably foreign to that nationality: instinctively we wish to have nothing in common with a man who looks like that."[122] All Aryans, no matter what their nationality, are members of the same race; the Jew alone is "foreign."

The revocation of citizens' rights for Jews in Nazi Germany relied both on this conviction and on the idea that citizenship had to be earned rather than automatically granted at birth. Both of these ideas intersect with the medicalization of legal contexts in *Mein Kampf*, in which Hitler applies medical criteria—health v. disease—to a legal state—citizenship. Hitler distinguished between two kinds of citizenship: "state membership" ("Staatsangehörigkeit"), which is awarded at birth, and "state citizenship" ("Staatsbürgerschaft"), which has to be acquired by submitting to an "education" designed to produce "a national comrade aware of the needs of race and nation." A young man's mandatory path to citizenship was sports activity aimed at the production of a super-fit body followed by a stint in the army (citizenship, Hitler announced, would be awarded upon completion of military service); a young woman's was marriage, where she would contribute to public health by producing strapping young national comrades.[123]

Analogies, no matter how compelling, are just that; they are not causes, origins or consequences. It would thus be incautious to cast the delinquent of criminal biology as a direct ancestor of the Nazis' Jew. It is also not necessary. The unjust imprisonment, sterilization and murder of people, suggested by pre–World War I criminologists as a solution for crime, and the same measures inflicted by the Nazis on Jews both drew water from the same well. The well, in this case, was a century-long process in which Embattled Man redefined himself as Superior Man and began to look around for inferiors. In the process, four conceptual boundaries were redrawn: that between the national and the non-national, between normal and abnormal, between individual and community, and between morality and amorality. From the moment the German state established itself (first as the Second German Reich, then as the Third), it began to formulate the terms of membership particularly by proposing principal exclusions. In both cases, criminals and Jews were among the first to be fingered, and based on similar criteria. The understanding of the criminal as congenitally "abnormal," the view of Jews as a degenerate race, pronounced their incompatibility to be immutable, inevitable and everlasting. For the biologically or racially "inferior," there was no conceivable way back into society. The privileging of society's rights over the individual's meant that society could decide who was a criminal and who was not—whether or not a crime had actually been committed—just as the Nazi State developed an elaborate system for the purpose of determining who was a Jew and who was not. And finally, the naturalization of crime and the criminal, that is, the misapplication of medical thinking to a legal context, amounted to a denial that moral considerations even applied. It amounted, in essence, to the smashing of the moral compass.

What Hannah Arendt has said about the deletion of the individual and his subsumption into the Mass under totalitarianism can be observed in the academic discussion of crime long before totalitarianism became a reality. Much like Himmler's SS men, criminal biologists were disinterested in "everyday problems"; they were out to solve "ideological questions of importance for decades and centuries."[124] The criminal's potential to become, at least in writing, the antithesis to Mass Man, the last vestige of individuality, was not fulfilled in criminology and even less in criminal biology. On the contrary: criminal biology rose to prominence because it promised blanket solutions, a silver bullet, a quick fix. Criminal psychology and criminal sociology failed because they offered only the long and arduous exploration of the human psyche or of social injustice. Both would have meant not only taking the context seriously, but also the individual.

As it was, the criminal "character" was never an "individual" in any but the most superficial sense. He was seen as an "individual" specimen to be poked, prodded and measured, but rarely, if ever, as an individual human entitled to judgment and treatment on a case-by-case basis. The part assigned to the criminal was that of "Mass Man," a template for the criminal community to which punishments could be assigned *en vrac*. Criminology before the World Wars fell victim to what we might call metonymic slippage; it set out to investigate the causes of crime and ended up writing a story of vice. It told a story that masqueraded as history. Its best efforts to bring about societal change ended in nothing more than an avowal of biological inevitability. In so doing, it moved the debate away from personal and public responsibility and helped to establish "a world of fatalities in which men find themselves entangled."[125]

Conflicts:
Crime Cases

A Conman Plays a Captain:
The Case of Wilhelm Voigt
(Berlin, 1906)

On October 10, 1906, a handful of soldiers commanded by a Captain occupied the Köpenick
City Hall[...], arrested the mayor and confiscated the money in the treasury. A few hours later
it emerged that this brazen, brilliant coup had been the work of an unknown perpetrator. The
soldiers were real, the Captain wasn't. … The entire world was laughing, the Emperor laughed
right along with them, and the police in Berlin toiled desperately to catch the perpetrator.
When he finally gave himself up, people couldn't believe their eyes. He was a pathetic little
man with a grey beard, a shoemaker named Wilhelm Voigt. He had bought the uniform from
a junk dealer.[1]

This is how Walther Kiaulehn, in his monumental history of Berlin, described what has
become known as one of the greatest criminal feats, and one of the most celebrated
criminals, in German history. The story Kiaulehn tells is inaccurate in several places:
the Captain's coup occurred on October the 16th, not on the 10th. The Emperor's amusement, while certainly well documented,[2] took a decided backseat to his grim determination not to have the Prussian State's authority ridiculed; he put considerable pressure
on the Berlin police to put the crook behind bars as soon as humanly possible. And
Voigt did not turn himself in, but led the police on a merry chase for ten days while
Germans laughed their heads off. But the details matter less than the sheer glee, the
delighted hero-worship of the brilliant conman that swept Berlin and Germany in 1906
and that still colored Kiaulehn's view of the affair half a century later. By that time, any
history of Berlin would have been unthinkable without according space to the cobbler
turned Captain. Far from a minor footnote in German history, he had turned into a
folk hero, a symbol of resourcefulness, hilarity and humanity pitted against injustice,
rigidity, humorlessness, militarism, and unthinking obedience—against everything, in
short, that was wrong with Imperial Germany.

Wilhelm Voigt: Life of a Jailbird

In symbolic terms, then, the shoemaker certainly had big shoes to fill. His significance for Germany's self-image exorbitantly surpassed the expectations one might have
attached to his personality (Kiaulehn was far from the only writer to describe him as
"pathetic"). Before the Köpenick Coup, he had been nothing but a minor crook. Born

in 1849 into a stereotypically broken family composed of an abusive drunkard father, an angelic mother, and suffering children, his first arrests—the first for begging, the second for stealing—date back to his school years. In his 1908 autobiography *How I Became the Captain of Köpenick* (*Wie ich Hauptmann von Köpenick wurde*), a work that, as the title already hints, seeks to contextualize and to some extent exculpate his life of crime, Voigt describes both arrests as twists of injustice and Fate. The confession of begging, he claims, was beaten out of him by the police: it is the first of many stories of mistreatment at the hands of Justice that wind their way through his autobiography, the constant refrain of his life.[3] Behind Voigt's first indictment for theft lurks an even more harrowing story: after a horrendous scene of domestic violence, then–14-year-old Voigt fled the house panic-stricken and half-naked, entered a neighbor's empty house, took some clothes to cover himself, and ran off. The neighbor, unaware of who had taken the clothes, reported the theft to the police, and Voigt was arrested. As a result of this, he was expelled from school just as he had made it to the final grade; his long-held dream of joining the military was also now out of reach because of his criminal record. The rest of his life is a merry-go-round of arrests and prison sentences: six arrests between 1864 and 1891—four for theft, two for document forgery—resulted in a total of more than 13 years of jail time.

Voigt always claimed to have been capriciously treated by the justice system, and while it is difficult to judge a case from this historical distance, the wildly varying lengths of his prison sentences do give one pause. June 1863: 14 days' prison for theft. September 1864: three months' prison for theft. September 1865: nine months' prison and one year's loss of civil rights for theft. Then, in April 1867 on a forgery charge: ten years' penal servitude (meaning imprisonment under considerably harsher conditions than in a regular prison) plus a 1,500 thaler fine or another two years' penal servitude added to the sentence in case of inability to pay.[4] At sentencing, Voigt was 18 years old. The much harsher 1867 sentence does not reflect a more serious charge, but the simple fact that the court, at that point, saw him as a "habitual criminal" from whom society had to be protected permanently, or as permanently as the maximum sentence for forgery allowed. Voigt clearly considered this sentence excessive—"*12 years penal servitude*," he wailed in his autobiography[5]—and claimed that "according to the presiding judge at my trial on December 1, 1906, such sentences would not be possible today."[6] And perhaps he was right: in 1922, Ella Klein and Margarethe Nebbe were respectively sentenced to four years in prison (Klein) and one and a half years' penal servitude (Nebbe)—for a jointly committed poison murder.[7]

Voigt's 12-year sentence for forgery, which does seem harsh by comparison, condemned him to what he termed "a living death" and by his own account permanently damaged his faith in justice.[8] Even allowing for Voigt's obvious attempts to rationalize his crimes and sentimentalize his fate, it is clear that this was a turning point in his life. He entered the penitentiary at the age of 18 and left it again at 29. While he was still inside, his beloved mother died and his father remarried. His relationship with his family was irrevocably ruptured: when he contacted his sister in 1906, shortly before embarking on his adventure in Köpenick, he had not had any contact with her for 34 years.[9]

Following his release in 1879, Voigt escaped the eagle-eye of the law for ten years by traveling abroad. In July 1889, he was sentenced to another year in prison for theft and in January 1890 again to one month's prison term for forgery.[10] These rather lenient sentences, given that Voigt had previously netted twelve years for the same offence, were undoubtedly due to the fact that Voigt had by now gotten wise to the courts' dim view of habitual criminals: he changed his first name to "Richard," thus successfully hiding his previous encounters with the law. During the 1889 stint for theft, he met Paul Kallenberg, who persuaded him to participate in an armed robbery upon their release. The two were promptly caught and Voigt was sentenced, in February 1891, to a further fifteen years' penal servitude.[11] This sentence is another story of judicial failure and injustice that looms large in Voigt's autobiography. To hear Voigt tell it, the civil servants investigating the case made off with part of the stolen money, thwarting Voigt's chances of showing remorse by returning all of the loot and throwing himself upon the mercy of the court. His gold watch was stolen by one or the other civil servant in charge and the case never investigated. His sentence was set after a mere half hour of deliberation and without calling any witnesses either for the prosecution or the defense.[12] There is some evidence that others as well considered his sentence excessive: Voigt cites a conversation with the Chief Prosecutor for the Province of Posen who, upon hearing of the length of his penitentiary sentence, assumed that Voigt must have committed murder in the course of the robbery.[13] Certainly, Judge Dietz, the presiding judge at Voigt's trial for the Köpenick affair, considered the severity of this sentence in the absence of witness testimony and after the briefest of deliberations highly irregular.[14]

Voigt was released from this fifteen-year stint in February 1906. He was now 57 years old and had spent nearly half of his life in prison. By his own account, he left prison a changed man, willing to abandon his bitterness, his sense of injustice, and his futile struggle against the law: "Hardly ever has a man entered freedom with greater determination to subordinate himself to society's requirements in all things!"[15] But his good intentions were eroded by his desperate yet futile attempts to obtain a passport, which he needed either to settle anywhere in Germany or to leave the country. Without papers, he was unable to accept employment and could be expelled, as an ex-con and danger to society, from any city or county at any time. (Documents submitted by the defense at the Köpenick trial showed that he was, in fact, deported no fewer than 30 times[16]). An intercession by the prison chaplain gained him employment with Court Shoemaker Hillbrecht[17] in Wismar, and a place at his family table. Hillbrecht later testified that Voigt conducted himself soberly, worked long hours, and proved trustworthy and honest even though he was placed in charge both of the cash till and of the master shoemaker's correspondence.[18] To all the world, Voigt in Wismar appeared exactly as he describes himself in his autobiography: a reformed elderly man, hard-working and penitent, industriously cobbling his way towards a quiet retirement. "This is when, suddenly and unexpected by all, my deportation order from Wismar arrived!"[19] The order, as he describes it, terminated his employment and ripped him from the bosom of a beloved second family; Hillbrecht later testified that Voigt, upon receiving the order, cried like a child.[20] All this "without offering any reason. [...] This was, essentially, the beginning of the Day of Köpenick!"[21]

Voigt's Coup

That day dawned on October 16, 1906, eight months after his release from prison and two months after his deportation from Wismar. Voigt rose early, scouted out the scene at Köpenick, returned to Berlin to have breakfast, requisitioned two separate guard troops off the street, and ordered them to follow him to Köpenick. He treated them first to beer and later to lunch. He did all this decked out in a uniform that was later variously described as "messy," "irregular," "not by the book." Voigt bridled at this disparagement of his perfect coup, insisting that his uniform had been "impeccable" and that indeed he had met a major at lunch who had accepted him as a captain without qualms.[22] Certainly, his freshly requisitioned troops never questioned his orders. Off they went to Köpenick, the false Captain in a second-class carriage, the troops in third class. Once arrived at around 2:45 p.m., Voigt posted guards at the city hall, allowing no one to enter or exit the building. He then proceeded, largely unopposed, with the arrests of the town's clerk Rosenkranz and its mayor, Dr. Langerhans, "on orders of His Imperial Majesty." Voigt ordered the city treasurer von Wiltberg to cash out and confiscated the entire treasury, writing von Wiltberg a receipt with an illegible name followed by a more decipherable "Captain of the First Guard Regiment." To avoid a forgery charge, which had previously netted him such long jail sentences, he later declared that he had told nothing but the truth on the receipt: his exact wording had been "from me, pretend–Captain in the First Guard Regiment" or, as he claimed on another occasion: "was never Captain in the First Guard Regiment." The court had the illegible signature deciphered as "v. Alassam, Captain of the First Guard Regiment" and booked him for both forgery and unauthorized assumption of authority.[23] In the end, Voigt made off with slightly more than 4,000 marks. As he calmly took the train back to Berlin, the soldiers and his arrestees were dispatched by coach to Berlin's main police station, where the non-plussed mayor and town clerk were finally informed that there was, in fact, no warrant for their arrest.

One thing is certain: Voigt enjoyed the masquerade hugely and took great pleasure in ordering everyone around. He executed his coup so perfectly that until he was unmasked as a lowly shoemaker at his arrest, numerous newspapers speculated that the perpetrator must have been an army officer.[24] The soldiers saw nothing amiss because he roared at them in exactly the same way that a true superior officer would have. From one soldier's court deposition: "The commands given by the accused were entirely military in style. If someone did not obey his orders, he yelled at them in a very brisk military tone of voice." And when anxious civil servants dared to peek out of their room, "the Captain barked at them: Back to your rooms, on the double, otherwise I'll have to use force!"[25] (As this and other passages in the court records show, the soldiers were so enthralled by Voigt's assumed authority that they insistently referred to him as the "Captain"—"der Herr Hauptmann"—even in court, where other appellations—"Herr Voigt," "the swindler," "the impostor" or, as they occasionally also called him, "the accused"—might have been more appropriate to the setting.) Neither did Police Inspector Jäckel see anything amiss. Awoken by the fake Captain from his afternoon nap, he was instructed to keep the peace in the town, but couldn't execute the order because Voigt's guards prevented him from leaving the building. Jäckel then begged leave to go home and take a bath, a request that Voigt, judging that Jäckel badly needed one, graciously granted.[26]

Whether the city mayor, Dr. Langerhans, saw something amiss was hotly disputed in court. Langerhans insisted that he suspected—based on Voigt's sloppy uniform—that he was dealing with either a prankster or a swindler; that he repeatedly asked Voigt for an arrest warrant or other legitimation and was harshly refused, and that he had only bowed to force since he could see that the soldiers were real even if the Captain wasn't and that they were willing to follow the Captain's orders to the letter.[27] Voigt, on the other hand, asserted that Langerhans had caused no trouble, even giving his word of honor as a reserve officer that he would not attempt escape (a detail that Langerhans confirmed in court). Voigt further related, with considerable glee, that Langerhans had most humbly begged his permission to speak with his wife, upon which he, Voigt, magnanimously sanctioned "undisturbed and unhindered contact" between husband and wife until Langerhans was carted off to Berlin.[28] In court, Voigt described his conduct as that of a "gentleman" and maintained that "no man could complain about him as a commanding officer."[29] Asked what he would have done in case of resistance, he told the court: "At the appropriate time, I would have acted as becoming an officer in such a situation!"[30] And he denied a witness account that at the Köpenick train station he had downed, very quickly, three glasses of beer: "That would have constituted conduct unbecoming an officer."[31] Clearly, Voigt not only played his part, he revelled in it, so much so that he ended up convincing not only others but also, to some degree, himself.

The fake Captain immediately became the subject of the largest manhunt Berlin had ever seen. Every senior police officer in Berlin's twelve districts was drafted to work on the case.[32] Rewards for his capture rose from 500 marks to 2,000—half of the Köpenick haul—and from there to 2,500 marks within days.[33] There were hundreds of Captain sightings, dozens of copycat Captains,[34] and dozens of erroneous arrests all over Germany.[35] Although Voigt practically gloried in his coup, loitering at advertising pillars where newspaper articles were posted about his coup and reading snippets out loud to bystanders, it took the police ten days to catch him. In the end, it was his former cellmate Kallenberg who gave him away, based on an incautious remark that Voigt had once made in his presence: "If you have a few soldiers, you can do good business."[36] Voigt, once again, recalls the scene quite differently: overhearing fellow prisoners hatching inept plans for a break-in, he claims to have told them: "You patsies, if I were to stoop to such things, I would simply get me some soldiers off the street!"[37] The difference is significant: one remark can be construed as indicating intent to commit a crime, the other cannot. There is good evidence, as this and other instances show, that Voigt was highly aware of his legal situation and crafty in his defense. In the end, though, the court, although clearly sympathetic, disbelieved the most central point of Voigt's defense: that he had not intended to rob the city at all, but staged the entire coup in search of a passport form that would have allowed him to settle and work, and that he had only accepted the money—after realizing that there were no passport forms to be had—because it was pressed upon him by the treasurer.[38] The court found him guilty of the unauthorized wearing of a uniform, the unauthorized assumption of authority, the unlawful detention of Langerhans, Rosenkranz and von Wiltberg, theft, and forgery (for putting a false name, "von Alassam," on the receipt he issued to von Wiltberg). For all this, he was awarded what must be regarded as a relatively mild sentence: four years in prison (significantly: not penitentiary). Extenuating circumstances recognized by the court included:

> the fact that the accused, after serving his last sentence, tried earnestly and—to the extent that this lay within his power—successfully to earn his living honestly, and was on track to become a useful member of society; that, however, these efforts were thwarted through no fault of his own, and that he was pushed back into a life of crime [...] For this reason, we recognize the presence of extenuating circumstances and decree for a prison rather than penitentiary sentence.[39]

Voigt, it seems, finally got a break in a court of law. That it could have been much, much worse is impressively argued in an article written by a criminalist who totted up Voigt's crimes and arrived at a potential prison sentence totaling 33 years; another newspaper article set his prospective penalty at a minimum of 20 years' imprisonment.[40] Later commentators confirm that Voigt, for once, got off easy: "The district court treated the accused with remarkable benevolence and clearly tried to curb his penalty."[41] As numerous newspapers reported, the presiding judge approached Voigt after pronouncing the sentence, wished him well and said in a low voice: "May God give you the strength to survive these four years!"[42] Understandably, this moving scene is somewhat embroidered in Voigt's autobiography:

> The presiding judge put down his beret, took off his gown, stepped down to the dock and wished God's blessing upon me, that I might survive my penalty in good health.
> I was so moved by this unexpected event that I could not even respond immediately. Once in prison, I wrote a letter to the presiding judge to apologize for my awkwardness, which had been caused by the commotion of the moment, and to thank him for his kindness, the deeper meaning of which I do appreciate.
> It was a sign of how difficult it must have been for the court to pass this sentence against me.[43]

Voigt's notion that the court would have preferred to let him off altogether is one with which most of his contemporaries would have agreed. Calls for his release abounded in the press, both before and after his arrest. Private citizens collected money for him or promised him employment or lifelong stipends upon his release. Some even proposed that he should be allowed to keep the loot: a small price to pay, the argument went, for providing the world with so much merriment.[44]

Voigt as Big Business

Merriment there certainly was. Voigt's coup became the biggest joke of the year—and big business. Even before Voigt's arrest, the coup spawned an entire cottage industry: comedians cracked puns; poets wrote witty couplets; cartoonists worked overtime. Satirical postcards commemorating the affair were quickly printed and sold like hotcakes at every street corner in Berlin[45]; literally hundreds of them were sent, certainly with malice aforethought, to the Köpenick city hall.[46] One of these—to cite just one example of the apparently endless stream of humorous creativity unleashed in the wake of Köpenick—showed Voigt's mugshot, in civilian clothes and in uniform with and without cap. The legend read: "Greetings from Voigt, Robber-Captain, now retired, earlier

Gruss vom Räuber-Hauptmann a. D.

Commemorative postcard from the "Robber-Captain, now retired," giving his current address as "Cell no. 15" (Reprinted in *Denkwürdigkeiten* [1906], 69).

from Köpenick, now residing in Cell no. 15."[47] A fake Imperial Decree, ordering all mayors in Germany to Berlin for closer study of a real Captain's uniform, made the rounds for days.[48]

Mere days after the coup, a comedy portraying a bunch of soldiers yelling "Yes, Sir!" to whatever absurd commands their Captain issued was staged at the Metropol Theatre in Berlin. On October 30, another comedy, *The Cobbler of Köpenick*, was performed to huge acclaim in Vienna, with the Captain being portrayed by Annie Calice, an actress known for her roles in humorous operettas, in a so-called "breeches role."[49] A third "sensational" play about the affair, to be performed in Dresden, was banned at the last minute because the police considered it an "endangerment to public order."[50] A longer literary work, "The Robber Captain of Köpenick, or, The Maltreated Mayor" was printed so quickly that the newspaper announcing its publication, a mere three days after the coup, did not have time to find out whether it was a play or a novel.[51] Hans Hyan, a well-known court reporter, teamed up with caricaturist Paul Haase to produce *The Captain of Köpenick: A Horrid and Torrid Tale of the Dim Wit of Obedient Subjects*, a work that lampooned unthinking obedience in cartoons and rhymes.[52] On October 28, the *Berliner Volks-Zeitung* complained that the realm of fiction was being swamped by Captain stories, including three novels at the time of writing, 12 days after the coup.[53] A Captain movie, the first of many, was announced two days earlier, coinciding, as it happened, with the day of Voigt's arrest.[54]

Even the nation's intelligentsia got in on the joke. While the easily amused watched the soldiers lockstep across the Metropol stage and the blue-collar crowds exchanged droll postcards at the pub, the erudite quoted Schiller's 1804 drama *William Tell*, whose archvillain, the Viceroy (in German: the *Vogt*), anticipated the modern Voigt by ravaging the land "on orders of His Imperial Majesty,"[55] or compared the Captain of Köpenick with the Captain of Capernaum, whose faith in Jesus saved the life of his sick subordinate[56]: "What was it that saved the Captain of Capernaum?—His faith. What was it that saved the Captain of Köpenick?—The faith of Herr Langerhans."[57] The *Frankfurter Zeitung* even brought an opinion piece in which a reader "well-versed in the Bible" provided proof positive that the (at the time of writing not-yet arrested) Captain of Köpenick was identical with the Captain of Capernaum:

> Finally the identity of the Captain of Köpenick has been discovered, although not by the Berlin police. Witness the Bible, where you read in Matthew 8:9: The Captain said to the Mayor: "For I have soldiers under me; and I say to this one, 'Go!' and he goes, and to another, 'Come!' and he comes, and to the third, 'Do this!' and he does it." Matthew 8:10: The Captain (to himself): "Verily, I have never yet found such great faith!"[58]

For the less spiritually inclined, there was Captain merchandise, which quickly expanded beyond postcards. Captain statuettes could be purchased from the Magdeburg manufacturer Gustav Köhler,[59] and a mere three days after the coup, Johann Bahr had already begun to market a "Captain of Köpenick" board game featuring a little tin Captain, 12 tin soldiers, and individual character-cards that described, in Wilhelm Busch–style, each character involved in the affair in cartoons and droll rhymes. Designed as a competitive boys' game that pitted the Mayor and the Treasurer against the Captain and his soldiers, it tended to end in a brawl because, as one newspaper reported, naturally "everyone wants to be the 'Captain.' The position of Mayor is in less demand!"[60]

Business boomed. Four days after the coup, on October 20, the *Berliner Tageblatt* estimated that the postcards and *The Maltreated Mayor* edition of *Lustige Blätter* alone had raked in at least 60,000 marks, fifteen times the amount with which the false Captain had absconded.[61] An enterprising manager pleaded with the Berlin police for permission to exhibit Voigt, offering, in addition to paying the police guards' salaries, the gigantic fee of 150,000 marks for the privilege.[62] The police declined the offer, but Voigt himself revived it, in his own way, after his release in 1908. He spent much of the rest of his life on an international "Captain of Köpenick" tour, exhibiting himself for money to his adoring public and selling postcards of himself and his autograph. Although the newspapers had, at that point, tired of him, the public never did. The Captain had become ubiquitous, inescapable, part of Germany's DNA. As one contemporary put it,

> unfortunately, you can't escape the Köpenick Captain anywhere. Not in the theatres, where comics have added a verse to the song every day since the Day of Köpenick. In brief, the old shabby Captain not only had the triumph of keeping Köpenick for an hour in a state of siege with His Majesty's grenadiers, he has also conquered Berlin itself. He will surely be honored with a statue in the *Tiergarten*.[63]

Voigt as Comedy

Why Voigt captured the imagination of his contemporaries to such a degree is perhaps easier to understand than why the joke has endured for so long: as the regular revival of the Köpenick Coup in film and fiction shows, Germans have been laughing

Double-sided ad for "The Robber Captain of Köpenick and the Purloined Mayor," board-
game (October 19, 1906) (Reprinted in *Denkwürdigkeiten* 95–6).

at it for well over 100 years now.[64] Part of the answer may be that Voigt was far more
than just a good joke; he was great comedy. In fact, he was the textbook exemplar of
Comedy as defined, a mere year before Köpenick, in Sigmund Freud's seminal *The Joke
and Its Relation to the Unconscious* (*Der Witz und seine Beziehung zum Unbewußten*,
1905). Comedy, Freud claimed, is distinct from jokes (or—as we might also translate
his titular *Witz*—distinct from "wit") because comedy is characterized by what he terms
"a diminished expediture of the imagination," as opposed to the "diminished expenditure
of inhibition" that characterizes the joke and the "diminished expenditure of feeling"
that characterizes humor.[65] Laughter in all three cases arises from the crucial dis-
similarity between producer and recipient, a discrepancy in terms of inhibition (jokes),
feeling (humor) or imagination (comedy). In the case of comedy, the disparity in imagination translates into a disappointment of expectations: in comedy, Freud claims, "the
definition of funny is an expectation that has come to nothing."[66]

This is precisely how the press portrayed Voigt. Voigt was not a great comic merely
because he was an impostor, even an imaginative one (as Erich Wulffen, one of the era's
most popular criminalists, wrote in his book *The Psychology of the Impostor*: "A successful impostor without imagination is impossible"[67]). Voigt was a great comic because,
in exercising his own imagination, he played upon the imagination of others (rather
than their inhibitions or feelings). By establishing a disparity between his imagination
and theirs, he created an expectation that came to nothing. The sheer audacity of the
coup naturally raised audience expectations of the impostor as portrayed in contem-

porary lore[68]: a former officer, perhaps (as surmised by the press and numerous witnesses who spoke to him on the day); certainly a dashing sophisticate, elegant and erudite, endowed with charisma and natural authority, conversant with the world into which he was inveigling himself and thus well able to impersonate one of its characters. That is the Impostor familiar from earlier cases, the Impostor as described in works by expert criminologists, the Impostor the audience expected. Instead, they got a grubby flat-nosed bow-legged bum with a bent back, cracked hands and rheumey eyes.

Once Voigt was arrested, the most overused word to describe him in the press was "disappointing."[69] But that disappointment was, as Freud had argued and as the papers also quickly realized, precisely what was so funny about the whole thing. "The scrubbier, the more drab and squalid this shoemaker appears, the more biting the satire and the more beautiful his deed. Wilhelm Voigt looks like a true cobbler, like meat rationing personified. And this is precisely what makes the satire perfect."[70] Or, as another commentator exulted: "That the city of Köpenick was not conquered by a gentleman, by an ex-officer or an impostor familiar with higher administration, but by a run-down tramp—that is the punch line of this splendid satire, and that is what should make us enjoy it all the more."[71]

Some gleefully pointed out that in Imperial Prussia, you couldn't go anywhere without having served in the army, certainly not into the civil service, which meant that everyone involved in the coup, from the soldiers Voigt commandeered to the civil servants he arrested, had extensive military experience—except, of course, Voigt himself.[72] While some commentators were scratching their heads to figure out how on earth "this cadaverous jaundiced face with its hollow cheeks and ugly crooked nose could strike fear into all of Köpenick, how these debauchery-reddened eyes could intimidate such courageous and self-confident civil servants,"[73] others hit upon the answer rather quickly: of course it wasn't him at all, it was the uniform. Voigt himself was nothing; the uniform everything. Had Voigt been the elegant impersonator everyone expected, there would have been confusion on this most central point. But because he wasn't, because he disappointed the universal expectation of who should and shouldn't be wearing an officer's uniform, Voigt was able to show up the actual joke: that Germans from all walks of life and with all levels of education and experience bowed and scraped before a uniform, and never mind its stuffing.

Accordingly, the press elevated the uniform to the status of a character, Voigt's co-star in the courtroom comedy that now unfolded. More often than not, the "triumph" of Köpenick was credited not to Voigt, but to his uniform,[74] and the capture of the "victorious uniform"[75] became almost as big an item in the press as that of Voigt himself. In the days leading up to Voigt's arrest, the papers fed the public a steady diet of interim reports on whatever bits and pieces of his uniform had been tracked down that day, always adding gleefully that the contents of the uniform were still at large.[76]

The uniform was also the source of considerable amusement when it had its day in court. Stripped of it, Voigt was a disappointment (indeed, some witnesses who had encountered him on the day of the coup could not recognize him without the uniform; Voigt had to have his mugshot retaken in uniform to be positively identified[77]). But the public attending his trial got its money's worth when the witnesses were called and

Wie der „Hauptmann" vor seiner
festnahme dargestellt wurde.

I.

„Lustige Blätter."

Wie der „Hauptmann"
vor seiner festnahme
dargestellt wurde.

II.

„Jugend."

Wie der „Hauptmann"
vor seiner festnahme
dargestellt wurde.

III.

„Kladderadatsch."

„Gott Uniform."

Preussische Disziplin I.

Scraping to an empty uniform. *(Left):* **"God Uniform,"** *Königsberger Illustrierte Zeitung;* *(right):* **"Prussian Discipline,"** *Ulk* **(reprinted in** *Denkwürdigkeiten* **29 and 44, respectively).**

> *seven brave soldiers in full uniform* marched, strapping and burly, into the courtroom. The Seven wore helmets on their heads, satchels and rolled-up military coats on their backs, and carried rifles in their nervy right hands. The window panes shook in their frames. Half of the audience strained in their seats. Wilhelm Voigt gazed with sorrowful envy upon the Seven who were permitted to appear in the splendor of the uniform, and the presiding judge, undeterred, continued to call the names of the witnesses. Each of the brave soldiers responded loudly and clearly with a snappy "Present!" And one Private roared his reply as if he meant to call out the guard at the Brandenburg Gate.[78]

The journalist to whom we owe this entertaining description was not alone in finding this funny: by all accounts, the public laughed so hard at this display of military might that the judge had trouble restoring order in the court.[79]

Comedy in Freud's sense could be had in spades at Voigt's trial, and Voigt himself became the darling of the nation by contributing to its amusement. Sometimes he simply cracked jokes: when asked by the investigating police inspector whether he had served (in the army), he responded: "Yes, 25 years in the pen."[80] But mostly, he entertained his adoring audience not with jokes but with comedy, by resorting to—in Freud's words—disparities of the imagination. Reduced to civilian clothes and looking to all the world like the down-and-out nobody that he was, he nevertheless continued to play the Captain. The press records of his interrogation in court and audience responses yield many passages, in addition to those already cited, in which Voigt mused on the

Opposite: **"Wilhelm Voigt looks like a true cobbler": Various contemporary "imaginations" of the Captain before Voigt's arrest (reprinted in** *Denkwürdigkeiten* **3 [***Lustige Blätter***], 5 [***Jugend***], 7 [***Kladderadatsch***], 65 [***Dresdener Rundschau***]).**

conduct becoming or unbecoming an officer, casually mentioned his jovial comportment towards his "inferiors," or told tall tales of the unquestioning obedience he inspired.[81]

Self-adulation it may have been, but much of it was confirmed by other witnesses. Mayor Langerhans, who became the butt of the national joke for allowing himself to be arrested by a fraudster, testified that when he asked Voigt politely to produce the arrest warrant, Voigt roared back: "'You don't have any demands to make! Any resistance from you and I'll stick you in the hole!' (Hilarity)."[82] Yet Voigt, rising to the mayor's defense, told Police Inspector Wehn that Langerhans actually did not deserve all that ridicule: "If Herr Wehn had come across him in the Köpenick City Hall, he *would have treated him in exactly the same manner*. Under no circumstances would he have entered into any dispute with him; if necessary, he would have ordered '*his soldiers*' to use their *weapons*."[83] At his trial, when asked what exactly he said to the town clerk Dr. Rosenkranz to convince him that he was arrested, Voigt thundered:

> "*By order of His Majesty, you are under arrest!*" This, he claims, he uttered in a non-threatening manner.—Judge: But previous to that, you spoke with considerable emphasis?—Accused: But that is the nature of the beast! (Hilarity.) Dr. Rosenkranz declared himself astounded and wanted to know the reason for his arrest. Well, I could hardly enlighten him. (Hilarity.)[84]

As many papers pointed out, the worse Voigt's disguise, the better the joke. Perhaps this is one reason why so many witnesses who had not questioned Voigt's authority on the day itself claimed afterwards that they had actually harbored serious doubts. Innkeeper Augustin, who served Voigt breakfast before the coup, testified, probably with the benefit of hindsight, that the "Captain" had looked as if he had come straight from the penitentiary.[85] One of the soldiers commandeered by Voigt, beset by doubts, kept looking out of the train window to see if the Captain got off without them (an admission that was greeted by the usual hilarity on the part of the audience), but added that he had worried about being made the victim of a prank rather than an accessory to a robbery.[86] But all doubts were dispelled when they got to Köpenick and observed how smartly the bureaucrats at the city hall clacked their heels at the Captain's barked orders. It was this behavior, perhaps more than the Captain in his shabby uniform, that convinced the soldiers that he was legitimate and that he had taken them to Köpenick on an important mission. Conversely, the civil servants only snapped to attention because the dubious Captain arrived with soldiers who were both indubitably authentic and willing to obey his orders to the letter. By himself and as himself, the Captain had no authority at all, but each group of his stooges legitimized him to the other.[87]

Voigt as an Indictment

The joke, in other words, had a butt, but even when he was in the dock, it wasn't the Captain. Other great impostors of the day excited public admiration, revulsion or sympathy, but usually public attention remained firmly focused on the case or the impostor as such and did not implicate society at large. The Köpenick affair did, because it needed two significant societal ingredients to occur at all: a penal system that made the rehabilitation of "habitual" criminals virtually impossible, and the rigid absolutism of the Wilhelminian age that expressed itself in the universal genuflection to the uniform. "Don a uniform in Prussian Germany, and you are the Almighty," declared one paper.[88] "Before the uniform, all crawl on their bellies," elaborated another, "the entire so-called 'society,' civil servants from ministers on down to the last night watchman, the bourgeoisie and the common folk. Anyone in uniform will conquer all, not because he is smarter or wiser than others but because he is in uniform."[89] The papers quickly designed an expressive (and, alas, intranslatable) term for this behavior: *Kadavergehorsam* (literally: "cadaver obedience"), a term that in its critical connotations and profound sarcasm goes well beyond "blind obedience" and that we might render as *doormatism.*

Both doormatism and the penal system, particularly the provision of placing "habitual" criminals under police surveillance after their release, attracted a good deal of criticism in the press. Even the Biblical Cain, the press lamented, was allowed to flee to foreign lands, whereas Voigt was allowed neither to stay nor to leave.[90] Heart-rending descriptions of Voigt as "a poor, miserable sod, hunted by the police and mistreated by the judiciary, trampled down whenever he tried to rise from the dust, systematically deprived of his human rights and his human dignity"[91] were quickly followed by calls for reform of the entire justice system: "This is where the Voigt case stops being an individual case and turns into an indictment of our entire judiciary and police system. We hope that the *Reichstag* and the Prussian House of Representatives will acknowledge this in the manner that it deserves."[92] The *Berliner Tageblatt* excoriated the "destructive effects of a still barbaric judiciary," adding that it was not so much Voigt in the dock as "the practice of police deportations"[93]; the *Berliner Volks-Zeitung* called directly for the abolition of police surveillance of former inmates.[94]

Paul Lindau's article "The Guilty One" ("Der Schuldige") is probably the era's most moving tribute to Voigt. Lindau portrays Voigt as a hunted, exhausted old man who was given no chance to rest or repent. To this, Lindau adds a passionate *J'accuse!*: "Not Wilhelm Voigt, our society belongs in the dock, indicted for its pitiless incitement of his crime!"[95] Lindau ended his piece with the well-known Aelianus fable of the wolf who, growing too old to hunt, tries to make peace with the shepherds: he promises to leave their flocks alone in exchange for being fed until his death. The shepherds chase him away, and the enraged wolf savages their herds before they finally succeed in killing him. "Then spoke the wisest of the shepherds: 'We were wrong to drive the old robber to the utmost and deprive him of the chance to reform, no matter how belated or forced by circumstance.'" Addressing himself to the judiciary, Lindau concludes: "Who among you will have the courage to admit, with Aelianus' wisest shepherd, that *we* drove the old robber 'to the utmost,' and that we would do well to begin our rehabilitation of released prisoners by improving our institutions and eliminating the cruel treatment of released inmates?"[96]

Like the penal system, Prussian militarism and resulting doormatism, while providing the press and the public with an extravagant abundance of mirth, also came in for its share of severe criticism. "Only the absolutist milieu in Prussia made this embarrassment possible," the *Berliner Tageblatt* avowed.[97] The *Berliner Volks-Zeitung* stated baldly that "blind obedience—*Kadavergehorsam*—[...] rules the army; it alone led to the *Uniform's* glorious victory over Reason."[98] The *Dresdener Gerichtszeitung* considered the "worship of the holy Uniform" the most dangerous phenomenon in Imperial Ger-

"Who is really the guilty one?" **Contemporary postcard, showing "The Ex-Captain in Moabit Prison" (left) and "Shoemaker Voigt in Wismar" (right), with the caption above reading "Police Surveillance!" and the hand-printed sign "Deportation Order" (reprinted in** *Denkwürdigkeiten* **33).**

many.[99] The *Wiener Arbeiterzeitung* castigated Prussia's military culture for "decimating, to the last little trace, any sense of civic self-worth and civic pride in vast swathes of the citizenry."[100] Colonel Gädke wrote an article that depicted in garish colors the horrors visited upon soldiers found guilty of insubordination,[101] and numerous newspapers ran articles on how the military generated unthinking obedience, telling appalling stories of hideous levels of physical abuse and personal humiliation regularly inflicted by officers on their subordinates.[102] And the town of Köpenick, after some deliberation, begged Mayor Langerhans, who had resigned in shame, to rescind his resignation, adding that they were disinclined to blame him for the debacle: "After careful consideration we have come to the conviction that the *excesses of militarism* are to blame for the mishap that has befallen our community."[103]

Köpenick, then, became not only a national joke, but also a discussion starter. It prompted, perhaps for the first time in an Imperial Germany still drunk on the success of the 1870 campaign and its recently achieved national unity, a certain level of introspection as to what kind of nation it wanted to be and how it appeared to others (both to German States outside of Prussia and to nations beyond the borders of Germany). Individual voices called for a major rethink of an absolutism reliant on military power and on the removal of undesirables from society. The practice of monitoring and deporting former inmates was earnestly debated in Parliament on February 19, 1907, with explicit reference to the Voigt case. Representatives cited expert testimony showing that the procedure proved both psychologically devastating and economically detrimental to former prisoners; others pointed out that the practice was applied unevenly across the German States. Who knows what might have happened had not Dr. von Bethmann-Hollweg, Minister of the Interior, nipped any chance at legal reform in the bud:

> Gentlemen: the criticism as expressed in the press following the case of the so-called Captain of Köpenick has, in my opinion, vastly overshot the mark.
> (Calls of "Quite right!" from the right.)
> The Captain of Köpenick is being celebrated like some kind of hero.
> (Hilarity.)
> The success of his coup did, after all, initially prompt a certain amount of sympathy with such a dashing fellow;
> (Hilarity.)
> but the conclusions drawn in the press in connection with this case as they relate to the practice of deportations go, in my opinion, too far. Perhaps I will be accused of a certain amount of cruelty, but to me the first consideration that must guide both the police and the judiciary must be to safeguard society from anti-social elements.
> ("Quite right!" from the right.)[104]

Debate there was, and introspection there was, but in the end, neither had anywhere to go. Blind obedience can be compelled by orders, but Reason, mental independence, and civic pride cannot. The State responded to a problem that had arisen because of blind obedience to orders by issuing more orders. If any shabby old bum with the gumption to snarl "On orders of His Majesty!" and to wave a piece of paper that vaguely looked like a Cabinet Order could arrest senior civil servants and make off with city treasuries, there was, the Emperor recognized, a flaw in the system. In response, demonstrating a characteristic inability to change his spots, the Emperor tried to solve the problem of the fake Cabinet order with a real one. "As recently announced, the Emperor, who had requested a detailed report on the deeds of the splendid Captain, intends to issue a Cabinet Order at the next Imperial Rescript of Recruits which will make events like those of Köpenick impossible."[105] On orders of His Majesty, the problem of *Kadavergehorsam* was now solved.

Voigt as a Folk Hero: The Press v. the Public

In the absence of an actual solution—which would have entailed a reconsideration of national priorities—Imperial Germans resorted to laughter. We don't know how close Parliament came to enacting penal reform in the wake of the Köpenick case, but we do know that they were not above appreciating its funny side. The Parliamentary Edition of the *Berliner Volks-Zeitung* cited a debate during which one Representative, when jesting that the re-election of a controversial colleague would necessitate an armed escort, was told, "We can't commandeer any; after all, we are not the Captain of Köpenick! (Excessive hilarity)."[106] But while the State could do no more than to issue fresh orders and, in some moments of condescension, join in the laughter at its own expense, that laughter sounded different coming from below. Voigt was Comedy, not merely a joke, and he was also more than a pitiable unfortunate hunted by a merciless justice system. He not only provoked people's laughter and pity, he stirred their gratitude. "Berlin, the whole world, has long not laughed so heartily. And humanity owes a debt of gratitude to every bringer of joy."[107] Voigt became the glue that united the multitudes: "It was a spectacle worthy of the Gods, this unity of an explosive and untamed hilarity!"[108] Voigt became a beacon of hope. "I ask you: can there still be a pessimist on German soil after this priceless joke tickled millions of German funny-bones? If you can laugh, you look at the world through rose-tinted glasses, and we owe this rosy perspective to him alone."[109] Voigt caused a sea-change in public behavior, in community feeling and interaction among ordinary Germans:

> In the trams, in the bars, in the theaters: wherever Germans now assemble they no longer found associations, they no longer give three cheers. Instead they grin at each other without saying a word. There is a telegraphing from brain to brain the likes of which we have not seen since time out of mind. Each believes of the other that he is thinking of Köpenick, that he cannot but be thinking of Köpenick.[110]

In the end, it is this that became the dominant narrative of Wilhelm Voigt, banishing others—for example, that of the broken old man advanced by his legal defense team[111]—to the shadows. The press and the public would have none of that: a man with one foot in the grave does not make a good folk hero. Voigt became, discursively at least, a slightly grubbier Robin Hood, a con not out to fleece individuals but to stick it to the State. Contemporary reporting turned him from an old crook into a brilliant con. "A crook is someone with a base disposition, and Wilhelm Voigt's deeds do not show a trace of it [...]. A scoundrel who steals 50 pfennigs from a poor woman seems much more vile and contemptible to us than a false Captain who cheats a city treasury out of a few thousand marks."[112]

But Voigt's appeal to the masses, while perhaps inaugurated in press reporting, did not end there. Once Voigt had been released from prison, he began his victory tour, exhibiting himself for money, offering fireside chats at inns, and conducting a riproaring trade, much of it without a license, with autographed Captain postcards. The press that had elevated his coup to the point of heroism in 1906 now fell all over itself to castigate the Voigt Cult:

> Have you all gone insane? [...] The man is in danger of becoming the national Saint of Little Germany. [...] First he is turned into the hero of the sensational press, which celebrates him in word and image, in rhymed and non-rhymed pathos, and nearly expires in humility when in the presence of his illustrious personality. Every aspect of his demeanor is added to the Daily Annals as the expression of a never-intuited greatness of his soul; all of his actions—when he leaves the house and where he goes, where and how he eats, how he sleeps, speaks, weeps and laughs—are recorded and reported faithfully...[113]

The *Berliner Allgemeine Zeitung* went so far as to say that Voigt's earlier modest demeanor and his hard-luck stories, including his many deportations and his vain attempts to gain identity papers, had been a sham to trick the courts into a clemency of which he was undeserving; his true character, they fumed, was the "old professional criminal's shamelessness" with which he "bragged about his robbery in Köpenick."[114] What stuck most in the press corps's collective craw was that Voigt was a huge success, and they never tired of rebuking him for his greed and tastelessness:

> Foolish curiosity is now celebrating veritable orgies. Barely arrived at the train station on Friday, he was received by a multitude, particularly by amateur photographers. There he sat, surrounded by a thick throng, eating and drinking and merrily conversing until dawn. "You have to strike the

iron while it's hot," he smirked, signing countless postcards with "Wilhelm Voigt, a.k.a. the Captain of Köpenick," of course only if paid an "author's royalty": 10 pfennigs per line.[115]

Clearly, the press vastly preferred Voigt, the ageing penitent shoemaker who might have lived out his life stitching shoes and accepting alms, to Voigt the celebrity, the cobbler who had grown too big for his britches. "Cobbler, stick to your trade," as a German proverb has it. Voigt had the temerity to refuse, opting instead to live out his life as an impostor. The press savaged him for it; the public adored him for it. In New York, as the *Berliner Morgenpost* reported furiously, the Captain held court in the Café Bismarck, selling postcards of himself in uniform for twice the price as postcards showing him in civilian clothes. "The owner of the café," the article fumed,

> had the effrontery to order the band to play German national songs in honor of the Captain of Köpenick, like "The Watch on the Rhine." Even worse were the guests. They practically fell all over themselves to get near the "Captain of Köpenick." He was treated at every table, and his postcards sold like hotcakes.[116]

In 1906, there had been a harmony of narratives between the press and the public. Voigt morphed from the genius impostor before his arrest to the poor old shmuck afterwards, until eventually both the press and the public settled on the narrative of Voigt as a folk hero who had valiantly and hilariously pitted his wits against a harsh and unyielding State. But after Voigt's release, from 1908 onward, the press and the public parted narrative ways. The papers insisted that Voigt return to his trade, his poverty and his obscurity. The public, however, refused to let go of its hero, just as Voigt himself refused to relinquish his role as the Captain. Press reporting of Voigt's exploits after 1908 may well be one of the best examples in German history of the papers misjudging the public mood. The new press narrative deprived Voigt of any meaning beyond himself that they had so readily accorded him in 1906. No longer was he a symbol of suffering, no longer a specific case that could give rise to more general and far-reaching reflections on police cruelty, injustice, militarism, or the subordination of civic prerogatives to blind obedience.

The press reduced him to a mere individual who had responded to clemency with greed and arrogance rather than the meekness and gratitude one had every right to expect. For the public, however, it was precisely this sassiness that kept their folk hero alive, and that also reminded them of Voigt's meaning beyond himself: to show that the authority structures we respect the most also tend to be the most predictable and the least flexible, and that they break all the more easily for refusing to bend. And so people kept grinning at each other without saying a word, knowing exactly what the person opposite was thinking of. They kept falling all over themselves to get near their Captain, paying good money for a chance to hear the famous tale straight from the horse's mouth and to walk off with his autograph. And why not? Conning, in any event, may well be the little man's most popular crime, for what little man does not dream of being a big man? Few act on the impulse, however. Voigt did, and in so doing demonstrated that a regime with an exceptional degree of self-importance also runs an exceptional risk of becoming a laughing-stock.

A Conwoman Nabs a Captain:
The Case of Tamara von Hervay
(Leoben, Austria, 1904)

Why Tamara von Hervay, a.k.a. The Black Baroness, ever became an "international sensation," as a recent account of her trial has correctly stated,[1] is not entirely clear. In the sisterhood of conwomen, which includes such illustrious names as "Big" Bertha Heyman (a.k.a. The Confidence Queen), Cassie Chadwick (a.k.a. The Lost Carnegie), and Sarah Rachel Russell (a.k.a. The Beautician from Hell), she appears rather humdrum. She was a woman of many names[2] and many husbands who told tall tales about her past, was sentenced for a petty crime, and ended by penning a tasteless, vindictive and badly written memoir on what she called her "martyrdom" in a disgraceful justice system. None of the primary sources we have left about her—the extensive press reporting on her case in dozens of newspapers; two contemporary novels; three essays by Karl Kraus, and said memoirs—portray her as either particularly funny, particularly clever, or particularly fascinating. Yet she apparently captivated men to such a degree that various witnesses attributed demonic powers to her, and Franz Preitler, the author of the most recent novel about her, told me that "she has transfixed me as much as she did her husbands."[3] Her allure seems as perplexing as her notoriety. Why should a bigamy trial in a small mining community ever have made it out of the local papers, let alone become one of Austria's most notorious trials and a *cause célèbre* causing bitter battles in rivalling newspapers across the country? Could it really merely be, as Alison Rose halfheartedly suggests, that "Frau von Hervay's Jewish background and her failure to behave according to accepted gender norms helped to fuel the controversy"?[4]

Fairy Tales: The Beginnings

On October 31, 1904, Tamara von Hervay was sentenced to four months in prison on charges of bigamy and false registration. Alison Rose, the most recent scholar to have written about the case, describes the counts of her indictment as "two minor legal matters—namely, that her previous marriage was not dissolved until shortly after her marriage to the district captain and that she had entered a false date for her birth year on her arrival and registration in Mürzzuschlag."[5] Rose's point that "these were relatively small, technical infractions"[6] can certainly be conceded regarding the false registration:

rather bizarrely, Hervay was formally charged with lying about her age by making herself 17 years younger when she registered at the hotel. She confessed to this non-crime in court, explaining the false registration somewhat incoherently as "a vanity, but not a lie."[7] The charge of bigamy, however, can hardly be dismissed as either a "minor legal matter" or a "small, technical infraction"; it was considered a serious crime in all Western nations and tended to attract harsher sentences in Catholic countries like Austria, where it could be punished with jail sentences of several years.[8] In fairness to Hervay, however, it has to be said that neither the court nor the public (nor, for that matter, some of the journalists covering the case) were inclined to give her a break. Context played a far greater part at her trial than substance; it was tinted by tragedy—the suicide of her fifth husband, Franz von Hervay, days after her arrest—and a sensationalism that ferreted out irrelevant facts about Hervay's past and mercilessly judged them in light of her fabrications.

Tamara von Hervay was born Elvira Leontine Bellachini on July 18, 1860, in Posen, the daughter of the Jewish conjurer Samuel Bellach, who adopted "Bellachini" as a stage name, and Helene Krüger. At the age of 16, she worked as a chorus girl at the Victoria Theater in Berlin. On November 22, 1880, she converted to Protestantism, although she denied both her parents and her Jewish ancestry all her life, claiming that she had been born a Christian and the child of aristocratic parents. Previous to her Mürzzuschlag marriage, she had been married four times: to the wine merchant Wilhelm Kuntz (married in Berlin on May 29, 1881; divorced at his request in February 1887), to the German military officer Karl von Lützow (married in Helgoland on April 24, 1888; divorced at his request on May 5, 1894); to First Lieutenant Ernst Artur von Schewe (married in Naples on January 29, 1895; divorced March 29, 1900), and finally to the squire and landowner Leo Meurin (married in London on June 7, 1900; divorced at his request on November 11, 1903). Her marriage to Franz Hervay von Kirchberg, District Captain of Mürzzuschlag, took place three months before her final divorce was granted, on August 9, 1903.[9]

Hervay arrived in Mürzzuschlag, a small resort town in Styria, on May 15, 1903, checking into a hotel as Tamara Baroness Lützow from Nice, born in July 1877, and accompanied by a Lieutenant Bartl whom she variously introduced as her cousin, brother, chamberlain or fiancé, but who was widely suspected of being her lover. Bedecked in magnificent gowns and jewelry, she represented herself as a noblewoman and the heiress to millions, the illegitimate daughter of a Russian princess and a German Count who was banned to Siberia because the royal family objected to his love affair with the Princess.[10] Both these stories and her account of how she met Franz von Hervay bear unmistakable traits of a fairy tale. As she told the story in court and later in her memoirs, she met Franz von Hervay while lost in the woods. Within minutes of finding her there, an instantly besotted Franz told Tamara that his family was about to force him into a marriage for money to an unloved girl and that he would rather kill himself than marry her. Within the hour, Franz ardently and tearfully embraced Tamara on a bench, begging her to marry him.[11] Within days, they were engaged. The official engagement ceremony took place precisely two months after her arrival, followed by the wedding three weeks after that, both over his family's ardent objections. Their marital life is rapturously described by Tamara as an ecstasy of bliss, the quintessence of a fairy tale. She may well have seen her entire life in these terms: in her 1905 memoirs, she announces her plan to write the story of her life in the form of a fairy tale entitled "How Suffering Walks the Earth."[12] Indeed, "fairy tale" ("Märchen," short for "Mara"/"Tamara"/ "Maria") was, as she never tired of pointing out, her husband's affectionate moniker for her.

Fairy Tales: Unhappy Endings

Then disaster struck in the form of another fairy tale. On April 30, 1904, the *Mürz-zuschlag Weekly* ran a feuilleton article entitled "An Ancient Fairy Tale" and signed by "I. Durchschaudi" ("I. Seethroughyou"). The fairy tale tells the story of a king seduced by a old witch who rides in on a broomstick and transforms herself into a beautiful young princess, fooling the king into dragging her out of the swamp in which she lives. Although the article did not mention her by name, it was clearly aimed at Tamara von Hervay, raising questions about her background and her age and claiming, among other things, that she was still married to a previous husband.[13] This opened the floodgates; from June 17 onward, she was constantly in the press. The Hervay family began an investigation into her past; the scandal grew; Franz von Hervay was asked to surrender his position and placed on extended administrative leave. On June 21, 1904, Tamara von Hervay was arrested on charges of fraud and bigamy and transferred to Leoben, the setting for the trial. On June 24, Franz von Hervay shot himself in the heart. On June 27, the *Grazer Volksblatt* ran the reprint of an extremely damning interview with Tamara's fourth husband, Leo Meurin, which had originally appeared in the *Leipziger Nachrichten*. Meurin names her as "Erni Leontini Elvira, daughter of the deceased magician *Bellachini*, whose real name

"Franzl" and "Märchen" on their wedding day (courtesy Franz Preitler/Wintersportmuseum Mürzzuschlag).

was *Bellach*," and details the reasons for her divorces as her marital infidelity in the first three cases and fraud in the fourth. He further claims that she was officially engaged to be married to someone else while still married to him, that she variously adopted her previous husbands' names for the purpose of conning others, that she had swindled a gentleman in Nice out of 5000 marks, that her "speciality" as a confidence trickster was divorcing wealthy men, and that while married to him she had spent four weeks in pretrial custody for fraud.[14]

The subject of all these revelations spent the next four months in a prison cell in Leoben, in the Stephanie Hospital in the same town (for a number of ailments that doctors described variously as both real and simulated), and in a mental hospital in Graz for an investigation of her mental state, while the court busied itself with the pretrial investigation of her earlier life, previous marriages, and career as a "marriage swindler." By the time her trial opened on October 29, 1904, the public—and certainly also the court—was well primed for it by a multitude of scandal stories detailing the love life and lies of this "curiously artful adventuress of 44 years who had gained by trickery the confidence and love of the 32-year-old man in the bloom of his beauty."[15]

An "artful adventuress of 44 years" and a "32-year-old man in the bloom of his beauty": Tamara von Hervay (March 1904) and Franz von Hervay (1903–4) (courtesy Franz Preitler/Wintersportmuseum Mürzzuschlag).

Guilt v. Innocence: Trivial Questions to the Court

Quite possibly the least interesting question about this trial is whether Hervay was, in fact, guilty. On this, recent scholars have given her the benefit of the doubt to a far greater degree than her contemporaries did, arguing that Hervay was innocent of bigamy because the priest had knowingly performed a sham marriage, a fact that was known to all three people involved—bride, groom, and priest.[16] But this does not in fact emerge clearly either from the trial records or from the extensive press reporting

on the case. What is clear is that both the accused and several witnesses for the prosecution offered statements in court that stretched credulity to the breaking point.

Hervay's defense was essentially that her husband, unable to wait any longer to
consummate his relationship with her, and the priest, Pastor Prangl, had jointly—and
initially without her knowledge—concocted a scheme to protect the couple from malicious gossip and to enable them, although legally unmarried, to live together as man
and wife. The plan was that Prangl would perform a sham ceremony designed to fool
the blabbermouths into believing that the two were married, whereas the marriage
would have no legal validity because Tamara was still, as both groom and priest knew
perfectly well, legally married to her fourth husband Meurin. To accept this statement
means to accept the preposterous idea that Prangl was willing to risk his position as a
Catholic priest, and quite possibly excommunication, by performing a sham marriage
and lying to his congregation, and moreover disrespected one of the most basic credos
of the Catholic church by condoning and enabling extramarital sex—for no reason other
than doing Franz von Hervay, his political superior, a favor.[17] Tamara paints Prangl as
a calculating and more than willing accomplice in the scheme, even claiming that the

**Tamara von Hervay, in full mourning with veil, in court on October 29, 1904; her defense
attorney, Dr. Obermayer, is seated to her right and inset image. Contemporary drawing,
originally published in *Mürzzuschlager Wochenblatt* (courtesy Franz Preitler/Winter-
sportmuseum Mürzzuschlag).**

priest counseled her to grease the mayor's palms with a few hundred crowns to bribe him into looking the other way.[18] When she told Prangl in no uncertain terms that her divorce from Meurin was not final and that she therefore could not enter into a marriage, the priest, by her testimony, offered her this practical advice to pave Franz's way to her bed: "Why don't you two travel to Vienna and when you come back, you just tell people you got married there."[19] Shortly after she dropped this bombshell in court, she admitted that she had, in fact, never told the priest that she was still married to Meurin, but claimed that she had withheld this crucial bit of information at Franz von Hervay's urging: "I didn't tell him [Prangl] because my husband pressed me and declared: *I can't live without you, make an end. You can withhold that one thing from the priest!*"[20]

Prangl, for his part, denied all of it. He said that the only previous marriage of which he had been made aware was the long-dissolved marriage to Lützow, Tamara's third husband. To get around the fact that Franz von Hervay, a Catholic, could not marry a divorced woman while her former husband was still alive, Tamara had told him that the marriage between her and Lützow had never been sexually consummated (which would, by canon law, invalidate it) and that Lützow was moreover missing and presumed dead (another reason to annul a marriage by canon law). Prangl further stated that he had been totally unaware of the still legally valid marriage to Meurin; and that he had performed a legal marriage for the Hervays, only neglecting to enter it into the church book because of missing documentation. The missing document in question, he clarified, was not a divorce decree from the Meurin marriage, of which he knew nothing, but a *Verschollenheitsurkunde*, a document from Lützow's home town proving that he was missing and presumed dead (as it turned out, Lützow was alive and well in Altona[21]). Prangl admitted that he should not have performed the wedding in the absence of this document, but that he had been pressured into this breach of Catholic protocol by the couple's threat that they would leave the Catholic church and marry in the Protestant church if he made any trouble.[22] Prangl's testimony that the document he was waiting for was Lützow's *Verschollenheitsurkunde* rather than Meurin's divorce decree must have made a considerable difference to the court's assessment of the case: if true, it meant that he had broken canon law (which does not allow a Catholic to marry a divorcée during the life of her former husband), but not the laws of the land (since there existed a valid divorce decree for the Lützow marriage).

The case naturally focused on the central question whether the Hervay marriage was lawful, and much was accordingly made in court of a handwritten addendum stating that "this marriage is not valid before the law."[23] Hervay claimed that this note referred to the marriage document of August 9 and constituted proof that it had been a sham marriage; Prangl implausibly insisted that it referred to the official engagement document from July 15.[24] A similar controversy erupted over the question whether Franz von Hervay had known of Tamara's still-valid marriage to Meurin—a relevant question, since penalties for bigamy were considerably harsher if it could be shown that the bigamist had concealed a previous marriage from the subsequent spouse. Letters from Franz von Hervay to a lawyer in Trier pressing for the swift sending of the documents regarding Tamara's former husband, to whom he apparently never referred by name, seemed to indicate that he knew of the Meurin marriage. Again, however, the court was offered different explanations. Tamara insisted that the letters referred to the

"Not valid before the law": Official wedding photograph, August 9, 1903 (courtesy Franz Preitler/Wintersportmuseum Mürzzuschlag).

divorce decree from Meurin and that her husband had, in fact, not cared whether she was still married or not. Conversely, both Karl von Hervay, Franz's brother, and his mother Henriette von Hervay testified that the letters had asked for a document showing that Lützow was missing, and that Franz was unaware of the fourth marriage to Meurin, let alone of the fact that it was still valid.[25]

In the end, when actual evidence proved insufficient to decide the only question that legally mattered—the lawfulness of the Hervay marriage—the court stooped to assigning significance to meaningless trivialities that were legally completely beside the point, unhelpful in deciding the question, and would have been thrown out as hearsay by any competent judge. Did those who attended the wedding *think* they were witnessing a true marriage?[26] Did the bride, as multiple witnesses claimed, wear myrtle blossoms in her hair as a symbol of her virginity, or were they, as she herself claimed, orange blossoms?[27] The fact that the court even entertained such nonsense shows the degree to which it had abdicated all standards of evidence and impartiality. If the crucial question of the validity of the Hervays' marriage could not be decided, untinted by the jaded perception of scandalmongers who clearly had it in for her, Hervay should have been— on the principle of *in dubio pro reo*—found innocent. Instead, the court sided with the priest's version of events, the family's anguished accusations, and the town tattletales, declared the Hervay marriage legally valid, and found her guilty of bigamy.[28]

Misogyny and Antisemitism: Serious Questions to the Press

More important than the question of Hervay's guilt or innocence is the question to what extent the court's view of her character, crime and punishment were steered by her representation in misogynistic or antisemitic coverage.[29] That there was anti-semitic reporting and—actually far more commonly—coverage that attacked Hervay because she "defied accepted gender norms"[30] is undeniable. But it is rather difficult to argue that the link between this coverage and Hervay's judgment by the court beats the standards of evidence at her trial, i.e.: that it is conclusive, rather than merely associative. What does seem likely is that the press coverage contributed significantly to the fashioning of a Hervay image for consumption by the public, even as reporters engaged in what they undoubtedly thought of as "unbiased" journalism.

Some papers took the liberty to editorialize heavily while also claiming to offer readers the facts of the case. Editorial comments are, however, normally sectioned off and presented as different articles under new headings, and thus clearly distinguished from actual trial reporting. Interrogation of the accused and witness testimonies are most often cited verbatim, in direct speech, less commonly paraphrased or offered in indirect speech. Deviations in the coverage between newspapers, including in verbatim quotations, are slight and usually limited to the word or syntactic level, such as might feasibly occur when reporters from different newspapers take down the same statement in shorthand as it was offered to the court. Although there are considerable variations in the interpretation of facts, the presentation of those facts themselves is astonishingly consistent across newspapers. In all this spilled ink, I have found few significant disagreement regarding dates, verifiable events, the content of documents read in court, Hervay's interrogation, or witness testimonies. On these points, the most forgiving and sympathetic papers diverged only in minor ways from the most obnoxiously nationalistic and antisemitic sheets, and these points of substantive agreement hold true even in cases where papers attacked each other fiercely over their respective coverage. Only one of the explicitly antisemitic papers, the *Deutsches Volksblatt*, not only introduced its coverage of the case with profoundly biased editorials (more on this below), but also editorialized within the coverage of the trial, mostly in the form of snide asides and unflattering descriptions of Hervay's mannerisms. Yet even its description of events and testimony in the courtroom is congruent with coverage in other papers.

My statements above and in what follows are based on 325 newspaper articles about the case and Hervay's subsequent appearances in public life, published in 35 different newspapers over the course of more than five years (April 30, 1904–July 10, 1909). I have classified this material in the following five categories: coverage that I perceive to be comparatively neutral (i.e., reporting on known facts and witness statements without editorializing or offering an opinion in one way or the other); sympathetic towards Hervay; critical of society or of the way the trial was conducted; judgmental or defamatory towards Hervay in a personal way (but without mention of her Jewishness), and either expressly or implicitly antisemitic. This final category includes coverage that makes explicit mention of Hervay's Jewish background in a manner that maligned her character, impugned her statements, or presumed her guilt (explicit antisemitism), or that refers to Hervay's Jewish background in an ambiguous fashion (for example: articles in which Hervay's Jewishness seems unrelated to the article's argument or content and it was thus unclear why it was even brought up).[31] The result:

Neutral	120
Judgmental of Hervay	106
Sympathetic towards Hervay	46
Antisemitic (explicit or implicit)	41
Critical of trial or society	12

Table 1: Coverage of Hervay news, based on a sample of 325 articles in 35 newspapers published from April 30, 1904 to July 10, 1909.

This breakdown permits several cautious conclusions. For one thing, it tells us that a relative (although not an absolute) majority of the journalists covering a trial where feelings ran extraordinarily high, a trial that Karl Kraus famously denounced as "The Witch Trial of Leoben,"[32] made at least an honest-to-goodness attempt at sober reporting: no name-calling, no nasty editorializing, no *a priori* presumptions of guilt, no ridiculing of Hervay's statements in court. Articles in the second-largest category are clearly biased against Hervay, showing that she was widely disliked; this coverage commonly denounced her as an "adventuress," a liar, a gold-digger, and a thoroughly unsavoury character, but not for her Jewishness. This slanted reporting is undoubtedly in part owed to her already shaky reputation (which was itself partly created in earlier press portrayals of her), but many of these articles also claim that Hervay did herself no favors in court, where she frequently contradicted herself, gave evasive answers, told transparent lies, cross-examined or harangued witnesses, and sometimes slandered them in the coarsest way imaginable. Nevertheless, she also found defenders: articles taking her side, expressing sympathy for her or pity for her plight, constitute the third-largest category (although interestingly enough, only twelve commentators before Kraus found anything wrong with the trial proceedings or with the moral worldview that led to her indictment).

Taken together, articles offering relatively neutral reporting, taking Hervay's side or objecting to her treatment (in total: 178) outnumber the 147 articles that denounce her either for her morals, her behavior, or

Tamara von Hervay accosts Pastor Prangl in court. Contemporary drawing of a courtroom scene. Originally in the *Mürzzuschlager Wochenblatt* (courtesy Franz Preitler/Wintersportmuseum Mürzzuschlag).

her Jewish background. Taken individually, articles rising to her defense (46) still outnumber those expressing antisemitic sentiments (41), which is the category that takes center stage in Rose's analysis, creating the impression that reporting on the case was predominantly antisemitic. The 41 antisemitic articles, which by my count constitute the second smallest category, are distributed across only six papers: the *Österreichische Land-Zeitung* (2 articles), *Deutsches Nordmährerblatt* (1), *Kikeriki* (1), *Reichspost* (2), *Grazer Volksblatt* (6) and the only paper that seems to have launched a consistent antisemitic crusade against Hervay: the *Deutsches Volksblatt* with 29 articles.

This crusade certainly merits further attention. The *Deutsches Volksblatt* was widely read; at a circulation of 45,000–55,000 in 1904, it got about half the readership of Austria's largest daily, the *Neues Wiener Tagblatt*, at a daily circulation of about 120,000 in 1904.[33] *Volksblatt* coverage of the trial begins with an antisemitic fanfare, an editorial whose title screams "Driven to Death by a Jewess!"[34] and that vilifies not only Hervay herself, but also the "Jew press" rushing to her defense:

> On the occasion of this distressing affair, our Jew press has once again demonstrated its full indecency and mendacity. Not only did it grind away at this case to the point of nausea for all decent Aryans, it also deliberately concealed the origins of *v. Hervay's* wife. While the latter was shrugged off with a few words of perfunctory regret, they practically tried to turn his wife into a heroine. She was portrayed as an extremely soulful (!) and spirited woman, as a "born lady" etc. etc.
>
> The reason for this deliberate deceitfulness lies in the fact that this scheming woman is by birth a — — *Jewess*, who entered the world as the daughter of a so-called "artist," a sleight-of-hand conjurer named Samuel *Bellachini*. This Jew might still be remembered by older Viennese citizens under the nickname "The *Jewish Magician.*"
>
> Today, the protégée of the international Jew press, Elvira Leontine *Hervay v. Kirchberg*, née *Bellachini* (!), must answer charges of *bigamy* and *false registration* at the local district court.[35]

This editorial precedes the actual coverage of the trial and is clearly separated from it, but there was obviously no chance at all that readers would have been able to read the following coverage in any way other than in light of these remarks. Nor were they meant to. While the trial coverage is less strident, the editorial is nevertheless a fairly representative sample of *Volksblatt* writing. Some of its most characteristic features, for example the sarcastic use of italicization, quotation marks, dashes and exclamation points in parentheses, appear in no other newspaper (including antisemitic ones), but permeate both editorials and trial coverage in the *Volksblatt*. On the second day of the trial, the paper followed this up with an even more repulsive editorial entitled "A Spoiled Child of the Jewish Press" on the front two pages of the morning edition and, separately, coverage of the trial itself, again under the header "Driven to Death by a Jewess!," in the evening edition.[36] The second editorial introduces Hervay to readers, just in case they had missed the first, as

> that Jewish monster [...] who had driven the much respected district captain of Mürzzuschlag, Herr *v. Hervay*, a man endowed with the most appealing virtues of a man and official, to his death. The affair has occupied the public incessantly for months, not only due to its tragic character arising from the suicide of the unfortunate victim of this devilish Jewish trollop, but even more so since the entire Jew press has turned a wench who lured five men into her net and cheated them out of their happiness into a Jewish National Saint...[37]

The *Deutsches Volksblatt*, it can fairly be said, is the only openly propagandistic newspaper in the sense that it alone (alone even among antisemitic papers) had dropped all pretense at objective reporting and had no interest in having its own coverage perceived as neutral. Yet even it spread its poison not through falsification of the actual data or testimony, but limited itself to three propagandistic methods: foul editorials preceding the actual coverage; editorial comments and snide asides within the coverage, and the sarcastic use of italicization or punctuation. Let us consider, side by side, the opening scene of Hervay's trial as presented by a paper that was attempting to be neutral and occasionally even sympathetic to her (the *Neues Wiener Tagblatt*) and the one that was clearly the most hostile, the *Deutsches Volksblatt*. Editorial comments are marked in **boldface**, significant divergences in formulation or representation are in ***boldface italics*** and factual divergences are in **boldface underline**.

Neues Wiener Tagblatt	Deutsches Volksblatt
Judge. Your name is Eleonore Leontine von Hervay?—*Accused* **(quietly)**: Yes.—*Judge: **I entreat you to speak up**.* You were born in Posen?—*Accused:* As far as I know, yes.—*Judge:* When?—*Accused:* As far as I've heard and as far as I was told, in the year 1860.—[...] *Judge:* I must advise you to tell the truth here as much as possible. In case you are sentenced, a confession would be considered an important extenuating circumstance.	*Judge. **You must stand when you are being addressed!—The accused is silent.**—Judge:* Where were you born?—*Accused* **(in an affected, whiny voice)**: As far as I know, near *Posen.*—*Judge:* When were you born?—*Accused:* As far as I know, in the year 1860.—[...] *Judge:* I advise you to tell the truth here. If you tell the truth, this would be considered an extenuating circumstance. ***Sit down!***
[The indictment is read.]	*[The indictment is read.]*
Judge. Well, accused, you have heard the indictment. Are you guilty?—*Accused:* No, certainly not.—	*Judge.* Accused, ***stand up!*** Do you confess yourself guilty?—*Accused* **(loudly, almost screaming)**: No, certainly not! **(In general, the entire demeanor of the accused has a theatrical air.)**—*Judge: **Answer the charge. We will begin with your youth. Who were your parents?**—Accused:* I can't say, because I don't know, since there was never a trace of affection between my so-called mother and me. Indeed, I've never been to her grave.—*Judge: **We have a document that is very definitive and offers information on both your parents and your birth.***
*Judge: **Let's talk about your relationship with your parents.**—Accused:* On this I cannot tell you anything. There was never any love or affection between me and my purported mother. I've never been to her grave.—*Judge:* You have a baptismal certificate from Posen, ***according to which you were registered in July 1860 as the daughter of the artist S. Bellachini.***	
—*Accused:* **My purported mother** wrote me a letter on her deathbed, in which she declared that I was *not her child*, that she had adopted me in Helsingfors and that I was the child of highly noble parents. ***I cannot say anything more about this.***	—*Accused:* **My father** wrote a letter on his deathbed: she is not our daughter, we adopted her in Helsingfors **in place of our deceased little daughter**, she is the daughter of noble parents. ***I don't consider it necessary to say more./The presiding judge then reads a birth certificate from the Jewish registry in Posen stating that the wife of Samuel Bellachini, née Krügel, bore a child at 2 in the morning on July 18, 1860, which received the names Elvira Leontine.*** [...]—*Accused:* I was educated in
—*Judge. **Your baptismal certificate clearly affirms otherwise. You were of the mosaic faith?**—Accused: **I don't know.*** I have been raised in the Protestant church and have always thought I was Protestant.	

Neues Wiener Tagblatt (continued)	*Deutsches Volksblatt* (continued)
	a Protestant school, I have always received Protestant religious instruction, and I have always gone to Protestant church services.
—*Judge.* There is a baptismal certificate showing that you converted in the year 1880, **before your marriage**, to Protestantism.—	—*Judge:* We have evidence that in 1800, **shortly before your first divorce from Cuntz**, you converted to Protestantism.—
Accused: **I did not convert.** I was merely accepted into the Protestant congregation.—	*Accused:* **I did not know** that this was a conversion. **I was told** that since I wasn't born in Berlin I had to be accepted into a Berlin church congregation in order to be able to marry in Berlin."[39]
Judge: **That wouldn't have been necessary if you had been a Protestant.**"[38]	

Table 2: Opening scene of Hervay's trial as reported in *Neues Wiener Tagblatt*, October 29, 1904 (L), and *Deutsches Volksblatt* of the same day.

To be sure, the same scene, as represented in politically diametrically opposed papers, shows divergences, but hardly of the kind that would seem to justify the bitter press wars that erupted between liberal and antisemitic papers over their respective coverage. Points of disagreement on actual facts are relatively rare: in one version, it is Tamara's mother who writes the letter confessing she is not her child, in the other it is her father; in one version, her conversion to Protestantism takes place immediately before a marriage, in the other immediately before a divorce. The first case (mother v. father) holds no perceptible propagandistic value and may be attributable to simple error on the part of the journalist recording the interrogation in shorthand. The second is a clearer case where a fact is not merely a fact but also an important point of representation: the *Volksblatt's* mention of her first divorce where the *Tagblatt* merely mentions a marriage serves as a reminder to readers that she was a serial divorcée, read: a loose woman. Even more crassly, the *Volksblatt* editorializes repeatedly, endowing her with an "affected, whiny voice" at a point where the *Neues Wiener Tagblatt* describes her, in a rather more dignified manner, as answering "quietly." Her "not guilty" statement comes across as neutral in the *Tagblatt* and as hysterical in the *Volksblatt* and is there followed immediately by a general denunciation of her "theatrical" demeanor. In the *Volksblatt*, her snarky little aside to the judge—"I don't consider it necessary to say more" (in the *Tagblatt*: "I cannot say anything more about this") was undoubtedly meant to indicate disrespect to the court at best and her generally impertinent character at worst.

Interestingly, Hervay is not the only character who appears in a different light in both versions. The judge in the *Tagblatt* version is far more benign and polite, "entreating" her to speak up, whereas the *Volksblatt* judge barks at her to stand up, sit down, and answer the charge. In the *Tagblatt*, the judge also offers facts about her background, merely asking her to confirm their correctness (as if reading them from documents on his desk: "You were born in Posen?"). Conversely, the formulations of the *Volksblatt* judge—"Where were you born? When were you born?" suggest an interrogation, or, as Kraus would later claim, an inquisitional trial. We might take this to mean that the *Tagblatt* either meant to represent or truly viewed the judge as a man in search of the truth, certainly as initially neutral (until he becomes impatient with her implausible statements at the close of the scene). In contrast, the triumphalist *Volksblatt* coverage shows us a judge who, from the moment he sat down at the bench, assumes her guilt as much as the paper itself does and who will, as the paper implies with more than a little *schadenfreude*, get this tramp exactly what she deserves.

Points of agreement between the two papers are no less interesting. Both present the accused as absolutely unwilling to admit to anything, even the most basic data about her birth and background. She downgrades the date and place of birth on her birth certificate to mere hearsay (in both versions) and claims not to know who her parents were, indicating, however, her absolute conviction that it wasn't the Bellachinis, who are in her speech demoted to "purported" or "so-called" parents (in both versions). She also did not know whether she had ever been Jewish (*Tagblatt*), nor was she aware that the ceremony she underwent in Berlin in 1880 constituted a conversion from Judaism to Protestantism (*Volksblatt*), whereas in the *Tagblatt* she denied unequivocally that a conversion had ever taken place.

From these and hundreds of other articles on the trial I would cautiously draw three conclusions. The first is that although antisemitic coverage was certainly loud and obnoxious, it was in the minority, and it would thus be unfair to characterize press reporting on Hervay's trial as predominantly antisemitic. Secondly, even the most zealously antisemitic reporters stopped short of perjuring themselves or falsifying agreed-upon facts. And finally, even the most rabidly antisemitic coverage (in contrast to antisemitic editorials preceding it) was, in many ways, not that far removed from reporting that attempted to remain neutral or even occasionally expressed some sympathy for the accused. The hostility with which various newspapers attacked each other over their respective coverage of the Hervay trial was hardly warranted by actual differences in the reporting. Clearly, these attacks had less to do with the trial itself and more with the general propaganda wars of the *völkisch* papers against what they called the "Jew press," and in this broader context, Hervay was never more than a decoy.

Press coverage of the trial, whether neutral, sympathetic, or hostile, also shows one thing beyond doubt or question: that the court squandered its time and credibility on irrelevancies rather than investigating the only question that mattered, namely, whether Hervay had entered into a legal marriage while still legally married to someone else. As Karl Kraus snarkily remarked, the question could have been decided in half an hour by placing the marriage certificate and the divorce decree side by side on a desk and comparing the dates.[40] Instead, the court spent four months investigating and then two days debating questions that were essentially beside the point: Hervay's family, religion, multiple marriages and divorces, her first encounter with Franz, her reputation in town, or the juicy question of her relationship with Lieutenant Bartl, who was seen by witnesses entering or leaving her room in various states of undress.[41]

Both the court and the press seem to have absolutely thrilled to these trifles. The *Grazer Volksblatt* published an account by Franz von Hervay's lawyer who had witnessed the final exchange between Franz and Tamara shortly after the unfortunate husband had been told that his wife was a marriage swindler and an impostor. This is the lawyer's description of the scene: "v. Hervay greeted his spouse with the words: You have deceived me most despicably. Frau v. Hervay replied with a theatrical gesture: I did not deceive you, I only lied to you. To this I replied: In this case it is beside the point whether you deceived or lied to your husband."[42] Here and elsewhere, the press abandoned the realm of tragedy, even that of the fairy tale, and strayed into that of involuntary comedy. Above all, it abandoned all recognition that none of these trivialities—whether or not Hervay was Jewish, whether she had been married four times or fifty, whether or not she had slept with Bartl, whether she had deceived or "only" lied to her husband—was relevant to or useful in determining the only question the court was entitled to ask: whether she had, in fact, committed bigamy.

Hervay's Defenders

Some commentators did pick up on this. The left-wing *Arbeiterzeitung*, which denounced the court as "a court of mores, not a court of law," asserted that "She was really only arrested for being an 'adventuress'—which, although in Mürzzuschlag it means being the dregs of humanity, does not have a place among the paragraphs of the penal code […]. In truth, this investigation was not about bigamy but about the brand-new crime of *having a past*."[43] *Das interessante Blatt* opined that for Hervay to get a fair trial, the Goddess of Justice would have to have her bandage adjusted to not only cover her eyes, but also her ears to render them "air- and gossip-tight."[44] The *Neues Wiener Tagblatt* castigated the court for its emphasis on irrelevancies from her past that "even the presiding judge described as merely illustrative."[45] And Karl Kraus, undoubtedly Hervay's wittiest and most eloquent defender, devoted two essays to the case in which he pulled absolutely no punches. Even before her trial, he defined the court's "investigation" in similar terms as the *Arbeiterzeitung*:

> An outcry for the "truth" rings through the Mürztal, and all Styrian mountain morons are united with all Viennese fountain-pen thugs in their demand for clarity. The truth must finally out: does the contentment in the Hervay marriage rest on a healthy or a morbid basis? The suspense can be borne no longer. […] For too long have people put up with this woman, with her better manners and her better underwear; for too long has she plunged the village into an uproar with impunity. Not only did she nab the dashing district captain, she is well on her way to turning the heads of other husbands.[46]

In his second essay on her trial, he starkly stated that "They called it an indictment of 'bigamy' because they could hardly call it a witch trial," which he goes on to lampoon as follows:

> Leontine von Hervay came riding through the air on a broom stick to Mürzzuschlag, showing her silk petticoat. A fustian spirit full of foreboding cried at once: "I Seethroughyou." What matter that she had made the district captain happy? A conjurer's daughter and familiar with foreign tongues! Urgently suspected of consorting with the devil. Some may have been afflicted by sick cattle; others, perhaps, by rotting grain. The entire village is in an uproar. She administered a love potion to the district captain; other dignitaries will follow; the most desirable women of Mürz-zuschlag must take second place. Shall we allow her "to prevent men from siring and women from birthing, to prevent men from rendering conjugal service to women, and women likewise to men"? […] Not only did she out-strip women seventeen years her junior in the affections of the snappiest town official, she also—conjuresses are capable of much—made herself younger by seventeen years.[47]

Kraus's essay essentially takes over two narrative strategies from the press reports: the couching of the entire story in the form of a fairy tale—here retold with a dark twist—

and the general perception of the Hervay affair as a symbol for something that far transcended the significance of the case itself. To him, this was the opening of the anti-semitic floodgates, that is, the antisemitic papers' open celebration of the persecution of an individual for her membership of a group, thinly disguised as her prosecution for an actual crime. The trial, Kraus asserts, showed its true colors clearly enough: it did not prosecute but persecute, it was not interested in the crime but in her questionable past.

> Hervay is accused of bigamy; that state of affairs, to which nothing is relevant but an existing marriage certificate and a missing divorce decree, could have been legally determined in half an hour. But Herr Labres, the witch inquisitor of Leoben, now proceeds to the interrogation "under torture" that is the true purpose of the trial. "I want to begin with your youth. Who were your parents?" "Did you not introduce one of your admirers as your foster brother?" "Did you not later have an affair with Colonel Goltsch?" "Was there not also another man in Mürzzuschlag that the accused was interested in?" A hotel valet confirms that First Lieutenant Bartel has entered the room of the accused in a state of undress. This is obviously the point where we may prove that the witch "consorted with the devil." "You truly did observe this?" "Can you swear an oath to this?" "Did you really see what you have just stated under oath?" "Did you notice his state of dress?" Herr Labres inquires after every detail; his curiosity, which will be satisfied today, recoils from the priest's marriage certificate but not from the First Lieutenant's underwear, and the sole question that is spared the accused witch is whether the "semen dia-bolicum calidum aut frigidum" [whether the "devil's semen was hot or cold"]. Thus was the "bigamy" established...[48]

Kraus was one of Hervay's rare defenders who was interested in the larger picture, just as the antisemitic press was, although obviously with diametrically opposed objectives. The antisemitic press presented Hervay's trial as an individual example of something much larger and more significant: the idea that the "Jew press," in its defense of a morally despicable and clearly guilty Jewess, demonstrated merely that Jews stick together no matter what, naturally for the sole purpose of sullying "Aryan" decency and ultimately overthrowing the Aryan world order. As a rule, Hervay's defenders responded to this on the *individual* level, as if these assertions merely pertained to Hervay alone. They avowed her innocence, protested her treatment in prison or in the hospital, declared that others—the priest, the mayor—had also gotten their hands dirty, objected to the enormous bail that was asked for her release, and so on.[49] Kraus, conversely, expressed his sense that the issue transcended Hervay herself by framing the affair in broader terms: not in terms of law but in terms of literature and history. His definition of the trial as a witch trial spells out that he was not really interested in Hervay or in the question of her guilt or innocence, but in the way in which she had become the unwitting impulse for the mobilization of a mob mentality and the resulting suspension of justice that was not only accepted but generally applauded by the press and the public. Kraus alone saw how short the path is from the unjust imprisonment of an indi-vidual to that of an entire people. He alone recognized that the fairy tale, the fictional form constantly evoked to tell the story—by the press and also by Hervay herself—is a story whose fantastical plot merely masks its potential to serve as an allegory for reality. He understood Hervay's treatment as not only wrong in and of itself, but as an object lesson, even a harbinger, for everything that could go wrong on a truly apocalyptic scale.

Hervay on Hervay

Hervay, on the other hand, didn't. Perhaps understandably, she defended herself as an individual, sticking to the story of her noble birth, romanticizing the fairy tale of her love story, swearing to high heaven that she was innocent, and attempting to gain pity by portraying her indictment as capricious, her sentence as unjust, and her treatment in prison and hospitals as cruel to the point of torture. Most tellingly, she fell into the same trap as the court, the press and the public: her grounds for self-defense were not legal but moral. To hear her tell it, tongues had not started wagging until the defamatory "Ancient Fairy Tale" in the *Mürzzuschlager Wochenblatt*; until then, she claimed, the entire town had perceived her as she really was: a woman of angelic character and unimpeachable morals, kind to her inferiors and charitable to the poor, loved by many and admired by all. Faced with stationmaster Simon Tschitschek's damning assertions, she declined to contradict them, instead derisively reminding him of his earlier declaration that he considered himself "your most ardent admirer"—a statement to which his response is not recorded.[50] In another scene reported by the *Deutsches Volksblatt*, Hervay similarly attempted to counterbalance, rather than deny, Karl von Hervay's devastating testimony: "Lieutenant, you yourself told me: 'You are a good and noble creature. You will not obstruct my brother's path.'—*Witness. 'I know nothing about a good and noble creature.'* (Hilarity)"[51]

All this was obviously as irrelevant to the case as Lieutenant Bartl's underwear. But vindicating herself morally was clearly more important to her even than being found innocent. "I was defeated before the strict justice of the law; I will triumph before the mild justice of morality!," is the opening statement of her autobiography *Tamara von Hervay: Her Life and Thought*, published the year after her trial.[52] Just like her trial and the press coverage it attracted, Hervay's memoirs concern themselves only in passing with her actual guilt or innocence and place the major emphasis on her character and her past. Why did she marry so many times? Because whenever someone asked "I just couldn't say no. I was filled with immeasurable charity towards Man... [...] A strong tendency towards self-sacrifice reigns within me... [...] I wanted to give, everything in me is so serene, so noble, not even the slightest trace of ugliness lives inside me."[53] Her relationship with her Franzi is described as seventh heaven, a sensual paradise tempered by the saintliness of her character:

> He could barely stand to be without me for a few hours. Certainly his love was also sensual, but sensuality for him was not the main thing and I practiced moderation. Even in the most intimate conjugal intercourse we never lost control of ourselves, everything was hallowed, and we always savored our passionate love as something new and sacred!
>   I will repeat for you his own words:
>   "Sweetheart, how sacred is everything between us, how endless the happiness I receive from your deep soul! But tell me, will you love me the way you do now when I, as may happen very soon, am only able to kiss you?"
>   I answered him very earnestly that what he meant was not the "main thing," that true love was completely uninfluenced by "it."[54]

Quite aside from raising again the recurring question of Hervay's truthfulness (how likely is it that a 32-year-old man would announce to his much older wife that "very soon" he might no longer be able to satisfy her sexually?), this tawdry passage is utterly beside the point if the point was legal, rather than moral, justification. It is also the passage that lost her the support of Karl Kraus, her staunchest defender thus far. He cites the conjugal-intercourse passage, followed by another in which she elucidates

Tamara von Hervay after her release from prison (1905) (courtesy Franz Preitler/Wintersportmuseum Mürzzuschlag).

her exquisite taste in underwear, with palpable distaste, adding that he saw her memoirs as a "tiresome publication," that he worried about his earlier defense of her as being "mistaken for approval of this nonsense" and that he felt "in duty bound to explicitly disrecommend" the book.[55]

Kraus certainly had cause for concern. Hervay's memoirs are a vile document in which she spends more time maligning Franz von Hervay's family even than touting her own saintly virtue. As she herself states in the introduction to the work, the Hervay family paid her 5,000 crowns in return for her solemn assurance that she would refrain from further calumnies against the family. For this substantial sum,[56] she promised, also in the foreword, not to make any "polemical or hostile" remarks whatsoever against any member of the family, "but to ignore them as, for me, non-existent."[57] And yet, the Hervays are the undisputed stars of her book. Even in the rare cases where a statement actually relates to the 1904 trial, it often serves the greater purpose of casting aspersions on one or the other member of the family. Hervay claims, for example, that although Franz insisted that he was not interested in her past, "I showed heroic courage and forced my fiancé to listen to the relation of my entire life."[58] In fact, everyone in the family, Hervay steadfastly claims, knew of her previous four marriages. But the statement that everyone knew all about her past is not only offered to show that she neither "deceived" nor "lied to" her husband, but also affords her a welcome opportunity to humiliate "Baroness Paula," a member of the Hervay family chronically unable to nab a husband:

> "Oh, Baroness Lützow, yesterday someone told me that you had been married four times—! But how dreadful!"—
>
> I responded to her, smiling: "Yes, indeed it is dreadful, Baroness. I alone had four legitimate husbands—and some would be so glad to get just one. The world is unjust, Baroness, isn't it?"
>
> If looks could kill, I would not have had to go through all the agony that followed![59]

While the book practically teems with malicious anecdotes like this one, its greatest odium is reserved for Franz's mother, Henriette von Hervay. Described in the press as an elegant and slender lady of 48 (a mere four years older than Hervay herself) with slightly graying hair,[60] she becomes, in Hervay's memoirs,

> a frightfully ugly woman with a colossal fat body, a haggard face disfigured by red spots, who looked as if she had a sour apple in her mouth; his father is a chevalier, his brother a vacuous man; his brother's wife—she reminds one vividly of a roasting goose—or what do you call the white birds on the Roman Capitol?
>
> The first word Frau von Hervay ever said to me was: "Mais, ma chère, il n'ya pas un sou de fortune!" ["But my dear, you don't have a penny in fortune!"]
>
> And I said, pale with shock about this tactlessness:
>
> "Oh, Madame, cela ne faire rien!" ["Oh, madam, that make [sic] no difference!"][61]

It was this woman's relentless, grasping greed, Hervay asserts, that destroyed her happiness and that also necessitated all deceptions that marred her fairy tale love affair, including the lies about her immense fortune and the fake marriage. Characteristically, she does not own these lies but attributes them to the one person no longer able to defend himself: her dead husband. As she tells it, Franz

> said to me: "My *Märchen*, last night I wrote to my parents telling them that we have secretly married. I told them, to finally stop the endless questioning and torment, that *you have deposited 300,000 marks* in my name and that I have the deposit slip in my pocket. After all, Mama only wants money, she couldn't care less about anything else!"
>
> I was horrified at what I heard! "How will you keep this up?" I asked him. "Your mother will want to see the deposit slip at once; the marriage certificate would have been a minor matter."[62]

It is difficult to read Hervay's memoir without suspecting that she endowed other characters, above all her dead husband's family, with the attribute that characterized herself best: insatiable greed. Much of her "martyrdom," as she describes her suffering, amounts to little more than being deprived of the comforts of home. "I furnished our house delightfully," she stated without a trace of false modesty, "I am, I believe, a good homemaker and very modest when it comes to myself."[63] In prison, she reminisced about her bygone happiness:

> I light the lamp and cast my eyes about the room. How dreadful for a person whose basic life requirements are beautiful and harmonious surroundings! Alas! Our sweet home: how lovingly we assembled everything; how the rooms in which I lived adopted my character: there was nothing obtrusive, no loud colors; moderate contrasts, cozy corners, fresh palms, blossoming flowers: "Hic habitat felicitas!" ["Here dwells happiness!"] Over now—all over; my God, how hard this suffering is to bear![64]

Such visions intrude even on the starkest descriptions of her most extreme suffering:

> The first days in Graz were horrifying. I could not choke down the prison food and suffered hunger. Oh, how agonizing was this time! In my sickly state I had visions, often I saw our cozy dining room, the charmingly decorated dining table—then I saw magnificent foods, I bolted towards them—and bashed my head against the wall. I roared with hunger like an animal.[65]

Her husband appears in her memoirs in the fairytale scene of their first meeting in the woods, in the conjugal-relations scene, and in some other passages where he either erupts in rapturous worship of her personal qualities or concocts lies and deceptions to get his greedy family off her back. Passages in which she professes to mourn his passing or to miss him remain rare, perfunctory and colorless. But there is real narrative energy invested in describing the things she missed during her time in prison and in the hospital: fragrant flowers, a cozy home, a table groaning under the weight of delicious food. On this issue, the most critical press coverage does not indict her any more severely than does her own self-representation. The *Grazer Volksblatt*, for example, reports that she was told of her husband's suicide on Monday, July 4, 1904, and spent the rest of the day and half the night screaming. On Tuesday, July 5, however, she was apparently sufficiently recovered to give a lady visitor an exact breakdown of the money she paid to cover her husband's debts (6000 crowns), how much her jewelry was worth (16,500 crowns), how many suits (50) and cravats (70) she purchased for Franz from her own money, and the things she bought for herself (her own needs being modest, she merely acquired one pair of shoes, one blouse and one hat, all the while eating nothing but rice and milk in order to save money). It is worth noting here that the *Grazer Volksblatt* mentions all of this not to attack her but as possible points in her *defense:* if she really paid her husband's debts, the paper elaborates, it is highly doubtful that she was a marriage swindler.[66] Yet the question remains: would a woman who had spent the previous day in hysterics over her husband's death have a head for such details, such trifles, the very next day? It is not easy to fend off the thought that to her, these were not trifles but the main issue. Her book, too, although largely untainted by mourning for her husband's death, invests pages and pages on the liquidation of her husband's effects: all the expensive gifts that she gave Franz and that Karl von Hervay falsely promised to return; all the costly wedding presents that should have been restored to her; her table silver, her hand-held fans, her petticoats, and—yet again—her underwear are listed fastidiously, along with their estimated value and the much lower prices the greedy Hervays paid for each item. "For my silver, which I bought *used* for 1000 crowns, the Hervays paid 350 crowns. A precious black hand-held feather fan that cost several hundred francs was bought by Frau Amy von Hervay for——5 *crowns*. Similarly [...] my personal underwear was sold for a song." At the end of the list, she cannot resist another jibe at her former mother-in-law: "Frau von Hervay got a bargain, don't you think?"[67]

Tamara von Hervay was certainly vocal in her own defense, both at her trial and in her memoirs. She presented herself as a woman of saintly character and sophisticated background and education, a "deeply unfortunate woman who must perish miserably because *her horizons are larger* than that of *a wash basin in Mürzzuschlag!*"[68] She described her martyrdom at the hands of the court, the prison and the hospitals in the most gruesome terms. She complained about anything and everything. Not having nice underwear. What she got to eat. What she didn't get to eat. Lack of medical care. Lack of interesting books in the prison library. Cold rooms and straw sacks. Brutal beatings and bugs everywhere.[69] The only thing she never complained about, not even once, was being the victim of an antisemitic crusade. What was, to Kraus and every modern historian who has so far written on the case, the most significant aspect of her case—the profoundly prejudicial view of her offered in the antisemitic press she herself did not think worthy of a single comment. Perhaps she felt unable to protest antisemitic attacks on her while also ardently denying that she had ever been a member of the "mosaic religion" or the child of Jewish parents. In her memoirs, she put more clear blue water between herself and Jewishness by linking, as the *Deutsches Volksblatt* also did, Jewishness with greed. And greed and consorting with Jews for money is the brush with which she tarnished the Hervays, above all her most hated enemies, Franz's mother Henriette and his brother Karl:

At the age of twenty-four, Karl married a Baroness Lütgendorf whose mother was named Löwen-feld and who was a Jewess. But she had a big sack full of money.

    The Halls of Troy were full of rejoicing, Mother Hervay swam in bliss and even put up with Grandmother Löwenfeld.[70]

Is this merely a case of (antisemitic) attack being the best defense (against the suspicion of being Jewish herself)? Or is it a sign of something worse? The passage, brief as it is, contains a number of aspects pointing in this direction. The name-change from Löwen-feld to Lütgendorf; the pejorative formulation of the "Jewess" having "a big sack full of money" (rather than a more respectful description of the Baroness as, perhaps, "a woman of considerable means"); the snide mention of the Halls of Troy (where rejoicing was cut short by the Fall of Troy—perhaps a hopeful allusion to the imminent downfall of the Hervay family?), and the clear implication that although the Hervays knew that consorting with a Jewess was the lowest one could sink, they were so blinded by greed that they put up not only with a camouflaged Lütgendorf but with an actual Löwen-feld…. It is a passage that could have appeared unchanged in the *Deutsches Volksblatt*, and one that betrays, as does the trial coverage in that and other papers, a deep-seated and unmotivated antisemitism, which, after all, neither requires nor offers any rationale beyond its own hatred.

The Conman and the Conwoman: Voigt on the Road to Immortality

On the face of it, the case of Wilhelm Voigt, the Captain of Köpenick, and the case of Tamara von Hervay, the Black Baroness, display many similarities. Sentenced within precisely two years of each other, in late October/early November of 1906 and 1904 respectively, both were the subjects of the most celebrated trials of their age. Both attracted broad press coverage and the attention of major writers such as Frieda von Bülow, Hermann Bahr, Hans Hyan, and Carl Zuckmayer. Both were impersonators using fake names and nobility degrees for the purpose of self-enrichment. Both were lifers, career confidence tricksters. Both had their sentence commuted by an Imperial pardon[71]; both were fleetingly the subjects of discussion in Parliament,[72] and both showed up the cracks in the societal structure. Both wrote autobiographies in which they justified themselves and their deeds.

But this is where the parallels end. Voigt continued, with public sanction, with an impersonation that had long been unmasked, turning his career as a conman into public theater. Hervay's subsequent career as a conwoman was dogged at every step: numerous articles in the years following her trial report that she had her sights on another innocent victim who was saved from marrying her in the nick of time.[73] Voigt was internationally celebrated while Hervay continued to be vilified. His moniker, the Captain of Köpenick, was coined on the day of his coup and has remained a household name for over 100 years. Her moniker, the Black Baroness, was not even invented until 2015, when it first appeared as the title of Preitler's novel.[74] Unless you have read one of the three novels about her, you would be highly unlikely to ever have heard her name. Given how few people so far have taken note of her, it is doubtful that the "Black Baroness" will ever achieve fame as one of history's great female impostors.

To the question why Voigt became the darling of the nation whereas Hervay was forgotten, there are several easy answers, none of which, however, hit the nail entirely on the head. First of all, the blindingly obvious and most often cited: she was a woman whereas he was a man. She was Jewish (and could thus be attacked as such) whereas he wasn't and couldn't. Then, less obviously, there is the matter of near-universal presentation of their respective stories: his as a comedy, hers as a fairy tale. Perhaps comedies hold their value better over time than fairy tales. Over a century later, we are still laughing at Voigt's escapades, but Hervay's fairy tale, once unmasked as a series of simple lies, has lost its magic. And finally, we might throw morals into the mix: Voigt had— or claimed that he had—a personal code of honor that forbade him from harming individuals[75]; like a shabbier Robin Hood, he was a robber of faceless institutions like banks and city halls. Tricking someone into marriage, as Hervay did, is also an attack on a societal structure, but it also involves individual harm. Both Voigt and Hervay attacked common societal beliefs: he the belief in the invincibility of the Prussian military and the idea that law-abiding citizens must be protected from ex-cons by serial deportations; she the sanctity of marriage. But unlike the dogmas he undermined, the sanctity of marriage had not attracted widespread criticism and was not seen as a sign that there was something wrong in the State of Austria.

These distinctions seem to me far more persuasive in explaining the difference in the reception of Voigt versus Hervay than simply citing her Jewishness or gender. The difference, in other words, lay not only in the perception of their personalities but also in that of their deeds. Unlike Hervay's multiple marriages, the Köpenick affair was seen as saying something far-reaching about Germany and Germans. "Yesterday's tragicomedy," wrote the *Daily Mail* hopefully,

> may occasion two cataclysmic changes in the life of the German people. First: the destruction of the principle that you must bow to the Emperor's uniform, as the Swiss had to bow to Gessler's hat. Secondly: the blind and thoughtless obedience that is drilled into the teutonic soldier as his most glorious virtue might see considerable mitigation. Without these traditions that have become ingrained in the German people, the tragicomedy of Köpenick, which now has exposed the *Reich* to the scornful laughter of both hemispheres, could not have occurred.[76]

This is also what Maximilian Harden meant when he wrote in *Die Zukunft* that Voigt had infringed a dozen legal paragraphs but in so doing had rendered the country an immeasurable service.[77] The Captain is not necessarily like "us," the contemporary argument went, but he says something about "us" and shows us how we might become a little less "us." The Captain's coup not only led to a broad discussion about the Prussian form of government and law enforcement, but also about the values and dangers of absolutist rule. And finally, the Captain made contemporaries see things about their society that they would not have been able to see themselves, without his help: "An impostor, a hustler, a robber had to come in order to make a mockery of one of our most wondrous State institutions!," rejoiced the *Berliner Volks-Zeitung*.[78] None of this was true about Tamara von Hervay. Once her case was over, she lost the historical meaning as a symbol of Jewish victimization in the antisemitic press that Kraus and others had assigned to her. She does appear in future coverage, right up to about 1909, but always as a mere individual—as a marriage swindler out to nab her next husband; as a cabaret performer or the author of her memoirs; as the beneficiary of a benefit soirée; as the plaintiff in yet another court case.[79] Never again did she mean anything beyond herself.

In view of these larger contexts, it seems to me somewhat dissatisfying to opt for the simplest (and so far most commonly offered) answer to the mystery of Hervay's unpopularity during her lifetime and her obscurity after her death: that Hervay was vilified as a Jew and as a woman who refused to play by the gender rules of her time. Yet while I am unconvinced that either her Jewishness or her gender constitute the whole answer, I would agree that both must be taken seriously as two factors (among several) that shaped her reception. Would Voigt have become a national treasure if he had been a Jew? In all the press coverage on Voigt, the possibility is mentioned only once, in an article by Paul Blook in the *Berliner Tageblatt*, where he mentions as a particularly delicious aspect of the national joke the fact that "ten grenadiers followed, without further ado, an improperly uniformed and bow-legged Captain with (as the *Staatsbürger-Zeitung* meaningfully remarks!) a *crooked* nose."[80] A *crooked* nose, in italics, would have been an unmistakable physiognomic signal indicating Jewishness. The *Staatsbürger-Zeitung* may have wanted to assign this further "meaning," but as Voigt's popularity increased, they dropped the subject in a hurry, along with everyone else. Even before Voigt's arrest, when nobody knew who he was and speculation about his identity were rife, the idea that this folk hero might be Jewish was never again so much as mentioned. It is the only black hole in the wide-ranging imaginations of the Captain before he was finally unmasked as the cobbler from Tilsit. Perhaps this does indicate how unthinkable a Jewish folk hero had become as early as 1906.

And what about Hervay, that Jewess whose entire life project was based on the rejection of her Jewishness, beginning with the denial of her parentage and of her conversion and ending in the disparagement of a rich Jewess in her memoirs? If there is one difference that emerges clearly from the press coverage of both trials, it is that Voigt was judged for his crime whereas Hervay was judged for something else. There really is no better word for that something else than Hannah Arendt's term for the category by which Jews are commonly judged, namely: "vice." As the press coverage demonstrates beyond doubt or question, and as was pointed out by a few brave souls, Karl Kraus among them, Hervay's trial did not focus on her crime but on her many vices: her multiple marriages; the fact that she was found at fault at virtually every divorce; her haughty behavior towards townspeople; her impersonation of a noblewoman. Little use that the *Neues Wiener Tagblatt* protested that "on all this, the High Court can only express a moral opinion, but its juridical sentence must remain uninfluenced by it."[81] Little use that the *Czernowitzer Allgemeine Zeitung*, after savaging Hervay for being a liar, an impostor, the daughter of a Jewish conjurer, a hussy and an adventuress, added this significant statement: "But is she a criminal? No."[82] The court failed to establish unequivocally that she was guilty of a crime and thus sentenced her for her vices, which is as much as to say: for her character. A "crime" is something you do and can thus stop doing; "vice" describes what you are and cannot stop being. Furthermore, "vice," unlike "crime," generalizes the individual and mistakes the specific for the general. It thus relieves the judger of the duty of judging a case on its merits. What happened at Hervay's trial was a symptom for a disease that Hannah Arendt has diagnosed as the abdication of responsibility. "In assimilating crime and transforming it into vice," Arendt wrote, "society denies all responsibility and establishes a world of fatalities in which men find themselves entangled."[83]

A Name—What's in a Name? Hervay on the Road to Nowhere

We may not be able to prove in a court of law that Hervay was railroaded, first by her contemporaries and later by history, because she was Jewish, whereas Voigt became a folk hero because he was not. Undeniably, however, contemporary ideas of Jewishness (often pejorative) and Germanness (often critical) affected how the stories of Voigt and Hervay were received by contemporaries and thus also the way in which their stories have come down to us. The same, we might suspect, is true of gender. It may not be as straightforward as saying that Hervay was condemned for being female or for confounding gender norms. And yet, Hervay's gender may well constitute one of the reasons—as important as her Jewishness—as to why Voigt became a household name whereas history took little notice of her. For being female means, above all, an unstable personal identity that expresses itself most often in multiple names. For a female impostor, this problem is vastly exacerbated.

At Hervay's trial, not even the most elementary facts—her name, her birth date, her parentage, her religion—remained uncontested. One difference between the impostor Tamara von Hervay and the impostor Wilhelm Voigt is simply that he pled guilty whereas she never did. For an impostor, an admission of guilt is an admission of his or her true identity. He confessed to being the cobbler Wilhelm Voigt, born in Tilsit on February 13, 1849, and when he reprised the Captain role after his release, he fooled no one: everyone knew who he was and went along with his little ruse. He served his time and took the con game above ground, launching a highly successful career as the only open and publicly approved impostor in German history. Not so Tamara von Hervay: after serving her time, she had to keep trying to ply her trade underground, with varying degrees of success. Both of her projects—first to assert her innocence and later to continue working as a conwoman—meant that she had to retain her disguises. Thus Tamara von Hervay insistently pitted her own reality of who she was—Tamara Baroness von Lützow-Hervay, daughter of a Russian princess and a German count, born in July 1877—against the general agreement that she was Elvira Leontine Bellachini, born in July 1860, as asserted in official documents, the court and the press.

This is the point where her femininity becomes an issue, for something as simple and heartbreakingly folksy as Wilhelm Voigt (or Elvira Bellach) would not have permitted a female impostor to have any kind of career. Female frauds are like female writers; they are women of many names. For that reason they are easier to hide, easier to suppress, easier to forget, and harder to research. Women writers changed their names with each husband and more often than not, at a time that harshly censured women's writing as inferior, trivial, even "unfeminine," used numerous pseudonyms.[84] Katharina (Kathinka) Rosa Therese Pauline Modesta Zitz or Halein (1801–77) sported, in addition to her multiple first and last names, fifteen pseydonyms.[85] Which name is the right one? Her birth name? The name of her first husband? The name of her last husband?

The name under which she published the most? The name that made her famous? Journalists covering Hervay's trial essentially ran into the same problem as modern scholars trying to research early women writers, for any kind of historical presence depends on the One True Name. A name like Goethe, Mozart, Wilhelm Voigt. Women, these people of many names, disappear into the tangled mass of history. We know that Tamara von Hervay married at least twice more, but nothing is known either about these two marriages or about the place and year of her death.[86]

For journalists covering her trial, the more immediate problem was that before you can shame, you must be able to name. This may, in fact, be Hervay's only victory. She was maligned, despised and ultimately found guilty, and she was called all sorts of names. But not the One True Name that could have denoted a reliable identity. She herself frequently changed both her first and last names. Journalists, whether they loved her or loathed her, never knew what to call her. "He no longer calls her Maria, he cooingly transforms her name to Mara, then Tamara [...] like her erstwhile father, a certain—what was his name again?—ah yes, Bloch, who then called himself Bellach—or Bellachini!"[87]—"The district captain's wife is not a née *Lützow* from Russia, but a *Jewess from Berlin* named *Singer* and has already been unmasked as such."[88]—"...she called herself Camera v. Lützow, but her documents show her name as Elvira Liontine v. Lützow."[89]—"She was born in Charlottenburg and her name as a girl was Maria *Bellach*. She is the daughter of a juggler."[90]—"Erna Bellachini, or, to call her by her real name, Hedwig Bellach or Bloch [...] is a genius impostor..."[91]—"Elvira Klementine is the daughter of the Jewish couple Bellach."[92]—"...the Jewess *Bellachini*-Murin-Lützow-Hervay [...] An officer came and saw this liberal *Märchen* who no longer called herself Bellachini or Lützow or Hervay but '*Baroness Kirchberg*,' and he was vanquished by her charms"[93]— "she impersonated a Baroness Tamara v. Lützow, although her name isn't Tamara but Leontine."[94]

Literally dozens of examples could be added to these. Over the five years in which Tamara von Hervay made regular appearances in the press, she was endowed with no fewer than 16 first names and 15 last names (not counting variable spellings). First names included Maria, Marie, Mara, Mora, Tamara, Märchen, Camera, Elvira, Leontine, Liontine, Leontini, Leonore, Erna, Erni, Hedwig, and Klementine; last names assigned to her were Bloch, Polak, Rachey, Bellach, Berlach, Bellack, Bellachini, and Bellami (all as birth names), Kunz, Cunz, or Cuntz (the name of her first husband), Schewe, Sheve, von Schewe, and Baroness de Shève (the name of her second husband, occasionally ennobled), Lützow or von Lützow (as either a purported birth or married name), Meurin, Murin (as either a married name or literary pseudonym), von Hervay, Hervay-Kirchberg, Hervay von Kirchberg, Baroness von Kirchberg, Baroness von Kirchbach (versions or bowdlerizations of her fifth husband's name), Singer (presumably meant to indicate her Jewishness), and de Belhair or Bellèr (also occasionally frilled up with a Baroness or a Dame). Further adding to the melee was the fact that it was apparently unclear which first name went with which last name: she herself insisted on Tamara as her first name, whereas the court called her by her last husband's name (von Hervay) but attributed to her the first names on her birth certificate (Elvira Leontine). The press, either understandably confused or in a further effort to discredit her, referred to her by virtually any random first name-last name combination concoctable from the options above, and sometimes invented numerous perplexing last-name combos: Lützow-Hervay (a composite of the last names of husbands no. 3 and 5), Lützow-Bloch (a merger of her third husband's last name and the name of her father before he changed it to Bellachini), or Bellachini-Lützow-Murin-Hervay (her father's assumed name followed by the last names of husbands 3–5).

Matters came to a head when, in January 1907, a court order robbed her of the name Hervay. The Hervay family, eager to prevent her from bearing the family name, not to mention cashing in on Franz's officer's pension as his widow, had the marriage declared invalid on the grounds that she had still been married to someone else when the wedding to Franz took place. As a result, she was ordered by the court to relinquish the name "von Hervay"—a dilemma for the press, since this was the name under which she had become notorious and thus also a money-spinner.[95] The press responded to this blow variously either by simply ignoring the court order, by inventing further creative name combos that camouflaged the now-forbidden name in several others, or simply by surrounding it with scare quotes: Frau von "Hervay."[96] And perhaps this last is not only a defamation, but also a way of attesting to her success as an impostor: Hedwig Marie Elvira Leontine Klementine Tamara Erna Leonore Bloch Bellachini Cuntz de Shève de Belhair Meurin von Lützow Baroness von Hervay-Kirchberg, or whatever her name was, never acquired an unequivocal, definable character.

A character, however, is an indispensable prerequisite for attracting sympathy, and Hervay's nebulousness may well be the most significant reason why even her most ardent defenders were limited to expressing anger rather than arousing compassion. A good example is Siegmund Bergmann's open letter to M. Ring, the senior editor of the *Österreichische Volks-Zeitung*, published in the *Wiener Montags-Journal* on January 29, 1906, in which Bergmann attacks Ring and his paper for having maligned Hervay. She had been, he claimed, innocently sentenced, her only crime that of having nabbed the smart captain, thus disappointing the hopes of the flowering womanhood of Mürzzuschlag, arousing their ire and giving rise to the malicious gossip that destroyed her reputation and her husband's life. But most of Bergmann's writing and clearly also most of his anger is reserved for the *Volks-Zeitung*'s claim that Hervay was Bellachini's daughter and Jewish, and the paper's insistence on calling her names that she had rejected:

> There is nothing juicy about this affair, nothing worthy of being ground out in public, except for the name. This name that awakens so many memories, that is known to so many, that is just about good enough to be thrown to the news hyena that you have been called upon to feed. And so you dragged the name back into the light, dressed it in a zesty sauce [...] and cooked it up to make the slop tasty. Even just the list of names! The woman denies ever having had any family- or other relations with Bellachini, and she'd have to be 57 years old today in order to be the daughter of this Berlin juggler. But in your *Volksblatte* [...] she must remain this daughter, the "Jewess," because this makes your paper "objective," distinct from the "Jew press" that is now being castigated by the *Deutsches Volksblatt*, although this woman has never been Jewish, nor is she descended from Jews. She is instead a devout Catholic, and for this, she is being martyred on the cross by her brothers and sisters in faith.[97]

Bergmann's defense is worth considering here because it fails so monumentally at its clearly earnest attempt to evoke pity for her plight. In other words: he failed to create for her a stable character, an identity that could be pitied or liked, focusing instead on the *rejection* of identities attributed to her in the press. Instead of telling readers who she was, he told them who she was not: not a Bellachini, not Jewish, not 57 years old. In so doing, he merely added to the confusion that had always surrounded the most basic data of her life: name(s), dates, religious confession(s). Why, for instance, did he claim that she would have to be 57 years old to be Bellachini's daughter? The date of birth on the certificate listing her as Bellachini's daughter, July 18, 1860, would have made her 45 years old at the time of his letter, not 57. The statement seems to imply that her father (or purported father) Bellachini died as early as 1847–48 (in other words: at least 58 years earlier), when it was well known even at the time that Samuel Bellachini, one of the most popular and celebrated 19th-century magicians, had died in 1885. (The Samuel Bellachini whose death was widely reported on in January 1908 and who was inevitably misidentified as Tamara's father was most likely one of the hundreds of conjurers who, in admiration for the original Bellachini's work, adopted his name.[98])

Bizarrely, Bergmann's defense of Hervay achieves the same effect as the plethora of names against which he tried to defend her: it made her appear insubstantial. Readers are told that she was a Catholic and younger than 57 years of age. Beyond this, she is shielded from the "list of names!"—most particularly from one name, Bellachini—but not assigned one (it is astounding how often Bergmann refers to her simply as "the woman"). Identities are denied, but nothing is ever put in their place.

Hervay herself employed a similar modus operandi, picking and choosing, but mostly rejecting names and identities at will, blithely disregarding birth certificates, registry documents or social conventions, or casting doubt upon their authenticity with her recurring "As far as I know." The engine of her world was inclination, not reality. As she explained in court, she called herself "Tamara" simply because she liked the name; she rejected the name Meurin, the name of her fourth husband when she arrived in Mürzzuschlag and thus, at the time, her legal name, "because that name was not sym-

Samuel Bellachini (1828–1885), internationally famous court conjurer and Tamara von Hervay's contested father (courtesy Franz Preitler/Wintersportmuseum Mürzzuschlag).

pathetic to me." Instead, she picked a name from the many in her past that sounded good to her, in this case, the name of her long-divorced third husband, von Lützow, no doubt without his knowledge or consent. Whether or not she was legally entitled to do this—the court told her that she actually was not[99]—made no difference to her. And although her entire defense rested on her claim that she had never been legally married to Hervay, she tried to secure her future ownership of his name, telling the astounded court that she and her husband "had an agreement that in case he died before our real wedding took place I would still have the right to bear his name."[100] Adopting and discarding identities at will, she remained nebulous, a woman of many names. In the writing of her detractors, this marked her as an adventuress, a sham and a fraud, a gold digger, a marriage swindler, an impostor. To her defenders, this made her a tantalizingly mysterious woman. Both ultimately define her as a woman without substance, a nobody. Everything about her, positive or negative—her nickname, *Märchen;* the "fairy tales" she was accused of telling in the town and later in court; the fairy tale as which she herself described her love affair with Franz—indicates her irreality. As one such fairy tale describes the magical moment during which Franz von Hervay first cast eyes on her: "She was—he knew not who. She came—he knew not whence."[101] And she went—we know not where.

A Tale of Two Thieves:
The Case of Franz and Erich Sass
(Berlin, 1920s)

For the most part, Gorski will turn out to be right. [...] As soon as safe cracking is no longer worth it in Berlin, most safe crackers will turn again to normal break-ins, into shops or apartments. Even now, this migration is already noticeable. [...] Only the very few who have the mettle to be truly great safe crackers [...] will, as Gorski did, use an oxygen apparatus or explosives for their break-ins. But their audacity will focus the criminal police's investigative zeal on them to such a degree that their doings will hardly last long.

On balance, aside from isolated occurrences, safe cracking will be at an end within the foreseeable future.—Erich Liebermann von Sonnenberg, "The Elite Among Burglars," 1912[1]

In 1929, the Sass Brothers worked following the model of the American safe crackers when they emptied the vault of the Disconto-Society on Wittenbergplatz in Berlin. Not a robbery that relied on speed and violence but a secretly and cunningly executed crime: Bank break-ins had come to Germany.—Marcel Boldorf, "The Invention of Bank Robbery," 2001[2]

In 1912, Erich Liebermann von Sonnenberg, a jurist (and later, under the Nazis, the Chief of the Berlin CID) and Max Gorski, himself a safe cracker of note, agreed that bank safe cracking as a profession was finished. Bank safes, Gorski lamented, had simply become too good for traditional tools of the trade like wrenches and drills. More modern methods such as oxy-fuel cutting or blasting open safe doors necessitated heavy and expensive equipment, things that were both hazardous and cumbersome to transport, like oxygen bottles, welding tools or explosives. Between the invention of more robust bank safes and increased police zeal, the job had become both too onerous and too dangerous. And so it was that barely six years after the first bank safe break-in had been recorded in Berlin,[3] a criminal mourned the passing of safe-cracking as a profession while a criminalist danced on its grave.

The Sass Sensation: A New Age Dawns

Nothing could have prepared either for the Brothers Sass, Germany's most gifted, daring, ingenious, persistent, and beloved thieves, destined to revive the profession in grand style. When Franz Sass was twelve and Erich was ten, they embarked on a criminal partnership that would ultimately turn them into "the first media stars, or the first pop stars of bank robbery."[4] This was in 1916, barely four years after Liebermann had pronounced Berlin's bank safes safe. The brothers' greatest coup, the Disconto bank job of March 1929, would come to be seen, by Boldorf (and historians and criminalists throughout the past 90 years), as the beginning of a new age in the history of modern crime.[5] Some see this sea-change already achieved two years earlier, when the sassy brothers attacked the Alt-Moabit bank in March 1927.[6] But no matter: whether we take their failed (but brilliant) attempt in 1927 or their successful (and brilliant) coup of 1929 as the starting pistol of the new era, there is universal agreement that pistol was fired by the Brothers Sass. Bank break-ins had come to Germany, and with a pizzazz heretofore unimagined.

Beyond a great deal of chutzpah and a staunch attachment to other people's money, Franz and Erich Sass had something else in common with Germany's other celebrity criminal, Wilhelm Voigt: they grew up dirt poor in a broken family. In their home quarter Moabit, one of Berlin's poorest, the local joke had it that you collect your rent with a revolver and the local legend traced the name of the quarter back to a contemptuous eighteenth-century French moniker: *la terre maudite*—a wretched country.[7] The Sass family's little slice of wretchedness was Birkenstraße 57, side entrance, four floors up, one room, one kitchen, toilet on the gangway outside shared with another family. When Ekkehard Schwerk wrote his seminal study of the Sass brothers in the early 1980s, the tiny apartment was occupied by one student. When the Sasses lived there, six people had to squeeze into its 430 square feet: mother Marie (1879–?) and younger brother Hans (born in 1914) slept in the kitchen; the tiny main room was shared by father Andreas (1868–1936), who slept on a cot while Franz (born in October 1904) and Erich (born in April 1906) shared the marital bed.[8] Where their older brother Max (born in 1903) slept is not recorded. Not crowding out the apartment was the eldest son Paul, born in 1902—a little too soon for decorum, which led to a permanent rift between the parents. (As soon as Paul was "legitimized" after his birth, he was farmed off to foster parents and had no further contact with his birth mother or her family; aside from the youngest son Hans, he was the only Sass brother who escaped a life of crime.) Max Fabich, the Detective Sergeant who spent much of his career on the brothers' trail, described their father as a Polish tailor who never learned German although he lived in Berlin for over 40 years, "a rather peculiar old codger who didn't much concern himself with his fellow man and considered his five boys [...] as simply non-existent."[9] Other than paying the rent, he refused to support his family in any way. Accordingly, Mother Marie was forced to put in long hours at her job as a washerwoman in the local hospital: up at 5 a.m., returning in the late afternoon, for a weekly wage of 35 marks.[10] Left completely unsupervised, the three middle brothers, Max, Franz and Erich, soon began to steal from department stores, leading to capture, a rap sheet, and a sentence of "corrective training" against all three. Erich was placed into training as a metal worker and locksmith by Child Protective Services. He only stayed for six months, but the training he received stood him in good stead in later years, when he was routinely faced with metal walls and doors to which he did not have a key. As Fabich ruefully states, "this, unfortunately, became the basis for his later criminal career. Due to a curious one-sided

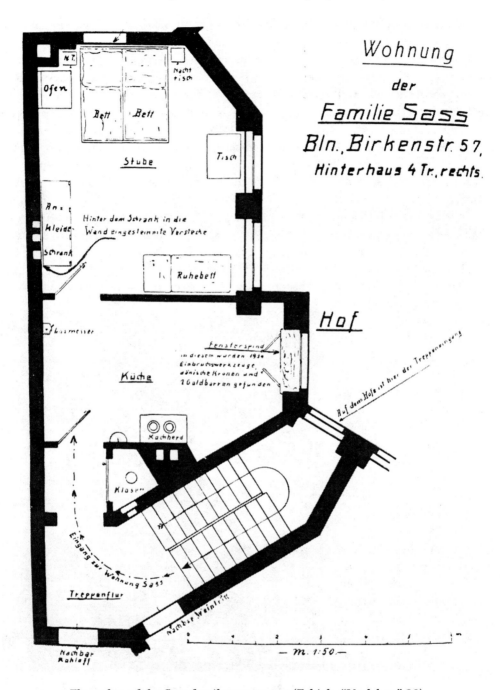

Floorplan of the Sass family apartment (Fabich, "Vorleben" 38).

technical talent he quickly learned how to use the locksmith's tools, which he knew to employ in a manner that would have been better devoted to different purposes."[11]

Child Protective Services and the police tended to blame the Sass brothers' lack of parental supervision for their lives of crime. That may well be, but they were certainly also born into a time when honest work didn't pay, or at least not nearly enough, for the vast majority of Berlin's poor. Part of the reason why Berliners identified with the Sass brothers to such a degree was that their family background and childhood story was hardly unusual. In Moabit and other poor quarters of the city, tiny apartments such as the Sass family occupied were normally home to eight or ten people. Fathers waited outside the front door until the children were asleep; people who had a balcony slept on it during the summers—anything for a bit of breathing space.[12] The Great Depression was already in the air and Berlin was swamped with an army of jobless workers. Discontent was in the air too, often expressing itself in the celebration of those who refused to accept the uneven distribution of money as god-given, foremost among them those who attacked faceless institutions like banks rather than resorting to robbing their often already impoverished fellow man. As Klaus Schönberger put it, "every bank robbery reminds us that societal conditions are historical and hence alterable, for bank robberies challenge the seemingly natural distribution of societal wealth."[13] Some went so far as to suggest that the era's true criminals were not bank robbers but those who kept the distribution of wealth uneven, and some of this sentiment can be linked directly with popular support for the Sass brothers' escapades. Everyone knows Bertolt Brecht's

famous accusation of society's real crooks in *The Threepenny Opera* (*Die Dreigroschenoper*, 1928): as Mac the Knife muses on the relative scale of criminal behavior, "how does robbing a bank even compare to founding a bank?"[14] Few remember, though, that this line was directly inspired by the daring feats of Franz and Erich Sass.[15]

Unlike their brother Max, whom they set up in a cigar shop (undoubtedly bought with money from one of their many breakins), neither Franz nor Erich ever held down a legitimate job. Max Sass was a part-time worker, both licitly and il-, whose law-breaking exploits never grew beyond the spotty and the ordinary.[16] Franz and Erich, conversely, went all in. Together, they founded what Schwerk has humor-

Franz (seated) and Erich Sass in the dock (1929) (ullstein bild).

ously called their own "Company of Crooks, Brothers Sass, Inc.,"[17] with themselves as directors, shareholders and the sum total of the workforce, and systematically set about securing for themselves a slice of the Golden Twenties. They were the Dream Team of crime: little Franz, 5'5", blond and blue-eyed with the gift of gab; tall, dark and handsome Erich, 6'1", the genius surveyor of the thickness of walls, the weakness of locks and the safest path to the safe.[18] In Moabit and soon all over Berlin, they became the stuff of legend, the epitome of the local boys who had made good. From 1925 onward, at the tender ages of 19 and 21, they began to live like kings: tailor-made suits and silk-lined overcoats, expensive motorbikes and fast cars, trips to Paris, London, Italy, Denmark, Monte Carlo and Helgoland, from where they dutifully sent postcards home to the dinky apartment in which they continued to live when not on vacation. Just like in *The Threepenny Opera*, everyone knew where the money came from. Legend had it that after each unsolved bank robbery in Berlin, 10-mark bills began to appear in the mailboxes of the Sass neighbors in Moabit. Although it makes for a wonderful story, there is, alas, little evidence for this charitable streak; it was not even confirmed by their attorney Dr. Müller-Stromeyer, who defended them to the end and cultivated their legend whenever it seemed expedient.[19] But the fact that the tale has persisted for so long (in the early 1980s, Schwerk interviewed their former next-door neighbor who swore that the Robin Hood story was true[20]) shows the degree to which the Sass brothers were admired, even adored.

The Criminal Working World

Franz and Erich's Company of Crooks was both unique and embedded within a specific context, namely that of an organized crime scene within which safe crackers ranked at the very top of the hierarchy. Safe crackers were more than mere thieves, they were experts of a trade and thus considered an elite, the "aristocrats of the world of crime."[21] Whereas a regular thief was near his goal by the time he had broken through the door, a safe cracker's work had barely begun at that stage. Safe cracking required talent, persistence, and skill, even "study" or a training period; several instances are recorded of people undergoing years of training for legitimate jobs (as locksmiths, welders or metalworkers, for instance) in order to qualify for a career in safe cracking.[22] Numerous statements from imprisoned offenders of the time attest that the contemporary criminal code of honor ranked crimes hierarchically (not dissimilar to the legitimate working world, where a lawyer's or a doctor's prestige outstrips a janitor's or a plumber's), with safe cracking considered the most noble profession and pimping the most vile. Crucially, nonviolent crimes were ranked more highly than violent ones. Crooks who used weapons were frequently panned both for unnecessary brutality and for incompetence. "And how often have I said to my friend Willi, whenever he bursts into a bedroom, gun in hand: Knock it off, Willi, we'll do proper break-ins!"[23]

That relations between the criminal underworld and the police were respectful, even cordial until at least 1914 is fairly well documented.[24] But even after the war, thieves rarely used violence against the police, even when caught *in flagrante delicto*. In all of Prussia, not only Germany's largest State but also home to Germany's largest, most populous, and most crime-ridden city, only four policemen died in the line of duty between 1925 and 1931.[25] In 1922, the Berlin Detective Hans von Tresckow reported that he was told by a burglar whom he had just arrested: "I don't have anything against you. My job is stealing and yours is catching me do it."[26] In 1929, a robber pragmatically declared that he considered the average cop a "colleague who, just like me, is doing it for a few dimes a day and doesn't want to lose his pension."[27] Similarly, as Liebermann noted with despair, the average thief "considers his trade, the appropriation of someone else's property, a regular job like any other."[28] Commentators throughout the age have claimed that most thieves were not actually rebelling against the social order but seeking to be part of it, trying to become "equal members of human society," which to them meant having access to "luxury items like beer, tobacco and a 'girl.'" According to Curt Elwenspoek, many planned to hang up their picklocks and open up a little business, perhaps a bar or a butcher's shop, just as soon as they had stolen the necessary capital.[29]

Given the decidedly bourgeois aspirations and behavior patterns of thieves (the desire for legitimacy; the establishment of professional hierarchies; the "we're-all-just-doing-our-jobs-here" attitude toward the police), it is not all that surprising that they imitated law-abiding society in terms of organizational structure as well. By 1918, there were five underworld unions in Berlin. By the end of the 1920s, there were more than 50; by the time the Nazis shut them down in 1934, there were 64. These thieves and robbers-unions, the so-called *Ringvereine* (Ring Associations), which would feature so prominently in Fritz Lang's 1931 film *M*, were neatly subdivided into union chapters with fine-sounding names like "Semper Fi," "Hand in Hand," "German Power" or "Mountain Eagle." Just like societies in the law-abiding world, these clubs were officially registered and had a strict honor code, charters and statutes. Applicants had to prove, by showing their prison release papers, that they had spent at least two years in jail and obtain recommendations from two existing members with solid, respectable criminal records. Murderers, manslaughterers, and sexual criminals were excluded from membership. Aspirant members had to serve as lookouts for several jobs before they were admitted to full membership in a formal ceremony. The unions provided legal advice and alibis, hired only the very best attorneys for members in trouble, and took care of the widows of those who died. There were even concerts and a yearly ball to which the police, including high-ranking inspectors, were invited. And why not? It is always a good idea to rub shoulders with the opposition. For their part, the police did not object to the crime unions, which brought together, in a nice and orderly fashion, nearly the entire "crème de la crème of the underworld," as Schwerk put it.[30] Having a pool of known suspects for each new crime neatly assembled in a room must have been of some comfort to the cops, even as the teamwork among union members made their capture and prosecution infinitely more difficult.[31]

Underworld unions made sense particularly in a criminal profession that centrally relied on collaboration with others, such as bank robbery. No safe cracker ever works alone, Liebermann explained, because you need at least one lookout and several people working on the safe. At absolute minimum, a single break-in gang had to contain three to five members, more likely six or seven. "Through this constant affiliation of several safe crackers in a gang that always works together, where each is working in concert with the other and knows he can rely on the other, safe crackers retain a trace of the old, genuine and authentic crime world. A safe cracker arrested alone will rarely betray his accomplices. Even threatening him with long prison terms will not bring him to do it."[32] When it comes to safe crackers and their code of honor among thieves, even Liebermann, a hard-nosed criminalist who spent much of his writing lamenting the free fall of morality and the rise of crime, sounds almost nostalgic.

Underworld Geniuses

Within this context, the Sass brothers were highly unusual. They were regulars at union festivities, where their exploits, even before the memorable 1929 Disconto bank job, quickly gained them superstar status.[33] But they never joined up, they always worked alone, and they raised the aspects of the job that made safe crackers the royalty of the underworld—planning, expertise, nonviolence, training, and skill—to an entirely new level. On Monday, March 28, 1927, employees of the Deutsche Bank in Alt-Moabit found all doors leading to the vault broken open and immediately alerted the police. Enter Max Fabich, who would become the Sass brothers' principal opponent for the next thirteen years. In 1927, he was a "man in his so-called prime, 42 years old, short, nimble and bald."[34] It was the first time he had seen a "hot" safe cracking job. The attempt failed because the robbers knew as little about the procedure as the cops did: they did not know, for example, that welding torches leach oxygen from the room. They got sick and had to stop, leaving "unsavoury remnants" of their last meal at the scene, but, crucially, no fingerprints.[35] Fabich, reconstructing the case in 1940, notes admiringly that:

> even these early break-ins are characterised by the Sass brothers' very unusual ability to correctly assess locks and other security measures and circumvent them[...]. Furthermore, their inconceivable talent to grasp architectural structures and use them and their weaknesses to develop a tactical plan of attack can only be described as clairvoyant.[36]

This would become the Sass brothers' signature style. Uncannily, inconceivably shrewd, skilled and patient, they prepared each break-in for weeks, if not months; they knew exactly where and how to get in; they were hardly ever heard or seen, even though they spent entire days or even weeks on a single job, and they never left finger- or footprints. Spurning hammers and chisels, they cut through the strongest walls by removing the mortar between bricks with a jigsaw, breaking out the bricks in complete silence, and hiding the holes with cleverly painted wooden panels that matched the color of bricks and mortar, even the dirt stains, on the wall. The art work was so effective that most observers missed it standing right in front of it. When Fabich was urgently called to the Dresdner Bank branch on Savignyplatz on December 4, 1927, he knew exactly, contemplating the two squares neatly cut out of the bank's safe, whose work he was looking at. The work being incomplete, he had the place staked out, hoping the Sass brothers would return. The police spent a very cold night waiting in vain: the brothers, alerted by we know not what, were watching the watchers.[37]

The papers, distracted by a sordid teen murder-suicide story with plenty of sex and plenty of blood, did not honor the March break-in with the attention it deserved—

it was, after all, the first time in recorded crime history that a welding torch had been used to open a safe.[38] On December 5, however, the press sat up and took notice. What baffled them was the sheer level of planning, preparation and determination that had gone into the job. The robbers had arrived with six large oxygen canisters, each weighing 220 pounds, and several canisters of gas, all of which they transported—unseen and unheard by anyone—over a wall separating the bank from the adjoining property and the train station at Savignyplatz. They then opened the bank's reinforced back door, without damaging it in the slightest, and secured an alternate exit route, in case they were surprised, by opening an iron grille securing a window. Only then did they turn their attention to the vault, where they first very carefully secured all their equipment. "It must have been a tremendous amount of work to carry all of this material, unnoticed, to the scene and over the wall; the attack on the vault was even more difficult. The criminals must have spent *many hours* smelting the vault open."[39] You can practically see the journalist describing all this scratching his head in baffled admiration: the criminals had timed their expedition to coincide with construction work at the nearby railway station, so that what little noise they had to make, cutting through an 80-cm-thick wall reinforced with steel and concrete and a similarly enforced 50-cm-thick door, would be attributed to that. Such a job, the paper surmised, necessitated a large gang, four men at absolute minimum. Happily, however, "this new attempt demonstrates once again that even specialists with the best tools and the greatest means are not capable of coping with bank safes. Their technique is simply not yet equal to the security measures of the banks."[40]

How right they were to qualify this overconfident verdict with the little word "yet." The Sass brothers obviously did not regard their unsuccessful attempts as failures but as valuable training. As Fabich grudgingly noted, "the Sass brothers made *technical* and *tactical* progress from case to case, in each attempted break-in and in all their criminal activities."[41] There were three more of these training exercises in 1928, the first on March 6, the second barely three weeks later, on the night of March 24; the third on May 20.

The March 6 attempt on the German Railway's main administration building, which contained a safe with the payroll for its employees—a potential haul of 1 million marks—was another exemplar of planning. How the Sass brothers even got into the building remains their secret to this day. Since the safe was not in the basement but on the first floor, they drilled through the ceiling from the floor beneath, hiding the hole, as usual, with a plaster square that perfectly matched the dirty grey ceiling paint. With a cunning that Fabich later described as "incomprehensible," they had once again correctly identified not only the precise location of the safe but also the building's only weak entry point.[42]

Coincidence—in this case, in the form of an unscheduled walk-by by a night watchman—foiled both this effort and the next, their attempt on the Dresdner Bank in Charlottenburg. On the night of March 24, Attorney Grzimek, returning home late, noticed the smell of burning and woke up the night porter Suleck. The smell led them to the elevator shaft of their building, which connected through a tunnel to the cellar of the bank next door. Men of the fire brigade called to the scene noticed two eyes peeking out at them from a slightly raised blind of the bank basement and notified the police.

Fabich arrived accompanied by an entire police brigade. High alert; rumors flying; a multitude—numbering, according to the *Berliner Tageblatt*, in the thousands[43]—gathered on the street to watch the show. Fabich reverently contemplated a neatly broken out hole in the wall, masked perfectly with a square of wood plastered and painted with the same kind of bricks and mortar to hide the hole. Crawling through it, Fabich found an identical hole in the cellar wall opposite, again masked to the point of invisibility, leading to the adjacent building. Nobody in the house had heard or seen a thing until the Sass brothers, cutting through iron grates to reach the safe, accidentally set alight a box containing check forms stored on the other side, causing the smoke noticed by Grzimek. Fabich knew perfectly well that this was the Sass's work, and so did everybody on the street, where rumors spread like wildfire: the thieves are still in the building. Indeed, Franz and Erich Sass spent the night squeezed tightly into a small cellar light shaft in a building that was by now crawling with cops. The cops turned the place upside down but couldn't find the robbers; they gave up after hours of searching. Early in the morning, the police long gone, Frau Gönne, wife of the bank's cash messenger, called them back: she had seen a man running up the back stairs to the attic. The police raced back, sirens howling and tires screeching; the neighbors settled in on their balconies to watch Act II of the night's entertainment. There were now so many people on the street that the police had to waste most of their efforts on crowd management. Frau Gönne pointed heavenward, and "the shadows of two agile men are seen over the roof of house number 10 on the roof of the adjoining building." Split seconds later, they were gone, leaving Fabich to tear his hair out for not having searched the building more thoroughly.[44]

The press, of course, had a field day, particularly with the vision of the thieves sitting in their hidey hole, waiting out the police and listening in on their conversations. Although Fabich knew as well as everyone on the street who the culprits were, they were not recognized, and their signature handiwork alone did not even merit a search warrant, let alone an arrest. Although only two men were seen fleeing, the press dutifully repeated the police-authored fable that only a large gang could have pulled off something like this. A "band of well-versed 'experts,'" proclaimed the *Berliner Börsen-Zeitung*, "one of the most cunning and best-equipped gangs ever."[45] A "robber gang," cried the *Berliner Tageblatt*, comprising at minimum "four or five men."[46] And in the *Volkszeitung*, defensively: "Police inquiry has established that we're dealing with members of a large ring of safe crackers."[47] Mere months after the confident proclamation that bank security will foil even the most determined thieves, this faith was now severely shaken. The recurring canard of the huge robber gang reads both as a justification that things could even get to this state and as an excuse for the police, who, faced with what sounds like an entire underworld army, had nothing to show for hours of desperate searching.

The police responded to this humiliation by placing the Sass brothers under surveillance. From March to May 1928, they watched the brothers' every move, noting where they went and making meticulous lists of everything they bought: black paint, spiral drills, screws, iron tools. It was not a subtle operation; everyone in the quarter knew who the watchers were and where they were hiding at all times, including, of course, the Brothers Sass. There is a lovely story on record in which the police, following the brothers to the Darmstädter- und Nationalbank at Nollendorfplatz and watching them disappear inside, observed the bank until it closed hours later. The brothers did not emerge, but the watchers stayed where they were, assuming the Sasses had allowed themselves to be locked in on purpose. After closing time they searched the bank—in vain. The brothers were long gone; they had simply strolled in the front door and immediately out through the back.[48]

When surveillance was finally canceled in the second half of May 1928, the Brothers immediately sprang into action with their most ambitious plan to date. On May 19, they came hauntingly close to stealing 9 million marks, earmarked for war reparation payments to France, from the safe of the Inland Revenue Office Alt-Moabit. The brothers had again chosen a circuitous route: over a fence, down a hill, through a window facing the railroad tracks, through a 100-meter corridor and then up a floor to the safe, all this weighed down with a heavy oxygen bottle. They had 1.5 hours, the time it took the nightwatchman Karl Lehmann to make his round, to get through the safe door, and began cutting the minute he left the porter's lodge. Erich disabled the alarm protecting the safe but could not prevent a brief lighting of the lamp, and Lehmann, returned before his time, saw it and called out. Franz, watching the watchman, ran to Erich, who was just opening the safe door, and the two fled through the corridor and the window, up the incline and out onto the street Alt-Moabit, where the first cop cars were already arriving. The brothers left behind 9 million now completely unprotected marks, a lot of expensive equipment, and no fingerprints.[49] Fabich, grudgingly: "The way in which they stalked up on the vault—averse as I am to use an honest hunting term for such criminal deeds, there is no word that can more adequately describe this act of sneaking up from a distance—was again made possible only through this peculiar talent to recognize spatial dimensions."[50] The press was strangely silent on this potentially greatest of all Sass coups: perhaps the national embarrassment of very nearly losing the country's entire war reparation payment to a "large gang" of two was too much for the police, and they managed to hush up the affair.

The Disconto Bank Job

After this, there were months of silence from the Sass brothers. It turned out to be the silence before the storm. The storm broke on Monday, January 28, 1929,[51] when Mr. Nürnberg, cashier at the Disconto-Society Bank on Kleiststraße, corner of Wittenbergplatz, tried to open the door of what was then the best-secured vault in Berlin. The key turned but the door did not open. He called his boss who called the bank director who called the firm who had installed the door. Nobody, including the firm's two burly locksmiths, succeeded in opening the door. Hours passed. The director objected to the police being called just because a door was jammed: imagine the scandal! Most likely, he suggested hopefully, the door was jammed because the Berlin underground train running directly beneath the bank had caused the entire building to settle.

After a day of fruitless shimmying and chiseling, the director commissioned two bricklayers for the following day to break open the cement wall next to the door. Fourteen hours of sweaty labor later, on the morning of Wednesday, January 30, they finally had broken out a square hole. The director took a flashlight and looked inside. "Those present heard him gasping, moaning, finally gagging. The record states that the Herr Director, faced with what he saw in the flashlight's beam, bequeathed his barely finished breakfast to the inside of the vault."[52] The vault was littered with valuables that the thieves hadn't bothered with, including an original score of Wagner's *Tristan und Isolde*, crumpled up and carelessly tossed into a corner. Of 181 safety deposit boxes, 179 had been opened—not broken open, but opened in a manner that could not be reconstructed, without any visible damage—and cleaned out. (The police later speculated that the thieves had scouted out the scene by renting safety deposit boxes,[53] to which we can add the reasonable suspicion that the two boxes left untouched belonged to the Brothers Sass.) Never had a pair of thieves taken more time over a haul; they had sorted through the loot in calm comfort and with all the time in the world. They left behind two empty wine bottles, needless to say bereft of fingerprints: celebrations had been in order, it seems.

To this day, nobody knows how high the Sass brothers' take was. The officially reported 150,000 marks is a ludicrously low estimate. The *Fehrbelliner Zeitung* was probably closer to the mark with its estimate of a loss of "many millions," with at least one million in cash.[54] The bank had no record of what the safe deposit boxes contained,

The scene of the crime. "They opened almost by themselves. The safety deposit boxes in the vault on Wittenbergplatz were barely damaged" (*Berliner Volks-Zeitung,* February 1, 1929, evening edition p. 1).

and their owners never specified their losses—for good reason: most of the valuables stashed there were things they were hiding from spouses, creditors or the taxman. That the Sasses must have walked off with millions is indicated not by what they took—the loot has, to this day, never been found[55]—but what they left behind, probably because they could not transport it all: gold bars, silver and platinum bars, whole bundles of money, and valuable jewelry. Or more concretely, the less valuable parts of valuable jewelry: they had broken out the precious stones and tossed the gold and silver settings aside.[56] The papers reported that the valuables they had not bothered with were later collected in 36 large boxes and that 100 bank employees had to be employed to sort through it.[57]

It goes without saying that this coup brought the entire police force to the scene, from the police president Zörgiebel and his vice president Weiß to the lowliest beat cop on the streets of Berlin. The streets were black with people, whom 100 policemen tried, with varying success, to keep away from the bank. As one paper put it: "The house on Kleiststraße 23 was besieged all morning by a vast crowd who admired the exacting work of the thieves with mixed feelings."[58] Windows and balconies of surrounding houses had become the best seats in the house. Meanwhile, inside the bank, detectives had begun the laborious job of reconstructing the bank robbery of the century. They crawled through the hole in the vault in order of seniority: Zörgiebel followed by Weiß followed by the ever luckless Fabich. Fabich was the first to discover that the

The fallout: anxious customers and curious bystanders assemble at the bank as word gets around (ullstein bild).

brothers had entered and left through the ceiling ventilator. He took the same path, leaving the others staring behind him as he disappeared through the hole in the ceiling. He traced the Sass's path through a tight light shaft protected by iron bars (now cut through), followed by a vertical shaft neatly carpentered out with wooden supports, walls and ceilings, directly beneath the sidewalk in front of the entrance to the bank. To get to the safe, the brothers had broken through two basement walls and tunneled through the frozen ground underneath the sidewalk for three meters: the painstaking work of several weeks. As Fabich later described it: "This difficult and complex 'pioneering' work must naturally have claimed many nights, for it necessitated moving no less than 2.5 cubic metres [= 88.28 cubic feet, TSK] of earth, taking further into account that the perpetrators couldn't, and didn't, leave any trace. No wonder, then, that the Brothers Sass had previously indulged in a few months of rest."[59]

Cops and Robbers

The police did their best to catch the thieves, barely aided by their exact knowledge of who they were: the problem was proving it. Endless interrogations of everyone living in Kleiststraße and the stratospheric reward of 40,000 marks yielded lots of gossip and over 1,000 tips, each of which had to be followed up carefully[60]—more busywork for the police—but no convincing leads. A host of multitudes claimed to have seen the Sass brothers at strange times of the day or night around the bank; everyone was certain of their guilt. A search of the Sasses' apartment produced items rarely found in the dwellings of the poor: expensive jewelry, gold watches and necklaces, bejewelled cravat pins, brooches and golden earrings—as well as tools, dirty gloves, and lock picks—and a gold dollar coin from the year 1858, which the safety deposit box holder who had lost one just like it could not definitively identify as hers.

On February 22, the brothers were duly arrested,[61] but their interrogation turned out to be a nightmare for the police. Dressed to the nines, Franz and Erich slouched on their chairs, acting bored, speaking in Berlin dialect and admitting nothing. They had bought the jewelry for their mother, from a street vendor, having no idea that it was genuine. They had found the coin at the tramway station near the bank—obviously, one of the thieves must have dropped it while fleeing. The tools were easily explained with a good dose of filial duty: there's always something to fix around the house, and what with father and mother working hard all day for so little pay...[62] The police tore their hair out and Berliners laughed their heads off; according to Schwerk, this was when the moniker "the beloved brothers" began to make the rounds.[63] On April 6, the police finally released the brothers for lack of evidence, in the wee hours, hoping for a minimum of fuss and fanfare. But they had not reckoned with the sassy brothers or their lawyer, Dr. Müller-Stromeyer. Marching from the prison cell straight to Lutter & Wegner on Gendarmenmarkt, Berlin's classiest restaurant, they threw a champagne breakfast for the press followed by a press conference full of boozy good cheer and tall tales from the brothers. Franz bragged that they had been contacted by a film company who wanted to shoot a caper movie based on their lives, and claimed police brutality, a claim that resulted in more busywork for the police: a lawsuit, a countersuit, and two appeals. The appeals were eventually thrown out of court—a minor victory for the police, if we're feeling generous—but the legal fallout from Franz's abuse claim ended up costing the cops time, money and energies that they would have undoubtedly preferred to spend on finally nailing the Brothers to the wall.[64]

The fallout from the Disconto job was immense. It was soon seen as a major "European criminalistic event," and upset papers reported that "even America," widely perceived in Germany as the undisputed Land of Crime, "was astounded at the audacity of these criminals."[65] In 1927, the press had confidently proclaimed the superiority of bank security over even the wiliest break-in attempt. In 1928, the Sass brothers dealt a severe blow to the faith in the safety of safes. In 1929, what little remained of that faith was utterly shattered, again by the Brothers Sass. Fabich, remembering the affair in 1940, saw this clearly:

> in the background lurked the anxious question whether *vaults even existed* that could withstand the modern break-in methods of skilled and ruthless robbers. [...] The Brothers Sass had also demonstrated that even so-called protective alarm systems could only be relied upon up to a point. Bank customers, banks and insurance companies were thus in an understandable uproar. In the eternal technological race between the security industry and break-in techniques, the former had been defeated in unexpected ways, and to such a degree that it seemed uncertain whether this defeat could be offset in the foreseeable future.[66]

This is presumably why not only the entire police force but also big political brass, including the Minister for Home Affairs Grecesinski and Undersecretary Hirschfeld,[67] were hastily called to the scene on the very morning the break-in was discovered. The following day, an emergency meeting of senior police, bank directors and representatives of the Central Association of German Bankers was convened, to discuss forming "a coalition for the joint fight against criminal activities." Impressed by the Sass brothers' demonstration of the inadequacy of their security measures, the attendees quickly approved some expensive decisions: "*Every vault must be guarded at all times by at least one guard, preferably two.* There also must be a telephone installed which the guard can use to call a police station or Central Watch at any time."[68] On February 1, the papers reported that the bank directors and Police Vice President Weiß planned to call a national conference to include "all multicorporate banks whose vaults are in danger, in order to win them over to joint defensive action against safe cracking gangs."[69] Gone entirely was the smugness of 1927: this was sheer panic combined with a facesaving exercise that refused to admit that this was now a matter involving a barn door and a horse. And it was not only the faith in bank security that was shattered, but also that in police competence. "Is this really the end of an investigation that has been watched by the entire world?," asked the *Vossische Zeitung*, clearly disappointed, after the Brothers' release. "Can this really mean that all the work of three months, in which hundreds of detectives did nothing but follow every trace that has emerged since the Night of the Vault Looting on Wittenbergplatz, has been wasted, in vain? If so, then the Berlin police force has suffered a defeat and a loss of prestige from which they will not recover for years."[70]

After the champagne-soaked press conference, the police returned to licking their wounds while Franz and Erich returned to living in the lap of luxury: elegant clothes, a new motorbike, a nice new car. It was a very fast car; the police, infamously under-

Franz and Erich Sass. Police mugshot, ca. 1929 (Fabich, "Vorleben" 39).

equipped,[71] would never be able to catch up with it. Almost exactly a year after the Disconto bank disaster, cops and robbers squared off again. Around Christmas of 1929, rumors began to circulate that the cemetery Luisenfriedhof in Charlottenburg was haunted. "It got to the point," Fabich reports, "that anxious neighbors no longer dared to go near their windows at night."[72] The cemetery's groundskeeper Geschwendt found disorderly piles of fresh earth, with human bones protruding, and confronted the grave diggers, who denied it all. This fruitless back-and-forth continued until New Years' Eve. Then the groundskeeper's nephew met a stranger in the yard of the school next to the cemetery who could not adequately explain his presence. And so the police were called again, on January 9, 1930. Fabich noticed a hand print in the dirt on the Geschwendts' chicken coop near the cemetery wall, and asked Detective Sergeant Jeschke to climb a ladder to check it out. Ladder and Jeschke sank slowly into the ground, which, at this time of year, should have been frozen solid. A bit of digging soon revealed a sizeable subterranean hideout: a shaft, 2 × 3 meters, neatly walled out with wodden planks, with a wooden ceiling created to protect the structure from collapse, followed by two similarly constructed larger rooms, 3.38 meters long by 2.38 meters wide by 2.30 meters high, filled with tools. There was even a sort of primitive stairwell leading down to the chambers. The wood had not been sawed but hand-drilled and broken off, a silent method of carpentry that eventually yielded an underground hideout not much smaller than the Sass apartment.[73]

Fabich knew immediately who had created this marvel, but kept his suspicions to himself as he ordered the force to stake out the scene. They were in for a bitterly cold night, miserably shivering in a ditch, their limbs stiffening because they couldn't move.[74]

Hours later their patience was rewarded with a Sass sighting. Fabich recognized Franz at once, but Franz realized even more quickly that the lock to his hideout had been tampered with and fled. The police in hot pursuit, Franz jumped up the two-meter-high cemetery wall, which had been outfitted with protruding wooden footholds to aid in quick escape, and was pulled over the wall by his brother's helping hand. On the other side, the policemen stationed there without being told why, were left wondering why the thieves of Disconto bank fame, whom they knew by sight, were running past them as if all the hounds of hell were at their heels. Now definitively identified as both the moles and the "ghosts" haunting the cemetery (Franz Sass wore white handkerchiefs to protect his hair while engaged in overhead digging), the brothers were arrested the next day. Shortly thereafter, they were released again, following an ironclad alibi provided by their lawyer and the cops' depressing realization that the Brothers, alibied or not, could not be indicted. For what? Trespassing, damage to property, disorderly conduct, lack of respect for the dead?[75] Later they were caught again while digging a hideout; they got a month for property damage and trespassing.[76] To the long-suffering cops, it must have seemed more anticlimactic than busting Capone for tax evasion.

Two more break-ins that netted the brothers nothing but more trouble with the law nevertheless show how utterly outmatched the police were in their struggle with the Sass brothers. In April 1930, they were finally caught in the act while breaking a hole through a cellar wall of a house on Werftstrasse that housed a cigar shop. The *Berliner Volks-Zeitung* triumphantly blared: "Brothers Sass finally caught! Caught in the act of a break-in and arrested!"[77] But the elation did not last. Some queried why the brothers took the trouble of breaking through the wall when only a dinky little lock separated them from the cash box in the tobacco shop,[78] but nobody ever wondered why the greatest bank robbers Berlin had ever seen, who had stolen and successfully hidden millions, would suddenly content themselves with the negligible amount of cash that a tobacconist might leave in his cash box overnight. We can only guess that the hole in the cellar wall of the house on Werftstrasse was the starting point of one of their long and circuitous routes, which would eventually, after weeks or months of painstaking labor, have led to a major bank with a big safe stuffed to the brim with cash. We can only guess, because the brothers, of course, were as tight-lipped as ever. During police interrogation, Franz and Erich confessed to their names and address and nothing else. Indictment was unlikely since they had not actually committed a crime, and the material damage they had done was so negligible that even the homeowner was unlikely to sue.[79]

As the police tied themselves into knots trying to exhort a confession, as prosecutors went quietly crazy trying to justify an indictment for theft, the brothers spent their pretrial imprisonment reading press clippings on themselves; apparently, they even took out a subscription with a newspaper clippings service that regularly sent them Sass news from the national and international press.[80] They went on trial for attempted theft on April 29[81] and were sentenced to time served—one month per brother, for property damage—and released immediately. Despite this—for them—ideal outcome, they had the nerve to appeal the sentence,[82] probably just on the general principle that prosecutors and police kept busy with such nonsense would not have the time to do much chasing, arresting and indicting. As Fabich furiously reported, although their initial appeal was denied, they stubbornly kept appealing until a higher court converted the remainder of their already ludicrously low prison sentence into a negligible fine.[83] Two years later, in the waning days of 1932, history repeated itself, minus the trial, sentence and appeals: two beat cops who did not know the brothers by sight caught them breaking into a cellar at Trebbiner Strasse and arrested them. At the police station, the detectives recognized their nemesis immediately, and their hearts sank. They knew how this would end: a use- and listless interrogation where every question netted no more than a bored shrug from the brothers, followed by their swift release. And that is, of course, precisely what happened.[84]

Nazi "Justice"

Had the Nazis not taken power and immediately set about demolishing the rule of law, the Sass brothers most likely would have outfoxed the police for another decade and then retired to their motorbikes and their millions. But it was not to be. On November 24, 1933, the "Law Against Dangerous Habitual Criminals" (*Gewohnheitsverbrechergesetz*) was passed, providing for indefinite confinement of any person deemed to be a "habitual criminal," regardless of whether or not a crime had been committed, and regardless of whether that person's sentence had already been served. Any criminal who had been charged at least three times, even if not convicted, could be placed in "security confinement" (*Sicherheitsverwahrung*) without trial for the rest of his life. Nazi criminalists, like Willy Fleischer and Hans Salaw, hastened to decree that safe cracking was "an activity intrinsic to professional and habitual criminality" and that therefore all safe crackers should be "inevitably assigned to the group of habitual criminals."[85] Worse, the Law Against Dangerous Habitual Criminals not only attacked their profession in general but was written specifically with the Sass brothers in mind. As Kurt Daluege, since 1932 Chief of the Prussian police, put it: "Cases like that of the Brothers Sass in Berlin, who repeatedly professed their intention to commit burglary and theft by their actions, but who had to be released every time because they did not fulfil the criteria for a criminal offense—resulting in the mockery of the authorities—shall become impossible in the National Socialist State."[86]

Even before this ominous announcement, the Sass brothers saw the writing on the wall and fled to Denmark,[87] with false passports: their passports had expired in 1932, but they knew that with their record, they would never be granted a renewal. They arrived in September 1933 in Copenhagen, a city blessed with many banks, and from the month of their arrival, Copenhagen's rate of bank break-ins shot up steeply. Since their technique had never been used in Denmark, Detective Sergeant Christian Bjerring suspected that foreigners were at work and sent word to all hotels and guesthouses in Copenhagen to notify him of suspicious foreigners. One of them told him that two of her guests, young German men, never left their room before 3 p.m., never returned before midnight, and avoided hotel staff and other guests like the plague. A search of their room in Copenhagen and coordination with Fabich in Berlin, who had their apartment in Birkenstraße searched yet again, yielded enough evidence to indict them in both countries. On June 5, 1934, they were sentenced to four years' imprisonment in

Copenhagen, for forgery (of their passports and visas to Denmark) and two attempted break-ins. Since Berlin had now also issued a warrant for their arrest (for the Disconto job of 1929, based on some valuables finally found in their flat in a heretofore undiscovered hidey hole), they were also sentenced to deportation back to Germany after serving their prison terms in Denmark.

Perhaps neither the Sass brothers nor their loyal attorney Dr. Müller-Stromeyer understood that deportation to Nazi Germany was as good as a death sentence. But they knew it meant that they would never see the light of day again. Müller-Stromeyer went so far as to travel to Denmark, where he explained to the judges in detail how German "justice" was now administered, and begged on his knees for the mercy of having his clients deported to any country on the globe, just not to Germany. To no avail. The Sass brothers, too, understood the danger: the records still contain a draft letter by Erich Sass, claiming that he and his brother were communists and wished to be deported to the Soviet Union after serving their sentences.

The prison term in Denmark must have been the hardest time the brothers had ever done. They spent the four years in solitary confinement, separated from each other for the first time in their lives. When Fabich received his captives at the Danish-German border, on March 3, 1938, he couldn't recognize them. "Franz is bloated, almost bald, taciturn. If he ever says anything, it's *'I'm innocent.'* He says: *'I.'* It used to be: *'we.'* Erich is hollow-eyed, gaunt, confused. He says to Fabich on the train that he wants to make a full confession."[88] In Berlin, they spent two years in pretrial imprisonment, again separated, constantly watched by guards, in cells that were brightly lit day and night, bound on hands and feet at all times except for the few minutes per day they were given to eat, shower and use the toilet.[89] Müller-Stromeyer, fallen from grace in the NS State, was not allowed to go near his clients, let alone defend them; he later committed suicide.[90] While Franz and Erich were still in pretrial torture, the chief of police sent a note to the district attorney: "Moreover, we ask to be notified in a timely fashion as soon as pre-trial and prison sentence are complete so that the necessary arrangements can be made for their intended transfer to a concentration camp."[91] It was clear, then, even before their trial or sentence, that this was where their path would end.

On January 27, 1940, Franz Sass was sentenced to thirteen years' imprisonment; Erich's sentence was reduced slightly to eleven years because he had confessed while Franz insisted on his innocence. They were again imprisoned separately, in windowless cells, brightly lit day and night, bound on hands and feet day and night. On March 27, 1940, both were turned over to the Gestapo and transferred to the concentration camp Sachsenhausen. On March 28, the newspapers reported that "the habitual criminals Franz and Erich Sass were shot on March 27, 1940 while resisting arrest."[92] Their execution was overseen by none other than Rudolf Höß, later commander of Auschwitz. Of the many state-sponsored murders he oversaw, that of the Sass brothers is accorded some space in his memoirs, which he wrote in 1946, the year before he was hanged for his role in the Holocaust:

> after their sentencing hearing, the RFSS (Reichsführer SS, Heinrich Himmler) had a special envoy pick the two up from prison and bring them to Sachsenhausen to be shot. They were to be shot immediately, without grace period. They were driven by car right up to the sand pit of the industrial yard. The officials who accompanied them said that they had conducted themselves in a fairly

brazen and defiant manner on the way and wanted to know where they were being taken. Once they arrived at the place of execution, I read the order to them: death by firing squad. Immediately they began to kick up a fuss: "That can't be real, how can you do this? First we want to see a priest," and much more. They absolutely refused to stand against the pole, and I had to have them tied up. They struggled with all their might. I was jolly glad when I could finally give the order to fire.[93]

One of the brothers was murdered at 8:05 p.m., the other five minutes later. Their death certificate produced in the camp reads: "shot on orders of the Führer"—a note that Günter Morsch, author of many books and exhibits on German concentration camps in general and Sachsenhausen in particular, takes literally. "We have death certificates from executions that read differently; they say: shot on orders of the *Reichsführer* [Himmler, TSK] or whatever. So we do have to assume that Hitler personally ordered the execution of the Brothers Sass."[94]

The Sasses, Synchronized

Arguably, the Brothers Sass died not because they finally reaped the fruits of their sins, and not only because they were explicitly targeted by the Nazis, but of *Gleichschaltung*, the process in which the Nazis "synchronized" ideas, opinions and utterances to establish total control over all aspects of society. In the course of "synchronization," Berlin's beloved brothers morphed into textbook incorrigible habitual criminals. Even in critical reporting, in articles that clearly recognized and condemned the Sasses as criminals, there is a world of difference in press attitudes between 1930 and 1940. From the *Berliner Volkszeitung* on May 1, 1930:

Under interrogation, both [Sass brothers] stated their names but pretended to know nothing about their previous convictions. Every question was answered with "We don't know anything and therefore decline to answer any question." Asked what they were doing late at night in the cellar, they responded: "Exercise." Finally the two men had to be returned to the police holding cell since their interrogation, by virtue of the Sass Brothers' old tactic, had yielded no result whatsoever. Today there will be another attempt to produce evidence against the suspects. If criminalists do not succeed in this, *the detainees will probably be released again in the course of the week...*[95]

And, a year earlier:

Of course, the value of the goods stolen from the broken-in safes is not yet calculable. On this, one would have to rely on the customers, but hardly anyone previously specified the nature and value of the things they had deposited. [...] During the entire morning, customers of the branch stormed the bank, asking bank officials anxiously to what extent they had suffered losses in the break-in and whether the Disconto-bank's insurance was liable. None of these customers could be reassured, and officials had to content themselves with consoling them and calming them down as best they could. Thus the relatively small cashier's room was the scene of some very agitated exchanges between safe-deposit box holders and bank employees who could only tell them that all questions of restitution, for which formally and juridically the bank was not liable, would be regulated by the Director and clarified after extensive scrutiny. The discussions were made particularly difficult by the fact that none of the customers knew the extent of the losses they had suffered [...]. On top of this, *even the bank did not know what had been stored in individual safety deposit boxes, since customers alone have access to these boxes and do not need to provide the bank with an inventory of the contents.*

The Disconto-Society, therefore, must rely on the assertions of deposit-box holders regarding their contents [...]. For this reason it has not been possible to determine the precise extent of the losses.[96]

How would Berlin's many jobless poor have read passages like these? How would they have responded to the news that the losses of the Disconto Bank, while certainly ranging in multiple millions, could not even be quantified because the "rightful owners," having themselves stolen, embezzled, misappropriated, or hidden these riches from the taxman, could not admit to what they had lost? Every journalist presumes a reader attitude and writes with it in mind. To readers of articles in which society's leeches lost some of their ill-gotten gains, or in which the Sasses deadpanned that they had been "exercising" in someone else's basement, watching cops and robbers square off against each other was a national sport. In 1930, the count stood at 7:0 for the Beloved Brothers.

Ten years later, the view of the Sass brothers had been synchronized. The Robin Hoods of Moabit had themselves turned into leeches and exploiters. "Franz and Erich Sass are two brothers who, with very brief interruptions, have never done honest work. They lived in grand style, traveled extensively, even to France and England, and knew how to elude the police's grasp."[97] Even their greatest coup, the Disconto bank job, is reduced to an average bank robbery. Not a word on the missing millions: "Here, at least 150,000 marks in cash and foreign currency fell into their hands."[98] And the sheer sass that had garnered the brothers the love of the entire city was recast as insolent lies: "One of the brothers, Erich Sass, even claimed to have found this gold coin circa two days after the break-in very near the scene of the crime, at the tramway stop! With such antics could criminals in the previous regime 'substantiate an alibi!'"[99] The transition of the Sass image from gentleman-scoundrels to Enemies of the People could not be clearer: it is not only the reporting that has changed here, but also the expectation of the readers' response.

One person who did not make the adjustment easily was Max Fabich. His three articles on the Sass brothers are odd hybrids of candid memoir and synchronized lip service to the Nazis' far greater efficiency in dealing with crime. Exasperated as he undoubtedly was, the many passages in which he describes the Brothers' skill as "inconceivable," "incomprehensible," or "clairvoyant" show that he had a healthy respect, even admiration, for their work. His daughter-in-law, Ruth Fabich, later quoted him: "He always said: they are not criminals, they are scoundrels. Good scoundrels."[100] And yet his Sass essays are also full of outrage—not irritation, which would be perfectly understandable, but churning, seething outrage—at the brothers' recalcitrance and at a justice system that gave them the right to remain silent. He fumes at their insolence—the Brothers sought to evade capture! they refused to confess as soon as arrested! They had a *lawyer!!*[101]—and sums up: "That *despite* the results of the painstaking police investigation the Brothers Sass were *not* indicted in 1929 is characteristic for conditions at the time."[102] In his essay on the Sass's criminal career, he praises what he calls the Nazi era's "special treatment" of "habituals" (i.e., the new laws permitting permanent imprisonment in the absence of an actual crime) and describes the previous regime's rule of law, which still allowed for such things as the right to remain silent and legal representation, as "reprehensible obtuseness" resulting in the "legally sanctioned emasculation of the police."[103] Thank God, he concludes, for rulers who are tough on crime:

After the National Socialists took power and finally took on the fight against habitual criminality in an efficient manner, when, for the first time, the law enabled preventive measures against habitual criminals, a fundamental reversal occurred in Berlin's underworld. [...] The entire guild of bank safe crackers is now behind bars [...]. Moreover, the extensive preventive measures no longer permit events and conditions as I have described them here to occur. They are, happily, a thing of the past.[104]

It is perhaps the strongest sign of the extent of Fabich's "self-synchronization" that he did not mention the gruesome conditions of the Brothers' imprisonment, or their murder, with a single word, although the first of his essays appeared mere days after their execution. Whether he knew that this would be the Sasses' fate when he dragged them back to Germany is unlikely: reportedly, he promised to help them find honest work after they had served their prison sentence. But he was certainly also a believer in the new strongman State, whether influenced by "synchronization" or by his own bitter memories of years of fruitless pursuit. "Everything has gotten much better," he told the terrified brothers as he picked them up at the border, "there is no unemployment anymore..."[105]

Genuine Rogues: Nostalgia

The Sass brothers were a riddle who had the bad fortune to survive into an era that eradicated all mysteries and murdered every myth. Their legend derived substantially from the fact that they were, to use a Fabich word, "incomprehensible." They were simultaneously enamored of their own fame and, understandably, given their chosen profession, camera-shy. Beyond police mugshots and courtroom photographs, not a single image of them exists: no childhood pictures—a testimony to the wretched poverty in which they grew up—but also no holiday snapshots, no photos from the press conference, no pictures shot of them by fans or private trophy hunters.[106] They were a mass of contradictions: camera-shy celebrity hounds, millionaires living in a rat hole, covetous but not greedy. They demonstrated several times that when threatened with capture, they were perfectly capable of walking away from an open safe containing millions, even after months of planning and preparation. Contradictions are a sign of character, and having a character is the sole province of individuals. The Sass brothers were individuals in an age that sought to erase individuality. Press reporting that routinely misrepresented them as an entire "gang" of robbers, when everyone knew perfectly well which two individuals had committed this brilliant coup, is perhaps an early indication of the desire to fold the individual into an anonymous mass. By 1940, in the court's written justification for their sentence, not being part of the anonymous mass was itself a crime. "A reform of these accused cannot be expected even following the most severe penalty. They are extremely antisocial elements, who have never consistently done honest work and will never, by the court's conviction, find their way into the community of the *Volk*."[107] And the court was undoubtedly right: the Brothers Sass could not be synchronized.

The many jokes about the Brothers Sass attest to their continued popularity even in the early NS years. In February 1933, when the SA (*Sturmabteilung*), the Nazi party's original paramilitary wing, and the SS jointly burned down the Reichstag building, a crime for which they guillotined a hap- and blameless Communist, the following joke made the rounds: "Who burned the Reichstag?—Of course: the Brothers SA-SS."[108] It was an apt comment on a regime that specialized in blaming others for their own crimes. Even more daringly, as the regime entrenched itself: "How do you spell Germany's most famous criminal gang?"—answer: "S-A-S-S."[109] We can certainly read these witticisms as expressions of nostalgia. In the age of mass men, the Sass brothers stood out. In a regime that reigned with unprecedented brutality, the Sass brothers, who had never carried a weapon or harmed a fly in their entire lives of crime, were throwbacks to a less violent age.[110] In a regime that systematically obliterated individual rights and flouted the rule of law, the Sass brothers' ability to wriggle out of every indictment was a last reminder of a constitutional State long gone. In a land ruled by criminals, they were rogues, or, to use Max Fabich's term, "good scoundrels." And rogues, as Peter Bamm has so aptly remarked, are "moralists, and this is why they are so rare. The main aspect of real roguery is that society is taught a moral lesson through an immoral act.... This is why true rogues enjoy the approbation of all well-meaning people.... How happy is the nation that still manages to produce a true rogue from time to time!"[111] Ekkehard Schwerk, to whose research we owe so much of our knowledge of the Brothers Sass, comments in tones of despair:

> How unhappy we are! For how long have we well-meaning people been forsaken by the "true" rogues! They no longer exist. They are, the Devil knows why, extinct, like the may bugs. They were, certainly, pests, but also a pleasure. And how a society responds to rogues, how it deals with them, mirrors its disposition.
>
>   The last truly genuine rogues existed in Berlin, in the so-called Golden Twenties, in the form of the Brothers Sass. Since then, nothing comparable has been on offer.[112]

Perhaps this is why their popularity endures to this day, why they were the subject of a novel and three films,[113] and why every online blog on the Sass brothers is filled with comments from people named Sass claiming to be their descendants.[114] In our neverending pursuit of Franz and Erich Sass, we may be chasing—even more than the still-missing millions from the Disconto haul, which have inspired treasure-hunts without number—the last vestiges of our own vanishing and compromised individuality. And perhaps the Sass brothers and how they were "dealt with" serve as a reminder that even today, when we look into the mirror that shows us our society's disposition, we often do not like what we see.

A Tale of Two Editors:
The Case of Hugo Bettauer and
Rudolf Olden (Vienna, 1920s)

The attempt on Bettauer's life greatly excited a "lady" who had been educated in a strictly Christian manner and thus thought and acted accordingly. It even wrested from her the aching regret that it was such a pity that the corrupter Bettauer had not been fatally injured. She thus took the Christian decision *to pray to God*, so that Bettauer would at least succumb to his wounds. As you can glean from yesterday's newspapers, God answered her prayer.—*Tagblatt*, March 28, 1925[1]

A big, burly man came into the office and refused to be turned away until he had had his say: He had heard that Bettauer could only be saved by a blood transfusion. He had come to offer his own blood to the wounded man. And when asked what had moved him to such a sacrifice, he said: "Bettauer had saved him and his family through his wise counsel and humane assistance."—Rudolf Olden, "Abschied von Hugo Bettauer," March 31, 1925[2]

Hugo Bettauer (1872–1925) was, to paraphrase Kleist, one of the most beloved and, at the same time, one of the most hated men of his day. To hear the contemporary press tell the story, you would hardly even notice that there were *two* men in the dock at the infamous "pornography trial" of 1924: Hugo Bettauer and his coeditor and friend Rudolf Olden (1885–1940). Both were journalists and progressive writers; both ran afoul of the right-wing and particularly the Nazi press; both were of Jewish descent, converted young and assimilated fully; both were indicted for coediting a journal accused of leading to the sexual corruption of youngsters; both were acquitted, and both ended up being murdered by the Nazis. But in the direct aftermath of the 1924 trial, Bettauer was hunted, vilified, threatened, assassinated and posthumously maligned while Olden was more or less ignored. The "immoral" journal coedited by Bettauer and Olden had always been and would forever be the "Bettauer Weekly." Controversies besieging it fed the "Bettauer scandal," led to the Bettauer assassination, and ended with a second "Bettauer trial" at which, for appearance's sake, his killer was indicted, but that in truth resuscitated the "pornographer" Hugo Bettauer and his "swinish" writings in order to get his murderer off.

Hugo Bettauer: A Professional Taboo-Breaker

One straightforward answer to the question that immediately arises—why Bettauer but not Olden?—is that Bettauer was, quite simply, a far more colorful character. He assimilated as a Jew but in no other way. He was a runaway, an adventurer, a deserter, a deportee, a repeated transatlantic emigrant and returner, a maniacal writer (it was not unusual for him to produce five best-selling novels in a single year), an author whose novels sold in the millions, were frequently turned into hit movies and whose runaway success was greeted by more "serious" authors with turned-up noses, a columnist and editor whose magazine editions reached dizzying heights never dreamed of by his competitors. From advocating the rights of women (a term that, to him, included prostitutes) to lobbying for the decriminalization of abortion and homosexuality, he never held an opinion that wasn't controversial, and millions of readers debated them, argued over them, cheered them or objected to them. To the right-wing press and the Nazi assassins, that made him the man to take down, while Olden was—temporarily—permitted to fade into the background.

The vilification of Hugo Bettauer as a filthy Jew was undoubtedly facilitated by the fact that he was born (in Baden near Vienna, and in 1872, not 1877 or 1878, as is variously claimed[3]) into a downright stereotypically wealthy Jewish family (his father, Arnold Samuel Aron Bettauer, worked for the stock exchange). Bettauer's career as "a professional taboo-breaker"[4] began at the age of sixteen, when he ran away from home. He made it all the way to Alexandria, Egypt, before he was caught and returned home. On

July 20, 1890, not quite 18 years old, he converted to Protestantism and volunteered for military service but deserted after five months because he could not tolerate military life. He fled to Zurich, where he married his childhood sweetheart Olga Steiner, with whom he emigrated to the United States and produced a son (Heinrich Gustav Hellmuth, born June 12, 1899). After losing his job as a journalist in New York, he moved to Berlin in early 1899 to take up the editorship of the local section of the *Berliner Morgenpost*, but his articles exposing police corruption scandals made him profoundly unpopular. Not quite two years after his arrival, in January 1901, he was expelled from Prussia as a troublesome foreigner; his brief sojourn in Berlin was marked by constant police surveillance, no fewer than twelve court

Hugo Bettauer (*Das interessante Blatt,* September 19, 1925, p. 4).

judgments against him (for libel), and one stint in jail (for the same reason).

After his divorce, he met sixteen-year-old Helene Müller, with whom he eloped, again to the U.S., marrying her on the journey across and eventually producing a second son (Reginald Parker Bettauer, born August 23, 1904). From 1907 onward, he wrote crime novels that, initially serialized in various U.S. newspapers, proved so popular that book versions had to be hastily published in large editions. By 1910, he was back in Vienna, writing for numerous papers. Between 1918 and his death in 1925, he wrote 23 Viennese novels—crime novels, satirical novels, society novels, morality stories. All touched upon controversial subjects; all were best-sellers, selling tens or hundreds of thousands of copies; nine were made into major films.[5] By any measure, Bettauer, whose work is now nearly completely forgotten, was one of the most popular, influential and successful authors in Austria after the First World War.[6]

Bettauer's novels are, by the standards of the day, provocations. His heroes are browbeaten people battling the daily grind of poverty, hunger, inflation, blackmail and sexual exploitation; liberated women openly living their sexuality; unrepentant criminals justifying their crimes and escaping justice. Probably his most famous work is his 1922 novel *The City Without Jews* (*Die Stadt ohne Juden: Ein Roman von übermorgen*), in which Vienna's mayor Schwertfeger ("a composite cameo of contemporary politicians Karl Lueger, Michael Mayr, and Ignaz Seipel"[7]) expels all Jews from the city. Jew-free Vienna promptly degrades from a cosmopolitan city to a boring little village. Its commerce, press and banking sector collapse; coffee houses and operas close; the lively sex economy crumbles because Vienna's "sweet girls" decide that their boorish Aryan clients can't hold a candle to their far more entertaining Jewish suitors of yesteryear. Even the Nazi party, deprived of its *raison d'être*, folds. Finally, faced with economic devastation, a cultural wasteland, sexual ennui and the lack of convenient scapegoats, the City Fathers ruefully beg the Jews to return.[8] The novel was enough to send Nazi ideologues like Herwig Hartner and Alfred Rosenberg into paroxysms of wrath,[9] and it earned Bettauer a place among the "degenerate writers" of the 1938 *Eternal Jew* exhibit in Munich.[10] But in the 1920s, it was not enough to attract death threats, public calls for the author's lynching, and assassination attempts.

He and She: The Bettauer Scandal

All of this was accomplished by a journal entitled *He and She: Weekly Magazine on Lifestyles and Eroticism* (*Er und Sie: Wochenschrift für Lebenskultur und Erotik*), which Bettauer and Olden began to coedit in February 1924. Its subtitle and the drawing of a naked "He" and "She" on the banner notwithstanding, it was hardly racy stuff,[11] not even by the standards of the day and certainly not compared to Bettauer's novels. For a mere 2,000 crowns (the price of an egg at the time), each issue offered a lead article by Bettauer (who alone signed as the magazine's editor) and accessibly written case studies of sexual woes, penned by gynaecologists, psychologists or sociologists, followed by erotic fiction, a section on reader letters and answers by the editors, and a personal ads section. Bettauer and Olden funded the magazine out of pocket, showing that this was an enterprise about which they cared deeply. The purpose of *He and She* was twofold: to offer readers, regardless of educational background, access to scientific but

Bettauer's novel *The City Without Jews* **(1922) and the first edition of** *He and She* **(February 14, 1924) (Wikimedia Commons).**

jargon-free articles on human sexuality, and to make readers aware that sex was not merely a personal affair, but also a social and political matter. *He and She* was where readers were told that sexual misery was not their personal fault but the result of social conditions and political intrusions. Of course, the magazine averred, the miserably constricted living conditions of the poor led directly to incest, teenage pregnancies, and unwanted children. Of course the government distracted attention from such conditions and its own failure to address them by ostracizing their victims: unwed mothers, girls driven to prostitution, and "illegitimate" children. Along with these politically charged statements, the magazine offered concrete advice to readers that sat ill with official recommendations. Masturbation was pronounced entirely safe. Pills and electric shock treatments did nothing to cure impotence. Flagellation, S/M sex, homosexuality, and adultery were absolutely fine, so long as all participants were of the age of consent and nobody was hurt or coerced. Along with personal empowerment and political critique, the magazine also offered concrete guidance on where to get practical help in sexual matters, be it medical, psychological, or spiritual.[12]

   He and She was an unprecedented success. Issue 1, comprising 12 pages, sold 20,000 copies; issue 2 had already been expanded to 16 pages and sold 60,000 copies, reaching an estimated 200,000 readers. Contemporary newspapers reported that readers practically ripped each new issue from the hands of news sellers.[13] Bettauer received several hundred reader letters per week. In addition to handling this vast correspondence, he held twice-weekly office hours, during which he offered not only advice but often also financial support to readers in need of help but too shy to write in. According to testimony offered by his employees at his killer's trial, not a day went by when Bettauer didn't give away hundreds of thousands of crowns of his own money, often borrowing money from his employees to help the neediest. Once, his secretary Ria Lang testified, he gave her his wallet for safekeeping so he wouldn't give all his money away.[14] Another secretary, Grete Grün, told the court that when she had met Bettauer, she was jobless, destitute, and desperate. Bettauer, she said, promptly gave her 200,000 crowns and followed this up by sending her a great number of job ads; as soon as he was able, he hired her himself.[15]

On the first day of its appearance, February 14, 1924, the police press bureau sent a copy of the first issue of *He and She* to Vienna's Youth Welfare Office, encouraging them to launch an application to have it suppressed.[16] At the time, there was officially no censorship in Austria, but there was a press law outlawing the sale of writings that "endanger the moral welfare of juveniles by exploiting youthful urges." Editors had to submit copies of their magazines to security services and the Prosecutor's office; if found to be morally degenerate, they could be banned from sale on the streets or through news vendors.[17] This was obviously the result the police press bureau wanted to achieve with regard to *He and She*, but they could not take action without an official complaint, and the magazine's readers were not complaining. The city's Youth Welfare Office, invited to do so, duly complied; its request to suppress the magazine arrived at the police press bureau on February 29 and was immediately approved, effectively outlawing the sale of *He and She* to anyone under 18 or by street or news vendors. Bettauer and Olden appealed to the mayor of Vienna, Karl Seitz, to rescind the suppression order, which Seitz did.[18]

On March 12, Ignaz Seipel, Chancellor of the Republic, held a flaming speech in which he claimed that "Red Vienna" (an allusion to the fact that the Social Democrats, Seitz's party, were, at the time, the strongest party in Vienna) was drowning in a "flood of pornography" and attacked Seitz for protecting people who were peddling filth to children.[19] Murray Hall has identified this speech as the one that turned Bettauer into fair game.[20] Seitz shot back that Seipel, as a Catholic priest, might have ideas on eroticism and immorality that differed somewhat from those that might be held by the population of a cosmopolitan city,[21] but the damage was done. Two days after Seipel's speech, assured of support from the highest office of the land, the Prosecutor's office drew up an indictment against Hugo Bettauer and Rudolf Olden for "coarse violations of public decency," procurement of sexual services, "public vilification of the institution of marriage, the family, private property, or approval of unlawful or immoral acts," vilification of the authorities, and instigation of seditious behavior.[22] As Bettauer and Olden waited for their trial date, dutifully supplying copies of each issue to prosecutors so they could search for instances of coarse violations, vilification, and instigation, the police busily confiscated every copy of *He and She* they could lay their hands on: 100 copies of Issue 1; 20 of issue 2; 1,300 of Issue 3; 480 of Issue 4 and 2,400 copies of Issue 5, after which the journal folded because—as Olden later explained—it could not financially absorb the confiscations.[23]

On March 18, Bettauer complained to the police about the confiscations, stating that if they had not been able to make a case in four weeks, this was an indication that there was nothing to find and therefore also nothing to confiscate.[24] Certainly, the prosecutors took their sweet time with the case. The official indictment was not published until June 24, three months after the magazine had been driven out of business by systematic police confiscations which were, given that the editors voluntarily supplied the Prosecutor's office with copies, unnecessary to make the prosecution's case. More than seven months passed between the first police action against *He and She* and the trial—plenty of time to launch both new businesses capitalizing on the success of Bettauer's idea and to keep the "Bettauer Scandal" boiling.

In April, the month after the demise of *He and She*, the first of several imitation magazines sprang up, many of which sported analogous titles (*I and You; The Two of Us; Both of Us; Adam and Eve; The Rendez-Vous*) and, more often than not, plagiarized Bettauer's subtitle (*Weekly Magazine on Lifestyles and Eroticism*).[25] Many of these were quite a bit more explicit than *He and She* had ever been, and some of them, particularly the first, *I and You* (*Ich und Du*), were constantly misattributed to Bettauer. Both Bettauer and *I and You* editor Josef Carl Schlegel repeatedly insisted that Bettauer had nothing to do with the new magazine. It was no use: *I and You* continued to be mistaken for another Bettauer product—by the press, by the police, even in court. Schlegel's intentions were probably no more sinister than capitalizing on the tremendous popularity of *He and She*, but his deliberate knockoff title invited misidentification and helped turn Bettauer's name into a synonym for any kind of "smut."[26] The press lapped it up. Drawings (notably: no photographs) were run on front pages showing small children perusing *He and She*, and Bettauer and his work were routinely defamed as a "professional pimp," a "Jewish swine," a "mud-wallower," a "two-legged swine," a "perverse Jew," an "infamous pornographer," "a greater criminal than a robber and murderer," a "perverse sewer animal," a "mangy Talmudic soul," a "horny monster" who published "Bettauer feces," a "literary cesspool," a "flood of muck," a "professional prostitution mag."[27] Months before the trial took place, the press routinely "explained" the success of *He and She* (or of whichever magazine they ascribed to Bettauer that day) with the "fact" that Bettauer had taken to peddling flesh:

> The secret of this success is the fact that Herr Bettauer has moved on from theory to practice. In each issue of his magazine [*I and You*, TSK] he publishes hundreds of ads for the purpose of procurement. Young girls offer themselves to rich old gents for use and sprightly young men seek mature, wealthy ladies. Every kind of normal and abnormal sexual satisfaction, in every price range, can be achieved with Herr Bettauer's help. [...] The man has joined the ranks of professional pimps. He conducts this business with a virtuosity that surpasses everything we've ever seen. The most cunning members of the guild of pimps and white slavers have to hand it to him. He has industrialized pimping.[28]

Eventually, the "Bettauer scandal" reached Parliament, where, in one session, the antisemitic Christian Social councilman Anton Orel went off topic to slander "the Jew Bettauer who wants to poison our children with Jewish poison and Jewish swinishness!" Orel went so far as to attack Mayor Seitz, who chaired the meeting, for having failed to "kick this Jew's ass and throw him out the door" (a remark that is recorded in the minutes of the meeting but went unreported in the right-wing press). The meeting ended in a scuffle.[29] Orel's speech was hardly the first or the last in the long history of Bettauer slander, but it was a crucial step in the antisemitic project of taking Bettauer down: now the affair was not merely about the pornographic pig Bettauer, but about the *Jewish* pornographic pig Bettauer.[30]

The "Bettauer" Trial

Six months into this fabricated "Bettauer scandal," on September 18, 1924, the "Bettauer trial" (coeditor Rudolf Olden was, at this point, already no more than an afterthought) finally got under way.[31] After months in which prosecutors and police had desperately tried to prove that the magazine was primarily read by juveniles and children, often basing what little "evidence" they could find on data obtained from *I and You*,[32] the actual indictment was a bit of a letdown. It accused Bettauer and Olden of intentionally "unsettling ethical standards and arousing sensual lust" for mercenary motives and claimed that the personal ad section aimed "almost exclusively at promoting extra-marital intercourse." The "justification of immoral and illegal acts" was found in the magazine's call for the decriminalization of homosexuality.[33] Mere minutes into Bettauer's defense speech, the prosecutor, Dr. Schwarz, leapt up to demand that the room be cleared because Bettauer had used the term "sexual suffering" (*sexuelle Not*). Bettauer's defender, Dr. Rosenfeld, ridiculed the idea: neither Bettauer nor Olden had used a single lascivious or obscene term (although, as he admitted sarcastically, Bettauer had once mentioned the word "lace panties"), and that the "court wasn't, after all, a girls' boarding school." Olden's attorney, Dr. Braß, added laconically that he couldn't understand why the mere mention of "sexual suffering" sent the prosecutor into such a tizzy. The audience responded with gales of laughter.[34]

While the trial thus began on a note that reflected the ridiculousness of the indictment, Schwarz's attempt to have the audience excluded significantly influenced trial reporting. The attempt to ban the public was made again and again throughout the trial; and since the judge concurred once, agreeing to have the room cleared for one session of the two-day trial, newspaper coverage was erratic at best. Some papers took the fact that the public was partially excluded as a pretext not to report on the trial at all. Particularly papers who were none too kindly inclined towards Bettauer jumped at the excuse to conceal from their readers the fact that the prosecution's case never looked better than silly and fell apart almost immediately. Instead, these papers often opted to omit the entire trial—including the full day to which the public, and therefore also the press, was admitted—skipping swiftly to the acquittal verdict, which sounded all the more outrageous if the paper had set up this "disgraceful" ruling with a good bashing of Bettauer literature. The "trial reporting" of the *Vorarlberger Wacht*, for example, spent paragraph after paragraph pontificating on the "obscenity" of Bettauer's writings, following this up with a curt (and inaccurate) single sentence on the trial itself: "The trial, which was, for the most part, closed to the public, so that we cannot report on it, ended with the acquittal of both of the accused."[35]

Both Bettauer and Olden—this, perhaps, another reason for many newspapers to avoid judicious reporting—made clear at trial that they perceived the indictment not as born of a struggle against immorality but as a concerted campaign against them personally. Olden stated it plainly: "We were unfortunate in the sense that our magazine fell into a *political atmosphere* and that a veritable *witch hunt* was unleashed against us."[36] Day 1 of the trial was spent in a useless public reading of all passages in the journal that might possibly be considered vaguely incriminating. The day ended with the summary acquittal of Rudolf Olden, who successfully argued that he had fulfilled no more

Hugo Bettauer and Rudolf Olden at trial. Courtroom drawings (*Der Tag,* September 19, 1925, p. 7).

than an administrative role for the journal and was not responsible for content, and the dropping of several points of the indictment against Bettauer (including the procurement charge that had relied entirely on the personal ads section, which turned out to be no more racy than that in any other major newspaper[37]). Day 2 ended with the acquittal of Hugo Bettauer, with the jury voting either overwhelmingly or unanimously for acquittal on all remaining 17 points of the indictment.[38]

In the press, this result was not reported as the total humiliation of the prosecution and the complete vindication of the accused that it was. Most newspapers shook their head in dismay that the jury had "*denied all points of the indictment with a large majority; the vote distribution was nearly consistently 9 to 3 or 8 to 4 [...] The Prosecutor, visibly surprised by this result, rose and declared that he could not battle against such a flood.*"[39] Much of the press took up the prosecutor's cue as to what Bettauer's acquittal meant: "This is how far we have come. Now the floodgates are open to smut and filth."[40] Some, ominously, advocated "self-help" against the "flood" of "pornography," given that, or so the argument went, the judicial system had abandoned the populace to its grave dangers.[41] In October 1924, Kaspar Hellering, a middle-school teacher and member of the Austrian Nazi party, published a hysterical article entitled "Towards Self-Help Against Bettauer," in which he claimed that it was "truly high time that all still decent folk—since the State has, in this case, failed utterly—resorted to ruthless self-help." His addendum "An eye for an eye, a tooth for a tooth!" left little to the imagination as to what, specifically, he had in mind.[42] In December, he wrote in the Nazi paper *The Brute* (*Der Grobian*) that Bettauer should have been "lynched long ago." In February 1925, he followed this up with a "taxonomy" of Bettauer as "*Bettauer*, sus silvaticus, scrofulous wild pig or common sow, wallows in cesspools and sewage, nourishes itself with women's flesh and other by-products of moral waste, spreads a pestilential stench—hence to be exterminated."[43] There is no evidence that the police responded to Hellering's calls to murder Bettauer in any way.

From then on, death threats against Bettauer regularly appeared in his mail and, often only thinly veiled, in the right-wing press. He was under constant police surveillance and "encouraged" not to speak in public. On an international lecture tour in November, if the Nazi press is to be believed, he faced empty halls in every town because local Nazis had "warned" the public to stay away.[44] Much of this was undoubtedly wishful thinking. The *Prager Tagblatt*, for example, reported that Bettauer, "one of the most popular and productive personalities in Vienna," had packed Prague's Urania Theater to the rafters and that his speech there had been a colossal success.[45] As this and other reports show, death threats and police cautions were hardly enough to shut Bettauer up. The follow-up magazine that he and Olden had started in mid–May 1924 to replace the now-defunct *He and She*, titled simply *Bettauer's Weekly* (*Bettauers Wochenschrift*), was similar in layout and content, enjoyed the same tremendous success with readers, and offered the same twice-weekly office hours to readers seeking advice and help.[46] With an average weekly circulation of 60,000 copies, it quickly became the most popular Austrian magazine on the national or international scene. In one issue, Bettauer wittily called out Hellering, albeit without mentioning his name: "This distinguished politician of the alehouse, the man who has called for my lynching, recently declared unequivocally, as the hour grew late and he was already a bit befuddled by his indulgence in the amber nectar, after vigorously belching a few times and yelling 'Howl!': *Bettauer's Weekly* has to disappear! This swinish rag is even more dangerous than the *Workers' News* and the *Evening* taken together!"[47] And yet, even as he continued his work and lampooned his assailants, Bettauer understood that he was in grave danger. He made a will on November 1, 1924, and in March 1925, days before his assassination, he canceled a lecture tour, telling his friends that "he had recently received several threatening letters and felt in peril of his life."[48]

Bettauer's Murder

On March 10, 1925, then 20-year-old Otto Rothstock, a jobless dental technician with Nazi leanings, arrived at Bettauer's office at 11 a.m. to call on Bettauer during his office hours. He was told to come back at 3 p.m. At 2:30 he was back, pacing until Bettauer arrived. Although there were already two or three people waiting to see Bettauer, Rothstock cut into line. He followed Bettauer to his office, gave him a faked letter of introduction, and locked the door. He was less than two feet away from him when he shot him five times, hitting him in the arms, chest and stomach. Bettauer tried to defend himself with his desk lamp and managed to unlock the door and escape. Rothstock locked the door behind him and proceeded to tear up writings on Bettauer's desk until the police arrived. Bettauer, still conscious, received first aid and pleaded with those present not to harm his attacker. By the time Bettauer was carted off to hospital, circa 200 people had assembled on the street in front of his office, some openly celebrating the assassination, hoping for Bettauer's death, and calling everyone who objected a "Jewish swine." Bettauer, shot through the lung and the liver, died 16 days later, on March 26, 1925.[49]

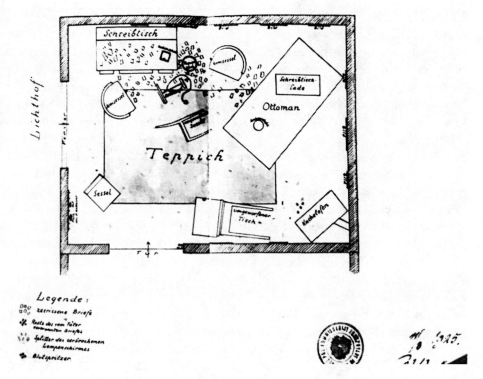

Police sketch of the crime scene. "Strafsache gegen Otto Rothstock" (Landesgericht für Strafsachen Wien I: Vr XXVII 1748/25).

Otto Rothstock's statements on every aspect of his deed were contradictory, confusing, transparently nonsensical and soon unmasked as lies, with two notable exceptions. On these two matters—that he had intended to kill Bettauer and the question of conspiracy—he stuck to the script so closely, not even varying formulations, that anyone with an actual interest in investigating this crime would have begun to wonder whether there *was* a script. But the police could not be bothered to check on the most basic elements of the crime: Rothstock's whereabouts immediately before the murder, where and from whom he had bought the murder weapon, with whom he had discussed his plans to murder Bettauer, or indeed his connections with other members of the Nazi party. On all of these crucial questions, the police simply took the killer's word.

Rothstock claimed that although he had never confided his plan to murder Bettauer to anyone, he had told others that Bettauer should die, but the police never asked him with whom he had discussed the desirability of Bettauer's death. Rothstock claimed variously to have received the gun from an acquaintance a year earlier, bought it around Christmas, or bought it from an unnamed person (someone he had known for a long time although he didn't know his name) in January. The police checked none of it and generally exhibited a supreme disinterest in the origins of the gun. Nor was the court particularly concerned: in the seven-page indictment of Rothstock, the weapon only takes up five lines, and the trial was concluded without any information as to where the gun had come from. And where was Rothstock immediately before the crime? He claimed to have passed the time until Bettauer's arrival at the Café Kronprinz, where he claimed to have been a regular, drinking coffee and reading newspapers from 11 a.m. to 2:30 p.m. Nobody at the café remembered seeing him, either on that day or ever before. The police were also disinclined to interrogate witnesses claiming to have seen Rothstock stake out Bettauer's office with four other Nazis immediately before the murder, or a neighbor stating that she had overheard Rothstock discuss the gun and a planned murder with several others. Both were only interviewed after a great deal of foot-dragging and after considerable pressure being brought to bear by the left-wing press.[50] Their testimony was swiftly dismissed in court based on no evidence beyond Rothstock's stubborn insistence that he had had no accomplices, which the police and the court took at face value.

Nor did anyone stumble over Rothstock's many contradictory statements on his reason for leaving the Nazi party mere months before the murder. The one he used most frequently was that he had planned to murder Bettauer (or another "pornographer") even then and did not want the party to be blamed for a murder for which he alone wanted to claim responsibility.[51] As Murray Hall has summed up: "Thanks to an incompetent bureau of investigation, Rothstock could simply say anything whatsoever since his statements were taken down without question."[52]

On the day of the assassination, March 10, and in an interrogation the following day, Rothstock stated unequivocally that Bettauer had never harmed either him or anyone he knew or had ever heard about, either in person or through his writings.[53] On March 12, Rothstock received a letter from Dr. Walter Riehl, a criminal defense attorney, former Head of the Austrian Nazis and now Head of the German National Association (*Deutschnationaler Verein*). Riehl offered to defend him *pro bono* since "I am utterly convinced and have also been

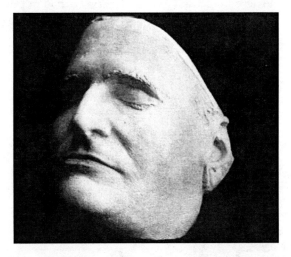

Bettauer's death mask, by sculptor Alexander Jaray (*Das interessante Blatt*, April 2, 1925, 5).

informed by persons who know you well that you performed the assassination of Bettauer for purely idealistic reasons; I further believe that you performed this deed under the impression of events in your very close circle of acquaintances."[54] The letter not only offers to defend Rothstock for free, but also hints that Riehl, who moved in Nazi circles, knew perfectly well that Rothstock's attack on Bettauer had been part of a Nazi conspiracy. (It goes without saying that no investigator ever asked either Riehl or Rothstock who these "persons who know you well" were, or followed up other possibilities to which the letter clearly opened the door. Was Riehl aware of the conspiracy to murder Bettauer *before* it took place? Nobody wanted to know.)

The day after Rothstock received this letter (and retained Riehl), Riehl's suggestion that Rothstock must have been laboring under "the impression of events in your very close circle" kicked in and Rothstock's statements about his own motives changed considerably. From March 13 onward, Rothstock began to claim that he had always been aware that Bettauer's writings led to moral devastation and lustful behavior particularly among young people; that he had personally observed the ruination of his friends and of "hundreds of thousands" of others, and that he had experienced these evil effects on himself as he read Bettauer's writings. He claimed to have shot Bettauer out of "pity" for young people and did not feel guilty "because I am of the opinion that if you eliminate a wrecker of society and of youth even in a way that the law disallows, this cannot be considered murder."[55] His statements following his retainer of Riehl are verbatim quotations of stock phrases published in the Nazi press, most particularly the *Deutsche Arbeiter-Presse, Jugendlicher Nationalsozialist* and *Der Grobian*, in which Hellering had repeatedly called for Bettauer's murder. Questioned in court, Rothstock's claim that he himself had been corrupted by Bettauer literature quickly fell apart. He could not name a single one of Bettauer's works until Riehl helpfully supplied some titles, and even then he confused titles and timelines, claiming, for example, that he had read Bettauer's *I and You* as early as 1921 or 1922. Nobody pointed out to him that Bettauer had never edited *I and You*, that Bettauer had not begun to edit any magazine before 1924, and that *I and You* had also not come into existence until 1924.[56]

Otto Rothstock. Left: *Das interessante Blatt* **(March 19, 1925); right: courtroom drawing** (*Der Tag,* **October 6, 1925, 5).**

The "Bettauer" Trial Reprised

Rothstock's attorney Riehl based his defense on two strategies: an insanity plea and retrying Bettauer at Rothstock's trial. Not only did he ask to see the court records of the 1924 "pornography" trial, but he also solicited, in a letter to his broad circle of Nazi acquaintances, "truly objective and useful letters containing actual proof of specific cases documenting the corrupting influence of Bettauer-literature, with names and addresses."[57] It was not a rich harvest. At trial, Riehl was more or less stuck with an undocumented statement by Otto Rothstock's father (!) that "many" (unnamed) young prostitutes with venereal disease had stated under questioning "that they had been ruined by reading *Bettauer's Weekly*."[58]

Riehl's second tactic was an insanity plea, his only hope of getting his client off since Rothstock had committed the murder in the presence of several witnesses. Court psychiatrists, who observed Rothstock briefly, leaned toward mental impairment, but concluded after a few days that they could not determine the issue and passed Rothstock on to the psychiatric faculty at the University, who observed and interviewed him for a month. They concluded that although Rothstock was a pathological liar to the point that none of his statements deserved any credence, there was no sign of mental disease. They added that Rothstock had admitted while still in their care that he had a clever "plan to regain his freedom through simulating a, as he himself said, mild mental illness."[59] Although the ultimate verdict—not insane and thus fully responsible—was entered into evidence, the university's statement that Rothstock was a habitual liar was not cited in court, where Rothstock's version of events continued to be accepted as gospel truth.

The second "Bettauer trial" began on October 5, 1925, the Honorable Dr. Ernst Ramsauer (who was *völkisch*, that is: populist/nationalist and typically antisemitic) presiding, Privy Councillor Dr. Franz Butschek (also *völkisch*, and more often defending Rothstock than prosecuting him) for the prosecution and Dr. Walter Riehl acting in Rothstock's defense.[60] Bettauer's widow Helene, understanding well that it was really her husband on trial again, had also retained counsel: Dr. Hugo Zörnlaib attended to defend Hugo Bettauer against the worst excesses of posthumous slurs and falsehoods. His role was mainly to remind the court—time and again—that the man in the dock was not Hugo Bettauer but Otto Rothstock. The trial began with a chance for the murderer to lay the groundwork for his twofold defense tactic: that he was slightly mentally confused and thus not responsible, and that it really had all been Bettauer's fault.

Judge. Do you plead guilty?

Accused. Your Honor, two thousand years ago…

Judge. Tell me first: yes or no.

Accused. I have forced the writer Hugo Bettauer *from this world into the next*, killed him, as people call it. However, I am not at fault.

Judge. So: not guilty.

Accused. Your Honor, two thousand years ago—a few minutes of Divine Time—the Son of God came into this world in order to lead the fight against these Jewish writers and scholars, since they are the Sons of lies and of Satan. I came into this world in order to continue this fight.

*What I have done is not treacherous murder. It is a **warning shot**, to wake up all peoples and above all the German nation, to continue the fight, brutally and ruthlessly, to protect themselves before it is too late.* Hugo Bettauer mocked all that is German. I am not at fault![61]

Throughout the trial, Rothstock represented himself as an "idealist" who had only wanted to protect youth from Bettauer's filth. Ever the devout Christian, he distinguished between "killing" Bettauer and sending him "to another world." According to his religious convictions, he explained, the soul was eternal, and thus it was never really possible to kill anyone. Since he had merely sent Bettauer's soul to a better world, he had really done him a favor.[62] His image as mentally confused was established by his statement that God personally had given him permission for the murder by sending Rothstock a vision in which, in Rothstock's confused account, figured prominently a rock, a burning sensation in his heart, a physical and ethical transformation, and Rothstock throwing books around.[63] Neither Rothstock's vision nor his divine "mission" to kill Bettauer had ever been mentioned in pretrial interrogation; both made their debut appearance in court. In cross-examination, Riehl led his witness constantly, suggesting answers that Rothstock only had to confirm ("Was it an inner voice that told you of your calling or did you receive a *sign?*"[64]). He did this so often and so shamelessly that one newspaper described Riehl as Rothstock's "prompter."[65] Naturally, Rothstock also continued to deny that he had had any accomplices, that he had told anyone of his intention to kill Bettauer, or that he was in the least "political." For reasons that remain unclear, Rothstock's mere say-so seems to have carried more weight with the court than witness statements that he had been overheard plotting the murder with other Nazis, or his former employer's testimony (who happened to be Jewish) that Rothstock was an avid Nazi who came to work with a swastika in his buttonhole.[66]

Bettauer's side was represented by heartbreaking testimony by his employees, who unanimously testified to his generosity, his kindness, his pleas that his attacker should not be harmed (when it looked like Rothstock, being led off immediately after the assassination, might be attacked by bystanders), and his decision in hospital, when he still hoped to recover, not to press charges against Rothstock.[67] Two social workers testified that although many of their charges, mostly girls who had gone off the straight and narrow, read *Bettauer's Weekly*, they could not point to a single concrete example of Bettauer's writings having resulted in harm to anyone. A woman's testimony claiming that her daughter had been prostituted with the help of an ad in *Bettauer's Weekly* fell flat when the offending ad was revealed to have appeared in *I and You*. The case against Bettauer, it is safe to say, was not going well, a fact that spurred Riehl to action: he appealed to the court to read publicly "countless" letters from "fathers, school directors and doctors" documenting the corrupting influence of Bettauer's writings (his request was denied). Medical expert testimony included the two warring psychiatric evaluations, one declaring Rothstock possibly insane, the other stating unequivocally that he was sane and fully responsible, and the coroner's report showing that all five bullets had been fired from the front. This moved the prosecutor to commute the indictment from "treacherous murder" to "common murder," probably on the assumption that a murder could only be "treacherous" if the victim was shot in the back.

Other than Rothstock's hypocritical testimony, Riehl's summation must have been the hardest part of the trial for Bettauer's friends and family to endure. It lasted three full hours and brimmed over with invective for the victim and worship of the murderer. As *Der Tag* paraphrased it:

Dr. Walter Riehl. Left: Stadtarchiv Wiener Neustadt, StAWN, Kt. 12/101440. Right: court-room drawing (*Der Tag*, October 6, 1925, p. 8).

> *Defense attorney Dr. Riehl* declared that Rothstock's deed had been committed with a *chivalry* that, given the boy's proletarian origins, could *hardly be surpassed.* Confronted with the buckets of filth that had been emptied on Rothstock after his deed, one could only cite the declaration on Rothstock in a letter: *This nation is not worthy of a Rothstock.*
>
> Dr. Riehl's remarks contain a flood of insults for the dead man. [...]. He pleads for the *acquittal* of the accused, who acted under almost irresistible compulsion and was not responsible for his deed.
>
> Dr. Riehl closed with an appeal to the jury to *judge only according to their conscience* and not allow themselves to be influenced by their fear of reporting in newspapers that *stand together in racial solidarity.*
>
> *After he had finished,* **loud applause** *could be heard from the corner of the room where the supporters of Rothstock and Riehl were seated.* [...] The prosecutor added a few sentences. He noted that the defender had not offered a speech in defense of his client but a speech indicting Bettauer.[68]

With unmatched duplicity, Riehl further used his summation to read out all of the letters claiming the corrupting influence of Bettauer's works that the court had explicitly disallowed to be offered into evidence. He finished with a flourish:

> The defense attorney emphasized that he, too, adhered to a Christian worldview and then quoted a passage from the Gospel according to Matthew: "But whosoever shall offend one of these little ones, even the least of them, it were better for him that a millstone were hanged about his neck, and that he were drowned in the depth of the sea. In one respect our Saviour knows no pity against him who *offends our little ones.* And Hugo Bettauer has given such offence." [...] Rothstock's defense attorney championed the *acquittal* of the accused in blazing words: he deserves it, since he had acted only from idealistic motives and had merely, as it were, expressed the sentiments of the people.[69]

That such a speech could be given in a court of law, barely challenged, shows that the court acquiesced to the narrative of Rothstock as a God-inspired knight and Bettauer as Jewish filth who had deserved to be drowned with a millstone around his neck. Press reporting occasionally claims that both the *völkisch* prosecutor, whose obvious sympathies for Rothstock visibly undermined his prosecutorial resolve, and the judge (also *völkisch*) allowed their partiality to show numerous times throughout the trial. The judge, by two accounts, told the jury as they went off to deliberate: "*At this trial* it is very important that there is not another *miscarriage of justice*; for such miscarriages of justice can lead someone who believes that the State has not, in this case, exercised its duty to punish, *to appoint himself judge* and act accordingly. This *really should come as no surprise*."[70] If true—the incident is reported only in two newspapers—Judge Ramsauer was guilty of a severe attempt to prejudice the jury, telling them essentially that Bettauer should have been found guilty at the 1924 "pornography" trial, and skating right up to the proclamation that Bettauer had brought his death upon himself by being acquitted.

Whatever the truth of this particular instance, Ramsauer was certainly guilty of allowing Riehl to lead witnesses, badger the jury, and declare the same evidence alternately conclusive or questionable, depending on how it suited his case at any given moment. In his summation, Riehl instructed the jury to disregard the verdict of university psychiatrists (who had had Rothstock under strict observation for a month and concluded that he was sane) in favor of the vague statement that he might be insane by court psychiatrists (who had studied him for a mere three days). And why? Because, Riehl argued, the university experts, "overwhelmed with other tasks, can hardly have had a chance to observe the accused closely."[71] But the minute the verdict came in—the jury declared Rothstock unanimously guilty of murder, but was evenly split on the insanity question, so that the question was decided in favor of the accused—Riehl leapt up again and declared the court psychiatrists' verdict that Rothstock was insane null and void, adding that for the purpose of sentencing, only the university verdict, which he had previously condemned as unreliable, should be considered. In essence, Riehl argued that his client was insane for the purpose of determining his guilt (so that he could escape a prison sentence), but perfectly sane for the purpose of determining his sentence (so that he could also escape being sent to a mental hospital).[72] In the end, Riehl almost got to have that cake and eat it: Rothstock was declared mildly "confused" and sent to a mental hospital, where he was placed into the care of the same psychiatrists who had declared him sane in the first place. Since they could not legally keep him there in the absence of an actual mental illness, Rothstock was, after some bureaucratic to and fro, released in May 1927. He had spent barely twenty months off the streets.[73]

The Myth of the Lone Gunman

More plainly even than the second "Bettauer" trial itself, the verdict against Rothstock expressed the paradoxical belief that while Bettauer was a Jewish pig and deserved to die, he was emphatically *not* the victim of a Nazi assassination plot. The reason for this was obvious: had it been established that Rothstock had planned Bettauer's murder for months with Nazi comrades, even—as he himself admitted freely—leaving the Nazi party months before the murder so that they would not be implicated, he would hardly have been able to plead mental "confusion." But the question mattered not only in terms of Rothstock's defense strategy. On March 12, two days after the assassination, *Die Stunde* reported that

> a rumor has emerged from Parliamentary circles that if a link can be established between the assassin *Rothstock* and the National Socialist Party, the dissolution of the National Socialist Party will be considered. This measure would be justified by the fact that recent murders have predominantly been committed by members of this party and that this party is therefore to be considered the cause of the brutalization and the indoctrination of adolescents.[74]

The stakes were thus high. Consequently, shrill denials that there had ever been a conspiracy to murder Bettauer permeated the pretrial interrogation, the trial itself, and the vast majority of press reports on the case. Only four newspapers declined to jump on the "nothing to see here" band wagon: the left-wingers *Arbeiterzeitung*, *Arbeiterwille*, *Die Rote Fahne* and *Der Tag*. Had they not so doggedly reported on the witnesses who had overheard conversations between Rothstock and others about a planned shooting or who had seen him in the company of other Nazis at Bettauer's door on the day of the murder, the public would never have heard of either. On March 11, the day after the murder and the day before Rothstock retained Riehl, the *Arbeiterzeitung* reported that Rothstock himself had "intimated that he was a member of a group that aimed to protect *German youth from all corrupting influence*, which included Bettauer's doings, a group that, as the assassin vaguely hinted, fought against all evil."[75] Three days later, the right-wing *Vorarlberger Wacht* confirmed that Rothstock had "banded together with like-minded comrades some months earlier to found an association whose mission was no more and no less than saving German culture and liberating German youth from all corruption. Hugo Bettauer was held by Otto Rothstock to be a corrupting influence and thus shot down."[76] Apparently, then, Rothstock himself had indicated that the deed had been planned in conjunction with others, before Riehl had a chance to instruct him that this should be denied at all costs. That there was a conspiracy to commit murder is also intimated clearly enough in Riehl's letter to Rothstock, in which he mentions that he knew of Rothstock's motives through "persons who know you well." Even dismissing eye- and ear-witnesses establishing the conspiracy, and even discounting the constant calls for Bettauer's murder in the Nazi press, the police had plenty to go on. Yet barely two days after the assassination, on the morning of March 12, the police declared that they had concluded their investigation into the conspiracy angle, had found no evidence of a plot, and were no longer pursuing leads in that direction.[77]

Rothstock's fervent insistence that he had acted alone (and inspired only by the noblest motives) was given major space in all press reporting on the case. Many newspapers misrepresented the shoddy police investigation of possible accomplices, which can have lasted barely 24 hours, as "extremely extensive."[78] In most articles, and not only those in the right-wing press, the denial that there was a plot to kill Bettauer is repeated too relentlessly not to arouse suspicion:

> An exhaustive search of his apartment brought nothing to light [that points to a conspiracy, TSK] but instead confirmed what Rothstock had stated: that he had acted on his own impulse in order

to free persons of his own age from the thoroughly reprehensible products of Bettauer's supposedly moral writings, and that he had no accomplices.

Two pages further on, in the same article:

> The assassin Otto *Rotstock* [sic] has, in another interrogation, declared anew that the attack on Bettauer has no connection whatsoever with any political group or with his own previous political activities; the deed arose from his own free decision as well as the conviction that such a *corrupter of the morals of youth* had to be eliminated; he had not acted on anyone's orders; he had not been incited to the deed by anyone else; nay, he never even spoke to anyone about his intention to attack Bettauer.

And a few lines further down, in the same article:

> He again resolutely denied having had accomplices or confidants. He declared that he had not spoken to a single other person about his deed...[79]

No connection whatsoever, no orders, no incitement, no single other person involved: it reads like an incantation. At least 58 lead articles on the matter, published in 37 newspapers spanning the political spectrum, hammered this message home to readers. The *Reichspost* alone ran no fewer than six major articles dedicated entirely to the denial of the "conspiracy theory."[80] In its stead arose two fables: the centrist press held that a poor, mentally disturbed youth—who had acted very much on his own—had made the horrible mistake of appointing himself judge, jury and executioner, while the right-wing press averred that a knight in shining armor—also, of course, acting very much alone—had arisen to do heroic battle with the Filth-Spewing Dragon. Rothstock was routinely praised and pitied as

Wir kommen still und nett,
Wir schießen frisch und flott,
Und sind wir auch komplett.
Sind wir doch kein Komplott.

Cartoon from the Nazi paper *Götz von Berlichingen* on the conspiracy theory. Citizens of all classes, armed with guns and knives, line up at the editorial office of *Bettauer's Weekly*. Legend: "We come here quiet and nice,/We'll shoot you in a trice,/And that we are a lot/Does not mean there's a plot" (March 14, 1925, p. 7).

> a murderer born of outrage about the *abuse of eroticism*, a murderer motivated by a *deep and profoundly violated chastity*. Today, as a victim lies bleeding on the ground, we do not wish to judge with *harshness*, we wish to let *compassion* raise its voice. Young Otto Rothstock has, in his life so far, been impeccably honest, he has never acted in a sensual manner, never lusted after profits, never sought his own advantage. Here it was not the beast in Man that overwhelmed him, *here a young man has acted, compelled by the command-*

ment of his outrage, from a searing, burning wrath—intensified to the level of criminality—*about abuses* that we, alas, already take for granted and that run off us like rinse water. How intense must this feeling have been, how it must have churned within the young Rothstock, what monstrous deeds he must have witnessed and experienced that he could decide to become the *avenger of aggrieved decency* and shoot down an opponent who *had, by his conviction, to be shot down in order to protect young souls from corruption*, so that profiteering could no longer touch the holiest things, things that the son of a machinist still holds sacred while the dregs of the city besmirch and defile them! Must we not all of us together *blush with shame in the contemplation of this crime?* Let all of Bettauer's followers take *warning* from Hugo Bettauer's fate! Let them all consider that one day things may *end differently* than their thousand-fold cynicism imagines! Let them know that the best things still left to this impoverished humanity are *not to be laughed at nor trifled with!*[81]

It is a perfect reversal—not only of the roles of evildoer and victim, but also of the roles of individual and mass men. Rothstock, in this tale, is the quintessential individual, which in itself stands in direct contradiction to the idea of Rothstock as part of a plotting group. Heroes can be admired only as individuals; victims can be pitied only as individuals. Rothstock is assigned the role of both. He is virtuous and chaste, a stranger to all sensuality, a pure innocent who has never lusted after women or profits—in a word: the very antithesis to the famously hedonistic, lustful and materialistic Bettauer. The "avenger of aggrieved decency" acts on his own truest impulses, compelled only by his own outraged decency, entirely uninfluenced by others. Bettauer, on the other hand, ceases to be an individual after the throwaway sentence in which he lies bleeding on the ground. Thereafter, he becomes part of an anonymous mass that comprises him, his followers, and the "dregs of the city," all of whom, motivated by greed and lust, commit monstrous deeds, corrupt and defile, and drag the holiest of holies through the dirt. Even though the article studiously avoids mention of the word "Jew," it relies centrally on easily recognizable antisemitic motifs, stock phrases, and rhetoric—that familiar feverish vision of sex, greed, and degeneracy that graced every *Stürmer* story on Jewish ritual murder, served up with a good dollop of righteous fury and ending in a direct threat—not against Bettauer, who was, after all, beyond the Nazis' reach at that point, but against an amorphous mass of (Jewish) defilers, besmirchers, and corrupters.

Bettauer on His Own: Jewish Coding

So how did Bettauer, but not his coeditor Olden, come to personify "Jewish swinishness"? If background and personal history are considered, Olden was every bit as "Jewish" as Bettauer. Just as Bettauer had converted to Protestantism at age 18, Olden decided to shed his Jewish background in order to enable his military career in the First World War. Born neither Rudolf nor Olden but Gunther Oppenheim (a name that suggested Jewish roots), he adopted his father's pen name, Olden, and the first name Rudolf (in homage to his uncle, Prince Rudolf of Liechtenstein), in 1916. Correspondence from August 1915 documents how urgently he pursued the alignment with his aristocratic relatives and the purging of any hint of Jewishness in his background. "Why do lawyers even exist?," the future lawyer Rudolf Olden wrote in exasperation to his aunt, Princess Hedwig of Liechtenstein. "This is not a matter for the civil registry office. Also the matter of the *Christian name* must be dealt with. Otherwise I'll never be a lieutenant."[82]

Mere months after the Nazis seized power, in June 1933, Olden was disbarred because he was a Communist, without any hint that he was also a Jew. Jewishness would not have been a legal reason for disbarment in 1933 (the racial laws banning Jews from practicing law and other professions were not passed until 1935). Still, the fact that the Nazis did not use Olden's Jewish roots to discredit him further may indicate that Olden's early efforts to distance himself from them were successful.

Be that as it may: both Bettauer and Olden perceived their Jewish roots, whether real or imagined, as undesirable or even career killers. Bettauer acted in 1890 (by converting to Protestantism); Olden in 1915 (by changing a Jewish-sounding name that could later come to haunt him). Yet when both embarked on the joint enterprise of coediting and funding *He and She*, Bettauer was turned into the "Jewish pornographer" while Olden was given a pass. It is reasonable to assume that this was not happenstance but a deliberate process, something we might think of in the terms suggested by Lisa Silverman: Jewish "coding." Silverman's investigation of several criminal cases involving Jews (or "Jews") as either criminals or victims describes Jewish coding as a method of identifying people as Jews "independent of whether the 'actors' involved in their roles were Jews. Ultimately, these trials show that codings of Jewishness were abstract, detachable, applicable to a range of individuals, and not necessarily contingent upon the degree to which they, or others, considered themselves as Jews, if at all."[83]

We can only speculate as to why this process was applied to Bettauer but not Olden, although some reasons readily suggest themselves. Bettauer, not Olden, had written countless novels in which heroes broke the law and got away with it and in which women gloried in their sexual freedoms, thus feeding the antisemitic stereotype of the Jews undermining societal mores and the very foundation of *Volk* and State. Bettauer, not Olden, had shown a consistent interest in sexuality throughout his career, thus inadvertently opening the door to being typecast as a Jewish sex fiend, a flesh-peddler, a pervert and a pimp. Bettauer, not Olden, had raised Nazi hackles by writing a novel ridiculing the Nazi dream of creating a city, or a country, without Jews. Silverman's analysis of what should have been the "Rothstock" trial but wasn't states it plainly:

> it was the intense focus on Bettauer's Jewishness *after* the murder that reveals the degree to which he was more or less "transformed" into a Jew by the context of the crime committed against him. In his case, sexual indecency and immorality were not deployed as superficial pretexts for killing a Jew; rather, these functioned as a way to buttress acceptance of the killer's crime and to make his act both explicable and politically "useful." [...] As a result, Bettauer's status as a Jew, first emphasized at his trial for public indecency, only increased after his death. Coding Bettauer as Jewish by associating him with pornography, prostitution, and sexual perversity helped the Viennese envision Rothstock as a hero and allow him only light punishment for the murder. Although sexual deviance, crime, and Jews had long been linked in Central European culture, in this urban context of politically useful antisemitism, Bettauer's Jewishness was more significant to the audience needing a "rational" reason for accepting his brutal murder than it had likely been for Rothstock, who needed few excuses to justify killing him.[84]

If Bettauer, as Silverman suggests, was "coded" as a Jew in order to help the Viennese accept his murder and Rothstock's acquittal, we have now left the realm of reality and entered the world of large-scale indoctrination. There is, in fact, a good deal of evidence for this. Both Murray Hall and Silverman have pointed out—and both court records and press coverage confirm—that Rothstock never once cited antisemitism as a motive, leaving Bettauer's Jewish "coding" entirely to Riehl and the press.[85] That Bettauer "became more Jewish for the purposes of the trial" is confirmed by Olden, who attended the first day of Rothstock's trial and "complained bitterly that the entire first day focused on Bettauer, Jews, and the 'immoral' media instead of on his murderer."[86] It is also true that Bettauer's Jewish coding set in the course of the 1924 pornography trial, where the press pounced upon Bettauer while ignoring his coeditor Olden. "A perverse Jew," trumpeted the *Christlich-soziale Arbeiterzeitung* on March 15, 1924,

> got the idea to turn Vienna into a literary pig trough in the hopes of making a killing. It is certainly not a stupid venture; every major city hosts a great herd of two-legged pigs, and that this should not be the case in Vienna [...] after its social life was poisoned by the morals of Jewish immigrants, would be a miracle. Thus the Jew *Bettauer* sat down and edited a new illustrated magazine with a title familiar in the pigsty: "He and She." Afterwards you could see the magazine advertised in the windows of tobacco shops and newspaper vendors; flocks of children and juveniles reveling in the pictures and buying the "pretty pictures" and "juicy anecdotes" if they could. A literary flood of slime oozed through the streets of Vienna...[87]

The point here is obvious: like hundreds of other articles, this one refers to *one* perverse Jew, not two. This *one* Jew, "the Jew *Bettauer*," is then made fruitful and multiplied: he is turned into the representative of a large group ("Jewish immigrants") and into a symptom for an apocalyptic development (the "flood of slime"). Fast forward a year and a half—past this trial and the next, past his murder and his murderer's acquittal—and you'll find Bettauer's coding in the press unchanged:

> Yes, Bettauer is dead, but not his work. It continues to eat away at a thousand poisoned hearts and in rivers of contaminated blood. Should one even believe that magazines like *I and You* were pressed into the hands of girls coming straight from school? [...] The newspaper Jew knows exactly what to write in order to shackle his readers. He sells his product, and the German people take in the poison. It becomes ever more docile, lustful, immoral—and thus ripe to be used for nefarious schemes. Thus the warning must resound again and again:
> "No Jewish papers in any German house!"[88]

Looking at the press coverage spanning both "Bettauer" trials and the fallout (Rothstock's acquittal in 1925, his release and inscription into the army in 1927, and his career under the Nazis), and casting our net wide (from October 1923 to May 1934), we encounter Bettauer as the main subject of 461 articles in 37 newspapers. In the same time span, Rudolf Olden is mentioned a mere 129 times, often in ways unrelated to either the "pornography"- or the murder case: as the author of a new work announced in the *Austrian Correspondence of Booksellers*, for example.[89] In the following table, I have again—as I did in Tamara von Hervay's case—classified articles by predominant attitude or obvious purpose. I have presumed that Nazi papers would evince strong antisemitic tendencies in all or most cases, and therefore, to avoid skewing results, excluded Nazi sources like *Der Hammer*, *Götz* or *Deutsche Arbeiterzeitung* from this count, but have included all prominent right-wing papers (such as *Reichspost*) as well as centrist and left-wing papers (such as *Arbeiterzeitung*). Where an article shows two main purposes and a predominant attitude could not be determined, I have listed it in both relevant columns (for example: antisemitic *and* criticizing the State for not taking action against Bettauer). The result:

Defending Bettauer or protesting his treatment	130
Maligning Bettauer without mention of his Jewishness	118
Neutral	92
Antisemitic	58
Criticizing the State for failing to protect Bettauer or take action against his killer	58
Criticizing the State for failing to take action against Bettauer	14

Table 3: Coverage of Bettauer news, based on a sample of 461 articles in 37 newspapers published from October 9, 1923 to May 12, 1934.

This breakdown allows us to draw some further (cautious) conclusions, both with regard to Bettauer's Jewish coding and with regard to how Austria's press scene changed in the two decades between Hervay's trial in 1904 and Bettauer's in 1924/25. In 1904, reporting that attempted to remain neutral was the largest category in Hervay coverage (120 articles of a total of 325); in the Bettauer sample, it has slipped to third place. The percentage of explicitly antisemitic reporting (again: in the mainstream press, excluding Nazi coverage) is almost exactly the same: 12.6 percent in 1904, 12.5 percent twenty years later. One could further argue that the Jewess Hervay got a tougher ride from her contemporary press than the Jew Bettauer: a total of 147 articles attacked her whereas only 58 rose in her defense. In Bettauer's case, articles maligning him—with or without reference to his Jewishness—(190) nearly hold the balance with those either defending him or criticizing the way in which he was railroaded (188).

And yet, the journalistic scene changed considerably in those two decades. Coverage of the Hervay trial could fluctuate considerably in terms of framing or nasty asides, but actually varied little in terms of content or verifiable facts, and either harsh judgment or ardent defense of Hervay could be found in newspapers of all political stripes. This is not true in Bettauer's case. Articles defending Bettauer or protesting his treatment are spread across only ten newspapers (out of a total of 37 examined), most on the left wing.[90] Bettauer's most frequent and ardent defenders, and also the sole promoters of the conspiracy theory, were the Socialist/Communist dailies *Arbeiterzeitung*, *Arbeiterwille*, and *Die Rote Fahne*. Whereas writings fighting Bettauer's corner thus reached only readers who were likely to be fairly left-wing, coverage maligning Bettauer, with or without antisemitic overtones, appeared across the political spectrum, in twenty-nine newspapers out of 37, reaching the vast majority of newspaper readers in Vienna and beyond.[91] Furthermore, coverage in papers that one might have regarded as Bettauer's natural allies—the Jewish or left-wing press—was by no means unswervingly positive towards him. Zionist papers like the *Wiener Morgenzeitung*, perhaps fearing that the pogrom against him could easily turn into a pogrom against Jews in general, refused to have the Jewish community, as they put it, "burdened with Bettauer."[92] In March 1924, the Zionist *Wiener Stimmen* ran an unpleasant article with the headline "The journalist as a professional pimp," in which they declared that "to sustain and pamper the scribbler Bettauer was tasteless and frivolous. To tolerate or support the pimp Bettauer would be a crime for which Jewish society would have to suffer bitterly."[93] Left-wing papers, too, often made it clear that they only cared about Bettauer as a victim of a Nazi assassination plot: "The pornographic scribbler Bettauer does not concern us, but what does concern us is the fascist murder organizations, because we know that if they kill Bettauer for 'moral' reasons today, they are merely 'consolidating,' all the better to 'dispatch' class-conscious workers tomorrow."[94]

To the best of my ability to discover, Bettauer was defended only in a very small corner of news reporting (the extreme left-wing) and attacked everywhere else. Nor was he safe from attacks from the left-wing or the Zionist press. Outside of the pages of his own magazine *Bettauer's Weekly*, which Olden and Bettauer's widow tried to redact for a short time after his death until it folded in September 1927,[95] there really was no safe space for him, no "Bettauer camp," in the entire broad field of Austrian reporting. This is what Olden meant when he said that although Bettauer himself was apolitical, his was the first political murder in Austria.[96] Or, to speak with Silverman: "emphasizing the Jewishness of one's victim was clearly how to get away with murder in Vienna in 1925."[97] Just as Bettauer was coded as a Jew (and therefore a natural victim), Rothstock was coded as a valiant slayer of Jews: "We'll find a Rothstock for you as well" ("Es wird sich doch ein Rothstock finden") became a popular threat against professors at the University of Vienna between 1934 and 1938.[98]

The Jewish Coding of Bettauer and the Overlooking of Olden are also highly noticeable in the works of Nazi propagandists. Herwig Hartner, who would later distinguish himself through writings that identified Jews as a criminal race,[99] cut his teeth in a book called *Eroticism and Race*, which was serialized in the antisemitic satirical magazine *Kikeriki* in 1926 and in which Bettauer played a starring role. *Eroticism and Race* casts Bettauer, who had abjured his Jewish faith at age 18 and from whom the Zionist press could not distance itself quickly enough, as a quintessential Jew and leader of the Jewish people. All of his books were coded as Jewish novels: *The Joyless Street* (*Die freudlose Gasse*, 1924) was nothing more than a "Jewish satire"; *The Battle for Vienna* (*Der Kampf um Wien*, 1923) merely "a *roman à clef* for the glorification of Judaism and the denigration of non–Jewish Vienna."[100] The scandal surrounding *He and She* is recast as a titanic struggle "that split Vienna into two camps, one of which—Jewish Social Democrats and Jewish freethinkers—took Bettauer's side while the other—Christians and nationalists—unleashed a storm against Bettauer."[101] Bettauer is elevated to a kind of sexual prophet for the Jewish people:

> In all, Bettauer was a Marxist Socialist, a Democrat and Jew who, while not racially motivated, was instinctively and consciously Jewish. The adulation he received particularly in Jewish circles [...], where he was adored like a prophet, shows that he spoke from the very depths of the soul of Judaism [...]. Bettauer was the first herald of the new sexual religion who was acknowledged and worshipped by a broad congregation of the faithful.[102]

As Hartner remarks, the disavowal of Bettauer by Zionist papers like the *Wiener Morgenzeitung* for fear that "the uproar about Bettauer [...] might turn against Jews in general" is an exercise in futility: "This simple denial cannot eradicate the fact that Bettauer, in his entire spirituality, in his strong libido and his consciousness, and in his business acumen and bustling activity is a true Jew, as can be shown flawlessly from his writings, just as the whole sexual revolution is dominated entirely by Jews."[103] And since Bettauer is not a mere individual but the Quintessential Jew, even his death does not solve the problem. As another antisemite once put it, Bettauer is dead, but not his work. So long as Jews like Anton Kuh and Sigmund Freud are allowed to continue writing,

Hartner concludes, the titanic struggle between Christians and Jews will continue.[104] In all of this coding of Bettauer as the Leader of His People and the Essence of all Jewishness, Rudolf Olden is not mentioned even once.

The year before Hartner weighed in, Alfred Rosenberg, who would go on to become one of the most significant propagandists of the Nazi movement and editor of the *Völkischer Beobachter*, dedicated an issue of his antisemitic biweekly magazine *World Struggle* (*Der Weltkampf*) entirely to *The Bettauer Case* as *A Classic Example of Jewish Attempts to Contaminate through Morally Corrupting Writings* (*Der Fall Bettauer: Ein Musterbeispiel jüdischer Zersetzungstätigkeit durch entsittlichendes Schrifttum*). Rosenberg's title, *The Bettauer Case*, is to be taken at face value: as usual, Rudolf Olden does not even rate a mention. Bettauer appears here as merely one of thousands of Jewish writers peddling pornography and filth, for "nowhere does the Jewish race feel more at home than in the production and distribution of literary smut, which—just like the stock exchange and white slavery—have almost wholly turned into a Hebrew monopoly."[105] After Bettauer peddled "deliberate Jewish race propaganda" in *The City Without Jews*, after the "half–Jew Seitz-Pollacksohn," in typical Jewish solidarity, had refused to shut down Bettauer's dirty business, "it is entirely understandable that an impotent rage came over the populace that had been mocked openly by impudent Jews. Young Rothstock certainly only did what hundreds of thousands of mothers wished on the tempter of their children."[106] Writing shortly before Rothstock went to trial, Rosenberg agitates for his acquittal, for

> the dead man was the representative of a race and a movement that day by day besmirches, degrades and mocks our people. The Austrian State government, in a dereliction of duty, stood idly by as the poison ate into hundreds of thousands. There is no German, no matter how much he objects to murder as a method, who does not feel the highest veneration for Rothstock's motive: to awaken his derided people. Public feeling clearly demands that the Austrian courts atone for the guilt incurred by the Austrian government and release Rothstock, ruthlessly suppress smutty literature, and imprison all brothel journalists.[107]

Rosenberg glories in the press attacks on Bettauer, gleefully citing from the worst examples. Nevertheless, he castigates even the most ardent Bettauer haters for failing to acknowledge that "Bettauer is, as cannot be emphasized enough, only one among thousands, many thousands, millions": "As correct as the onslaught on the scribbler Bettauer was in some papers that have not yet been Judaized, we still miss the characterization of this 'journalist's' pernicious doings as quintessentially Jewish."[108] Clearly, coding Bettauer as an *über*–Jew, as one among millions yet also "representative" of his race, mattered far more to Rosenberg, Hartner and other propagandists even than getting Rothstock off. In the end, the answer to the question "why Bettauer but not Olden?" may be quite simply: because Olden was not needed in the coding process. A single "representative" sufficed to signify the entire race. And just as Bettauer was coded as representative of and one among millions, the celebration of his murder became easily decodable as the barely veiled public advocacy of the massacre of those other millions.

Fond Memories and Holes of Oblivion

Adorno once famously said that after Auschwitz it was impossible to write poetry because—given that Auschwitz had been possible and remained possible into what he called "the unforeseeable future"—no "cheerful artform" could be imagined.[109] Is it possible to say that Nazi "justice" made true rogues like Wilhelm Voigt and the Sass Brothers impossible because—given that the criminalization and murder of rogues or complete innocents had been possible—no "cheerful criminal" could be imagined? And if so, what does this have to do with antisemitism? Can the lovable criminal, the "rogue" of real life or literature, adored, pitied, and cheered by an audience of millions, ever be a Jew?

The four trials investigated here, spread across two decades, yield three concrete results and one surprise. First off: neither of the Jewish accused, Tamara von Hervay or Hugo Bettauer, were ever traded as the lovable rogue of Germanic culture, although both were types that practically exemplified the part: openly hedonistic, strong-willed, insubordinate, *bons vivants* and vociferous in their own defense. Secondly and surprisingly: the percentage of explicitly antisemitic reporting in mainstream newspapers did not increase in the 20 years between 1904 and 1924. And finally, less surprisingly: both of the later cases, the case of the Brothers Sass and the case of Hugo Bettauer, were settled out of court, by shooting the accused and exculpating the killer. In 1904, courts and trials still decided the question of what constituted justice; in the later cases, the court's role was limited to confirming decisions taken at an extra-judicial level. In the Sass brothers' case, there was an "orderly" progression from their railroading in court to their State-ordered murder in a concentration camp; in the Bettauer case, the execution preceded the trial, which was then left scrambling to justify it retrospectively. These disparities, however, are differences in degree only. What happened to the Sass Brothers shows us a society completely divested of the authority—moral or judicial—of its court system; what happened to Bettauer shows us a society well on its way there.

Court records and press reporting suggest strongly why Hervay and Bettauer were ineligible for the role of the lovable rogue: both were coded as Jews, and the tale of the lovable rogue cannot be told in the language of antisemitism. Explicitly antisemitic mainstream press reporting on their cases, to which both were subjected to a similar degree, does not tell the whole story. The story is both more subtle and more far-reaching than the press coverage of a few years can capture. As Shulamit Volkov has shown, it amounts to an entire culture of perception being created by an endless series of "wrong metaphors" and "associative mergers" that equate Jews and Judaism with all the ills of modernity and in which "a quick turn of the pen made a single problem [Judaism, TSK] stand for all others."[110] The associative merger in both Hervay's and Bettauer's case was that between sex, greed and Jewishness; their defiant advocacy of a free sexuality turned them into proponents of a hated modernity. In both cases, this emerges, exactly as Volkov has described it, in a process of conceptualization and verbalization. Much of this process can be traced distinctly in (although it is hardly limited to) court records and press coverage. In this process of conceptualization and verbalization, whether explicitly antisemitic or not, Hervay and Bettauer were not treated as individuals but coded as "symbols of the time," even in articles in which the word "Jew" does not occur once. Press reporting shows time and again that it had already become virtually impossible to distinguish attitudes toward Jews from what Volkov has termed "the rest of one's ideological and cultural 'package deal,'"[111] in this case: moral outrage about sexual licentiousness, materialism or depravity. Volkov further claimed that there is rarely an attempt to distinguish between separate issues—between, for instance, objections to Jews and objections to materialism. The press coverage on both Hervay and Bettauer seems to confirm this: in a total of 786 articles, the only such attempt I have been able to find is the lone article in *Die Rote Fahne* that stated its interest in Bettauer only as a victim of a Nazi plot (whereas the pornographic hack Bettauer could go to hell for all they cared).[112]

Distinctions between issues are, of course, only relevant in a context where we still distinguish between *people*, and the absence of this distinction is perhaps the most significant reason why Hervay and Bettauer could not be traded as lovable criminals. The court verdict at the Sass trial, which stated that it was inconceivable that they would ever find their way into the *Volksgemeinschaft*—the "people's community"—because they had never really been part of it,[113] speaks volumes in this regard. Just as the Captain of Köpenick was deemed unique, the Sasses were judged to be individuals, even by a court that condemned them to death for it. Their individuality enabled both their adoration by the populace and their extermination as—in Nazi lingo—"anti-social elements." Hervay and Bettauer, conversely, were de-individualized, totalitarianized. To speak with Hannah Arendt: they were turned into Mass Men, simultaneously part and representative of "millions" of Jews. Coded in this way, they were no longer perceived as "criminals": not because neither had actually committed a crime in the sense of doing something illegal, but because a crime is seen as the act of an individual, and the response usually considered appropriate is punishment of the individual. Instead, Hervay and Bettauer were tarnished with the brush of vice. Unlike crime, vice is not a deed but a state of being; it cannot be punished, only exterminated.

To understand the difference between the treatment of Jewish and non–Jewish accused in the courts and in the press, we need to read "vice" in the broad sense intended by Arendt, not in its limited legal meaning (which might truthfully but irrelevantly point out that only Hervay's and Bettauer's crimes, but not Voigt's or the Sass brothers,' were linked with sexuality). The accusation that figured most prominently in all four cases was that of materialism, and in writings of the time that link crime with either Judaism or modernity, the "vice" of materialism plays a far greater role even than sex.[114] On the face of it, then, it makes little sense to perceive the Captain's or the Sass brothers' blatant materialism as individual "crimes" while totalizing the materialistic desires of which Hervay and Bettauer stood accused (sleeping one's way into a moneyed marriage, or profiting financially from peddling smut) into something that "Jews" do for money. Voigt and the Sass brothers were undoubtedly guilty of materialism, but their exploits were always perceived as individual acts, never as a "vice" or a state of being. Neither the Captain nor the Sasses were ever turned into a symbol "of the time," seen as representing "millions," or held responsible for all the ills of modernity. Yet this, in the process of Jewish coding, is precisely what happened to Hervay and Bettauer. And in Bettauer's case, we can point to concrete examples where his extermination in speech acts or acts of writing prefigures not only the extermination of Bettauer in real life, but also more than hints at the desirability of the extermination of the "millions" he was made to represent.

And what of Adorno's disturbing thought that such acts of extermination not only were possible but also remained possible into "the unforeseeable future"? Totalitarian States, Arendt explains, do not leave behind corpses like individual murderers do, and while individual murderers have no power to erase their victims' memories from the surviving world, totalitarian States create "veritable holes of oblivion into which people stumble by accident and without leaving behind them such ordinary traces of former existence as a body and a grave."[115] But traces of former existence, the memory of a person, can be found not only on a tombstone but also in the writing that constitutes collective memory and culture. The Captain of Köpenick is still one of Germany's most beloved folk heroes. The Sass brothers have been resuscitated in online blogs, where they are as celebrated as ever they were in Berlin in the 1920s. Both Voigt and the Sasses are now the heroes of several movies. Hervay and Bettauer, conversely, have fallen into that hole of oblivion. Our memory of them today is limited almost entirely to the scandals that brought them to trial. We know very little of what became of Hervay after that, and that Bettauer, who was unquestionably one of the most successful, widely read and controversial authors of his age, could be so comprehensively forgotten is bewildering, to put it mildly. Some of his novels were reprinted more than half a century after his death,[116] but he still hardly figures in scholarship on Austrian literature, and much of what there is begins with a statement about what a hack he was, as if the authors were embarrassed to be talking about him at all.[117] Almost nothing that Bettauer had created survived very long. His work, which had sold like hotcakes during his lifetime, was promptly forgotten after his death, partially and belatedly reprinted, and still awaits rediscovery. His journal *Bettauer's Weekly*, once Austria's most popular magazine, outlived him by only a year and a half. His oldest son Helmuth did not survive the Second World War; he was murdered in Auschwitz in 1942.

Rudolf Olden, too, did not last long. One of the earliest writers to see through Hitler, in his monumental biography *Hitler the Conqueror: Debunking of a Myth* (*Hitler der Eroberer: Entlarvung einer Legende*, 1933), he was also one of the earliest targeted by the Nazis. In February 1933, on his way to court, he was warned by friends that the Gestapo were waiting for him in the courtroom, and barely managed to escape. He spent his exile in Britain, where, although classified as a Category C refugee—that is: totally loyal and reliable—he was, as were all German exiles even in that category, interned in a camp. In 1940, following the intervention of friends and colleagues, he was released and allowed to accept a professorship in New York on the condition that he never return to Britain. The *City of Benares*, the ship that should have brought him to America, was torpedoed by the Nazis, and Olden died together with his wife Ika, who fought not to be forced into a rescue boat without him, and 77 children who were being evacuated to Canada. That Olden, who had escaped in 1925 because of Bettauer's towering presence, had belatedly achieved a similar status as a Nazi hate figure, is recorded in Goebbels's claim that the *Benares* had been sunk because Olden was on it.[118]

The murderer Otto Rothstock was dealt better cards. Interned as "insane" in October 1925 and released as "cured" in May 1927, he applied to join the army in December of that year. He was promptly enlisted, following a police report testifying as to his good character and unblemished legal record. Only because the press reported on this absurd development—some even critically[119]—were the police forced to explain themselves. They claimed that providing positive character references was standard procedure for all who had not been sentenced for a crime, which Rothstock, after all, hadn't. (They failed to explain why they had told the army repeatedly that Rothstock had never been *under investigation* for a crime, which was emphatically untrue.) Rothstock went on to have a stellar career, first in the army and then in the SS. In 1938, he had the nerve to apply to the City of Vienna for financial compensation for his "illegal imprisonment" following the Bettauer murder, claiming that he had only been sent to the mental hospital "based on forged papers that later disappeared; I was also, as I was told, only held there because the Jewish lobby demanded it."[120] After the war, he got away with denying his SS record, settled in Hanover, married three times, and lived out his life as a well-respected dentist.

Fifty years after he murdered Bettauer, he was still absolutely remorseless, as documented by his correspondence with Murray Hall, the author of the most seminal Bettauer study to date, and a TV interview the following year. In his 1976 letter to Hall, he repeated that he had not had any accomplices but admitted that he had simulated insanity to escape punishment.[121] In his 1977 interview with Peter Huemer, Rothstock, then aged 73, still insisted that what he had done to Bettauer could not be considered murder, that he had only acted from noble motives, and that, given another chance, he would do it again—except that this time he would not go after the "pornographers" with a mere gun but with a "ton of dynamite." And he had nothing but praise for the Nazis' record on crime:

> Well, you've got to admit, so many crimes weren't even possible, because the notorious and pathological criminals were disappeared, kept in so-called concentration camps, and everybody knew: woe betide him if he falls into the hands of the police. So everything was a bit better then. [...] Well, it was definitely a more moral time. Look at this sex magazine that you've given me here. If someone had done that then and had gotten caught—that man would never have done it again. Only when the liberators of the German people arrived in 1945, that's when sex was once again declared to be the main point of the people's education.[122]

That Arendt's "hole of oblivion" was not filled in after 1945 is expressed not only in the extermination of the victims from life and literature but also in the honors, the impunity, the peace and long life enjoyed by so many of their killers. It is expressed in conceptualizations and verbalizations after 1945 that employ much the same coding as before. It is expressed in the *space* a society gives to some ideas and not to others. Fifty years after his murder, Otto Rothstock was afforded the public space to yearn for "a more moral time" when anything and anybody who offended him was conveniently "disappeared." In 1977, Otto Rothstock had more of a voice than Hugo Bettauer. Even after decades of "coming to terms with the past," of "memory boom" and "historians' quarrel," the course for much of our writing and thinking about the Nazi period, much of our *memory* of that period, was set during the period itself. How a society responds to its criminals defines that society no less than the question to whom it grants the dignity of individuality and whom it lumps together as an amorphous "mass," who is fondly remembered and who is flung into the hole of oblivion. Our continued toleration of the fact that Hervay and Bettauer were disappeared characterizes us as much as our lasting amusement at the escapades of the Clever Captain and the Sassy Brothers—in the past, present and into the unforeseeable future.

Plots:
Crime Stories

Tragic Criminals and
Farcical Justice (1890s–1914)

"Good and evil often lie so close together in the human heart."—Auguste Groner, *The Case of the Pool of Blood in the Pastor's Study* (1891)

"You can only truly understand a criminal if you know his entire life. Particularly the parts of it that he spent out of jail."—Hans Hyan, *Bad Boys* (1907)

The Rise of Pop Culture

Germany, that self-styled "Land of Thinkers and Poets," did not become a Land of Readers until about 1870, coinciding neatly with its unification into a politically integrated nation State under Emperor Wilhelm I. Just a decade earlier, in the 1860s, the so-called "lower" classes, which comprised at least 90 percent of the population, had had no greater exposure to books than their great-grandparents in the early 1800s, limiting themselves, provided they could read at all, to religious tracts, calendars and practical handbooks. Just a few short years later, in the early Empire years, at least 70 percent of the laboring classes could read to some degree and professed a sudden interest in fiction. The causes commonly cited for this extreme and rapid change—urbanization, advancements in print technology, and a higher degree of education among the laboring classes—serve to explain the sudden growth in the pool of lower-class readers and, in the 1870s, the swift creation of an enormous book market catering specifically to them.[1] Yet such explanations tend to ignore a vital conceptual change that was no less significant in shaping the literary marketplace: the desire, in a vast majority of Germany's new readers, to read not for edification—either intellectual or religious—but for entertainment. The new literary form that indulged this new desire was the colporteur novel, which we might think of as second cousin to the English "penny dreadful."

Christened after the traveling booksellers who sold them door to door, colporteur novels dominated the literary marketplace throughout the 1870s, selling in the millions and increasing their share of the market seven-fold within the decade.[2] But their significance cannot be reduced to a matter of marks and pfennigs. Colporteur novels were more than just another genre; they were a literary earthquake: "the first great expression of modern popular culture in Germany,"[3] and certainly the first literary genre ever to cater to anyone but the eight or nine percent that made up Germany's educated elite.

That elite naturally derided them as "trashy literature" or "'back stairs novels,' the latter name derived from the widely accepted supposition that the books were sold furtively to servants on the back stairs by sinister characters,"[4] but this did not diminish their popularity one bit. Understandably so, since "every aspect of the 'colporteur novel' was calculated to appeal to the tastes and desires of the ill-educated people who made up at least 90% of Germany's population,"[5] and who by sheer force of numbers also constituted, after 1870, a hefty percentage of Germany's *reading* population. The colporteur novel savvily accommodated their financial limitations by allowing them to subscribe at 10 pfennigs per chapter rather than forcing them to hand over 10 or 15 hard-earned marks for the novel entire. And it indulged their "tastes and desires" for entertainment, unadorned by philosophy, ponderousness or proselytizing of any kind, with a focus on crime.

Crime Stories: Traditions

Crime stories had been known and popular well before colporteur novels arrived at the scene. François Gayot de Pitaval's collection of *Causes célèbres*, originally published in 1734–43 in twenty volumes, was translated into German in the late eighteenth century. One hundred years later, its successor, *The New Pitaval*, had mushroomed to sixty volumes; the original author's name had become synonymous with the genre, and dozens of *Pitaval* imitations vied for a share of the market. But these tales were offered not to the uneducated 90 percent for the purpose of entertainment but to the educated elite for the purpose of edification. No less august a writer than Friedrich Schiller edited one of the eighteenth-century *Pitaval* translations, and the learned legal scholars and writers Anselm von Feuerbach, Julius Eduard Hitzig and Willibald Alexis jumped on the *Pitaval* bandwagon in the nineteenth. Tone, form and content of their tales confirm that they addressed themselves to readers of a similar class and worldview. They presented the criminal as an interesting aberration to be studied; they invited reflection on the part of the reader on the rectitude of the judicial system, the dangers of rising above one's station, and the regrettable necessity to reaffirm the strength and solidity of law-abiding society through its ritual expulsion and excision of the criminal.[6]

Colporteur novels, conversely, addressed themselves to a different class of readers and had no truck with erudite musings on what Kleist once called "the imperfect state of the world."[7] They were, as Otto Glagau put it in 1870, tales of

> murder and manslaughter, for the masses have a burning craving for simple facts, [for] compact and unadorned incident, for an uninterrupted and relentless pace, for a riot of ever-new twists and turns of plot, the wilder and more improbable the better. They don't want to be given the opportunity to linger and reflect, but rather want to be perpetually surprised and dazzled, to be dragged through a labyrinth of incident, and to be shocked and stunned by ceaseless, explosive, and unexpected swerves in the plot.[8]

Glagau's view of the colporteur novel, condescending as it may sound, has been confirmed by many producers of the genre. "Your broad, cozy description of family life doesn't appeal to the tastes of our readers at all," wrote an incensed publisher to a hack writer who had veered from the formula for success. "The end of the seventh installment must have a detailed, exact description of a murder or other gruesome act, which will be further developed in the eight installment and concluded in the ninth."[9] Publishers, who alone determined content and style and merely contracted assemblyline writers to do the actual writing, were crucially aware that "the masses' appetite for these subjects was insatiable" and that "Germans could devour installment after installment detailing the horrid details of crime."[10] Thus colporteur novels tended to make the most of murder most foul, both historical (for instance the exploits of the killer Schentz, serialized in several novels) and fictional (such as the racily titled *The Killer of Women and His Victims/Der Frauenmörder und seine Opfer*, 140,000 copies sold).[11] Robbers and murderers from Germany's colorful past were routinely resurrected as heroes of the genre. The poacher Matthias Klostermeyer, executed in 1771, rose from his grave as *Hiesel* [nickname for "Matthias," TSK], *A Robber and Yet, a Folk Hero* (*Der Hiesel. Ein Räuber und doch ein Volksheld*); similarly *Arno Kraft Called Goliath, the Greatest German Robber Captain of the Nineteenth Century* (*Arno Kraft, genannt Goliath, der größte deutsche Räuberhauptmann des 19. Jahrhunderts*), *Johann Christian Messerschmied, Called the Scourge of the Rhineland* (*Johann Christian Messerschmied, genannt die Geißel des Rheinlandes*) or *Heinrich Anton Lichtweis, the Reckless Robber and Poacher* (*Heinrich Anton Lichtweis der verwegene Räuber und Wilddieb*). The infamous outlaw Johannes Bückler a.k.a. "Schinderhannes" ("Torturing Jack"), guillotined in 1803, enjoyed a vigorous literary afterlife in any number of colporteur novels as *Torturing Jack, the Greatest Robber Captain of the Nineteenth Century* (*Schinderhannes, der grösste Räuberhauptmann des 19. Jahrhunderts*).[12] Victor von Falk's *The Hangman of Berlin* (*Der Scharfrichter von Berlin*), a 3,000-page thrill ride comprising "an orgy in a bandit hideout, a patricide, the hanging of an innocent maiden, an attempted poisoning, a revolt, and a grave robbery; [...] espionage, the hypnotism of a maiden, the kidnapping of a child and preparations for its murder, a train crash, divorce, a trapeze artist's fall, vows of vengeance, the burial of a living person, a duel—and more," sold over a million copies and made its publisher a profit of three million marks.[13] For publishers, the recipe for riches was simple: if it bleeds, it leads.

Rising costs and hostile legislation took a bite out of the colporteur novel's absolute dominance of the market in the 1880s and '90s,[14] but this in no way diminished the new readership's thirst for entertainment, their interest in crime, or the publishers' skill at turning these predilections into a gold mine. Around the turn of the new century, colporteur novels gave way to dime novels (*Groschenhefte*), colporteur copycats in all but name, with a predominant readership in the laboring classes, a predominant focus on crime, and staggering subscription numbers. Weekly editions ranged from tens of thousands all the way to 100,000 copies per issue.[15] "Never before and never since have there ever been so many series and such high circulation. Contemporary experts claimed that since the invention of the printing press, no literary genre has attracted so many readers in such a short time."[16] At the outset of the First World War, there were at least 100 different dime novel series whose profit margins reached 50 million marks each.[17]

In dime novels, the colporteur formula still held but was varied on occasion. Its traditional hero, the criminal—pirates, robbers, shady adventurers and gentleman thieves[18]—retained pride of place; some variations featured his opposite number, the detective, as main protagonist. Many of these, particularly adaptations of American or

Cover of Issue 5 of *Torturing Jack, the Greatest Robber Captain of the Nineteenth Century* (Berlin: W. Grosse, 1890).

British imports, from Nick Carter to Nat Pinkerton to Sherlock Holmes, were wildly popular. Publisher Adolf Eichler landed a coup when he acquired the translation rights to the Nick Carter stories in 1906; by 1908, he had sold 250 of them at a circulation of about 45,000 pamphlets per week.[19] Nick Carter dominated the market to such a degree that his name became a byword for trashy literature; Prussia seriously considered passing a "Lex Nick Carter" by the end of the decade.[20] Sherlock Holmes, not to be outdone, was accorded the dubious honor of having a mental illness named after him. The main symptom of "Sherlockism," diagnosed in the June 1908 edition of the *Stock Exchange Gazette of German Booksellers* as "a literary disease similar to Werther-Mania and Romantic Byronism," was the reading public's obsession with "a detective who can see through three waistcoats whether you have a mole on your fifth rib, three millimeters in diameter."[21]

Such an obsession naturally inspired homegrown imitations by the fistful, from *Rolf Brand, the German Sherlock Holmes* to *Ethel King, the Female Nick Carter*. Homegrown originals also flooded the market. From 1876 onward, the *Library of Entertainment and Knowledge* (*Bibliothek der Unterhaltung und des Wissens*) appeared in 13 volumes per year, publishing crime and detective stories by German and Austrian authors like Ludwig Habicht, E. H. v. Dedenroth, Carl Adolph Streckfuß, Auguste Groner, Balduin Groller and many others.[22] All of these authors also published independently and were widely read.[23] Mirko Schädel's illustrated crime literature bibliography identifies over 800 new and original works by German-language authors first published between 1900 and 1933, and also notes that the number of new works steadily grew over that time, year on year.[24] By the beginning of the First World War, the film industry had caught on, and German-authored detectives with Anglo-Saxon names like Joe Deebs, Harry Higgs or Joe Jenkins began to chase, kick, punch and shoot their way across Germany's movie screens. Stuart Webbs, the most popular of these, was the hero of many films, from *The Mysterious Villa* (*Die geheimnisvolle Villa*, 1913) and *The Man in the Basement* (*Der Mann im Keller*, 1914) to *The Dead Rise* (*Die Toten erwachen*, 1915) and *The Striped Domino* (*Der gestreifte Domino*, 1915).[25] On the eve of the First World War, at least three crime or detective films became box office hits in Germany: Max Mack's *Where Is Coletti?* (*Wo ist Coletti?*), Joseph Delmont's *The Mysterious Club* (*Der geheimnisvolle Club*) and Franz Hofer's *The Black Snake* (*Die schwarze Natter*, all 1913). Joseph Delmont developed an entire series of crime films, the "Miss Nobody" series; and foreign productions (Nordisk's Sherlock Holmes series, Éclair's Nick Carter films, Pathé's Nick Winter films, and Eclipse's Nat Pinkerton series) were staple cinema fare throughout Germany and Austria.[26]

Crime Stories: Lost Traditions

With such a literary and cinematic maelstrom swirling around the criminal and his archnemesis, the detective, it is difficult to comprehend how the academic credo that there was no German-language tradition of detective or crime fiction until the 1960s was able to persist, amazingly unchallenged, until well into the 1990s.[27] But then, our knowledge of literature is so often mediated by the educated elite, whose attitude towards the crime genre has, for the most part, ranged from neglect to antagonism. From the very beginning of its meteoric rise, popular literature in all of its forms fell foul of such Arbiters of Taste. After victory in 1871, censors opined that only German war heroes should grace kitsch literature, henceforth to be cleansed of redskins, pirates, sympathetic crooks and foreign detectives. Antitrash writing, from brochures to academic works, lamented *The Sordidness of Our Youth Literature* (Heinrich Wolgast's 1899 book *Das Elend unserer Jugendliteratur*).[28] From its first issue onward, Germany's educated classes subjected the Nick Carter series to a veritable crusade seeking its legal prohibition.[29] "By 1910 a vast array of individuals and organizations were engaged in the war to promote Good Literature at the expense of the pamphlet series. The movement reached its emotional apogee in 1912 with the death of Adolf Eichler [who had brought Nick Carter to Germany, TSK], an event cheered hysterically by the Good Literature groups."[30]

State governments began to look into the possibility of enacting outright bans, and occasionally did. Bavaria outlawed "trashy literature" in 1908; Württemberg banned its sale in train stations in 1909; and the much-loved gentleman thief Lord Lister, a.k.a. "Raffles," fell victim to the censors in 1911.[31] Dime novels were banned completely during the First World War.[32] The antitrash movement reached such heights of absurdity that it was occasionally lampooned in the works of crime writers. In Hans Hyan's *Sherlock Holmes, Educator* (*Sherlock Holmes als Erzieher*, 1909), to cite just one example, two crooks, about to be arraigned in court, plan a genius defense: tell the judge, accompanied by a requisite amount of breast-beating and crocodile tears, that your addiction to detective stories led you to stray from the path of virtue.[33] Other writers, too, identified this "cause" of crime as the dumbest excuse most likely to go down the gullets of gullible judges and lawmakers unwilling to recognize crime as the complex social phenomenon it was. When faced with criminality, blame Sherlock.

Whether the war on "trash" was prompted by the fact that it far outstripped "good" literature in terms of popularity and sales, or by a more principal objection to the fact that the "lower" classes had begun to read in overwhelming numbers, we can no longer determine. But certainly, the hostility of the educated elite to crime fiction is a 20th-century constant, whether expressed by commission (attempts to suppress it during the early 1900s) or omission (attempts to ignore its existence for the rest of the century and well into the next). In the foreword to his extensive bibliography of crime literature (*Illustrierte Bibliographie der Kriminalliteratur 1796–1945*, 2006), a compendium of over 9,000 texts, Mirko Schädel understandably wondered why so few scholars were even aware of these texts. He concluded that this ignorance was owed partly to the disposability of the materials themselves—since most colporteur and dime novels were produced in the form of flimsy pamphlets—and partly to a good dose of cultural arrogance that *perceived* these materials as disposable. Crime fiction, after all, is trash, and trash is taken to the dump. "Sometimes I heard from sellers that they had just dumped *Krimis* by the boxful from an old lending library into the paper recycling."[34] To this, Karolle-Berg has added a sobering analysis of how a literary tradition that once swept entire nations can go missing in scholarship: "literary scholars after 1945 would review early *Kriminalromane*, find them to fall short of generic expectations, and thus use them as proof that no 'real' tradition existed."[35]

The Sympathetic Criminal in "Elite" and "Trashy" Literature

Another aspect of crime and detective fiction that may well have stuck in the craw of the educated classes was a recurring plot device: the sympathetic criminal. Some modern scholars have begun to see him as a progressive character that embodies simultaneously the socially oppressive criminalization of "aberrant" behavior and the dignity of resistance. Because such a character, or so the scholarly argument so often goes, can only appear in complex, "elite" literature, his existence in crime fiction is routinely denied. Expressionist literature like Kaiser's drama *From Morning to Midnight* (*Von morgens bis mitternachts*, 1912) or Realist novels like Fontane's *Under the Pear Tree* (*Unterm Birnbaum*, 1885) or Raabe's *Horacker* (1876) and *Tubby Schaumann* (*Stopfkuchen*, 1891) are routinely extolled as exemplars of critical treatments of human deviance, profound and groundbreaking thought-experiments where criminality is no longer seen as "deviant acts" but as "existentially and societally contingent—'conditio humana' (as a space enabling defensive violence, protest and rebellion). This perspective is further enhanced by the fact that the authors stylize themselves as 'outsiders of society' and view criminalized and excluded societal groups as 'allies.'"[36] But crime fiction? Cheap, trivial, and oblivious of any social dimension:

> In German literature, [the detective story] loses, in its continual alignment with Anglo-Saxon series, its relation to reality and what little critical substance it ever had. Within the borrowed literary schemes, the precepts for the criminalization of an act and the punishment of the culprit are meaningless. The consequences are a foregone conclusion. A crime has been committed, the criminal must be detected and punished. [...] In the realm of elite literature, however—in contrast to the detective story—morally and socially reflexive portrayals of crimes are developed and differentiated. Complex determinants of criminal behavior are foregrounded: links between crime, insanity and social declassification. The criminal appears as a victim of society and as a configuration of social conditions.[37]

In the literary scholarship of the 20th and early 21st centuries, where the criminal has become presentable to the elite—as an outsider, as embodying social victimization or the human condition per se, or simply as sympathetic or personable—denials that such a thoughtfully crafted character ever existed in trashy literature are sure to follow. Yet in the waning years of the nineteenth and the early years of the twentieth century, the complex, noble or sympathetic criminal was perceived not only as undeniably present in detective fiction, but in fact as one of the most defining aspects of the genre:

> The detective finds the criminal, with whom he is obsessed and tries to empathize, sympathetic; he considers him superior; he even secretly agrees with him and doesn't want to catch him, and when he does he feels profoundly guilty. The criminal, for his part, shows him that he could very well function as a detective himself, and sometimes demonstrates this role either for fun or in the service of a shared morality.[38]

A century before this criminal became the darling of the elite (and was consequently excised from the detective genre), he was seen as a major problem. His sympathetic characterization and the closeness between criminal and detective resulted in a blurring of the lines between criminality and morality, and in a yawning chasm between justice and the law, that presented readers with a major conundrum. That the detective novel put such ideas into the heads of the "masses" seemed, to many members of the elite, tantamount to inciting social unrest. As Paul Dehn put it:

> I don't want to claim that the thriller pursues Social Democratic tendencies directly. But it does abet them. The poor man in these novels, often in real life too, is noble, helpful and good, but mostly he is alone in this, in contrast to those moving in higher social circles [...]. On occasion you can see this tendency already in the titles: "Noble criminals," "An innocently sentenced workman" etc. [...] Ultimately thrillers arouse discontent and envy in their readers and so pave the way for Social Democratic agitation.[39]

This was also the view of a parochial organization in Berlin that, in 1892, lobbied home owners to forbid salesmen of colporteur novels entry into their homes, for this literature, they claimed, "was designed to estrange our people from God, to help increase murders and suicides, to augment immorality, to raise up Social Democracy, and to incite 'class hatred.'"[40]

Auguste Groner's Redeemable Criminals

It was in this context that the Austrian author Auguste Groner (1850–1929), one of the most famous, prolific and successful crime writers of her day, published her numerous novels and novellas. Her work, comprising 18 crime stories and 25 novels published between 1890 and 1927,[41] is one of the best responses to the elite accusation that detective fiction was socially unaware. In fact, as Tannert and Kratz have recognized,

> pre–World War I detective stories from the German and Austro-Hungarian empires are [...] characterized by a unique and complex set of questions about the nature of justice in a classed society [...]. For German and Austrian writers of the nineteenth and early twentieth centuries, the socially detached approach of a Dupin, an Inspector Bucket or a Sherlock Holmes was dangerous: the detective's very survival in a rigidly classed society depended on his awareness of the way others viewed his work, and he could not afford to behave as if he did not care whom he alienated or exposed.[42]

Auguste Groner undoubtedly qualified as "morally and socially reflexive"; she was also "more popular than Sir Arthur Conan Doyle"[43] and the recipient of many awards.[44] Yet even at the height of her fame, she remained far beneath the lordly gaze of the educated elite. Isabel Colbron, one of her earliest reviewers and translator of several of her stories and novels, noted with disbelief in her 1910 review that "Her name is never mentioned in the magazines that set a standard of criticism, and the essayists who discourse on modern literature know not her fame. This is natural, for detective stories are not literature, according to German ideas."[45] This may also be why Groner still awaits rediscovery today.[46]

Groner's crime stories are remarkable in particular for the near-total absence of irredeemable characters. Her tales practically teem with the innocently accused, but are notably free from habitual criminals of any kind. No chronic offenders, no hardened criminals, no recidivist robbers, no white-collar bankers ruining thousands, no serial killers. Almost all of her criminals—if they turn out to be guilty at all—fall from grace only once; almost all are portrayed as noble, repentant and relieved to be caught. The result is a highly human(e) and understanding relationship between criminals and the law that characterizes Groner's tales more than anything else.

Auguste Groner at the beginning and end of her career, ca. 1890 (left) and 1925 (left: Wikimedia Commons; right: *Wiener Bilder* 16 [April 19, 1925], 4).

The law is represented above all by Detective Josef Müller, Groner's most famous creation and the star of fifteen of her texts. Described as small and frail, plain, unassuming and of indeterminate age, Müller is a genius detective and a master of disguise. Although he is a low-ranking member of Austria's Secret Police, his superiors, well aware that his talents vastly outstrip that of the rest of the Department, leave him free rein. Thus Müller, much like Sherlock Holmes, is left to solve cases on his own, bringing in his colleagues only at the end, to perform the arrest and take the credit for his work. On the chase, he is a bloodhound who does not rest, eat or sleep until he has cornered the criminal. But

> when he has this victim in the net, he will sometimes discover him to be a much finer, better man than the other individual, whose wrong at this particular criminal's hand set in motion the machinery of justice. Several times that has happened to Muller, and each time his heart got the better of his professional instincts, of his practical common-sense, too, perhaps, ... at least as far as his own advancement was concerned, and he warned the victim, defeating his own work.[47]

Indeed, Groner's stories consistently upset moral certainties. The victim in *The Case of the Golden Bullet* (*Die goldene Kugel*, 1892), found sitting at his desk with the titular golden bullet in his heart, is immediately and harshly judged:

> "He was a coward," said the detective coldly, and turned away. Horn repeated mechanically, "A coward!" and his eyes also looked down with a changed expression upon the handsome, soft-featured face, framed in curly blond hair, that lay so silent against the chair-back. Many women had loved this dead man, and many men had been fond of him, for they had believed him capable and manly.[48]

If the victim is not entirely innocent, is it any wonder that the murderer turns out to be less than guilty, a man betrayed by his wife (one of the many who had fallen to the coward's dubious charms), a man who then, rather poetically, shot his betrayer with a bullet smelted from his own wedding ring? Of course, Müller deeply regrets catching the killer, for, as he tells him, "you are a thousand times better than the coward who stole the honour of your wife and who hid behind the shelter of the law." Rather than dragging this "stately man," as the murderer is described, through the humiliation of a court trial and following execution, Müller gives him the opportunity to commit an honorable suicide. The noble killer thanks the detective profusely: "'I thank you, indeed, thank you,' he said with the first sign of emotion he had shown, and then added low: 'Do not fear that you will have trouble on my account. They can find me in my home.'" He leaves Müller a substantial sum of money and a letter confirming the detective's moral judgment:

> Yes, I have committed a crime, but I feel that I am less criminal than those two whom I judged and condemned, and whose sentence I carried out as I now shall carry out my own sentence with a hand that will not tremble. That I can do this myself, I have you to thank for, you who can look into the souls of men and recognise the most hidden motives, you who have not only a wonderful brain but a heart that can feel.

That the shared morality and kinship between murderer and detective expressed in this letter exists not only in the killer's but also in the detective's mind is confirmed in one of the story's final sentences: "Muller kept this letter as one of his most sacred treasures."

The criminal who is less guilty—or at least more moral—than his victims is a recurring character in Groner stories. In Groner's most tragic tales, it usually emerges that the criminal is not even guilty of a crime, neither in the legal nor in the moral sense. Some of these focus on the severe consequences of unjust accusation, such as *The Registered Letter* (*Der Brief aus dem Jenseits*, 1896), in which John Siders is prevented from marrying his lady love by her guardian Graumann, who unjustly suspects him of a crime based on flimsy circumstantial evidence. Outraged and out to teach the guardian a lesson, Siders commits suicide, leaving circumstantial evidence pointing to Graumann's guilt for his murder. Graumann would indeed have gone down in flames, had Siders not exculpated him by posthumous registered letter sent to a friend with instructions to have it made public if Graumann were in danger of being found guilty. The purpose of the morality tale is less to exact revenge than to teach the overly judgmental Graumann (and, of course, the reader) a lesson about the insufficiency of circumstantial evidence to establish someone's guilt.

Another morality tale masquerading as a crime story is *Twenty Years Later*, alternatively titled *The Old Gentleman* (*Nach zwanzig Jahren/Der alte Herr*, 1898). Set in 1881 and 1901, *Twenty Years Later* tells the story of 87-year-old Herr Winkelmann, known in the neighborhood only as "the old gentleman," who, having no family of his own, has decided to leave his stately home to his loyal housekeeper Josefa Müller for her decades of devoted service. Josefa has a secure position and hopes of a generous bequest, but is embittered that Winkelmann, due to his unreasonable fear of death, has long delayed making a will, even as she watches her son Hans, a talented but successless actor, his new wife Helene and their baby Gottfried sinking into penury. The next thing we know, Josefa and Hans bury the old man in the garden, burn bloodied pillowcases, and assure each other that their love for each other will help them bear what they have done: "Thus a mother's love—or, if you prefer, the madness of a mother's love—remains the strongest, the most magnificent love, incomprehensibly great even after it has been sullied by crime."[49] Mother, son and son's family settle in Winkelmann's house, but wracked by remorse, they suffer immeasurably. Their entire lives revolve around the necessity to pretend that Winkelmann is still alive. Hans's acting career is reduced to playing the old man sitting at a window for the neighbors' benefit. Josefa continues to wash Winkelmann's clothes and hang them to dry in the garden; she continues to order the delicacies that he liked, but cannot bring herself to eat them and gives them to the dog.

Twenty years of harrowing guilt later, things finally unravel. After the death of Winkelmann's doctor, his nephew, going through his papers, is made suspicious by finding Winkelmann, supposedly now 107 years old, listed as an active patient, and young Gottfried, now in his early twenties, comes to suspect his parents and grandmother of murder and attempts suicide, which prompts his family to confess all. Surprisingly, however, all criminals are exculpated: the old man, it emerges, died of a stroke, and Josefa and Hans desperately and vainly tried to call for a doctor to save his life. Fearing destitution in the absence of a will and bequest, Josefa, Hans and Helene decide to bury the old man and live in his house, but their lives are made miserable by remorse and the emotional distance from Gottfried, who, growing up, cannot understand their strange behavior. Not only are the three elders innocent of the murder to which, in a paroxysm of guilt, they falsely confess, they are not even guilty of stealing a legacy: when Winkelmann's corpse is exhumed, the will leaving the house to Josefa is found in his pocket. Two decades after the murder for gain that never was, it emerges that the tale's three "criminals" stole from nobody but themselves and ruined nobody's life but their own. They are further punished by the early death of guilt-ridden Helene and a permanent rift between father and son. At the end of the tale, Hans Müller, who has played Winkelmann for the neighbors' benefit for decades, becomes him. Grown old at barely forty, silent and white-haired, he confines himself to Winkelmann's chair at the window, and passersby asking his name are told what he were told about Winkelmann two decades earlier: "People only call him the old gentleman."[50]

Much like *The Registered Letter, Twenty Years Later* is one of Groner's several crime stories bare of a crime. Tragedy trumps criminality: there is a body and a grave, but no murder. There is no crime but lots of punishment: decades of guilt, four ruined lives, a dead mother, and a lost son. Groner leaves the reader to believe to the very last that a murder has been committed, only to yank back the curtain at the very end to reveal the true horror: the lives of an entire family utterly destroyed—all because a loyal servant and loving mother gave in to a momentary resentment of her flawed but gentle employer; all because she was unable to believe in his capacity for kindness.

Similarly, *The Red Mercury (Der rote Merkur,* 1910), one of Groner's most significant crime novels, teems with noble characters and erring humans. Both of the novel's criminals are defined principally by the characteristic that also drives *Twenty Years Later:* abject remorse. The cast of characters includes two pairs of thwarted lovers, "honest man" Otto[51] and his fiancée Anna, who, too poor to marry, must await the promised 4000 crowns from Anna's rich but stingy Aunt Resi, and Baroness Simonetta, engaged to the handsome and kind nobleman Alfons Eck von Pachern but secretly in love with the middle-class Dr. Malten. There is Otto's step brother Fritz, who has embezzled a large sum from his firm and begs Otto for help to return the money, upon which

Otto gives Fritz everything he has and borrows from a number of sources. Instead of returning the money to his firm, however, Fritz gambles Otto's money away and disappears, leaving Otto to hold the bag.

When Aunt Resi is found murdered, suspicion naturally falls first on Otto—who was seen leaving the victim's house and admits to having had a falling out with her over the marriage—and then on Fritz, who has fled to his mother's and sister Hanna's house, where his brother-in-law, village teacher Joseph Tilgner, confronts him with the murder. "'Joseph,' cried Fritz, 'I have become a man without morals, without honor, but I have not sunk this low! For the mercy of God, believe me—I am no murderer!'"[52] Fritz's depraved mother and his upright brother-in-law briefly wage battle for his soul, until Fritz, taking Joseph's more moral advice, decides to turn himself in:

> Fritz stood up. His handsome face was very pale and very serious. He stood up straight, gazed firmly into the eyes of his brother-in-law and then his sister's, and said: "I want to go back to Vienna. Joseph, Hanna, forgive me for disgracing you. I believe that from this day forward I will be a different person. [... To his mother]: Go away, Mother, otherwise I might stray again from the path of virtue and truth."[53]

Fritz, one of Groner's many redeemable criminals, does indeed turn himself in, and it hardly needs to be added that he also turns out to be innocent of Resi's murder.

Josef Müller, genius detective and friend of the innocently railroaded, plays a significant part in clearing Otto's name and recovering the inheritance—an extremely valuable postage stamp, the Red Mercury of the title—the sale of which enables Otto and Anna to marry. With this most central matter taken care of (in Groner stories, flushing out the guilty always takes a back seat to protecting the innocent), Müller can now finally focus on discovering Resi's murderer. It turns out to be the noble Alfons von Eck, one of the novel's most sympathetic and tragic characters. Eck is a melancholy figure, although exceedingly favored by Fortune: he is as rich as Croesus, handsome beyond measure, engaged to the beautiful Baroness and universally beloved; his servants sing his praises and village children follow him everywhere. As it turns out, his nobility of spirit vastly exceeds the nobility of his birth. A servant's child, he was placed into the arms of the dying Bianka von Eck after her own baby had died in childbirth; the fake son was then adopted by Bianka's husband for making her last moments happy. But Resi, then a servant in the household, knew the truth of his low birth and threatened to reveal all, and Eck killed her in the heat of the moment while looking for the letters that could have ruined him. Like most caught criminals, Eck responds to Müller's discovery of the truth with "noble calm," thanking him profusely for catching him: "I thank you. You have taken an unbearable burden from my soul."[54] Like the tragic criminal of *The Golden Bullet*, he opts for suicide: "There is a sympathy, genuine sympathy, between us, isn't there? You do feel that I am no scoundrel, that I cannot drag the name I bear into a prison."[55] Müller, however, persuades him to serve his prison time with dignity. Eck is granted extenuating circumstances, sentenced to a mere two years and, much like Fritz, spends the rest of his life making it up to society, his heart filled with gratitude to the detective who sent him to prison: "I thank you that you advised me to do the only right thing. The horror I felt for myself has left me. My thanks, then, profound thanks!"[56] While Eck, having "atoned both externally and inwardly," decides to spend his life in the service of "all who are in need of charitable love,"[57] the former thief Fritz, similarly rehabilitated, is immediately rehired into his former position upon his release from jail. "'I'll even give Fritz Stegmann control over the cash box again,' said Leibner. 'I think he will now do good for the rest of his life.'"[58]

Groner's earliest Josef Müller story, *The Strange Shadow* (*Der seltsame Schatten*, 1891), reveals how Müller became, "as paradoxical as it may sound, both the most feared enemy and the most loyal friend of all criminals."[59] The tale introduces a theme that Groner later revisits in *The Registered Letter* and many other stories: how often justice becomes a farce, railroading the innocent for no better reasons than prejudice, convenience or laziness. The story also establishes Müller's most central characteristics as a detective: his sympathy for the criminals he pursues and his principal scepticism toward circumstantial evidence. For it was just such evidence that was deemed good enough to convict one Josef Holzer—Müller's real name—of a crime he did not commit and send him to prison for ten years.

When *The Strange Shadow* opens, Holzer has been out of prison for four months. He is desperately looking for work, but inevitably and promptly fired as soon as his past is discovered. As Holzer bitterly reflects:

> Prisoners, too, are human beings, humans who, at times, try their hardest to rehabilitate, but they are forcibly flung back into a life of crime. [...] I had seven masters within three weeks. All sent me away. Not because I worked less well or less hard than others. Oh no! Nobody has ever been able to say anything against me other than that I was a former inmate. And the last one, he even sicced the dog on me. This happened on *that* night. At the time, for two cents I might have killed the next best man on the street—because everyone, everyone was my enemy. For nobody wanted to enable me to remain an honest man.[60]

That night is the night on which Anton Werner, the policeman responsible for the travesty of justice that resulted in Holzer's imprisonment, is murdered. Naturally, Holzer is immediately picked up as his murderer, on no evidence other than the fact that he is an ex-jailbird with good reason to bear a grudge. The police, convinced they have their man, are inclined to dispense with further investigation:

> "You were so good in prison," the Chief Inspector addressed him, "you conducted yourself so well in there that it's quite a surprise how quickly you have fallen again."
> "Did I? Sir! Do you have any evidence?," the former inmate erupted.
> "What evidence we still need will turn up. In the meantime it's enough for us that you have been slinking around Werner's house since the murder, in disguise, and that we arrested you there today."
> "Is that all you have, Chief Inspector," the prisoner said calmly.
> People began to consider him impertinent.[61]

That the jobless and homeless Holzer was reduced to sleeping under a bridge with a good view of the victim's house on the night in question provides him with vital clues the cops have ignored. Well aware that the only way to exonerate himself is to catch the real killer, he escapes with the help of a forged pass purportedly signed by the prison warden and solves the case by posing as Josef Müller, a low-ranking member of the Austrian Secret Police. Fully vindicated, he is promptly hired by the police under that name and in that capacity, not only because he is a genius detective but because detective work, and most importantly undercover work, is the only career option left open to him.

Thus Groner quite possibly delivered her most explosive social critique in the very first Josef Müller story she ever penned: the admission that for former inmate Josef Holzer—innocent or not, vindicated or not—there can be no way back into regular society. Josef Holzer sheds his bourgeois identity and goes permanently underground, working as Josef Müller or sometimes Franz Schmid, possibly the most common names in German-speaking lands. These names do not, as names are usually charged to do, identify a person, but erase identity. Society's inability to admit that justice is, at times, a farce, leads to a preposterous situation where justice has to be done sneakily and secretly. The absurdity is neatly encapsulated in Müller's names: common as mud and eminently forgettable, they signify both Everyman and Nobody, enabling him simultaneously to remain unrecognized as the former inmate Josef Holzer and to scale the pinnacles of fame as Austria's answer to Sherlock Holmes. Rarely does Müller introduce himself to others without a fine irony that hints at his paradoxical existence as both Anonymous and Austria's most famous detective, as both ordinary and exceptional, as both enforcer and victim of the Law: "I am called Müller, like so many others."[62]

Hans Hyan's Caged Beasts

The closest thing to Groner that Germany ever produced, in terms of both social progressiveness and sheer productivity, was the court reporter, writer, actor and cabarettist Hans Hyan (1868–1944). A liberal social critic, Hyan authored more than 100 novels and stories focusing predominantly on crime and spanning nearly fifty years, from 1899 until his death.[63] Hyan was an early representative of the True Crime genre, an author whose texts comprise social criticism, pop psychology and fictional elements without allowing themselves to be categorized as any of the above. At a time when crime "literature" could include anything from criminology to fiction and genres blurred constantly, this was not unusual. Some people we would today consider criminalists (for example, Erich Wulffen) routinely based their analyses on criminal characters from fiction, not real life. Others we would today consider primarily literary authors (for example Theodor Lessing or Alfred Döblin) also worked as psychologists or psychiatrists in the court system, and often served as expert witnesses in criminal trials.[64]

Hyan, too, was a hybrid. Drawing on his extensive experience as a court reporter and many interviews with

Hans Hyan (ullstein bild).

inmates, his tales purport to relate criminal careers straight from the horses' mouths, peppered with critical commentary on the social conditions that got these offenders into trouble and on the justice system that kept them there. Although Hyan saw his own crime stories as contributions to criminal psychology, he considered the science to be fatally undermined by the penal system. He once compared prisoners with caged beasts of prey: unlike animals, he claimed, criminals quickly learn to dissemble in captivity, becoming useless as objects of psychological study.[65] He railed against the idea that criminals should be punished at all, an idea that he considered a mere belief or even borderline superstition. His goal was to increase understanding of criminality, and resocialize criminals, to such a degree that "crimes of necessity" would ultimately disappear, leaving only the "*crimen pathologicum,* or crimes of passion."[66]

Hyan's tales are a skillful mix of socially aware tear-jerkers about youngsters or the poor driven to delinquency and humorous adventure stories in which flamboyant types converse in a quaint criminal argot that is barely comprehensible to the law-abiding reader and thus often necessitates a lengthy glossary at the end of the book.[67] His collection *Bad Boys* (*Schwere Jungen*, 1907), for example, begins with the heartbreaking tale of young Fritz Neumann, whose wretched stages of life (orphanage, joblessness, penury, robbery, prison, murder, prison and possible death sentence) are traced in a story acerbically titled "How to Produce Criminals."[68] Other stories in the same collection transport the reader right into the "dive" ("Kaschemme") in which shady types with colorful nicknames like "Vat Willy" ("Bottenwilhelm," so called because he always wears shoes several sizes too big), "Revolver Fred" ("Revolverfred"), "Scarface Emil" ("Narbenemil"), "Snotnose" ("Schniefneese") and "Red Emmi" ("Die rote Emmi") plan their next heist.[69] Readers of these tales, like all readers struggling through texts in a foreign language in which they are not well versed, are likely to spend more time looking up words in the glossary rather than losing themselves in the action. For these tales are told largely in "Chochem loschen" ("thieves' language"), a mix of Yiddish, Berlin dialect, and alleyway idioms, some of which would have been comprehensible to the average reader and most of which would not. The "Chawrusse" (community of thieves), even the "bust cadets" (those who have no money at all) dress up in "swell rags" (decent clothes) before they go out "swiveling" (stealing) or "pushing pads" (breaking into a bank). After that they "bury the ashes" (hide the money) and either "crash" (sleep) in a "breezy kip" (a half-decent inn) or "rip tiles" (spend the night outside). But don't "blab" (talk about) your "score" (success) to any "Clambering Hanna" (woman), even if you're "on flannel watch" (variously: courting, in love, just married). For if she "whistles" (speaks) to the "graspers" (police) you'll "go to crash" (be arrested) and end up straight in the "calaboose" (prison). Unless, of course, you "got doves" (get lucky).[70]

In many tales, extensive direct speech–passages and exquisite attention to milieu and argot serve to drag the law-abiding reader right into the midst of the criminal gang, for one obvious purpose: to confront readers with the reality of a world right next door that they know nothing about, a social and linguistic space that is as different from their own as a country on the other end of the world. Other tales read more like adventure stories, with extensive elaborations on the thieves' MO or descriptions of actual crimes, from deed to flight to capture.[71] Often there are helpful hints to householders describing specialized criminals and their *modi operandi:* some thieves scout out your apartment by pretending to be gas meter readers; "Sunday Drivers" ("Sonntagsfahrer") ring your doorbell and break in if nobody answers, "Flutterers" ("Flatterfahrer"), often people who also work legitimately as chimney sweeps, will break in through your roof or skylights, and so on.[72] And always—with one notable exception—there is a narratorial commentary outlining the consequences of the story just told and the preconditions that made it possible: how society got to this point and how it might get out. Hyan's "In Stir" ("Im Kittchen"), a heart-warming tale of how inmates support each other in jail, offers highly sympathetic portrayals of prisoners based on the author's personal interviews with them. The story concludes that punishments meted out for most crimes are excessive, and that school and work provisions in prison grant inmates not only the tools to obtain honest work after their release, but also enable them to imagine, often for the first time, a life beyond crime.[73]

In one of Hyan's most affecting tales, entitled simply "To Death" ("Zum Tode"), the reader is transported into the prison cell where 22-year-old Friedrich Bewer awaits execution for murder. Bewer is muddled, confused, hapless, and totally uneducated. He doesn't understand why he committed the murder and he didn't at the time he committed it. He couldn't follow his own trial, and can't grasp that he'll die on the guillotine. "Good God!," exclaims the narrator, "he can't even read or write! The only thing he knows, because he has memorized it, is the Ave Maria and the Our Father. Besides that he's spent his life in neverending dull labor, pushing a raft and carting dirt. The booze bottle and a dirty woman's body were his only pleasures."[74] Bewer is portrayed as barely human, more akin to "one of those strong Masurian bulls that has taken a human on its horns and killed her, and that will soon be taken away by the butcher."[75] Hyan's point about Bewer the Bull is the same as his point about "criminal" children: although Bewer is held responsible for his crime, he is not responsible because society has not afforded him a sufficiently human life, a life that would have enabled him to assume responsibility. Assuming responsibility presupposes an education able to engender a level of understanding, both intellectual and ethical, that transcends memorization. Because Bewer doesn't understand, he cannot feel remorse, even as he eats his last meal and sleeps his final sleep:

> But in the evening the roast potatoes—roast potatoes!!—and the beefsteak, the red wine and the cigars, oh, how good! … Bewer smiles. That night he sleeps, sleeps deeply and dreamlessly like a man with the best conscience in the world… […] In the prison courtyard he flings himself against the guards. The executioner's assistants come running—a struggle. His last. For the enemy is stronger…
> Ha! … Something glittering comes down through the air! … The screaming stops. Abruptly. And the executioner, approaching rapidly: "Mr. Prosecutor, the sentence has been carried out!"[76]

What is the purpose of punishing someone who cannot understand why he is being punished, who can neither regret his actions nor atone for them? For Bewer, atonement is neither moral nor religious but purely physical, as indeed was his entire life, which, composed of eating, drinking, sleeping, and screwing, in no way transcends that of a bull. For Friedrich Bewer, the tragedy lies not merely in his awful death but in the life that precedes it. For Hyan's readers, the tale intimates, the tragedy lies in a society that tolerates the reduction of humans to the level of beasts and then punishes them for their inability to behave otherwise. "To Death" is the only story in the *Bad Boys* collection that is entirely bare of social commentary: Hyan allows the misery, the inhumanity and senselessness of Bewer's life and death to speak for themselves.

The question of criminal responsibility, both individual and societal, is at the heart of most of Hyan's writing. His criticism of society's myriad ways of abdicating the responsibility for crime and shifting it onto the shoulders of individuals—usually the weakest shoulders—is at its most scathing in the stories involving children and juveniles. Hungry beggar children, he claims in "Lookouts and Flutterers" ("Baldower und Flatterfahrer") are often inducted into a life of crime, for example by being used to scout out houses for robberies. For the children, the consequences are severe: most fail to develop to such an degree that they seem younger than their years; at the same time, disease carries them off long before they reach maturity. Hyan's description of a lookout of his acquaintance is an anguished sketch of someone who was cheated out of both youth and adulthood, "an urchin that nobody would assume to be as old as fourteen. Only his withered face, grazed by every debauchery, indicates that he is older than he looks. As for the rest, looking at his small, narrow-chested, rickety body, you wouldn't give him ten years to live."[77] The theme of childhood at death's door is expanded in a story called "Juveniles" ("Die Jugendlichen"), where Willy and Otto, aged 14 and 16 respectively, reminisce about how they became fledgling killers by killing animals, beginning with insects and birds and graduating to kittens, which one of them took apart with a knife at the age of seven or eight. Willy, the younger of the two, comes from a brutal background; his father decapitated a servant girl to steal the money she had just inherited and killed himself in jail. Willy tells this story with detached amusement, as if it were a joke. Otto, son of a drunkard father and a mother who went insane, is terrified of being caught for the murder they just committed, but Willy takes it all in stride: because of their youth, he argues, the death penalty does not apply, and the most they can get for it is fifteen years in prison. He'd still be younger than 30 when released, he muses, with his whole life of crime still ahead of him.[78]

What do you do after hearing a story like that? For Hyan, there is only one thing to do: rise to the defense of the child. Even children growing up in ideal conditions, he asserts, have no affect control: "Even the smallest child on its mother's arm reaches for the moon and wants to take down the pretty silver coin."[79] By how much, he asks, would the distance between seeing and wanting be diminished for children who grow up in penury, saddled with alcoholic, insane or even murderous parents? How would a child living with dirt, disease and abuse at home respond to seeing others live in safety and comfort, an "envious comparison" that awakens "in this poor little soul the wild desire to live, to indulge in the same way"?[80] Society does nothing to alleviate such desires, but punishes those who help themselves by means of a penal law that assumes a degree of accountability from children of which social custom deems them incapable:

> A child cannot be the object of legal punishment. [...] A child cannot conduct a legal transaction, it cannot represent itself, it is subject to the custody of its parents or guardians and cannot escape from it. Parents are liable for damage to the property of others caused by their child. Children are not required to swear oaths; their witness testimony [...] is ignored in courts. But the moment that a child breaks a criminal law that is so obviously made for adults, it is considered an independent person that must receive what today's society calls "justice" and what, particularly in this case, constitutes the most bitter injustice imaginable.[81]

That these bitter injustices legally perpetrated against children weighed heavily on Hyan's mind is documented by the regularity with which they appear in his writing. Much of his treatise *Sherlock Holmes, Educator* is dedicated to statistics of children in Germany punished legally for crimes: 30,000 of them in 1882, 50,000 in 1904 and 55,000 in 1906, tendency: rising steeply.[82] Particularly illuminating is the list of offenses for which these children were locked up. People too young to enter into legal contracts were apparently routinely sentenced for forging documents, "lèse majesté" (in other words: insulting the sovereign) or blasphemy.[83] Hyan argues that these children, some less than 13 years old, were probably not even capable of understanding the crimes for which they were being jailed, and ultimately throws up his hands in despair: "What kind of a God or a King could possibly be insulted by a child?"[84]

That the children imprisoned for these nonsensical offenses were, without exception, proletarian children goes almost without saying, although Hyan does say it—angrily, vehemently, and repeatedly.[85] *Sherlock Holmes* is one of Hyan's many texts in which he encourages his readers to see crime in a social context rather than merely through the eyes of the law. For criminality, as he claims in *Bad Boys*, is "merely the last and strongest expression of that discontent that festers everywhere, that threatens the very idea of property, that—thinking it can bring about a fairer distribution of goods—rattles the pillars of capitalism with ever-increasing strength."[86]

Human Beasts and Human Beings

Groner and Hyan, perhaps the most popular crime writers of their respective Empires, wrote in a context in which the sympathetic, tragic or innocent criminal became the crime story's most significant character. In both of their works, too, this character takes pride of place. But if both Hyan and Groner tend to absolve the criminal, they do so for very different reasons. While Hyan views the criminal as less guilty than the society that first turns him into one and then prevents his rehabilitation, Groner tends to see the criminal as less guilty than the individuals he has harmed. Hyan's criminals are produced by social circumstance, Groner's are what they are by nature and character. Hyan's end point is social critique and legal reform, Groner's a curious mixture of that and physiognomic and classist essentialism.

Groner's *The Case of the Lamp That Went Out* (*Warum sie das Licht verlöschte*, 1899) shows this most clearly. The novel contrasts three criminal characters: the evil blackmailer and murder victim Leopold Winkler; the useless tramp Johann Knoll, suspected of his murder, and the noble, kind and talented Herbert Thorne, who—of course—turns out to be Winkler's killer. Groner's description of these three central characters speaks volumes. Leopold Winkler, as is quickly established, is no great loss to the world. Even before he turns to blackmail, he is presented as untrustworthy and greedy, a shoddy worker, a drunk who has no friends and spends all of his free time with ladies of easy virtue. In life, nobody liked him; after his death, his landlady and coworkers struggle vainly to speak well of the dead. The tramp who is booked for his murder—on circumstantial evidence that doesn't stand up to Müller's scrutiny—is described as an idle, lazy vagabond of questionable morality.

But even a man who has spent forty years in useless idling need not be all bad. There must have been some good left in this man or he could not have lain there so quietly, breathing easily, wrapped in a slumber as undisturbed as that of a child. It did not seem possible that any man could lie there like that with the guilt of murder on his conscience.[87]

Watching Knoll sleep the slumber of the just is quite enough in and of itself to convince Müller of his innocence. Even more bizarrely, Müller, that ardent critic of circumstantial evidence, turns out to be a firm believer in physiognomy: "there was a softness in his [Knoll's] eyes that showed there was something in the man which might be saved and which was worth saving."[88] But Knoll's possible rehabilitation, rather than being celebrated as a victory of humanity over the cold mechanism of the law, poses a problem for the detective, since he now has to turn his attention to the only other suspect, Herbert Thorne. Merely considering the possibility of his guilt causes Müller paroxysms of anguish as "All the charm of Herbert Thorne's personality" comes flooding back to his mind. The contrast between his two suspects—the worthless tramp and the "attractive, sympathetic figure" of Thorne—catapults Müller into what may be the most profound existential crisis of his entire career. In his mind's eye

He saw the little anxious group around the carriage in front of the Thorne mansion. He saw the pale, frail woman leaning back on the cushions, and the husband bending over her in tender care. And then he saw Johann Knoll in his cell, a man with little manhood left in him, a man sunk to the level of brutes, a man who had already committed one crime against society, and who could never rise to the mental or spiritual standard of even the most mediocre of decent citizens.

If Herbert Thorne were to suffer the just punishment for his deed of doubly blind jealousy, then it was not only his own life, a life full of gracious promise, that would be ruined, but the happiness of his delicate, sweet-faced wife, who was doubtless still in blessed ignorance of what had happened. And still one other would be dragged down by this tragedy; a respected, upright man would bow his white hairs in disgrace. Thorne's father-in-law could not escape the scandal and his own share in the responsibility for it. And to a veteran officer, bred in the exaggerated social ethics of his profession, such a disgrace means ruin, sometimes even voluntary death.

"Oh, dear, if it had only been Knoll who did it," said Muller with a sigh that was almost a groan.[89]

The dangers of such reasoning are apparent, and the tale pursues it quite a bit further. Both Müller and his boss, the chief inspector, are united in their opinion that "Winkler was a miserable scoundrel" and that "Thorne did only what any decent man would have felt like doing in his place."[90] Thorne, as it happens, agrees completely: "In his own eyes he had only killed a beast who had chanced to bear the form of a man. But of course in the eyes of the world this was a murder like any other."[91] In the end, Müller does his duty, but it is a hard-won victory: Müller, arresting Thorne, "had seldom found his official duty as difficult as it was now. His words came haltingly and great drops stood out on his forehead."[92]

The Case of the Lamp That Went Out is by no means the only Groner story where humans are assigned a principal value, even a ranking, based on physiognomy and class. Inevitably, as it does in *The Lamp*, the law prevails; the case is decided on demonstrable guilt or innocence. But there is more than a hint here that "justice" would have been able to take into account aspects that the law has to ignore, namely the moral distance between Theodor Winkler, "a beast who had chanced to bear the form of a man," Johann Knoll, "a man sunk to the level of brutes," and the charming, attractive, accomplished and admirable *Übermensch* Herbert Thorne. Hyan would have attributed this difference to a distribution of "goods" (money, education, opportunity) that enables the nobility of the Herbert Thornes and flings the Johann Knolls down into the pit with the other brutes. Groner, conversely, never really makes up her mind about what causes the difference between *The Lamp*'s three criminals. She does ultimately allow the legal facts to determine the story's outcome, but grudgingly and clearly implying that there should be more to "justice" than this. On occasion, she skates right up to the suggestion that while the law must punish deeds, justice should punish or exculpate people based on intrinsic value, irrespective of what they have done.

In this, Groner was hardly alone. In 1904, barely five years after the publication of *The Lamp*, the jurist and law reformer Franz von Liszt introduced a bill providing for the preemptive and indefinite imprisonment of people who had not committed a crime, from the mentally ill to people classed as "incorrigible" repeat offenders. An argument could certainly be made that the distinction between human "beasts" and human beings plays a significant part both in Groner's story and in Liszt's bill, and that this distinction ultimately resulted in biological arguments being brought to bear on legal contexts, with all the consequences this entailed.

Voigt Volumes: The Conman in Literature

Perhaps one of the strangest gaps in crime fiction before the First World War is that of Wilhelm Voigt and Tamara von Hervay, the subjects of the most famous criminal trials of the age and of interminable coverage in the contemporary press, appear nowhere in it. You would think that Voigt, who in the press practically symbolized the sympathetic criminal railroaded by a merciless society, would have slotted perfectly into the growing body of crime fiction that focused on just such a character. You would also think that the tragic tale of the Hervays, widely touted in the press as that of a noble young captain "Driven to Death by a Jewess!," might have given antisemitic writers great scope to portray her as a Black Widow, surely one of crime literature's most enduring characters. Nevertheless neither Voigt nor Hervay ever made an appearance in proper crime fiction, although both were the subject of literary texts in other genres.

Voigt, like many other famous conmen of his day, made a big splash in a new literary genre christened in honor of the sympathetic conman: *Hochstaplerliteratur*, or Fraudster Literature.[93] Economic, psychological and sociological conditions around 1900 offered fertile ground for the growth of a literary genre that hacked away at the granite of social structure by creating a world in which a waiter could become a Count and a shoemaker a Captain. The conman's wit, sass, nonviolence and the fact that—at least in literature—he only ever harmed either the filthy rich or faceless institutions like banks or insurance companies qualified him for both the role of the noble criminal and that of society's victim. Fraudsters became not only the stars of witty poems, political satires or memoirs by real-life frauds—from Harry Domela to Ignatz Strassnoff and, of course, Wilhelm Voigt[94]—they also made a frequent appearance in elite literature, for example in Heinrich Mann's satire *In the Land of Milk and Honey* (*Im Schlaraffenland*, 1900), Frank Wedekind's *The Fast Painter or Art and Mammon* (*Der Schnellmaler oder Kunst und Mammon*, 1886) and *The Marquis of Keith* (*Der Marquis von Keith*, 1901); Carl Sternheim's satirical comedies *The Underpants* and *The Snob* (*Die Hose* and *Der Snob*, 1910–15) and Erich Mühsam's *Fraudsters* (*Die Hochstapler*, 1906).[95] But with the exception of the memoirs penned by the fraudsters themselves, these texts focus not on the criminal but on the ills of the society he has harmed (Sprecher has actually termed these texts "Medical Histories of Society"[96]), and they were perceived not as crime fiction but as either satirical or stern societal critique. Erich Mühsam's 1906 comedy *Fraudsters*, to cite a prominent example, characterizes his heroes as bohemian societal outsiders whose crimes only impact the wealthy bourgeoisie and whose motivation is split between obtaining the funds for a long-dreamed-of trip to India and railing against the hypocrisy of the Empire.[97]

All the *Köpenickiaden*, the satirical poems, riotous farces, verses, songs, poems and ballads on Voigt's exploits that flooded the market between 1906 and 1912, rely on a similar mixture of witticism and criticism. Portraying Voigt as a sympathetic criminal was not the point but a mere side effect; the point was to revel in the fact that Prussian militarism and discipline had become the butt of Voigt's joke.[98] This is why so many of these texts do not even focus on Voigt as a criminal but take the perspective of one of the other players, usually that of one of Voigt's rubes. Leo Leipziger's poem "The Grenadier of Köpenick" ("Der Grenadier von Köpenick") is written in the voice of one of the soldiers commandeered by Voigt, who—despite the fact that the jig is up—steadfastly defends his unquestioning obedience to the false Captain's orders. The refrain of each stanza explains his rationale, if such it can be called: "All Prussia's greatness will come to naught/If ever I permit myself a thought."[99] Of all of the plays and poems commemorating Voigt's coup, the only one I've been able to find that mentions criminality in any way is a poem published by someone called "G.H." and entitled "Aye, aye, Sir!" ("Zu Befehl!"), which refers to the false Captain as "Crook X" and jokes that whereas the robber bands of earlier ages had to steal their weapons, today's version (the army) is fully equipped by His Majesty's government and sent on a mission to fleece the unsuspecting populace. While this is one of the very rare poems that even considers Wilhelm Voigt an honest-to-goodness criminal, the poem's main point, once again, targets not crime or Voigt as a criminal but lampoons, as Voigt literature tends to do, unthinking militarism and blind obedience to a uniform. The poem's final joke is a vision of Voigt's trial, where the judges not only acquit him but stand at attention while doing so, clicking their heels and saluting with his dossier.[100]

Societal critique was also the point of Hans Hyan's illustrated poem *The Captain of Köpenick: A Horrid and Torrid Tale of the Dim Wit of Obedient Subjects* (*Der Hauptmann von Köpenick: Eine schaurig-traurige Geschichte vom beschränkten Untertanenverstande*, 1906).[101] Published in book form with illustrations by Paul Haase, the story relates the Captain's exploits from the perspective of the hoodwinked: four grenadiers under his command; the mayor and his wife, and the policeman managing the crowd so the Captain can complete his robbery undisturbed. The point of Hyan's tale is, once again, not to portray Voigt as a criminal—much like Wulffen, Hyan considered Voigt less a criminal than a poet, someone who tried to force his own resocialization on a society that would have none of him[102]—but to lampoon a society that would have responded no differently to Voigt if he had been a true criminal:

Cover of Hyan/Haase, *Der Hauptmann von Köpenick* **(1906).**

Even if he is a killer,
If he wears a uniform,
He's boss to civilian rabble,
He commands and you conform!

Some were loath to grasp the matter,
But most understood the deal:
Our people have one duty—
Scream "Hooray!" and click your heels...[103]

Tamara-Texts: The Conwoman in Literature

Like Voigt, Tamara von Hervay makes no appearance in contemporary crime fiction. Unlike Voigt, she also plays no part in the fraudster literature of her time, probably because her deeply unsympathetic press portrayal as a sinister conwoman clashed fatally with the literary perception of the conman as a lovable rogue. Both of the contemporary texts in which she plays a significant part, the German writer Frieda von Bülow's (1857–1909)[104] *Inside the Witch's Circle* (*Im Hexenring*, 1901) and the Austrian modernist Hermann Bahr's (1863–1934)[105] *The Witch Drut* (*Drut;* republished as *Die Hexe Drut*, 1909), are society novels. Bülow wrote hers three years before the 1904 Hervay trial, basing her character on her personal acquaintance with Tamara von Hervay, with whom she spent a summer in the country; Bahr's novel, inspired by the press coverage of her trial, was written five years afterwards and is a despairingly critical assessment of how Austrian society treats its outsiders, a sorrowful text in which both that society and Klemens Furnian, the character based on Franz von Hervay, play a far greater role than his Tamara rendition.[106]

Certainly after the trial, contemporary readers of either novel would have had no trouble at all in deciphering Bülow's Susi von Tschirn and Bahr's Gertrud Baroness Scharrn as fictionalizations of Tamara von Hervay. The aspects taken from Hervay's biography that played such a prominent part in the press—the multiple marriages; the bigamy; the faux aristocrat later unmasked as the daughter of a sideshow actor—are simply too stark in both novels to mistake the original. And yet, despite the similarity of genres and the surprising affinity of the titles, the novels could not be further apart in their portrayal of the Hervay character. In Bülow's novel, Susi is a selfish, vain and childish swindler, a pathological liar who only lives for her own self-aggrandizement. She marries a country gentleman under false pretenses, subjects him and his family to a series of exhausting escapades, and would have destroyed them all had she not been exposed and expelled as a fraud at the novel's end.[107] In Bahr's novel, Drut is a tragic character, a conwoman against her will. Swept off her feet by the handsome and tumultuously passionate Captain Klemens Furnian, she is cajoled into chasing after a bit of happiness, always suspecting that it will go horribly wrong, and is proven right in spades at the end when a mob stones her to death.

Despite these diametrically opposed characterizations, both novels define their Hervay characters by recourse to two types: the swindler and the witch. These identical images document better than any contrast could the enormous distance between Bülow's contemptible Susi and Bahr's tragic Drut. The witch theme ended up in both Bahr's and Bülow's titles, but the role it plays in either novel is both figurative and negligible. In Bülow's *Inside the Witch's Circle*, the theme describes the poisonous atmosphere Susi creates in the house. Observing a circle of poisonous mushrooms colloquially known as a witch's circle, Wolfine, the story's main character, reflects: "Susi has drawn just such a witch's circle around Mervisrode, [...] everyone is now bound by a spell that cripples their will, that forces them to tumble helplessly from one state of commotion to another and that suffocates the wish to free oneself from this poisonous atmosphere."[108] In Bahr's *The Witch Drut*, the witch theme is based largely on Drut's nickname, for Drut or Trud is both short for Gertrud and an old designation for a witch. As Klem-

Frieda von Bülow (1902).

**Hermann Bahr (painting by Emil Orlik,
1908, Wikimedia Commons).**

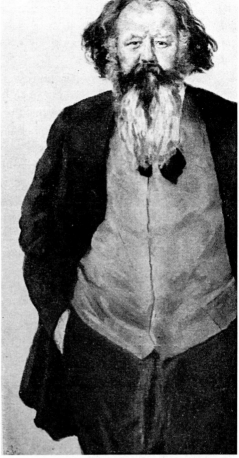

ens flippantly tells Drut: "Do you know what we call a Trud? A Trud comes in the night and sits on your heart until you can't breathe and suffocate miserably. She is an evil witch."[109] That the witch theme mattered to Bahr we can surmise from his renaming the novel, originally simply titled *Drut*, as the more explicit *The Witch Drut* in the 1929 re-edition. And yet, the witch plays no greater part in the 1929 version, where she is limited, as she was in 1909, to the figurative and the colloquial (Drut has "bewitched" Klemens). Beyond this and the conversation in which Klemens explains to Drut the meaning of her name in the Austrian rural vernacular, the witch is reanimated only once, in a brief passage in which Klemens shudderingly contemplates Drut's old servant, a sinister black-clad elderly woman: "She seemed as eerie to him as an old black raven"[110] (in witch lore, ravens were considered the most common animal familiar of a witch).

The fraudster theme is, in both novels, far more central, and taken quite literally in Bülow's book. Written in 1901, it prefigures the Hervay case of 1904 to a remarkable degree, so much so that readers are practically forced into a choice: either life in 1904 imitated the art of 1901, or Bülow based her account on swindles Hervay perpetrated in 1899/1900, when Bülow made her acquaintance, that were virtually identical to the swindles for which Hervay was locked up in 1904. In Bülow's novel, these lies and frauds constitute both most of Susi's characterization and most of the plot. Just as Hervay did in her 1905 memoirs and in court, Susi claims to have married her husband out of mere pity and to be beset from all sides by rich aristocratic lovers who either commit suicide for her sake or ardently beg her to leave her husband. Just as Hervay did in her memoirs, Susi presents herself as a loving and devoted wife, harping endlessly on her skills as a housekeeper, her exquisite taste and sense of beauty, and the self-sacrifice with which she works herself into the ground for others who never give her a word of thanks. Just as Hervay was accused of doing in Mürzzuschlag in 1903, Susi sneaks her lover into the household, pretending that he is her brother. And like Hervay, Susi pretends to be an illegitimate child from the high aristocracy and heiress to millions, but is then exposed as a woman with a checkered past that has led her from touring with her father, a Jewish pimp/ juggler/ magician/ third-rate actor, to numerous marriages entered into under false pretenses and ending inevitably in divorce. The only thing that saves Bülow's novel from being read as a rather snide *roman-à-clef* about a sleazy society scandal is that the novel predates the scandal by three years.

Bahr's novel offers a far more interesting take on the fraudster theme: it is used figuratively, as a code for the characters' wishes and suspicions. When Klemens is hesitantly in love with Drut, his insistence to think of her as a "swindler" is a cipher for his secret conviction that she is simply too good to be true. Drut rows like a sports pro, plays piano like a concert pianist, wraps all men around her little finger with her wit and charm, and socializes as easily with peasants as she does with aristocrats and cardinals: "No doubt at all, he thought, that she's a fraudster!"[111] Yet it is clear that Klemens's suspicion is merely a way of guarding against his already strong feelings for Drut.

As their love story progresses, the swindler theme constantly appears in loving conversation between them, as an inside joke. "Fraudsters always have secrets,"[112] she giggles at him whenever she wants to appear charmingly mysterious. Elsewhere she laughs off his ever-more-ardent proposals of marriage: "I'm just one of your adventures. Think of it: a conwoman!" As Drut is well aware, her main attraction consists precisely in her ability to embody this playful sense of illicitness and adventure for Klemens, a young man beaten down by his loveless family, asphyxiated by the rigidity of Austrian class society, and shamed by the daily deceptions necessary to climb his career ladder. "I wish you were a conwoman!," he bursts out when she has rejected him once again, "I want only you, just as you are! Whether you're a baroness or a fraudster makes no difference to me. And after all, who isn't a fraud these days? Most people just aren't very good at it."[113]

Things change when playful banter turns into harsh reality. Barely three months into the marriage that Klemens has begged, pleaded and coaxed her into, Drut the charming "conwoman" is unmasked, in a scandal sheet of dubious reliability, as a real swindler—a fake aristocrat, the daughter of a pimp and gambler, a bigamist who married Klemens while still married to a man serving a prison sentence for her father's murder. This is, of course, Klemens's crucible, the point where he might decide either to run away with Drut—opting for romance and adventure in action as well as words—or to return to the corseted, suffocating society that raised him. As it turns out, the former possibility never even enters his mind. Desperate to keep his job as a civil servant, a job that he has often derided in Drut's company, Klemens betrays her instantly, offering the authorities a prompt divorce and degrading the love of his life to a wanton flirt. But there is no way back into society's good graces. In a clear signal that his career as a civil servant in Austria is finished, Klemens is told either to kill himself or emigrate to America. Thus the heroic Captain dies as a cowardly suicide while Drut, the novel's fraudster, is accorded the genuine tragedy of a martyr's death.

The Missing Jew: Literary Lacunae

One of the most interesting aspects of Bahr's novel is that while adapting many other aspects of Hervay's biography for his character, he never identifies Drut as Jewish. Bahr's novel simply ignores this aspect of Drut's real-life original; in fact, it seeks to elide the issue, draw attention away from it in ways that taken individually seem minor but are too numerous to count. To cite just one example, Bahr describes Drut physically as recognizably Hervay-esque—a short curly-haired woman, not pretty but inexplicably enticing, slender and agile, with strong eyebrows and tiny hands—with one notable exception: Drut is a blonde. Given how obsessively some press coverage of Hervay's trial, which must have formed part of Bahr's research, hashed and rehashed her Jewish background, this must have been a deliberate decision on the author's part.

We can't be certain why Bahr, an outspoken opponent of antisemitism,[114] chose to ignore Hervay's Jewishness in his crafting of Drut (and thus also as a possible aspect of her victimization[115]), but we can hazard some reasonable guesses as to the consequences of this decision. In fact, a brief glance at contemporary reviews reveals how much of Drut's character had to be elided to arrive at a view of the novel as a lovingly drawn comedic portrait of Austrian society, which was—despite the horrible ending the novel reserves for both main characters—a popular interpretation in the year of its appearance. Jewish or not, Drut is the one character that doesn't fit, either into the Austrian society portrayed in the novel or with readers' view of that society as funny in its absurdity or lovable in its tragedy. True, Bahr's title stands in tension with the novel in many ways; the title character is not the novel's main character, and she certainly is not a "witch," as the 1929 title styles her. The most important point about Drut—important enough to Bahr to turn it into the novel's title—is that she triggers the disease of ostracism in a classed society, a disease that is initially dormant but that flares up with her arrival and ends up killing both her and Klemens, the novel's main and most lovingly crafted character.

It was precisely Drut's function as society's "witch," as symptom and trigger for a permanent and malign societal condition, that reviewers committed to a patriotic view of Austria practically tied themselves into knots to deny. In such reviews, Drut is downgraded to a minor figure, often also to the novel's weakest and least interesting character,

> although Bahr staged her with all his might. But he merely staged her: the theatrical nature of the character [...] has proven too brittle even for this writer, and it is even more brittle for the reader. The exotic, the mysterious, intrigues for a while, but then the effect fails. Even the sentimentality of her exit into death, which Bahr invented feeling that the Baroness's character needed more touching up, cannot help the novel past this, its dead point.

> But Drut doesn't even matter. She is the only person in the novel who is not Austrian, and the author has written a human comedy from Austria, which he succeeded in portraying as merry and as sad as Life itself, and what is more: it is precisely the kind of merriment and sadness that weeps and laughs in Austria and nowhere else.[116]

Clearly, Hervay is present in this review, as a real-life original even less interesting than Drut. Bahr's major addition to the Hervay story is explicitly given space: Drut would have been just as trivial as Hervay, the reviewer implies, if Bahr had not pimped her up a bit by granting her a tragic death. But Bahr's major omission, Hervay's Jewishness, is passed over in silence. We can guess why. Would it have been possible to read the novel as a human comedy if Bahr had, in addition to Hervay's physique and biography, also imported her Jewishness as a central aspect of his character? Would the mob-perpetrated stoning of Drut the Jewess have mattered to readers in a different way than that of Drut the fraudster? It is difficult to avoid wondering to what extent Bahr himself opened the door to readings of his book as a human comedy, for the excision of Hervay's Jewishness changes not merely the title character but the Austria portrait that is the novel's main point. What that portrait shows us is a society castigated as gossipy, spiteful, malicious, prejudiced and ultimately murderous, but not as antisemitic.

Crime fiction before the First World War has one thing in common with Hermann Bahr's novel: it is characterized by the near-total absence of Jews or Jewishness, either as authors, characters or themes. I have been unable to find any German-Jewish or Austrian-Jewish authors of crime fiction writing and publishing in the run-up to the First World War. Katharina Hall and the scholars assembled in her edited volume *Crime Fiction in Germany* (2016) couldn't find any in the entire 20th century. That this came as a major surprise is documented by the fact that Hall keeps returning to this point in her introduction:

> When surveying German-language crime fiction of the twentieth century, there is a lack of readily identifiable texts by Jewish-German, Jewish-Austrian or Jewish-Swiss authors. [...] the question of whether there has ever been a tradition of crime writing by Jewish authors in the German-speaking world remains largely unexplored. [...] A recent German encyclopedia that surveys *Juden und Judentum im Detektivroman* (Jews and Jewishness in the Detective Novel), but contains neither entries for Jewish German-language crime novels nor a recognition of this absence in its introduction, suggests that a further academic focus on this area is required [...] Research for this volume has not identified any contemporary Jewish German-language crime authors who have produced significant numbers of texts, although the possibility that some exist but do not identify themselves publicly as Jewish cannot be excluded.[117]

Hall offers some valid conjectures as to why this may be. Perhaps the absence of Jewish crime writers in German-speaking lands after 1945 can be attributed to the mass murder of Jews and its effect on European culture, or perhaps Jewish crime writers did exist but, for reasons readily understandable, assimilated too well to be recognized.[118] Given that academics believed until fairly recently that there was no German-language crime fiction at all before ca. 1960, an assumption that has now been laid to rest by Mirko Schädel and others, we should take the latter possibility seriously. But until someone steps into Schädel's shoes and produces a crime literature bibliography for German-Jewish writers, speculation is all we have.

The same void that describes the German-language Jewish crime writer applies to the Jewish crime genre: there is no subgenre within crime fiction written in German that takes Judaism or Jewishness as its major theme, is set in a Jewish community, or casts Jews as major characters. This, too, should surprise us, certainly after 1945, when crime fiction became so amorphous that it branched out into many specific subgenres. To the best of our knowledge, an age that saw the rise of women's crime fiction, Turkish crime fiction, even Allgäu crime fiction (crime novels set in the prealpine region of Swabia and Austria) produced no Jewish crime fiction.[119]

The Antisemitic Jew: The Creation of a Chimera

Jews do (very) occasionally appear as (often minor) characters in crime fiction before the First World War. Auguste Groner's many novels and stories are as *judenrein* as Drut's family tree. Hyan's literature yields little: there is a Jewish character (named, of course, Kohn) in his short story "In a Dive" ("In der Kaschemme"), but Kohn's sparse characterization permits no distinction between him and the story's non–Jewish criminals.[120] In Hyan's hommage to Wilhelm Voigt, *The Captain of Köpenick*, one of the four grenadiers pressed into Voigt's service, Baruch Cohn, is recognizably Jewish and quite a bit more clever than the three Aryan soldiers with whom he serves. He is the only one of the four who thinks for himself, immediately recognizing the fake Captain as "treyf." Cohn thus becomes a vehicle to indict Prussian society not only for its brainless militarism but also for its unthinking antisemitism:

> Griping, carping, grumbling
> Are a typical Hebrew trait,
> Consequently antisemites
> Are the pillars of our State![121]

In the literature surveyed here, Bülow's Susi von Tschirn stands out as the sole Jewish character who plays a significant part in the text, more specifically: whose *Jewishness* plays a significant part in it.[122] Much like her real-life model Tamara von Hervay, Susi is herself a fervent antisemite and zealously denies her Jewish roots. What initially gives her away in *In the Witch's Circle* is her physiognomy. The novel's main character Wolfine contemplates Susi shortly after meeting her, still thinking that she is looking at a gentlewoman hailing from the Prussian aristocracy:

> Strangely, she looked Jewish. A fine-boned, narrow-shouldered, narrow-hipped little figure was she, with a flat chest and a wasp waist. Her little head small, full of black, frizzy hair combed deeply into her naturally high forehead. Beneath beautifully painted, fine dark eyebrows flashed narrowly shaped and rather small black eyes; beneath them a slightly crooked, longish little nose and above the short and weak chin a mouth crooked upwards, quite large, with thin and pinched lips.[123]

Wolfine's suspicions, based on Susi's stereotypically "Jewish" features, turn out to be well-founded when Susi is unmasked as the daughter of the Jewish actor Barukinsky, whose original name is, of course, Baruch. But her Jewishness is not primarily defined as either a matter of birth or physiognomy but by her principal incompatibility with gentile society. Linking the novel's main plot—the story of a woman who fraudulently insinuates herself into a noble family and proceeds to suck it dry—with the antisemite's most basic view of Jews in "Aryan" societies is not, after all, a huge leap, and one that is repeatedly suggested to the reader. "Wolfine sensed: she does not belong with us. She suppresses her true nature in order to assimilate to us. Sometimes she succeeds, more often not. And sometimes her suppressed nature may rebel against this constraint. At bottom, in those moments she hates and despises us."[124] Although this passage, like most others in the novel, is linked explicitly not to Susi's Jewishness but to her mendacious character, the allusion could not be clearer: Susi is nothing more than a badly assimilated Jewess, forced to conform to a society she secretly hates and seeks to destroy. Most disturbingly, the term applied to her most often throughout the novel is one that later figured prominently in Nazi antisemitic propaganda: "parasite" ("Schmarotzer"), with often graphic figurative speech advocating that such "epitomes of the absolutely malign," such "parasites of the most noxious kind" out to destroy "lives that are worth a hundred times more" than hers should be "annihilated without scruples, like poisonous reptiles."[125] By far the most rabid of antisemitic ravings are placed into the mouth of the novel's only other Jew, Dr. Mayer:

> I am a Jew, want to be a Jew and am proud to be a Jew, proud to be part of a people that has produced the greatest of all humans. I maintain that this is a badge of honor that nobody can surpass. But I have never deceived myself about the fact that we Jews are a senile people, despite the tenacity and strength that is still apparent. And that our senility produces apparitions of such pernicious character that I would compare them to gangrene. I would count [... Susi] von Tschirn amongst these symptoms of putrefaction and decay, people who, utterly bereft of the strength to truly live, enable themselves to lead a sham existence by deliberately feigning that they have a purpose in life. Instead of living they juggle with life, not believing that life is serious, and feed their bloodless souls with delusions of superiority over their much simpler, much less aware, more childlike and hence also more gullible victims. I consider these members of my race as the putrefaction of a corpse! They poison the blood of all healthy life they touch, a poison that must, unless immediate and vigorous action is taken, lead to death and decay. In the interest of my people, first and foremost, I want to see them extinguished from the Earth with fire and sword![126]

Dr. Mayer's speech would have been quite at home in the mouth of Dr. Goebbels. All the sentiments later expounded *ad nauseam* in *The Stormtrooper* are here: the deterioration of the ancient Jewish "race" whose achievements, if any, are banished to the dimmest recesses of ancient history; the view of modern Jews as vampiric "bloodless" parasites too weak to live on their own and hence reduced to sucking the blood of healthier, stronger races; the depiction of such bloodsucking as a deliberate attack on the superior race, with an aim to poison it; the idea that Jews perceived themselves as superior to Aryans and cunningly convinced their much more honest and hence gullible "victims" of the same; the visualization of the social body as an actual (decaying) body; the filthy rabble-rousing vocabulary that wallows in blood and soil, death and decay, poison and putrefaction; the fanfare at the end, advocating the extinction of these parasites as a sacred duty using the preferred weaponry of avenging angels—fire and sword. And how better to avoid the charge of antisemitism than to put these extermination fantasies into the mouth of the book's only sympathetic Jewish character, one who, moreover, self-identifies as an ardent defender of his people?

For a novel that mostly deals with household intrigues and childish tantrums, bike rides and female fashions, sumptous meals and tepid love stories, it is an astonishing conclusion. It is difficult to imagine its wellspring as anything other than a searing, fanatical hatred of Jews that informs Bülow's entire characterization of Susi, even though the character's Jewishness is left implied more often than not, in the many passages describing her crooked nose, her parasitic character, or simply the way in which she poisons the world. Indeed, Susi's departure from the novel is presented as a healing of the world, "as if a deliciously tangy, purifying air from the beloved sea were blowing through the village."[127] Mother Earth, having been cleansed from Jewish poison, exudes "a wonderful sense of peace [...]. Just as a violent thunderstorm batters the Earth in sultry summer days and cleans the stuffy air, so it was in Mervisrode: a deep breath of infinite relief!"[128] Susi is not merely expelled but *disappeared*, dissolved, as disembodied as smoke from the chimneys of a concentration camp. "Nobody ever heard of her again. She seemed dispersed and turned to nothing, like a shimmering soap bubble."[129] And just as the Nazis would endlessly juxtapose the dirty, money-grasping Jew with the wholesome hard-working Aryan peasant, Bülow's novel visualizes a Jew-free paradise in the image of a strong young peasant girl bailing hay. Observing the idyllic scene from afar, Wolfine is beset by two consecutive thoughts: "How hard she has to work!" immediately followed by: "And yet she is happy."[130]

Would it be a step too far to read Bülow's book as an inverse society novel? "With uncanny clairvoyance, the then-imminent collapse [of Austrian society], which has since come to pass, is experienced and suffered through in the form of a civil servant's tragedy from Antiquated Austria," wrote a critic about Bahr's novel *Drut*.[131] Turn-of-the-century society novels, from Theodor Fontane's *Effi Briest* (1894/95) to Thomas Mann's *Buddenbrooks: The Decline of a Family* (1901), are so often about societal decline. Even as they assess the mechanisms with which society chews human beings to rags, they mourn the passing of that society as much as they pity the individuals destroyed by it. This is precisely what Bahr wrote: a novel of a world now gone. Not so Bülow. Where Bahr looks back at the end of an era, she looks forward to a brave, new and Susi-free (Jew-free) world. Where Bahr offers a forlorn document shot through with biting sarcasm, Bülow revels in a sunny fantasy of Aryanization. Bahr's main mood is melancholy, Bülow's is triumphant. Her ending shows that Bülow fell into the same trap as Auguste Groner occasionally did; that she surrendered to the same flawed thinking as mars the work of so many criminologists of her time.

In all three cases, the recipe for Utopia involves two egregious failures of both logic and humanity. The first is what we might call metonymic slippage: the flawed substitution of an attribute for a thing that it cannot possibly mean, as tends to happen, for example, when we apply biological arguments to social contexts. The second failure results directly from the first: a principal distinction is dreamed up between Jews and Aryans, between human beasts and human beings, between criminals that may yet be resocialized and so-called "incorrigibles," usually followed by feverish fantasies of social "cleansing" and "purification." In such a world, as many crime novels of the time acknowledge unequivocally, the criminal cannot be anything other than a tragic character; he is railroaded like Joseph Müller, executed like Friedrich Bewer, disappeared like Susi or stoned to death like Drut. In such a world, justice cannot be anything but a farce.

Criminology and crime fiction before the First World War already exhibit early symptoms of the State to come, a State in which "justice" and the "law" are skipped over in a rush to "punishment" in its most extreme form: annihilation. Even before the First World War, the language of extermination transcends propaganda, invading texts ostensibly written and read for reasons other than crass indoctrination. Criminological treatises, crime and society novels begin to speak in this apocalyptic tongue: Blood and Soil; Root and Branch; Lock, Stock and Barrel; Fire and Sword. In adopting such language; in its inability to imagine the tragic, noble, witty, clever or lovable criminal as a Jew; in its ranking of humans by intrinsic worth; and sometimes in its outright anti-semitism, much crime fiction in the run-up to the First World War gives voice to a chimera: the idea that some humans are less human than others, and that this justifies their exclusion from the protections of the law, that it voids their right to justice. Different authors treat the chimera in different ways—Hyan rails against it while Groner struggles with it; Bahr savages it while Bülow embraces it—but the chimera was a constant theme in fiction decades before the NS State turned it into reality. Fiction is, of course, the chimera's natural home; concocted entirely of fantasy and language, it has no basis in social, historical or any other reality. Yet perhaps it is precisely its antithetical relationship with reality that ultimately gave the chimera the power to supplant it, for reality, as the novelist and Hitler biographer D. Harlan Wilson once said, is shaped by the forces that destroy it.

Farcical Criminals or
Tragic Victims (1926–1939)

"a comic dramatic work using buffoonery and horseplay and typically including crude characterization and ludicrously improbable situations."—*Dictionary definition of "farce"*

"You are the biggest ratfink ever created by the Devil in his fury. Why, unhappy man, did you not stay that way?"—*Message found in a murder victim's buttonhole in Walter Serner's story "Yellow Terror"*[1]

"Only in the form of forgery does art still make sense. My paintings and drawings are rotting in a box. But people will scramble and bay for these prints! [...]
    The unification of all artistic styles has been achieved. Futurists, Expressionists, Cubists, New Objectivists, Neopointellists, Light-Color-Sound-Sensitives: everyone will love my prints and collect them! Everything is a racket!"—*Speech of a money forger and failed artist in Paul Gurk's novel* Safe Cracking[2]

The Criminal Arrives: Trauma Culture
in the Weimar Republic

The Weimar Republic (1919–1933) not only has the distinction of having been Germany's first experiment with democracy, but also became known as its heyday of crime. This is the assessment offered during the Nazi era, which supplanted Germany's first Republic and had an obvious interest in depicting it as a State in permanent turmoil, as a cesspool of crime with a police force emasculated by a corrupt and incompetent government now happily vanquished by a strong and stable regime.[3] The evidence for the Nazis' summary condemnation of the period is partly fabricated—such as the often falsified crime statistics of the time published during the Third Reich—and partly real, such as the Weimar era's undeniable obsession with crime and criminals, which dominated its art, literature and film. NS-era defamation aside, the Republic itself "understood itself through its criminals. The traditional distinction between law and outlaw, criminal and noncriminal, the normal order of society and the moments at which that order breaks down no longer seemed to make sense in post–World War I Germany."[4]

This self-image, and more generally what later came to be known as the Republic's "trauma culture,"[5] had far more to do with fictional than with real-life crime. Contemporary crime statistics do show a significant rise in the crime rate during the first five years after the First World War, which then, however, drops sharply—to below prewar levels—after 1924.[6] But plummeting crime rates did little to diminish contemporary interest in the subject. During the Weimar Republic, the criminal finally "arrived"; he became a main subject of elite culture, in the works of major writers (such as Bertolt Brecht, Alfred Döblin, and Robert Musil), artists (e.g., George Grosz, Max Beckmann, and Otto Dix), and filmmakers (among them Fritz Lang, Robert Wiene, and Georg Wilhelm Pabst). The spotlights of Culture as well as culture homed in on the criminal and on him alone, all but erasing his main opponent, the detective, from the story. Herzog has explained this with a general disinterest of the period in what the detective represented, namely order: "The German *crime* novel, in contast to the English, French, and American *detective* novel, situated itself in a realm outside of reason, logic, and order."[7] Brecht, one of the era's most astute observers (and also one of its most significant crime writers) made a related point in his 1938 essay "On the Popularity of the Crime Novel" ("Über die Popularität des Kriminalromans"), in which he claimed that the detective novel portrays people "as actors, whose actions have definite and identifiable consequences," whereas in real life, people rarely leave traces.[8]

If the criminal and his newly recognized ability to make grand philosophical statements on the human condition and the state of the world appealed to the era's sophisticates, less erudite readers found other things to appreciate in crime fiction, which they devoured in considerable numbers. Statistics of new crime literature published between 1900 and 1938 show not only an upward but an inflationary trend. Crime fiction's best year, with 743 new publications, was 1920—the year after the foundation of the new Republic—its weakest year 1901 with 27. In the year 1901, crime fiction, with 0.8 percent, made up the lowest percentage of all fiction on the market; by 1930/1932, this had risen to a stunning 12.7 percent.[9] Specific criminal types, particularly the "sex killer" (*Lustmörder*), commanded a great deal of attention, and they, too, are more at home in the realm of the imagination than in real life.

To be sure, the era did produce its fair share of notorious sex- or serial murderers, among them Carl Großmann (arrested 1921), Karl Denke (1924), Fritz Haarmann (1924), Peter Kürten (1926), and Adolf Seefeldt (1936). Yet their relationship to the sex killers ubiquitous in art, film and fiction is not as straightforward as art imitating life. As Götz von Olenhusen has shown, the "sex-killer" craze in art and literature took off during the First World War, years before these real-life murderers were arrested, tried and dragged through the press, and reached its apex earlier as well, between 1919 and 1924.[10] The psychological and social studies of real-life serial killers undoubtedly built as much on the momentum of serial-killer fiction as on the lives and deeds of their actual subjects. Fritz Haarmann, the "Werewolf of Hanover," was the subject of several of these (Theodor Lessing's *Haarmann: Story of a Werewolf*, 1925; Hans Hyan's *Mass Murderer Haarmann: A Criminalistic Study*, 1924, and Richard Herbertz's *Twilight of the Criminal: Psychological Interpretation and Philosophical Perspectives of the Recent Murder Cases Haarmann, Angerstein, Denke, etc.*, 1925). Poison murderesses, the stars of Alfred Döblin's *Two Female Friends and Their Poison Murder* (1925) and Ernst Weiss's *The Vukobrankovics Case* (1924) ran a close second to sex murderers in terms of their eligibility for sympathetic portrayals in true crime accounts by well-regarded writers.[11] Three of these books appeared in the series *Societal Outsiders* (*Außenseiter der*

Gesellschaft), a series of fourteen books published in 1924–25 that critically linked criminality with social deviance and sought to show how societal and psychological factors combine to produce "the criminal."[12]

Certainly, the *Outsiders* series is one place where real life and the imagination crossed paths. Another was critical court reportage, another distinct subset of crime writing that rose to prominence during the Weimar Republic.[13] Its most illustrious names included Paul Schlesinger, an authority among court reporters, writing for the *Vossische Zeitung* under the pseudonym "Sling"; his successor Moritz Goldstein a.k.a. "Inquit," and Gabriele Tergit (bourgeois name Elisa Hirschmann), writing for the *Berliner Tageblatt*, as well as Theodor Lessing, Hans Hyan, Siegfried Kracauer, and Rudolf Olden. Often pleading for a psychological understanding of crime based on Freud's theories, most of these writers followed murder trials and asked probing questions about crime's social and psychological causes. Some did not shy away from political causes, either, with particularly Tergit and Inquit reporting on Nazi terror from 1929 onward.

Some titles, like Sling's "The Little' Man's Great Anger" ("Die große Wut des kleinen Mannes," *Vossische Zeitung*, May 20, 1928), and Tergit's "The Deed of a Desperate Man" ("Die Tat eines Verzweifelten," *Berliner Tageblatt*, March 1, 1928) already show where their principal sympathies lay: with the man or woman in the dock. The criminal, not the crime or even its victims, takes pride of place in their writing. Tergit ran a long series of articles focusing on lower-class girls accused of either abortion or infanticide. Sling's recurring metaphor for the criminal was "Exploding Man" ("der explodierende Mensch"): "A man who shoots someone else is as innocent as a boiler that explodes."[14] Criminals were routinely cast as "fallen angels" (*gefallene Engel*), "impeded humans" (*verhinderte Menschen*) or victims. Victim, *Opfer*, became the most frequently employed term to describe the criminal; he appeared as a victim of inflation, as a victim of the "dagger thrust" at the home front, as a victim of the Versailles Treaty, as a victim of class-based justice.[15] The direct rapport such reportages sought to establish between criminals and readers finds further expression in the tremendous contemporary demand for, and success of, autobiographical memoirs written by criminals, among them Albert Bertsch's *Twenty Years in Jail* (*Zwanzig Jahre Zuchthaus*, 1926), Rudolf Bussmann's *The Law Commits Murder* (*Das Gesetz geht morden*, 1921) or Carl Hau's *Death Sentence* (*Das Todesurteil*, 1925).

That even the era's most feared criminals, its sex murderers and serial killers— real or fictitious—garnered their share of sympathy is well documented by their frequent protrayal as the opposite of dangerous or even deviant in both fiction and press reporting, where they commonly appear as weak, childlike or effeminate, as confused or disturbed, or as far closer to the law-abiding bourgeois or common man than one might think. As Lessing described Fritz Haarmann: "A figure, not at all unsympathetic, appears before us. Seen from the outside: a simple man of the people."[16] Similarly, Siegfried Kracauer has described Hans Beckert, the child murderer in Fritz Lang's film *M* (1931), as "a somewhat infantile petty bourgeois who eats apples on the street and could not possibly be suspected of killing a fly. [...] He is fat and looks effeminate rather than resolute."[17] Although Haarmann and Beckert were possibly the era's most iconic real-life and fictitious murderers respectively, they are routinely either feminized or infantilized.

"A simple man of the people": Fritz Haarmann (center, in prison uniform) poses for the camera days before his trial in November 1924 (Bundesarchiv Bild 102-00824).

Both Erich Wulffen and Theodor Lessing have described Haarmann as a woman[18]; Beckert's "babyface" and his "girlish" behavior permeate all discussions of Lang's killer[19]; and press reporting, psychological profiling and reminiscences by people centrally connected with the Haarmann case, such as prosecutors and defenders, routinely bring up the defendant's homosexuality as evidence that he was "less than a man."[20]

Infantilization, feminization and normalization are all ways of diminishing the terror these criminals inspired, of defining them not as opposites but as outgrowths of law-abiding society, and of pointing out the role that society played in their creation. Peter Kürten, who, much like the "Werewolf" Haarmann, had been saddled with a dehumanizing moniker ("the Vampire of Düsseldorf"), regained some of his humanity in the story, widely circulated in the contemporary press, of his childhood and youth in a family devastated by poverty, alcoholism, and domestic abuse that ran the gamut from the father's wife- and child-beating to his death threats against the children. Karl Denke, the "Cannibal of Münsterberg," who killed, ate and was rumored to have sold the flesh of 30–40 victims, was exonerated in a 1924 article in the *Frankfurter Zeitung*, which offered the most compassionate explanation imaginable for the containers full of human flesh and fat found in Denke's kitchen: hunger.[21] Contemporary observers found this anything but implausible. "It is possible that as a small bourgeois living on his property, he had become maddened by the starvation and hardships entailed first by the war and then by the inflation,"[22] wrote Margaret Seaton Wagner in her rather sympathetic biography of another serial killer, the "monster" (as per her title) Peter Kürten.

If even the age's most terrifying real-life murderers were given an occasional break, compassion and understanding was showered in abundance on its fictional criminals. Birgit Kreutzahler, who has written the most extensive account of crime novels of the Weimar Republic, has found that the vast majority of them defended their criminals as unjustly accused, framed, driven to crime, victimized, or pathetic rather than evil. Her chapter titles, which are dedicated to criminal types, speak volumes: crime fiction during the Weimar Republic portrays the criminal "as an outsider"; "as a symbol for the fundamentally tainted Republican civilization"; as an "ambivalent figure"; "as a rebel and as a citizen"; as an "innocent sex offender"; as a "gentleman criminal"; as a "little man"; "from a psychological viewpoint"; "as a victim"; as situated "between innocence and responsibility"; "from a critical-judicial viewpoint," or "as a bourgeois."[23]

The Criminal Co-Exists: Third Reich Crime Fiction and Propaganda

This trend ended as abruptly during the Nazi era as the tradition of critical court reportage. The reasons for this relate to Nazi propaganda, but that relationship is surprisingly complex and indirect. Crime fiction was hardly suppressed during the Nazi period, where it continued to be, just as it had been throughout the Weimar Republic, among the most popular literary genres. Even during the 1940s, the years of the most extreme direct censorship, virtually every German publisher printed and sold both German and foreign crime novels in huge numbers. In the four months between November 1938 and February 1939, more than 200 new titles appeared on the market,[24] and a number of publishing houses specializing in crime fiction—Deutscher Verlag, Wilhelm Goldmann, Paul Zsolnay, Werner-Dietsch, Freya, and Ullstein—published more than 1,000 new titles in 1939 alone.[25] Nor did NS-era crime literature conform to or disseminate any propagandistic self-image of the regime; it is not awash with Hitler images, SS uniforms, swastikas or ideological haranguing. In fact, commentators have found it "difficult to find in these texts a specific National Socialist personality profile, however conceived,"[26] so much so that some have claimed that most NS-era crime novels are indistinguishable from those published in the 1920s or 1950s.[27]

But perhaps we should not rush to conclude from this that "literature does not lend itself to propaganda."[28] More and more crime writers of the prewar Nazi period set their tales not in their contemporary present but in the preceding era, simultaneously avoiding trouble with the new regime and adding to the lore of the Weimar Republic as a period steeped in crime.[29] A time setting before 1933 became so ubiquitous that it is now commonly considered "typical" for Third-Reich crime fiction.[30] The crime story's most basic attitude toward crime and the criminal also shifted noticeably during these years. Slowly but inexorably, crime fiction moves from the depiction of the likeable or pitiable criminal ground up by a chaotic world to that of a well-run industrial State endowed with a highly efficient and competent police force.[31] Police officers or detectives in early NS-era crime stories don't bore the reader with Nazi propaganda; they don't describe their work as a "cleansing" of the *Volkskörper* or as part of the struggle against the Eternal Jew. But they make it clear that their quarry, once caught, can expect neither understanding nor mercy. The criminal of these texts is no longer the sympathetic, tragic or victimized lawbreaker of earlier ages, he is a "hardened" and repeat offender, characterized by nothing but his crime, and what happens to him after his arrest remains unstated in the text.[32] None of these developments can be shown to have been the direct result of State-imposed propaganda. Yet they are clear signposts on the road from a liberal to an illiberal society, and perhaps also symptomatic of that mental state for which Germans have coined the incomparable expression *vorauseilender Gehorsam*— preemptive obedience.

Just as there was little obvious propagandizing within crime fiction before the war, there were also few direct state-sponsored attempts to steer the reception of pop culture.[33] Propaganda before 1939 busied itself not with suppressing the undesirable but with adding to the already existing, leaving established cultural traditions to survive in the company of new and strange bedfellows. Dime novel series with run-of-the-mill detectives or robber heroes continued to exist, but were now joined by new series subtitled "Brown Library" ("Die braune Bibliothek") or "The Brown Series" ("Braune Reihe") that featured titles like *A Hitler Youth's Adventures* (*Ein Hitlerjunge erlebt*), *The Flag on High* (*Die Fahne hoch*), and *Sieg Heil*.[34] Antisemitism, not exactly mandated "from above" but subtly encouraged by sponsorship and positive reviews, increasingly crept into crime stories.[35] Defamation of "trashy" literature by the Arbiters of Taste continued as it always had, but was now increasingly spiced with references to "Niggerization" ("Verniggerung"), "Judaification" ("Verjudung") or "Cultural Bolshevism" ("Kulturbolschewismus") dragging German culture through the mud.[36] Germany's "invasion" by a "foreign genre," the detective novel, was deemed by one commentator "comparable to the invasion of a foreign spirit."[37] Others maligned lending libraries as platforms from which "the Jew," feeling close to "his goal of the Bolshevization of the world," could "hurl his poisonous thought, unhindered and beyond measure, into a spiritually wrecked humanity."[38]

The years between 1933 and 1939 appear as a time when pre–NS conventions and practices were allowed to co exist, uncomfortably to be sure, alongside an increasingly belligerent and antisemitic body of propagandistic writing. As the clouds of war began to gather, this *laissez-faire* attitude ceased. In 1939, the Propaganda Ministry published, for the first time, concrete guidelines for fiction authors, issued a ban on all crime literature that propagated English institutions and "English ways," and ordered the "cleansing of entertainment literature from the influences of hostile nations."[39] The same year, the Propaganda Ministry's Siegwalt Benatzky wrote a widely read report on trivial literature, in which he blamed the flood of crime stories, Wild West tales, and women's novels for all sorts of horrifying consequences ranging from lechery to "antisocial instincts" to—naturally—a rise in crime. While this sounds like a standard diatribe as it might have been written in the early 1900s, Benatzky added some ominous and distinctly 1939-ish thoughts: he claimed that such trash was a holdover from a bygone "liberal-individualistic time" that directly opposed the principles of the new regime, and recommended the internment of authors of trashy literature in concentration camps for the purpose of "re-education."[40]

Certainly, censorship tightened during the war years; literature was more often suppressed and authors imprisoned with greater regularity after 1939 than before. But even these measures did not produce a crime literature standardized in any propagandistic sense, either in terms of form or content, and even during the war years, explicitly National Socialist or antisemitic crime stories were in the minority.[41] Goebbels himself commented on this state of affairs in May 1943, when he confided to his diary his dearest wish to see "a series of antisemitic novels written by authors of note, even if they are not as unreserved in their support of National Socialism as our garden-variety writers whose attitude is laudable but who aren't terribly competent."[42] Perhaps literature does lend itself to propaganda—if not imposed from above, then "voluntarily" adopted from below, by preemptively obedient authors who knew on which side their bread was buttered. But there was still, as Goebbels noted with annoyance, a discernible difference between the fictions of fiction and those peddled in propaganda. In fact, the "normality" of much of crime fiction published during the Nazi era has led at least one observer to an uncomfortable suspicion: that precisely its *lack* of flag-waving and Jew-baiting helped to promote greater acceptance of the new regime. Its very ordinariness, the fact that even looking back in today's cold light, we might mistake an NS-era crime novel for one written in the 1920s or in the 1950s, may have served to uphold the illusion of the Nazi state as a society that was

> perhaps not democratic, and perhaps reliant on the rule of law only to a limited extent, yet fundamentally decent, as was confirmed by every successful solving of a crime. As long as there was still a possibility to understand this fiction as vaguely corresponding to one's personal reality, the effect had to be that of stabilizing Nazi rule, from which the National Socialists could only benefit.[43]

Walter Serner's Underworld Figures

Even conceding that crime fiction retained a measure of independence even at the height of Nazi rule, it is difficult to imagine some of the Weimar Republic's weirder and more unfettered creative minds flourishing after 1933. One of the most inspired of these was undoubtedly Walter Serner (born in Carlsbad in the Austro-Hungarian Empire in 1889, subjected to a Nazi ban of his works in 1933, and murdered in a makeshift gas chamber near Minsk in 1942).[44] Born an Austrian Jew (as Walter Eduard Seligmann) but later converting to Catholicism and a rather determined nomadic cosmopolitanism—he lived in, or rather traveled through, Carlsbad, Greifswald, Zurich, Geneva, Paris, Naples, Barcelona, Berne, Vienna, and Prague, among others—he wrote one crime novel, one crime play, and exactly 100 crime stories between 1918 and 1926.[45] At their core is a radically original character: the Farcical Criminal.

Serner's crime stories are among the most eccentric written even in a literary epoch that had no shortage of peculiar crime fiction. The heroes of his tales are, without exception, on the wrong side of the law, bearing names that sound outlandish in any language: Flou and Pepino; Kaudor, Sasso and Lusi; Moo, Gibsi and Lapu; Öchsli and Jukundus; Wutschka, Schicketan and Fidikuk. All stories are dominated by totally decontextualized dialogue into which the reader is flung without any information about who is speaking, how these people know each other, where they are, what prompted the conversation, what preceded it or what happens afterwards. Some, like "A Strange Conversation" ("Eine eigenartige Konversation") feature hardly anything but dialogue;

others, like "Yellow Terror" ("Der gelbe Terror") are dominated by lengthy monologues. When the Censorship Office in Berlin tried to determine, as early as 1931, whether to place Serner's crime literature on the register of "trashy and obscene writings" (*Schund-und Schmutzschriften*), they found it difficult to say anything about these stories other than that they were thoroughly objectionable:

> It is not only difficult to provide a plot summary of individual stories—since some are barely comprehensible—, it is also unnecessary, since they all, clad in various forms and guises, always have one content—the milieu of criminals and prostitutes [...], and offer variations on only *one* basic theme: the portrayal of a heroic criminal who unscrupulously asserts his superiority over his fellow men "dumbed down" by feeling, considerateness, even goodness. These downright disgusting tales are told with a slick coolness and objectivity which ultimately seems ironic and thus provocative.[46]

Serner's censors were right about one thing: it is not plot but intangibles like mood, milieu and tone that make Serner stories what they are. They are short stories, but only in the sense that they are short, varying in length between two and six pages. Beyond that, they follow none of the short story's generic rules and feature none of its characteristics. Setting, characterization, plot, and conflict are in short supply; resolution nonexistent. All stories are set in major cities—Berlin, Vienna, New York, London, Lisbon, Barcelona, Nice, Paris, Munich, Lyon—but unless Serner is kind enough to drop us the name of a café or a bar, we can only deduce the story's setting from dialogue snippets written in English, French, Italian, Spanish, Yiddish or Berlin, Bavarian, Austrian, or Swiss dialects.[47]

All of Serner's main characters are criminals, but they cannot justly be described as being in "conflict" with the law. A conflict implies an opponent, and in Serner stories, the other side barely rates a mention. On the very rare occasions when detectives and policemen even appear, they are cast firmly in the victim role (like the detective murdered in "The Kaff Gang"[48]) or as dupes: in some stories, the criminal, after flabbergasting the cops with his Sherlockian genius in solving crimes he himself has committed, is hired onto the police force.[49] Other stories openly ridicule the clever-detective formula. In "A Strange Conversation" one character brags to another of the astuteness with which he has deduced his age and is promptly asked whether he's read too many detective stories; in "The Fateful Camel Cigarette" ("Die verhängnisvolle Camel"), the detective's clever reasoning and insufferable overconfidence nets him nothing but the wrong guy.[50] Not one of Serner's characters appears in more than one of his 100 fragmentary tales, and if a link can be drawn between one story and another, it would be neither a common frame story (like those of the *Arabian Nights* or the *Decameron*) nor recurring plot strands, characters, developments or socially critical "commentary" of any kind,[51] but merely the merciless exactitude with which Serner, in all of them, draws an image of a crime milieu solely through conversations between prostitutes, fraudsters and thieves.[52]

A "typical" Serner story, if there is such a thing, begins *in medias res:* "It was on a Sunday on the street 'Among the Tents' in Berlin when Miss Anna suddenly heard next to her the lisped words [in Berlin dialect, TSK]: 'I am really in favor of not using cucumber salad to polish one's shoes.'"[53] It will end "with both of them tearing each other's hair out, smashing dishes and rolling around screeching on the stone floor."[54] What happens in between is as trivial, as irrelevant, as unintelligible, as frivolously *non sequitur*, but also as unaccountably intriguing as the story's (if that is what it is) beginning and end. Similarly, "Bucket Fever" ("Lampenfieber") features no plot beyond the determination of three weirdly named criminals, Spinach-Emil ("Spinat-Emil"), Nun-Japoll ("Nonnen-Japoll") and Arable Käthe ("Acker-Käthe") to commit a crime. Their plan is not shared with the reader, but delights Arable Käthe to such a degree that she swings Spinach-Emil around the room screaming "Kitz-kitz-kitz-kitz-kitz-kitz!," then proceeds to nearly suffocate him by pressing him tenderly to her bosom. Nun-Japoll saves Emil's life by smacking Käthe on the head so lustily that her glass eye jumps out and rolls under the wardrobe, from where Käthe retrieves it, licks it clean, and reinserts it. And that, aside from a brief sex scene between Emil and Käthe and repeated references to Emil's fear of the police (the title's "bucket fever") is all he wrote.

A recurring setup in Serner stories—to speak of an overarching link between them would be stretching it—features a pimp and a prostitute teaming up to defraud a male victim of money (for example in "Kuhle's Very Rare Hour"; "The Hedonist"; "Doctor Sahob"[55]). The Hedonist Schülle is in love with Sima, but she objects to his plans to create a sound financial basis for their lives together. He pretends to be insanely jealous of her (in reality nonexistent) flirtatious behavior toward Dr. Kandismayer, which of course immediately propels the previously totally uninterested Sima into Kandismayer's arms. Schülle then meets up with the doctor under an assumed name to give him an earful about Sima's jealous boyfriend Schülle and informing Kandismayer that the best way to Sima's heart would be to play the very opposite, to pretend a studied indifference toward Sima's amorous encounters with other men. "If Madame dances with another, walk past the pair, smoking lackadaisically, and airily call out to them: 'Children, straighten your backs!' or: 'Sima, what a wonderfully firmly held figure you make today!' or even more simply: 'Listen, you should really clean off first after you're finished!' And so. That'll make the best impression."[56] Sima's lucrative love affair with Kandismayer, punctuated by her lover's weekly debriefings with Schülle, lasts until the doctor tires of her, at which point she steals his money and disappears. Knowing that Sima has by now learned to appreciate an opulent lifestyle, Schülle now re-enters the scene as her lover and handler. "Listen up!," he tells her, "I don't mind at all that you're tricking rich idiots out of money. But I have to know about it. I have to know all. If not, you might end up being their sucker."[57] The story's Happy End provides for everything that makes an ending happy in fairy tales and Serner stories: sex and money. "The pecuniary basis categorically necessary for every enduring love affair was established. And Sima was almost even more in love than her little Schülle."[58]

"Kuhle's Very Rare Hour" proceeds from the same point of departure. Sasso and Marja progress from a paid to a romantic entanglement and team up to swindle Kuhle, a rich trader in antiques whose main flaw is his profound morality and who is repeatedly ridiculed for his moral principles as the story's "High Ground Man" ("Höhenmensch"). After Sasso tells Kuhle of Marja's criminal background, representing her as a "fallen woman," Kuhle immediately decides to save her. A—for Marja very lucrative—love affair ensues, and Marja expresses her gratitude to Sasso in currency of money and sexual favors. Kuhle labors under the illusion that Marja is madly in love with him and spurns Sasso's ardent advances. Feeling indebted to Sasso for enabling his own bliss and perturbed by Sasso's presumed unhappiness in love, Kuhle persuades Marja to sleep with Sasso—just once, to make him happy. "She should do it as a favor to him [Kuhle]. It was her duty as a woman. As a human being."[59] This bizarre act of sexual charity enables Marja to carry on her love affair with Sasso—which is real and whose purpose is to fleece Kuhle—in full view of Kuhle, just as she carries on her pretended love affair with Kuhle under the watchful eyes of her actual lover Sasso.

The arrangement falters when Marja gets tired of Sasso's art history lessons: "And then, to be honest, I'm really sick and tired already of taking classes from you two hours a day in order to play the educated woman to this old jackass. It's almost like I'm really going to university. A disgrace! Quite apart from wasting time that I could be using for business."[60] Sasso agrees that the arrangement has run its course and writes Kuhle an anonymous letter whose author accuses Sasso of sleeping with Kuhle's wife and black-mailing Marja. But the letter does not have the hoped-for effect: Kuhle, ever taking the moral high ground, asks Sasso to help him locate the author of the letter, in order to save his soul. Marja, who has just slept with Sasso, overhears this conversation from the next room, decides to pull the plug on this ridiculous story, and emerges scantily clad, thinking that Kuhle would now finally understand that she is Sasso's lover and that he's been duped by both her and Sasso all along. The story ends as any farce must—with shock, disgust, a surprise and a joke:

> But lo! nothing like she expected actually happened.
> 　Kuhle approached her, smiling, embraced her like a father and whispered to her, deeply affected: "I knew you'd have the strength to do it. I knew it…. And you, Sasso, I beg your forgiveness that I ever distrusted you. Yes, even now I have distrusted you…" With these words, passionately moved, he tore up the anonymous letter that he held in his twitching hand. "O, what a very rare hour! What an uplifting hour!" And he incessantly kissed Marja's hand and began to weep.
> 　Sasso, despairing, threw himself onto a chair.
> 　Marja, disgusted, sank back onto the pillows.
> 　Finally, Kuhle discovered his sense of tact, said the most philanthropic goodbye imaginable, and left, his head held high…
> 　Sasso and Marja left Lyon on the evening speed-train, but not until they had forged one of Kuhle's checks that Marja had stolen just in case for a very high sum. They hoped that this would prevent Kuhle from committing further crimes on the Moral High Ground.[61]

Is Kuhle's Very Rare Hour the one in which he recaptures his faith in the goodness of humanity after a brief period of doubt, salvaging his view of the world as a happy place inhabited by noble creatures? Or is it the one in which he fools himself beyond any crook's ability to fool him, becoming the old jackass as which Marja has seen him all along? It all depends on how wedded to reality or morality the reader wants to be. Readers who see themselves as inhabiting Kuhle's moral high ground may opt for one version, others who are more interested in clever gameplaying for the other. For game-playing, claims Sabine Kyora, is what this is all about. All three players in "Kuhle's Very Rare Hour" play games and make up the rules as they go along. Kuhle is an amateur in the game because he doesn't understand that his story is invented; he confuses imagined and playacted love with his faith in "true love." Sasso, too, is vulnerable because he believes in his own and sole authorship, whereas in reality his story depends on the cooperation of both a reader (Kuhle) and a main character (Marja). That Marja might walk out of his story or develop as a character in a way that tells the story differently never occurs to him. Marja, finally, is merely the material—an actor in, not an author of—both the stories dreamed up by Kuhle and Sasso. This is why, in the end, she is happy to abandon the game and return to reality, to what actually matters, to the only business there is: the exchange of sex for money.[62]

It is this awareness of the difference between game playing and reality (or "business") that informed Serner's ideas about what he called the "Verism" or "Sincèrism" of his own stories and that led him to claim that he was the most honest author ever to have written about crime. "True love," if such a thing exists, precludes any game playing because the players would be subject to their feelings, or rather: "true love" can never be more than a losing game because the players play it unknowingly and unwittingly. Honesty—"Sincèrism"—must remain aware that love is artificial, a fiction, a game enacted by someone for a specific and usually mercenary purpose. But what is "Sincèrism"? Should we read it as Serner's expression of allegiance to the New Sincerity movement of the early twentieth century, or is it merely a game he played to ridicule the era's addiction to "isms"? Serner's early work suggests the former—he was, after all, the author of the Dada manifesto *Final Relaxation* (*Letzte Lockerung*)—; his unmistakably approving portrayal of game playing in his crime stories seems to imply the latter.

For the very few critics who have, so far, tried to make sense of Serner stories, the idea of game playing has become a cornerstone concept. Like Kyora, André Bucher has suggested that Serner's criminals play games with the moral code of the law-abiding middle class; they lead an "As-If-existence that relies on the playful adaptation of a code of behavior belonging to a class alien to them."[63] These are not "naturalistic" tales like Hyan's crime stories, and unlike Hyan, Serner is totally uninterested in political protest, social criticism, or awareness-raising of any kind. Serner stories are, as Bucher has said, closer to slapstick in silent movies or George Grosz's grotesque art than to naturalist storytelling.[64]

While all this certainly has the ring of truth, neither game playing nor slapstick entirely capture Serner's world of crime. Both slapstick and game playing are aspects of *content* used to describe tales that are largely content free, and both ignore Serner's unique form of storytelling. For this reason, I would like to offer another possibility— not, God forbid, as a "system" of "interpretation" (Serner would probably be horrified at the very idea), but as one mental ball we might juggle as we descend into Serner's world of crime: we might think of Serner's stories as farces. For farce, it seems to me, comes closest to describing Serner's indescribable tales.

Every single dictionary definition of "farce," whether understood literally or figuratively, as describing a literary genre or an absurd situation, could be applied seamlessly and without modification to Serner's literary world. Both farce and Serner's crime tales "use buffoonery and horseplay and typically include crude characterization and ludicrously improbable situations"; both are "a light, humorous play in which the plot depends upon a skillfully exploited situation rather than upon the development of character"; both are "a light dramatic composition marked by broadly satirical comedy and improbable plot" describing "an empty or patently ridiculous act, proceeding, or situation."[65] Serner's farces would be games if they weren't so wedded to a dreadful reality; they would be slapstick if they weren't so unfathomably serious; they would be absurdist theatre if they weren't so uproariously funny; they would be crime stories if they showed even the slightest interest in motive, circumstance, punishment or justice.[66] As it is, farce is the only glove that seems to fit. And if we surmise that Serner wrote crime farces, it is doubly appropriate to consider him the Father of the Farcical Criminal, for the Farcical Criminal rules Serner's world refreshingly unencumbered by all context. Having stripped his tales of setting, plot, characterization, conflict, and resolution, Serner leaves us only the criminal's words, in dialogue or monologue, as the most direct and undiluted testimony to the farcical games he plays.

The "Criminal" Walter Serner

Although Serner was clearly one of the most innovative authors of his time, he remained unknown for decades. After the Nazis banned and burned his books in 1933, none of his titles appeared in any publisher's catalogue for the next thirty years.[67] In part this may be due to his contemporaries' inability to make sense not only of his literature but also of his life—a life of which we know very little, even today. We merely know enough of both to say that neither conformed in the least to the traditional formula of what a crime story, or a writer's life, should look like. Serner had a high school diploma (passed on the second attempt in 1909) and a law degree (passed on the second attempt in 1913). Immediately after obtaining his hard-fought-for high school diploma, he converted from Judaism to Catholicism and changed his name from the recognizably Jewish Seligmann to Serner.[68] Immediately after obtaining his hard-fought-for law degree, he announced his decision never to use it but instead to spend the rest of his life touring Europe by train. Until the Nazi advance made travel through Europe difficult for Jews, that is what he did, and nobody had the slightest idea what Serner actually lived on.

It was this mystery, coupled with the minuteness with which he described the world of crime and Serner's own claim that he was intimately familiar with criminals and their milieu, that led to the persistent myth that Serner himself was a professional criminal. The author of these rumors was Serner's own publisher, Paul Steegemann, who sent a fictitious Serner bio to the Jewish writer Theodor Lessing. Lessing did not hesitate to spice his 1925 review of Serner's crime stories with these "biographical" details and adorn them with a Serner mugshot that, in stark contrast to the anaemic doe-eyed insurance salesman type that peers out uncertainly from other Serner portrait photos, presents him as a hardened criminal glaring at the observer with an unmistakable air of menace. "You won't find his address in literary calendars," Lessing wrote, "but you will find it in the files of the criminal investigative police. He is an international conman of the highest order. His books contain nothing that he hasn't experienced. You're welcome to say all this out loud. Herr Serner doesn't give a damn. Currently he is traveling through the orient, the owner of several grand brothels in Argentina."[69] This bio led Alfred Rosenberg, one of the Nazi's most prominent antisemitic propagandists, to denounce both Lessing and Serner as Jewish peddlers of female flesh and "brothel natures" whose work showed "the blood-curdling abyss that separates Jews from human beings."[70] Even Serner, the most miserly of authors when it came to autobiographical statements, felt moved to comment:

The many faces of Walter Serner. Left: signed author photograph dedicated to Christian Schad, ca. 1925 (Wikimedia Commons). Right: mugshot of the "criminal" accompanying a Serner-bio (*Börsenblatt des deutschen Buchhandels*, 1927, p. 11609).

I find it annoying that people constantly attribute to me the most tasteless motives. I therefore solemnly declare that I am neither a brothel owner nor the right hand of Boris Ssawindow, whom I've never, alas, known in person; that I love the N-Boy from Berlin but consider the German double mocha a disgusting brew; that I consider human interaction a type of psycho-dance and Lichtenberg's aphorisms and Flaubert's "November" good basic training [...]; that politics makes me barf but that I find the Italian Lazzo [a stock comedy routine of the *commedia dell'arte*, TSK] sympathetic; that I am tender, lazy, curious and coarse; [...] that I travel neither for Skoda [the car manufacturer, TSK] nor the Emperor of the Sahara but for my personal pleasure; and that I have a Czechoslovakian passport and, fortunately, a thick skin.[71]

In inimitable Serner fashion, the essay, while lampooning the biography written by Steegemann and parroted by Lessing, refuses to offer a single concrete revelation about the life that his readers, at this point, must have been on tenterhooks to hear more about. Instead, it offers a wealth of useless and contextless snippets that taken together amount to nothing at all. Like his crime fiction, his "autobiography" is peopled with farcical fictitious characters whose entire purpose in the tale is to throw the reader off the track, from the mysterious Boris Ssawindow (a Russian spy?) to the intriguing N-Boy to the preposterous Emperor of the Sahara. Even the essay's title, "Who is Walter Serner???," with its triple-question-mark send up of his readers' curiosity, is a joke, an announcement that that question would not be answered.

In another response to Lessing and Rosenberg, "Theodor Lessing and the White Slavetrader" ("Theodor Lessing und der Mädchenhändler," 1926), Serner is both more serious and more concrete, but continues to play his biographical cards close to his chest. Once again, the only details of his life on offer are negative ones:

Herr Steegemann has claimed that there was nothing in my books that I haven't lived through.
That is correct. Every line I write is based on things I saw, heard or physically experienced. But
the identification of my life with the facts used in my books is hardly as irrefutable as many claim.
True, it would be difficult to discover an author who knows Europe's crime circles better and has
described them more honestly than I, but is the possibility that someone traverses these circles
without doing more than traversing them so terribly fantastical? It seems so. Even the criminalists
who for the past six years have subjected me to surveillance in every country of Europe prove, in
so doing, that they don't believe in this possibility either: someone who knows criminals and
police work as well as I must be either a criminal himself or a secret policeman from a hostile
nation. That someone could acquire such knowledge merely by observation seems out of the
question to every criminalist. And yet it is so. The fact that I don't have a criminal record and that
there is no concrete evidence against me is thus merely seen as proof of my criminal mastery.
That is flattering but untrue.

  What is, however, true is that I've never been a pimp, never an international conman, never a
white slave trader. It would be easy for me to prove what I've lived on until today. And it is practically a tragicomic joke that the few irregularities in my biography were actually caused by the
duress that the police has seen fit to subject me to.[72]

Much like Serner's literature, his biography is dominated by negatives: all we know
is what it *isn't*. It isn't a crime story, a detective story, or something with a discernible
plot line, let alone a "message." He wasn't a criminal mastermind, a pimp, or a white
slave trader. Even those who knew him best knew next to nothing. The painter Christian
Schad, whom Serner once called in a letter "my only and best friend,"[73] was so uncertain
about the provenance of Serner's exquisite knowledge of crime milieus and argot that
he finally broke down and asked:

I remember that once I asked him the confidential question without further ado. I received a
smile and an extensive explanation that culminated in the sharply formulated sentences: "Must
someone who seeks out the most awful environments and has contact with the lowest of men
necessarily be part of that milieu and participate in those acts? Must someone who encounters in
that milieu [...] the most hideous honesty necessarily feel scandalized by it? Must someone who is
disgusted by the hypocrisy and the innate lies everywhere else not feel better there? Must even
someone who feels like that necessarily feel good there?"[74]

In the absence of concrete information, we are left only with questions to consider.
Serner's texts are so engaging and so disturbing because they really offer nothing else.
And so, in sheer self-defense, we spin our own stories—about his texts or his life. Serner
the criminal mastermind is certainly the one that had the most traction. Even Christian
Schad, who knew him best, was occasionally seduced by it, for myth flourishes in the
absence of facts. In 1927, immediately after the publication of his Collected Works edition, Serner fell silent as a writer; 1927 is also the date of his final brief letter to Schad.
44 years after they lost contact, in 1971, Schad became conscious that his personal
memory was the sum total of historical memory of Walter Serner, and fearing its loss
with his own death, he began to write his Serner memoirs. Much like Serner's own
statements on his life, Schad's account amounts to tales, words and the near-total
absence of even the most basic biographical data. Until 1981, when Thomas Milch, the
scholar who rediscovered Serner in the 1980s, dug up the records and told him, Schad
had no idea that Serner had perished in a makeshift gas chamber somewhere near
Minsk in 1942. In his memoirs, originally published in 1971 and re-edited in 1980, he
muses idly where Serner might have ended up after the war: perhaps he emigrated to
the U.S., or maybe he wound up in South America?[75] As his widow Bettina Schad states

in her afterword, he left the passage unchanged even after Milch told him the awful truth; he did not want to add to his memories of Serner, which are obviously not only memories of Serner but also imagined stories about Serner.[76] Thus Serner was allowed to live on in Schad's memoirs, even after Schad knew better, as a "breezy clever conman who could survive even the Holocaust."[77] The Walter Serner who defended himself against the myth of Serner the criminal mastermind might have been horrified. The Walter Serner who judiciously withheld from the world even the most basic biographical data might have approved.

And, indeed, why not? Who wouldn't choose the intriguing witticism of a half-sentence casually flung our way by a criminal in a Serner story over a boring explanation of the same criminal's motives? Who wouldn't prefer Serner's biographical denials, his declaration of what his life *wasn't*, to a tedious year-by-year chronology of where he lived, with whom he lived, and what he lived on, like those available about practically every single major writer the world has ever produced? Who wouldn't choose the questions with which he left us over a catalogue of answers that might not be nearly as vivid or intriguing? And who wouldn't treasure the fantasy of Walter Serner living his scandalous life of terrible honesty, perhaps in South America, over the sordid horror of Serner gassed in a modified Volkswagen van?

Hugo Bettauer's Non-Art

At least biographically speaking, Hugo Bettauer (1872–1925) has much in common with Walter Serner. Like Serner, he was an Austrian Jew, a Christian convert straight out of school, a cosmopolitan, a frequent traveler, a victim of Nazi terror, and an extraordinarily prolific writer. As a writer, however, he might be considered Serner's polar opposite. Unlike Serner, who was barely read and gave up writing in frustration in 1927, Bettauer's books sold in their millions, and nine of his 23 novels were adapted for the screen. Predictably concluding that such success must mean triviality, contemporary Arbiters of Taste and later scholars inevitably begin any discussion of Bettauer's works by stating what a hack he was. "Nobody will claim that these and other narratives are great literary achievements," such apologetic prejudgements commonly read, for "These were simple stories, entertaining *Trivialliteratur*, not great literature" and "not particularly valuable from a literary viewpoint."[78]

This is both misleading and an underestimation, for it implies that Bettauer tried to gain admission into the august circles of taste and was spurned for his lack of talent. Rather, the opposite was the case: Bettauer spurned their company, and for good reason. Günter Nenning, in his article on the 60th anniversary of the author's murder, got it but didn't know what to make of it: "I have to think for a long time before I can come up with a comparable author who *intentionally writes non–Art*—masterful, sensationalistic, insolently topical and topped with a mix of progressive engagement and timeless horniness."[79] Anton Kuh, an Austrian-Jewish essayist and Bettauer's contemporary, got it and did know what to make of it. He claimed that the great literati of Bettauer's time despised him not because he discredited himself linguistically and intellectually, but simply because he invited his readers in, as opposed to writing in an obscure and incomprehensible style that would have rendered his works the "secret property of a small circle of intellectuals." To the great literati of his day, Kuh muses, Bettauer's straightforward style seemed such a "betrayal of content and form" that, if it could have been done in a seemly manner, they would have openly celebrated, even conspired in his murder:

> Yes, this was the reason for their hatred; this is why they spat in his face in essays and articles even after his death! For nothing is less forgivable to an intellectual than to see someone spread truths demagogically among people that they themselves cultivate, separate from real life and away from other people. Nothing is less forgiveable to the Man of Letters than to see his own more liberal thoughts on the streets. He then pretends to himself that it is not the publication of these ideas that enrages him but the street dirt in which they roll. But he is lying: he only ever means himself.
>
>   And this is the point at which [...] the literati and the swastika-bearers, the snob and the mob obligingly shake hands.[80]

Bettauer often prided himself on writing like his readers would if they could put their meanings into words,[81] and he deliberately offended not only literary but also social and moral sensibilities. Crime novels like *Law of the Jungle* (*Faustrecht*, 1919) and *Unscrupulous* (*Hemmungslos*, 1920) are full of criminals whose inner urges (for survival, riches, sexual satisfaction) is presented as justifying any crime, including murder. "Not the murderer but the murder victim is at fault" is the motto often attributed to these works; their focus is not the reprehensibility of the crime but that of the victim who, it usually turns out, deserved no more than he got. Crimes remain unpunished; the role and rule of law are negligible, and what few court trials there are usually end in acquittal. Criminality is presented as a way, sometimes as the only way, of solving otherwise intractable conflicts.[82]

Hugo Bettauer's Faustian Killer

Bettauer's novel *Killer of Women* (*Frauenmörder*, 1922) follows this pattern with a twist. Its genius detective Joachim von Dengern essentially has the same history as Auguste Groner's Joseph Müller: innocently sentenced for a crime he didn't commit, he spends long years in prison and exonerates himself after his release by solving the crime for which he was sentenced. Impressed by his spectacular genius and feeling guilty, Dr. Clusius, formerly the detective whose flawed evidence convicted Dengern and now Chief of Berlin's Criminal Investigative Division, hires Dengern as a detective. Much like Müller, Dengern abandons his name and aristocratic title in favor of one of the most common names in the German language and solves the Division's most difficult crimes as modest Detective Krause. He is naturally also entrusted with the case that now shocks Berlin and baffles the police.

Four young women, all aged 22 to 26, have disappeared. They vary in appearance and geographical origins—slender or buxom, blond, brunette or red-headed, they hail from Berlin, Hamburg or Bavaria—but the rest of their stories are remarkably similar. All four rented a room, paying ahead for a month; all four were, to judge from their clothes, dirt poor and yet owned some valuable jewelry (rings, a gold watch, a diamond brooch); none had any friends or family; all disappeared after informing their landladies that they were going on a two-day trip with their respective fiancé in order to look at an estate they were considering for purchase. The fiancé was described, in all cases, as tall, blond, slender, clean-shaven and wearing a pince-nez. And finally, all four victims were endowed with "the most banal and common names you could imagine. Müller, Möller, Jensen, Pfeiffer! There are tens of thousands of those in the German Reich."[83] Just as the investigation gets going, a fifth girl disappears (24 years old; no family; poor but able to pay a month's rent ahead; freshly engaged to a blond, slender gentleman with a pince-nez). This one, for variety's sake, is Jewish and raven-haired, and her last name is (deeply unsurprisingly) Cohen.

Krause soon hits on the idea that the blond bridegroom must have had access to a broad range of women to pick out the ones whose circumstances matched his requirements best, and quickly traces him through the personal ads section of a newspaper. Following the blond monster home, he discovers that he is the writer Thomas Hartwig who rents a room in an apartment in one of Berlin's poorest quarters; after Hartwig has left, Krause succeeds in renting another room from the same landlady and thus gains a key to Hartwig's living quarters. From journalists of his acquaintance, Krause finds out that Hartwig is an unsuccessful writer who has written a voluminous novel that was published by a minor press and that nobody on earth has read. Because both Hartwig's newspaper columns and his general comportment inspire a great deal of sympathy in Krause, as well as severe doubt that Hartwig could be a killer, Krause resists Clusius's prompts to arrest him. Instead, he interviews Lotte Fröhlich, a beautiful young girl rumored to have an affair with Hartwig, who gives him Hartwig's novel, says that Hartwig has also written a play that nobody wants to perform, and concludes despairingly that Hartwig will never become famous: "He isn't part of the clique. And he hasn't got it in him to play to the gallery and find sponsors."[84] Krause's reading of Hartwig's novel confirms his impression of the man as a literary genius and a profoundly moral man, but a search of Hartwig's room yields the answer letters from Müller, Möller, Jensen, Pfeiffer and Cohen, the missing girls with the eminently forgettable names. A conversation with Hartwig, in which Hartwig expresses bitter disappointment at the universal humiliating disregard for his work, throws Krause into a maelstrom of contradictory feelings: "Krause wavered, confused: compassion, sympathy, horror overwhelmed him. The motive for the execrable deed of snuffing out five human lives? Ambition, craving for recognition, the urge to become someone at all costs."[85]

After Hartwig's inevitable arrest, he immediately rockets to stardom as the most horrible serial killer of all time. "But the real sensation wasn't even that. The real sensation was his novel *Souls in Struggle*. Has anyone ever heard of an honest-to-goodness serial murderer who wrote a novel that was even published? No, that was unheard of."[86] Hartwig's novel is first serialized in the papers, then quickly reprinted in huge editions, widely read, enthusiastically reviewed, and translated into every major language on Earth. Its author, in custody awaiting trial and refusing to either confess or deny his crimes, becomes a superstar and a millionaire. Then Director Hohlbaum, whose theater is going broke, digs out the play submitted earlier by the now world-famous Thomas Hartwig. Before the author's rise, Hohlbaum could not even be bothered to read it, but now he hastily prepares it for immediate production. The author grants his permission but stipulates that the premiere must be on the evening of the first day of his two-day trial. All of Berlin now feverishly seeks to secure tickets for both sensational events.

As Hartwig's fame and his bank account expand into the stratosphere, both his defender and his prosecutor find themselves flummoxed. Hartwig's defender, who is as sure of his client's guilt as everyone else, recommends an insanity defense, in a line eerily prophetic of the future fate of Bettauer's own murderer: "They won't sentence you, they will bring you to Dalldorf [a city-owned lunatic asylum, TSK] and then release you as cured a year later."[87] Hartwig's prosecutor, conversely, agonizes over the contrast between Hartwig's indubitable guilt and the fact that extensive searches have yielded no bodies, no body parts, and no concrete evidence of any kind that anyone was, in fact, murdered. The trial nevertheless goes ahead, with courtroom tickets and theater tickets for Hartwig's play the same evening selling out in record time.

At trial, Hartwig declares his innocence but refuses to say anything else. The five landladies recognize him as the mysterious bridegroom; the prosecutor points out that only violence could have kept the five impoverished girls from using a room they had already paid for. Character witnesses for the accused describe him as a kind, gentle and ethical man utterly incapable not only of crime but of any dishonorable act whatsoever, but the jury nods in agreement with the judge's casual statement that time has passed and people change. It is clear that Hartwig's guilt is assumed as established by everyone in the room. The court adjourns early because everyone involved, including the judge, both attorneys and all jurors, have tickets to the Hartwig theater premiere that evening, which is an unprecedented triumph: thundering salvoes of applause, weeping viewers, gushingly exuberant reviews. Only the fact that its author is a soon-to-be-executed criminal prevents the crowd from breaking out into shouts of "Long live Hartwig!", and critics unabashedly praise the play to the skies. As the narrator sardonically remarks, "After all, you don't always get a chance like this—to write exactly as you feel. With a living author, there are all kinds of considerations, concerns, and personal matters that you can't quite overcome. But Hartwig was dead, or as good as dead—"[88]

When the trial resumes the following morning, Detective Krause drops the bombshell: Hartwig has not committed murder, but written a farce, posing as a serial killer to draw attention to a novel that otherwise would never have been read and a play that would never have been performed. The five victims were played by his fiancée Lotte Fröhlich, the sinister bridegroom by himself, and the story practically wrote itself, aided greatly by people's willingness to believe the worst of others. "It's easy to say," Hartwig explains to the stunned court,

> that Genius blazes trails! We only know of those who blazed trails, but not of the many that got stranded along the way, the victims of often ridiculous tribulations. Had I labored on patiently, my novel would probably only ever have served as cheese wrapping, and my drama would have lain in Director Hohlbaum's cupboard until the mice had gnawed it to bits. I was neither willing nor able to wait. I preferred to be dragged into daylight by a frivolous rogue's trick than to shrivel away patiently in the dark.[89]

The storm that greets these revelations is perhaps not far removed from that which raged around Bettauer's literature; it is a tempest of mixed feelings, a cyclone of confusion. "Thunderous laughter, sobbing, shouts of outrage were heard. Some people applauded Hartwig, others hissed at him. The Prosecutor ceaselessly screamed the word 'Blasphemy!'; the Presiding Judge screamed 'Quiet!'; the Defense Attorney stood pale and bewildered, trembling like a leaf..."[90] Hartwig's audience, much like Bettauer's, is divided, unsure what to make of this most daring of all authors.

Like so much of Bettauer's work, *Killer of Women* is an indictment of the arrogance and privilege of the upper classes and the grovelling deference with which they're treated by everyone else, for no reasons other than those prescribed by convention. Yet Bettauer's novel cannot be reduced to mere societal critique. The novel is a farce within a farce: Hartwig's farce, in which, refusing to die as the Author who was never read, he turns himself into a Killer who has never killed, and Bettauer's farce, in which he lampoons above all one aspect of his contemporary class society: its wearisome, plodding, mind-numbingly insipid predictability. In the end, Hartwig emerges as the tale's hero rather than its villain only because the Reich's Chancellor, who has attended both performances—the tragedy authored by Hartwig and performed at the theater and the farce authored by Hartwig and performed in the courtroom—finds the courtroom farce deliciously funny. Since disagreeing with the Reich's First Public Servant is, of course, unthinkable, everyone swiftly subordinates their own opinions of the matter to the Chancellor's, and the pendulum of public opinion swings in Hartwig's favor. Only in a ploddingly, painfully predictable societal "order," only in a profoundly unimaginative and unsurprising world, can Hartwig's farce succeed. His insistence, for example, that the premiere of his play should fall on the evening of the first day of his two-day trial is owed to his understanding of the immutable laws that rule behavior in both the literary and the judicial sphere. Since no Arbiter of Taste ever takes a chance on a new author, you have to be dead to be positively reviewed. And since everyone accused of a crime is considered guilty until proven innocent, it is entirely predictable that his reviewers, like his judge and jury, would consider him as good as dead.

And so Thomas Hartwig, one of Bettauer's rare innocently accused criminals, takes his place among the many guilty ones who are just as clear-eyed about the chances society is about to give them but do not hesitate to kill in order to get what they want. They all are cut from the same cloth: perpetual malcontents, resentful geniuses, people who desire powerfully and untiringly, people who move heaven and earth to achieve their desire, people who, like Hartwig, are beset by "the urge to become someone at all costs." On their deathbeds, we imagine, these characters might sum up their lives as follows: "I sped through the World that's there:/Gripped by the hair every appetite,/And let go those that failed to delight,/Let those fly that quite escaped me./I've desired, achieved my course,/Desired again, and so, with force,/Stormed through life..."[91] Thomas Hartwig and his brothers are nothing but Goethe's Faust masterfully, sensationalistically, insolently catapulted into a work that is *intentionally* "non–Art." Dragged from the Olympian heights of the greatest work ever written in the German language, he rolls in the dirt of the street, where even readers bereft of a literary education can contemplate the possibilities of desiring, struggling, achieving, and stopping at nothing to do so.

Carl Zuckmayer's Lovable Conman

While Bettauer's crime novels observe bourgeois society from within its exceedingly narrow walls, and while Serner's stories look beyond them, German crime fiction of the late Republic and early NS years was engaged in looking back. The two texts that embody this nostalgic attitude best are also—hardly coincidentally—among the most adored, widely read and enduring crime stories ever written in Germany. One is the play that later became the definitive and iconic literary account of the Köpenick farce, Carl Zuckmayer's (1896–1977) drama *The Captain of Köpenick.*

Yet Zuckmayer's text did not acquire its nostalgic overtones until after the fall of the NS regime. Writing the play at its dawn, nothing could have been further from the author's mind than nostalgia. The play was published two years before the Nazis assumed power, banned Zuckmayer's works and expatriated the author for his Jewish grandfather and his criticisms of the new regime. As Zuckmayer made clear, his *Captain* was not conceptualized as a misty-eyed glance back at the good old days but as a good hard look at his own time, when

> the Nazis were entering the Reichstag as the second-strongest party and thrusting the nation into a new craze for uniforms. The story was an image, a farcical mirror image, of the evils and dangers that were growing in Germany, but also of the hope that they could be overcome as the shoemaker had overcome his difficulties by native wit and humane insight.[92]

That the author himself defined his play as "a farcical mirror image" of the present and immediate future rather than the past is seemingly belied by the play's subtitle, *A German Fairy Tale in Three Acts*, and the Brothers Grimm quotations with which the play opens and closes. And yet, these quotations themselves hint at the critical potential of Zuckmayer's farce. The opening quotation, affixed before the *dramatis personae*, is taken from Rumpelstiltskin, that foul dwarf who, no longer content with gold rings and other trinkets, ultimately blackmails the miller's daughter into selling him her firstborn child, for "something alive is dearer to me than all the treasures in the world."[93] The closing quotation, appended without comment after the final curtain, is taken from the Grimms's "The Bremen Town Musicians," a tale of a four farm animals who, grown too old to work and destined for slaughter by their ungrateful masters, run away to Bremen to become the town's musicians. "We are going to Bremen," said the donkey to the cockerel, "You can find something better than death anywhere."[94] Voigt, too, is a fairy tale character: like the donkey, he is now too old to work; destined for the scrap heap, he embarks on a journey to see if he can find something better than death. Like Rumpelstiltskin, he lives in a barter economy where human life ranks no higher than lifeless objects and is usually valued only when adorned by trinkets. The trinket that assigns worth to a human life in his society is, of course, the uniform.

Zuckmayer's description of his text as a "farce" should be taken seriously, even if the vast majority of it reads like a tragedy. For 16 of the play's 21 scenes, Voigt wanders the Earth: in and out of prison, in and out of police bureaus where he begs in vain for a residence permit that would allow him to stay (which, he is told, he cannot get without a job) or a passport that would allow him to leave (which he is refused due to his criminal record); in and out of and shoe factories where he unsuccessfully applies for work (which, he is told, he won't be offered without a residence permit or a passport). Desperation drives him to burglarize a police station to obtain the forms for forging the papers he needs; he is caught and slapped with another ten-year prison sentence. After his release he is taken in by his sister Marie Hoprecht and her husband Friedrich, but this brief respite is shattered by a deportation order. Voigt, who has just returned from the funeral of a young girl who died of tuberculosis and whose final days he sweetened by reading to her and comforting her, tells Friedrich Hoprecht that he heard a voice at her gravesite:

> Man, it said—at some point, everyone will fall flat on their ass. You, too, it said. And then, then you'll stand before God the Father, you will, who made everything, before him you'll stand, and he'll ask you to your face: Willem Voigt, what didya make of your life? And then I have to say— doormats, I have to say. I plaited them in prison, and then everyone stepped all over them, I have to say. And at the end, you'll wheeze and choke for that little bit of air, and then you're done. That's what you'll tell God, man. And he's gonna say to you: get outta here! he'll say! Deport this guy! he'll say! I didn't give you your life for that, he'll say! You owe it to me! Where is it? What didya do with it? (*Very calmly.*) And then, Friedrich—and then it'll be nothing doing again, about that residence permit.[95]

This speech clearly marks the end of the line for Voigt, the height of his tragedy (in Richard Oswald's 1931 film,[96] the incomparably hangdog Max Adalbert, who played Voigt, begins by whispering the speech and gradually ramps up volume and emotional intensity until he screams it at the top of his lungs, straight into the camera). Turning the end of the line into a crossroads means, of course, going off to see if you can find

Carl Zuckmayer (Wikimedia Commons) and his most famous creation, the Captain of Köpenick: Max Adalbert in the title role in Richard Oswald's 1931 film.

something better than death somewhere. In the following scene we see Voigt buy the uniform that will transform him, both from a nobody to a respected member of society and from a tragic character to a farcical one.

As others have pointed out,[97] Voigt is not the only main character of Zuckmayer's play, the other, of course, being the uniform, which assumes a life of its own. Like that of the tragic character Voigt, the story of the uniform is one of gradual decline. Originally destined to provide new glamour for a Captain of an elite regiment who then cannot use it because he has to resign his commission following a tavern brawl, it is sold used to a mere lieutenant of the reserves, who, grown to fat to close it, rips it accidentally and consigns it to a pawn shop. This is where the discarded, unwanted uniform and the discarded, unwanted cobbler find each other and the play turns from tragedy to farce. Significantly, Voigt assigns as much responsibility for his Köpenick coup to the uniform as to himself: "Any child knows that if you're in the military you can do whatever you want. I've known that all my life. ... I didn't really do all that much. A uniform can do it almost all by itself."[98] And the play proves him right: while the genuine Captain von Schlettow is disgraced in the tavern scene simply because he is out of uniform and thus not recognized as an officer, Voigt gets all the respect in the world once he dons a fake uniform and is no longer recognized as a civilian.

But what are we to make of the play's final scene, the one in which this illusion is seemingly debunked? The police director, to whom Voigt has willingly confessed over port wine, asks him to model the uniform for the amusement of the police force. The sight has him crying tears of laughter: "Gentlemen," he says, wiping his eyes, "this is the most wonderful hour of my thirty-year long career."[99] Only Voigt, the object of all this mirth, is not in on the joke. When Voigt says timidly that he's never seen himself in uniform, the Director asks for a full-length mirror. The play ends with precise stage directions:

> *Voigt steps in front of the mirror, the port wine glass in his hand. He stands with his back to the audience. The director steps aside with the others, watching him. Voigt, at first, stands quietly— then his shoulders begin to twitch, without a sound—then his entire figure begins to shake and tot- ter, so that the port wine slops out of the glass—then he slowly turns around—laughing—laughing harder and harder, laughing ear to ear, with his entire body, with his entire essence—laughs until he's out of breath and tears run down his face. From this laughter a word emerges—at first low, almost inaudible—then ever stronger, more clearly, more definitive—finally subsuming all in another great, liberating and powerful burst of laughter:* Impossible!![100]

Zuckmayer's final scene does, of course, invite a Lombrosian reading: what is so funny, even to the author of the joke, is the contrast between Voigt's "proletarian" body and the "upper-class" uniform.[101] But there is more to it than that, for it is the literal reinsertion of humanity, in the form of Voigt's body, that saves the play from ending as a tragedy. That Voigt, in the end, does not recognize himself as an officer does not change the fact that everyone else did. It even less changes the fact that they could do so only by looking exclusively at the uniform and disregarding the human body inside, just as they were unable to see Voigt as a human being when he came to them begging for work or papers. A world in which the discarded can find nothing better than death, in which "something alive" is routinely discounted in favor of "treasure," like a gold ring or the epaulettes on a uniform, is tragic. Farce, in the end, intervenes, destabilizing tragedy by creating a brief moment in which the human becomes visible. For what we see in the mirror is not only Voigt's misshapen body but also a refracted worldview both blinded by treasure and blind to the humans on the scrapheap: a view of a misshapen world that is, as Voigt's final word has it, not merely cruel and absurd, but "impossible."

Perhaps unsurprisingly, given all it implies, Zuckmayer's farce was quickly turned into mere comedy. Richard Oswald's 1931 film does more than merely omit the famous mirror scene; it *reverses* it. Zuckmayer's farce mitigates the tragedy in its final "liberating and powerful burst of laughter," but otherwise leaves it very much intact. In the film, conversely, the Happy End of comedy simply wipes the slate clean. Even tragedy's most obvious visual image, militarism, is recruited in the service of this ending: Voigt, freshly released from prison, marches in front of a military band, perfectly in step with the marching soldiers, happily waving his Imperial pardon and the all-important, finally granted passport in time to the music.

Zuckmayer's drama has long since overpowered not only all other literary adaptations of the Köpenick myth, but also the original story of Wilhelm Voigt. All feature films (1931, 1941, 1956, 1960, 1997, 2001 and 2005); all radio plays (1945, 1947, 1951, 1954, 1955, 1962, 1964), even pop songs (by Drafi Deutscher, 1968) refer not to the historical case but to Zuckmayer's play. And yet, these adaptations often alter the original play's genre, mood and context even if they closely follow its plot. Zuckmayer's original, a bittersweet concoction of two thirds tragedy and one third farce, often re-emerges after the Second World War as the sugary cocktail of nostalgic comedy, and Zuckmayer's "intensely humane, helpless, and naive underdog"[102] became the blueprint for the lovable criminal of a thousand witty postwar tales. It goes without saying that this Captain is only vaguely related to either his historical original or to Zuckmayer's character.

Heinrich Spoerl's "Originals"

If ever there was a text that reached the popularity of the nostalgic-comedic Captain of Köpenick, it would have to be Heinrich Spoerl's comic crime novel *The Muzzle* (*Der Maulkorb*). *The Muzzle* portrays the exact opposite of Serner's seedy underworld; it is set in Wilhelm Voigt's time but in a Wilhelminian age that has little to do with that portrayed in Zuckmayer's play. Spoerl's unabashedly nostalgic novel portrays a German idyll full of cobblestoned streets, charming villages and sunlit vineyards, untainted by National Socialism, World Wars, and violent crime. As attested by its stunning sales figures, its incarnation as a hit play touring Germany in 1938–39,[103] and the five feature films made of the novel over the course of the next six decades (1938, 1958, 1963, 1980, and 1997), this nostalgia turned *The Muzzle* into one of the most enduringly popular texts ever produced in the German language.

Written in 1936—after the Reichstag fire (1933), the Night of the Long Knives (1934), and the Nuremberg Laws (1935)—Spoerl's lighthearted tale portrays an endearing image of State authority that is about as far removed from Nazi Germany as is imaginable. Set some time in the Imperial era, Spoerl's never-identified "Most Gracious Sovereign" might or might not have been inspired by Emperor Wilhelm II. Certainly, however, the "Sovereign's" laissez-faire bonhomie stands in extreme contrast to the steely strength Germany's new Chancellor sought to project in propaganda films like Riefenstahl's *Triumph of the Will*, which appeared the year before Spoerl's novel. Similarly, Spoerl's policemen, jovially named or nicknamed Bristle Batons (Drahtschnauz), Gunpowder Gourd (Pulverkopp), In-the-Thick-of-It (Mittenmang), Criminal Inspector Drudge (Kriminalkommissar Mühsam), or Law Clerk Doornail (Referendar Thürnagel) are no SA- or SS-men, or even the stern big city cops of the Weimar Republic: "These weren't sinewy characters with iron faces and incorruptible objectivity, but well-nourished people with red lapels on blue cloth and shiny spiked helmets; individuals, maybe even originals."[104] They are, in other words, all that's needed to police Spoerl's fictitious small town ca. 1900, where an entirely asexual bohemianism is about as seedy as it gets, where a bit of drunk-and-disorderly is the worst crime on the books and all conflict can be boiled down to mere misunderstandings and entirely forgivable all-too-human weaknesses.

The novel's action begins when a political bomb is flung into this sleepy idyll. The Most Gracious Sovereign has seen fit to give a speech in which he publicly criticizes certain unnamed "Smarty-Pants" and "Mischief-Makers." Although nobody in town has heard or read the speech, gossip about it spreads like wildfire. "The populace seethed, here and everywhere,"[105] particularly because this clearly inflammatory speech has been carefully kept out of the newspapers, which smacks of censorship. Amidst all this public uproar about freedom of expression and state control, Crown Prosecutor Herbert von Treskow is roundly teased by his drinking buddies because as a public servant he is not permitted the luxury of an independent opinion. He gets vicarious satisfaction by drinking them all under the table, then pontificates, drunk as a skunk, to his dog August: "We are n-no mischief-makers, August, and we w-won't allow them to m-muzzle us, muzzle us!"[106]

The next morning, to the shock and horror of the entire town, the marketplace statue of Our Most Gracious Sovereign is adorned with a muzzle. Police, sniffer dogs, and prosecutorial office immediately spring into action to investigate this most execrable lese majesty, executing search warrants on every dog owner in town and interrogating countless witnesses attracted by the enormous reward. The investigation of the town's crime of the century is entrusted to the capable hands of Crown Prosecutor von Treskow, whose career, it is made clear, will be made or broken by this high-profile case. And were it not for his clever wife Elisabeth and his even cleverer daughter Trude (who secretly replace the muzzle he has lost somewhere), and were it not for the young painter Rabanus (an eyewitness to the dastardly deed who has a vested interest in saving Treskow because he has fallen in love with Trude), the comic idyll might well be shattered by both farce and tragedy. A Crown Prosecutor who feels muzzled by the authorities, gives voice to this feeling in an inebriated state by committing a crime (if such it can be called), does not remember having done so, and then chases himself: that is a farce. A Crown Prosecutor who might actually catch himself, have his career ruined, and—as a good civil servant à la Franz von Hervay—escape the scandal by shooting himself: that would be a tragedy.

Fortunately, Rabanus salvages the situation. He plants the idea of claiming the reward into the heads of two jobless lower-class layabouts, who agree to play perp and denouncer respectively and split the reward. At trial, Bätes the pretend-perp claims that he didn't recognize the statue as that of Our Most Gracious Sovereign; the charge of lese majesty is reduced to mere disorderly conduct, and Bätes is sentenced to a three mark fine. The novel ends happily for all. Wimm and Bätes gleefully split the 3000 mark reward. Treskow is joyfully promoted to Chief Crown Prosecutor. Rabanus merrily waltzes off (literally, in the last scene which features a ball at the Treskows) with Trude. The novel's coda returns briefly to the Imperial Speech that started all the trouble: Our Most Gracious Sovereign breaks down in a fit of hysterical laughter about his speech, which never appeared in the newspapers and never could—because he never gave it.

Spoerl's novel incorporates several farcical elements: a speech that never was; an investigator who chases himself; a culprit who is innocent but condemned and, in being condemned, rewarded instead of punished; and—in the courtroom scene—an accuser who refuses to accuse, a confessed criminal who refuses to confess, and a crown witness who first refuses to testify and then informs the court that his testimony will be false. Because the representative of the law, Crown Prosecutor von Treskow, is also the potential victim were the law to take its course, the bureaucratic machinery of justice must be temporarily disabled so that justice can be done.

The 1938 film (dir. Erich Engel) stages this conflict between the letter and the spirit of the law even more explicitly. In a scene in which von Traskow (a slight name change from Spoerl's original) confesses to his wife that he himself is the culprit he's been chasing, she argues that his confession would undermine the authority of the state by opening up its judicial branch to public ridicule. But von Traskow, ever the correct official, will have none of a perfectly rational argument if it benefits himself: "Every civil servant, every government agency, has one most supreme obligation: absolute honesty. If this principle is ever—even once, at any point—subverted, faith is destroyed, and with it the government's reputation and authority."[107]

Clearly, this is an admirable stance that would, equally clearly, lead to catastrophe. It also reveals a further aspect that characterizes Spoerl's work as a farce, namely, the consistent portrayal of directly opposite characteristics or paradoxes as unproblematically compatible. Treskow is the story's "criminal" (this, as it turns out, is hardly a disaster) and simultaneously its most upright citizen (this, as it turns out, might well be). He is saved by a man who can only be described as his polar opposite—Rabanus, simultaneously the story's devil-may-care bohemian and its Voice of Reason. Rabanus is described as leading what, around 1900, would have been considered a highly dissolute lifestyle; he "slept when he didn't feel like working, worked when he had had enough sleep, and didn't give a damn about bourgeois and astronomical day- or night-time; he received friends when it suited him and threw them out again when he was sick of them."[108] Asked what he did for a living, he prevaricates: "that's a bit complicated— painters think I'm a good musician; musicians think I'm a good writer, and writers think I'm a good painter. I don't know which of them is right—I'm afraid it might be all three."[109]

Paradoxically, it is this nonconformist and flippant proponent of Cheerful Chaos who comes to the rescue of Order. In court, he refuses to testify because he knows that Treskow would be destroyed by the truth, and is promptly threatened with six months' imprisonment for withholding testimony. His response is characteristic: "I am not well served by six months in prison. But if I testify, justice is even less well served."[110] In the end, Rabanus perverts the course of "justice" in the cause of Justice, or perhaps simply because "I don't feel like ruining a human being and destroying his future because of a stupid statute."[111]

Central to Spoerl's farce is the understanding that although Crime, Punishment, the State, the Law, Justice, Authority, and Order are often seen, and wish to be seen, as absolute and immutable, their perception actually varies greatly, depending on "individuals, maybe even originals." The dissolutely bohemian but rational Rabanus shrugs off a "stupid statute" over which the exemplary bourgeois but emotional Treskow would have killed himself. Evidently, the same crime may have different consequences depending on its perpetrator; more concretely: depending on the perpetrator's *class*. For Treskow/Traskow, being unmasked as the criminal would result in public ridicule, a major scandal, and the loss of his job, status and social esteem. What he fears most, as per his traumatized speech in the 1938 film, is "the funny papers. I will be a figure of fun. The perpetrator his own prosecutor; the prosecutor his own perpetrator. No matter how this ends: I have to resign. And then I can sell wine door to door or peddle pencils."[112] But for the casual laborer Bätes, who would cheerfully peddle pencils if he could get the work, and who is already—by virtue of his class, his total lack of education, and his thick Rhenish dialect—defined as "a figure of fun," being found out as the culprit is hardly a tragedy.

As Germans have known since at least Johann Christoph Gottsched and his infa-

"The prosecutor his own perpetrator": Ralph Arthur Roberts as Crown Prosecutor von Traskow in Erich Engel's *Der Maulkorb* (1938).

mous "estates-clause," only lower-class characters like Bätes or Wilhelm Voigt play comedy parts, and only their crimes are funny. But a respected Pillar of the Community like Crown Prosecutor von Treskow, pitched from the pinnacle of High Drama, flung down into the pit of Comedy with the likes of the unemployed laborer Bätes and the unemployed shoemaker Voigt? Unthinkable. Only a farce can avert such a tragedy. That the tragic character Treskow and his inner conflict mattered to Spoerl a great deal more than the comedy and its folksy types emerges from the author's strict instruction to the director of the dramatic adaptation of his novel: "Above all and at all costs I want to prevent this from being turned into a folk play. The focus lies on the Crown Prosecutor and the conflict. Wimm and Bätes are folk-types, but ultimately peripheral characters, two quasi-Shakespearean fools who criss-cross the plot and unconsciously fulfil the role decreed for them by Fate."[113]

All Things Human: Spoerl's Fictitious Germany

Reading *The Muzzle* in the context of its time throws up quite a few problems. Should we see it as a nostalgic text written at a time when many Germans began to lose the will to look around and had no optimism left to look forward? Where else to look than backward to a kinder, gentler era when even politics and crimes were still humane, even funny? Or should we see it as a document of resistance against the Nazi regime, however oblique? After all, *The Muzzle* starts out with a free speech issue (a population enraged by a Head of State's attempt to "muzzle" it; the 1938 film begins with the confiscation of newspapers by the police) and ends with the explosive statement that justice can only be done by subverting the rule of law. Depending on the individual (or original) doing the reading, both interpretations could be made to sound perfectly plausible. What is certain is that the novel, written right in the middle of the peacetime Nazi era, became such a riproaring success that it permitted Heinrich Spoerl to give up his failing legal practice in Düsseldorf and move to Berlin, into a large house on the Wannsee with a secretary, a domestic servant, and a boat.

Spoerl's first career as an attorney may not have been implicated in the NS regime— or no more than his second career as one of the Nazi era's most popular humorists— but certainly it was perceived, by family and friends, as needing a bit of postwar polish. Spoerl's entire law career, particularly during the NS years, is regularly presented as an aberration, a minor detour on the way to his true vocation as a writer, or even dismissed as coincidental. Supposedly Spoerl's decision to study law was not owed to any calling but merely to the fact that his extreme shortsightedness did not permit him, as originally planned, to study engineering. As his son Alexander explained:

> Unavoidably, my father became a defense attorney. Not a good one. He sent some people away because he said their case was hopeless. Others because he said he couldn't defend them with conviction. My mother said he should for once think of his family and not only of the "dignity of his office." And so my father became an honorable man, but not a rich one.[114]

Another testimonial of Spoerl's law career comes down to us from his childhood friend Hans Müller-Schlösser, who remembered a courtroom summation by Heinrich Spoerl as follows:

Heinrich Spoerl wanted to make a lot of money as a defense attorney. But that didn't work out because his spontaneous whimsical ideas, against which he was utterly defenseless, got in the way. I witnessed his first defense speech in court. He wanted to get a crook off. The judge, the assessors and the public split their sides laughing. The poor sinner was sentenced, but to the absolute minimum.[115]

Both the upright character described by Spoerl's son and the hilarious courtroom speech described by his childhood friend could have come straight out of one of Spoerl's novels. We can read this as life imitating art or as art imitating life. Perhaps Spoerl did indeed base the courtroom scenes at the end of most of his novels on experiences from his practice. Or perhaps Spoerl's novels were later used as blueprints for the author's life, as a way of presenting the author as truly at home in the quaint, just and humane world he created and—by obvious extension—as a stranger to the unjust, inhumane and deeply unfunny world created by the NS regime. No matter which of these interpretations we favor, we should assume that during the Nazi period, a legal career, however unsuccessful, and unquestionably a highly successful writing career would have had to rely on the regime's forbearance, if not support.

Both Alexander Spoerl and Lovis Wambach have claimed that Spoerl gave up his legal career once he saw how arbitrary Nazi "justice" had become.[116] Yet several aspects make such a disinterested move seem unlikely. Among them are the fact that Spoerl's abandonment of his legal practice and his move to Berlin, the Nazi headquarters of power (in 1937) followed swiftly upon the publication and financial success of *The Muzzle* (in 1936); that Spoerl joined both the Reich's Literature and its Film Chamber (*Reichsschrifttumskammer* and *Reichsfilmkammer*)—although, granted, never the Nazi party; and that he seems to have been on cordial terms with the Nazi regime's most important cultural agencies. He regularly wrote for Goebbels's militant paper *Attack* (*Angriff*), recommended the propagandistic use of positive reviews of his work published in the Nazi party's weekly *Völkisch Observer* (*Völkischer Beobachter*), rejoiced when Goebbels invited him to an official function, and thanked Goebbels in person for giving him the idea for *The Gasman* (*Der Gasmann*, 1940), one of his most beloved novels.[117] All this seems to indicate that Spoerl made his arrangements with the regime, perhaps even "more than was necessary for survival."[118]

Were that to be the case, it would not be devoid of irony, for Spoerl's tremendous success rests largely on his creation of a literary world carefully cleansed of the historical horrors he lived through. The author's priorities may have lain with Treskow and his tragic inner conflict, but consumers of *The Muzzle*, be it novel, movies or plays, seemed far more interested in comedy. Much like *The Captain of Köpenick* (some reviews of the 1938 hit play *The Muzzle* actually referred to it as a "Köpenickiade"[119]), this comedy pits the natural wit of lower-class characters against the State, resulting in a minor and hilarious infraction of the State's authority to which the State responds with a wag of the finger and an indulgent smile. It goes without saying that this view of the State made great fodder for Nazi propagandists. As the *Völkisch Observer*, party organ of one of the most repressive regimes the world has ever seen, put it in its review of the 1938 *Muzzle* play, "This play is about all things human. It is about the people's profound and primal desire to mouth off."[120]

If Spoerl's "human" stories enabled the Nazi State to misrepresent itself as one in which people could safely "mouth off," it is surely also significant that public interest in these tales continued unabated for decades after the fall of the regime (the last cinematic adaptation of *The Muzzle*, so far at least, appeared in 1997). The wholesome, humanitarian Germany originally created by Spoerl is being constantly recreated by his readers, and what that world conceals is as significant as what it portrays. To retain access to that land to which no war, no Nazi terror, no concentration camp has ever come, readers must disregard the degree to which its creator was willing to turn a blind eye to all of it in order to recreate this German idyll in one book after the other. Entering Spoerl's fictitious Germany required and still requires reading his books as humorous sketches of "human nature" and simultaneously holding "human nature" incapable of starting World Wars or gassing other humans. From the promo blurb of a 1960s edition of *The Muzzle*: "Spoerl, that witty connoisseur of human nature, does not whitewash, he only presents everything in its proper light, gifting to the reader liberating laughter and a pensive smile about forgiveable human weaknesses."[121]

Paul Gurk's Uncrackable Safe Crackers

A final work that deserves honorable mention as an exemplary crime farce is Paul Gurk's 1935 novel *Safe Cracking (Tresoreinbruch)*, not only because it is partly based on the career of the Brothers Sass but also because it is one of the most innovative crime novels of the period. *Safe Cracking* is a big city novel where buildings and objects are endowed with life and humans are atrophied to the point of thingness, a vivid eccentric work that could proudly take its place next to Döblin's *Berlin Alexanderplatz* or Dos Passos's *Manhattan Transfer*[122]—if anyone still knew about it. Like the equally brilliant, equally unconventional, equally prolific and equally unsuccessful Walter Serner, Paul Gurk, author of 30 novels, 53 novellas, and innumerable poems, fairy tales, grotesques, paintings and drawings, was forgotten because "even during his lifetime (1880–1953) he fell through the cracks of all stylistic trends, wasn't ranked by the quickly-adjudicating critics, couldn't be made available to posterity for cheap consumption."[123] Today, about half of his novels are still available in their original editions from the 1920s–40s; and three were reprinted as part of a failed attempt at rediscovery in the 1980s.[124] At the time of this writing (2017), the Darmstadt publisher Agora is planning a 15-volume collected works edition, of which only one volume (consisting of his novel *Berlin*, orig. 1934) has appeared so far.

That Gurk was a major anthropophobe probably didn't help his sales. Most of what we know about his life comes from his own autobiography, which he wrote in the third person in 1944, and from a brief text called "Self-Encounter" ("Selbstbegegnung"), in which he described the writing process as follows:

> I write exclusively for myself, in ghastly conditions, lonely and anthropophobic to the point of exclusivity, to the point of physical pain. For years my soul has wandered the streets, and I suppose my body will end up on the streets as well. The life of a true writer, with a secretary, a telephone, a house in the country and public philanthropy is so far beyond my imagining that I couldn't bear it anymore. I am frightened by each of the very rare letters I still receive because I always sense that life will play a dirty trick on me.... At times I am asked how my works are written, to which I can only say: I don't have a library or a desk. I write on my knees and with great speed... but what does that explain? Nothing![125]

Gurk's *Safe Cracking* follows a similar path: it wanders the streets and in the end explains nothing. Surrounded by many subplots about crimes both major and minor, its main plot is inspired by the career of the Brothers Sass. Gurk endowed his characters Albert and Otto Maas with the same nonchalant genius and shrewd wit that characterized Franz and Erich Sass. Like the Brothers Sass, the Brothers Maas are profoundly unconflicted about their choice of profession. They worry that their younger brother Robert, who doesn't quite have the talent for the job, might end up as a law-abiding person; they regret that the gifted juggler Jussuf wastes his talents on the circus instead of using his nimble fingers to steal wallets and watches. Nothing against the Maas brothers can ever proven, but everyone knows what they do for a living (indeed, they openly list "Safe Crackers" as their official occupation on forms). On the job, the Brothers are endlessly patient, aware that their investment of time and effort will eventually pay off: "No vending machine will give you anything if you don't first put in your dime," says Albert.[126] As individuals, too, the Brothers Maas are distinctly characterized in ways highly reminiscent of the Brothers Sass: Albert is the taciturn genius planner who oversees every job and its execution, Otto the silver-tongued devil who bamboozles the police and charms the public. And like the Sass Brothers, the Maas Brothers carry no weapons: "The Brothers did not work with knives and revolvers. Blood doesn't pay. Much better to bust out of jail at the right time or, if it couldn't be avoided, to allow the police and the Penal Code to score a goal in the soccer game of their lives."[127]

The man playing center-forward on the opposing team is Detective Franz Steppmann, whose baldness not only recalls that of his real-life original Max Fabich, but also saddles him, in the novel, with an affectionate nickname: Bowling Ball ("Schusterkugel"). Bowling Ball ardently pursues the Brothers and has made it his life's ambition to nail them, but is also, much like his real-life original, full of admiration for their work and capable of cordiality towards them, even during interrogations. "No formalities, dear Otto! It's not like we've been pummeling or ratting on each other! To you, I'm simply Bowling Ball, and I'm on informal terms with every honest safe cracker."[128] Like Fabich did, Steppmann even offers the Maas Brothers his assistance if they would ever consider retirement, and he ceaselessly wonders why the Brothers, who are neither liars nor idiots, have opted to lead a life of crime: "At bottom, you are quite bourgeois and you lead bourgeois lives. You are together, you help each other. Why don't you want to lead honest lives, Albert, be a part of the *Volk*, join in with the Great Community?" Albert's contemptuous response is eerily prescient of the 1940 court verdict against the Sass Brothers, in which—five years after the publication of Gurk's novel—the judge voiced his conviction that the Brothers would never "find their way into the community of the *Volk*." "I *am* honest!," Albert tells Steppmann. "This is why I can't be part of the *Volk* or the Community. Sometimes I read the papers. They always talk a lot of community, especially when people beat each other up.—Be honest, Bowling Ball, and think about it: Have you ever seen a Community?"[129] Bowling Ball, in the end, concludes that the Maas Brothers can't be cracked open: "You are put together like a good, new safe. Your steel walls are smooth and seamless. No drill and no crowbar will pry you open!"[130]

The Maas Brothers' greatest break-in in the novel obviously harks back to the Sass's greatest coup, the March 1929 attack on the Disconto bank. Widely seen as the age's most sensational bank robbery, it would certainly still have lodged clearly in the minds of readers when Gurk's novel appeared six years later. Much of Gurk's account could have been lifted straight from 1929 news reporting: the shouty headlines—"*Safe Cracking!!!,*" in bold face and adorned with multiple exclamation points; reports on panicked customers and baffled policemen; the underground tunnel; the unmarked vault door; the safe doors that seemed totally untouched but swung open by themselves; the speculation that there must have been a large gang of safe crackers at work. Bowling Bawl takes one look at the scene and pronounces it to have been "Maas Work" (the German original, "Maasarbeit!," is a play on words with "Massarbeit," precision work). Of course he interrogates the Brothers, knowing well that "Only Albert Maas has the brains for this!,"[131] and of course he gets nowhere.

The Brothers, released for lack of evidence, unwind from their arduous labor on a seaside holiday; their last appearance in the novel shows them bronzed, relaxed, and retrieving their enormous loot from its clever hiding place. Bowling Ball, conversely, sees his entire career invalidated by his failure to convict the clever Brothers. Watching Albert and Otto drive past in a luxury car, each with two pretty blondes on their knees, is the last straw. "Society, the State, Order seemed to him a cracked vault, its safe long since emptied. And he stood in front of it and risked his life to guard broken locks and empty deposit boxes!"[132] In despair, Bowling Ball resigns his commission, even giving up his police pension. "Perhaps," the novel concludes, "someone should have come to tell him that a renewal of the myth must happen, a Community composed of Difference, an Order composed of living Nobility, and that he should wait and hope for the Great Reversal. But there was nobody like that in the police station—or maybe he was on vacation that day."[133]

Breaking In and Breaking Out

As the novel's final sentence indicates, its author was every bit as suspicious as the Maas brothers of the newly established *Volksgemeinschaft*, an ignoble "community" that suppressed all difference (unsurprisingly, Gurk's novel was outlawed and existing copies pulped after the Nazis came to power[134]) and pronounced itself irreversible, a Thousand-Year Reich. The greatest crime committed in Gurk's world—and in this, it resembles the criminal underworld of Walter Serner's stories—is its failure to acknowledge its own quintessential criminality. Much like the criminals of Serner's underworld, only criminals in Gurk's novel are truly free. The story of the brilliant Maas Brothers is really no more than a point of departure to make this point; they are just two swimmers in the sea of humanity portrayed in the novel.[135]

With the notable exception of Bowling Ball, all characters in the novel are major or minor criminals. There is Jussuf, the brilliant juggler, who knows the Maas Brothers are criminals but doesn't mind a bit because he's never met an honest person in his entire life. There is the beautiful prostitute, commonly referred to as the "Sex Seller" ("Geschlechtsverkäuferin"), who describes herself as a student of physics and chemistry, which seems like a salacious joke until it turns out to be literally true: when not making money on her back, she is a genius physicist working on splitting the atom. There is Frau Lehmann who performs abortions on demand with a lucrative sideline as a soothsayer and palm reader. There is the criminally disgraced former lawyer Ottomar Zeckau, who runs a thriving practice as a "Corner Consultant" ("Winkelkonsulent") for other criminals and sleeps in a coffin like a vampire. There are the five money forgers who only know each other as A, B, C, D and E. B, a gifted but failed artist, knows that while his drawings and paintings will rot away in a box, unseen and unappreciated by anyone, his outstanding forgery of a 100 mark bill will be bought, appreciated and collected by thousands. After the band of forgers has moved out, a religious sect moves in, turning the apartment into its headquarters to fleece the faithful. There are the customers of the bank robbed by the Brothers who smell an ideal opportunity to vastly overestimate their losses and defraud the insurance company: "The breakdown of their losses offered by the robbed customers and their indemnity claims peculiarly laid bare the human soul, or rather the soul-replacements common at the time."[136] Beyond Bowling Ball, the novel's most honest person is the poor cobbler Lambert, who is, paradoxically, also the only character who actually has a criminal record. Released from prison, he tries to make an honest living, but is spurned by all for his past and finally murdered by another ex-con. The murderer escapes with all of Lambert's worldly possessions, amounting to the grand total of 1.80 marks, which, in a paroxysm of remorse, he spends on a wreath for the cobbler's grave.

Just as the novel portrays nearly all humans as criminals, safe-cracking and break-ins become metaphors for all human activity,[137] an easy cipher for what Goethe's Faust would have called "striving." Bowling Ball vainly tries to crack the impenetrable safe that is the Maas Brothers. The unsuccessful writer and later suicide Titus Lamm longs to "break into the nine-times bolted Vault of Language, to free it, to become a poet."[138] The Sex Seller asks Jussuf whether he plays with balls because he's no longer capable of "breaking into a woman."[139] She herself dies the moment she realizes her dream of splitting the atom: "Now the obsessed woman cleaved open the door of the vault and broke into the most secure treasure chamber in the world! The atom is split and has released the treasures of its superhuman powers!"[140] And Frau Lehmann views her side-line of card-laying and palm-reading as a "break-in into the future."[141] All human strife is criminal activity, and all criminal activity, labelled as a "break-in," is really the act of breaking out, for honesty leads to total subordination under and subsumption into a "community" bare of both myth and nobility and intolerant of difference. The only life it permits is a kind of living death—waiting for change, guarding empty safes. All honest men, like Bowling Ball or Titus Lamm, or those who try to reform, like the ex-jailbird Lambert, fail to survive in this community; in the end, they resign their commission, shoot themselves, or have their heads bashed in for a mark and eighty pfennigs. No wonder that the elder Maas brothers contemplate the death of their younger brother Robert, killed by a stray bullet, with equanimity: "It is better this way. He would never have been more than an honest man."[142]

Much like Serner's stories, Gurk's novel shows how porous the border is between the "lawful" or "decent" and the lawless or illicit. Both, in the end, portray candid criminality as far more honest than the hypocritical decency of the law-abiding *Volk*. Both authors also take a step beyond the common view of the criminal as an archetype of freedom—although this is undoubtedly a major part of their portrayal of any criminal character. "I am no Jumping Jack whose strings you can pull," Albert tells Bowling Ball in the scene in which the detective tries to convince him of the virtues of an honest life.[143] In the end, Paul Gurk, writing in 1935, makes explicit what Serner, writing around 1925, constantly implied: that terms like honesty and criminality are themselves farcical—in the sense of meaningless—when their meanings are determined by a criminal society. The "myth" for whose renewal Bowling Ball cannot wait would be the return of these terms to a fixed and reliable meaning.[144] The Great Reversal would occur when what is "criminal" and what is "honest" is not defined by a State that is itself run by criminals, but rooted in a moral worldview on which a "community of difference" can agree. Until that reversal happens, all you can do is wait for it while doing your bit of dishonest work and steadfastly refusing all attempts to integrate you into the honest community of the *Volk*. For resistance against an oppressive State is criminality—or will, inevitably, be defined as such by that State—and the goal of criminality is simple survival. "Why are people so hopelessly honest if in the end they die of consumption anyway?," asks Otto, and Albert has the answer: "You're not supposed to be honest. You're supposed to be alive."[145]

Art v. Propaganda: Literary Criticism, Nazi-Style

How did literature and film stay "alive" in a State that was not only built on the idea of racial superiority but also increasingly advocated the destruction of racial "inferiors"? Can we conceive of literature written, or films produced during such a regime, yet somehow untouched by its most principal philosophy? The regime itself liked to pretend so; it distinguished clearly between propaganda versus art or entertainment. Hitler himself is on record as insisting that never the twain should meet:

> I want to exploit the film as an instrument of propaganda, but in such a way that every theatregoer may be clearly aware that on such and such an occasion he is going to see a political film. It nauseates me when I find political propaganda hiding under the cloak of art. Let it be either art or politics. The subject matter strikes me as immaterial. The artistic effort must be 100%. The saccharine gruel that has been put on the screen lately has been enough to chase away every person of judgement.[146]

Most of what the NS regime produced in terms of literature and film fell, apparently, under the heading of art (or at least entertainment), not politics. We don't have to take the regime's word for this; the Allies that shut it down and postwar scholars overwhelmingly agree. There were few card-carrying Nazis in the movie industry, which was, in fact, considered "a hotbed—however passive—of limited resistance to the government."[147] Of 1,363 feature films made between 1933 and 1945, only 208 were banned after the Second World War for containing Nazi propaganda, and a 1951 catalogue of 700 proscribed films published by the Allied Control Commission claims that even of those 700 considered dangerous enough to be blacklisted, "only 141 were politically objectionable."[148] That Goebbels, as late as 1938, had to instruct the German film industry to start producing overtly antisemitic films, with each studio ordered to contribute one such film,[149] may well have meant either that studios were not voluntarily snapping to it or that they weren't doing so fast enough for Goebbels's taste. Even during the war years, which obviously saw an increased production of outright propaganda films, their total share of the cinematic market never exceeded 25 percent.[150]

And yet it is difficult to argue with Siegfried Kracauer when he states categorically that "all Nazi films were more or less propaganda films—even the mere entertainment pictures which seem to be remote from politics."[151] Kracauer's implication—that a "remoteness" from politics, real or pretended, does not mean neutrality or disinterestedness—applies to literature every bit as much as it does to cinema. All of the texts and films discussed so far understood themselves as, and were read by others for the purpose of, "mere entertainment"; all presented themselves as suitably "remote from politics." Yet the regime, while not explicitly requiring pro–NS propaganda or rabid antisemitism in every literary work, had a way of expressing its displeasure. Literary criticism, NS-style, could result in the destruction of both the work and its author. Writers like Heinrich Spoerl, whose works presented a worldview that either complemented that of the Nazis or could be made functional in that context, flourished. Works that could not or would not were banned, pulped or burned (including works by Bettauer, Zuckmayer, Serner, and Gurk); their authors silenced like Serner and Gurk, driven into exile like Zuckmayer, or murdered like Bettauer and Serner. The closer Germany inched towards war, the more untenable the spurious distinction between "art" and politics became, and the more often the façade was dropped: mere months before Germany's invasion of Poland, the critic Erich Langenbucher expressly called for more antisemitic crime fiction.[152]

Antisemitic Crime Caper: Hans Zerlett's Farcical Criminals

It is worth casting a passing glance at two texts that complied: Hans H. Zerlett's film *Robert and Bertram* (*Robert und Bertram*) and Pieter Coll's crime novel *The Nagotkin Case* (*Der Fall Nagotkin*, both 1939). *Robert and Bertram*, the Nazi era's only antisemitic musical crime caper, is routinely listed among the regime's most egregious antisemitic films, in the company of *Linen from Ireland* (*Leinen aus Irland*, 1939), *The Rothschilds* (*Die Rothschilds*, 1940), *Jew Süss* (*Jud Süss*, 1940), and the infamous *Eternal Jew* (*Der ewige Jude*, 1940).[153] *Robert and Bertram* pits the lovable, farcical and witty Aryan criminal against the sinister repulsive Jewish crook who, it goes without saying, commits the real crimes of exploiting and defrauding the German people. Released in 1939, the film is set precisely 100 years earlier, in an idyllicized preindustrial 1839 in which German villagers wear traditional costumes, speak plainly, eat and drink heartily, and dance folk dances with childlike abandon.

All characters except for Robert and Bertram themselves bear descriptive names: there is the German Michel, a shy, softhearted and whiney man-child based on the "allegorical figure 'German Michel' with his sleeping cap, who since the sixteenth-century peasant wars has symbolized Germany's good-natured but sleepy People unable to forge a successful revolution"[154] (the film's Michel is gratifyingly turned into a "real man" by Prussian military discipline). There is the innkeeper's daughter Lenchen Lips, who loves Michel and only waits for him to "man up" in order to marry him, and whose Aryan credentials are established by virtue of her blue eyes, blond braids, and her act of gifting a huge ham to Michel's mother. There is Herr Biedermeier, whose name simultaneously signifies an upright citizen, a petty bourgeois, and the Biedermeier period in which the film is set and which was later caricatured for its avoidance of politics and its withdrawal into petty philistinism and materialism. And there is the immeasurably rich and grasping Jew Nathan Ipelmeyer, whose name simultaneously indicates wickedness (just as "Bieder" means "good," "'Ipel' is a South German variation of *übel*, meaning 'evil'") and Jewishness (*meyer* being the more conventional spelling for Jewish names).[155]

If characters like Michel, Lenchen and her father Lips represent the honest German peasantry whose livelihoods and happiness are being destroyed by greedy and exploitative Jews, Biedermeier represents the duped "inferior Aryan" and "Jew-lackey"[156] collaborating in this destruction. Biedermeier's quest to force Lenchen to marry him leads him to borrow money from Ipelmeyer (at shameless interest rates, of course) in order to buy up Lips's mortgage and thus force his hand. Robert and Bertram, the film's two lovable rogues and genius thieves, overhear Biedermeier's scheme and vow to repay Lips and Lenchen for their kindness by saving them from the misguided Aryan and the grasping Jew. Posing as a Count and a famous Professor, they manage to snag an invitation to a masked ball at Ipelmeyer's palace, where they relieve all the guests of their money and jewels. They send the loot to Lenchen and her father, instructing them to turn it over to Biedermeier in repayment of their mortgage, knowing that Biedermeier will have no choice but to return the jewels to Ipelmeyer, who is now pressing Biedermeier for repayment of the loan. The story ends happily: Michel, who has traded his sleeping cap for a handsome Prussian uniform and his childlike demeanor for suitable machismo, marries Lenchen; Ipelmeyer and his entire *mishpocheh* are ridiculed; Robert and Bertram float off in a hot air balloon, straight to heaven, where their minor crimes are forgiven and their greater virtues rewarded.

While films like *Jew Süss* and *The Eternal Jew* seek to portray Jewish "infiltration" of Aryan societies as a menace, *Robert and Bertram* spends much of its time ridiculing failed Jewish attempts at assimilation. Jews in the film are all too easily recognized by virtue of their crooked noses, flat feet, Yiddish accents, and hoity-toity airs. At the café, where Robert and Bertram instantly recognize Ipelmeyer by his profile, Ipelmeyer orders the financial gazette, caviar and champagne, whereas Bertram feasts, like any "real" German, on a ham sandwich and beer while reading the *Königlich Privilegirte Zeitung*, Berlin's oldest newspaper. Much of the film's representation of Jews is a literalization of Hitler's claim that Jews are limited to bad imitations of their host-peoples' cultures because they do not possess a culture of their own.[157] When Robert introduces himself to Ipelmeyer as the Count of Monte Cristo, Ipelmeyer is deeply impressed: "Famous line, ancient nobility," he says in his thick Yiddish twang, simultaneously displaying his bad German and his ignorance of Dumas's famous novel.[158] The ball scene practically teems with jokes playing on "Jewish" ignorance of "Aryan" cultures: Ipelmeyer, dressed up as "Louis Quatorze the Fifteenth" and his wife, dressed as "Madame Pampadour" (Pompadour), tell their daughter Isidora, who is costumed as "Queen Cleptomania" (Cleopatra), that she looks like the "Venus of Medicine" (Venus de Medici) and instruct the orchestra director to play the "Ofentüre" (oven door, as opposed to the overture). The saddest object of ridicule is Isidora's suitor Samuel, who, dressed in a knight's armor, clatters helplessly around the ball, unable to sit, dance or kneel to propose to his lady love. Samuel the Tin Man not only symbolizes the inherent contradiction of a

Jewish "man at arms"[159] (in all-too-obvious contrast to the masculinization of Michel in the army), but also amplifies the point made about all the other masqued Jews: Jews, the message is, may don the trappings of Aryan culture, but they'll never understand its deeper meanings.

"Jewish" corruption also comes in for its share of lampooning, for example in Ipelmeyer's lascivious pursuit of the lead ballet dancer, his stern orders to his daughter not to marry anyone for less than a million, and in a conversation with his Jewish attorney, whom he sternly informs that he knows he's been stealing from him and sleeping with his wife, and that he'll be fired if there's even one more thing. When one (Aryan) guest, surveying the lavish palace stuffed to the rafters with opulent kitsch, remarks to another that the place must have cost Ipelmeyer a fortune, another retorts that "It's even cost several fortunes,"[160] implying, of course, that Ipelmeyer's wealth rests on the misfortune of others whom he has defrauded and ruined.

As farcical characters, the film's lovable rogues Robert and Bertram are an uncomplicated blend of contradictions. They are thieves but refreshingly unconcerned with money. Their lives of crime are dedicated to the higher cause of justice. They are aware of the ills of the world: in a scene towards the end, they read an 1839 newspaper, commenting with sadness on wars, rebellions and upheavals everywhere but assuring each other that "it'll all be very different in a hundred years."[161] But they are also carefree and cheerful, ready to break into a song and dance with minimal provocation. They take occasional imprisonment with a sense of humor: "I'll take this room," says Bertram as he's shoved rudely into a prison cell, while Robert, interned in the cell above him, bangs out a melody on the bars of his window.

Robert and Bertram are the film's only characters who are not endowed with a "descriptive" name, but arguably, they do not need one, since they hark back all too obviously to the amiable rascals of literature and lore, from Til Eulenspiegel to Robin Hood to the amiable Good-for-Nothings of the German Romantic tradition.[162] They are ciphers, not characters, and thus they are neither required to undergo a development nor charged with finding their place in society. As characters, they would have represented a vagabondism and indolence that would have jarred harshly with the regime's work ethic: they did, after all, skip and dance across Germany's screens at a time when the Nazis routinely denounced "beggars" and "tramps" just like them as "work-shy" and deported them to concentration camps.[163] As symbols, however, they were simultaneously assigned the role of saving the German *Volk* from Jewish greed and granted license to refuse integration into the German *Volksgemeinschaft*. "You are a washed-up genius, and I am a drop-out bourgeois, one who would rather be a tramp than a conformist," says Bertram to Robert.[164] The film grants them special dispensation to remain lovable nonconformists in the penultimate scene, which shows them behind bars again. The audience is briefly allowed to think that they are back in jail, until the camera pans back to reveal them gazing through an iron bar fence at a sculpture garden, with Bertram stating pensively: "You see, Robert, that's life. Bars everywhere. The only difference is that some look out through the bars and others look in. I'd rather look out." Robert responds laconically: "Well, then just let 'em lock you up again."[165]

This is more than merely a joke on the "farcical view of incarceration," which jokes that the "advantage to being locked up is that the view is better,"[166] it is also an admission that for incurable rascals like Robert and Bertram, going back "inside" is the only way to be "included" in society. Ultimately, the understanding of Robert and Bertram as ciphers rather than characters is also the reason for the film's ending, which sends them to heaven while still alive, thus confirming that there is no place for them on Earth, that they cannot be subsumed into the *Volk*. (A planned alternate ending, which called for just such an integration—Robert and Bertram join the military and end up serving the *Volk* under Michel's command—was never realized.[167]) Instead, Robert and Bertram find their place not in the community of the *Volk* but in that of the angels, looking down (and, of course, out) from on high. Heaven, the only place where being "inside" does not mean imprisonment, is therefore also the only proper home for the lovable rogues, a point made visually as the heavy iron bars of the Pearly Gates clang shut behind them.

The film's most central point is not its contrast between Jewish criminality and corruption with Aryan/German forthrightness, honesty, simplicity and so forth, but its juxtaposition of the Jewish and the German criminal. *Only* the German criminal can be funny or lovable, the film asserts; all "true" crime, conversely, is committed by Jews, who are portrayed as "an 'abstract' force of modern capitalism, creatures whose very identity is counterfeit."[168] But this depiction is not contrasted with that of the German criminal as an individual, on the contrary. The sympathetic German rascal is equally "abstract," a creature whose identity is, if not counterfeit, then at least make-believe.[169] That Robert and Bertram are not meant to be characters but symbols banishes them from contemporary "reality" and propels them into the realm of both myth and farce. This is precisely how Tobis Studios, the film's production company, marketed and advertised the film: "So get into the refreshing bath of genuine cheerfulness, the great German film farce of Tobis, *Robert und Bertram*."[170] Yet in 1939, the year of the film's appearance, farce was on its way out, documented not only by the film's miserable box office numbers, but also by the many reviews that flatly denied the film's farcical nature by emphasizing its "realistic" portrayal of Jewish characters (played, without exception, by gentile actors).[171] Hitler, too, refused to see *Robert and Bertram* as a farce, complaining to Goebbels that it "maligned" Germans.[172] In a spectacular failure to view the film in any way but literally, he misread the Robin Hood–types Robert and Bertram—and even Michel and Biedermeier, whose very names define them as allegories—as actual characters, stand-ins not for myths but reality. Later critics have speculated that Hitler's humorlessness may have been to blame for the fact that *Robert and Bertram* remained the Nazi era's only antisemitic comedy. Henceforth, only "bitter satire was allowed for the purpose of ridiculing 'sub-humans,'"[173] and film and literature dutifully buckled down to a generic depiction of Jews as treacherous monsters whose evil machinations, uncovered only on the brink of global apocalypse, imperil the world.

Antisemitic Crime Fiction: Pieter Coll's Tragic Victims

The rise of the monstrous Jewish criminal (and the concomitant demise of the lovable, farcical German crook) is aptly documented by Pieter Coll's[174] (pseud. for Heinz Otto) novel *The Nagotkin Case* (*Der Fall Nagotkin*). Written in the year in which *Robert and Bertram* appeared and praised at the time for its appealing "combination of political-philosophical attitude with a gripping adventurous plot and the victorious struggle against the Jewish global enemy,"[175] it is a weakly plotted, badly written, sluggishly paced tome that reads more like an antisemitic tirade than a crime story. Jan Leumac, a young reporter in Paris and eye witness to the brutal murder of a man, easily identifies the killer—by virtue of "two narrowly spaced, piercing black eyes and broad cheekbones beneath a low forehead"[176]—as a Jew. The victim turns out to be the Russian immigrant Nagotkin, an economist and erstwhile director of a Jewish-owned bank. When Jan teams up with Inspektor Blun to solve the crime, they discover that the bank covered up Jewish fraud in the service of a sinister international crime organization called the All-Jewish Combat League ("Alljüdischer Kampfverband"), whose crime portfolio includes scamming the civilized world out of billions, selling Aryan girls into slavery and prostitution, and, of course, countless murders. When Jan publishes an article in which he claims, based on no evidence whatsoever, that Nagotkin's murder was the work of an international crime organization, he is promptly abducted and tortured by the evil Jews. The novel ends with Jan's rescue, the gratifying destruction of the Jewish crime organization in Paris, and a call to all civilized governments worldwide to follow suit. "I can only hope," Blun sermonizes at the end of the novel, "that the Gentlemen in our Government—now that we can prove the criminal activities of Jews—will finally learn their lesson and stop consorting with this rabble! [...] As long as ever new criminal impulses originate from Judah, our work will never be done."[177]

Coll's book fails miserably as a crime story because it subordinates everything that makes a story—setting, plot, conflict, resolution, and especially characterization—to antisemitic diatribes. The book's criminal is not an individual (and therefore also not subject to characterization of any kind) but a global conspiracy. Its members include the fake Russian emigrant, bogus military hero and phony aristocrat Captain von Sodonoff (later unmasked as the criminal mastermind Herschel Wallach Silberstein); his underling, the fat and gluttonous Jew Schwarzbart; the sadistic torturer Pjotr, who has learned the business as the apprentice of a Rabbi whom he assisted in performing ritual slaughters; and, of course, Nagotkin's murderer, a scary Scarface who earns his money as a fiddling clown in a seedy bar. All are typified by simple physiognomy (low foreheads, piercing black eyes, extreme obesity, crooked noses, and nasty scars), seedy surroundings (strip clubs, pots of money, tasteless kitsch, expensive champagne by the bucketful, and jazz music) and offences ranging from financial crimes and document forgery to drug-dealing, white slavery, torture and murder. The All-Jewish Combat League is all-powerful and blessed both with limitless funds and the backing of the misguided French government. (This is why, as Blun repeatedly fumes, he can't even get a search warrant for Jewish-owned properties; in one scene, he instructs his police force to just go in shooting since he knows that no Jew will be convicted in a court of law.)

Coll's novel paints a world in which all criminals are Jews, all Jews are criminals and guilt can therefore be safely assumed from the outset. Paranoia, it logically follows, is a perfectly rational response, even if it is consistently debunked: Blun (incorrectly) suspects Jan of being a Jewish co-conspirator; Jan (falsely) suspects Nagotkin's daughter Anja, with whom he is in love, of the same; Frau Nagotkin (wrongly) sees an evil Jewish agent in every policeman investigating her husband's murder. Victims are individuals but criminals aren't. All this means that Coll's book cannot play by the rules of the traditional crime novel, which assumes that criminals are individuals, that individuality implies some sort of motive, and that motive necessitates at least some characterization. In the absence of individual criminality, the novel can dispense with such niceties as motive, evidence, and character portrayal and simply base its investigation on the insinuation of "common knowledge" about Jews. The combination of the Jews' certain guilt and their total imperviousness to prosecution deletes most options open to the traditional crime novel: there can be neither a Whodunit nor questions about motive. Nor can there be an evidence-based investigation rooted in a comprehensible logic, a logic on which not only criminal investigation normally depends, but on whose reconstruction the pleasure of reading a crime novel depends as well.

The deletion of this logic and its replacement with tortured psychology and antisemitic bias yields a reading experience that is simultaneously baffling and boring. No rationale is offered for the assumption that Nagotkin was murdered by a crime organization rather than a simple robber: readers are simply expected to surmise, as Jan and Blun do, that only a worldwide Jewish conspiracy would have the clout to conceal a killer. How is Joco the Clown first suspected as Nagotkin's killer? Because Blun thinks it unlikely that someone extroverted enough to perform on stage at night would spend his days out of the limelight, which to him means as much as: in hiding. And how does Blun arrive at the conclusion that Schwarzbart, who dies of poison mid-interrogation, was murdered? Because everyone knows, of course, that Jews are too cowardly to commit suicide. Protected globally by the powerful worldwide Jewish lobby and locally by the French government, all criminals are totally untouchable by the police, mock their efforts and glory in their own crimes. The novel's constant refrain is that the "adversary" (its most common designation for its Jewish criminals) "is strong and works with the craftiest means."[178] And yet, these wily and invulnerable criminals inevitably blanch in terror whenever a cop appears on the scene (readers who think that there is a contradiction here are clearly not paranoid enough). Sodonoff turns pale whenever Blun shows up to ask him a few (not particularly probing) questions; Joco the Clown—Nagotkin's murderer—starts visibly at the sight of Jan and later practically faints in terror when the police enter the bar where he works; Schwarzbart turns pasty-white when Blun appears at the door. Such feeble clues are inevitably elevated to the status of incontrovertible proof: Jan knew that Joco had murdered Nagotkin when he noticed that he "was startled at the sight of him"[179]; Blun, asked how he knew that Schwarzbart had ordered a co-conspirator's murder, answers that "He was so surprised and scared when I appeared in the bar that his manner betrayed him."[180] In the absence of actual evidence for any crime, it's a jolly good thing that these criminal masterminds have their countenances so badly under control.

Jews in the novel are painted as a danger to civilized society not only because of the extreme brutality of their crimes, but also because of their ability to delegitimize civilized identity. When Blun breaks into the offices of the All-Jewish Combat League, he finds himself wading knee-deep in forged passports of all nations, adorned with the counterfeited signatures of every civil servant worldwide entrusted with signing passports, in addition to fake birth and baptismal certificates, identity cards, work books, insurance cards, even train tickets. Forgery, of course, not merely enables infiltration, but also spells the invalidation of the "true" (documented) identity of Aryans. The scene reads like a bureaucratized visualization of the Hitlerian adage that Jews rely on imitating their host nations' cultures because they don't have a culture of their own. Just as in *Robert and Bertram*, all Jewish identity is counterfeit.

Coll's novel does not straddle the fine line between fiction and propaganda, it smudges it. Within the text, the transition is most clearly marked by the elimination of one of the characters most central to the period's crime fiction, the farcical criminal—and the introduction of another: the tragic victim. The farcical criminal and the tragic victim are mutually exclusive; they cannot inhabit the same crime story. There are no tragic victims in Zuckmayer's and Spoerl's tales, whose farcical criminals do not harm anyone. It is impossible to identify or sympathize with, much less fear for, the dupes of Serner's farcical criminals. In Bettauer's novel, there is no victim: its farcical "criminal" has not actually committed a crime. The victim of the crime caper described in Gurk's novel is a faceless institution, not an individual for whom one might feel pity.

Robert und Bertram can be seen as a transitional text between fiction and propaganda, in that it attempts to combine a crime caper featuring two farcical crooks with a tragic victim story: Lips might be ruined financially; Lenchen might end up forced to marry the Jewish lackey Biedermeier. In Coll's work, finally, the farcical criminal has lost his place. He is supplanted by his polar opposite, the tragic victim. The novel's tragic victims include the pitiable banker Nagotkin, who leaves his post in remorse for his collaboration with Jews and is brutally stabbed in the back; his grief-stricken wife and daughter, whose distress and terror of the crime organization are granted extensive narrative space; and Jan as a victim of sadistic torture and potential murder victim (the scenes in which Jan's captors describe to him the fate they have planned for him, in lascivious and pornographic detail, are among the most sickening in the novel). And yet, despite all the lip service paid to their suffering, Coll barely bothers with characterization. In a propaganda novel, this makes sense, for the tragic victim is nothing but the counterpart to the faceless, evil organization that serves as the new criminal. Characterizing the victim is senseless in a work that seeks to evoke not pity but panic: "We have taken out a hornets' nest that was damned dangerous for our city and our country," Blun lectures at the end. "But I fear that this will not do us much good; for if you cut off one head of this hydra, two, three and even more heads will grow in other places."[181]

The propagandistic crime novel spurns the farce's buffoonery and horseplay, but retains the genre's ludicrously improbable situations and crude characterizations. Crimes are assumed, not proven; insinuation takes the place of evidence; paranoia is not irrational but a perfectly sensible response; victims are defined as tragic but too crudely characterized to arouse pity. It is partly this lack of characterization that makes the tragic victim the polar opposite of the farcical criminal. A farcical criminal must be sufficiently individualized to earn the audience's sympathy and mirth. The tragic victim, conversely, is insipid enough to be anyone, and it is this very blandness that marks him as a cast member central to any propagandistic crime story. For just as the individual criminal is replaced with a faceless global conspiracy, the tragic victim is merely a cipher for an all-encompassing victimhood to which we can respond neither with laughter nor pity but only with terror: the downfall of nations, the decay of civilization, the annihilation of culture.

Resolutions?

Neverending Stories
(1950–2001)

Firsts and Fissures

> "I understand how. I do not understand why."—Winston Smith in George Orwell's *Nineteen Eighty-Four* (1948)

> "...under conditions of terror most people will comply but *some people will not,* just as the lesson of the countries to which the Final Solution was proposed is that 'it could happen' in most places but *it did not happen everywhere.*"—Hannah Arendt, *Eichmann in Jerusalem* (1963)

All normality establishes itself by reference to whatever it defines as abnormal. On the other side of the abnormal—in this case, writing about criminals and Jews—is, or should be, the idea of normal: an articulation of what it meant to be a citizen whose compact with his or her nation involved accepting its protections and consenting to its laws. Normality, however, requires a modicum of stability to establish itself as such, and in the time period under discussion, normality was repeatedly torpedoed by a quick succession of "never-befores" and "first-time-evers." The Empire (1870–1918) was Germany's first experience in centuries as a unified nation, the Weimar Republic (1919–33) its first democratic experiment, and the early years of the Third Reich (1933–39) its first experience of dictatorship. Austria meanwhile morphed from a dual monarchy (Austria-Hungary, 1867–1918) to a First Republic (1919–34) to a first Fascist dictatorship, initially on its own (from 1934 onward), after annexation in 1938 under German rule.

In these times of "firsts" and neverending changes to national self-definition in both countries, views of crime and antisemitism remained remarkably stable. When we ask ourselves what the relationship might be between the (self-)definition of the law-abiding citizen on the one hand and contemporary ideas involving crime or antisemitism on the other, the first thing to note is that at these critical historical junctures, notions of "normal" and "abnormal" seem to have moved at different speeds. The theoretical debate about both crime and antisemitism emptied into a philosophy of permanence. From the late nineteenth century onward, arguments advocating change (like sociological ones) were increasingly discarded in favor of biological arguments that presupposed immutability and inevitability. Ideas of national self-definition, conversely, changed repeatedly, rapidly, and radically. The end of particularism after 1871 turned regional Bavarians, Westphalians and Hessians into Germans, only to transform these newly minted Imperial subjects, less than a half-century later, into democratic citizens who then, barely a decade and a half on, mutated into dictatorial followers, opponents, perpetrators or victims. All this within sixty-three years—the historical version of lightning speed.

In both prewar periods, there are distinct signs that practical crime writing (news reporting of court cases and crime fiction) and crime theory (criminological treatises) went their separate ways. Theorizing about the criminal entailed thought processes entirely dissimilar from judging him in court or imagining him in fiction. As the lovable, tragic, hilarious, ingenious or misunderstood criminal became the darling of the press and one of the most popular heroes in the history of crime fiction, criminology found itself in a quandary. Should the criminal be seen, as the eighteenth century had, in an anthropological and social context—that is, as a human being who can be understood and possibly even "cured"? Or was the criminal, as late nineteenth-century writings suggested, biologically predestined for crime, himself a symptom of a "disease" that threatened the healthy body of the *Volk* and left "hygiene" in the form of the criminal's segregation or eradication as the only option? Practice—court reporting and crime fiction—retained some ability to entertain complexities, while theory—criminology—was initially caught between just two main ideas and eventually settled for just one. Practice doesn't always do as theory bids it, and thankfully so, since theory often works with a narrower menu of ideas from the outset. Criminology of the prewar periods was never an independent science but always charged to "cure" crime; it was a medical discipline in the service of the law. Nothing leads more easily to either-or thinking and to cause-and-effectism (the idea that if there is a relationship between two things, it must be a causal one) than the search for a cure. When criminology turned into criminal biology, it abandoned the question "why" for a mere understanding of "how." As we know from Winston Smith, "I do not understand why" is the most basic phrase in a dictatorial citizen's lexicon: not only because the answer is withheld, but because the subject of totalitarianism does not even get to ask the question. Neither does science in a totalitarian age, or science in a society on its way there.

Aside from that between crime theory and practical crime writing, the other great fissure to be noted is, of course, that between the Jewish and the non–Jewish criminal in these works. To be sure, sensible criminologists and statisticians before the First World War (far less so before the Second) tried to present Jewish criminality in its proper social context, a battle that was as hopeless as the broader struggle of criminal sociology against the ultimately victorious criminal biology. But if there were similarities between criminology's view of Jewish v. non–Jewish offenders, both of whom were finally defined in biological terms, no such parallels emerge in journalism or fiction. The humanity of the lovable criminal, the hilarious chutzpah of a Wilhelm Voigt, the sheer sass of the Sass brothers, the quiet despair of the innocently railroaded in Auguste Groner's tales, the quaintly bureaucratic honorability of Spoerl's von Treskow, the witty impudence of Serner's underworld figures, the admirable willpower of Bettauer's or Paul Gurk's lawless heroes—none of it was replicated in news reporting on court cases in which the accused was Jewish, or in crime fiction featuring Jewish offenders.[1] One reason for this was that the lovable criminal had a specific part to play over a time period when the nation's view of itself was profoundly unbalanced. As Germany and Austria stumbled from Empire to Republic and from there to dictatorship, the sympathetic criminal became a humanistic self-image of the law-abiding citizen, a symbol of decent "Germanness,"[2] and simultaneously an accessory to the Nazi crime of assigning the idea of serious criminality to Jews.

More Captains, More Muzzles, More Beloved Brothers

The phase that began in 1945 is obviously yet another period of national self-definition, one that obliges denazified Germans and Austrians continually to measure the distance between a pre–1945 dictatorial subject and a post–1945 democratic citizen. In the Federal Republic,[3] postwar pop culture continues to teem with lovable non–Jewish criminals, many of them recycled from the pre–Nazi or Nazi periods. The escapades of Wilhelm Voigt and Prosecutor von Treskow have become postwar Germany's never-ending stories of crime. All post–1945 *Captain of Köpenick* films adopt Zuckmayer's original title *Der Hauptmann von Köpenick* and follow the play closely, which means that all confirm Zuckmayer's whitewashing of the historical original that turned the Captain into a German folk hero. In all versions, Voigt is not, as the historical Voigt undoubtedly was, after the money, but merely yearns for a passport or identity papers that would allow him to survive as an honest man in an increasingly uncaring and bureaucratized world. While the films' portrayal of Voigt as the lovable unlucky devil is virtually identical, they do differ subtly in their portrayal of society's response to him, imprinting on the film's historical setting (1906 or 1910) concerns of the period that produced the film (1956, 1960, 1997).

The 1956 version (dir. Helmut Käutner), which became the most iconic postwar *Captain* and Germany's first postwar success in the U.S., lightens the mood considerably. The first scene shows Voigt's legs, only his legs, trying in vain to keep time with a parade of marching soldiers. Just these shots of Voigt's lower half—his worn-out shoes, his ratty cardboard suitcase, the constant comments from his buddy Kalle about his bow legs—indicate the extent to which Voigt is literally out of lockstep with his militarized society. That society is one that pretends to take people in but simultaneously rejects them. The homeless shelter in which Voigt spends the night is called "Homeland Shelter" ("Herberge zur Heimat"), a name instantly ironized by the sign over Voigt's bunk quoting Eichendorff's song "The Happy Wanderer": "He whom God would show true favor/He sends him out into the wide world."[4] The line is, of course, intended as a whitewashed expulsion order, and although Voigt doesn't notice the sign, he agrees that there can be no way back for him into his society: "All I want is to get out," he says ("Ich will nur raus").

The film's solution to the dilemma seems to suggest that the new German society is liberal enough to tolerate even individuals who cannot march to the common tune. Voigt turns himself in and clarifies that in his entire criminal career, he has never harmed an individual, he has only struggled with "the authorities" ("die Behörden"). In response, he is showered with love and acceptance everywhere—at the police station, in prison, and after his release. Discharging him following the Imperial pardon, the prison director ceremonially bestows upon Voigt his longed-for passport, simultaneously telling him that he no longer needs it, for he is now the Captain of Köpenick. Voigt, in other words, no longer needs to "legitimate" himself in the sense of establishing his identity through papers; he is enough of an individual to be recognized and accepted wherever he goes. The film's final scene confirms this assessment: it shows Voigt dancing around, not attempting to march with, a military parade. Clearly, he is not with them, but tolerated alongside, until finally, the parade crosses Voigt's path, marching off in one direction as Voigt hobbles off in the other, more Chaplin than Captain.

Other *Captain* films have taken issue with this rather cheery image of a new Germany that affably allows even the quirkiest individuals to march whichever way they choose. Rainer Wolffhardt's TV version of 1960, with its extreme emphasis on Zuckmayer's original theme of militarism, can be read as an indirect commentary not only on this vision but also on the re-establishment of the German armed forces in November 1955 (a development on which Käutner's film, released in August 1956, remained silent). Wolffhardt's version puts far greater emphasis on society's ways of raising servile individuals, and on the ways in which individuals participate in their own degradation and that of others. The manager at the shoe factory insists on hiring only ex-soldiers because of "Social Democratic seditious agitation" ("sozialdemokratische Wühlarbeit"). Wolffhardt's film further grants extensive space to the prison scenes in which the Battle of Sedan is ludicrously re-enacted by the prisoners, who look like five-year-olds hopping about, clop-clopping to imitate horses, or pretending to crawl through mud as the Warden shouts orders like "Crawl! Crouch down! Well done!"[5] (the German verb used, "ducken," is commonly used to mean both "ducking down" in the literal sense and to cower before someone in the figurative).

Wolffhardt's portrayal of the old (and new?) German society as one that drills prisoners (and citizens?) to buckle under and like it is expressed in numerous other scenes in which ancient trimmings of German culture are pressed into that service. What could be more acerbic than a slow pan over a choir of prisoners in their grey stripes full-throatedly bellowing the Lutheran hymn "The Lord hath helped me hitherto/By his surpassing favor"?[6] If the point of Käutner's *Captain* was to propagate a newfound tolerance in which society and even oddball individuals can come to a mutual arrangement, the point of Wolffhardt's film is to show that even the most tolerant democratic societies are built on their citizens' obeisance and enforce it with harsh punishments. His film ends with yet another military march to the tune of the German patriotic anthem "The Watch on the Rhine." Over the sung line "Dear Fatherland, no fear be thine," we see Voigt being led off by a guard, to prison. There is no pardon, no release, no passport, and no happy ending, just a closeup of Voigt's abandoned uniform over the closing credits.

Closer to our own time, *Captain* films became increasingly uncomfortable with having to choose between Käutner's cheerful and Wolffhardt's sinister visions of the new Germany. The most popular solution toward the end of the twentieth century seems to have been a fudge. Frank Beyer's 1997 *Captain* film places more emphasis on the immense contrast between society's self-image and the way in which the individual, in this case Voigt, experiences it. The new Germany presents itself as healed from "corruption," as "healthy," but also as a society that builds this integrity on absolute inflexibility. "Germany is built on firm ground," Hoprecht tells Voigt. "We are completely healthy. At the top and at the bottom. And that which is healthy is also right, Wilhelm. This society is built on rock."[7] This self-righteous pride in a functional system ignores, of course, that this same system is in the process of devastating Voigt, who cannot get a job without the proper papers and cannot obtain the papers he needs without proving employment: "That's the way it is all over Germany. Because order prevails."[8] In an orderly society, an individual's options are extremely limited, as Voigt understands all too well. When told by his friend and ex-cellmate Kalle that he is on the wrong track, he replies: "You can only go where the track leads."[9]

The track leads him inexorably to the final irony: Voigt looking at himself in the mirror and laughing out loud at the absurdity of it all. In this version, however, the Inspector does not—as he does in Zuckmayer's original play, and as he also does in all earlier cinematic versions that reinstate the mirror scene cut in the 1931 film—join him in laughter. Instead, he reads Voigt chapter and verse on his horrible crimes, sternly ordering him to stop laughing and berating him that he isn't fit to wear a Prussian uniform. "What you have done this time," he lectures Voigt,

> is worse than all your previous crimes. You have impudently usurped the power of military command. You have undermined the authority of the uniform. You have played fast and loose with the trust in the God-given order of the monarchy. You have dragged eternal values through the dirt. That is akin to high treason, Voigt. You will be harshly judged for this.[10]

Instead of being harshly judged, of course, Voigt gets away courtesy of the Emperor, who laughs his head off and grants him a pardon. Obviously, audiences are meant to side with laughter and leniency rather than self-importance and sermonizing. Equally obviously, the Inspector's moralizing—which is not part of the iconic mirror scene in any previous version—throws up yet another vision of the new Germany: like an autocracy, it continues to cling desperately to an inflexible "order," but like a democracy, it can no longer blame the man at the top for all of its ills. That the film's bureaucrats are far more humorless, and do far more damage, than its Emperor means that the autocratic values on which the new democratic Germany is built are no longer imposed from above but have taken on a life of their own. It is no longer an oppressive regime that grinds individuals to dust, but other individuals who perceive themselves as people in power, as representatives of a superstructure—the "State," or simply "Order," however understood—that has long since stopped taking itself as seriously as it is taken by its bureaucrats. In such a society, the film concludes, individuals are more or less unmoored. As if to demonstrate, the final scene shows Voigt, freshly released, in front of the prison gates—all alone. There are no crowds to greet him and bear him in triumph on their shoulders; there are no military marching bands he could either join or cross. In fact, Beyer's is the *only* Köpenick film that does not open and close by showcasing Voigt's fraught relationship with a military marching band.

A quick glance at other postwar films that recycle the lovable criminals of earlier ages confirms that the portrayal of the liberal and democratic post–1945 (West) Germany was predicated on the question of how to deal with its predecessor. For a while, at least, the choice seems to have been that between directly, and critically, referencing the Nazi period or ignoring it entirely. One example should suffice for each of these diverging paths.

Wolfgang Staudte's musical comedy *The Muzzle* (*Der Maulkorb*, 1958) changes the plot somewhat. Whereas in Spoerl's novel, His Gracious Sovereign's speech never took place, this film supposes that the speech was real and received critically, upon which the government orders an immediate crackdown on free speech and new stiff jail sentences for lese majesty. The law is pushed through without Parliament's input or a vote. In the film's opening scene, worried ministers agonize that this would prevent newspapers from printing the truth, only to be shouted down: "We decide what the truth is! If everyone wanted to sharpen his dirty beak on our Highest Sovereign, that would be opposition! Unthinkable!"[11] The free speech issue recurs in a song sung by Rabanus, in which he suggests that citizens are muzzled—they are only kept around to pay taxes, die in wars, and bow and scrape to their "betters." Wrongful imprisonment is a routine punishment for those who engage in constitutionally legal political opposition or even the mildest criticism of the authorities. Of course, the very fact that the film flaunts its own ability to voice such radical reproach defines the society in which it is shown as a more liberal one than the one in which it is set. Its denigration of an oppressive government long gone is nothing more than a foil for the film's present tense, a new, happier, freer society. Whether we understand that now-defunct oppressive State as the Imperial Germany the film portrays or as the Nazi period it implies is actually immaterial.

And yet, *The Muzzle* also defends "order," largely by refusing to ridicule von Treskow. In Spoerl's original novel and Erich Engel's 1938 film, Prosecutor von Treskow was the lovable criminal, the conscientious criminalist who errs on the side of bureaucratic correctness and can only be prevented from being chewed up by the machine because his inflexibility is balanced by Rabanus's humanity and irreverence. Twenty years later, Staudte transfers the role of the lovable criminal to Wimm and Bätes, or rather: to the Captain of Köpenick, who, by the time the film aired, had already become practically synonymous with the type.

The Captain is here referenced in two ways. The first is the renaming of Wimm and Bätes as Wilhelm (Voigt's first name) and Kalle (Voigt's cellmate in prison, Paul Kallenberg a.k.a. Kalle, a character well known from Voigt's memoirs, Zuckmayer's play and almost all cinematic versions of the Köpenick tale). The second is the casting of Rudolf Platte, who played Wilhelm Voigt in the *Captain of Köpenick* film of 1956—a mere two years before this version of *The Muzzle*—as Inspector Drudge. Both moves seem to imply that in the new liberal Germany, crime, punishment and "order" are actually not taken all that seriously. The face that viewers would remember as that of the quintessential lovable criminal in the 1956 *Captain* film has now been pasted onto a representative of order, a policeman who is engaged in the fruitless pursuit of lovable criminals and in the solving of ludicrous "crimes." And the insertion of Wilhelm and Kalle, two characters from a different crime story, into *The Muzzle* is another tangible hint that every lovable criminal is a Captain of Köpenick and every crime is a *Köpenick-iade*. On the gaping wound of repressive totalitarianism—raised in the film's portrayal of the revocation of freedom of speech, the confiscation of newspapers and the unjust imprisonment of citizens—*The Muzzle* slaps the soothing salve of the Köpenick myth.

In the end, the film leaves us with both the image of a benevolent State (the Sovereign, amused by the caper, revokes the law forbidding free speech) and with that of a strong "order" (the film ends, like Käutner's *Captain* film did two years earlier, with a military parade marching past a statue of the Sovereign).

The other path taken—that of simply brushing aside Germany's repressive past— is best represented by Hans Deppe's film *Robert und Bertram* (1961). Based on the same 1856 Gustav Räder play as the antisemitic 1939 film, Deppe's version is sanitized of all controversy, which means above all cleansed of both its criminals and its Jews. The film, a musical comedy and typical representative of the *Heimatfilm* of the 1950s and 60s,[12] portrays a (West) Germany defined not by its past, but by its glorious scenery and the economic miracle. While most of the film seems to advertise the simple pleasures of walking and love of landscape, it ends with a nod to a utopia both more modern and more materialistic when Robert and his wife Klara finally achieve their long-held dream of homeownership. The film does its best to present this uncomplicated marriage of progress and nature, of simplicity and wealth, as the new Germany's core values. As part of an advertising stunt for a shoe firm, Robert and Bertram are paid to walk 500 kilometers through an idyllic landscape entirely free from cities and bare of Hitler's *Autobahn*, but instead, much like one might imagine pre–World War I Germany, dotted with cookie-cutter villages and crisscrossed by country roads. Car ownership, if not exactly universal, is common, but not so common as to present a problem (traffic is only ever held up by sheep or baby ducks crossing the road). The film's Germany is not only thoroughly unacquainted with city life and traffic jams, but also utterly amnesic about such unpleasant realities as war, crime and concentration camps. The former two are mincingly alluded to; the third is elided altogether. The war, for instance, appears only as a joke: Robert quips that for someone who once walked 2,000 kilometers (from Moscow to Cologne, returning from the Second World War), 500 kilometers is a cake walk.

Like the war, politics has no place in the new Germany, not even in the news. "If people only ever read about politics, they'll choke on their four-fruit jam,"[13] says Bertram's boss, ordering Bertram, a journalist, to write something funny for the paper. In fact, so little happens in this idyllic Germany that Robert and Bertram, just for walking, make the front page of every newspaper every single day. Given the absence of more exciting frontpage news, viewers must surmise that this Germany is entirely crime-free, and the film confirms it for us by presenting even the possibility of crime as unreal. For example, Robert and Bertram are accused of being marriage swindlers—falsely, of course. And when Robert's wife calls the police on him for breaking into his own house and stealing her money, she is told by the police that since legally spouses own everything together, no crime has been committed. Crime in the film is presented as simultaneously faux and fun, relegated to the realm of false accusations and puns. When asked where he has spent his life so far, Robert answers: "Imprisoned. 20 years in an office. But now I've had enough."[14]

It is almost ironic, then, that the ending negates the film's celebration of Germany's "free" outside spaces by putting its characters back "inside," inside, that is, a brand new suburban home. Yet the ending expresses more than the simple sentiment that materialism trumps nature after all. Everything on the street on which Robert's new house sits, from its smooth and pothole-free asphalt, its identical red-roofed houses with their fresh paint, its manicured lawns, cone-shaped hedges and lattice fences, is brand-spanking new. Germany, the final shot tells us, has been rebuilt from the ground up. From what devastation, the film leaves unsaid.

Postwar Sass movies became another vehicle to comment on the state of the new Federal Republic. The earliest of these, Werner Klingler's *Bank Vault 713* (*Banktresor 713*, 1957), was written by Herbert Reinecker, whose writing credits include several propaganda films during the Nazi era as well as the two single most successful TV crime series ever to screen in postwar West Germany, *The Inspector* (*Der Kommissar*, 1969–76) and *Derrick* (1974–98). *Bank Vault 713* retells the story of the Sass brothers' famous Disconto bank heist from the perspective of a *Wirtschaftswunder*–West Germany that has cast its war veterans aside and tempts its lower middle-class workforce with a "good life" that remains financially out of reach for most. The film is neither a historical account nor a biopic of the Sass brothers, much less a film about genius criminality and its implied middle finger to State authority, but ultimately about poverty and its hopeless-yet-envious stare at abundance. In fact, the film references the story of Wilhelm Voigt even more extensively than the story of the Brothers Sass.

The film's two brothers, Klaus and Herbert Burkhardt, have been left behind by the economic miracle. Older brother Herbert was drafted into the Second World War in the middle of his university studies. Damaged by his war experiences, his six years as a POW in Siberia, and the long walk home, Herbert returns to a Germany he doesn't recognize and that no longer requires his services. Because he has begun a university course, he is overqualified for minimum-wage work; because he couldn't complete his degree, is underqualified for anything else, and his inability to find work prevents him from saving money to complete his university studies. It is a precise recap of Voigt's dilemma: Herbert can't get a job without the right papers and he can't obtain those papers without a job. As Herbert runs Voigt's bureaucratic gauntlet, his younger brother Klaus, who has escaped the draft due to his age, works at the car wash, although he is presented as clearly more intelligent than his job requires.

While the war has left its traces on both brothers, they live in a country on which it seems to have had absolutely no effect. Long camera sweeps show us a fully recovered Berlin rebuilt in steel and glass, a city in which glittery banks and "insurance palaces" ("Versicherungspaläste") spring from the ground like mushrooms. "When you look at that," says Klaus, pointing at the Disconto Bank gleaming in the sun, "you could really get furious. They do have money for that."[15] The film even features an homage to the first scene in Zuckmayer's *The Captain of Köpenick*, in which Voigt enviously presses his nose to the display window of an elegant uniform tailor's shop. Klaus's girlfriend Margot works as an advertising model for a car company, parading chic clothes and valuable jewelry in front of a luxury car. As Klaus looks on, the car's owner asks Klaus nonchalantly whether he's ever washed a car like that, and Margot, at the end of the shoot, is immediately stripped of her gown and jewels. In the next scene, we see Klaus windowshopping for cars and watches that he wouldn't be able to afford even if he washed cars for the next half-century. Such humiliations make Klaus susceptible for Herbert's suggestion to break into the Disconto Bank to take what he argues they're owed.

The humiliations of Herbert and Klaus are presented as excruciating, but since the film leaves them dangling—without drawing from them any conclusions that implicate the State—they serve not as expressions of societal critique but merely as motivation for the robbery. Thus the film's main tension, in the end, is not that between the brothers and the State, but that between the brothers—between Herbert, who has given up on his society ("I don't believe in anything anymore," he tells his girlfriend Vera, "neither in the law nor in morality"[16]), and Klaus, who goes along hesitantly and seems more willing to believe that he will eventually get his chance in the new Germany. Shortly before the brothers reach the vault, they are surprised by a third bankrobber who has overheard their plans and blackmails them for a cut. In the ensuing scuffle, the blackmailer is killed, but his death shocks Klaus back into reason. Klaus leaves the scene, unbeknownst to Herbert, who jumps down into the vault room from which he cannot climb out without help. The film ends abruptly, with Klaus staggering despondently through the streets of Berlin and Herbert trapped in the vault, screaming his brother's name.

The story of *Bank Vault 713* is not the story of two brothers cast aside by their society, but the story of the transition from a dictatorial State that decides what its citizens owe to the State (and what, in turn, they are owed by it) to a democratic State that has untethered its citizens to pursue their own happiness, neither helped nor hindered by the State. As Klaus totters through Berlin's streets, he runs into Vera, whose role in the film is limited to her repeated and vain attempts to stabilize Herbert. Klaus, still traumatized from his brief criminal career and aware that he and his brother will now go to prison, tells her what Herbert has repeatedly told her as well: "I can't go on. It's all over. Everything is lost." But she holds out hope: "No, not everything. He won't lose me, no matter what he's done."[17] In a State that no longer oppresses its citizens but also no longer takes responsibility for their well-being, the solution to social problems like unemployment and failed integration are shifted onto the individual. The film clearly admits that the new society is marred by problems: Klaus in his car wash, Margot in her borrowed jewels are obvious images of the painful distance between the haves and the have-nots (or perhaps, if we're feeling hopeful, the haves and the have-not-yets), and Herbert's fruitless job search is shown to be as bitter and unjust as Voigt's once was. But while Voigt is rejected by representatives of the State (police commissioners, passport officials and the like), Herbert is given his marching orders by private employers. The State, the film seems to say, is no longer the problem. Nor is it part of the solution: the answer to Herbert's dilemma, the film argues, was not to attack the State's institutions (in the film aptly represented by banks), but to accept Vera's repeated offers to finance his studies. Thus *Bank Vault 713* tosses the baby of social solidarity out with the bathwater of State authority. If there is hope for an individual in the new West Germany, it lies not in the solidarity between a State and its citizens, but in that among individuals, here expressed in Vera's offer to stand by Herbert that represents the film's final, and only, ray of hope.

Two later films, Rainer Wolffhardt's *Shot on Orders—The Sass Brothers, Once Berlin's Great Crooks* (*Auf Befehl erschossen—Die Brüder Sass, einst Berlins grosse Ganoven*, 1972) and Carlo Rola's *Sass* (2001) offer slightly different perspectives on the Beloved Brothers. Both films grant extensive space to the Sass myth: the Brothers' wit and genius, their incredible popularity with the press and the populace, the degree to which they managed to exasperate the police, and their wretched end at the hands of Nazi butchers. But while Wolffhardt's is a historical-biographical film shot through with fictional elements, Rola reimagines the story of the Brothers Sass as a gangster film with only passing nods to historical background. Much like *Bank Vault 713*, Rola's *Sass* spans the enormous distance between the haves and the have-nots, whereas Wolffhardt's film focuses on that between a free and an oppressive State.[18]

Shot On Orders sets in after the 1929 Disconto Bank heist, at the height of the Sass Brothers' fame. One of its earliest scenes features the infamous press conference after the brothers' release from investigative custody, in which Reporter Backhaus asks an uncomfortable question, namely: why the Sass Brothers, although nobody harbors the slightest doubt as to their guilt of many crimes, are the people's darlings while everyone makes fun of the police and the courts, who are, after all, charged with the protection of that same populace. He is immediately shouted down, accused of being a Nazi, and invited to emigrate to Mussolini's Italy. At this point Bendix, the Sasses' lawyer, takes the floor. His ensuing lecture, surely the most significant speech in the film, informs the assembly that the people's hero worship of the Brothers and the police's helplessness to bring them to book symbolize nothing less than the two pillars of a free and democratic society:

> For this is what makes our Beloved Brothers special, isn't it, that our young liberal Democracy stops at nothing anymore. [...] Instead, Justice finally emerges from the dark back rooms of the court houses, into the bright light of the public realm, and tells us: I punish the guilty, but I protect the innocent! And he against whom there is no proof is innocent![19]

Clearly, this scene is where the audience's alignment with the Sasses' adoring fans in the film breaks down. The lawyer's sophistry not only outrageously equates a basic democratic right (the right to be presumed innocent until proven guilty) with a ludicrous idea (that democracy depends on undermining the police's ability to nab criminals), he also as good as says outright that actual guilt or innocence are beside the point. But what is the way out of this moral dilemma? The film does not offer one, but merely pits one extreme—the utter lawlessness of the Weimar Republic and its reckless celebration of criminality—against another. Criminal Inspector Fiebach, barely renamed from his historical original Fabich, shakes his head in despair at Bendix's speech, but responds with the same despondency when a judge draws a swastika on a piece of paper, asking him: "Have you ever seen this? [...] Trials will be a lot shorter then." Fiebach's response: "They'll leave us nothing to do."[20] The law, in other words, has no role to play in either a liberal or a restrictive society: a liberal one will defang it, a repressive one bypass it.

One of the film's most significant questions is how long the idea of a functional justice system will endure after its eradication in real life. This faith is portrayed as particularly difficult to let go of, persisting long after all other illusions are gone. Bendix's girlfriend, for example, who has never wanted children, responds enthusiastically to the Nazi advocacy of universal motherhood and suddenly harbors no greater desire than to "give the Führer a child." She berates Bendix to fire Silberstein, the Jewish partner of his law practice: "I don't want a child from someone working for a Jew."[21] Silberstein, overhearing this through the door, bursts in and informs Bendix that he is quitting of his own accord: "Tell your wife that she will bring a child of pure German blood into the world. I have applied for emigration for myself and my family. I don't want to shake your hand, Bendix. Your child might reproach you later."[22] The reality of antisemitism, in other words, is not in doubt; it is accepted as an indisputable fact by both its perpetrators and its victims. But when it comes to the integrity of the law, the film's characters vacillate endlessly and painfully between clear-eyed certainty and despairing disbelief.

Two scenes show this most clearly. In the first, Bendix tries to convince the Danish Inspector Mundte to revoke the Sasses' deportation order to Germany after completion of their jail sentence in Denmark. Bendix informs Mundte that there is now a German policy of extra-judicial murder of "habitual criminals," only to be told that Mundte fully agrees with it: "If you want to remove dirt, you have to start at the floor,"[23] he tells a horrified Bendix. In the second scene, Fiebach picks up his captives at the Danish-German border and is told by Franz Sass: "Don't trouble yourself on our account, Inspector. Why don't we do it right here?" Fiebach, who could no longer muster a faith in the law in the scene with the judge, now seems to have rediscovered it: "There are still judges in Berlin, Franz."[24] In both scenes, there is a clear understanding—in the first, on Bendix's part, in the second, on Franz's—that neither justice nor mercy have any further part to play in deciding the fate of Franz and Erich Sass.

And yet both Bendix and Franz make a last-ditch effort to revive faith in the integrity of the law and in its capacity for mercy. In a final conversation between Bendix and the doomed brothers, Franz—who in the border scene had given up on the law—pins his last hopes on legalities while Bendix—whose pleas for mercy were so harshly rejected in Denmark—hopes for clemency from the Nazi State. Franz tells Bendix that the police, still unable to prove that the money found at their apartment belonged to the Disconto Bank, don't have any more actual evidence now than they did in Weimar Republic days. "You can build an entire defense on that, Herr Bendix. No proof—end of story! They won't even get preventive detention with what they have."[25] But Bendix, who knows that the law is no longer worth the paper it is printed on, and who doesn't even have the heart to tell his clients that he can't represent them because they no longer have the right to an attorney, advises them to throw themselves on the mercy of the court. He even has their begging speech at the ready: "We trust in the healthy public feeling of the German *Volk*, in its sense of justice," he drones in an exhausted monotone that is the precise opposite of his energetic press conference speech in defense of unpunished criminality as a sign of democracy. "We know that we are guilty, but we beg the German community of the *Volk*: do not cast us out forever! Accept us back into your ranks in the not too distant future!"[26]

Franz, unimpressed, insists on having his day in court. His trial merely confirms the prescience of his sarcastic suggestion to Fiebach at the border that perhaps they should simply be shot without bothering with the pretense of a trial. Numerous audience members express exactly the same sentiment: "Why don't you make short work of them!"—"Hang him now!"—"Off with their heads!"[27] Complicating the scene, in which such hateful outbursts express the audience's disdain for the fact that even a charade of due process is permitted to remain, is the fact that this is the same public who had, once upon a time, rejoiced in the law's inability to bring the clever criminals to justice. Public opinion, in other words, never comes down on the side of the law, neither in the democratic Weimar Republic nor in the oppressive fascist regime. And yet, the law, ever unloved and reviled, remains the final straw desperately clutched by people who are wrecked by their societies, which indiscriminately includes the law's servants like Fiebach, its breakers like the Brothers Sass, and its benders like Bendix. In one way or the other, all behave as if the law's integrity, its power to protect and its capacity for mercy existed outside of its social and political context.

Fiebach, the inspector who told a doomed Franz Sass at the Danish border to put his faith in the good judges of Berlin, holds on to this illusion longer than anyone else. Toward the end of the trial, when it is already clear that the Brothers' fate is sealed, he tells Bendix that he is not happy about how all this ended: "I'd much rather have caught them back then, in 1930. They'd already be out again today."[28] But of course, this is another misconception, one that ignores entirely the new Nazi laws allowing for the permanent imprisonment of anyone deemed a "habitual criminal," even in the absence of any crime. Fiebach, that lifelong and loyal servant of the law, is undoubtedly the film's most morally upright character. And yet, his vision of justice is no more advanced than that of lawyer Bendix, who represents the corruption of the Weimar Republic's legal system.[29] Essentially, Fiebach confuses justice with his own frustration about his fruitless pursuit of the Brothers back in 1930. If Bendix is guilty of advocating a society that thinks itself above the law, Fiebach is at fault for believing that the law is above the society that wields it. In Wolffhardt's film, then, the lovable criminal does not, as he so often does, simply represent heroic resistance against an oppressive society or its restrictive laws. Instead the film poses a series of questions: about the ability of the law to exist in a space beyond interpretation, either by individuals or States; about the tendency of both individuals and States to bend the law to their purposes; and finally whether, given this endless instability, the law even has the power to fulfil its most central function: to define and regulate the relationship between individuals and society.

Rola's *Sass* (2001), finally, simplifies matters considerably by returning to what was also the main theme in Klingler's 1957 Sass film: the question of how to get ahead (financially) in modern society. "A person who no longer has any hope also no longer has a future," the film's introductory voiceover informs us. "These were the prospects of everyone born in Berlin at the beginning of the twentieth century. There was no such thing as a childhood. Only anxiety, beatings, and hunger."[30] In this dire context, Franz and Erich Sass are cast as heroic figures who refuse to buckle down to misery. Unlike their historical originals (and also unlike the characters of Wolffhardt's film), they are not portrayed as career criminals but as frustrated workers who cannot get ahead with honest work. In an early scene, Franz asks Erich how long he's been wearing the same pair of shoes. Erich can't remember; he only remembers that they were hand-me-downs from Franz, who himself got them handed down by their father. "We work like idiots, day and night, and what do we have then? Nothing," Franz tells Erich. "We have no chance, no matter how much we slog." Erich tells him that honest work is a good thing, and maybe, in a few decades.... But Franz cuts him short: "I don't feel like waiting 30 years, only then to get sick and kick the bucket at 55."[31] And so they embark on their crime spree, captivating their audiences (both diegetically and, in intention at least, extra-diegetically) with their waggish jocularity, their criminal genius, their refusal to use weapons, their unmistakably Germanic work ethic, and their unfailing generosity to their poor neighbors and the local hospital.

While the historical Sass brothers avoided capture for years because they had no entanglements other than with each other—no confidants to betray them for a reward—Rola's film endows its heroes with an extensive social context, largely to accommodate the basic generic requirements of a gangster caper. Each brother is embroiled in a love story, and both are partly characterized through their relationship with their father, an honest man who knows what they do for a living but loves them anyway (the historical senior Sass, it will be remembered, was an abusive drunk who barely supported the family and had no contact with any of his five sons). Most importantly for the crime story, the brothers are placed within a community of both cops and other robbers. Whereas all other criminals are portrayed as ruthless and malicious (Father Sass is brutally murdered by a rival gang after the Brothers refuse to make common cause with them), the representatives of the law come in both honest and corrupt versions, with correspondingly divergent ideas about how to handle the ever-elusive brothers. One inspector on the Sass case tells honest Inspector Fabich: "We'll just frame them for something. We all know, after all, that they're dirty. All of Berlin knows it!" Honest Fabich's simple response: "If you do that, I'll report you."[32]

This seems to indicate that we may be headed for a Wolffhardt-esque conundrum about what the law can achieve while it insists on remaining honest. In the end, however, the problem is solved more directly. The Sass brothers are indicted and tried for the Disconto bank job, which, in the film, nets them about 8 million marks of NSDAP money. The court fulfils the letter of the law, pronouncing the brothers not guilty for lack of evidence. But of course, the Nazis will not let them escape, and Franz and Erich are shot dead by swastika armband-wearers, dying hand in hand on a snowy staircase after affirming to each other that it was all worth it because they lived life as they chose. In this way, *Sass* offers a simple answer to all the problems Wolffhardt raised: the film's dying (but now happily revived) democratic society is represented by the rule of law, which functions as it should; its coming period of Nazi terror by a murderous "street justice" that bypasses the courts entirely.

Sass is thus a great deal simpler than *Shot on Orders*, dodging Wolffhardt's difficult questions about what it might mean when a society still living under the protection of law celebrates its criminals. *Sass*'s attitude toward its heroes is, in fact, unabashedly celebratory. Rola defined his own film as "The story of two brothers who adamantly stick together against their time, against their circumstances, and enjoy their life, no matter what." He further offers an exculpatory motive for their lives of crime: "I think that they were simply two proletarians [...], they were, actually. They had no chance, they had no dough, didn't know what to do. And so they advanced themselves, made something of their misery."[33] All of the film's lead actors, Ben Becker (who played Franz), Jürgen Vogel (who played Erich) and Henry Hübchen (who played Fabich) went on record as being enthusiastic Sass fans, citing the same qualities: their cleverness, their nonviolence, their wit, their persistence, and their refusal to play the hand Fate had dealt them.[34] In *Bank Vault 713*, the answer to poverty, however lukewarm and unconvincing, is working hard, staying honest and grasping the helping hands of other individuals (although not the State's). Barely 30 years later, *Sass* disputes the idea that anyone can work his way out of poverty. "They said: we don't feel like doing this anymore, we're not letting them screw us over anymore, we're now taking this thing in hand ourselves."[35] These and other comments in interviews with the film's director and cast express, or rather map onto the historical Sass brothers, a sense of betrayal. If there is no way of escaping poverty through hard work, society's advocacy of hard work is no more than a large-scale swindle. Criminality, in this context, becomes synonymous with creativity, an attribute that distinguishes the world's (criminal) masterminds from its poor schmucks.

Of course this is the basic attitude of many a gangster movie, and thus it is no wonder that *Sass*, in adapting the historical material to that genre, adopts it as well. Yet in doing so, the film simultaneously relinquishes the possibility of societal critique and that of societal rehabilitation. The film portrays the Sass brothers' poverty as universal and inevitable, but feels no obligation to delve any further into its causes. The only possible escape from poverty is creativity (criminality). And yet, the society that has somehow (we are never told how) caused both the Brothers' misery and deprived them of a legal remedy for it is ultimately let off (after all, it delivers the "correct" judicial verdict at the end). The Happy Ending is tantalizingly close: if only it weren't for those pesky Nazis—who, far from representing a vision of a repressive State, are portrayed as little more than street thugs—the clever brothers would have made it safely to America with their loot and their ladies. *Sass*, in the end, celebrates resistance, the brothers' refusal to be "screwed over," without clarifying what is being resisted, or who, if anyone, is doing the screwing.

From the 1950s to the early 2000s, cinema endlessly recycled Germany's most famous lovable criminal stories. There are now six Captains (three filmed after the year 2000),[36] four Muzzles,[37] and three renditions of the Sass story. The enduring lure of these stories undoubtedly lies as much in their symbolic as in their entertainment value. All of these films followed the lead of their source stories in casting the lovable criminal as an emblem for the fraught relationships between justice and the law, between individuals and their State. A half-century after the beginning of this postwar tradition, Rola's film became the first to subordinate the heroes' symbolic meaning to the generic requirements of a pop genre. By letting the State off the hook, the film leaves its lovable criminals to enter the twenty-first century alone: untethered from their prime antagonist, deprived of context, symbolizing nothing.

Symbols, Scapegoats, Silences

But can and should the criminal actually represent anything beyond himself? This is, to return to Hannah Arendt, one major question of *Eichmann in Jerusalem: A Report on the Banality of Evil*. She raises it in a series of adamant denials of what her book is *not*: not a history of the Holocaust, not an account of totalitarianism, not a history of the German people during the Nazi period, "nor is it, finally and least of all, a theoretical treatise on the nature of evil,"[38] its suggestive subtitle notwithstanding. Instead, she defined her book as a mere trial report and its subject Adolf Eichmann as no more than a criminal:

> It can be held that the issue is no longer a particular human being, a single distinct individual in the dock, but rather the German people in general, or anti–Semitism in all its forms, or the whole

of modern history, or the nature of man and original sin—so that ultimately the entire human race sits invisibly beside the defendant in the dock. All this has often been argued, and especially by those who will not rest until they have discovered an "Eichmann in every one of us." If the defendant is taken as a symbol and the trial as a pretext to bring up matters which are apparently more interesting than the guilt or innocence of one person, then consistency demands that we bow to the assertion made by Eichmann and his lawyer: that he was brought to book because a scapegoat was needed, not only for the German Federal Republic, but also for the events as a whole and for what made them possible—that is, for anti–Semitism and totalitarian government as well as for the human race and original sin.[39]

The logic is as simple as it is inescapable. Only Eichmann the individual can be tried and found either guilty or innocent. Eichmann the symbol would have to be judged both innocent and framed. What Arendt indicts here is the common idea that we can't judge individuals but only groups, creating a moral universe in which all cats are grey, we're all equally guilty, and we all accept that nobody could have acted differently from the way they did. Constructs are thought up that "'explain' everything by obscuring all details," among them "such notions as the 'ghetto mentality' among European Jews; or the collective guilt of the German people [...]. All these clichés have in common that they make judgment superfluous and that to utter them is devoid of all risk."[40]

Does Arendt's insistence that turning a criminal into a symbol eliminates both our ability to judge and responsibility for the crime cast new light on postwar Germany's enduring partiality to the lovable criminal tales of earlier ages? Considering this question might begin with a reminder of four (interrelated) facts: that Germany's fondness for its lovable criminals is as undiminished post–1945 as it was in both prewar periods; that the lovable criminal of German history and fiction is always conceptualized as an individual; that he is inevitably conceptualized as *German*—never as Jewish—and that his continued popularity does not document fondness for the historical individual but for the symbol he became.

Antisemitic writing, in its usual sloppy use of terminology, tends to talk about the "symbolic" role of Jews[41] when all it aims for is sweeping generalizations, rather than the symbol's power to express the immaterial, the intangible, or the ideal. In the latter sense, the Jewish criminals of criminology, crime reporting or crime fiction were never eligible for a symbolic role. True symbolism depends on individuation; stories are told about individuals whereas "masses" or groups are relegated to history. Jews, whether "criminal" or law-abiding, are inevitably "massed" in writing of the time (as members of a herd, a race, "Jewry"; "vermin" and so forth[42]). As antisemitic criminology perverted real-life crime statistics to avoid characterizing Jewish criminals as individuals harming other individuals, crime reporting and crime fiction of the 1920s and 1930s took a similar line, casting the Jewish criminal as a member of a worldwide conspiracy out to destroy entire nations. Bare of individuality and hence also of all symbolic value, the Jews of these texts are simply ineligible to serve as the material for a "story." Because Tamara von Hervay and Hugo Bettauer were perceived as part of an amorphous mass, a "people" or even a "race," they were never able to symbolize anything, and thus they were silenced. They are now part of history, from where they can be retrieved by those who are interested, but they have not, like Voigt or the Sass Brothers did, achieved the timeless status of beloved symbols. We should gratefully acknowledge historians' insights on Hervay and Bettauer, but we should also remain aware of the level of research this required. Theirs are not stories that are offered unbidden to a vast populace of non-experts on a near-constant basis, before, during and after the World Wars and right into the next century.[43]

It is, at this point, worth reminding ourselves of Berkowitz's insight that the Nazis' attribution of criminality to Jews was no more than "institutionalized hypocrisy."[44] The Nazis did not exterminate Jews because they thought them criminals but because they thought them subhuman, and the entire literature that branded Jews as criminals was nothing but a distraction to conceal this elementary fact. Thus when we assess the postwar era's continued adoration of the Captain or the Sass brothers and, by contrast, its thundering silence on Hervay or Bettauer—which should come as a surprise at least in Bettauer's case, given that he was the era's best-selling author—we are no longer talking about criminality but about commemoration. And commemoration is where history seems to draw the short straw compared to storytelling.

Telling stories, such as that of the German lovable criminal, is a chatty affair; commemorating history, such as that of the Holocaust, more often than not takes the form of respectful silence. Likewise, retelling the story of the individual German criminal takes symbolic form, whereas commemorating the "mass" of Jewish victims is a singularly literal act. The statue of the Captain of Köpenick in front of Köpenick's city hall honors neither the individual Wilhelm Voigt nor the "Captain" he played, but what the Captain character symbolizes—wit, ingenuity, creativity and ultimately humanity. The Holocaust Memorial in Berlin, conversely, re-enacts literally, with its rows upon rows of blank tombstones, the namelessness of thousands of Jewish victims flung into their graves. As a literal structure it is, as its architect Peter Eisenman once called it, a "place of no meaning," and its very lack of symbolic value is usually greeted with relief. "'Place of no meaning,' Eisenman once called the site, thus immediately taking the wind out of the sails of all critics who feared that it was meant to visualize the Holocaust in a monumental symbolic graveyard."[45] Remembering Arendt's warning that symbolism merely enables us to create a moral universe in which we are all equally guilty, which is to say that nobody is, certainly justifies such a fear of symbolism. On the other hand, if we consider that repudiating symbolism also means rejecting individuality, we must wonder what it means to strip Holocaust victims of both. Does not our "massing" of the Jewish dead, even in honoring them, echo the acts of de-individualization, in crime writing and other forms of writing, that led to their deaths in the first place? "The totalitarian state lets its opponents disappear in silent anonymity," wrote Arendt.[46] Does the respectful commemoration in democratic States that have now superseded totalitarian ones offer the Jewish dead more than silence and anonymity?

Where the Bodies Are Buried

Long stretches of postwar history, in Germany more than in Austria, were marked by concerted efforts to eradicate antisemitism in both official institutions and the population. Signposts along this path are academic terms so overused that they have made it into common parlance: Denazification ("Entnazifizierung"), Coming to Terms with the Past ("Vergangenheitsbewältigung"), Historical Repression ("Geschichtsver-

drängung"), Historical Falsification ("Geschichts-
fälschung"), Interpretational Sovereignty ("Deu-
tungshoheit"), and Historians' Dispute
("Historikerstreit"). Public discourse in both Germany and Austria today harshly disowns explicit
antisemitism, as is documented by the panicked
haste with which the press brands antisemitic
remarks by public officials as "isolated cases"
("Einzelfälle"[47]) whenever they occur. And yet,
while Nazism and antisemitism are officially "out,"
the lovable criminal is here to stay, and he is still
an Aryan. We should therefore invest some
thought into the role this character had to play in
German society, both in the 20 years of peace preceding the two World Wars and in the decades of
postwar peace since then.

The sympathetic criminal has been one of
the most beloved characters ever conceived in
either journalism or fiction, garnering the adora-

**Statue of the Captain of Köpenick in front of
Köpenick's City Hall (Wikimedia Commons);
Holocaust Memorial, Berlin Mitte (Wikimedia
Commons, CC BY-SA 2.5, photograph by Klaus
Brandstetter).**

tion of vast audiences over a considerable time span. Such enduring popularity is partially owed to the comic genre and to a character that offers ample scope for identification. Yet it is doubtful that either would have been sufficient to keep the pot boiling for decades, let alone, in the Captain's case, for well over a century. The millions of Captain or Sass fans read their stories not only for their comedic or empathic, but also for their symbolic value. What these characters symbolized was both the possibility of remaining a decent person in times of turmoil and *a subversiveness that stops short of meaningful criticism of or opposition to the State.* These may well have been the precise qualities required of citizens transitioning from a chaotic to an organized and vastly more powerful State: first from particularism to the Second German Reich, and then, within a few short years, again from a fragmented Republic to the Third Reich. In the postwar era, with its emphasis on "coming to terms with the past," that self-image lost none of its attraction. "[U]nder conditions of terror most people will comply but *some people will not*," wrote Hannah Arendt.[48] Retelling stories of lovable German criminals, endlessly chortling at their witty ways of non-compliance, may be our way of turning Arendt's *"some"* into a *"most,"* maybe even, via the power of the symbol, into an *"all."*

If "[t]he point of any reconstruction lies in the present,"[49] we should query whether the continued popularity of the lovable criminal after 1945 is linked with what he symbolized before, and—if that turns out to be the case—ask ourselves why these old symbols still serve us today. Of all of the character's many symbolic functions, three seem to have made it seamlessly into the postwar period: the criminal as an *individual*; the criminal as a symbol of *navel-gazing*, and the criminal as a *foil.*

The first symbol, that of the lovable criminal as an individual, returns us to the point Arendt made about totalitarian States replacing individuals with "mass men" who are both expendable and aware of it.[50] This context might answer the question why the criminal, of all imaginable literary types, became a symbol for individualism: if "normality" expresses itself in the mass, individuality can only be perceived as deviant. Simultaneously Arendt's thought might account both for the new mass-citizen's yearning for individuality *and* the effectiveness of Nazi propaganda describing Jews as a "mass." Just as the individual might well become an object of nostalgia for Mass Man, Mass Man might also easily be induced to fear an amorphous mass (Jewry, World Conspiracy) because part of an amorphous mass is precisely what he himself is becoming. Arendt saw the "massing" of human beings realized in the death camps, but the lovable criminal indicates that at least on a conceptual level, the process of de-individualization that turned individuals into a mass and defined the individual in terms of deviance from the norm began much earlier. The enduring popularity of the lovable criminal in postwar fiction naturally raises the question whether it also lasted longer. Do we, postwar citizens of democratic nations, still define the mass as the norm? Are we still unable to see individuality as anything but deviant? How are these ideas expressed in mass media and popular (that is: mass) culture (why, for example, have superhero movies assumed absolute dominance over the Hollywood landscape?)? And finally: how might such ideas influence political processes (particularly those that pit the "individual" against the "masses")?

The second symbol, the criminal as an emblem of national navel-gazing, belied the degree to which Germany was contemplating outward aggression. It does seem significant that both pre–World War periods were marked by both war preparations on the one hand and an obsession with crime on the other. Criminology as a science, just like portrayals of the lovable criminal in journalism and fiction, was inward-looking; it was meant to express something about Germany as a society, not about her attitude toward the outside world (that was the job of diplomacy, foreign correspondence, and propaganda). Attacks from the outside (by "foreigners"), even attacks by "foreign" elements within society (Jews), left society's view of itself unscathed. But talk of crime and criminals goes to the heart of society's self-image, defining how it functions under the law, how it enacts justice, and how it treats its outsiders. Criminology's relentless focus on the criminal (in psychology, psychiatry, and biology) rather than crime and its social causes (in sociology) is, of course, another example of turning inward, for if the causes of crime were contained within the criminal himself, crime has nothing to say about society as a whole. Both the analysis of the criminal—but not the crime—and the lovable criminal as a symbol of "Germanness" constitute acts of navel-gazing. The first deprived the criminal of his social, the second the country of its international context. Perhaps this was the greatest success of Nazi propaganda: not so much to teach its citizens to hate the "foreign," but to instill in them a near-total inability to look beyond their front doors. Indisputably, this kind of national navel-gazing is making a comeback in Germany, Austria and elsewhere, as a response to the effects of globalization, mass migration and multiculturalism.

Finally, the lovable criminal as a foil forces us to ask what contemporary thinking about crime, particularly the serial celebration of the lovable German criminal, has to do with antisemitism and ultimately the Holocaust. At this point, it is worth reminding ourselves of Shulamit Volkov's understanding of "culture," which she declared to be antisemitism's natural home, as a realm that both subsumes and far transcends smaller mental jurisdictions like "ideology" or "world view." Only "culture," Volkov claims, can produce "the total interconnected ways of thinking, feeling, and acting" that operate, "in society as well as in individuals, both on the intellectual-rational level and on that of implicit values, norms, lifestyle and thought, common ambitions, and emotions."[51]

Culture, not merely ideology, is the realm in which the lovable German criminal emblematizes a celebration of freedom, individualism, decency and opposition (although never actual resistance). This explains not only his prominence in radically different text types—from court reporting and sentencing documents to fiction—but also accounts for his survival in various societies that espoused radically different ideologies, from the Second Reich to the Weimar Republic to the NS dictatorship, and from there to postwar Germany. Culture is also the domain where the lovable criminal serves as a foil for "true" (that is: Jewish) criminality. As a cultural code in Volkov's sense, he became a vehicle of mass identification, and as a vehicle of mass identification, he encouraged ordinary Germans to see themselves as distinct from both the "authorities" and from Jews. The lovable criminal, in other words, was the useful idiot enabling a positive German self-image at a time when that should have been nigh-well impossible. He was a way of sidelining humanity, of reserving compassion for some so that it could be withdrawn from others.

The truth is that no society can exist without its outsiders. But whereas we usually think in binary terms—in terms of in and out, authority and resistance, individuals and masses—the lovable criminal suggests that societies have a vested interest in creating at minimum *two* kinds of outsiders. One allows society to demonstrate its tolerance and sense of humor, the other permits it to show its steely side (to cite an Americanism: being "tough on crime"). In the run-up to the Nazi era, German criminals were clearly assigned one role and Jews the other, and thus Hannah Arendt's assertion that there was a principal incompatibility between the idea of a "criminal" and the idea of a "Jew" makes perfect sense.

The changing status of different out-groups in different societies suggests that postwar societies continue to turn to this way of "resolving" social conflicts. To cite a well-known example from a different country: under President Reagan, the most vilified out-group in U.S. society were the poor. Under President Trump, they have a different role to play: they serve as a foil for race-based persecution. Unemployed, underemployed and underpaid blue-collar workers wondering how to hang on to their healthcare can easily be mobilized to demonize immigrants, particularly illegal immigrants. It is no longer possible, in Trump's America, to speak of "welfare queens" the way Reagan did[52]—not when you need the indigenous poor as a foil to justify antiimmigration policies and deportations.

In the end, the lovable criminal tells us that binaries only tell us half of the story. There is never a simple contrast between the criminal and the law-abiding, between authority and opposition, between accepted and persecuted groups, between in and out. There always have to be at least two out-groups, one of which is tolerated to allow for the persecution of the other. That the worship of the lovable criminal continues unabated in today's Germany shows that we remember one of his symbolic meanings—that of German decency—but not the other: his complicity in the Nazi crime of casting Jews as the "real" criminals. Our continued adulation of the lovable criminal, our obsession with stories about him, also throws up the question of why we still need him. Perhaps he has yet a part to play, as a foil for some other group to be demonized in the future.

Chapter Notes

Criminals and Mass Men in Pre-Totalitarian Peace Time

1. Throughout this book, all translations from primary or secondary sources are my own unless indicated otherwise.

2. The most extensive account of the case is *Three Weeks in October*, coauthored by Charles A. Moose, the primary official in charge of apprehending the serial snipers, and Charles Fleming.

3. These and other possible motives are listed by Daniel Pipes in his *New York Post* article "The Snipers: Crazy or Jihadists?" (October 29, 2002).

4. Mentioned by Gordon Duff in "Forgotten Terror—The DC Sniper," *Veterans Today* (July 10, 2012).

5. See the interview between Curt Autry and Mildred Muhammad.

6. Liptak, "Virginia Justices Set Death Sentence in Washington Sniper Case," *New York Times* (April 23, 2005).

7. The exhibits are listed by Cawthorne in *Spree Killers* (unpag.); the statement by Muhammad's unnamed friend is cited by Daniel Pipes.

8. See Peter Bergen's entry "September 11 Attacks" in the online *Encyclopaedia Britannica*.

9. Favouring the jihad-theory in addition to Pipes's article in the *New York Post* are Pierucci, "California Links Beltway Snipers to Jamaat Al Fuqra," *Christian Action Network* (December 16, 2013) and Paul L. Williams, "Beltway Snipers Exposed as Muslim Terrorists," *Canada Free Press* (Sept 17, 2009). The theory is also given credence and space in Sperry's inflammatorily titled *Infiltration: How Muslim Spies and Subversives Have Penetrated Washington* (see, for example, p. 209–10).

10. See, for example, Schmid: "the American public's relief was almost palpable when the D.C. snipers were finally arrested and turned out to be not terrorists but good old-fashioned serial killers" (*Natural Born Celebrities* 27).

11. On this phenomenon, see Schmid, *Natural Born Celebrities: Serial Killers in American Culture.*

12. The quotation is taken from Schmid's "Serial Killing in America After 9/11," 61.

13. I am using this spelling rather than the more common hyphenated form ("anti–Semitism") to indicate that I do not consider "Semite" or "Semitism" on its own as meaningful, i.e.: that I do not consider "Semites" to be a "race." Shmuel Almog has explained in succinct terms what the inclusion or omission of the hyphen may indicate.

14. These include the works of Sander Gilman (*Freud; The Jew's Body; Jewish Self-Hatred*) as well as works by Gilman and Katz; Gliksman; Erb ("Zur Erforschung" and *Die Legende*); Hoppe; Jeggle; Lichtblau, and Lindemann.

15. Vyleta, *Crime* 46 and 47.

16. These two are Hans Gross's *Archiv für Criminalanthropologie und Criminalistik* and Gustav Aschaffenburg's *Monatsschrift für Kriminalpsychologie und Strafrechtsreform*; see Vyleta, *Crime* 47.

17. Vyleta, *Crime* 49.

18. Vyleta, *Crime* 46–7.

19. Vyleta, *Crime* 221.

20. Vyleta, *Crime* 221.

21. Vyleta, *Crime* 50.

22. Vyleta, *Crime* 50.

23. Vyleta, *Crime* 225.

24. Berkowitz, *The Crime* xiii.

25. See his Chapter 2.

26. Berkowitz, *The Crime* xvi.

27. Berkowitz, *The Crime* 39.

28. Berkowitz, *The Crime* 18, 26.

29. See Berkowitz, Chapter 3.

30. Berkowitz, *The Crime* 30.

31. Berkowitz quoting a memo from the NS Periodical Service (Zeitschriftendienst), January 9, 1942 (*The Crime* 37).

32. Citation and discussion in Berkowitz, *The Crime* 44.

33. Berkowitz, *The Crime* 224 and 226 respectively.

34. Elon viii.

35. Most of all Daniel Goldhagen with *Hitler's Willing Executioners* (1996).

36. Marcel Stoetzler, *The State, the Nation, and the Jews* (2009); Stoetzler and Christine Achinger, "German modernity, barbarous Slavs and profit-seeking Jews" (2013).

37. Lars Fischer, *The Socialist Response* (2007) and "The Social Democratic response" (2009).

38. Achinger, "Allegories of Destruction" (2013), "Antisemitismus und 'Deutsche Arbeit'" (2011), *Gespaltene Moderne* (2007), "Threats to Modernity" (2012); Robertson, *The Jewish Question* (1999).

39. Gerhard Scheit, *Verborgener Staat, lebendiges Geld* (2006).

40. See the collection of essays in Fraenkel's *The Jews of Austria* (1970); Silverman, *Becoming Austrians* (2012); the essays in Wistrich's *Austrians and the Jews* (1992); van Arkel, *Antisemitism in Austria* (1966);

Kluger, "The Theme of Anti-Semitism" (1991); Pauley, *From Prejudice to Persecution* (1992); Lichtblau, "Die Debatten" (1993); and the works of Daniel Vyleta.

41. Lars Fischer, "*A difference in the texture of prejudice*" (2016).

42. See the works of Friedman, Gliksman, Arnd Müller ("Streicher und die Juden"), Pätzold, Pöggeler, Varga, Bytwerk, Showalter and especially Roos on Julius Streicher; and the works of Stephan, Wunderlich, Bade, Bärsch, Bramstead, Fest, Fraenkel and Manvell, Fröhlich ("Joseph Goebbels"), Heiber, Höver, Jungnickel, Kessemeier, Krause, Michel, Michels, Moeller, Hans-Dieter Müller, Neuhaus, Oppermann, Pol, Reiman, Reuth, Riess, and Schröder on Joseph Goebbels (a number of these works focus on Goebbels as an author of fiction, in addition to his role as the Nazi State's premier propagandist).

43. Lars Fischer again: "Anti-'Philosemitism'" (2011), "Social Democratic Response" and *Socialist Response*.

44. Central here, among many others, are the works of George Mosse (*Towards the Final Solution*, 1978), Moishe Postone ("Anti-Semitism and National Socialism," 1986) and Michael Berkowitz.

45. Levy, *The Downfall of the Anti-Semitic Political Parties in Imperial Germany* (1975); Pulzer, *The Rise of Political Anti-Semitism in Germany & Austria* (1988).

46. Jochmann, *Gesellschaftskrise und Judenfeindschaft in Deutschland 1870–1945* (1988) and "Struktur und Funktion des deutschen Antisemitismus" (1976); Mosse, *Towards the Final Solution* (1978).

47. The book is an expanded and revised version of her earlier *Jüdisches Leben und Antisemitismus* (1990). All quotations from the latter that have no direct equivalent in her later *Germans, Jews, and Antisemites* are rendered in my translation.

48. Volkov, *Germans, Jews, and Antisemites* 82.

49. Volkov, *Germans, Jews, and Antisemites* 84.

50. Volkov, *Germans, Jews, and Antisemites* 88.

51. "*Die soziale Frage ist die Judenfrage*"; cited in Volkov, *Germans, Jews, and Antisemites* 86; emphases original.

52. Volkov, *Germans, Jews, and Antisemites* 99–100.

53. Rürup, "Die 'Judenfrage' der bürgerlichen Gesellschaft" (1975).

54. Mosse, *Towards the Final Solution* (1978).

55. In both *Gesellschaftskrise* (1988) and "Struktur und Funktion" (1976).

56. Volkov, *Germans, Jews, and Antisemites* 110.

57. Volkov, *Germans, Jews, and Antisemites* 110–1.

58. Vyleta, *Crime* 223.

59. Vyleta, *Crime* 224.

60. "Der Antisemitismus war keine direkte Reaktion auf reale Umstände. Tatsächlich reagieren Menschen auch nicht direkt auf Ereignisse. In einem Prozeß der Konzeptualisierung und Verbalisierung konstruieren sie sich eine Interpretation ihres Welt-Erlebens, und nur auf diese selbstgemachte Konzeption der Wirklichkeit können sie reagieren" (Volkov, *Jüdisches Leben* 25, my translation).

61. Volkov, *Germans, Jews, and Antisemites* 117.

62. Volkov citing Theodor Barth in *Germans, Jews, and Antisemites* 118.

63. Volkov, *Germans, Jews, and Antisemites* 118.

64. Volkov, *Germans, Jews, and Antisemites* 117.

65. Arendt, *Origins* 35–6.

66. Arendt, *Origins* 25.

67. Arendt, *Origins* 403.

68. Arendt, *Origins* 316 ("gigantic massing of individuals"); 441 ("inanimate men"); 407 ("atomized individuals"), and 467 ("One Man").

69. Arendt, *Origins* 316.

70. Arendt, *Origins* 316.

71. Arendt, *Origins* 349.

72. Arendt, *Origins* 83–6 on the Dreyfus affair; the quotations 86.

73. Arendt, *Origins* 80–1.

74. Arendt, *Origins* 83.

75. Arendt, *Origins* 87.

76. Arendt, *Origins* 447.

77. Arendt, *Origins* 448.

78. Arendt, *Origins* 434–5.

79. Arendt, *Origins* 434.

80. Arendt, *Origins* 316.

81. Arendt, *Origins* 352.

82. "Sie treten meist in großen Scharen auf [...]—nicht anders als die Juden unter den Menschen" (Fritz Hippler, dir., *Der ewige Jude*, 1940).

83. Vyleta, *Crime* 104.

84. She claims this briefly, without explaining further, in *Eichmann in Jerusalem*: "It was not until the outbreak of the war, on September 1, 1939, that the Nazi regime became openly totalitarian" (68). In *Origins*, she elaborated: "it was only during the war, after the conquests in the East furnished large masses of people and made the extermination camps possible, that Germany was able to establish a truly totalitarian rule" (310–1), and elsewhere: "The radicalization began immediately at the outbreak of war; one may even surmise that one of Hitler's reasons for provoking this war was that it enabled him to accelerate the development in a manner that would have been unthinkable in peacetime" (410).

85. Arendt, *Eichmann in Jerusalem*, the argument on 291–2, the citation on 292.

86. Vyleta, *Crime* 3.

87. The citation is taken from the second balcony speech of Emperor Wilhelm II, delivered on August 1, 1914 (full text available in "Die Balkonreden," *Frankfurter Rundschau* of July 22, 2004).

88. See the scholarly literature cited in note 41.

89. Vyleta, *Crime* 8.

90. Sardar and Wyn Davies, *Why Do People Hate America?* 46.

91. Vyleta, *Crime* 10.

92. Turner, *The Anthropology of Performance* 21.

93. Turner, *Anthropology* 22.

94. Turner, *Anthropology* 22, 24.

95. I owe these terms to Helmut Walser Smith, who has taken a similar approach to his "cameo history" of antisemitism, told through the lens of the murder of Ernst Winter in 1900 (cf. his *The Butcher's Tale* 177 on rehearsed and spontaneous elements of cultural performance).

96. This marks one of my most central disagreements with the (nevertheless seminal) work of Michel Foucault, who, in *Discipline and Punish*, has famously described *The Birth of the Prison* at the outset of modernity. Foucault reads crimes and punishments as social and political events and texts, including literary texts, as social signs; I consider the literary aspects of social and political events, including criminal trials, and read all texts as more or less "literary," no

matter what their provenance or self-presentation. Foucault's watchwords are "political technology" (24), mine are "cultural coding."

97. Koepnick, *The Dark Mirror* 17.

Compulsion v. Conspiracy

1. Gerteis 87.
2. Wetzell, *Inventing the Criminal* 31–2.
3. Galassi has offered an overview of perceptions of the criminal in German discourse from antiquity until early modern society, showing that during that time criminals were overwhelmingly seen in theological, moral or legal terms: the scientific discourse about criminality, she claims, did not begin until ca. 1880 (39–80). Psychiatry "in the nineteenth century was often conceived of as a scientific, deterministic discipline that left little room for free will and moral responsibility. In contrast, the law was portrayed as a system which took free will as its essential axiom. Such categorical appraisals fuelled the struggle between the two professions and promoted a powerful myth of incompatibility" (Harris 321). On this development, see also Weindling 81: "from the 1850s a shift of values from free will, moral responsibility and justice to the naturalist categories of biological evolution occurred: biological heredity rather than the social environment was seen as the cause of pathological behaviour."
4. Peter Becker, *Verderbnis* 21–5.
5. One of his students' counts listed 26,886 criminals and 25,447 normal subjects (Gerteis 90).
6. Lombroso, "Introduction" xxiv.
7. Wetzell, *Inventing the Criminal* 30; Baumann 37; Galassi 147.
8. Lombroso, *Criminal Man*; on these and other traits see also Gerteis 91–2 and Galassi 153–5, 157.
9. Wetzell, "Criminology" 407–8. Many have offered competent analytic overviews of the response to Lombroso in Germany and his influence on discussions about criminology and penal reform; among them are Wetzell, *Inventing the Criminal*; Lees, *Cities, Sin, and Social Reform* (Chapter 4), and Bondio.
10. "dass alle echten Verbrecher eine bestimmte, in sich kausal zusammenhängende Reihe von körperlichen, anthropologisch nachweisbaren, und seelischen, psycho-physiologisch nachweisbaren, Merkmalen besitzen [...], deren Besitz ihren Träger mit unentrinnbarer Notwendigkeit zum Verbrecher— wenn auch vielleicht zum unentdeckten—werden lässt, ganz unabhängig von allen sozialen und individuellen Lebensbedingungen. Ein solcher Mensch ist zum Verbrecher geboren, er ist, wie Lombroso sagt, 'delinquente nato'" (2).
11. Galassi 145–7. For a useful overview of what changed in the various editions of *Criminal Man,* see Matt DeLisi's entry "Cesare Lombroso" in *Oxford Bibliographies*. For an extensive overview of Lombroso's reception in Germany, see Bondio, *Rezeption*.
12. "Man solte meinen, es wäre selbstverständlich, dass bei einer psychologischen oder anthropologischen Untersuchung nicht blos derjenige und nicht jeder als Verbrecher zu gelten hat, der auf einer gesetzwidrigen Handlung ertappt worden ist" (Bleuler 3).
13. He claimed, among other statements, that the brain of a criminal was closer to that of an ape than to that of Man (*Naturgeschichte* 72–3); that the hands of pickpockets were commonly long and narrow, "like

those of gibbons or orang-utans" (*Naturgeschichte* 90), and that the prominent jaws and lower foreheads of criminals revealed their far greater interest in chewing than in thinking or feeling ("An solchen Gesichtern gewinnt man sofort den Eindruck, dass für ihre Besitzer Kauen ein viel wichtigeres Geschäft ist, als das hinter der engen, sich nach hinten versteckenden Stirn sich abspielende Denken und Fühlen"; *Naturgeschichte* 45).
14. "ein fast sechsjähriger Aufenthalt in Dörfern und Kleinstädten des preussischen Ostens, mitten unter den Tagelöhnern der östlichen Latifundien hat mich überzeugt, dass auch die elendesten Löhne, dass eine lebenslange Ernährung mit Kartoffeln und Sauerkraut, eine tiefe Erniedrigung in hoffnungslose Abhängigkeit, Verachtung und Schmutz nicht genügen, um aus normal veranlagten Menschen Verbrecher zu machen. Wohl aber wirken diese Zustände in andrer Weise auf die Kriminalitätsziffer. Die elende Ernährung bedingt [...] im Lauf der Generationen ihre Wirkungen anhäufend eine Degeneration der Nachkommenschaft dieser beklagenswerten Bevölkerung, und aus diesen degenerierten Kindern schlechtgenährter Eltern rekrutiert sich das Verbrechertum" (Kurella, *Naturgeschichte* 170).
15. On degeneration, see Wetzell, *Inventing the Criminal* 46–50.
16. See Bondio, *Rezeption* 110.
17. Kraepelin, "Das Verbrechen als soziale Krankheit," 22–44.
18. Bondio, *Rezeption* 140.
19. Quoted in Wetzell, *Inventing the Criminal* 38.
20. Pointed out by Wetzell, *Inventing the Criminal* 67, among many others.
21. See Wetzell's summation of Aschaffenburg's findings in *Inventing the Criminal* 63–7.
22. For this aspect of Aschaffenburg's work, see also Bondio, *Rezeption* 215–8.
23. "Society must protect itself against incorrigible criminals, and since we do not want to decapitate or hang them and cannot deport them, the only course remaining is internment for life (or for an indefinite period of time)."—"Gegen die Unverbesserlichen muß die Gesellschaft sich schützen; und da wir köpfen und hängen nicht wollen und deportieren nicht können, so bleibt nur die Einsperrung auf Lebenszeit (bezw. auf unbestimmte Zeit)" (Liszt's original quoted in Christian Müller 132).
24. The quotation ("infolge günstiger äußerer Umstände noch nicht zur Begehung eines Verbrechens gekommen ist") is taken from von Liszt's "Entwurf eines Gesetzes betreffend die Verwahrung gemeingefährlicher Geisteskranker und vermindert Zurechnungsfähiger" (1904); qtd Galassi 349.
25. On Liszt, see Wetzell, *Inventing the Criminal* 31–7 and "Criminology" 402; Bondio, *Rezeption* 224–9 and 231–8; Baumann 51; Gerteis 92–3.
26. Wetzell, *Inventing the Criminal* 74–5 and 96; see also Galassi 190 and 360 on the subject of preemptive imprisonment.
27. On this discussion, see Galassi 377–94.
28. According to Bondio, hardly anyone spoke in favor of these models (*Rezeption* 146).
29. Wetzell, *Inventing the Criminal* 97–9; citation and discussion 99.
30. Wetzell, *Inventing the Criminal* 100–5. On Näcke and Groß, see also Christian Müller, particularly 152–5.

31. Bondio has claimed that in 1911, racial hygiene and eugenics were among the most discussed subjects among criminologists (*Rezeption* 146); see also Bondio, *Rezeption* 165 and Galassi 402–3.

32. "Wenn es dem Menschen gelungen ist, hornloses Rindvieh (Suffolkcattle) und Pflaumen ohne Kern dadurch zu züchten, daß man eine günstige Variante aufgriff und festhielt, die gekernten Pflaumen und die gehörnten Rinder aber aus dem Fortpflanzungsprozeß ausschaltete, so weiß ich nicht, warum es nicht ebenso gelingen sollte, einen moralischen Menschenschlag systematisch zu züchten. Solange wir noch keine ganz genaue Kenntnis der Vererbungsgesetze haben, wird uns das große Mittel der Auslese diesem Ziel näher zu bringen haben" (Hentig 13).

33. "Es handelt sich um Individualelimination, wenn die Einzelperson künstlich Umweltbedingungen unterworfen wird, denen sie sich nicht mehr anpassen kann, ohne in der Regel sogleich oder nach Verlauf einiger Zeit zugrunde zu gehen" (Hentig 24).

34. "Die schwere Gefahr liegt darin, daß die lebensschwachen Individuen nur für ein paar Monate oder Wochen sich von den Strafanstalten beherbergen lassen und dann frisch gestärkt in die Freiheit hinausgehen, ihr Schädlingsdasein fortsetzen und womöglich noch ihr verdorbenes Keimplasma an die Zukunft weitergeben" (Hentig 167).

35. Wetzell, *Inventing the Criminal* 10.

36. See Weindling; Bondio, *Rezeption* 151.

37. "Alle Kriminalpsychologen sind darüber einig, daß den Verbrecher eine gewisse geistige Minderheit kennzeichnet, als deren Ausfluß unter anderem eben das Verbrechen erscheint" (Wulffen, *Gauner- und Verbrechertypen* 8).

38. "Im allgemeinen ist der Verbrecher nur wenig originell. Er betätigt vielfach nur einen simplen Nachahmungstrieb. Er wiederholt immer nur dasselbe, was er von Jugend auf getan hat, was er von gleichgesinnten Genossen gehört und gesehen, was er in den Zeitungen gelesen hat usw. Selbst das große Verbrechertum läuft sich die Kinderschuhe nicht ab" (Wulffen, *Gauner- und Verbrechertypen* 10).

39. "Der Zustand des Somnambulen, des Nachtwandlers, ist eine Steigerung dieser Verfassung in das Pathologische, in das Krankhafte. Wie der Nachtwandler sicher über die Dächer steigt, so sicher verübt der Instinktverbrecher seine Tat" (Wulffen, *Gauner- und Verbrechertypen* 15).

40. "Uns aber erfaßt am Schlusse dieses Buches das beruhigende Gefühl der Sicherheit [...]. Der Gedanke an das Unentrinnbare, in das der Verbrecher seinen zerbrechlichen Nachen steuert, kommt über uns" (Wulffen, *Gauner- und Verbrechertypen* 313).

41. On this case, see Vyleta, *Crime* 1–2, 178–217, 223 and the excerpts from trial records published by Paul-Schiff.

42. On the murder of Ernst Winter and its consequences, see Helmut Walser Smith and Christoph Nonn.

43. Arkel, for example, considers "the large-scale use made of the ritual murder charge," given that it had previously been virtually forgotten, one of the most interesting features of *fin-de-siècle* Austrian antisemitism (14). On the popularity of the accusation around the turn of the century, see, among others, Jeggle, Lichtblau, Erb and Hopp 28. Johannes Schwarz has traced the theme in the frequent contemporary cartoon portrayal of Jews as vampires.

44. See Rainer Hering 199.

45. See, for example, the edition of 28 September 1897, p. 6.

46. Gilman, *The Case of Sigmund Freud* 170.

47. Gilman, *Jewish Self-Hatred* 68–83. On the criminal argot, see also Kurella, *Naturgeschichte* 220–3, who traces its origin to the "reception of Hebrew words into Yiddish" ("Rezeption der hebräischen Worte des Judendeutsch") but claims that Yiddish traces in criminal language are gradually being replaced by aspects of Berlin dialect, since Berlin contained by far the largest concentration of crooks (223). In other words: even to Germany's greatest defender of biologically determined criminality, the similarity between Yiddish and criminal argot are not a racial but a historical category and thus subject to historical and geographical change.

48. Vyleta, *Crime* 41–52, the citation 41.

49. Vyleta, *Crime* 41, his list of attributes 40.

50. Vyleta, *Crime* 161.

51. Vyleta, *Crime* 9.

52. Vyleta, *Crime* 161.

53. "In 1892, twenty-seven traffickers—all Jewish—were tried in a Lemberg court for the charge of transporting twenty-nine females (twenty of these themselves Jewish) to various destinations abroad. Ten days of hearings resulted in twenty-two convictions, and gave antisemitic publications plenty of time to rehearse the theme" (Vyleta, *Crime* 58). On the white slavery discourse and specifically Berg's treatise, see Vyleta, *Crime* 57–61.

54. I am using Vyleta's translation of the citation in *Crime* 60. Berg's original reads: "dank dem von den deutschen Sicherheitsbehörden bisher nur zu wenig gehinderten Wüten dieser Seelenverkäufer befindet sich das gesamte Ausland, die niedrigsten Rassen und der Abschaum der ganzen Menschheit, der Neger und Chinesen, der Kulis und Mulatten, der Hottentotten, Kaffern und Samojeden in der Lage, ihre tierischen Gelüste an den verratenen und verkauften Töchtern gerade der deutschen Nation befriedigen zu können" (36).

55. Berg 28–9.

56. "Daran beteiligt sich die ganze Bande ohne Unterschied von Stand und Bildung, von gesellschaftlicher Stellung und Beruf" (Berg 10).

57. "Hinterlistigste Niedertracht, grausamste Unmenschlichkeit, skrupellose Verübung von Verrat und Vertrauensbruch, das sind die für diesen Handel erforderlichen unentbehrlichen Seelenrequisiten./Irgendeinem anderen Volke ist es nun schlechterdings unmöglich, solche Ungeheuer zu erzeugen. [...] allein auf Grund ihres allgemeinen niedrigen Rassencharakters. Das ist ein unbestrittenes Privilegium dieser Rasse" (Berg 11).

58. For example: "ein rückständiges fremdes Volkes" (*sic*; Berg 39).

59. Berg 29–30.

60. Although Berg does not specify, he is most likely referring not to Samuel Richardson's 1748 novel but to an eponymous novel published originally in Paris in 1892 by the pseudonymous "Lord Monroe" and followed by a German edition in the same year (see Berg 18 and 26). Josef Schrank, whom Berg cited as liberally as Schrank quoted him, cites the same novel on p. 15.

61. Berg 36.

62. Berg 19–20.

63. Berg 37–8.

64. "hoffen wir, daß trotz der jahrzehntelangen Entnervungs- und Betäubungs-Versuche der jüdischen Preßkünste, der deutschen Nation noch soviel Rache-Energie geblieben ist, um über die Köpfe der Advokaten ihrer in Menschenfleisch machenden Rassegenossen hinweg endlich Das in Angriff zu nehmen, was schon lange eine Forderung des nationalen Ehrgefühls und wahrer Menschlichkeit gewesen ist, und was schon lange hätte geschehen müssen, nämlich einen erbarmungslosen Vertilgungskrieg gegen dieses semitische Raubgesindel zu beginnen, das die ganze Nation vor sich selbst im Innern und vor dem gesamten Auslande so schmachvoll entwürdigt" (Berg 41–2).

65. "Verfasser vermied hiebei alles, was der Schrift einen tendenziösen Charakter in politischer, konfessioneller oder nationaler Richtung geben könnte" (Schrank, "Vorrede" iii).

66. "Der Export von Mädchen findet aber nur mit wenigen Ausnahmen, aus den europäischen Staaten statt" (Schrank 10); "fast durchweg sind dies Juden" (29).

67. Schrank 26–7.

68. For example: "In der *Türkei* wird hauptsächlich in Konstantinopel und fast ausschließlich von Juden der Mädchenhandel betrieben. Die verhandelten Mädchen sind meist christlicher Religion" (Schrank 58, emphasis original). Or: "Die Polizei in Buenos-Ayres, kümmert sich wenig oder gar nicht um den Mädchenhandel, welcher großartig organisiert ist und meist von Juden betrieben wird" (Schrank 70).

69. Presentation of research, in fact, makes up the bulk of his book; see, among others, his lengthy passages on international laws (104–35) and conference reports (135–245).

70. "In Folge des wirtschaftlichen Druckes, unter dem die Juden in den russischen Provinzen stehen, kommt es vor, daß sie selbst ihre eigenen Töchter an die Mädchenhändler verkaufen" (Schrank 57). Even more fervent is his claim "daß die Mädchenhändler mit Vorliebe ihre Opfer aus der jüdischen Bevölkerung der ost-europäischen Länder suchen und ihr verbrecherisches Vorgehen hauptsächlich in der rücksichtslosen Ausbeutung der wirtschaftlichen Notlage dieser Klasse der Bevölkerung besteht" (Schrank 231).

71. "Die europäische Prostitution in Indien und Ostasien rekrutiert sich vorzugsweise aus Jüdinnen aus den Balkanstaaten, Österreich-Ungarn und Rußland. Diese, bereits von Jugend auf der Unzucht ergeben, waren vorher in der Levante und in Ägypten in Bordells, sind daher als Opfer nicht mehr zu bezeichnen" (Schrank 77).

72. "Es wurde von einem Wiener Tagblatt behauptet, daß die christlichen Arier um den Mädchenhandel in Österreich sich nicht zu sehr erhitzen brauchen, da von den aus Österreich exportierten Mädchen nur 1/10 Christinnen sind, es sich daher zumeist um Jüdinnen handelt. Verfasser ist der Meinung, daß nicht nur die Regierung, sondern jeder Einzelne, der in der Lage ist, gegen diesen sozialen Aussatz etwas tun zu können, welcher Religion, Nation oder Rasse die Opfer angehören den Mädchenhandel zu vernichten trachten soll" (Schrank 253).

73. "Bis jetzt hat sie durch ihre unermüdliche Tätigkeit Großes geleistet" (Schrank 175). Schrank lists a number of international organizations and committees dedicated to the struggle against white slavery (193); he himself headed one of them, the Aus-

trian League for the Repression of White Slavery (Vyleta, *Crime* 58).

74. "daß gerade der jüdische Mädchenhandel die teuflischste Blüte jüdischer Geldsucht zeigt" (Schrank 92).

75. Vyleta, *Crime* 59.

76. I am quoting Vyleta's translation (*Crime* 60) of Schrank's statement; in the original: "Die [...] exportierten Mädchen sind zum größten Teile (bei 90%) Jüdinnen, viele sind darunter, die sich freiwillig den Mädchenhändlern überliefern, um durch die Prostitution im Auslande sich soviel Geld zu verdienen, daß sie in ihre Heimat zurückgekehrt, sich verheiraten oder ein Geschäft etablieren können" (Schrank 42).

77. Vyleta, *Crime* 60.

78. "Diese Unwissenheit erklärt sich in erster Linie daraus, daß die Christen in der Regel sich sehr wenig um die Religionsgesetze und die rituellen Gebräuche des talmudischen Judentums kümmern und dasselbe meistenteils in einen Topf mit der mosaischen Religion werfen" (Mommert v).

79. The appendix is on pp. 97–106.

80. The case is described at length on 25–49 and includes a graphic description of the murder itself followed by extensive quotation of interrogation records of all killers involved.

81. Mommert 46.

82. Mommert 50.

83. Mommert 69–71.

84. "Viel einfacher und richtiger wäre es, wenn die Juden sich alle taufen ließen und Christen würden" (Mommert 47).

85. "Die Bluthändler [...] verkauften es um sehr hohen Preis an *solche Glaubensgenossen, die keine Gelegenheit hatten, selbst Christenknaben abzuschlachten*" (Mommert 110, emphasis original).

86. Mommert 112–3.

87. Mommert 107.

88. Mommert v, 46, 78 and elsewhere on secrecy towards Jews; towards non-Jews 16–9; 23.

89. "als ob die Juden damit *Kraftproben* geben und uns zeigen wollten, welche Macht sie durch ihr Geld, ihr Zusammenhalten und ihre in einflußreiche Stellen geschobenen Freunde besitzen, und wie wehrlos die "Zweifüßler" (Nichtjuden) aller Länder ihnen gegenüber stehen" (Mommert 106, emphasis original).

90. For a brief assessment of this work, see Greive 88–9.

91. "Und doch ist der heißentbrannte Kampf gegen den kapitalistischen Moloch, der Kampf für die Erhaltung des Christentums unzertrennlich mit der Bekämpfung des Judentums verbunden. [...] Die Aufklärung über die Errungenschaften der Juden soll ein Ansporn sein zur Nacheiferung [...]. Abkehr von den Schädlichkeiten des Judentums, Aufschwung zur Kulturhöhe des Judentums im Geiste Christi, das sei die Richtlinie für den Kampf der Gegenwart, die Losung für die Zukunft!" (Rost 3–4).

92. "Das dritte Grundübel ist das *Judentum*. Seit Jahrtausenden sitzt dieser Völkersplitter den Nationen im Nacken, wie ein unabwendbares Verhängnis" (Rost 6).

93. "Heute sind sie eine furchtbare Macht im Wirtschaftsleben der Nationen, welche tonangebenden Charakter beansprucht" (Rost 10–20, the citation 20).

94. Rost 23–48.

95. Rost 53–6 ("Zuwiderhandlungen gegen das

Gesetz über die *Sonntagsruhe und den Ladenschluß"* 55; emphasis original); 58.

96. Rost 58.

97. "Diese Sucht, auf kapitalistisch-spekulativem Wege die Arbeit des Lebens auszufüllen, ist eine unleugbare Rasseneigenschaft des Judentums. Wie ein unwiderstehbarer Zwang lastet der Drang auf dem Judentum, durch Handel und Geldgeschäfte sich zu bereichern" (Rost 21).

98. Rost 19.

99. "Die jüdische Rasse [...] ist nach einer Seite ihrer Veranlagung gleichsam die Inkarnation kapitalistisch-kaufmännischen Geistes" (Rost 30).

100. Rost 93–8.

101. "Der Rassenantisemitismus hat als letzte Konsequenz die Ausweisung der Juden aus den Staatsgrenzen zur Folge" (Rost 90).

102. Wulffen, *Der Sexualverbrecher* 302–3 ("jüdischer Unternehmungsgeist").

103. Hellpach as cited in Gilman, *Sigmund Freud* 177.

104. "Daß die den Schluß des Flugblattes bildende Behauptung, der Jude dürfe zu *gottesdienstlichem Zwecke* Nichtjuden ermorden, eine böse Unwahrhaftigkeit ist" (*Jews: Can They Be Called "Criminals for Religious Reasons"?—Die Juden, dürfen sie "Verbrecher von Religions wegen" genannt werden?*, 1893, 8, emphasis original); more generally on the ritual murder accusation in his *Blood Superstitions (Der Blutaberglaube*, 1892).

105. On some of these writers, see Lipphardt 127–8 and Vyleta, *Crime* 116, 150–5, 218–21.

106. Fuld 4–5.

107. "Pflegt ja doch nicht der einzelne Schuldige einer religiösen Minorität für eine schandhafte That *allein* verantwortlich gemacht zu werden, wird doch im Gegentheil jedes Verbrechen eines Anhängers derselben benützt, um auf die gesammte Glaubensgemeinschaft den Stein zu werfen, sie als eine 'Gaunerbande,' als ein Konglomerat verbrecherischer und depravirter Menschen hinzustellen, gegen welche nur strenger Zwang und Ausnahmegesetzgebung schützen könne" (Fuld 6).

108. Fuld 7–8.

109. Fuld 9–11.

110. On crime statistics, 22–33; on perjury specifically, 19–22.

111. "In der antisemitischen Bewegung spielt die Behauptung eine grosse Rolle, dass die Juden durch eine ganz besondere Veranlagung zum Verbrechen eine Gefahr für jene Länder seien, in denen sie sich aufhalten. Wie so viele Behauptungen von verwandter Art wird auch diese Angabe meist ohne jeden Beweis ausgesprochen; und ist sie nur häufig genug ausgesprochen, so gilt sie auf Grund der ewigen Wiederholungen schon als Wahrheit; sie wird schliesslich als Thatsache hingenommen. [...] Die nachstehenden Zusammenstellungen bringen nackte Zahlen mit kurzen Erläuterungen dazu, die nicht für Fanatiker geschrieben sind, sondern für solche Leute, welche die objective Wahrheit zu suchen wünschen" (Comite vii).

112. Comite viii.

113. Comite ix.

114. Comite 19.

115. Comite 38–41; see also their statistics showing that a large number of acquittals could be linked to false accusations (37).

116. Comite xv–xvi.

117. Comite xii.

118. Comite 15.

119. Comite 47–56.

120. Wassermann, *Beruf* 46.

121. Wassermann, *Beruf* 92.

122. Liszt, "Das Problem" 7.

123. *"Der Mädchenhandel ist ein spezifisch jüdischer Erwerbszweig.* Die Mädchenhändler sind in allen Staaten fast durchwegs Juden" (Rost 60–1; emphasis original).

124. "So kann man denn im Anklang an das bekannte Schlagwort von Franzos ["Jedes Land hat die Juden, die es verdient"] den Satz aufstellen: Jedes Land hat die Kriminalität der Juden, die seinen politischen und wirtschaftlichen Verhältnissen entspricht, d. h. die *Kriminalität der Juden eines Landes ist nichts festes,* sie ist nicht bedingt durch die Rasse und wurzelt nicht im Wesen einer jeweils mehr oder minder ausgeprägten jüdischen Eigenart. Sie ist *vielmehr* das *Produkt sozialer Verhältnisse, auf das Rasseneigentümlichkeiten, wenn überhaupt, nur in einem ganz geringen Masse einwirken"* (Wassermann, *Beruf* 92, emphases original).

Incorrigibles v. Inferiors

1. "Die Kriminalbiologie ist *die Lehre von der Persönlichkeit in ihren ursächlichen Beziehungen zum Verbrechen"* (Antonow 10, emphases original).

2. Simon, "Einleitung" 11.

3. "The most striking aspect of the development of the sociological study of crime in Germany before the First World War is the virtual absence of sociologists or other social scientists working on the subject." This disinterest continued in the Weimar Republic. The 1931 *Handwörterbuch der Soziologie* contained no entry on crime: "sociologists showed almost no interest in the subject" (Wetzell, *Inventing* 107–8; see also his remarks on 295–6).

4. Reik 33–4, 36.

5. "Nein, ich wünsche nicht, daß die Psychoanalyse in den Gerichtssaal 'hereingelassen' werde."— "Ist von seiten der Psychologie in absehbarer Zeit keine Hilfe in der Lösung dieser Aufgabe zu gewärtigen? Ich glaube: nein" (Reik 40 and 36 respectively).

6. Citation and discussion in Finder 448 and 465.

7. Wetzell, *Inventing* 299. Elsewhere, he states that "[...] psychiatrists became increasingly concerned with the welfare and protection of society as a whole rather than the individual patient [...]. psychiatrists' interest in identifying the genetic factors in criminal behavior was related to their general enthusiasm for eugenics, which many began to see as a panacea not only for mental illness but for crime as well" (Wetzell, *Inventing* 125–6).

8. "Die NS-Diktatur förderte erbbiologisch orientierte Kriminologen ebenso, wie sie deren eher soziologisch ausgerichtete Gegner diskriminierte, ja teilweise aus dem Land trieb. [...] Die kriminalbiologische Lehre war rassistische Wissenschaft, da sie Gruppen von Menschen aufgrund ihrer Gene als minderwertig klassifizierte" (Patrick Wagner, *Volksgemeinschaft* 270).

9. One example of many is Max Mikorey's article "Judaism in Criminal Psychology" ("Das Judentum in

der Kriminalpsychologie," 1936), in which he denounces Lombroso, Aschaffenburg and Liszt as agents of this nefarious scheme and calls criminal psychology "the Categorical Imperative of Political Jewry to gain messianic world domination!" ("der kategorische Imperativ des politischen Judentums zur messianischen Weltherrschaft!"; citation 82). Mikorey also delivered a lecture at the 1936 conference on "Jews and Crime" of the NS Association of Lawyers (Rechtswahrerbund), in which he claimed that Jewish criminal psychology had a vested interest in explaining crime sociologically rather than by reference to biology or race (Wetzell, *Inventing* 187–9).

10. Antonow 13.

11. Wetzell, *Inventing* 126–7. On the elimination of criminological disciplines other than criminal biology, see also Simon, "Kriminalbiologie," particularly 79–80, and Baumann 69–70.

12. On Viernstein's work, see Christian Müller 247–63.

13. Baumann 14.

14. Wetzell, *Inventing* 133. On the nature of the questions, see Christian Müller 244–5 and Liang 441–2.

15. On the numbers of questionnaires and the spread of the system to other states, see Liang 425; Baumann 57–64; Christian Müller 231–6; Simon, "Kriminalbiologie" 84–6.

16. Christian Müller 251; 238–9.

17. Wetzell, *Inventing* 136.

18. Christian Müller 263–4.

19. "Ausmerzung der für Volkstum und Rasse als unerwünscht erkannten Volksgenossen" (Viernstein quoted in Simon, "Kriminalbiologie" 80); see also similar statements by Viernstein quoted in Christian Müller 250 and Wetzell, *Inventing* 130.

20. Wetzell, *Inventing* 134–5.

21. Simon, "Einleitung" 10.

22. Reulecke 205.

23. Christian Müller 173–4; Wetzell, *Inventing* 238.

24. Weindling 391; for further examples of calls for eugenic measures throughout the early 1920s, see Weindling 396 and Schwartz, particularly 29–60.

25. "Wir stellen es als eine Forderung der Kriminalpolitik auf [...] dass jedes Verbrechen, wenn es wirksam bekämpft werden soll, aus der Persönlichkeitsstruktur des Täters abgeleitet werden muss" (cited in Baumann 68).

26. See Binding and Hoche and discussions of their work in the anthology edited by Riha, the analysis by Hafner and Winau, Weindling 394–6 and Christian Müller 172–3.

27. Lange 96; on his work, see Baumann 65; Dölling 199; Wetzell, "Criminology" 407 and 409 and *Inventing* 161–6.

28. "Unter Berücksichtigung aller Einzelheiten kommt man zwangsläufig zu der Schlussfolgerung, dass rassehygienische Maßnahmen gerade bei Schwerkriminellen unbedingt zu fordern sind" (Stumpfl, *Erbanlage* 299). On his work, see Antonow 25, Baumann 93; Wetzell, *Inventing* 191–200.

29. Quoted in Wetzell, *Inventing* 192.

30. Wetzell, *Inventing* 198.

31. Wetzell, *Inventing* 154–7.

32. Wetzell has diagnosed the new definition of abnormal character traits as congenital as the major difference: "This view marked a change from the prewar

years, when most psychiatrists had subscribed to the theory of degeneration, which attributed such abnormalities to a combination of genetic and environmental factors" (*Inventing* 175). On the disappearance of 'environment' from the discussion, see also Baumann 16.

33. "Wenn ein Verbrecher oder Asozialer Vorfahren hat, die ebenfalls verbrecherisch oder asozial lebten [...], ist nach den Ergebnissen der Erbforschung erwiesen, daß sein Verhalten erbbedingt ist. Ein solcher Mensch muß [...] in anderer Weise angepackt werden, als ein Mensch, der [...] einer anständigen Familie entstammt [...] Der Verbrecher wird nicht mehr als Einzelperson, seine Tat nicht mehr als Einzeltat angesehen. Er ist vielmehr als Sproß und Ahn einer Sippe, seine Tat als Tat eines Sippengliedes zu betrachten." The quotation is taken from a manifesto published in 1938 by Paul Werner, SS-Oberführer and Head of Legal Administration at the Central Office of Security Police, and quoted by Patrick Wagner, *Volksgemeinschaft* 266.

34. "[W]er kann denn überhaupt unterscheiden, wer ein Berufsverbrecher und wer ein Gelegenheitsverbrecher ist? Na? Das wissen nur wir, und wir werden es nicht sagen." The passage, purportedly a transcript of the words of a recidivist robber, is taken from Artur Landsberger's *The Underworld Speaks* (*Die Unterwelt spricht*, 1929) and cited in Wagner, *Volksgemeinschaft* 411–2.

35. On these developments, see Baumann 94–8; on feeble-mindedness in particular, a category that was immensely expanded during the NS-years and that served as the basis for most sterilizations, see Baumann 80–3; Weindling 533; Wetzell, *Inventing* 260–8.

36. "Die *künftige Strafrechtspflege* wird ihr oberstes Ziel darin sehen, dass sie sich in den *Dienst der Volksaufartung* zu stellen hat. Dieses Ziel aber schließt *zwei Aufgaben* in sich: die Wiederherstellung der *Verantwortlichkeit des Einzelnen* gegenüber der Volksgemeinschaft und die *Ausscheidung volks- und rasseschädlicher Bestandteile* aus letzterer" (Mezger 203, emphasis original). On Mezger, see Baumann 98–106, Dölling 202–9.

37. "Kampfrecht zum Schutze und zur Entfaltung des Volkes" (citation and discussion in Dölling 209).

38. The psychiatrist Hans Otto Luxenburger had claimed that predilection was a far more significant causal factor for crime than environment, that education could not improve on criminal predilection, and that punishment was essentially powerless to deter or rehabilitate, leaving only permanent imprisonment or sterilization as punitive options (on Luxenburger's work, see Baumann 70–9). Identical arguments were advanced throughout the 1920s by Oda Olberg and others; see Schwartz 40–8 and 53–60.

39. As expressed, for example, in the 1939 report of the Center for Criminalistic Family Research (Zentralstelle für kriminalistische Sippenschaftsforschung, founded in 1938); see Wagner, *Volksgemeinschaft* 271.

40. Concrete examples, to which undoubtedly many more could be added, are offered in the following sources: Dölling 201 and 205–9; Baumann 51–3, 78–84, 88–9; Weindling 391–6 and 450; Wetzell, *Inventing* 177–80, 183–5, 237–44, 255–8; Wagner, *Volksgemeinschaft* 264–6, 269, 271; Christian Müller 172–3. The suggestion for the pre-emptive death penalty came from Karl Astel (1898–1945), a racial scientist and rector of the University of Jena. The

ideas he presented to Hitler in 1937 "included a preventive death penalty for would-be murderers. He set
to work to build up a data bank of index cards by
means of which he could sift out the "antisocial" and
"pathologically degenerate" from the supposedly
racially valuable elements of the population. He
hunted for homosexuals, criminals and the mentally
subnormal, while praising the value of the peasant
stock for the regeneration of the Volk" (Weindling
529).

41. Wetzell, *Inventing* 183–4.

42. The Imperial German Penal Code, the *Reichs-
strafgesetzbuch*, took effect in 1871. A first reform
commission was appointed in 1906; a first revision
draft was published in 1909 and a second planned for
1914 when reform efforts were abandoned due to the
First World War. Reform efforts picked up again in
the 1920s, with a first draft debated by parliament in
1927 (Wetzell, *Inventing* 74–6 and 121).

43. Christian Müller has provided a good overview
of parliamentary discussions and failed penal law reform measures during the Weimar Republic; see particularly 181–223.

44. Wetzell, *Inventing* 249–51; Schreiber 166.

45. On the use of eugenics in these and other NS
laws, see Wetzell, *Inventing* 255–73; Weindling 525,
and Simon, "Kriminalbiologie" 95–9; on the indebt-
edness of these laws to criminal biology, see Wetzell,
Inventing 235–6; Schreiber 167–8.

46. Schreiber 158–9; the quotations ("Erhaltung
des Blutes, die Bewahrung der völkischen Treue und
der Gemeinschaft an die Spitze der Ziele des
Strafrechts [...] Die Strafbarkeit habe zu beginnen,
sobald der verbrecherische Wille in Erscheinung getreten sei") 158. In the end, the reformed Penal Law
was never enacted, probably because World War in-
tervened, as it had in 1914 (Schreiber 166). On penal
law reform under the Nazis, see also Christian Müller
276–82.

47. "Das Strafgesetz sei nicht mehr als Magna
Charta des Individuums vor regelwidrigen Angriffen
der staatlichen Strafgewalt zu verstehen, sondern es
habe die Gesamtheit der Volks- und Staatsinteressen
zu schützen" (cited in Schreiber 157). On this development, see Rüping 181.

48. "Der SS-Richter dient der Gerechtigkeit.
Gerecht ist allein diejenige Entscheidung, die den
Willen der Volksgemeinschaft ausspricht. Der
Wille der Volksgemeinschaft aber ist der Wille [ihres]
besten Mannes, des Führers" (cited by Rüping 191).

49. Baumann 105.

50. For a discussion of this work, see Wagner,
Volksgemeinschaft 20–36, 136 and *Hitlers Kriminalisten* 21–2.

51. Heindl's tables are on 185–88.

52. Heindl 140–1.

53. Heindl 142–55.

54. Heindl 158–60.

55. See Wagner, *Volksgemeinschaft* 31–6.

56. "Und damit gelangen wir zu der Maxime, daß
es sich sehr wohl mit der Gerechtigkeit verträgt, über
das nach allen Regeln der Juristenkunst für eine bestimmte *Tat* ausgerechnete Strafmaß hinauszugehen
und einen *Täter*, der sich nach seinem ganzen Vorleben als besonders gefährlich erwiesen hat, noch
länger, ja sogar lebenslänglich hinter Schloß und
Riegel zu halten. Er hat eben durch sein *Gesamt*verhalten eine solche Behandlung verdient und notwendig

gemacht."—"Denn von 1885 bis zum Weltkrieg hat
sich *kein einziger* Sicherungshäftling der Wiederent-
lassung würdig gezeigt" (Heindl 374 and 392, emphases original).

57. Theodor Viernstein had similarly claimed that
an offender's level of corrigibility depended on his
"Gesinnung" and that discovering this was "less a
matter of logical deduction than of ... a sense
[*Empfinden*] that one is dealing with a good or a bad
person, a sense that often cannot be explained"
(quoted in Wetzell, *Inventing* 136).

58. Wagner, *Volksgemeinschaft* 183–99.

59. See Daluege 12 (on Weimar Republic crime statistics), 22–3 (on imprisoning owners of suspicious
tools), 32–42 (on protective custody), 45–56 (on surveillance and curfews), and 59 (on the plummeting
crime rate in the NS-state).

60. See Antonow's genealogical table for Heinrich
Keil, 167. Similar arguments were advanced by Robert
Ritter, who called for the imprisonment of law-
abiding "asocials" based on the possibility that—to
cite just one of his examples—a mother's vanity might
combine with a father's profligacy to produce a son
destined to become a marriage impostor (Wagner,
Hitlers Kriminalisten 96–8).

61. Wagner, *Hitlers Kriminalisten* 51–2; on crime
statistics of the age and Nazi claims, see also his
Volksgemeinschaft 214–7.

62. Daluege 42; point made by Wagner, *Volksgemeinschaft* 219.

63. On this development, see, among others, Baumann 75; Wagner, *Volksgemeinschaft* 226 and 254–
5.

64. Wagner, *Volksgemeinschaft* 254–5.

65. On this and other crackdowns on homeless
shelters in these two years, see Wagner, *Volksgemeinschaft* 279–92.

66. Wagner, *Volksgemeinschaft* 295–300.

67. Wagner, *Volksgemeinschaft* 227–32.

68. For numbers and a breakdown per year, see
Baumann 86–8; similarly for numbers of people imprisoned pre-emptively: Wagner, *Hitlers Kriminalisten* 90–2.

69. New crimes that were assigned the death
penalty in the NS-years are listed by Schreiber 170–
4 and Baumann 102–3.

70. See Richard Wetzell's caution against this; *Inventing* 10.

71. On the Nazi phenomenon of "Gleichschaltung," see Bracher.

72. "Im anderen Falle bezeichnet er [the Jew, TSK]
das menschliche Wirken, sofern es dem Selbsterhal-
tungstriebe ohne Rücksicht auf das Wohl der Mitwelt
dient, als Diebstahl, Wucher, Raub, Einbruch usw."
(Hitler, *Mein Kampf* 326–31, the citation 326). On
Hitler's distinction between "Mammon" (identified
with Jews) and "idealism" (as an Aryan trait) in *Mein
Kampf*, see also Vuorinen, particularly 47–51.

73. Exner's *Kriminalbiologie* described as "Wesens-
züge der jüdischen Straffälligkeit: Zurücktreten der
Gewaltverbrechen, Hervortreten der Gewinnsuchts-
verbrechen," and thought that this "Gesamtbild der
jüdischen Straffälligkeit [stimmt] ganz auffallend mit
den Grundzügen des jüdischen Wesens überein."—
"Im Sozialen wie im Antisozialen ist er von mächtig-
stem Gewinnstreben beherrscht und verfolgt oft be-
denken- und rücksichtslos seine materiellen Interessen"
(Exner, *Kriminalbiologie*, 47–50 and 67 respectively).

On Exner's work, see also Dölling 210–1, Baumann 102, and Wetzell, *Inventing* 213–6.

74. Mezger 146–7 (1942 ed.). On the differences between the first and second editions of Mezger's work, see Baumann 101–2; on Mezger's work in general, see Wetzell, *Inventing* 210–3.

75. See Wetzell's remarks on the papers given by Max Mikorey and Johann von Leers at the 1936 conference of the Association of Lawyers (Rechtswahrerbund), *Inventing* 187–9.

76. Wetzell, *Inventing* 190–1; Wagner, *Hitlers Kriminalisten*.

77. Michael Berkowitz has offered an overview of interpretations of Jewish criminality in various areas of public life during the Nazi era (see both his *The Crime of My Very Existence* and "Unmasking Counterhistory").

78. Iwo 21–6.

79. On reporting in the *Völkischer Beobachter*, see Dennis.

80. Both citations from the cover of no. 7, September 1937. On *Der Stürmer*, see Roos, Showalter (particularly *Little Man*), Julia Schwarz on cartoons, and Hahn particularly on letters to the journal.

81. On the index, see Hahn 117.

82. Showalter, *Little Man* xii.

83. Dennis 459.

84. "[...] bei dem es nicht unter Anwendung eines modernen Strafgesetzbuches zu Zuchthaus und Aberkennung der bürgerlichen Ehrenrechte reichlich 'langen' würde" (Leers, "Die Kriminalität des Judentums" 6).

85. Leers, "Die Kriminalität des Judentums" 5–13, the citation ("in der zeitgenössischen Literatur die Klagen über jüdisches Verbrechertum") 13.

86. Leers, "Kriminalität" 9–10.

87. Leers, "Kriminalität" 54–7, the citations ("wesenhaft kriminell"/"das 'arimanische Tier', der Streiter der Finsternis gegen das Licht") on 55 and 57 respectively.

88. "So glaube ich heute im Sinne des allmächtigen Schöpfers zu handeln: Indem ich mich des Juden erwehre, kämpfe ich für das Werk des Herrn" (Hitler, *Mein Kampf* 69–70).

89. Keller and Andersen 10 (on Bolshevism), 15–6 (on language), 10 (on the essential criminal nature of Jews), 11 and 22 (on world domination), 12 (on Jews as Lucifer).

90. Keller and Andersen 17–9.

91. "Das Bezeichnende und Wesenseigentümliche des jüdischen Verbrechers ist, daß er seine Verbrechen so begeht, daß sie meist unentdeckt bleiben. Werden sie jedoch entdeckt, so versucht er, seiner Überführung und Verurteilung durch zahllose Machenschaften zu entgehen" (Keller and Andersen 20).

92. "Es ist nicht jüdische Art, jemand aus Eifersucht, aus Wut zu töten; die Juden verstehen es auf andere Art, einem mißliebigen Menschen ans Leben zu gehen. Der jüdische Mörder tötet aus Berechnung und mit kalter Überlegung" (Keller and Andersen 159).

93. Keller and Andersen 160.

94. Keller and Andersen on American gangsters (162–74) and the Russian Revolution, Bolshevism and the murder of the Tsar and his family (10, 21–24, 186 and elsewhere).

95. Keller and Andersen 22.

96. "Ich habe geschossen, weil ich Jude bin. Ich bin mir meiner Tat vollkommen bewußt und bereue sie auf keinen Fall" (Keller and Andersen 207; in that chapter, the authors claim that Jews routinely confess to major crimes referring to their own race as the sole motive).

97. "So richtet sich seine 'Religion' gegen Gott, sein Gesetz gegen das Recht, seine Moral gegen die Sittlichkeit. Seine Natur ist widernatürlich, sein Volksbewußtsein ist anti–völkisch, sein Nationalismus ist internationalistisch und seine Politik ist das Verbrechen. So ist der Jude der wahre *Gegenmensch*, das verdorbene Glied einer unterrassischen Mischung. Er ist der geborene Anführer des Untermenschentums" (Keller and Andersen 11, emphasis original).

98. Hartner-Hnizdo, *Das jüdische Gaunertum* xi, 1–10.

99. Hartner-Hnizdo, *Das jüdische Gaunertum* 17–8.

100. Hartner-Hnizdo, *Volk der Gauner* 15–21.

101. Hartner-Hnizdo, *Das jüdische Gaunertum* 355–62.

102. Hartner-Hnizdo, *Das jüdische Gaunertum* 28–32 and 263; see also his interpretation of Jewish mugshots on 176–7.

103. Hartner-Hnizdo, *Volk* 71.

104. "Die Judenfrage ist eine Fieberkrankheit, die immer neu die arische Kulturwelt durchrüttelt; Krankheiten aber soll man heilen" (Hartner-Hnizdo, *Volk* 4).

105. "Das Judentum selbst krankt am Judentume und es ist—von der durch scharfe Judengegnerschaft geschaffenen künstlichen Einheit abgesehen—nur so weit einigermaßen vor einer Selbstzersetzung geschützt, als sich der arische Ordnungsgeist durchsetzt" (Hartner-Hnizdo, *Das jüdische Gaunertum* 365).

106. Hartner-Hnizdo, *Volk* 3–4.

107. ***"Es wird aber auch klar, daß der 'Gott der Rache' die jüdische Hemmungslosigkeit ist, die jede Art von Sittenlosigkeit und Verbrechertum in einem Maße groß werden und sich auswirken läßt, daß sie zuletzt das eigene Volk züchtigt und zugleich zur Erhebung der arischen Welt wider Israel führt"*** (Hartner-Hnizdo, *Das jüdische Gaunertum* 365, bold-face italicization original).

108. Berkowitz, *The Crime* 36 and elsewhere.

109. The term used by Galassi to describe the beholdenness of criminology to penal reform (427); Peter Strasser has also pointed out that criminology in the service of penal reform was robbed of its ability to do disinterested research.

110. Wetzell, *Inventing* 299. Wetzell has pointed out this dilemma numerous times. For example: "it might have been genuinely comforting to attribute criminal behavior to biological rather than social causes because this explanation relieved society of responsibility and distanced the supposedly abnormal criminal from the rest of society" (*Inventing* 71). And: criminology "focused on the individualization of punishment, that is, on the transformation of the offender rather than social change. From this perspective, criminal biology was welcome because it promised the knowledge about individual criminals that was crucial for an offender-oriented reform effort" ("Criminology" 422).

111. This is, of course, one of the most central insights of Foucault's work, particularly *Discipline and*

Punish, succinctly summarized by Daniel Vyleta: "Foucault suggests that the emerging new scientific discourse on crime, criminals and their punishment constituted a distinct system of knowledge that aimed at securing exclusionary power over those it identified as deviants. The identification of criminals as distinct from the general population, in other words, allowed for their surgical removal from society; the medicalisation of criminology went hand in hand with its potential and ambition for social engineering. Criminological knowledge is thus connected to eugenic measures such as forced sterilisation in the early and mid-twentieth century" (*Crime* 15).

112. Citations ("Massenpsychiatrie"; "seelische Volksgesundheit"; "Entartung des Volkes") and discussion of Kraepelin's works in Bondio, *Rezeption* 196–8.

113. Citations ("Träger eines gefährlichen Infektionsstoffes"; "gesellschaftlichen 'Organismus'"; "sittliche Gesundheit [...] der Gesamtheit") from Kraepelin, *Die Abschaffung des Strafmaßes* [1880], 71–5; discussion in Galassi 85–8.

114. "dauerhafte Quarantäne [...] Ausmerzung der infektiösen Elemente aus der Gemeinschaft der Besserungsfähigen in den Strafanstalten" (Kraepelin, *Abschaffung* 73).

115. I am using here the Kantian terms of moral law and natural rights as established in his *Metaphysics of Morals*.

116. Broszat, "Plädoyer" 384.

117. In his *Crime* 41–52 and elsewhere.

118. Wetzell, *Inventing* 187.

119. Peter Becker, *Verderbnis* 335.

120. "Als nunmehr *minderwertige* Menschen hatten sie keine Wahlmöglichkeit für oder gegen eine Integration in die Gesellschaft. Aufgrund ihrer psychophysischen Defekte galten sie zum abweichenden Verhalten bestimmt."—"Erst mit der Durchsetzung eines neuen Erzählmusters, das die Delinquenten als Nicht-Bürger begriff, konnten die gesellschaftlichen Außenseiter mit voller Berechtigung diskursiv von den Partizipationsrechten der bürgerlichen Gesellschaft ausgeschlossen werden. Diese neuen Denkansätze trugen außerdem zur Ent-Tribunalisierung von Individuum und Gesellschaft bei, indem sie die Nicht-Bürger als Menschen beschrieben, denen die innere Entwicklung zum Bürger für immer verwehrt blieb" (Peter Becker, *Verderbnis* 34 und 254 respectively).

121. On this part of Lombroso's work, see Galassi, particularly 153.

122. The *VB*-articles on cultural greats and their hatred of Jews are listed in Dennis 86–102; the citation is taken from Wagner's *Judaism in Music* and quoted in Dennis 102.

123. Hitler, *Mein Kampf* 490–1, the citation ("Erziehung zum rassen- und nationalbewußten Volksgenossen") on 490.

124. Arendt, *Origins* 316.

125. Arendt, *Origins* 80–1.

A Conman Plays a Captain

1. "Am 10. Oktober 1906 besetzte eine Handvoll Soldaten unter Führung eines Hauptmanns das Rathaus von Köpenick bei Berlin, verhaftete den Bürgermeister und beschlagnahmte die Stadtkasse. Ein paar Stunden später wurde bekannt, daß es das freche Bravourstück eines unbekannten Täters gewesen sei. Die Soldaten waren echt, der Hauptmann war falsch gewesen.... Die ganze Welt lachte, der Kaiser lachte mit, und die Berliner Polizei gab sich verzweifelte Mühe, den Täter zu finden. Als er sich dann schließlich selber stellte, traute man seinen Augen nicht. Es war ein mickriger kleiner Mann mit grauem Bart, ein Schuster namens Wilhelm Voigt. Die Uniform hatte er beim Trödler gekauft" (Kiaulehn, *Berlin* 528).

2. See, for example, "Der Kaiser und der 'Hauptmann von Köpenick,'" *Berliner Tageblatt und Handels-Zeitung*, November 2, 1906, Abend-Ausgabe 6; "Der Kaiser und der 'Hauptmann von Köpenick,'" *Berliner Volks-Zeitung*, November 2, 1906, Abend-Ausgabe 3; *Berliner Börsen-Zeitung*, November 3, 1906, 1. Beiblatt 5.—When citing newspaper articles, I will not designate morning-editions for those newspapers who ran them but will specify evening-editions ("Abend-Ausgabe") and supplements ("Beiblatt"); where those designations do not appear, readers should assume that the article cited appeared either in the morning edition or in the only edition of the day.

3. Voigt 5.

4. Voigt's criminal history is exceedingly well documented. The best collections of court documents are Heidelmeyer's *Der Fall Köpenick*, which contains excerpts of court documents, Voigt's autobiography, press reporting on the case, and many other contemporary documents, and *Wilhelm Voigt der Hauptmann von Köpenick*, a collection of court documents pertaining to the Köpenick-case. Voigt's various sentences are listed in documents republished in Heidelmeyer 48.

5. Voigt 10–13, the citation "*12 Jahre Zuchthaus*" 13, emphasis original.

6. "Nach Ansicht des Vorsitzenden der Strafkammer vom 1. Dezember 1906 wären heute solche Urteile nicht mehr möglich" (Voigt 13).

7. Siebenpfeiffer, "Nachwort" 119. The Klein/ Nebbe case is analyzed at length in Claßen 148–97.

8. Voigt 13 ("Lebendig tot").

9. As per Voigt's court testimony on December 1, 1906. Numerous newspapers covered the case in detail; Voigt's statement cited above was reported, among many others, in "Der Hauptmann von Köpenick vor Gericht," *Berliner Börsen-Zeitung*, December 1, 1906 (4. Beiblatt 9–10, the reference to his renewed contact with his sister on 10).

10. See the court documents cited in Heidelmeyer 54.

11. Court documents cited in Heidelmeyer 54.

12. Voigt 29–31.

13. Voigt 36.

14. The judge is quoted as saying: "*It is true that of the six witnesses called in the case, none was questioned in court. The minutes also do not state that either you yourself or the prosecutor had waived evidentiary hearing. Thus the sentence was certainly contestable*" ("*Es ist richtig; von den sechs damals geladenen Zeugen ist keiner vernommen worden. In dem Protokoll ist auch nicht vermerkt, dass der Staatsanwalt oder Sie selbst auf weitere Beweisaufnahme verzichtet haben. Das Urteil ist tatsächlich anfechtbar gewesen*.") "Der Hauptmann von Köpenick vor Gericht," *Berliner Börsen-Zeitung*, December 1, 1906 (4. Beiblatt 9–10, the citation 9–10, emphasis original).

15. "Wohl kaum ist jemals ein Mensch mit festerem Entschluß, sich den Forderungen der Gesellschaft in

allen Dingen anzubequemen, der Freiheit entge-
gengegangen!" Voigt 39.

16. Documentation in "Der Hauptmann von
Köpenick vor Gericht," *Berliner Tageblatt und Handels-
Zeitung,* December 1, 1906, Abend-Ausgabe 1–2 and
4; documents cited on 4. Some of Voigt's deportation
orders are reprinted in Heidelmeyer 60–2.

17. The spelling of his name in the press is variously either "Hilbrecht" or "Hillbrecht"; I am following Voigt's spelling of the name with a double l.

18. Hillbrecht's testimony is recorded verbatim,
among others, in "Der 'Hauptmann von Köpenick'
vor Gericht," *Berliner Börsen-Zeitung,* December 2,
1906, 1. Beiblatt 6–8; 2. Beiblatt 9; the testimony 1.
Beiblatt 7.

19. *"Da kam, allen unerwartet, plötzlich mein
Ausweisungsbefehl aus Wismar!"* Voigt 41, emphasis
original.

20. Hillbrecht's testimony, verbatim: "Voigt wept
bitterly and showed that he was deeply affected because he so badly wanted to remain with me. The witness also confirmed that Voigt had tried his very best
to obtain papers in Wismar. This, however, turned out
to be impossible for unknown reasons" ("Voigt hat bit-
terlich geweint und gezeigt, daß ihm dies sehr nahe
ging, weil er so gern bei mir bleiben wollte. Der Zeuge
bestätigt auch, daß sich Voigt in Wismar redlich bemüht habe, Papiere zu bekommen. Dies sei ihm jedoch
aus irgend einem Grunde nicht möglich gewesen.")
Berliner Börsen-Zeitung, December 2, 1906, 1. Beiblatt
6–8; 2. Beiblatt 9; the testimony 1. Beiblatt 7.

21. *"ohne Angabe des Grundes. [...] Hier beginnt
eigentlich schon der Tag von Köpenick!"* Voigt 41–2,
emphases original.

22. Voigt 47: "Auch das bürgt zur Genüge dafür,
daß die so sehr bemängelte Uniform in durchaus
tadellosem Zustande war."

23. For Voigt's claims about the receipt, see
Berliner Börsen-Zeitung, October 27, 1906, 8 ("war
niemals Hauptmann im 1. Garde-Regiment") and October 27, 1906, Abend-Ausgabe 4 ("von mir als
Hauptmann im 1. Garderegiment").

24. For example: "Der Handstreich des Pseudo-
hauptmanns," *Berliner Tageblatt und Handels-Zeitung,*
October 17, 1906, Abend-Ausgabe 3 and again on 4;
Berliner Börsen-Zeitung, October 18, 1906, 6; "Auf den
Spuren des falschen Hauptmanns," *Berliner Tageblatt
und Handels-Zeitung,* October 18, 1906, 3; *Berliner
Börsen-Zeitung,* October 19, 1906, 4.

25. "Die Kommandos des Angeklagten waren ganz
militärisch. Wenn jemand seinem Befehl nicht
nachkam, so herrschte er ihn in ganz strammem militärischen Ton an. [...] schnauzte sie der Herr Hauptmann an: Scheren Sie sich schleunigst in Ihre Bureaus
zurück, sonst lasse ich Gewalt anwenden." *Berliner
Börsen-Zeitung,* December 2, 1906, 1. Beiblatt 6–8; 2.
Beiblatt 9; the citations 1. Beiblatt 7.

26. The story of the smelly Police Inspector is gleefully told in various papers, for example in *Berliner
Tageblatt und Handels-Zeitung,* October 17, 1906, 4;
again in the same paper on October 26, Abend-
Ausgabe 3; as well as in "Der 'Hauptmann' von
Köpenick verhaftet!," *Berliner Volks-Zeitung,* October
26, Abend-Ausgabe 1.

27. As reported in Langerhans's court testimony;
see, for example, *Berliner Börsen-Zeitung,* December
2, 1906, 1. Beiblatt 6–8; 2. Beiblatt 9; Langerhans's
testimony cited verbatim on 1. Beiblatt 7.

28. "Dann wünschte er seine Frau zu sprechen.
Auch diesen Wunsch erfüllte ich ihm. [...] ich teilte
ihr in höflicher Weise mit, daß ich genötigt sei, ihren
Herrn Gemahl nach Berlin zu schaffen, daß sie aber,
solange er noch hier wäre, ungestört und ungehindert
mit ihm verkehren dürfe." Voigt 52.

29. "Kein Mann werde sich über ihn als Komman-
deur beschweren können./Auch die Herren von
Köpenick müßten, wenn sie gerecht sein wollten, an-
erkennen, daß er sich wie ein Gentleman benommen
habe." Voigt's testimony is quoted verbatim in *Berliner
Börsen-Zeitung,* October 27, 1906, 4.

30. Voigt 49: "Im gegebenen Augenblick würde ich
eben gehandelt haben, wie es für einen Offizier in
solcher Lage geboten ist!"

31. The story is reported in *Berliner Börsen-
Zeitung,* October 27, 1906, 8; Voigt's testimony, as
quoted in indirect speech: *"Das hätte sich für einen
Offizier nicht geschickt.* Eine solche Dummheit habe
er nicht gemacht. In Köpenick habe er nur eine Tasse
Kaffee getrunken" (emphases original).

32. As reported in *Berliner Börsen-Zeitung,* October 25, 1906, 1. Beiblatt 5; see also the report in the
Lokal-Anzeiger of the same day, cited in Heidelmeyer
28.

33. As documented in an ad in the *Deutsches
Fahndungs-Blatt,* 8/2306 no. 33, October 22, 1906,
cited in Heidelmeyer 101–3.

34. Copycat crimes, not only in Germany but
world-wide, are reported in: *Berliner Börsen-Zeitung*:
November 30, 1906, Beiblatt 7; December 1, Beiblatt
7; *Berliner Tageblatt und Handels-Zeitung*: "Köpenick
in Königsberg," October 25, 1906, 1. Beiblatt; "Voigts
Epigonen," November 19, Abend-Ausgabe 4;
"Köpenickiade in Paris," November 26, Beiblatt 1;
"Der Hauptmann von Schöneberg," November 30, 1.
Beiblatt 2; *Berliner Volks-Zeitung*: October 25, 1–2
and Beiblatt 2; "Ein Streich à la Köpenick in Amerika,"
November 4, 2. Beiblatt 2; "'Köpenick' in München,"
November 11, 1. Beiblatt 2; "Eine 'Köpenickiade' in
Posen," November 13, Abend-Ausgabe 3; "'Köpenick'
in Hamburg," November 27, 3; "Ueber die 'Köpenick-
iade in Hamburg,'" November 29, Beiblatt 2; "Der
Hauptmann von Schöneberg," November 30, 4.

35. Such arrests were reported, among others, in
Berliner Börsen-Zeitung (October 19, 1906, 4; October 21, 6; October 22, 3; October 23, 5; October 24,
Abend-Ausgabe 4; October 25, 3); *Berliner Tageblatt
und Handels-Zeitung* (October 19, 1906, Abend-
Ausgabe 4 and Beiblatt of the same day; October 20,
4; October 22, 1. Beiblatt and Abend-Ausgabe 4; October 24, Abend-Ausgabe 3); *Berliner Volks-Zeitung*
(October 19, 1906, 3 and Abend-Ausgabe 2; October
21, Beiblatt 3; October 22, Abend-Ausgabe 2; October
23, Abend-Ausgabe 2; October 24, Abend-Ausgabe
3; October 25, 2).

36. Kallenberg's testimony as reported verbatim in
"Der Hauptmann von Köpenick vor Gericht," *Berliner
Tageblatt und Handels-Zeitung,* December 1, 1906,
Abend-Ausgabe 1–2, 4; the testimony ("Wenn man ein
paar Soldaten habe, dann könne man gute Geschäfte
machen") 4.

37. "Ihr Einfaltspinsel, wenn ich mich zu derartigen Sachen hergeben wollte, dann würde ich mir einfach Soldaten von der Straße holen!" Voigt 59.

38. Stargardt seems to be the only modern commentator on the case who actually took Voigt at his
word; see 2.

39. "Aber andererseits verdiente eine weitgehende Berücksichtigung der Umstand, daß der Angeklagte nach Verbüßung seiner letzten Strafe ernst und—soweit es an ihm lag—erfolgreich bemüht gewesen ist, sich seinen Lebensunterhalt ehrlich zu erwerben, und auf dem besten Wege war, ein nützliches Mitglied der bürgerlichen Gesellschaft zu werden, daß aber dieses Bemühen ohne seine Schuld vereitelt und er wieder auf den Weg des Verbrechens gedrängt ist. [...] Aus diesem Grunde sind mildernde Umstände als vorhanden angenommen und ist deshalb nicht auf Zuchthaus, sondern auf Gefängnis erkannt worden." The sentence is quoted in full in *Wilhelm Voigt der Hauptmann von Köpenick,* unpaginated handwritten facsimile followed by the court's typescript of 15 pages; the quotation on 14–5.

40. Dr. Richard Alexander-Katz, "Der falsche Hauptmann," *Berliner Tageblatt und Handels-Zeitung,* October 21, 1906, 2. Beiblatt 1–2; "Der 'Kommandant' von Köpenick," *Berliner Tageblatt und Handels-Zeitung,* October 18, 1906, 2. Beiblatt 1–2.

41. "Das Landgericht war auffallend wohlwollend mit dem Angeklagten umgegangen und ersichtlich bemüht, die Strafe begrenzt zu halten" (Rosenau 287; see also his analysis of the ratio of indictments to penalties on the same page).

42. As reported, for example, in "Die Verurteilung des Hauptmanns von Köpenick," *Berliner Tageblatt und Handels-Zeitung,* December 2, 1906, 1. Beiblatt 1–2, the quotation ("*Möge Gott Ihnen die Kraft verleihen, die vier Jahre zu überstehen!*") on 1 (emphases original).

43. "Der Vorsitzende legte sein Barett ab, zog seinen Talar aus, trat zu mir an die Schranken und wünschte mir Gottes Segen, daß ich meine Strafe gesund überstehen möge./Ich selbst war von diesem unerwarteten Vorgange so betroffen, daß ich im Augenblick gar nicht darauf zu antworten vermochte. Erst aus meiner Haft heraus schrieb ich einen Brief an den Herrn Gerichtsdirektor, um mich für mein damals fast tölpelhaftes Benehmen, das durch die Erregung des Augenblicks hervorgerufen war, zu entschuldigen und für eine Freundlichkeit zu danken, deren ganze Bedeutung ich wohl ermesse./War es mir doch ein Zeichen, wie schwer es dem Gerichtshof geworden sein mußte, dieses Urteil gegen mich zu fällen." Voigt 66–7.

44. Calls for his immediate release or Imperial pardon in: "Der Kaiser und der 'Hauptmann von Köpenick,'" *Berliner Tageblatt und Handels-Zeitung,* November 2, 1906, Abend-Ausgabe 6; "Ein Opfer: Nachwort zum Voigt-Prozeß," *Berliner Tageblatt und Handels-Zeitung,* December 3, 1906, 1; reports on or suggestions for collections and job offers: "Die Verurteilung des Hauptmanns von Köpenick," *Berliner Tageblatt und Handels-Zeitung,* December 2, 1906, 1. Beiblatt 1–2; "Der Vorläufer des Helden von Köpenick," *Berliner Volks-Zeitung,* October 18, 1906, 1; "Was der Hauptmann von Köpenick wert ist," *Berliner Tageblatt und Handels-Zeitung,* November 3, 1906, 1. Beiblatt 2; *Berliner Börsen-Zeitung,* November 4, 1906, 1. Beiblatt, 6; *Lähner Anzeiger,* December 1, 1906, 2; "Der 'Hauptmann von Köpenick' vor Gericht," *Berliner Volks-Zeitung,* December 2, 1906, 2. Beiblatt 2; suggestions that he should be permitted to keep the Köpenick money in: Paul Blook, "Der Hauptmann von Köpenick," *Berliner Tageblatt und Handels-Zeitung,* October 17, 1906, Abend-Ausgabe 1.

45. Reported widely; see, for example, *Berliner Börsen-Zeitung,* October 28, 1906, 8.

46. As reported in "Der Räuberhauptmann von Köpenick," *Berliner Tageblatt und Handels-Zeitung,* Abend-Ausgabe 3–4, the story of the postcards 4.

47. "Gruß von Voigt, Räuber-Hauptmann a. D., früher Köpenick, jetzt Zelle 15." The card is reprinted in *Denkwürdigkeiten* 69.

48. Cited in *Denkwürdigkeiten* 37.

49. As reported in *Berliner Volks-Zeitung,* October 30, 1906, Abend-Ausgabe 2.

50. "'Der Hauptmann von Köpenick' verboten," *Berliner Volks-Zeitung,* November 6, 1906, 4.

51. "Auf den Spuren des falschen Hauptmanns," *Berliner Tageblatt und Handels-Zeitung,* October 18, 1906, 3. The work, as it turned out, was a special edition of the satirical magazine *Lustige Blätter;* see "Auf der Suche nach dem Hauptmann," *Berliner Volks-Zeitung,* October 19, 1906, Abend-Ausgabe 2.

52. The publication is announced in *Berliner Tageblatt und Handels-Zeitung,* November 6, 1906, 1. Beiblatt 1.

53. "Volksliteratur," *Berliner Volks-Zeitung,* October 28, 1906, Beiblatt 2.

54. Announcement in *Berliner Volks-Zeitung,* October 26, 1906, Beiblatt 3.

55. In the article, the words of Schiller's character Stauffacher are humorously attributed to Mayor Langerhans: "Comes me the Viceroy [Vogt] riding with his train;/Before this house he halted in amaze;/Straightway I rose, and with submission due/Advanced to greet the man who personates/The Kaiser's over-lordship in the land" ("Da kam der *Vogt* mit seinen Reisigen (geritten)./Vor diesem Hause hielt er wundernd an;/Doch ich erhub mich schnell und unterwürfig/Wie sich's gebührt, trat ich dem Herrn entgegen/(Der uns des Kaisers richterliche Macht/Vorstellt im Lande)." The English translation is taken from Schiller, *William Tell,* trans. Patrick Maxwell; the German original as quoted in "Der gefangene Hauptmann," *Berliner Volks-Zeitung,* October 27, 1906, Abend-Ausgabe 3.

56. The story of the Captain of Capernaum is told in Luke 7.1–10.

57. "Was hat dem Hauptmann von Kapernaum geholfen? Sein Glaube. Was hat dem Hauptmann von Köpenick geholfen? Der Glaube des Herrn Langerhans." Der Werwolf, "Ein Erfolg," *Berliner Volks-Zeitung,* October 21, 1906, 1.

58. "Ein bibelfester Leser schreibt uns: Der Hauptmann von Köpenick identisch mit dem bekannten Hauptmann von Kapernaum! Endlich ist es gelungen—aber nicht der Berliner Kriminalpolizei—die Identität des Hauptmanns von Köpenick festzustellen. Man überzeuge sich davon in der Bibel und lese:/Evang. Matth. Kap. 8. Vers 9./ Der Hauptmann zum Bürgermeister: "Siehe, ich habe unter mir Kriegsknechte. Und wenn ich zu dem ersten sage: "Gehe hin!" so geht er, und sage ich zum andern: "Komme her!," so kommt er, und zum dritten: "Tue das, so tut er es!"/Evang. Matth. Kap. 8 Vers 10./Der Hauptmann (für sich): "Wahrlich, ich habe noch niemals gefunden einen solchen Glauben!" The article from the *Frankfurter Zeitung* was reprinted in *Denkwürdigkeiten* 54.

59. See the ad for the statuettes reprinted in *Denkwürdigkeiten* 93.

60. The game is described in "Auf der Suche nach

dem Hauptmann," *Berliner Volks-Zeitung,* October 19, 1906, Abend-Ausgabe 2 ("Zum Schluß entwickelt sich jedoch meist eine Prügelei, weil jeder 'Hauptmann' sein will. Der Bürgermeisterposten ist weniger gesucht!")

61. "Die Jagd auf den Räuberhauptmann," *Berliner Tageblatt und Handels-Zeitung,* October 20, 1906, Abend-Ausgabe 3–4, the statistics 4.

62. As reported in "Was der Hauptmann von Köpenick wert ist," *Berliner Tageblatt und Handels-Zeitung,* November 3, 1906, 1. Beiblatt 2.

63. "dem Köpenicker Hauptmann entgeht man leider nirgends. Auch in den Theatern nicht, denn dort singt jeder Komiker seit dem Tage von Köpenick eine Strophe mehr. [...] Kurzum, der alte schäbige Hauptmann hat nicht nur den Triumph gehabt, die Stadt Köpenick mit den Grenadieren seiner Majestät für eine Stunde lang im Belagerungszustand zu halten, er hat auch Berlin selbst erobert. Er wird sicherlich noch ein Denkmal im Tiergarten bekommen." The citation is taken from a letter sent by August Spanuth from Berlin to the New York paper *Sonntagsblatt der N. Y. Staats-Zeitung* and is reprinted in *Denkwürdigkeiten* 12.—The *Tiergarten* refers both to Berlin's parliamentary, government and diplomatic district and to its largest and most popular inner-city park, both, naturally, brimming over with statues of famous personalities. This writer was not the only one calling for a statue of the Captain; an article in *Berliner Tageblatt und Handels-Zeitung* (October 29, 1. Beiblatt) considered it only fair that the city of Köpenick erect a statue to the "ingenious" Captain for putting Köpenick on the world map and for "launching a new epoch in the History of Köpenick" ("Möglich, daß sie einmal gerechterweise dem ingeniösen Herrn Voigt ein Standbild dafür errichten müßten, daß er eine neue Epoche in der Geschichte Köpenicks eröffnete."). In 1996, the Captain of Köpenick was indeed honored with a statue in front of Köpenick's City Hall.

64. "Captain of Köpenick" films were shot and aired throughout the 20th century and into the 21st: in 1906 (twice), 1908, 1931, 1941, 1956, 1960, 1997, 2001, 2005, and 2012. For a discussion of some of them, see "Plots" and "Resolutions" respectively.

65. Freud, *Witz* 192–93: "ersparter Vorstellungsaufwand" (comedy); "ersparter Hemmungsaufwand" (joke); "ersparter Gefühlsaufwand" (humor).

66. Freud, *Witz* 162: "das Komische ist eine in nichts zergangene Erwartung."

67. "Ein erfolgreicher Hochstapler ohne Phantasie ist unmöglich." Wulffen, *Die Psychologie des Hochstaplers* (unpag.).

68. On that character, see Claßen 18–19; Claßen also discusses the Voigt case on 87–93.

69. See, for example, *Berliner Tageblatt und Handels-Zeitung,* December 1, 1906, Abend-Ausgabe 1; *Berliner Börsen-Zeitung,* October 26, 1906, 7 and October 27, 4. Voigt's physical exterior featured prominently in this universal disappointment and is thus described in exquisite detail in virtually all papers. See, for instance, *Berliner Tageblatt,* October 17, Abend-Ausgabe 4; October 20, 1. Beiblatt; October 26, Abend-Ausgabe 2; December 1, Abend-Ausgabe 1; *Berliner Börsen-Zeitung,* October 18, 6 and 26, 7; *Berliner Volks-Zeitung,* October 18, Beiblatt 2; October 20, 3, and October 26, 7.

70. "Je kümmerlicher, glanzloser und armseliger dieser Schuhmacher aussieht, desto beißender ist die Satire, und desto schöner ist die Tat. Wilhelm Voigt sieht aus, wie ein richtiger Flickschuster und wie die Verkörperung der Fleischnot, aber gerade dadurch wird die Satire vollkommen." "Der Hauptmann von Köpenick vor Gericht," *Berliner Tageblatt und Handels-Zeitung,* December 1, 1906, Abend-Ausgabe 1–2, 4; the citation 1.

71. "Daß die Stadt Köpenick nicht etwa durch einen Mann der besseren Stände, durch einen ehemaligen Militär oder einen in allerlei Verwaltungssachen erfahrenen Hochstapler, sondern durch einen ganz heruntergekommenen Pennbruder beherrscht wurde, das erst ist ja die Pointe, die der glänzenden Satire noch fehlte und deren wir uns freuen sollten." *Berliner Börsen-Zeitung,* October 27, 1906, 4.

72. Noted, among others, in *Berliner Volks-Zeitung,* October 26, 1906, Abend-Ausgabe 2.

73. "Aber wie konnte dieses ausgemergelte, gelbliche Antlitz mit den hohlen Wangen und der häßlich eingebogenen Nase ganz Köpenick in Schrecken setzen, und wie konnten diese geröteten Jungerleideraugen eine mutige und selbstbewußte Stadtverwaltung einschüchtern?" "Der Hauptmann von Köpenick vor Gericht," *Berliner Tageblatt und Handels-Zeitung,* December 1, 1906, Abend-Ausgabe 1–2, 4; the citation 1.

74. For example in: "Fetischuniform," *Berliner Tageblatt und Handels-Zeitung,* October 17, 1906, Abend-Ausgabe 1.

75. For example in "Die Jagd nach dem Räuberhauptmann," *Berliner Tageblatt und Handels-Zeitung,* October 19, 1906, Beiblatt: "We have the sabre, the pants and the cap, so that the victorious uniform will soon be completely in the hands of its captors. But the peerless bearer of the uniform and the 4000 marks have yet to surface" ("Den Degen hat man, die Hose und die Mütze hat man, so daß die siegreiche Uniform bald vollständig in den Händen ihrer Häscher sein wird. Aber den einzigartigen Träger und die 4000 Reichsmärker hat man noch nicht.").

76. For example: "Sporen, nicht Spuren," *Berliner Tageblatt und Handels-Zeitung,* October 23, 1906, 1. Beiblatt 1–2; "Der verschwundene 'Hauptmann,'" *Berliner Volks-Zeitung,* October 23, 1906, 3; "Der verschwundene Räuberhauptmann," *Berliner Tageblatt und Handels-Zeitung,* October 22, 1906, 1. Beiblatt; "Der Räuberhauptmann von Köpenick," *Berliner Tageblatt und Handels-Zeitung,* October 19, Abend-Ausgabe 3; "Die Jagd nach dem Räuberhauptmann," *Berliner Tageblatt und Handels-Zeitung,* October 19, Beiblatt.

77. As reported in "Der 'Kommandant' von Köpenick," *Berliner Tageblatt und Handels-Zeitung,* October 18, 1906, 2. Beiblatt 1–2, witness testimony on 2.

78. "dann marschieren, stramm und wuchtig, *sieben brave Soldaten in voller Uniform* in den Saal. Die Sieben tragen auf dem Kopfe den Helm, auf dem Rücken den Tornister und den gerollten Mantel und in der kräftigen Rechten das Gewehr. Die Scheiben erzittern, die Hälfte der Zuschauer recken sich, Wilhelm Voigt blickt mit leidvollem Neid auf die Sieben, die hier mit dem Prestige der Uniform erscheinen dürfen, und der Vorsitzende fährt gleichmütig fort, die Namen der Zeugen aufzurufen. Jeder der braven Soldaten antwortet laut und vernehmlich mit einem kurzen "Hier!" Und ein Gefreiter äußert sich so dröh-

nend, als gälte es, die Wache am Brandenburger Tore herauszurufen." "Der Hauptmann von Köpenick vor Gericht," *Berliner Tageblatt und Handels-Zeitung*, December 1, 1906, Abend-Ausgabe 1–2, 4, the citation 1, emphasis original.

79. Reported in various papers; for example: "Der Hauptmann von Köpenick vor Gericht," *Berliner Börsen-Zeitung*, December 1, 1906, 4. Beiblatt 9–10; the citation 9.

80. "Als der 'Hauptmann' heute früh verhaftet wurde, antwortete er auf die Frage des Kriminalkommissars, ob er *gedient* habe: '*Fünfundzwanzig Jahre im Zuchthause.*'" "Der 'Hauptmann' von Köpenick verhaftet!," *Berliner Volks-Zeitung*, October 26, 1906, Abend-Ausgabe 1–3, the citation 1, empases original.

81. All widely reported; see, for instance, "Der Hauptmann von Köpenick vor Gericht," *Berliner Tageblatt und Handels-Zeitung*, December 1, 1906, Abend-Ausgabe 1–2, 4.

82. "'Sie haben überhaupt nichts zu verlangen! Bei dem geringsten Widerstand werde ich Sie in Arrest stecken lassen!' (Heiterkeit.)" "Der 'Hauptmann von Köpenick' vor Gericht," *Berliner Börsen-Zeitung*, December 2, 1906, 1. Beiblatt 6–8; 2. Beiblatt 9, the testimony 1. Beiblatt 7.

83. "Wäre der Herr Wehn ihm im Köpenicker Rathaus entgegengetreten, würde er *genau so mit ihm verfahren* haben. Auf irgendeine Auseinandersetzung hätte er sich mit ihm keineswegs eingelassen, sondern gegebenenfalls '*seine Soldaten*' aufgefordert *von der Waffe Gebrauch zu machen*." "Der Räuberhauptmann gefangen," *Berliner Tageblatt und Handels-Zeitung*, October 26, 1906, Abend-Ausgabe 2–3, the citation 3, emphases original.

84. "*Im Namen Se. Majestät, Sie sind verhaftet!*" Auch dabei will er nicht sehr pathetisch gesprochen haben.—Präs.: Aber Sie haben doch vorher sehr bestimmt gesprochen?—Angekl.: Das liegt doch in der Natur der Sache! (Heiterkeit.) Dr. Rosenkranz erklärte seine Verwunderung und wollte den Grund wissen. Na, ich konnte ihm doch keine Aufklärung geben. (Heiterkeit.)" As reported in "Der Hauptmann von Köpenick vor Gericht," *Berliner Börsen-Zeitung*, December 1, 1906, 4. Beiblatt 9–10; the citation 10.

85. As reported in *Berliner Volks-Zeitung*, October 17, 1906, 3.

86. From the testimony of Private Clapdohr: "On the train to Köpenick I frequently looked out of the window since a comrade said to me: watch out in case he gets off the train. (Hilarity.)"—"Nur auf der Fahrt nach Köpenick habe ich öfter zum Fenster hinausgesehen, da ein Kamrad zu mir sagte: Du paß mal auf, daß er nicht aussteigt. (Heiterkeit.)" "Der 'Hauptmann von Köpenick' vor Gericht," *Berliner Börsen-Zeitung*, December 2, 1906, 1. Beiblatt 6–8; 2. Beiblatt 9, the testimony 1. Beiblatt 6.

87. See, for example, the portrayal of the affair in the article in *Berliner Börsen-Zeitung*, October 18, 1906, 6, whose author arrives at exactly that conclusion.

88. "*Umkleide dich in Preußen-Deutschland mit einer Uniform und du bist allmächtig.*" "Die Komödie von Köpenick," *Berliner Volks-Zeitung*, October 17, 1906, 1, emphasis original.

89. "Vor der Uniform liegen alle auf dem [B]auch, die sogenannte 'Gesellschaft,' die Behörden vom [M]inister bis zum letzten Nachtwächter, das Bürgertum [u]nd die Masse des Volkes auch. [...] Wer die

Uniform trägt, der siegt, nicht [w]eil er besser oder klüger oder weitsichtiger wäre als die [a]nderen, sondern weil er uniformiert ist." "Fetischuniform," *Berliner Tageblatt und Handels-Zeitung*, October 17, 1906, Abend-Ausgabe 1.

90. "Er trug das Brandmal Kains auf seiner Stirn, 'unstet und flüchtig' wie dieser, aber er hatte es noch schwerer als Kain. Denn wenn der Brudermörder der Bibel wenigstens in ein fernes Land fliehen und dort sich eine neue Heimat schaffen durfte, so war es dem Voigt selbst verwehrt, in die Fremde zu ziehen. Er brauchte einen *Paß*, und diesen Paß bekam er nicht, obgleich er sich bei allen möglichen Behörden darum bemühte." "Ein Opfer: Nachwort zum Voigt-Prozeß," *Berliner Tageblatt und Handels-Zeitung*, December 3, 1906, 1.

91. "Aus dem lustigen Hauptmann ist ein armer, elender Mensch geworden, gehetzt von der Polizei, mißhandelt von der Justiz, niedergetreten, so oft er sich aus dem Staube erheben wollte, systematisch um sein Menschenrecht und seine Menschenwürde gebracht." "Ein Opfer: Nachwort zum Voigt-Prozeß," *Berliner Tageblatt und Handels-Zeitung*, December 3, 1906, 1.

92. "Hier hört der Fall Voigt auf, ein Einzelfall zu sein, hier wird er zu einer Anklage gegen unser ganzes Justiz- und Polizeisystem. Wir hoffen, daß man ihn im *Reichstage* und im preußischen *Abgeordnetenhause* so würdigt, wie er es verdient." "Ein Opfer: Nachwort zum Voigt-Prozeß," *Berliner Tageblatt und Handels-Zeitung*, December 3, 1906, 1, emphases original.

93. "Diese gleiche Affäre, die wie ein herrliches Spottgedicht die schwächliche Unterwürfigkeit und den Mangel an Bürgerstolz geißelt, zeigt mit geradezu tragischen Akzenten die zerstörenden Wirkungen einer oft noch barbarischen Justizgewalt. [...]. So stand in diesem merkwürdigen Prozesse neben dem rückgratlosen 'Respekt' die *polizeiliche Ausweisungspolitik* an dem Pranger." "Die Verurteilung des Hauptmanns von Köpenick," *Berliner Tageblatt und Handels-Zeitung*, December 2, 1906, 1. Beiblatt 1–2, the citation 1, emphases original.

94. "Das Ende der Hauptmannsaffaire," *Berliner Volks-Zeitung*, December 2, 1906, 1.

95. "Nicht Wilhelm Voigt, unsere Gesellschaft gehört auf die Anklagebank als Hauptangeklagte: als mitleidslose Anstifterin!" Paul Lindau, "Der Schuldige," *Berliner Tageblatt und Handels-Zeitung*, November 28, 1906, 2. Beiblatt.

96. "Da sprach der weiseste von ihnen: 'Wir taten doch wohl unrecht, daß wir den alten Räuber auf das äußerste brachten und ihm alle Mittel zur Besserung, so spät und erzwungen sie auch waren, benahmen.' [...] Wer wird den Mut haben, mit dem weisesten Schäfer des Aelianus einzugestehen, daß *wir* den alten Räuber 'auf das äußerste gebracht' haben, und daß wir gut daran tun werden, bei unserer Fürsorge um die Besserung entlassener Strafgefangener mit der Besserung unserer Einrichtungen, der Beseitigung der Grausamkeiten gegen entlassene Sträflinge den Anfang zu machen." Lindau, "Der Schuldige," unpag.

97. "Der *Köpenicker Gaunerstreich* hat auch im Auslande das Zwerchfell erschüttert. Zugleich fühlt man aber dort sehr wohl heraus, daß nur durch das absolutistische Milieu in Preußen der blamable Vorgang ermöglicht wurde." *Berliner Tageblatt und Handels-Zeitung*, October 19, 1906, 1.

98. "In unserer gestrigen Betrachtung über die *tiefernste Seite der Köpenicker Komödie* [...] hatten wir als den springenden Punkt den *blinden Gehorsam*—Kadavergehorsam—bezeichnet, der in unserem Heere rechtens ist und dem allein es zu verdanken ist, daß die *Uniform* einen glänzenden Sieg davongetragen hat über alle Vernunft." "Der Vorläufer des Helden von Köpenick," *Berliner Volks-Zeitung,* October 18, 1906, 1, emphases original. See also its article "Die Komödie von Köpenick," October 17, 1.

99. "Der heilige Rock von Köpenick," *Dresdener Gerichtzeitung,* reprtd. in *Denkwürdigkeiten* 40.

100. "Eine alle Schichten durchdringende 'militärische Erziehung,' die selbst die höchsten zivilen Funktionäre in der Würde des Reserveleutnants die vornehmste Auszeichnung erkennen läßt und die den Vorzug des Militärischen in allem willig zugesteht, hat in der Tat in den weitesten Kreisen des Bürgertums bürgerliches Selbstgefühl und bürgerlichen Stolz bis zum letzten Restchen ausgetilgt." "Der 18. Brumaire in Köpenick," *Wiener Arbeiterzeitung,* reprtd. in *Denkwürdigkeiten* 44. On the co-optation of the middle classes through their incorporation in the reserve officer corps, see Stargardt, especially 11–12, 47.

101. "Der militärische Gehorsam im Lichte des Gaunerstreichs von Köpenick," by Oberst Gädke, *Berliner Tageblatt und Handels-Zeitung,* October 18, 1906,1–2. Another article tells the story of a company of soldiers who, for refusing an order from a clearly insane superior that would have resulted in all of their deaths for no gain, were condemned to life-long penitentiary sentences ("Fetischuniform," *Berliner Tageblatt und Handels-Zeitung,* October 17, 1906, 1).

102. For example: "Der Soldatenpeiniger," *Berliner Volks-Zeitung,* October 26, 1906, Beiblatt 3. On militarism in Imperial Germany, see the respective works of Stig Förster and Bettina Musall. Bernhard Neff has offered a good account on the critique of militarism from within the army itself, which tended to focus on the military's overemphasis on drills and parades at the cost of actual combat training (Neff 134–6).

103. "Wir sind nach reiflicher Überlegung zu der Ueberzeugung gekommen, daß die *Auswüchse des Militarismus* das über uns *hereingebrochene Mißgeschick* verursacht haben." The resolution of the Köpenick city fathers is cited in "Kundgebung für den Köpenicker Bürgermeister," *Berliner Tageblatt und Handels-Zeitung,* October 21, 1906, 1. Beiblatt, emphases original.

104. "Meine Herren, im Anschluß an den Fall des sogenannten Hauptmanns von Köpenick ist die Kritik, wie sie sich in den Zeitungen dokumentiert hat, meiner Überzeugung nach zum Teil weit über das Ziel hinausgeschossen./(Sehr richtig! rechts)/Man hat den Hauptmann von Köpenick als eine Art von Helden gefeiert./(Heiterkeit.)/Der gute Erfolg seines Handstreichs legte es ja sehr nahe, daß man im ersten Moment eine gewisse Sympathie mit einem so schneidigen Kerl hatte;/(Heiterkeit.)/aber die Folgerungen, welche dann in der Presse an diesen Fall in bezug auf die Ausweisung geknüpft worden sind, gehen meiner Überzeugung nach zu weit. Man wird mir vielleicht eine gewisse Grausamkeit vorwerfen, aber für mich ist doch der allererste Gesichtspunkt, den die Polizei und auch die Strafrechtspflege zu befolgen hat, der, daß wir die Gesellschaft gegen die unsozialen Elemente sichern./(Sehr richtig! rechts)." Excerpt from the stenographic minutes of the debate in the Prussian House of Representatives, 20th legislative period, 3rd session 1907, reprtd. in Heidelmeyer 160–9, the quotation 162.

105. "Wie verlautet, soll der *Kaiser,* der sich eingehend die Taten des famosen Hauptmanns schildern ließ, beabsichtigen, bei der nächsten Rekrutenvereidigung eine *Kabinettsorder* zu erlassen, durch die Vorgänge, wie sie sich jetzt in Köpenick ereigneten, unmöglich gemacht werden sollen." "Auf den Spuren des falschen Hauptmanns," *Berliner Tageblatt und Handels-Zeitung,* October 18, 1906, 3, emphases original. The *Berliner Volks-Zeitung* similarly reported that the Emperor was planning to issue new instructions to army recruits in order to forestall such embarrassing incidents in the future; see "Der 'Hauptmann' von Köpenick," October 24, 1906, Abend-Ausgabe 3.

106. "Wir können doch nicht abkommandieren; wir sind doch nicht der *Hauptmann von Köpenick!* Große Heiterkeit.)" *Berliner Volks-Zeitung, Parlaments-Ausgabe,* October 17, 1906, 1, emphasis original.

107. "So herzlich hat Berlin, Deutschland, hat die ganze Welt lange nicht gelacht. Und jedem Freudenspender ist die Menschheit dankbar." Paul Lindau, "Der Schuldige," *Berliner Tageblatt und Handels-Zeitung,* November 28, 1906, 2. Beiblatt.

108. Der Werwolf, "Ein Erfolg," *Berliner Volks-Zeitung,* October 21, 1906, 1: "Es war ein Anblick für Götter, diese Gemeinsamkeit in der Explosion einer ungebärdigen Heiterkeitsstimmung!"

109. "Und ich frage Sie: kann es noch einen Schwarzseher auf deutschem Boden geben, nachdem dieser gelungene Jokus Millionen deutscher Zwerchfelle erschüttert hat? Wer lacht, sieht rosig in die Welt, und diese rosige Perspektive danken wir allein ihm." "Ein Plaidoyer für den Räuberhauptmann," *Denkwürdigkeiten* 78.

110. "In den Straßenbahnwagen, in den Kneipen, in den Theatern, überall, wo Deutsche versammelt sind, gründen sie jetzt nicht mehr einen Verein, bringen sie jetzt nicht mehr ein Hoch aus, sondern sie grinsen sich an, ohne ein Wort zu sagen. Es ist ein Telegraphieren von Gehirn zu Gehirn, das sich da vollzieht, wie man es seit Menschengedenken nicht erlebt hat. Jeder glaubt vom anderen, er denke und könne nur denken an Köpenick." Der Werwolf, "Ein Erfolg," *Berliner Volks-Zeitung,* October 21, 1906, 1.

111. See above all the summation by Defense attorneys Schwindt and Bahn, cited in Heidelmeyer 138–9.

112. "Zum Gauner gehört doch wohl die niedrige Gesinnung, und davon ist in den Handlungen, die wir von Wilhelm Voigt seit seiner letzten Entlassung aus dem Zuchthause kennen, keine Spur wahrzunehmen. Eher das Gegenteil. Und es liegt kein Grund vor, seiner Versicherung, daß es ihm nie einfallen würde, von einem einzelnen unrechtmäßig auch nur einen Pfennig zu nehmen, den Glauben zu versagen. [...] Ein Lump, der eine arme Frau um fünfzig Pfennig bestiehlt, erscheint uns viel gemeiner und verächtlicher als der falsche Hauptmann, der einer städtischen Kasse ein paar Tausend Mark widerrechtlich entzieht." Paul Lindau, "Der Schuldige," *Berliner Tageblatt und Handels-Zeitung,* November 28, 1906, 2. Beiblatt.

113. "'Seid Ihr denn alle verrückt geworden?' [...] Der Mann läuft Gefahr, zu einem Nationalheiligen des Micheltums zu avancieren. [...] Zunächst ist er

der Held der Sensationspresse geworden, die ihn in Wort und Bild, mit gereimtem und ungereimtem Pathos feiert, und sich fast entleibt in Ergebenheit vor seiner illustren Persönlichkeit. Jeder Zug in seinem Auftreten wird als Ausfluß einer kaum je geahnten Seelengröße den Tages-Annalen einverleibt; über jede seiner Handlungen, wann und wohin er ausgeht, wo und wie er ißt, wie er schläft, spricht, weint und lacht, wird getreulich Buch geführt und Bericht erstattet." *Die Post*, August 18, 1908, reprtd. in Heidelmeyer 157–8, the citation 157.

114. "Voigt, der eine Zeitlang durch die Maske des Biedermannes das Publikum täuschte und den Anschein erweckte, als ob er durch Schicksalsschläge auf den Weg des Verbrechens gedrängt worden sei, zeigt jetzt, daß er die sehr milde Beurteilung, die er vor Gericht und noch mehr im Publikum fand, nicht verdiente. Er hat die Schamlosigkeit des alten Berufsverbrechers und reist in Ost und West herum, um sich mit seinem Köpenicker Räuberstück zu brüsten." *Berliner Allgemeine Zeitung*, June 19, 1909, reprtd. in Heidelmeyer 178–9, the citation 179.

115. "Die blöde Neugier feiert wahre Orgien. Auf dem Bahnhofe am Freitag wurde er schon von vielen Leuten, insbesondere von Amateurphotographen empfangen. Dann saß er, umringt von einer dichten Menge bis zum Morgengrauen in einem größeren Restaurant bei Speise und Trank in fröhlicher Unterhaltung. 'Man muß das Eisen schmieden, so lange es warm ist,' meinte er schmunzelnd und unterschrieb vergnügt zahllose Ansichtskarten mit 'Wilhelm Voigt, gen. der Hauptmann von Köpenick,' natürlich nur gegen 'Schriftstellerhonorar,' die Zeile 10 Pfennige." *Berliner Neueste Nachrichten*, September 28, 1908, cited in Heidelmeyer 171. Further press articles critical of the Voigt-cult include *Die Post*, August 18, 1908 (cited in Heidelmeyer 157–8); *Vorwärts*, August 21, 1908 (cited in Heidelmeyer 158–9), *Deutsche Tageszeitung*, January 1909 (cited in Heidelmeyer 175–6); *Berliner Börsen-Zeitung*, 1909 (cited in Heidelmeyer 177); *Wormser Zeitung*, 1909 (cited in Heidelmeyer 178–9); *Berliner Allgemeine Zeitung*, June 19, 1909 (cited in Heidelmeyer 179), and others. Some of this opprobrium is reproduced in the assessment of later scholars; see, for example, Heidelmeyer 30–2.

116. "Der Besitzer dieses Lokals entblödete sich nicht, die Kapelle anzuweisen, zu Ehren des Hauptmanns von Köpenick die deutschen Nationalweisen, wie die 'Wacht am Rhein,' zu spielen. Aber noch schlimmer trieben es die Gäste. Sie rissen sich förmlich um den 'Hauptmann von Köpenick.' An jedem Tische wurde er bewirtet, und seine Postkarten gingen ab wie warme Semmeln." *Berliner Morgenpost*, April 26, 1910, reprtd. in Heidelmeyer 179–80, the citation 179.

A Conwoman Nabs a Captain

1. Rose 157. The two main secondary sources on the case are Alison Rose's "Bigamy and Bigotry," which situates the case in the context of contemporary Austrian antisemitism, and Barbara Pachler's M.A. Thesis "Der Fall Hervay," which reconstructs the court case based on trial records. Vyleta briefly discusses the case in *Crime, Jews and News* 131–5.

2. On the problem of Tamara von Hervay's names, see the final section of this chapter.

3. Franz Preitler in an Email to Susanne Kord, January 26, 2017: "ich habe mich über sechs Jahre mit Tamara beschäftigt und sie hat mich ebenso in Bann gesetzt, wie ihre Männer." Preitler's novel *Die schwarze Baronin* (*The Black Baroness*) appeared in 2015.

4. Rose 157.

5. Rose 157.

6. Rose 165.

7. Her testimony on this is quoted verbatim by various newspapers. For example: "Die Sache war so. Ich kannte die österreichischen Verhältnisse nicht. Der Hotelier drängte aber, daß ich mich in das aufliegende Fremdenbuch eintrage. Ich schrieb dann die Zahl hin, das war eine Eitelkeit von mir, gelogen war es nicht." "Der Prozeß gegen Elvira von Hervay," *Grazer Volksblatt*, October 30, 1904, 5–7, the citation 6.

8. See Hans Schwarz on the legal situation and Hehenberger on the legal history of bigamy in Austria.

9. Rose 161–2.

10. Hervay's stories about her past were the subject of intense scrutiny by the press and re-told at length in many papers, for example in "Der Eheroman des Bezirkshauptmanns von Mürzzuschlag," *Grazer Volksblatt*, June 18, 1904, 4; "Verhaftung der Frau v. Hervay," *Neues Wiener Tagblatt*, June 21, 1904, Abendausgabe 11; "Die Ehe eines Bezirkshauptmanns," *Mährisches Tagblatt*, June 23, 1904, 5–6; "Verhaftung einer Bezirkshauptmannsgattin," *Salzburger Chronik*, June 23, 1904, *Beilage* 2–3; "Der Selbstmord des Bezirkshauptmanns Hervay v. Kirchberg," *Das interessante Blatt*, June 30, 1904, 12–13, and many more.

11. Hervay told the story of her fairy tale love affair with Franz von Hervay many times, most extensively in her memoirs, *Tamara von Hervay*, 16–19.

12. "Ich habe jetzt vor, ein Märchen zu schreiben, welches von meinem Leben handelt und 'Des Leidens Erdengang' betitelt ist. Es wird am 22. d. M. in der hiesigen 'Morgenzeitung' erscheinen." Hervay, *Tamara von Hervay* 141.

13. I. Durchschaudi, "Ein uraltes Märchen," *Mürzzuschlager Wochenblatt*, April 30, 1904, 1–2.

14. "Ein ehemaliger Ehemann der Frau v. Hervay schreibt den 'Leipziger Nachrichten': 'Sie ist die Tochter Erni Leontini Elvira des verstorbenen Zauberers *Bellachini*, der mit seinem richtigen Namen *Bellach* hieß. Erster Ehemann: Weinagent K., Scheidungsgrund: eheliche Untreue ihrerseits. Zweiter Ehemann: Freiherr v. L., Scheidungsgrund wie ad 1. Dritter Ehemann: v. Sch., Scheidungsgrund wie ad 1 und 2. Vierter Ehemann: M., meine Wenigkeit, Scheidungsgrund: Betrug und Hochstapelei. Zwischen Ehe 1 und 2 nannte sie sich *de Belhair*, zwischen Ehe 3 und 4 Bareness *de Shève* und gab sich als illegitime Tochter der Großfürstin Wladimir aus; wie Sie sehen, hat sie inzwischen sich selbst schon erniedrigt. Noch ehe unsre Scheidung ausgesprochen war, hatte sie sich mit einem Leutnant v. L. verlobt, welche Sache auseinanderging, da der Kommandant des Herrn auf die Schliche der Schwindlerin kam. Ein Herr v. E. ist von ihr in Nizza um zirka 5000 Mark betrogen worden. Als meine holde Gattin hat sie vier Wochen in Untersuchungshaft wegen Betrugs gesessen und ist nur wegen Mangels an Beweisen nicht verurteilt worden.'" "Der Fall Hervay," *Grazer Volksblatt*, June 27, 1904, Abendausgabe 1–2, emphases original.

15. "Eine seltsam raffinierte Abenteurerin von 44

Jahren war es, die sich das Vertrauen, die Liebe des 32jährigen blühendschönen Mannes erschlichen hatte." "Der Selbstmord des Bezirkhauptmanns Hervay v. Kirchberg," *Das interessante Blatt*, June 30, 1904, 12–13, the citation 12.

16. Rose 164–5.

17. This is precisely what Tamara von Hervay claims in her memoirs, *Tamara von Hervay* 60–1.

18. "Die Affaire der Frau v. Hervay," *Neues Wiener Tagblatt*, October 30, 1904, 12–14, the story of the recommended bribe on 12. The story is repeated by Hervay in *Tamara von Hervay* 64.

19. The testimony is cited verbatim as follows: "Angeklagte: 'Ich habe dem Pfarrer ausdrücklich gesagt, daß ich nicht heiraten kann. Darauf hat er mir erwidert: Reisen Sie nach Wien und wenn Sie zurückkommen, sagen Sie den Leuten, Sie haben in Wien geheiratet.' (Heiterkeit im Auditorium.)/Zeuge schüttelt verneinend den Kopf./Vorsitzender: 'Sagen Herr Zeuge ausdrücklich: Hat die Angeklagte gesagt, daß sie *keine* Ehe eingehen kann? Ja oder nein.'/Zeuge: 'Wenn sie das gesagt hätte, würde ich auf keinen Fall die Eheschließung vorgenommen haben.'" "Der Prozess gegen Elvira von Hervay," *Grazer Volksblatt*, October 30, 1904, 5–7, the citation 7, emphases original. Other newspapers relate the scene with negligible deviations.

20. "Ich habe es ihm nicht gesagt, weil mein Mann gedrängt hat und erklärte: *Ich kann ohne dich nicht leben, mach' ein Ende. Das eine kannst du dem Pfarrer schon verschweigen!*" "Die Affaire der Frau v. Hervay," *Neues Wiener Tagblatt*, October 30, 1904, 13, emphases original.

21. This was actually known as early as July; see the notice on Lützow's whereabouts in *Mährisches Tagblatt*, July 4, 1904, 5.

22. Prangl's testimony is reported verbatim in "Der Prozess gegen Elvira von Hervay," *Grazer Volksblatt*, October 30, 1904, 7; "Die Affaire der Frau v. Hervay," *Neues Wiener Tagblatt*, October 30, 1904, 12, and many others.

23. The exact formulation, as cited in several papers, reads: "Um der Braut zu ermöglichen, wegen der Anfechtung und Verleumdung eine Unterkunft unter dem Schutze ihres zukünftigen Mannes zu finden, nehme ich dieses Eheverlöbnis in der Form einer Hochzeit vor, *doch hat diese Ehe vor dem Gesetze keine Gültigkeit.*" The formulation "Eheverlöbnis" (engagement to marry) seems to point to the July engagement; the formulation "in der Form einer Hochzeit" (in the form of a wedding) to the August wedding. The note is cited, among many others, in *Deutsches Volksblatt*, October 29, 1904, Abendausgabe, 1–2, the citation 2, emphases original.

24. See his statements as reported in *Grazer Volksblatt*, October 30, 1904, 7; *Neues Wiener Tagblatt*, October 30, 1904, 12, and elsewhere. Why such a note should have been added to an official engagement document, i.e., a mere promise of marriage, remains mysterious: doing so would have achieved nothing beyond stating the obvious. Conversely, the notation would make sense on the August marriage certificate if the aim was to invalidate it legally. Prangl did not explain these oddities but merely claimed that the statement was added, at Franz von Hervay's insistence, to the engagement document from July after it had been invalidated anyway by the August marriage.

25. Tamara's testimony on this matter is reported in, among many others, "Die Affaire der Frau v. Hervay," *Neues Wiener Tagblatt*, October 30, 1904, 12; public reading of the letter by her defense attorney in the same article, 14; Karl von Hervay's testimony on the matter in *Deutsches Volksblatt*, October 31, 1904, Abendausgabe 5; Henriette von Hervay's testimony in *Grazer Volksblatt*, October 29, 1904, 13.

26. A series of townspeople and members of the Hervay family were paraded through the court; all testified that they had taken the marriage to be real. Reporting in *Deutsches Volksblatt*, October 30, 1904, Abendausgabe 8–11; *Grazer Volksblatt*, October 30, 1904, 5–7, and elsewhere.

27. Ardently debated in court, as reported in, for example, *Grazer Volksblatt*, October 29, 1904, 13; *Deutsches Volksblatt*, October 30, 1904, Abendausgabe 9, among many others.

28. The prosecutor's summary statement, in which he misrepresents hearsay as substantiated fact numerous times, is another instance that shows how low the standards of evidence were at the trial. It is cited verbatim in *Grazer Volksblatt*, November 1, 1904, 6–7, and with few deviations in *Neues Wiener Tagblatt*, November 1, 1904, 10.

29. Several times, Alison Rose has come very close to claiming this. "Gender stereotypes and stereotypes about Jewish sexuality contributed to the negative reactions to Frau von Hervay and fed into the sensation caused by the 'Hervay affair'" (169). It seems, on the face of it, an uncontroversial statement, and it makes sense to surmise that misogynistic and antisemitic literature influenced the general context in which the trial took place. Yet Rose does not, in fact, base her statements on actual reporting on the case, but on the existence of general antisemitic literature depicting Jews as "possessing overabundant sexual drives" (169) and on misogynistic literature: "The view of women as criminal, duplicitous, and purely sexual was promoted by Otto Weininger's 1903 bestseller, *Sex and Character*. With her multiple marriages and mysterious past, Frau von Hervay seemed to support Weininger's argument that women were by nature polygamous and predisposed to prostitution" (170). Of the hundreds of articles that I've read about the case in the contemporary press, including in the expressly antisemitic press, not a single one mentions either Weininger's book or the stereotype of the sexualised Jewess.

30. Rose 170.

31. While I have made every attempt to keep these criteria simple and unequivocal, I make no claims as to my own objectivity. Historians, in my view, have a duty to attempt fairness while admitting their own partiality. I readily admit that my view of the Hervay case was colored by some writing about her, most crucially her own. In cases where two or more categories overlap in an article—for example, coverage that is both sympathetic towards Hervay and critical of proceedings at her trial—I have assigned it to the topic on which the article places the greater emphasis or to which it accords the most space. For antisemitic articles, I have used more stringent criteria, grouping all articles that make even passing mention to Hervay's Jewishness in either a derogatory or ambiguous fashion (see definition above) in the antisemitic camp.

32. Kraus, "Der Hexenprozess von Leoben."

33. On distribution of both, see https://de.wikipedia.org/wiki/Deutsches_Volksblatt and https://

www.wien.gv.at/wiki/index.php/Neues_Wiener_Tag
blatt. On the general press landscape in Austria at the
turn of the century, see Skalnik.

34. "Durch eine Jüdin in den Tod getrieben!,"
Deutsches Volksblatt, October 29, 1904, Abendausgabe 1–2.

35. "Anläßlich dieser erschütternden Affäre hat
sich unsere Judenpresse wieder in ihrer ganzen
Schamlosigkeit und Verlogenheit gezeigt. Dieselbe
schrotete diesen Fall nicht nur bis zum Ekel aller
anständigen arischen Elemente aus, sondern sie ver-
schwieg auch absichtlich, wessen Ursprungs die Gattin *v. Hervays* eigentlich ist. Während letzterer mit
einigen Worten flüchtigen Bedauerns abgetan wurde,
versuchte man die Gattin desselben fast zur Heldin
zu stempeln. Sie wurde dargestellt als ein äußerst see-
lenvolles (!) geistreiches Weib, als die 'geborene Dame'
ec. ec./Die Ursache dieser planmäßigen Verlogenheit
lag eben darin, daß dieses ränkevolle Weib von
Geburt——*Jüdin* ist, und als die Tochter eines sogenannten 'Künstlers,' eines Prestidigitateurs namens
Samuel *Bellachini,* das Licht der Welt erblickt hatte.
Dieser Jude dürfte älteren Wienern noch unter dem
Spitznamen der *"Judenzauberer"* in Erinnerung
sein./Heute hat sich nun der Schützling der internationalen Judenpresse, Elvira Leontine *Hervay v. Kirchberg,* geborene *Bellachini* (!), wegen *Bigamie* und
Falschmeldung vor dem hiesigen Kreisgerichte zu verantworten." "Durch eine Jüdin in den Tod getrieben!,"
Deutsches Volksblatt, October 29, 1904, Abendausgabe 1–2, the citation 1, emphases original.

36. "Ein enfant gâté der jüdischen Presse," *Deutsches
Volksblatt,* October 30, 1904, 1–2; "Durch eine Jüdin
in den Tod getrieben!," *Deutsches Volksblatt,* October
30, 1904, Abendausgabe 8–11.

37. "Vor dem Kreisgerichte in Leoben stand gestern
jenes jüdische Scheusal als Angeklagte, die den allgemein geachteten, mit den schönsten Tugenden des
Mannes und Beamten geschmückten Bezirkshauptmann von Mürzzuschlag, Herrn *v. Hervay,* in den Tod
getrieben hat. Die Affäre hat seit Monaten die Oeffentlichkeit stets in Atem gehalten, und zwar nicht
nur wegen des tragischen Charakters, den dieselbe
infolge des Selbstmordes des unglücklichen Opfers
eines teuflisch gearteten Judenweibes annahm, sondern noch mehr, weil die gesamte Judenpresse das
Frauenzimmer, das fünf Männer in ihre Netze zu
locken verstand und um ihr Glück betrog, förmlich
zur jüdischen Nationalheiligen stempelte..." "Ein enfant gaté der jüdischen Presse," *Deutsches Volksblatt,*
October 30, 1904, 1, emphasis original.

38. From *Neues Wiener Tagblatt,* October 29, 1904,
Abendausgabe 2–4, all emphases original: *Präs.:* Sie
heißen Eleonore Leontine v. Hervay?—*Angekl.* (leise):
Jawohl./*Präs.:* Ich ersuche Sie, lauter zu sprechen. Sie
sind in Posen geboren?—*Angekl.:* So viel ich weiß,
ja./*Präs.:* Wann?—*Angekl.:* So viel ich gehört habe und
so viel mir gesagt wurde, im Jahre 1860. [...] *Präs.:* [...]
Ich muß Sie aufmerksam machen, möglichst wahrheitsgemäß sich zu verantworten, denn im Falle einer
Verurteilung bildet das Geständnis einen wichtigen
Milderungsgrund. [...] *Präs.:* Nun, Angeklagte, Sie
haben die Anklage gehört. Sind Sie schuldig?—*Angekl.:*
Nein, gewiß nicht.—*Präs.:* Wir wollen nun von den
Beziehungen zu den Eltern sprechen.—*Angekl.:* Da
kann ich nichts sagen. Zwischen meiner angeblichen
Mutter und mir war nie von Liebe oder Zuneigung
die Rede. Ich war noch nie an ihrem Grabe.—*Präs.:*

Sie haben einen Taufschein aus Posen, nach welchem
Sie im Juli 1860 als Tochter des Künstlers *S. Bellachini*
in die Register eingetragen wurden.—*Angekl.:* Meine
angebliche Mutter hat mir von ihrem Sterbebette
einen Brief geschrieben und darin erklärt, daß ich
nicht ihr Kind sei, daß sie mich in Helsingfors aufgenommen und daß ich das Kind sehr vornehmer Eltern
sei. Mehr kann ich darüber nicht sagen./*Präs.:* Ihr
Taufschein lautet aber sehr bestimmt. Sie waren mo-
saisch?—*Angekl.:* Das weiß ich nicht. Ich bin in der
evangelischen Schule erzogen worden und habe mich
immer für eine Protestantin gehalten./*Präs.:* Es liegt
ein Taufschein vor, daß Sie im Jahre 1880 vor Ihrer
Ehe zum evangelischen Glauben übergetreten sind./
Angekl.: Ich bin nicht übergetreten. Ich bin nur in die
evangelische Gemeinschaft aufgenommen worden./
Präs.: Das wäre nicht nötig gewesen, wenn Sie evan-
gelisch gewesen wären."

39. From *Deutsches Volksblatt,* October 29, 1904,
Abend 1–2, all emphases original: "*Vors.:* Wenn Sie
angesprochen werden, haben Sie aufzustehen!—Die
Angeklagte schweigt.—*Vors.:* Wo sind Sie geboren?—
Angekl. (mit affektierter, weinerlicher Stimme): So viel
ich weiß, bei *Posen.*—*Vors.:* Wann sind Sie geboren?—
Angekl.: So viel ich weiß, im Jahre 1860. [...] *Vors.:* Ich
mache Sie aufmerksam, sich wahrheitsgemäß recht-
fertigen zu wollen. Im Falle Sie die Wahrheit sagen,
haben Sie einen Milderungsgrund—setzen Sie sich!
[...] *Vors.:* Angeklagte, stehen Sie auf! Bekennen Sie
sich schuldig?—*Angekl.* (laut, fast schreiend): Nein,
ganz gewiß nicht! (Ueberhaupt trägt die ganze Verantwortung der Angeklagten das Gepräge des Theatralischen an sich).—*Vors.:* Verantworten Sie sich
über das, was Ihnen zur Last gelegt wurde. Wir werden mit Ihrer Jugend beginnen. Wer waren Ihre Eltern?—*Angekl.:* Das kann ich nicht sagen, denn ich
weiß es nicht, da nicht eine Spur von Zuneigung zwischen meiner sogenannten Mutter und mir bestanden
hat. Ja, ich war nie auf ihrem Grabe gewesen.—*Vors.:*
Wir haben ein Dokument, das ganz bestimmt lautet
und sowohl über Ihre Eltern als über Ihre Geburt
Aufklärung gibt.—*Angekl:* Mein Vater hat auf dem
Sterbebette einen Brief geschrieben, sie ist nicht unsere Tochter, wir haben sie in Helsingfors aufgenommen
und an die Stelle unseres verstorbenen Töchterchens
gesetzt, sie ist die Tochter vornehmer Eltern. Mehr
zu sagen halte ich nicht für nötig./*Der Vorsitzende*
verliest hierauf einen Geburtsschein aus dem Register
der Juden in Posen, in diesem steht, daß die Ehefrau
Samuel Bellachinis, geborne Krügel, am 18. Juli 1860
um 2 Uhr Früh ein Kind geboren habe, welches die
Vornamen Elvira Leontine erhielt [...]—*Angekl.:* Ich
bin in einem evangelischen Institute erzogen worden,
habe stets evangelischen Religionsunterricht erhalten
und stets evangelische Kirchen besucht.—*Vors.:* Wir
haben den Beweis, daß Sie im Jahre 1880, kurz vor der
ersten Ehescheidung mit Cuntz, zur evangelischen Religion übergetreten sind.— *Angekl.:* Ich wußte nicht,
daß dies ein Uebertritt ist, sondern es wurde mir
gesagt, weil ich in Berlin geboren bin, muß ich in
einer Berliner Kirchengenossenschaft aufgenommen werden, um in Berlin getraut werden zu können."

40. Kraus, "Der Hexenprozeß von Leoben" 89.

41. Reported, among others, in *Deutsches Volksblatt,* October 30, 1904, 8–11, the episode 10–11;
Grazer Volksblatt, October 30, 1904, 5–7, the episode
7; *Neues Wiener Tagblatt,* October 30, 1904, 12–14,
the episode 13–14.

42. "v. Hervay begrüßte seine Lebensgefährtin mit den Worten: Du hast mich schnöde betrogen. Frau v. Hervay erwiderte mit einer theatralischen Geste: Ich habe dich nicht betrogen, sondern nur belogen. Darauf antwortete ich: In diesem Falle bleibt es gleichgültig, ob Sie Ihren Mann betrogen oder belogen haben." *Grazer Volksblatt*, July 2, 1904, Abendausgabe 3.

43. "Man hat sie wirklich nur verhaftet, weil sie eine 'Abenteurerin' ist—was zwar in Mürzzuschlag so viel wie Auswurf der menschlichen Gesellschaft bedeutet, aber in der Reihe der Paragraphe des Strafgesetzbuches keine Stelle hat [...]. [...] in Wahrheit hat man nicht eine Untersuchung wegen Bigamie, sondern wegen des funkelnagelneuen Deliktes *Vorleben* geführt." "Die Tragödie Hervay," *Arbeiterzeitung*, November 1, 1904, 1–2, the citations 2, emphases original.

44. "Man begreift, daß, um der unsterblichen Ansprüche der wahren Gerechtigkeit willen, der Göttin der Justiz jene berühmte Binde so umgelegt werden müßte, daß auch ihre Ohren luft- und klatschdicht verschlossen würden." *Das interessante Blatt*, November 10, 1904, 11.

45. "Trotzdem die Stimmung der hiesigen Bevölkerung fast durchgängig eine für Frau v. Hervay sehr ungünstige ist, rief der Verlauf der Verhandlung sehr viel Verwunderung hervor, da so viele Dinge zur Erörterung gelangten, die der Vorsitzende selbst als bloße Illustrationen bezeichnete." *Neues Wiener Tagblatt*, October 31, 1904, 10.

46. "Ein Schrei nach 'Wahrheit' dringt durch das Mürztal, und mit allen steirischen Gebirgstrotteln vereinigen sich alle Wiener Tintenstrolche in dem Verlangen nach Klarheit. Es soll endlich an den Tag, ob die Zufriedenheit im Hause Hervay auf gesunder oder morscher Grundlage ruht. Die Ungewißheit ist nicht länger zu ertragen. [...] Zu lange hat man sich diese Frau mit ihren besseren Manieren und ihrer besseren Unterwäsche gefallen lassen, zu lange hat sie ungestraft den Ort rebellisch gemacht. Nicht nur, daß sie den feschen Bezirkshauptmann gekapert hat, ist sie auch auf den besten Wege, den anderen Ehemännern die Köpfe zu verdrehen." Kraus, "Der Fall Hervay," 76–7.

47. "Anklage auf 'Bigamie' hieß es, weil man's Hexenprozeß nicht nennen konnte [...]. Leontine von Hervay war auf einem Besenstiel nach Mürzzuschlag durch die Luft geritten, wobei ihr seidener Unterrock sichtbar wurde. Ein ahnungsvolles Barchentgemüt rief sofort: 'I Durchschaudi.' Was nützte es, daß sie den Bezirkshauptmann glücklich gemacht hatte? Eine Zaubererstochter und fremder Sprachen mächtig. Als 'teuflischer Buhlschaft' dringend verdächtig. Dem einen erkrankte wohl das Vieh, dem andern verdarb vielleicht das Getreide. Der ganze Ort wird rebellisch. Dem Bezirkshauptmann hat sie einen Liebestrank eingegeben, andere Honoratioren werden folgen, die begehrtesten Mürzzuschlagerinnen müssen zurückstehen. Soll man es dahin kommen lassen, daß sie 'die Männer verhindert zu zeugen, und die Weiber, zu gebären, und die Männer, daß sie den Weibern, und die Weiber, daß sie den Männern die ehelichen Werke leisten'? [...] Sie hat nicht nur Frauen, die um siebzehn Jahre jünger sind, in der Gunst des saubersten Beamten der Stadt ausgestochen, sondern—Zauberinnen sind manches imstande—sich auch selbst um siebzehn Jahre verjüngt." Kraus, "Der Hexen-

prozeß von Leoben," 84–6. Kraus's sarcastic quotations are taken from the 1484 Papal Bull of Innocent VIII, the Church's endorsement of witch hunting and inquisitional trials and now widely regarded as the inaugural document of the 'Burning Times' in Germany.

48. "Die Hervay ist der Bigamie angeklagt, in einer halben Stunde wäre der Tatbestand, zu dem eine vorhandene Trauungsurkunde und ein fehlendes Scheidungsdekret gehören, rechtlich festgestellt. Herr Labres aber, der Hexenrichter von Leoben, geht zur 'peinlich Frag' über, die den eigentlichen Zweck des Verfahrens bildet. 'Ich will mit Ihrer Jugendzeit beginnen. Wer waren Ihre Eltern?' 'Haben Sie nicht jemandem einen Ihrer Verehrer als Milchbruder vorgestellt?' 'Haben Sie nicht später mit dem Oberleutnant Goltsch ein Verhältnis gehabt?' 'War nicht auch noch ein anderer Mann in Mürzzuschlag, für den sich die Angeklagte interessiert hat?' Ein Hoteldiener bestätigt, daß der Oberleutnant Bartel sich in unvollständiger Toilette in das Zimmer der Angeklagten begeben hat. Hier ist offenbar der Punkt, wo man der Hexe die 'teuflische Buhlschaft' wird nachweisen können. 'Das haben Sie tatsächlich beobachtet?' 'Können Sie das auf Ihren Eid aussagen?' 'Haben Sie das bestimmt gesehen, was Sie jetzt unter Eid ausgesagt haben?' 'Haben Sie seine Toilette wahrgenommen?' Nach allem erkundigt sich Herr Labres, seine Neugierde, die heute einmal befriedigt sein will, schreckt wohl vor der Trauungsurkunde des Pfarrers, aber nicht vor den Unterhosen des Oberleutnants zurück, und nur die Frage bleibt der Inquirierten erspart, ob das 'semen diabolicum calidum aut frigidum' gewesen sei. So ward die 'Bigamie' bewiesen..." Kraus, "Der Hexenprozeß" 89.

49. See, for example: *Grazer Volksblatt*, July 8, 1904, Abendausgabe 4; August 14, 1904, 6; August 20, 1904, 3; September 3, 1904, 3; *Neues Wiener Tagblatt*, July 8, 1904, 7; July 15, 1904, 7; July 24, 1904, Abendausgabe 3; October 31, 1904, 10; November 3, 1904, 9–10; *Das interessante Blatt*, November 10, 1904, 11; *Österreichische Kronen-Zeitung*, July 15, 1904, 5–7; *Arbeiterzeitung*, November 1, 1904, 1–2, and many more.

50. "Die Angeklagte stellt sich kokett vor den Zeugen und ihn höhnisch anblickend, sagt sie: 'Haben Sie mir nicht gesagt, Herr Stationschef: *Ich bin Ihr eifrigster Verehrer!*'" *Deutsches Volksblatt*, October 30, 1904, Abendausgabe 8–11, the citation 9, emphases original.

51. "*Angekl.:* Herr Oberleutnant, Sie haben ja selbst zu mir gesagt: 'Du bist ein gutes und edles Geschöpf. Du wirst meinem Bruder nicht hinderlich sein.—*Zeuge: Von gutem und edlem Geschöpfe weiß ich nichts.* (Heiterkeit.)" *Deutsches Volksblatt*, October 31, 1904, Abendausgabe 5–6, the citation 5, emphases original. The story is re-told by Hervay in her memoirs, *Tamara von Hervay* 108.

52. "Vor dem strengen Rechte des Gesetzes bin ich unterlegen, vor dem milden Rechte der Moral werde ich siegen!" Hervay, *Tamara von Hervay: Ihr Leben und Denken* v.

53. All quotations in this and the following are taken from her memoirs, *Tamara von Hervay: Ihr Leben und Denken:* "da konnte ich nicht nein sagen. Es war ja so grenzenlose Menschenliebe in mir" (8).— "In mir ist ein starker Zug Opferfreudigkeit ... Ich wollte ja auch geben, in mir ist alles so klar, so

edel, kein auch noch so kleines Häßliches lebt in mir" (69).

54. "Er hielt es kaum wenige Stunden ohne mich aus. Gewiß war seine Liebe auch eine sinnliche, nur war ihm die Sinnlichkeit nicht Hauptsache und ich hielt Maß. Auch im intimsten ehelichen Verkehr ließen wir uns niemals gehen, alles hatte eine gewisse Weihe und stets genossen wir unsere heiße Liebe als etwas Neues, Heiliges!/Ich will Ihnen seine eigenen Worte wiederholen:/'Schatzerl, wie ist bei uns doch alles so heilig, was gibt mir dein tiefes Gemüt für grenzenloses Glück! Aber sag,' wirst du mich auch lieben, so wie jetzt, wenn ich, was vielleicht bald sein wird, dich nur noch küssen kann?'/Ich habe ihm sehr ernst geantwortet, daß das, was er meint, doch nicht die 'Hauptsache' ist, daß die wahrhaftige Liebe 'davon' doch ganz unbeeinflußt sei" (Hervay 75).

55. "Sowie ich heute nicht in der Lage bin, die Memoiren, die Frau v. Hervay kürzlich erscheinen ließ, zu empfehlen. Ich fühle mich sogar verpflichtet, sie ausdrücklich nicht zu empfehlen, weil Stillschweigen mir, der nun einmal als Verfechter der Hervay-Sache akkreditiert und auch in dem Buche selbst gepriesen ist, als Billigung des Unfugs ausgelegt werden könnte. [...] Ein Buch unter dem Titel 'Tamara v. Hervay. Ihr Leben und *Denken*' ist eine lästige Erscheinung" (Kraus, "Die Memoiren der Frau v. Hervay" 98, emphasis original). The citation of the conjugal-intercourse passage follows on 99.

56. In 1904, the average middle-class salary, for example that of a cashier in a bank, was about 4000 crowns per year.

57. "Ich gebe Ihnen hiermit das aufrichtige Versprechen ab, daß ich gegen den Herrn Oberleutnant Karl von Hervay, dessen Vater und Großvater und sonstigen Verwandten, dann gegen dessen Gattin, gegen deren Großeltern und sonstigen Verwandten in keiner Weise, sei es nun polemisch oder anfeindend, aufzutreten, sondern dieselben als für mich nicht existierend ignorieren werde. Ich anerkenne, daß infolge dieser Zusage Herr Oberleutnant Karl von Hervay Sie ermächtigt hat, mir *ausgleichsweise* zur Befriedigung meiner *Ansprüche* den Betrag von 'fünftausend' Kronen auszubezahlen!" (Hervay vi–vii, emphases original).

58. "Ich hatte aber den Heldenmut und zwang meinen Verlobten, mein ganzes Leben anzuhören" (Hervay 33).

59. "'Ach, Baronin Lützow, gestern erzählte mir jemand, Sie seien viermal verheiratet gewesen—! Nein, wie schrecklich!'—/Lächelnd antwortete ich ihr: 'Ja, es ist in der Tat schrecklich, Baronin, ich allein hatte vier legitime Männer—und manche wären doch über einen schon so froh. Es ist ungerecht in der Welt, Baronin, nicht wahr?'/Könnten Blicke töten—ich hätte die ganze Qual nicht zu erleben brauchen!" Hervay 47–8.

60. In *Neues Wiener Tagblatt*, for example, Henriette von Hervay is described as "Die schlanke Dame mit leicht ergrautem Haare"; October 30, 1904, 12–14, the citation 13; see also the corresponding description in *Grazer Volksblatt*, June 25, 1904, 3.

61. "Die Mutter, eine furchtbar häßliche Frau mit einem unförmig dicken Leib, einem hageren, von roten Flecken entstellten Gesichte, sah aus, als ob sie einen sauren Apfel im Munde hätte; der Vater ist Kavalier, der Bruder ein nichtssagender Mann; seine Frau—sie erinnert lebhaft an den Martinsbraten—

oder wie nennen Sie die weißen Vögel vom Kapitol? /Das erste Wort, welches Frau von Hervay zu mir sprach, war: 'Mais, ma chère, il n'ya pas un sou de fortune!'/Und ich sagte, bleich vor Entsetzen über diese Taktlosigkeit:/'Oh, Madame, cela ne faire rien!'" (Hervay 36)

62. "Als Franz dann in der Frühe in mein Hotel kam, sagte er zu mir: 'Mein Märchen, ich habe noch heute Nacht an meine Eltern geschrieben, daß wir uns gestern heimlich haben trauen lassen; und damit die ewige Fragerei und Quälerei endlich aufhört, habe ich ihnen mitgeteilt, daß *du 300.000 Mark für mich deponiert hast* und ich den Depotschein in der Tasche habe. Mama will ja nur *chère*, alles andere ist ihr 'Wurscht'!'/Ich war über das Gehörte entsetzt! 'Wie willst du denn das nur aufrecht halten?' fragte ich ihn. 'Deine Mutter wird doch sofort den Depotschein sehen wollen, der Trauschein wäre wohl Nebensache gewesen.'" (Hervay 62–3, emphases original)

63. "Entzückend richtete ich unser Haus ein, ich bin, glaube ich, eine gute Hausfrau und für meine Person sehr bescheiden" (Hervay 11).

64. "Ich stecke die Lampe an und mein Blick schweift im Zimmer umher. Gräßlich für einen Menschen, dem eine schöne und harmonische Umgebung Lebensbedürfnis geworden ist. Ach! Unser süßes Heim, mit welcher Liebe haben wir alles zusammengetragen, wie nahmen die Räume, in denen ich lebte, meinen Charakter an; da war nichts Aufdringliches, keine schreienden Farben; gemäßigte Sezession, trauliche Ecken, frische Palmen, blühende Blumen: 'Hic habitat felicitas!' Vorbei—alles vorbei; mein Gott, wie ist es schwer zu ertragen, dieses Leid!" (Hervay 21)

65. "Die ersten Tage in Graz waren entsetzlich. Ich konnte die Gefängniskost nicht hinunterwürgen und litt Hunger. Ach, qualvoll war diese Zeit! Ich hatte Visionen in meinem krankhaften Zustande, oft sah ich unser gemütliches Eßzimmer, den reizend arrangierten Eßtisch—dann wieder sah ich herrliche Speisen, ich stürzte darauf los—und schlug mit dem Kopfe an die Wand. Ich habe vor Hunger gebrüllt wie ein Tier" (Hervay 121).

66. "Einer in Leoben zum Besuche einer Patientin weilenden Dame gegenüber machte Frau v. Hervay im Spital Mitteilungen über ihre Ehe, die, wenn sie der Wahrheit entsprechen würden, die Affäre in einem neuen Lichte erscheinen lassen könnten." The itemized list of things bought and purchase price follows. *Grazer Volksblatt*, July 6, 1904, Abendausgabe 3.

67. The list of things sold at the liquidation and prices they fetched are in Hervay 143–5. The quotations: "Für mein Silber zum Beispiel, welches, *alt* gekauft, mit 1000 Kronen gezahlt worden ist, gaben Hervays 350 Kronen./Ein kostbarer schwarzer Federfächer, der mehrere hundert Franken gekostet hat, ist von Frau Amy von Hervay für——5 Kronen gekauft worden, ebenso ist beim Konkurse über das Vermögen *meines Mannes*, meine Leibwäsche für Spottpreise verkauft worden" (Hervay 144, emphases original).— "Frau von Hervay hat billig eingekauft, nicht wahr?" (145)

68. "ich selbst bin eine tief unglückliche Frau, die, weil ihr *Horizont größer ist* als eine *Mürzzuschlager Waschschüssel*, elend zugrunde gehen muß!" (Hervay 1, emphases original)

69. Her complaints about the conditions of her im-

prisonment are reported, among others, in: *Grazer Volksblatt*, July 8, 1904, Abendausgabe 4; August 14, 1904, 6; August 20, 1904, 3; September 3, 1904, 3, and October 31, 1904, Abendausgabe 5–7; *Neues Wiener Tagblatt*, July 8, 1904, 7; July 24, 1904, Abendausgabe 3, and November 3, 1904, 9–10; *Deutsches Volksblatt*, October 31, 1904, Abendausgabe 5–6, and November 1, 1904, 7–8; *Das interessante Blatt*, November 10, 1904, 11; and *Österreichische Kronen-Zeitung*, July 15, 1905, 5–7.

70. "Karl heiratete als er vierundzwanzig Jahre alt war, eine Baronin Lütgendorf, deren Mutter Löwenfeld hieß und eine Jüdin war. Sie hatte aber einen großen Geldsack./ In Trojas Hallen herrschte eitel Freude, Mutter Hervay schwamm in Seligkeit und nahm selbst die [...] Großmutter Löwenfeld mit in den Kauf" (Hervay 45).

71. The Austrian Emperor commuted Hervay's sentence from four months' imprisonment to one. See *Österreichische Kronen-Zeitung*, July 14, 1905, 7–8.

72. Hervay's case was briefly discussed in a session of the Viennese Parliament on November 4, 1904, in connection with the "protectionism" that permitted Franz von Hervay to force both the mayor and the priest to suspend important rules. As reported in *Neues Wiener Tagblatt*, November 5, 1904, 7.

73. *Deutsches Volksblatt*, January 24, 1906, Abendausgabe 2; *Grazer Volksblatt*, January 24, 1906, 12 and January 27, 1906, 4; *Salzburger Volksblatt*, January 24, 1906, 6; *Linzer Tagespost*, January 24, 1906, 3 and January 30, 1906, 3; *Österreichische Kronen-Zeitung*, January 24, 1906, 5.

74. As a moniker for a female impostor, it is a great one. Preitler explained that he wanted to call his novel *The Conjurer's Daughter*, but that the press objected. *The Black Baroness* was chosen by his publisher in consultation with the author. Email from Franz Preitler to Susanne Kord, February 7, 2017.

75. Voigt's personal "principles" that prevented him to steal even a penny from a private person were widely commented on in the press, for example in *Berliner Börsen-Zeitung*, October 26, 1906, 7: "Nach seinen 'Grundsätzen' brachte er es, wie er sagte, auch nicht über das Herz, einer Privatperson auch nur einen Pfennig wegzunehmen."

76. The comment is quoted in German translation in *Denkwürdigkeiten* 18: "Die gestrige Tragikomödie kann für das deutsche Volksleben zwei umwälzende Änderungen haben. Erstens: die Zerstörung des Grundsatzes, daß man vor des Kaisers Rock den Kotau machen muß, wie einst die Schweizer vor Geßlers Hut. Zweitens: der blinde, gedankenlose Gehorsam, der den teutonischen Soldaten als die ruhmreichste Tugend eingeprägt wird, kann eine erhebliche Abschwächung erfahren. Ohne diese Traditionen, die dem deutschen Volke in Fleisch und Blut übergegangen sind, könnte sich die Tragikomödie von Köpenick nicht ereignet haben, die das Reich dem Hohngelächter beider Hemisphären preisgibt."

77. "Was hat er getan? [...] Gegen ein halbes oder ganzes Dutzend Paragraphen verstoßen. Dem Land aber unschätzbaren Dienst erwiesen" (quoted in *Denkwürdigkeiten* 50).

78. "Die Komödie von Köpenick," *Berliner Volks-Zeitung*, October 17, 1906, 1: "Ein Hochstapler, ein Gauner, ein Räuber mußte kommen, um dergestalt eine der wundersamsten staatlichen Ordnungseinrichtungen ad absurdum zu führen!"

79. For example: *Neues Wiener Tagblatt*, January 15, 1905, 6 and July 15 of the same year, 7; *Österreichische Buchhändler-Correspondenz*, July 19, 1905, 12; *Deutsches Volksblatt*, January 24, 1906, Abendausgabe 2; *Grazer Volksblatt*, January 24, 1906, 12; *Linzer Tagespost*, January 25, 1906, 3; *Grazer Volksblatt*, February 28, 1906, Abendausgabe 4; *Neues Wiener Tagblatt*, March 2, 1906, Abendausgabe 4; *Innsbrucker Nachrichten*, March 54, 1906, 10; *Grazer Volksblatt*, August 8, 1906, 4; *Prager Tagblatt*, August 9, 1906, 6; *Grazer Tagblatt*, September 27, 1906, 3; *Innsbrucker Nachrichten*, October 16, 1906, 7; *Neue Schlesische Zeitung*, October 21, 1906, 2; *Neues Wiener Journal*, December 7, 1906, 8; *Grazer Tagblatt*, January 2, 1907, 4; *Linzer Tagespost*, January 31, 1908, 5, and many more.

80. "Aber daß zehn Grenadiere einem unvorschriftsmäßig gekleideten Hauptmann mit gebogenen Beinen und (wie die "Staatsbürger-Zeitung" andeutungsvoll bemerkt!) einer *krummen Nase* ohne weiteres folgen, wenn es gilt, das Köpenicker Rathaus zu stürmen und etwa gar den armen Bürgermeister aufs Bajonett zu spießen: das ist eine Lektion auf die Weisheit unserer militärischen Erziehung, wie sie kein Witzblatt besser erfinden könnte." Paul Blook, "Der Hauptmann von Köpenick," *Berliner Tageblatt*, October 17, 1906, Abendausgabe 1, emphasis original.

81. "Allein darüber kann der hohe Gerichtshof nur seine moralische Ansicht äußern. Die juristische Ueberzeugung kann und darf dadurch nicht beeinflußt werden." *Neues Wiener Tagblatt*, October 31, 1904, 10.

82. "Eine Abenteurerin ohne Zweifel. Aber eine Verbrecherin? Nein." *Czernowitzer Allgemeine Zeitung*, January 11, 1908, 1–3.

83. Arendt, *Origins* 81.

84. On this issue, see Kord, *Sich einen Namen machen*.

85. See the entries for her in Kord, *Ein Blick*, 440–1 and *Sich einen Namen machen* 198.

86. Rose 168.

87. "Er nennt sie nicht mehr Maria, er formt ihren Namen kosend in Mara um, dann in Tamara. [...] wie ihr Vater, ein gewisser—wie hieß er doch gleich?—ach ja, Bloch, der sich dann Bellach—oder Bellachini!" J. Lorm, "Verbrecherische Liebe," *Czernowitzer Allgemeine Zeitung*, January 11, 1908, 1–3, the citation 1.

88. "Die Gattin des Bezirkshauptmanns ist nämlich keine geborne von *Lützow* aus Rußland, sondern eine *Berliner Jüdin* namens *Singer* und auch schon als solche entlarvt." "Eine Affäre des Bezirkshauptmanns von Mürzzuschlag," *Grazer Volksblatt*, June 17, 1904, Abendausgabe 2.

89. "sie nannte sich Camera v. Lützow, hieß jedoch nach ihren Papieren Elvira Liontine v. Lützow"; "Der Eheroman des Bezirkshauptmannes von Mürzzuschlag," *Grazer Volksblatt*, June 18, 1904, 4.

90. "Sie ist aus Charlottenburg gebürtig und hieß als Mädchen Maria *Bellach*. Sie ist die Tochter eines Taschenspielers." "Verhaftung der Frau v. Hervay," *Grazer Volksblatt*, June 22, 1904, Abendausgabe 2.

91. "Die Verhaftete ist die Tochter des bekannten Hofzauberkünstlers *Bellachini*... Erna Bellachini oder, wie ihr richtiger Name lautet, Hedwig Bellach oder Bloch, ist eine kleine, schlanke, zierliche, eigentlich nicht hübsche Person und von bestrickenden Um-

gangsformen. Sie ist geradezu ein hochstaplerisches Genie, und die Zahl der Männer, die sie auszubeuten verstand, ist Legion." "Das Ende des Bezirkshauptmannes v. Hervay," *Neues Wiener Tagblatt*, June 25, 1904, Abendausgabe 3.

92. "... daß Elvira Klementine die Tochter des jüdischen Ehepaares Bellach sei." *Deutsches Volksblatt*, October 31, 1904, Abendausgabe 6.

93. "...die Jüdin *Bellachini*-Murin-Lützow-Hervay [...] Ein Offizier kam und sah das liberale Märchen, das sich nicht mehr Bellachini und nicht mehr Lützow oder Hervay, sondern *'Baronin Kirchberg'* nannte und war besiegt von seinem Reiz und seinen schönen Erzählungen." "Das 'Märchen' der Wiener Liberalen," *Reichspost*, January 25, 1906, 3.

94. "Auffällig ist es auch, daß die Verurteilte das Silberzeug, die Wäsche u. s. w. mit den Buchstaben 'T.L.' und der Freiherrenkrone versehen ließ, woraus doch hervorgeht, daß sie ihrem Manne die Ehe mit Meurin und auch die übrigen Ehen verschwiegen hat und sich als eine Freiin Tamara v. Lützow ausgegeben hat, obwohl sie gar nicht Tamara, sondern Leontine heißt." "Eine Unterredung mit Frau v. Hervay," *Grazer Volksblatt*, November 9, 1904, Abendausgabe 2.

95. The court order was widely reported on, for example in *Neue Freie Presse*, January 23, 1907, 13; *Arbeiterwille*, January 24, 1907, 5; *Österreichische Kronen-Zeitung*, January 24, 1907, 10; *Prager Tagblatt*, January 25, 1907, 10; *Linzer Tagespost*, January 31, 1907, 5, and many others.

96. For example in: *Linzer Tagespost*, January 25, 1905, 3 and again on January 30, 3; *Österreichische Kronen-Zeitung*, January 25, 1906, 5; *Grazer Volksblatt*, January 7, 1907, 3.

97. "Nichts ist an der Sache pikant, wert, ausgeschrotet zu werden, als der Name. Der Name, der so viele Erinnerungen weckt, der so vielen geläufig sein muß, der gerade gut genug ist, der Neuigkeitshyäne, die zu füttern Sie berufen sind, vorgeworfen zu werden. Und da haben Sie denn auch den Namen an das Licht gezerrt, mit der pikaten Sauce verbrämt, der ohne jede Rücksicht den Traditionen Ihrer genialen kleinen Ausgabe Rechnung trägt, und zugerichtet, daß der Fraß auch mundet. Schon diese Namensaufzählung! Zwar bestreitet die Frau, jemals mit Bellachini in irgend welchen Beziehungen gestanden zu haben, und sie müßte ja heute auch 57 Jahre alt sein, wenn sie diese Tochter des Berliner Taschenspielers sein sollte. Aber in Ihrem 'Volksblatte'—daß die Seiten nicht rot werden, wenn sie diesen Titel tragen!—muß sie diese Tochter bleiben, die 'Jüdin', weil sie dadurch 'objektiv' werden, nicht zu den 'Judenblättern' gehören, welche das 'Deutsche Volksblatt' nun geißelt, obzwar diese Frau nie eine Jüdin war, noch auch von Juden abstammt, sondern ein eifrige Katholikin ist und darum von ihren Mitgläubigen ans Märtyrerkreuz geschlagen wird." Siegmund Bergmann, "Journalisten als Banditen," *Wiener Montags-Journal*, January 29, 1906, 3–4.

98. Samuel Bellachini's reputation as a magician was Europe-wide; he was famous, among other things, for amusing and astounding Emperor Wilhelm I. to such a degree that he named him his court magician. The man who achieved this fame is uniformly identified as Tamara von Hervay's father. The death notices of 1908 misidentify the deceased as the genuine article, attributing to him both the Emperor-Wilhelm anecdote and parentage of Tamara von Her-

vay. The *Neue Schlesische Zeitung* inadvertently debunks its own misidentification by stating that the Bellachini who died in 1908 reached the age of 62. If that is true, Bellachini's birth year would have been either 1845 or 1846, which would have made him 14 years old in 1860, the year of Tamara von Hervay's birth. 1908 death notices for Tamara's father include "Das Ende des Zauberers," *Linzer Volksblatt*, January 8, 1908, 7; *Deutsches Volksblatt*, January 7, 1908, 5; "Das Ende eines Zauberkünstlers," *Neue Schlesische Zeitung*, January 12, 1908, 4. Alison Rose gives 1885 as the year of the original Samuel Bellachini's (and Tamara's father's) death (161), and sources on the famous conjurer list his life dates as 1828–1885 (see, among others, the Magicpedia entry on him at http://geniimagazine.com/magicpedia/Samuel_Bellachini).

99. As reported in *Deutsches Volksblatt*, October 29, 1904, 1–2; the citation from her testimony on 2 (emphases original): "Da mir aber dieser Name nicht sympathisch war und ich in *Nizza* eine deutsche Pension errichtet hatte, nannte ich mich aus Geschäftsrücksichten *Lützow*."

100. "Wir haben eine Vereinbarung getroffen, daß, für den Fall er sterben sollte, bevor die wirkliche Heirat stattfindet, ich trotzdem berechtigt sei, seinen Namen zu führen.—*Präs.*: Aber das ist ja unmöglich." *Neues Wiener Tagblatt*, October 30, 1904, 12–14, the citation 12.

101. "Sie war—er wußte nicht wer. Sie kam—er wußte nicht woher." J. Lorm, "Verbrecherische Liebe" 1.

A Tale of Two Thieves

1. "Im wesentlichen wird Gorski mit seiner Ansicht recht behalten. Wahrscheinlich wird es so kommen: Sobald in Berlin sich der Geldschrankeinbruch nicht mehr lohnt, wird der größere Teil der Knacker sich den gewöhnlichen Einbruchsspezialitäten, dem Geschäftseinbruch und dem Wohnungseinbruch, wieder zuwenden. Schon jetzt macht sich diese Abwanderung bemerkbar. [...] Nur einige wenige, die das Zeug zu Einbrechern großen Schlages in sich haben, und solche gibt es entgegen Gorskis Auffassung noch sehr wohl in Berlin, werden mit Sauerstoffapparat oder mit Sprengstoffen Einbrüche Gorskischer Art ausführen, aber durch ihre Verwegenheit den kriminalpolizeilichen Spüreifer in dem Maße auf sich konzentrieren, daß ihr Treiben kaum von langer Dauer sein wird./Im großen und ganzen wird es aber, von Einzelerscheinungen abgesehen, in absehbarer Zeit mit dem Knackertum zu Ende sein" (Liebermann von Sonnenberg, "Die Elite" 191–2).

2. "Nach dem Vorbild der amerikanischen Safeknacker arbeiteten 1929 die Brüder Sass, als sie den Tresor der Disconto-Gesellschaft am Berliner Wittenbergplatz leerten [...]. Kein Raub, der mit Schnelligkeit und Gewaltandrohung vorging, sondern ein heimliches, geschickt ausgeführtes Verbrechen: Der Bankeinbruch hatte Deutschland erreicht" (Boldorf 22).

3. If criminalist Max Fabich, who specialized in bank safe cracking in the 19-teens and 20s, has his facts right, the first such incident in Germany took place in Berlin on October 6, 1906. It was a "hot break-in" (i.e., one that employed means like explosives or smelting). The robbers tried to open the safe

door with explosives, with mixed success: the door hit one of them, Otto Preuß, on the head, killing him instantly. His comrades laid the dead thief out in state and left the safe door open but its contents untouched. Deterred by this tragedy, safe crackers subsequently turned to "cold work" such as working with the "Knabber" (basically a can opener for safes, enabling crackers to open metal up to 4 mm thick). The Otto Preuß case is described by Fabich, "Geldschrankeinbrecher" 61 and Liebermann, "Elite" 176–7.

4. The formulation is Klaus Schönberger's: "Historisch gesehen sind die Gebrüder Sass vielleicht die ersten Medienstars gewesen, oder die ersten Popstars des Einbruchs" (cited in Gabi Schlag's *SWR*-feature "Ehrenwerte Gauner").

5. Schlag reports that "Das große Verbrecher Lexikon" ("The Great Crime Lexicon") considered it "the most sensational bank robbery of German criminal history" ("Das große Verbrecher Lexikon bezeichnet diesen Bruch der Sass-Brüder als sensationellsten Bankraub der deutschen Kriminalgeschichte"), unfortunately without specifying whether this was Borrmann's *Das große Lexikon des Verbrechens* (2002) or Sinn's *Das große Verbrecher Lexikon* (1984).

6. To Patrick Wagner, for instance, this break-in marked "a leap in the modernization of the trade: for the first time bank robbers tried not to break into a free-standing safe but to penetrate the vault of a bank" ("einen Sprung in der Modernisierung des [...] Gewerbes. Zum ersten Mal versuchten Einbrecher nicht nur einen freistehenden Geldschrank aufzubrechen, sondern in den Tresorraum einer Bank einzudringen"; *Hitlers Kriminalisten* 42). Similarly Mahn: "Smelting open the vault doors was a previously unknown technique and initiated a turning-point in the history of safe cracking" ("Das Aufschweißen der Tresortüren war zuvor nicht bekannt gewesen und leitete eine Wende in der Geschichte der Geldschrankkriminalität ein," 25).

7. The saying "Moabit, da wird die Miete mit nem Revolver kassiert" is cited in Schlag; the story of the French origin of the name "Moabit" in Schwerk, *Meisterdiebe* 10.

8. The family background, apartment and sleeping arrangements are described in Fabich, "Vorleben" 39; Völklein; Schwerk, *Meisterdiebe* 12 and 19–20; Habbe; Dannenbaum; "Das Spiel ist aus."

9. Fabich, "Vorleben" 37: "Er war ein recht eigenartiger Kauz, der sich um seine Mitmenschen wenig kümmerte, auch seine fünf Jungens, die aus der Ehe hervorgingen, einfach als nicht vorhanden betrachtete." A similar description of Andreas Sass is offered in "Das Spiel ist aus."

10. Schwerk, *Meisterdiebe* 20.

11. "Gleichwohl aber war damit unglücklicher Weise der Grundstock für seine spätere verbrecherische Laufbahn gelegt. Infolge einer eigenartigen einseitigen technischen Begabung hatte er schnell gelernt mit dem Schlosserwerkzeug umzugehen, was er in einer Weise zu nutzen verstand, die für andere Zwecke besser angewendet gewesen wäre" (Fabich, "Vorleben" 38).

12. Conditions described in Schlag.

13. "Jeder Bankraub erinnert daran, dass gesellschaftliche Verhältnisse historisch und damit veränderbar sind, denn der Bankraub stellt die scheinbar naturgegebene Verteilung des gesellschaftlichen Reichtums in Frage" (Schönberger cited in Schlag).

14. Bertolt Brecht, "Was ist ein Einbruch in eine Bank gegen die Gründung einer Bank?" *Die Dreigroschenoper* 267.

15. See Schlag.

16. According to the 1949 retrospective "Das Spiel ist aus," Max Sass left the family in 1913, at the age of ten, and spent the next 15 years in Halle. In 1928 he returned to Berlin; from then on, he ran the cigar shop bought for him by his brothers but also frequently ran afoul of the law. Caught *in flagrante delicto* while breaking into an apothecary's shop, he killed himself in prison in 1935. Ekkehard Schwerk tells the story of his life somewhat differently: he seems to imply that Max spent the years between 1913 and 1928 in Berlin, where he had a long rap sheet even as a youngster, where the police knew him better than his elementary school teachers and his baby-faced photograph was included in the criminal file. Schwerk claims that Max was "last imprisoned" in 1928 and thereafter tried to make it as an honest man, opening a cigar shop (*Meisterdiebe* 13). Max's suicide in prison is well documented, but I have been unable to reconcile the differing accounts of his life.

17. The term is, of course, intended to be read figuratively, not literally: "Erich und Franz gingen einen besonderen Bruderbund ein, gründeten gewissermaßen die Gaunerfirma Gebrüder Sass" (*Meisterdiebe* 15).

18. A physical description of the Brothers is offered in Schwerk, *Meisterdiebe* 22, and *Berliner Volks-Zeitung*, February 19, 1929, 2.

19. Schwerk, *Meisterdiebe* 17–18; descriptions of their enormous popularity and Robin-Hood legend also in Völklein and Kuhrt.

20. Schwerk, *Meisterdiebe* 16; a similar story is cited in Schlag: Horst Kupferschmidt, a neighbor's descendant, claimed that his grandmother had once found 10 marks in her mailbox after a bank robbery. "It can only have been them. Who has so much money in such a poor neighborhood that he can give other people 10 marks?"

21. Wagner, *Volksgemeinschaft* 45 ("Aristokraten der Verbrecherwelt"); Liebermann, "Elite" 167.

22. Wagner, *Volksgemeinschaft* 45–6, 167.

23. Wagner, *Volksgemeinschaft* 70; the remark quoted there is an anonymous robber's: "Und wie oft habe ich zu meinem Freund Willi gesagt, wenn er immer wieder mit dem vorgehaltenen Revolver in die Schlafzimmer eindrang: 'Laß das Willi [...], wir wollen Einbrüche machen, wie es sich gehört!'"

24. See, for example, the account in Liebermann, "Elite," and Wagner, *Volksgemeinschaft* 68–73.

25. Wagner, *Volksgemeinschaft* 71.

26. Story and citation in Wagner, *Volksgemeinschaft* 71: "Gegen Sie habe ich gar nichts. Mein Geschäft ist, zu stehlen und Ihres, mich dabei zu erwischen."

27. Story and citation in Wagner, *Volksgemeinschaft* 71: "Kollegen, der ja auch doch nur für seine paar Groschen da sitzt und seine Pension nicht verlieren will."

28. "Er hält sein Gewerbe, das Nehmen fremden Gutes, geradezu für einen Beruf so gut wie jeden andern" (Liebermann, "Elite" 166).

29. The desire to be a "gleichberechtigtes Mitglied der menschlichen Gesellschaft," defined as "'behaglich leben zu können,' über Genußmittel wie Bier, Tabak und ein 'Mädchen' [sic!] zu verfügen," was expressed by the same 1929 robber who considered the cops his

"colleagues"; the statement and Elwenspoek's assessment are cited in Wagner, *Volksgemeinschaft* 72.

30. On the history of the *Ringvereine*, see Feraru; they are also described in Schwerk, *Meisterdiebe* 40–2 (the citation 41); Schlag, and Fabich, "Geldschrankeinbrecher" 61.

31. The clearance rate for theft and robbery in Berlin lagged far behind the clearance rate for murder, although the police force in Berlin increased tremendously over the years: from 202 policemen in 1890 to 607 in 1908 to 2205 in 1931. In that year, the cops solved 108 of 114 murders committed in the city, but only 52 percent of robberies, 49.8 percent of thefts, and 24.1 percent of grand larcenies (Wagner, *Volksgemeinschaft* 86).

32. "Durch diesen dauernden Zusammenschluß mehrerer Einbrecher einer Kolonne, die stets zusammen arbeitet, in der jeder auf den andern eingearbeitet ist, wo jeder weiß, daß er sich auf den andern verlassen kann, erhält sich in dem Knackertum noch ein Zug des alten, echten und rechten Verbrechertums. Der Knacker verrät, allein festgenommen, selten seine Komplizen. Selbst eine drohende schwere Zuchthausstrafe kann ihn dazu nicht veranlassen" (Liebermann, "Elite" 169). The collaboration among safe crackers is also described by Fabich in "Geldschrankeinbrecher."

33. As described, for instance, by Schlag.

34. Physical description in Schwerk, *Meisterdiebe* 24 ("Er war in jenem Jahr 1927, der Wende von der kalten zur heißen Geldschrank-Arbeit, im sogenannten besten Mannesalter von 42 Jahren, ein kleiner, beweglicher Mann, kahlköpfig"), and Schlag.

35. Citation in Schwerk, *Meisterdiebe* 24: "Den Einbrechern war übel geworden, worauf unappetitliche Spuren hinwiesen."

36. "Schon bei diesen Einbrüchen trat immer die ganz besondere Fähigkeit der Brüder Saß zutage, Kunstschlösser und sonstige Sicherungsanlagen technisch richtig zu beurteilen und ihren Absichten entsprechend außer Kraft zu setzen. Unbegreiflich ist ferner eine nur als geradezu hellseherisch zu bezeichnende Begabung, architektonische Raumverhältnisse richtig zu erfassen und ihnen entsprechend, ja von ihnen und ihren schwachen Punkten ausgehend, den Angriffsplan taktisch aufzubauen." Fabich, "Straftaten" 85–6.

37. The Sass brothers' 1927 break-ins are described in Schwerk, *Meisterdiebe* 24–30 and Fabich, "Straftaten" 85–6.

38. Schwerk, *Meisterdiebe* 26.

39. "Es muß schon eine schwere Arbeit gewesen sein, alles Material unbemerkt heran und über die Mauer herüberzubringen; noch schwieriger aber war der Angriff auf den Tresor selbst. Die Verbrecher müssen *viele Stunden lang tätig gewesen* sein, um den Tresor aufzuschmelzen" (*Berliner Börsen-Zeitung*, December 5, 1927, 3). Similar coverage of the break-in, in similar tones of bafflement, is offered in *Berliner Tageblatt und Handels-Zeitung*, December 5, 1927, evening edition 6 and *Berliner Volks-Zeitung*, December 5, 1927, evening edition 3.

40. "Von den Verbrechern ist noch keine Spur gefunden. Nach den Feststellungen am Tatort sind es sicher *vier Mann* gewesen. Zwei haben mit dem Schweißapparat geschnitten, einer hat draußen und einer an der Kellertreppe, die zum Tresor führt, aufgepaßt. Dieser scheint zeitweilig einen Sessel oder einen Hocker benutzt zu haben, um es sich bequem zu machen./Ein ähnlicher Anschlag wurde bereits in der Nacht zum 18. März auf eine Bankfiliale in der Turmstraße verübt, auch damals ohne Erfolg. Der neue Versuch beweist wieder, daß die Spezialisten auch mit den besten Werkzeugen und den größten Mitteln nicht imstande sind, der Banktresors beizukommen. Ihre Technik reicht an die Sicherungen der Banken doch noch nicht heran." *Berliner Börsen-Zeitung*, December 5, 1927, 3.

41. "Es ist nun kriminalistisch und kriminaltaktisch außerordentlich interessant und aufschlußreich zu verfolgen, wie die Brüder Saß von Fall zu Fall bei den von ihnen unternommenen Einbruchsversuchen in ihrem verbrecherischen Tun *technische* und *taktische* Fortschritte entwickelten" (Fabich, "Straftaten" 85, emphases original).

42. "Es ist unverständlich, wieso es gerade den Gebrüdern Saß gegeben war, diesen schwachen Punkt der durch ihre bauliche Lage aufs schwerste gefährdeten Tresoranlage zu entdecken" (Fabich, "Straftaten" 87).

43. *Berliner Tageblatt und Handels-Zeitung*, March 26, 1928, evening 6: "Die nächtliche Aktion der Schutzpolizei hatte eine nach Tausenden zählende Menschenmenge herbeigelockt, die mit Neugierde das Suchen der Polizei nach den Knackern verfolgte."

44. The March 1928 break-ins are described at length in Fabich, "Straftaten" 87–8, Schwerk, *Meisterdiebe* 31–40, and "Das Spiel ist aus"; the citation ("und himmelwärts, nämlich über das Dach von Nummer 10 hinüber auf das Dach des angrenzenden Hauses, wurden schemenhaft zwei behende Mannsbilder gesehen: Die Gebrüder Sass, soviel hatte sich schon herumgesprochen, waren entkommen") in Schwerk, *Meisterdiebe* 39–40. The *Berliner Börsen-Zeitung, Berliner Tageblatt und Handels-Zeitung*, and *Berliner Volkszeitung* all offer a blow-by-blow account of the March 24 affair (all in their March 26-editions: *Börsen-Zeitung* evening 6; *Tageblatt* evening 6; *Volkszeitung* 3).

45. "Kriminalkommissar Bünger und die Beamten des Sonderdezernats der Kriminalpolizei, die an den Tatort gerufen wurden, stellten nun fest, daß der Einbruchsversuch von einer Bande routinierter '*Fachleute' an Hand eines wohlvorbereiteten Planes* verübt worden sein mußte" (*Berliner Börsen-Zeitung*, March 26, 1928, evening 6, emphases original); and: "Die Vorbereitungen und die Ausführung lassen erkennen, daß man es mit einer der *raffiniertesten und best ausgerueten* [sic] *Bande* zu tun hat" (January 31, 1929, 1, emphases original).

46. "*Dennoch gelang es der Einbrecherbande, über die Dächer der Häuser zu entkommen*" (*Berliner Tageblatt und Handels-Zeitung*, March 26, 1928, evening 6, emphases original) and: "Nach den bisherigen Feststellungen handelt es sich um eine Bande von vier oder fünf Mann" (March 21, 1928, 7).

47. "Die Ermittlungen der Kriminalpolizei haben dann noch ergeben, daß es sich um Mitglieder einer großen Geldschrankknackerkolonne handelt" (*Berliner Volks-Zeitung*, March 26, 1928, evening 3).

48. The story is recorded in Schwerk, *Meisterdiebe* 45–6, among others.

49. Fabich, "Straftaten" 88–9; Schwerk, *Meisterdiebe* 46–8.

50. "Die Art, wie sie sich an den Tresorraum 'heranpirschten'—so sehr es einem widerstrebt, für ein solches verbrecherisches Handeln einen ehrlichen

waidmännischen Ausdruck zu gebrauchen: es gibt keinen, der dieses aus der Ferne Beschleichen besser verdeutlichen könnte—war wiederum nur bei der eigenartigen Begabung, Raumzusammenhänge zu erkennen, möglich" (Fabich, "Straftaten" 88).

51. The Disconto bank job, the Sass brothers' greatest success, is described in Schwerk, *Meisterdiebe* 50–69 and "Brüder" 196–9; Fabich, "Straftaten" 14–17; "Das Spiel ist aus"; Dannenbaum, Habbe, Schlag, and Kuhrt. Every newspaper in Berlin covered the story extensively and over several weeks; see, for example, *Berliner Börsen-Zeitung* (January 31, 1929, 1, 5 and evening edition 4; February 1, 1929, 6 and evening 4); *Berliner Volks-Zeitung* (January 31, 1929, cover, 2, evening 1, 3; February 1, 1929, 1. Beilage 2; evening 1 and 3; February 19, 1929, 2; February 21, 1929, 2 and evening 3); *Fehrbelliner Zeitung* (February 2, 1929, 2 and February 5, 1).

52. Schwerk, *Meisterdiebe* 52: "Die Umstehenden hören es röcheln, stöhnen, schließlich auch würgen. Es ist überliefert, daß der Herr Direktor angesichts dessen, was sich ihm im Scheine der Taschenlampe in der Silberkammer darbot, sein soeben eingenommenes Frühstück ins Innere der Silberkammer geopfert hat."

53. As reported in, for instance, *Berliner Börsen-Zeitung,* January 31, 1929, evening edition 4, and *Berliner Volks-Zeitung,* February 1, 1929, 1. Beilage 2.

54. *Fehrbelliner Zeitung,* February 2, 1929, 2, and February 5, 1.

55. See, among others, Schwerk, *Meisterdiebe* 77 and Völklein. Max Fabich's son, also named Max, told Schwerk that his father had once seen Franz Sass emerge from the Grunewald, a shovel slung over his shoulder, and that he had remained convinced until his death in 1963 that the brothers had buried the loot somewhere nearby (Schwerk, *Meisterdiebe* 50; Schlag). The missing Sass millions have inspired many treasure hunters to search particularly in that area, some armed with metal detectors. So far, nothing has turned up. For a brief account of the treasure hunts, see Völklein.

56. "Die Beute war so groß, daß die Diebe schließlich Gold- und Silbersachen gar nicht mehr mitgenommen haben, sondern aus ihnen *nur die Steine herausbrachen und das Edelmetall selbst wegwarfen*" (*Fehrbelliner Zeitung,* February 5, 1929, 1, emphases original).

57. *Berliner Volks-Zeitung,* February 1, 1929, 1. Beilage 2 and February 2, 1. Beilage 2; *Berliner Börsen-Zeitung,* February 2, 1929, 4.

58. "Das Haus Kleiststraße 23 wurde während des ganzen Vormittags von einer zahlreichen Menschenmenge umlagert, die die exakte Arbeit der Einbrecher mit gemischten Gefühlen bewunderten" (*Berliner Börsen-Zeitung,* January 31, 1929, evening 4).

59. Fabich, "Straftaten" 15: "Diese schwierige und umständliche 'Pionier'arbeit muß naturgemäß viele Nächte in Anspruch genommen haben, denn es mußten nicht weniger als 2 1/2 cbm Erde bewegt werden, wobei zu berücksichtigen ist, daß von den Tätern keinerlei Spuren hinterlassen werden durften und auch nicht wurden. Nicht umsonst gönnten sich daher die Brüder Sass zuvor einige Monate Ruhe." The *Berliner Börsen-Zeitung* estimates that the Brothers had actually moved 15–20 cubic meters of earth (between 530 and 707 cubic feet); their description of the crime appears in the issue of January 31, 1929, 5.

60. According to Fabich in "Straftaten" 16.

61. Although three brothers were arrested—Max,

Franz and Erich—it seemed fairly clear to both the police and the press that Max was not involved. Subtle signs of this can be found throughout the reporting, as, for example in the *Berliner Volks-Zeitung,* which reports on February 19 on the arrest of all three brothers but only offers a physical description of Franz and Erich (2).

62. Wagner quotes some of the exasperated comments by Kommissar Alfred Zopfe, one of their interrogators, in *Hitlers Kriminalisten* 44–5. On their interrogation, see the also *Berliner Volks-Zeitung,* March 2, 1929, 2; March 7, 1929, 2, and April 7, 1929, 3, and *Vossische Zeitung,* April 7, 1929, Beiblatt 5–6, which quotes some Franz Sass testimony that must have driven the police to the edge of despair (5).

63. Schwerk, *Meisterdiebe* 66.

64. The press conference and Franz Sass's abuse claims are described in "Das Spiel ist aus"; Schlag; Lars Koch 153 and the contemporary press: *Berliner Volks-Zeitung,* April 7, 1929, 3; *Vossische Zeitung,* April 7, 1929, Beiblatt 5–6 and April 8, 1929, 1; *Berliner Börsen-Zeitung,* April 8, 1929, 4 and April 9, 1929, 4. On the lawsuits and appeals, see *Berliner Volks-Zeitung,* April 9, 1929, 1 and evening 3; April 24, 2; and *Berliner Börsen-Zeitung,* April 10, 1929, 5.

65. *Vossische Zeitung,* April 7, 1929, Beiblatt 5–6: "der Tresorraub am Wittenbergplatz mit allen seinen Begleitumständen, dem unterirdischen Gang unter der Straße, an dem tagelang gegraben wurde, der Sprengung des Panzergewölbes war zu einem kriminalistischen europäischen Ereignis geworden, und selbst Amerika war von der Kühnheit der Verbrecher überrascht" (5).

66. Fabich, "Straftaten" 17: "im Hintergrunde erhob sich die bange Frage, ob es *überhaupt noch Tresore* gäbe, die den modernen Einbruchsmethoden geschickter und rücksichtsloser Einbrecher Widerstand leisten könnten. [...] Daß auch auf die sogenannten *Raumschutzanlagen* nur ein bedingter Verlaß war, hatten die Gebrüder Sass ebenfalls bewiesen. Bankkunden, Banken und Versicherungsgesellschaften waren daher in begreiflicher Aufregung. Man sah im ewigen Wettlauf der Technik der Sicherungsindustrie mit der Einbruchstechnik die erstere unerwarteter Weise geschlagen und zwar in einem Maß, daß es zweifelhaft erschien, ob diese Niederlage in absehbarer Zeit wieder ausgeglichen werden könne" (emphases original).

67. *Berliner Börsen-Zeitung,* January 31, 1929, evening edition 4.

68. "Augenblicklich findet bei dem Vizepolizeipräsidenten Dr. Weiß eine Konferenz dieser Kreise statt, die über einen Zusammenschluß zur gemeinsamen Bekämpfung des verbrecherischen Treibens berät. [...] *In jedem Tresorraum sollte ständig mindestens ein Wächter sich aufhalten, besser aber noch zwei.* Auch müßte eine Telephonanlage vorhanden sein, durch die der Wächter jederzeit von einer Polizeistation oder einer Bewachungszentrale Hilfe herbeirufen kann." (*Berliner Börsen-Zeitung,* January 31, 1929, evening 4, emphases original).

69. "Es wurde der Beschluß gefaßt, auch andere Bankkonzerne, deren Tresore ebenfalls der Gefahr ausgesetzt sind, für eine gemeinsame Abwehraktion gegen die Geldschrankknackerbanden zu gewinnen. In den nächsten Tagen wird deshalb noch einmal eine Konferenz einberufen werden, zu der auch andere Banken ihre Vertreter entsenden werden" (*Berliner Börsen-Zeitung,* February 1, 1929, 6).

70. "Soll das das Ende einer Untersuchung bedeuten, an deren Fortschritt die Augen aller Welt gerichtet waren? Soll das bedeuten, daß alle Arbeit in den drei Monaten, in denen Hunderte von Kriminalbeamten nichts anderes taten, als jeder Spur nachzugehen, die seit der Nacht der Plünderung der Stahlkammer am Wittenbergplatz sichtbar wurde, fruchtlos vertan war? Wäre es an dem, so hätte die Berliner Polizei eine Schlappe und einen Prestigeverlust erlitten, von dem sie sich in Jahren nicht wieder erholen könnte" (*Vossische Zeitung*, April 7, 1929, Beiblatt 5–6, the citation 5).

71. Many police stations at the time did not even have police cars or telephones installed at the station, so that crime fighters were routinely forced to "rush" to crime scenes on local transportation. Fabich, for example, was notified of the December 4, 1927 break-in at home and took the streetcar to the scene. See, for instance, Schwerk, *Meisterdiebe* 28, and Schlag.

72. Fabich, "Straftaten" 66: "Es kam sogar soweit, daß sich ängstliche Anwohner während der Nachtzeit nicht mehr an ihre Fenster wagten."

73. As reported in *Berliner Börsen-Zeitung*, January 11, 1930, evening 3 and January 12, 1930, 7; *Berliner Volks-Zeitung*, January 11, 1930, 2.

74. Colorfully and rather pitilessly described in *Berliner Börsen-Zeitung*, January 11, 1930, evening 3.

75. The story is recounted in Fabich, "Straftaten" 64–7; Schwerk, *Meisterdiebe* 71–6; *Berliner Börsen-Zeitung*, January 11, 1930, 5; *Berliner Volks-Zeitung*, January 11, 1930, 2 and evening 2; the story of their alibi and release in *Berliner Volks-Zeitung*, January 16, 1930, 3.

76. Schwerk, *Meisterdiebe* 77.

77. "Gebrüder Sass endlich gefasst. Beim Einbruch ertappt und verhaftet" (*Berliner Volks-Zeitung*, April 30, 1930, 2).

78. For example, *Berliner Volks-Zeitung*, April 30, 1930, 3.

79. *Berliner Volks-Zeitung*, May 1, 1930, 1, and May 3, 1930, evening 3.

80. *Berliner Volks-Zeitung*, June 21, 1930, 3.

81. Trial reporting in *Berliner Volks-Zeitung*, May 24, 1930, evening 3, and May 27, 1930, Beiblatt.

82. Both sides appealed, the prosecutor in an attempt to prosecute the brothers for actual robbery. Both appeals were struck down. On the appeals, see *Berliner Volks-Zeitung*, June 5, 1930, Beiblatt; September 24, 1930, 3, and September 25, 1930, Beiblatt.

83. Fabich, "Straftaten" 67: "Wie immer bestritten die beiden in arroganter Weise, mit dieser Tat etwas zu tun zu haben. [...] Wegen Sachbeschädigung und Hausfriedensbruchs wurden sie zu nur einem Monat Gefängnis verurteilt. Die von ihnen und der Staatsanwaltschaft gegen dieses Urteil eingelegte Berufung ist durch Urteil des Landgerichts I Berlin vom 24. 9. 1930 verworfen worden. Später erreichten sie noch, daß ein Rest dieser Strafe im Gnadenwege in eine geringfügige Geldstrafe umgewandelt wurde."

84. *Vossische Zeitung*, December 31, 1932, 1 and evening 4; the story is retold with great glee in "Das Spiel ist aus."

85. Fleischer's statement about safe cracking as "das eigentliche[n] Betätigungsfeld des gewerbs- und gewohnheitsmäßigen Verbrechertums" and Salaw's that safe crackers were "stets der Gruppe der gewohnheitsmäßigen Täter zuzuordnen" are cited in Wagner, *Volksgemeinschaft* 42.

86. The passage is quoted in Wagner, *Volksgemeinschaft* 200: "Fälle, wie die der Gebrüder Saß in Berlin, die wiederholt ihre Absicht zur Begehung von Einbruchsdiebstählen durch die Tat bekundet haben, jedoch jedesmal mangels der Erfüllung eines strafrechtlichen Tatbestandsmerkmals—zum Spott für die Behörde—frei ausgehen mußten, sollen im nationalsozialistischen Staat unmöglich werden" (see also Wagner, *Hitlers Kriminalisten* 50).

87. The story of the brothers' capture, imprisonment, deportation and execution is told in Fabich, "Straftaten" 124–6 (his account ends with their capture in Denmark) and in Schwerk, *Meisterdiebe* 78–91.

88. The paraphrase in Schwerk, *Meisterdiebe* 90: "Franz ist aufgeschwemmt, fast kahlköpfig und schweigsam. Wenn er etwas sagt, dann: '*Ich bin unschuldig.*' Er sagt '*ich.*' Früher sagte er immer '*wir.*' Erich ist hohläugig, hager, verwirrt. Er wolle, sagt er auf der Bahnfahrt zu Fabich, ein umfassendes Geständnis ablegen..." (emphases original).

89. Schwerk quotes from the warden's instructions for the prison on Lehrter Straße in Moabit, where Franz Sass was imprisoned, in *Meisterdiebe* 91; a letter by Erich cited on the same page documents that the same conditions applied to his prison in Plötzensee. See also Schwerk, "Brüder" 187.

90. Schwerk, *Meisterdiebe* 91 and "Brüder" 189.

91. Quoted in Schwerk, *Meisterdiebe* 91–2: "Ferner wird bei Beendigung der Untersuchungs- bzw. Strafhaft um rechtzeitige Benachrichtigung gebeten, damit wegen der beabsichtigten Unterbringung ... in einem Konzentrationslager das Erforderliche veranlaßt werden kann."

92. Quoted in Schwerk, *Meisterdiebe* 92: "Der Reichsführer SS und Chef der Deutschen Polizei teilt mit: Am 27. März 1940 wurden bei Widerstand die Berufsverbrecher Franz und Erich Sass erschossen."

93. "*... nach der Verurteilung ließ der RFSS* (Reichsführer SS, Heinrich Himmler) *auf Grund eines Sonderbevollmächtigten die beiden aus dem Untersuchungsgefängnis abholen und zur Erschießung nach Sachsenhausen bringen. Sie sollten ohne Frist sofort erschossen werden. Im Wagen wurden sie bis an die Sandgrube des Industriehofes gefahren. Die Beamten, die sie brachten, sagten, daß sie unterwegs sich ziemlich frech und herausfordernd benommen hätten und wissen wollten, wohin sie kämen. An der Exekutionsstelle angekommen, las ich ihnen den Erschießungsbefehl vor. Sofort begannen sie zu lärmen: 'Das gibt es ja gar nicht, wie kommt ihr dazu? Wir wollen erst einen Pfaffen haben,' und anderes mehr. Sie wollten sich absolut nicht an den Pfahl stellen, und ich mußte sie festbinden lassen. Mit aller Gewalt wehrten sie sich dagegen. Ich war heilfroh, als ich den Feuerbefehl geben konnte.*" The passage is quoted in Schwerk, *Meisterdiebe* 93–4; emphases original.

94. "Auf den Todesurkunden, die das Lager geschrieben hat, steht als Zusatz bei beiden auf Befehl des Führers erschossen. Dieser Zusatz ist meines Erachtens ernst zu nehmen. Wir haben auch andere Todesurkunden bei Exekutionen, die anders lauten, da steht auf Befehl des Reichsführers erschossen oder was auch immer. Also man muss schon davon ausgehen, dass Hitler ganz persönlich die Exekution der Brüder Sass angeordnet hat." Morsch's statement is quoted in Schlag.

95. "Bei ihrer Vernehmung gaben die beiden ihre

Personalien an, wollten aber von ihren Vorstrafen nichts wissen und gaben dem Beamten auf jede Frage die Antwort: 'Wir wissen von nichts und verweigern deshalb jede Aussage.' Auf die Frage, was sie denn eigentlich in später Abendstunde in dem Keller zu suchen hätten, erwiderten sie: 'Wir haben Sport getrieben.' Schliesslich mussten die beiden Männer wieder nach dem Polizeigefängnis zurückgebracht werden, da die Vernehmungen durch die alte Taktik der Brüder Sass völlig ergebnislos verlaufen sind. Man will nochmals im Laufe des heutigen Tages den Versuch unternehmen, etwaiges Beweismaterial gegen die Verdächtigen herbeizuschaffen. Gelingt dies den Kriminalisten nicht, *so wird man die Festgenommenen wahrscheinlich im Laufe dieser Woche wieder entlassen*" (*Berliner Volks-Zeitung*, May 1, 1930, 1, emphasis original).

96. "Der Wert der aus den erbrochenen Safes gestohlenen Sachen läßt sich natürlich auch jetzt noch nicht übersehen. Darüber müßten erst alle Kunden gehört werden. Die wenigsten geben vorher die Art und den Wert der von ihnen untergestellten Sachen an./*Ansturm der Safe-Inhaber.*/Während des ganzen heutigen Vormittags war ein großer Ansturm der Kunden dieser Bankfiliale zu verzeichnen, die in großer Besorgnis die Bankbeamten um Auskunft baten, inwieweit sie selbst durch den Einbruch in Mitleidenschaft gezogen würden, und wie es mit der Haftpflicht der Diskonto-Gesellschaft stünde. Allen diesen Kunden konnte jedoch keine Gewißheit gegeben werden, und die Beamten mußten sich darauf beschränken, die Geschädigten zu vertrösten und einigermaßen zu beruhigen. So war der verhältnismäßig kleine Kassenraum den ganzen Vormittag über der Schauplatz von zum Teil ziemlich erregten Auseinandersetzungen zwischen den Safe-Inhabern und den Bankbeamten, die nur die Auskunft geben konnten, daß alle Fragen der Entschädigung, für die nach formal-juristischen Gesichtspunkten für die Bankleitung eigentlich keine Verpflichtung bestehe, von der Direktion geregelt und nach eingehender Prüfung geklärt werden würden. Besonders schwierig gestalteten sich die Auseinandersetzungen dadurch, daß keinem der Kunden darüber Gewißheit wurde, inwieweit er geschädigt ist, da die Einbrecher bekanntlich alle Tresorfächer geöffnet, den Inhalt zusammengeworfen und nur diejenigen Wertgegenstände mitgenommen haben, deren Veräußerung nicht allzu große Schwierigkeiten biete. Hinzu kommt noch, *daß die Bank selbst nicht weiß, was in den einzelnen Tresorfächern untergebracht war, da die Kunden über die Fächer verfügen können und kein Verzeichnis über den Inhalt der Bank zugänglich zu machen brauchen.*/Die Diskonto-Gesellschaft muß sich also auf die Versicherungen des Safeinhabers hinsichtlich des Inhalts der Fächer verlassen und diese müssen selbst aus den noch übrig gebliebenen Wertsachen ihr Eigentum reklamieren. Aus diesem Grunde war es bisher auch nicht möglich, die Höhe des Gesamtschadens genau zu ermitteln." *Berliner Börsen-Zeitung*, January 31, 1929, evening 4, emphases original.

97. "Franz und Erich Saß sind zwei Brüder, die in ihrem Leben mit ganz kurzer Unterbrechung nie ehrlich gearbeitet haben. Sie lebten auf großem Fuße, machten große Reisen, auch nach Frankreich und England, verstanden sich den polizeilichen Zugriffen zu entziehen" (*Hamburger Neueste Zeitung*, January 19, 1940, 2).

98. "Hier sind ihnen mindestens 150 000 RM in Geldsorten und Devisen in die Hände gefallen" (*Hamburger Neueste Zeitung*, January 19, 1940, 2).

99. "Der eine der Brüder, Erich Saß, behauptete, dieses Goldstück etwa zwei Tage nach dem Einbruch ganz dicht in der Nähe des Tatortes, nämlich an der Straßenbahnhaltestelle gefunden zu haben! Mit solchen 'Mätzchen' konnten Verbrecher in der Systemzeit 'ihr Alibi nachweisen'!" (*Hamburger Neueste Zeitung*, January 19, 1940, 2).

100. "Er hat immer gesagt, das sind keine Verbrecher, das sind Ganoven. Gute Ganoven." Ruth Fabich's statement is cited in Schlag.

101. For example in Fabich, "Vorleben" 38.

102. Fabich, "Vorleben" 37, emphases original: "Daß *trotz* des in mühsamer Kleinarbeit von der Kriminalpolizei zusammengetragenen Ermittlungsergebnisses 1929 Anklage gegen die Gebrüder Sass *nicht* erhoben wurde, ist für die damaligen Verhältnisse kennzeichnend."

103. Fabich, "Straftaten" 67: "Die vorstehend berichteten Tatsachen [...] legen aber weiter auch Zeugnis ab von der geradezu sträflichen Uneinsichtigkeit, die man in den Jahren vor der nationalen Erhebung dem Gedanken einer Sonderbehandlung gefährlicher Gewohnheitsverbrecher gegenüber zur Schau trug, ein Gedanke, der die unter den damals geltenden Bestimmungen trotz aller Anstrengungen und aller Tüchtigkeit zu einem aussichtslosen Kampfe verurteilte Kriminalpolizei aus ihrer gesetzlich sanktionierten Machtlosigkeit befreien wollte und der durch das Gesetz vom 24. November 1933 endlich Wirklichkeit geworden ist."

104. Fabich, "Geldschrankeinbrecher" 37; 63: "Als nach der nationalsozialistischen Machtergreifung der Kampf gegen das Berufsverbrechertum endlich in wirksamer Form aufgenommen wurde und erstmalig auch Vorbeugungsmaßnahmen gegen Berufsverbrecher auf Grund gesetzlicher Bestimmungen ermöglicht wurden, trat in der Berliner Unterwelt ein grundlegender Umschwung ein. [...] Die Zunft der Berliner Geldschrankeinbrecher befindet sich hinter Schloß und Riegel [...], außerdem lassen die umfangreichen Vorbeugungsmaßnahmen Vorkommnisse und Zustände, wie sie hier geschildert wurden, nicht mehr zu. Sie gehören erfreulicherweise der Vergangenheit an."

105. "'Es ist alles viel besser geworden, es gibt keine Arbeitslosen mehr', erzählte er den Brüdern Erich und Franz und versprach, ihnen nach Strafverbüßung zu einer Anstellung zu verhelfen..." (quoted in Schwerk, "Brüder" 204).

106. See Schwerk's "Editorische Notiz" in *Meisterdiebe* 4.

107. "Eine Besserung dieser Angeklagten ist auch durch den schärfsten Strafvollzug nicht zu erwarten. Bei ihnen handelt es sich um in höchstem Maße asoziale Elemente, die noch niemals nachhaltig ehrlicher Arbeit nachgegangen sind und nach der Überzeugung des Gerichts auch niemals den Weg in die Volksgemeinschaft finden werden" (cited in Schwerk, "Brüder" 189, and Schlag).

108. "Noch einmal flackerte der Berliner Witz, bezogen auf unsere Meisterdiebe, auf. Wer hat denn den Reichstag angezündet? Natürlich die Brüder SA-SS" (Schwerk, *Meisterdiebe* 78).

109. Joke quoted in Lars Koch 162: "'Wie buchstabiert man Deutschlands bekannteste Verbrecher?'—Antwort: 'S-A-S-S.'"

110. This is a suspicion indirectly voiced by Schwerk: in the exceptionally violent NS-regime "waren die Gebrüder Sass mit ihren Gaunerstücken, mit ihren Fingerübungen an den Tresoren aufs Ganze gesehen Ausnahmen wie Juwelen unter viel Thalmi" (*Meisterdiebe* 45).

111. "*Moralisten, deshalb sind sie so selten. Das Merkmal einer echten Gaunerei ist, daß der Gesellschaft auf eine unmoralische Weise eine moralische Lehre erteilt wird... So genießen die echten Gauner ... seit je den Beifall aller Gutgesinnten... Wie glücklich muß man ein Volk schätzen, von Zeit zu Zeit noch einen echten Gauner hervorzubringen...*" Peter Bamm cited in Schwerk, *Meisterdiebe* 8, italicization original.

112. "Wie unglücklich sind wir! Wie alleingelassen sind wir Gutgesinnten von 'echten' Gaunern seit langem. Es gibt sie nicht mehr. Sie sind, weiß der Teufel warum, ausgestorben wie die Maikäfer; Plagegeister ganz gewiß, aber eben auch Pläsier. Und wie eine Gesellschaft auf solche Gauner reagiert, mit ihnen umgeht, spiegelt eben ihre Gesinnung./Die letzten wirklich echten Gauner kamen in den sogenannten goldenen zwanziger Jahren in Berlin als Gebrüder Sass daher. Seitdem wurde uns Vergleichbares nicht mehr geboten" (Schwerk, *Meisterdiebe* 8).

113. Paul Gurk, *Tresoreinbruch* (1935, novel); films: *Banktresor 713* (feature film, dir. Werner Klingler, 1957); *Auf Befehl erschossen: Die Brüder Sass, einst Berlins größte Ganoven* (TV-film, dir. Rainer Wolffhardt, 1972); *Sass* (feature film, dir. Carlo Rola, 2001). On literary versions of the story, see Göpfert; Wolffhardt's film has been analyzed by Lars Koch. See also my remarks in *Plots* on Gurk's novel and in *Resolutions?* on the films.

114. See, for example, Kuhrt's blog on them in *Moabit online*.

A Tale of Two Editors

1. "Das Attentat auf Bettauer hat eine sehr christlich erzogene und daher so denkende und handelnde 'Gnädige' stark in Aufregung gebracht und ihr sogar das schmerzliche Bedauern entrissen, daß es schade sei, weil der Volksverderber Bettauer nicht zu Tode getroffen worden sei. Sie faßte daher den christlichen Entschluß, *zu Gott zu beten,* daß Bettauer wenigstens an den Folgen der Verletzungen erliege. Wie aus den gestrigen Zeitungsnotizen entnommen werden kann, hat Gott ihr Gebet erhört" (*Tagblatt,* March 28, 1925, 3, emphasis original).

2. "Da kam ein grosser, stämmiger Mann in die Redaktion und ließ sich nicht abweisen, bis er sich Gehör verschafft hatte: Er habe gehört, dass Bettauer nur durch eine Bluttransfusion gerettet werden könne. Er sei gekommen, um dem Verletzten sein Blut anzubieten. Und als man ihn fragte, was ihn zu diesem Opfer bewogen habe, sagte er: 'Ihn und seine Familie habe Bettauer durch seinen klugen Rat und seine menschliche Hilfe gerettet.'" (Rudolf Olden, "Abschied von Hugo Bettauer," 5)

3. Botz (*Gewalt* 131) and others got Bettauer's birth year wrong, a common error that Murray Hall attributed to the fact that during the trial of 1924, Bettauer himself forgot, or chose to forget, his actual birth year, claiming that he was born in 1878 (*Der Fall Bettauer* 9). On Bettauer's biography, see Murray Hall, *Der Fall Bettauer* 9–19; Hacker 13–17; Werner Koch 255–6 and McEwen 145–6.

4. Silverman 72.

5. On Bettauer's novels, see particularly Murray Hall, *Der Fall Bettauer* 12–39; Höyng; Hacker 18–23; McEwen 145–6, and Noveck, "1925: Hugo Bettauer's assassination" 440; Murray Hall also offers an annotated list of the films based on Bettauer novels and their sometimes loose connection to the novels (*Der Fall Bettauer* 187–92). For an interpretation of Bettauer's crime novel *Killer of Women* (*Frauenmörder*), see the *Plots* chapter in this volume.

6. This is the assessment particularly of scholars who have written about his literature, for example Höyng: "Bettauer, unknown in literary circles today, was one of the key figures in Austria's capital after the downfall of the empire" (40).

7. Noveck, "1925: Hugo Bettauer's assassination" 441. Karl Lueger (1844–1910): prominent antisemite and mayor of Vienna; Michael Mayr (1864–1922): member of the Christian Social Party and Chancellor of Austria from 1920–1921; Ignaz Seipel (1876–1922): prelate and member of the Christian Social Party, who served as Federal Chancellor twice during the 1920s.

8. *The City without Jews* is, to this day, Bettauer's most written-about book; see, among others, Werner Koch 255–62; McEwen 146 and 170; Noveck, "1925: Hugo Bettauer's assassination" 440–5; Botz, *Gewalt* 131; Silverman 67–93, and Höyng.

9. See particularly Hartner, "Erotik und Rasse" and Rosenberg, *Der Fall Bettauer* (Rosenberg, the Nazis' chief ideologue, dedicated an entire issue of his antisemitic journal *Weltkampf* to Bettauer).

10. Novek, "1925: Hugo Bettauer's assassination" 441.

11. All scholars who have analyzed the magazine agree on this. See, for instance, McEwen: "Bettauer's erotica was at times titillating but largely tame" (147); Hacker: "Hugo Bettauer's remarks are hardly erotic and by no means pornographic" ("Hugo Bettauers Ausführungen sind wenig erotisch, keinesfalls pornographisch," 155) or Murray Hall: "It is quite possible to differ as to whether some passages in *He and She* are in bad taste, but you'd have to have an oversensitive nose to discover 'obscenity in word and image,' 'coarse violations of shame and decency' or anything 'causing public nuisance'" ("Man kann sehr wohl geteilter Meinung sein, ob manche Passagen in *Er und Sie* von schlechtem Geschmack zeugen, muß aber eine überempfindliche Spürnase haben, um 'Unzucht in Wort und Bild,' 'gröbliche Verletzung der Schamhaftigkeit und Sitte,' oder 'Erregung öffentlichen Ärgernisses' [...] zu entdecken," *Der Fall Bettauer* 68). See also Werner Koch, who considers *He and She* considerably less explosive than revelations in Bettauer's novels (263).

12. On *Er und Sie,* see Hwang; Murray Hall, *Der Fall Bettauer* 40–69; McEwen 146–70; Hacker 123–9 and 155; and Silverman 52–3 and 72.

13. "Der Erfolg übertraf alle Erwartungen. Das neue Blatt wies eine Riesenauflage auf und die Nummern werden den Verkäufern aus den Händen gerissen" (*Ybbstal-Zeitung,* August 16, 1924, 6).

14. Testimony about Bettauer's generosity in *Prager Tagblatt,* October 6, 1925, 6; *Der Tag* of the same day, 7, and elsewhere; the story of the secretary holding on to Bettauer's wallet is related in press reports cited by Murray Hall, *Der Fall Bettauer* 80–1.

15. Grün's testimony is reported in *Der Tag,* October 6, 1925, 7.

16. A day-by-day account of the process that ensued is offered by Murray Hall, *Der Fall Bettauer* 43–65; see also McEwen 148–50; Hacker 96–8.

17. § 12 of the *Pressegesetz* states that "Auf Antrag einer Unterrichtsbehörde oder eines Jugendamtes kann die Behörde (§ 7) für ihren Amtsbereich bestimmte Druckwerke oder Druckwerke bestimmter Art, die durch Ausnützung der jugendlichen Triebe das sittliche Wohl der Jugend gefährden, von jeder Verbreitung an Personen unter achtzehn Jahren ausschließen und ihren Vertrieb durch Straßenverkauf oder Zeitungsverschleißer überhaupt untersagen" (quoted by Murray Hall, *Der Fall Bettauer* 42).

18. Press reporting on the ban and its revocation: *Reichspost*, March 11, 1924, 6; *Wiener Zeitung, Amtsblatt*, March 13, 1924, 1; *Christlich-Soziale Arbeiterzeitung*, March 15, 1924, 3.

19. Excerpts from Ignaz Seipel's speech, as reported by the *Reichspost*, are reprinted in Murray Hall, *Der Fall Bettauer* 48.

20. Murray Hall, *Der Fall Bettauer* 48.

21. Seitz's speech, also widely commented on in the press, is reprinted in excerpts in Murray Hall, *Der Fall Bettauer* 165–6.

22. The indictment is quoted by Murray Hall, *Der Fall Bettauer* 48–9; and quoted directly or commented on extensively in the contemporary press. On the Seipel-Seitz exchange, see also McEwen 150–2, Hacker 98–100.

23. Numbers in Murray Hall, *Der Fall Bettauer* 52 and 59–60; Olden's statement is cited in the same source on 55.

24. Murray Hall, *Der Fall Bettauer* 52.

25. Most of these imitation-magazines folded very quickly (see Murray Hall, *Der Fall Bettauer* 139).

26. This is the conclusion arrived at by Murray Hall (*Der Fall Bettauer* 63).

27. The front-page drawing appeared in the "Bettauer number" of the magazine *Zitterrochen;* the defamation of Bettauer as a pimp in the Zionist newspaper *Wiener Stimmen* (Hall 54–5). With some exceptions ("two-legged swine"/ "zweifüßigen Schweine" and "perverse Jew"/"ein perverser Jude" are taken from *Christlich-Soziale Arbeiterzeitung*, March 15, 1924, 3; the "infamous pornographer"/"den berüchtigten Pornographen Hugo *Bettauer*" appears in *Reichspost*, July 5, 1924, 8), the insults were condensed by Murray Hall from various newspapers with sources: "'Fachzeitschrift für das Liebesgewerbe' (*WMZ*); 'Schandblatt' (*Wiener Stimmen*), 'Schweinereien,' 'Schlammwühler,' 'ein größerer Verbrecher als ein Raubmörder,' 'jüdisches Schwein,' 'Schweinehund,' 'Schandkerl,' 'Lügen- und Sudelblätter,' 'perverses Kloakentier,' 'räudige Talmudseele,' 'geiles Untier,' 'Bettauersche Fäkalien' (alle *DAP*), 'Sudelflut,' 'literarische Kloaken,' 'Schmierantenblatt,' 'Sudelliteratur,' 'Ungeziefer,' 'Schandliteratur,' 'gewerbsmäßiger Pornograph' (alle *RP*)," Murray Hall, *Der Fall Bettauer* 65.

28. "Das Geheimnis dieses Erfolges ist in dem Umstande gelegen, daß Herr Bettauer von der Theorie zur Praxis übergegangen ist. Er bringt in jeder Nummer seiner Zeitung Hunderte von Kupplerannoncen. Da bieten sich junge Mädchen reichen alten Herren zum Gebrauch an und rüstige Jünglinge suchen reife, wohlhabende Damen. Jede Art von natürlicher und widernatürlicher geschlechtlicher Befriedigung in allen Preislagen kann mit Hilfe Herrn Bettauers erlangt werden. [...] Der Mann ist unter die erwerbs-mäßigen Kuppler gegangen. Er betreibt das Handwerk mit einer Virtuosität, welche alles Dagewesene übersteigt. Die gewiegtesten Angehörigen der Zunft der Kuppler und Mädchenhändler müssen ihm die Palme reichen. Er hat das Kupplergewerbe industrialisiert" (*Ybbstal-Zeitung*, August 16, 1924, 6).

29. Press reporting on the affair: *Arbeiter-Zeitung*, March 22, 1924, 8; *Reichspost*, March 22, 1924, 8–9 and April 1, 8, among many others; *Arbeiterzeitung* quotes Orel's initial outburst as "Wir lassen uns nicht durch den Bürgermeister den Juden Bettauer aufdrängen, der unsere Kinder versauen will mit jüdischem Gift und jüdischer Schweinerei!" (March 22, 1924, 8). Orel's second statement, "Wenn der Bürgermeister gewußt hätte, was er zu tun hat, dann hätte er diesem Juden einen Fußtritt versetzen und ihn zur Türe hinauswerfen müssen," is quoted in the Nazi paper *Der Volkssturm* (March 30, 1924) but missing in mainstream coverage. Murray Hall has analyzed the meeting based on the stenographic minutes and press reports (*Der Fall Bettauer* 56–59) and reprinted a *Volkssturm* article describing the meeting (in the same source, 166–8). On Orel's speech, see also McEwen 152–4.

30. See Murray Hall's comment on this session: "*Er und Sie* wird Vorwand für eine Auseinandersetzung, bei der die Vertreter verschiedener politischer und ideologischer Richtungen eine seltsame Einmütigkeit an den Tag legen: im Kampf gegen den Juden Hugo Bettauer" (*Der Fall Bettauer* 51). Numerous commentators on the case have pointed out that this rhetoric drew on the common identification of rape, white slavery and other sexual crimes as "typically" Jewish; see, among others, Botz, *Gewalt* 131; Höyng 40; Silverman 56, Noveck, "1925: Hugo Bettauer's assassination" 444, and others.

31. Press reporting on the trial in: *Die Rote Fahne*, September 19, 1924, 8 and September 20, 1924, 3; *Prager Tagblatt*, September 20, 1924, 5; *Reichspost*, September 19, 1924, 8, September 20, 1924, 7 and September 26, 1924, 5; *Tagblatt*, September 20, 1924, 6 and September 21, 1924, 5; *Tages-Post*, September 19, 1924, 9; *Der Tag*, September 19, 1924, 7–8; *Ybbstal-Zeitung*, September 20, 1924, 1–2; *Arbeiterwille*, September 21, 1924, 7; *Christlich-soziale Arbeiterzeitung*, September 27, 1924, 3, and many others.

32. Murray Hall, *Der Fall Bettauer* 70.

33. The court records "Strafsache gegen Hugo Bettauer und Rudolf Olden" are at the Landesgericht Wien. The indictment is quoted verbatim in *Der Tag*, September 19, 1924, 7–8.

34. The exchange is quoted in *Der Tag*, September 19, 1924, 8: "*Dr. Rosenfeld* protestiert energisch dagegen, sagt, daß das Gericht doch schließlich kein *Mädchenpensionat* sei und daß Bettauer auch nicht ein Wort gebraucht habe, noch gebrauchen werde, das irgendwie lasziv oder obszön sei. Allerdings habe Bettauer von *'Spitzenhöschen'* gesprochen. [...] Die Angeklagten und ihre Verteidiger hätten das Recht, *ernst über ernste Dinge* zu sprechen./Die von der Staatsanwaltschaft so gefürchteten Artikel, die jetzt im Saal nicht verlesen werden dürfen, weil sie die Sittlichkeit gefährden könnten, seien zum Teil *fünf Wochen und drei Tage unbeanständet* geblieben, dann erst habe der Staatsanwalt, *und zwar aus einem Grunde, den er hier noch nicht erörtern wolle*, die Konfiskation ausgesprochen. [...] Dr. Braß [...] sagt, er verstehe überhaupt nicht, daß der Herr Staatsanwalt

bei der Erwähnung der 'Sexuellen Not' *gleich so nervös* geworden sei./Diese Bemerkung rief im Auditorium *Heiterkeit* hervor."

35. *Vorarlberger Wacht,* September 19, 1924, 6: "Die Verhandlung, die zum größten Teil mit Ausschluß der Oeffentlichkeit geführt wurde, so daß über sie nicht berichtet werden kann, endete damit, daß beide Angeklagte freigesprochen wurden."

36. "Wir hatten das Unglück, daß unser Blatt in die *politische Atmosphäre* geraten ist und daß gegen uns ein wahres *Kesseltreiben* entfesselt wurde." *Der Tag,* September 19, 1924, 8; emphases original.

37. On the "procurement"-indictment and the personal ads-section specifically, see Murray Hall, *Der Fall Bettauer* 69, and the court testimony by employees of the magazine, several of whom testified that *He and She* had refused to run ads that they perceived as "improper" ("anstößig") and got in trouble with advertisers who ran exactly the same ad without problems in other "respectable" Viennese newspapers (*Der Tag,* September 19, 1924, 8).

38. The vote count revealed that most indictments were struck down with 12, 11, or 10 majority votes; all counts were struck down with a minimum distribution of 9:3 in favor of acquittal ("Strafsache gegen Hugo Bettauer und Rudolf Olden"; see also Murray Hall, *Der Fall Bettauer* 73).

39. "Dieses war derart, daß selbst die Anhänger Bettauers überrascht waren, wie aus ihren Mienen deutlich zu lesen war, denn *die Geschworenen verneinten alle vorgelegten Fragen mit großer Majorität;* das Verhältnis der Stimmen war fast durchwegs 9 zu 3 oder 8 zu 4, nur bei zwei Fragen hielten sich die abgegebenen Stimmen die Wage./Sichtlich überrascht von dem Ergebnis war auch der *Staatsanwalt,* der sich daraufhin erhob und erklärte, *gegen eine derartige Flut nicht ankämpfen zu können.*" *Reichspost,* September 20, 1924, 7; emphases original.

40. "So weit sind wir jetzt./Nun sind dem Schmutz und Schund Tür und Tor geöffnet" (*Ybbstal-Zeitung,* September 20, 1924, 2).

41. Calls for "self-help" ("Selbsthilfe") in, among others: *Ybbstal-Zeitung,* September 20, 1924, 2; *Reichspost* (September 20, 1924 and March 12, 1925), and others; see Murray Hall, *Der Fall Bettauer* 73–5.

42. "... fürwahr die höchste Zeit, daß alle noch anständigen Menschen—da die Staatsgewalt hier völlig versagt—zu rücksichtsloser Selbsthilfe greifen. [...] Aug' um Aug', Zahn um Zahn!" Kaspar Hellering, "Auf zur Selbsthilfe gegen Bettauer," *Deutsche Arbeiter-Presse,* October 18, 1924, 6; on his subsequent calls for Bettauer's murder, see citations and discussion in Murray Hall, *Der Fall Bettauer* 78–9. Hellering's article is quoted and discussed in *Arbeiter-Zeitung,* March 11, 1925, 6, and *Arbeiterwille,* March 12, 1925, 2.

43. "*Bettauer, sus silvaticus,* skrofuloses Wildschwein oder gemeine Sau, wühlt in Sumpf und Jauche, nährt sich von Weiberfleisch und anderen moralischen Abfallsprodukten, verbreitet pestilenten Gestank—daher auszurotten" (Kaspar Hellering in "Das Eindrucksvolle!" *Faschingsblatt des Grobian,* Salzburg, February 1925, 2, emphasis original). On Hellering's hate-campaign against Bettauer, see Botz, *Gewalt* 132–3.

44. On Bettauer's hounding after the acquittal, see Murray Hall, *Der Fall Bettauer* 76–9; Botz 131–2.

45. *Prager Tagblatt,* November 9, 1924, 8: "Hugo Bettauer, eine der populärsten und produktivsten Persönlichkeiten Wiens."

46. On the similarities between *He and She* and the new journal, see McEwen 163–6.

47. "Dieser bedeutende Wirtshauspolitiker, derselbe, der Lynchjustiz gegen mich beantragt hat, sagte es neulich in vorgerückter Stunde und schon ein wenig benebelt vom Genusse des Gerstensaftes, nachdem er einige Male kräftig gerülpst und 'Heul' gerufen hatte, rund heraus:/*Bettauers Wochenschrift* muß verschwinden! Dieses Saublatt ist ja gefährlicher als die *Arbeiter-Zeitung* und der *Abend* zusammengenommen!" (Bettauer, "Ein neuer Anschlag" 1).

48. Murray Hall, *Der Fall Bettauer* 78, 81; the quotation "er habe in letzter Zeit wiederholt Drohbriefe erhalten und fühle sich seines Lebens nicht mehr sicher" 81.

49. The description of the murder in Murray Hall, *Der Fall Bettauer* 81–85 and numerous contemporary papers, most extensively in *Arbeiter-Zeitung,* March 11, 1925, 1, 6 and 7; *Arbeiterwille,* March 11, 1925, 1; *Illustriertes Wiener Extrablatt,* March 11, 1925, 1; *Prager Tagblatt,* March 11, 1925, 4; *Reichspost,* March 11, 1925, 7; *Vorarlberger Landeszeitung,* March 11, 1925, 3; *Wiener Zeitung,* March 11, 1925, 4, 6.

50. Reports on the hallway conversation in: *Arbeiterzeitung,* October 6, 1925, 8; *Arbeiterwille,* October 6, 1925, 4; *Der Tag,* October 6, 1925, 7; reports on Rothstock and other Nazis lounging around in front of Bettauer's office on the day of the murder in: *Arbeiterwille,* March 12, 1925, 7 and March 14, 1925, 7; *Arbeiterzeitung,* March 14, 1925, 7; *Die Rote Fahne,* March 24, 1925, 1; March 27, 1925, 2; March 29, 1925, 2; April 1, 2. I have been unable to locate any mention of these witnesses in any centrist or right-wing newspaper.

51. See Murray Hall's analysis based on court records and reporting in *Der Fall Bettauer* 85–98.

52. "Dank einer inkompetenten Untersuchungsbehörde konnte *Rothstock* einfach irgendetwas erzählen, da seine Aussagen kritiklos zu Papier gebracht wurden" (Murray Hall, *Der Fall Bettauer* 91–2, emphasis original). On the quality of the pre-trial investigation, see also Pauley 105.

53. Cited and discussed in Murray Hall, *Der Fall Bettauer* 91–2.

54. "Ich bin vollständig überzeugt und auch durch Personen, welche Sie kennen, informiert, daß Sie lediglich aus idealen Gründen das Attentat gegen Bettauer begangen haben und glaube, daß Sie auch unter dem Eindruck bestimmter, Sie sehr nahe treffenden Erscheinungen Ihres Bekanntenkreises die Handlungsweise vollführten." The letter is reprinted in full in Murray Hall's document section, *Der Fall Bettauer* 178, and quoted verbatim in Botz, *Gewalt* 406–7.

55. "Ich fühle mich auch des versuchten Mordes nicht schuldig, obwohl ich weiß, daß das Gesetz die Tat als solche mit Strafe belegt, denn ich bin der Meinung, daß wenn man einen solchen Schädling der Gesellschaft und der Jugend auch auf eine im Strafgesetz verbotene Weise beseitigt, dies nicht als Mord bezeichnet werden kann." Rothstock's statement is quoted in Murray Hall, *Der Fall Bettauer* 92, and in much press reporting.

56. For this and other statements on Rothstock's supposed familiarity with Bettauer's writings, see the minutes of the trial from October 5, 1925, p. 10 ("Strafsache gegen Otto Rothstock").

57. "...für wirkliche sachliche und zweckdienliche Zuschriften mit wirklichen Beweisen über spezielle Fälle von entsittlichenden Folgen der Bettauer-Literatur mit Namen und Adressen dankbar" (quoted by Murray Hall, *Der Fall Bettauer* 96).

58. Statement in the court records ("daß sie durch Lesen der *Bettauer'schen Wochenschrift* ins Verderben geführt wurden") quoted and discussed in Murray Hall, *Der Fall Bettauer* 96.

59. Statement by investigating psychiatrist Dr. Julius Wagner-Jauregg: "Plan, jetzt durch Vortäuschung einer, wie er sagt, leichten Geisteskrankheit, bald wieder in Freiheit zu kommen." On the psychiatric evaluation, see Murray Hall, *Der Fall Bettauer* 112–16, the quotation 114.

60. Trial reporting, often with extensive verbatim quotes from judge, defendant and attorneys, in: October 5, 1925: *Arbeiterzeitung*, Mittagsblatt, 1; *Reichspost* 2, 4; *Wiener Neueste Nachrichten* 2; October 6, 1925: *Arbeiterzeitung* 1–2 and 7–8; *Arbeiterwille*, Beilage and 3–4; *Prager Tagblatt* 5; *Reichspost* 6–7; *Der Tag* 5–8; *Tages-Post* 11; *Vorarlberger Landeszeitung* 2; *Vorarlberger Tagblatt* 3; *Vorarlberger Volksblatt* 1; October 7, 1925: *Arbeiterwille* 2; *Prager Tagblatt* 3; *Tagblatt* 6; *Tages-Post* 1–2; October 10, 1925: *Triestingtaler Wochenblatt* 1; *Vorarlberger Wacht* 1; *Ybbstal-Zeitung* 2; October 11, 1925: *Volksblatt für Stadt und Land* 5–6; October 23, 1925: *Tagblatt* 1. On the background and biases of the principals at the trial, see Pauley 105 and Botz, *Gewalt* 136.

61. The exchange between Rothstock and Judge Ramsauer is quoted, with small variations, in nearly every press account of the trial. I am quoting it here from *Der Tag*, October 6, 1925, 5 (all emphases original): "*Vors.:* Bekennen Sie sich schuldig?/*Angekl.:* Hoher Gerichtshof, vor zweitausend Jahren.../*Vors.:* Sagen Sie mir zunächst: Ja oder Nein./*Angekl.:* Ich habe den Schriftsteller Hugo Bettauer *aus dem Diesseits in das Jenseits gedrängt*, getötet, wie man das nennt. Jedoch ich trage kein Verschulden./*Vors.:* Also nicht schuldig./*Angekl.:* Hoher Gerichtshof, vor zweitausend Jahren—einigen Minuten göttlicher Zeit—kam der Sohn Gottes auf diese Welt, um den Kampf zu führen gegen diese jüdischen Schriftsteller und Gelehrten, weil sie die Söhne der Lüge und des Satans sind. Ich kam auf diese Welt, um diesen Kampf weiterzuführen./*Was ich getan habe, ist kein Meuchelmord. Es ist ein Alarmschuß, um aufzuwecken alle Völker und vor allem die deutsche Nation, fortzuführen den Kampf brutal und rücksichtslos, um sich zu schützen, bevor es zu spät ist.* Hugo Bettauer verhöhnte alles, was deutsch ist. Ich habe keine Schuld!"

62. This particular statement is cited in many newspapers, among others in *Der Tag*, October 6, 1925, 5–6. Some newspapers were shameless enough to echo Rothstock's vile rhetoric, for example the *Tages-Post* on October 7, 1925, in an article entitled "Not the murderer, but the murdered man is guilty!" ("Nicht der Mörder, der Ermordete ist schuldig!"), in which they argued that whereas Rothstock had murdered only one body, Bettauer had murdered thousands of souls, and that the gun had been put into his hands by the moral outrage of hundreds of thousands (1–2, the citation 2).

63. The religious vision in *Der Tag*, October 6, 1925, 5–6.

64. "*Verteidiger.* War es eine innere Stimme, daß Sie berufen sind, oder haben Sie ein *Zeichen* bekom-

men? Wie haben Sie diese Stimme vernommen?— *Angekl.:* Ich habe eine *Vision* gehabt" (*Arbeiterzeitung*, October 6, 1925, 7, emphases original).

65. Murray Hall, *Der Fall Bettauer* 118.

66. Both in *Der Tag*, October 6, 1925, 6.

67. *Der Tag*, October 6, 1925, 6–7.

68. "*Verteidiger Dr. Riehl* erklärt, die Tat Rothstocks sei mit einer derartigen *Ritterlichkeit* vollführt worden, daß sie, wenn man die proletarische Herkunft dieses Burschen in Betracht zieht, *kaum übertroffen* werden könne. Gegenüber dem Kübel von Schmutz, mit dem Rothstock nach seiner Tat überschüttet wurde, könne man nur das Wort anwenden, das in einem Brief über Rothstock gebraucht wurde: *Dieses Volk hat einen Rothstock gar nicht verdient.*/Dr. Riehls Ausführungen sind eine Flut von Beschimpfungen des Toten. Er spricht mit Karl Kraus vom 'Prinzipiellen Fallotentum,' mit Mommsen vom 'Ferment der Dekomposition,' um dann zu eigenen Kraftausdrücken überzugehen. Er plädiert für den *Freispruch* des Angeklagten, der fast unter unwiderstehlichem Zwang handelte und für seine Tat nicht verantwortlich sei./Dr. Riehl schließt mit dem Appell an die Geschworenen, nur *nach ihrem Gewissen* zu *urteilen* und sich nicht von der Furcht vor den Zeitungen, die in *rassischer Solidarität* zusammenstehen, beeinflussen zu lassen./*Nach seinen Worten ertönt aus einem Teil des Saales, wo die Anhänger Rothstocks und Riehls sitzen, lauter Applaus.* [...] Der Staatsanwalt spricht noch ein paar Sätze. Er stellt fest, daß der Verteidiger keine Verteidigungsrede, sondern eine Anklagerede gegen Bettauer gehalten hat." *Der Tag*, October 6, 1925, 7 (all emphases original).

69. "Der Verteidiger betonte, auch er stehe auf dem Boden der christlichen Weltanschauung und zitierte sodann eine Stelle aus dem *Evangelium Matthäi:* 'Wer aber solches Kind ärgert, und wäre dieses der Geringsten eines, dem wäre es besser, man hienge ihm einen Mühlstein um den Hals und versenkte ihn ins Meer, wo es am tiefsten ist.' In einem Punkte kennt unser Heiland kein Erbarmen gegen den, *der Aergernis gibt unseren Kindern.* Und dieses Aergernis hat Bettauer gegeben." [...] Der Verteidiger Rothstocks trat in flammenden Worten *für die Freisprechung* des Angeklagten ein: Er verdient es, denn er habe aus idealen Beweggründen gehandelt und gleichsam, dem Empfinden unseres Volkes Ausdruck gegeben." Quoted in *Volksblatt für Stadt und Land*, October 11, 1925, 5 (all emphases original).

70. "Wir stehen jetzt *vor einer Verhandlung*, wo es sehr wichtig ist, daß nicht wieder ein *Fehlurteil* gefällt wird; denn durch so ein Fehlurteil geschieht es dann, daß sich jemand, der glaubt, daß der Staat in diesem Falle seine Strafpflicht nicht erfüllt hat, *selbst zum Richter aufwirft* und danach handelt. Darüber darf man sich gar nicht wundern." Ramsauer's statement is quoted in *Arbeiterzeitung*, April 19, 1925, 5, emphases original, and *Die Rote Fahne* of the same day, 3 (all emphases original).

71. The statement in full, as reported in *Reichspost:* "*Dr. Riehl* erhebt entschieden Protest dagegen, daß man dem Gutachten der jahrzehntelang erprobten Gerichtspsychiater, die Gelegenheit gehabt haben, den Angeklagten genauestens zu studieren, weniger Glauben schenken wolle, als dem Gutachten der medizinischen Fakultät, deren Mitglieder, überhäuft mit anderen Geschäften, kaum Gelegenheit gehabt

haben könnten, den Angeklagten genau zu beobachten" (October 6, 1925, 7, emphasis original).

72. See the analysis of Riehl's argument in Murray Hall, *Der Fall Bettauer* 121–3.

73. On the verdict, see Murray Hall, *Der Fall Bettauer* 127–8, as well as press reporting in the following papers: *Arbeiterzeitung*, October 6, 1925, 1–2 and 7–8; *Reichspost*, October 6, 1925, 6–7; *Der Tag*, October 6, 1925, 5–8; *Vorarlberger Landeszeitung*, October 6, 1925, 2; *Vorarlberger Tagblatt*, October 6, 1925, 3; *Vorarlberger Volksblatt*, October 6, 1925, 1; *Arbeiterwille*, October 7, 1925, 2; *Prager Tagblatt*, October 7, 1925, 3; *Tagblatt*, October 7, 1925, 6; *Tages-Post*, October 7, 1925, 1–2; *Triestingtaler Wochenblatt*, October 10, 1925, 1; *Vorarlberger Wacht*, October 10, 1925, 5; *Ybbstal-Zeitung*, October 10, 1925, 2; *Volksblatt für Stadt und Land*, October 11, 1925, 5–6; *Tagblatt*, October 23, 1925, 1; *Wiener Sonn- und Montagszeitung*, November 9, 1925, 7.

74. "In parlamentarischen Kreisen ist heute das Gerücht verbreitet, daß wenn ein Zusammenhang zwischen dem Attentäter *Rothstock* und der nationalsozialistischen Partei festgestellt werden sollte, die Auflösung der nationalsozialistischen Partei in Erwägung gezogen werden wird. Diese Maßnahme würde damit begründet werden, daß die in der letzten Zeit begangenen Morde zumeist von Mitgliedern dieser Partei verübt wurden, daß diese Partei demnach als Quelle der Verrohung und der Verhetzung der halbwüchsigen Jugend zu betrachten ist" (*Die Stunde*, March 12, 1925, 5, emphasis original).

75. "Er ließ aber duchblicken, daß er einer Gruppe angehöre, die *die deutsche Jugend vor verderblichen Einflüssen*, zu denen er auch die Tätigkeit Hugo Bettauers zählt, fernhalten und, wie der Attentäter unklar sagte, alles Böse bekämpfe" (*Arbeiterzeitung*, March 11, 1925, 6, emphases original).

76. "[Rothstock] schloß sich vor einigen Monaten mit Gesinnungsgenossen zu einem Verein zusammen, der nicht mehr und nicht weniger in seinem Programm stehen hatte, als die Rettung der deutschen Kultur und die Befreiung der deutschen Jugend von allem, was ihr schädlich ist. Hugo Bettauer wurde von Otto Rothstock für schädlich gehalten und deshalb niedergeschossen" (*Vorarlberger Wacht*, March 14, 1925, 6).

77. See the critical comment in the *Arbeiterzeitung* of the following day: "Die Polizeikorrespondenz beeilt sich, mitzuteilen, daß sich *keinerlei Anhaltspunkte* für die *Existenz von Mitschuldigen* ergeben haben. Das ist ein *erstaunlich* rasches Urteil, so rasch, daß es allgemein Kopfschütteln erregen wird. Wir wenigstens sind keineswegs so schnell überzeugt wie es bei der Polizei in diesem Falle zu sein scheint!" (March 13, 1925, 6, emphases original).

78. For example in *Reichspost*, October 6, 1925, 6: "Der Vorsitzende konstatiert aus den Akten, daß *alle, sehr umfangreichen Erhebungen über eventuelle Mitwisser oder Mitschuldige ergebnislos verlaufen seien*" (emphasis original).

79. "Die genaue Durchforschung der Wohnung förderte nichts dergleichen zutage, sondern bestätigte, was Rothstock angegeben hatte, daß er aus eigenem Antrieb gehandelt habe, um seine Altersgenossen von durchaus verwerflichen Erzeugnissen angeblich ethischer Schriftstellerei Bettauers zu befreien, und keinerlei Mitwisser hatte. [...] Der Attentäter Otto *Rotstock* hat in einem neuerlichen Verhör abermals

erklärt, daß der Anschlag gegen Bettauer mit keiner politischen Gruppe oder mit seiner früheren politischen Betätigung in irgendeinem Zusammenhang stehe; die Tat sei seinem eigenen freien Entschluß entsprungen sowie der Überzeugung, daß ein solcher *Schädling der Sittlichkeit der Jugend* beseitigt werden müsse, er habe in niemandes Auftrag gehandelt und sei zur Tat von niemand verleitet worden, ja er habe nicht einmal mit jemand über die Absicht eines Anschlages gegen Bettauer gesprochen. [...] Er stellte wieder entschieden in Abrede, Mitschuldige oder Mitwisser gehabt zu haben. Er erklärte, daß er mit keinem andern Menschen vorher über die Tat gesprochen hätte" (*Wiener Zeitung*, March 11, 1925, 4 and 6 respectively, emphases original).

80. *Reichspost*: "Der Anschlag gegen Hugo Bettauer. Die Tat eines Einzelnen.—Die Ausschrotung in der Skandalpresse" (March 12, 1925, 7); "Das angebliche Komplott gegen Bettauer" (March 14, 1925, 5); "Das 'Komplott' gegen Hugo Bettauer.—Wie Sensationen gemacht werden.—Nachklänge zum Anschlag in der Langegasse" (March 15, 1925, 6); "Das 'Komplott' gegen Hugo Bettauer" (March 18, 1925, 7); "Der Attentäter Bettauers vor den Geschworenen" (October 4, 1925, 13).

81. From *Neue Freie Presse*, March 11, 1925: "Der Mörder aus Empörung über den *Mißbrauch des Erotischen*, der Mörder aus *tiefverletzter innerer Keuschheit*. Wir möchten heut, da ein Opfer blutend am Boden liegt, nicht *mit ganzer Schärfe* urteilen, wir möchten *das Mitleid* sprechen lassen [...]. Der junge Otto Rothstock ist tadellos ehrlich in seinem Vorleben, er hat niemals genußsüchtig gehandelt, niemals der Brunst nach Gewinn, nach raschem Auffangen des Vorteils gehorcht. [...] Hier ist nicht die Bestie im Menschen zur Uebermacht erwachsen, *sondern hier hat im Jüngling aus dem zwingenden Gebot seiner Empörung heraus gehandelt*, aus der bis ins Verbrecherische gesteigerten *brennheißen Wut über Mißbräuche*, die wir leider schon wie etwas Selbstverständliches empfinden und die wir an uns abfließen lassen wie Spülwasser. Wie heftig muß diese Empfindung gewesen sein, wie muß es in dem jungen Rothstock gewühlt, welche Ungeheuerlichkeiten muß er gesehen und erlebt haben, daß er sich entschloß, der *Rächer der beleidigten Moral* zu werden und einen Gegner niederzuknallen, der nach seiner Ueberzeugung *niedergeknallt werden mußte, damit Verderbnis von jungen Seelen abgewehrt werde*, damit sich Spekulation nicht länger an die heiligsten Dinge wage, an Dinge, die der Sohn eines Maschinenschlossers noch als heilig empfindet, während der Abschaum der Großstadt sie besudeln und entweihen läßt! Müssen wir nicht eigentlich alle zusammen *schamrot dastehen vor diesem Verbrechen?* Sie alle (die Anhänger Bettauers, Red.) mögen *Warnung* schöpfen aus dem Schicksal Hugo Bettauers. Sie alle mögen daran denken, daß *es einmal anders ausgehen* kann, als der tausendfach erprobte Zynismus sich einbildet. Sie alle mögen wissen, daß *sich nicht spaßen und scherzen läßt* mit dem Besten, was dieser entgüterten Menschheit noch geblieben ist." The passage is cited, with critical commentary, in *Arbeiterzeitung*, March 12, 1925, 2, all emphases original.

82. Rudolf Olden in a letter to his aunt, Princess Hedwig of Liechtenstein, dated August 21, 1915: "Der Stammrolle in Stettin hätte man durch einen Rechtsanwalt schreiben lassen sollen. Selbst schreiben ist

ganz verfehlt. Wozu giebt es Rechtsanwälte? Um das Standesamt handelt es sich nicht. Und auch die Sache mit dem <u>Vornamen</u> muss besorgt werden. Sonst werde ich nie Lt." The letter is cited in Asmus and Eckert, "Rudolf Olden," 15–16, emphasis original.

83. Silverman 31.

84. Silverman 55–6, emphasis original.

85. Murray Hall, *Der Fall Bettauer* 205; Silverman 56–8 and 217.

86. Silverman 59 and 56 respectively. For Olden's observations on the trial, see also Hacker 116–7.

87. "Hat da ein perverser Jude die Idee gefaßt, für die Wiener einen literarischen Sautrog zu schaffen, in der Hoffnung, damit ein glänzendes Geschäft zu machen. Dumm ist diese Spekulation gewiß nicht, jede Großstadt beherbergt eine große Schar zweifüßiger Schweine, daß dies in Wien nach der Schmutzwelle, die der Umsturz aufgewühlt hat und nach der Vergiftung seines gesellschaftlichen Lebens durch die Moral der zugewanderten Juden anders sein sollte, das wäre doch ein Wunder. Also setzte sich der Jude *Bettauer* hin und gab eine neue illustrierte Zeitschrift heraus mit dem, dem Schweinstall vertrauten Namen: 'Er und Sie.' Dann sah man in den Fenstern der Tabaktrafiken und der Zeitungsverschleißlokale das Blatt ausgehängt und Rudel von Kindern und Jugendlichen weideten sich an dem Anblick der Bilder und so weit sie konnten, kauften sie sich die 'schönen Bilder' und die 'saftigen Sprüchlein.' Eine literarische Schlammwelle wälzte sich durch Wiens Straßen" (*Christlich-soziale Arbeiterzeitung,* March 15, 1924, 3, emphases original).

88. "Ja, Bettauer ist tot, sein Werk aber nicht. Das frißt fort in tausend vergifteten Herzen und in Bächen verpesteten Blutes. Soll man es glauben, daß Mädchen, die aus der Schule kamen, Zeitschriften wie 'Ich und du' in die Hand gedrückt wurden? [...] Der Zeitungsjude weiß ganz genau, was er schreiben muß, um seine Leser an sich zu fesseln. [...] Seine Presseerzeugnisse setzt er ab und das deutsche Volk nimmt das Gift auf in sich. Es wird immer gefügiger, lüsterner, schlechter—und reif damit für dunkle Ziele. Immer und immer wieder muß daher der Mahnruf tönen:/'Judenzeitungen hinaus aus dem deutschen Haus!'" (*Niederösterreichischer Grenzbote,* October 25, 1925, 3).

89. See the Bibliography for a list of newspapers and date ranges consulted.

90. These papers are: *Arbeiterzeitung, Arbeiterwille, Die Rote Fahne, Prager Tagblatt, Tagblatt, Triestingtaler Wochenblatt, Der Tag, Volksbote, Vorarlberger Wacht,* and *Wiener Sonn- und Montagszeitung.*

91. I have found no articles critical of Bettauer in the following papers: *Arbeiterwille, Das interessante Blatt, Neuigkeits-Weltblatt, Prager Tagblatt, Tagblatt, Der Tag, Triestingtaler Wochenblatt, Volksbote,* and *Wiener Sonn- und Montagszeitung.*

92. *Wiener Morgenzeitung,* March 18, 1925: "daß das Judentum mit Bettauer belastet werde" (cited in Murray Hall, *Der Fall Bettauer* 101).

93. See Murray Hall on Bettauer coverage by the *Wiener Morgenzeitung* (*Der Fall Bettauer* 35) and *Wiener Stimmen* (54). The quotation from *Wiener Stimmen* from March 18, 1924 is on 54: "Den Schreiber Bettauer zu fördern und zu hätscheln, war geschmacklos und leichtfertig. Die Duldung und Förderung des Kupplers Bettauer wäre ein Verbrechen, das die jüdische Gesellschaft würde bitter büßen müssen."

94. "Zwar geht uns der pornographische Schmierfink

Bettauer nichts an, wohl aber die faschistischen Mordorganisationen, denn wir wissen, daß diese, wenn sie heute Bettauer aus 'Sittlichkeitsgründen' umbringen, sich gleichsam nur 'einschließen,' um morgen desto besser klassenbewußte Arbeiter zu 'erledigen'" (*Die Rote Fahne,* May 26, 1925, 3).

95. On the fortunes of Bettauer's magazine after his death, see Murray Hall, *Der Fall Bettauer* 135–8.

96. "Daß es in Deutschland *Erzberger* und *Rathenau* waren, die der Hakenkreuz-Fahne zum Opfer fielen, in Österreich aber Bettauer: das ist ungemein charakteristisch für die Verschiedenheit beider Länder (...). Bettauer, der als Gegner ermordet wurde, stand mit der Politik nur in losester Verbindung. Trotzdem ist das der erste politische Mord in Österreich gewesen" (from an article in *Die Weltbühne,* 1925, cited in Murray Hall, *Der Fall Bettauer* 109, emphases original).

97. Silverman 59–60.

98. Silverman 219.

99. Hartner-Hnizdo, *Das jüdische Gaunertum* and *Volk der Gauner* (both 1939).

100. Hartner, "Erotik und Rasse," *Kikeriki,* April 11, 1926, 7: "jüdische Satire"; "ein Schlüsselroman zur Verherrlichung des Judentums und zur Herabsetzung des nichtjüdischen Wien."

101. "[Er und Sie] rief so viel Erregung und Empörung hervor, daß es zu einem förmlichen Kampf um 'Er und Sie' kam, der Wien in zwei Lager spaltete, von denen eines für Bettauer Stellung nahm—die jüdisch-sozialdemokratischen und jüdisch-freisinnigen Kreise—, während das andere—die christlichen und die völkischen—gegen Bettauer Sturm lief" (Hartner, "Erotik und Rasse," *Kikeriki,* April 25, 1926, 7.

102. "Bettauer war, im Ganzen gesehen, marxistischer Sozialist, Demokrat und Jude, wenn auch nicht völkisch überzeugter, so doch triebhaft bewußter Jude. Die Verehrung, die er gerade in jüdischen Kreisen [...] gefunden hat, wo er wie ein Prophet verherrlicht ward, zeigt, daß er gerade dem Judentume zutiefst aus der Seele gesprochen hat. [...] Bettauer war nun der erste von einer breiten Masse von Gläubigen anerkannte und verehrte Verkünder der neuen geschlechtlichen Religion" (Hartner, "Erotik und Rasse," *Kikeriki,* April 11, 1926, 7).

103. "So lag also, wie ja auch die 'Wiener Morgenzeitung' hervorgehoben hat, die Befürchtung nahe, daß sich die Erregung über Bettauer und seine Wirksamkeit gegen das Judentum überhaupt kehren könnte./Die einfache Ableugnung kann jedoch die Tatsache nicht aus der Welt schaffen, daß Bettauer in seiner ganzen Geistigkeit, in seiner triebhaft starken, bewußten Art sowie in seiner Geschäftstüchtigkeit und Betriebsamkeit ein echter Jude ist, was sich aus seinen Schriften einwandfrei nachweisen läßt, wie denn auch die ganze geschlechtlich revolutionäre Richtung durchaus von Juden beherrscht wird" (Hartner, "Erotik und Rasse," *Kikeriki,* June 9, 1925, 7).

104. Hartner, "Erotik und Rasse," *Kikeriki,* June 9, 1925, 7.

105. "Er war einer jener, heute schon nach vielen Tausenden zählenden jüdischen Schriftsteller, welche sich in die durch Krieg und Revolution hervorgerufenen Wunden Europas eingefressen haben, sich der richtungslosen Seelen des Asphaltpublikums der Großstädte zu bemächtigen suchen, um ihr ewiges Wesen als das 'Ferment der Dekomposition'

(Mommsen) restlos auswirken zu können. Ueberall in den demokratisierten Ländern wuchert das Unkraut ungehindert [...] nirgends fühlt sich die jüdische Rasse wohler als in der Produktion und im Vertrieb von Schmutzliteratur, die—gleich dem Börsengeschäft und dem Mädchenhandel—heute schon fast ganz ein hebräisches Weltmonopol geworden ist" (Rosenberg, *Der Fall Bettauer* 2).

106. Rosenberg, *Der Fall Bettauer* 4 (on *The City without Jews* as "bewußt jüdischen Rassenpropaganda") and 10 ("Seit Monaten hat die völkische Presse Oesterreichs auf die Schmach und Schande Wiens aufmerksam gemacht, energische Abhilfe gefordert. Umsonst; weder der Staat noch der Stadtmagistrat mit dem Halbjuden Seitz-Pollacksohn an der Spitze legten dem Bettauer sein schmutziges Handwerk./Es ist deshalb verständlich, daß eine ohnmächtige Wut sich der offen von dreisten Juden verhöhnten Bevölkerung bemächtigte. Der junge Rothstock tat sicher nur, was Hundterttausende [sic] von Müttern dem Versucher ihrer Kinder gewünscht haben").

107. "Der Tote war der Vertreter einer Rasse und einer Bewegung, die Tag für Tag unser Volk beschmutzte, zersetzte und verhöhnte. Ihrer Pflicht vergessend, stand die österreichische Staatsregierung tatenlos daneben, während sich das Gift in Hunderttausende einfraß. Es gibt keinen Deutschen, möge er den Mord als Mittel noch so ablehnen, der nicht für die Motive Rothstocks—sein verspottetes Volk aufzurütteln—die größte Hochachtung empfindet. Das klare Volksempfinden fordert, daß die österreichischen Gerichte die Schuld der österreichischen Regierung gutmachen, d. h Rothstock freisprechen, die Schmutzliteratur rücksichtslos unterdrücken und die Bordelljournalisten ins Zuchthaus sperren" (Rosenberg, *Der Fall Bettauer* 12).

108. Rosenberg, *Der Fall Bettauer:* "Bettauer ist, wie nicht genug betont werden kann, nur einer unter Tausenden, Abertausenden und Millionen" (13); "Wie gesagt, so richtig in einigen noch nicht verjudeten Blättern die Beurteilung des Angriffs auf den Schmierfinken Bettauer ist, so sehr vermissen wir doch die Kennzeichnung des verderblichen Treibens dieses 'Journalisten' als etwas durchaus Jüdisches" (15–16).

109. "Der Satz, nach Auschwitz lasse kein Gedicht mehr sich schreiben, gilt nicht blank, gewiß aber, daß danach, weil es möglich war und bis ins Unabsehbare möglich bleibt, keine heitere Kunst mehr vorgestellt werden kann" (Adorno, *Noten zur Literatur IV, Gesammelte Schriften* vol. 11, 603).

110. Volkov on Treitschke in *Germans, Jews, and Antisemites* 99–100; see discussion in "Settings."

111. Volkov, *Germans, Jews, and Antisemites* 117.

112. *Die Rote Fahne,* May 26, 1925, 3.

113. See Schwerk, "Brüder" 189, and Schlag.

114. See, for example, many of the essays assembled in the anthology by Hook, O'Neill and O'Toole.

115. Arendt, *Origins* 434.

116. These include: *Unscrupulous (Hemmungslos,* orig. 1920, reprinted in 1988); *The City without Jews (Die Stadt ohne Juden,* orig. 1922, reprints in 1988 and 1996); *The Joyless Street (Die freudlose Gasse,* orig. 1923, reprints in 1988 and 2011); *The Gentleman on the Scaffold (Der Herr auf der Galgenleiter,* orig. 1922, reprint 2014); *The Blue Stain* (English translation of *Das blaue Mal,* 2017), *Killer of Women (Der Frauenmörder,* orig. 1922, reprinted 2016), and, in

1980, a 6-volume *Collected Works*-edition (*Gesammelte Werke*) containing six novels: *The Battle for Vienna (Der Kampf um Wien,* orig. 1922); *Vienna Unchained (Das entfesselte Wien,* orig. 1924); *The Joyless Street; The City without Jews; Law of the Jungle (Faustrecht,* orig. 1920), and *Unscrupulous.*

117. See, for example, Werner Koch 261–2, Murray Hall, *Der Fall Bettauer* 12 and 14; Egon Schwarz, and many others.

118. On Olden's life and death, see Asmus and Eckert and Sufott.

119. Press reporting on Rothstock's inscription in the army and the positive character reference from the police in: *Arbeiterzeitung,* January 5, 1928, 1–2; *Arbeiterwille,* January 5, 1928, 1 and 2; *Das kleine Blatt,* January 5, 1928, 2; *Die Rote Fahne,* January 5, 1928, 3 and January 6, 1928, 3; *Vorarlberger Landeszeitung,* January 5, 1928, 1; *Vorarlberger Tagblatt,* January 5, 1928, 1–2 and January 6, 1928, 1–2; *Vorarlberger Volksblatt,* January 5, 1928, 3 and January 12, 1928, 2; *Wiener Zeitung,* January 5, 1928, 2 and January 6, 1928, 1; *Volkspost,* January 7, 1928, 3; *Vorarlberger Wacht,* January 10, 1928, 1–2; *Reichspost,* January 15, 1928, 2–3.

120. Rothstock's letter, dated April 20, 1938, is cited in Botz, *Gewalt* 407–8; the citation 407 (emphases original): " Ich wurde tatsächlich *mit einem gefälschten Parere* [sic; should read: *Papiere*] im Steinhof eingeliefert, das später verschwunden ist. Ich wurde dort, wie man mir erklärte, nur gehalten, weil die jüdische Macht es wollte."

121. Murray Hall has reprinted excerpts from Rothstock's letter to him, dated September 6, 1976, in *Der Fall Bettauer* 182–3.

122. Otto Rothstock, interviewed by Peter Huemer for the show "Teleobjektiv," ORF, aired on February 23, 1977. The interview is transcribed in Hacker 181–6: "Mit meinem heutigen Verstand würde ich wohl so einen kleinen Schriftsteller nicht mehr aufs Korn nehmen. Ich müsste die Verantwortlichen für solche Entwicklungen mir vorknöpfen und dazu wäre vielleicht so eine Tonne Dynamit nötig" (Hacker 185). And: "Also eins muss man zugestehen, so viel Verbrechen waren nicht möglich, weil man die notorischen, die krankhaft veranlagten Rechtsbrecher kassiert hat, in den so genannten Konzentrationslagern festgehalten hat und dann wusste jeder: wehe wenn er in die Hände der Polizei kommt. Also war alles doch ein bisschen besser. [...] Also mehr Moral war ja doch auf alle Fälle. Schauen Sie sich doch dieses Sexheft an, das Sie mir da her gelegt haben. Wenn das jemand damals gemacht hätte, man hätte den Mann erwischt—der hätt's nie wieder getan. Erst 1945 als die Befreier des deutschen Volkes wieder im Land waren da wurde wiederum der Sex wieder zum Hauptpunkt der Volkserziehung erklärt" (Hacker 186).

Tragic Criminals and Farcical Justice (1890s–1914)

1. Fullerton, "Creating a Mass Book Market" 265. On these developments, see also his essay "Toward a Commercial Popular Culture in Germany," the works by Maase and Schenda, and Kosch and Nagl 23. Critical or bibliographical overviews of "trivial" or "mass" literature of the 19th and 20th centuries

have been offered in the collection of essays published by Kaes and Zimmermann, and by Mittelberg, Peter and Seiffert.

2. Many titles published between 1850 and 1960 are listed in the excellent bibliography by Kosch and Nagl.

3. Fullerton, "Creating a Mass Book Market" 275–7, the citation 277. On the response of the educated classes to this phenomenon, see also his "Toward a Commercial Popular Culture" 489.

4. Fullerton, "Creating a Mass Book Market" 267.

5. Fullerton, "Creating a Mass Book Market" 267.

6. On the *Pitaval*-tradition, see particularly Linder, "Deutsche Pitavalgeschichten."

7. Kleist, *Michael Kohlhaas* 45.

8. Otto Glagau is cited in Fullerton, "Creating a Mass Book Market" 268.

9. Cited in Fullerton, "Creating a Mass Book Market" 268.

10. Citations in Fullerton, "Creating a Mass Book Market" 276 and 271 respectively.

11. Materials and discussion in Fullerton, "Creating a Mass Book Market" 270–1.

12. All examples in Galle, *Lesestoffe* 45; on noble robbers as the heroes of colporteur and dime novels, see also Galle, *Groschenhefte* 37–9.

13. Citation and discussion in Fullerton, "Creating a Mass Book Market" 271; see also his statistics on sales of colporteur novels on 272–3.

14. On the decline of the colporteur novel, see Fullerton, "Creating a Mass Book Market" 275–6.

15. Maase 46–90.

16. "nie vorher und nie wieder hat es so viele Serien und so hohe Auflagen gegeben. Experten behaupteten damals, daß seit der Erfindung der Buchdruckerkunst keine Literaturgattung in so kurzer Zeit einen solchen Leserkreis gefunden hat!" (Galle, *Groschenhefte* 46).

17. Galle, *Groschenhefte* 46.

18. For examples ranging from Captain Morgan to Störtebecker, see Galle, *Groschenhefte* 47–53 and 35–6 on the "Lord Lister"-stories.

19. Fullerton, "Toward a Commercial Popular Culture" 498–9. On the wild success of the Carter-stories, see also Galle, *Groschenhefte* 24.

20. Galle, *Groschenhefte* 84.

21. Galle, *Groschenhefte* 29–33, the citation from *Börsenblatt des deutschen Buchhandels* on 29: "Der Sherlockismus. Es ist sicher, daß das gegenwärtige Europa an einer Krankheit leidet, die man Sherlockismus nennt. Der Sherlockismus ist eine literarische Krankheit ähnlich der Werther-Manie und dem romantischen Byronismus. Das Publikum begeistert sich für den Detektiv, der durch drei Westen hindurch sieht, ob man an der fünften Rippe einen Leberfleck von drei Millimeter Durchmesser hat."

22. Hügel, *Untersuchungsrichter* 207.

23. See, for example, Streckfuß's crime novel *The Will* (*Das Testament*) and his novella *Wild Girl Toni* (*Die wilde Toni*), both 1899; and Habicht's crime novel *The Legacy* (*Die Erbschaft*), 1897. Groner penned numerous crime novels and novellas, won a number of awards, and became famous particularly for her Detective Josef Müller-series (see below).

24. See Schädel's introduction and Karolle-Berg 435.

25. On Stuart Webbs films and other detective films of the era, see Kracauer, *Caligari* 19–20; Knops, and Hesse.

26. Hesse 145.

27. Noted by many, for example in Hickethier and Lützen 285–6; Hügel, *Untersuchungsrichter* 201; Knops 132; Katharina Hall, "Crime Fiction in Germany" 1–2, Tannert and Kratz, "Introduction" 1–5, Götz von Olenhusen 107; Kutch and Herzog 6, and Karolle-Berg.

28. Galle, *Groschenhefte* 84.

29. Hesse 144.

30. Fullerton, "Toward a Commercial Popular Culture" 502.

31. Galle, *Groschenhefte* 36. On censorship and the anti-"trash"-campaign, see also Schenda 104–6 and 242–7; Kosch and Nagl 43–5.

32. Götz von Olenhusen 115.

33. Hyan, *Sherlock Holmes* 7–12.

34. Schädel 7; cited and discussed in Karolle-Berg 435.

35. Karolle-Berg 436.

36. Schönert, *Kriminalität erzählen* 37–9, the citation 39: "abweichendes Verhalten [...] existenziell und gesellschaftlich bedingte—'conditio humana' (als Handlungsraum von Gegengewalt, Protest, Rebellion). Diese Perspektive wird auch dadurch verstärkt, daß sich die Autoren als 'Außenseiter der Gesellschaft' stilisieren und ihre 'Verbündeten' in den kriminalisierten und ausgegrenzten Gruppen der Gesellschaft sehen."

37. Schönert, *Kriminalität erzählen* 94–5: "In der deutschen Literatur verliert sie in fortschreitender Orientierung an angelsächsischen Serien ihre Realitätsbezüge und die ohnehin geringe kritische Substanz. Im übernommenen literarischen Schema sind die Vorgaben für die Kriminalisierung einer Handlung und die Bestrafung des Täters ohne Bedeutung. Die Konsequenzen stehen von vornherein fest. Es ist ein Verbrechen geschehen, der Täter muß ermittelt und bestraft werden. [...] Im Bereich der Elite-Literatur wird jedoch—in Distanz zur Detektivgeschichte—der Typus der moral- und sozialreflexiven Darstellung eines Verbrechens ausgebaut und differenziert. In den Vordergrund rücken die komplexen Determinanten kriminellen Verhaltens: Bezüge zwischen Verbrechen, Wahnsinn und sozialer Deklassierung. Der Verbrecher erscheint als Opfer der Gesellschaft und als Figuration des sozialen Zustandes."

38. This is Sprecher's description of the standard detective story around 1900: "Der Detektiv findet den Täter, mit dem er sich obsessiv befasst, in den er sich einzufühlen versucht, sympathisch, hält ihn für überlegen, gibt ihm innerlich sogar recht und will ihn gar nicht stellen, und wenn er es dann doch tut, hat er dabei ein tiefsinnig-schlechtes Gewissen. Der Täter zeigt umgekehrt, daß er durchaus auch Detektiv sein könnte, und führt diese Rolle mitunter zum Spaß oder im Dienste einer gemeinsamen Moral sogar vor" (63–4). On the tradition of the sympathetic criminal, see also Claßen 324.

39. "Ich will nicht behaupten, daß der Schauerroman unmittelbar sozialdemokratische Tendenzen verfolgt. Allein er leistet ihnen Vorschub. Edel, hilfreich und gut ist in diesen Romanen, oft ja auch im Leben, der arme Mann, aber zumeist dieser allein im Gegensatz zu den höheren Kreisen, aus denen vorzugsweise, wenn auch nur zur Verstärkung romanhafter Gegensätze und Effekte, Schwindler, Betrüger und Schurken vorgeführt werden. Gelegentlich zeigt sich diese Tendenz schon in den Titeln: 'Vornehme Verbrecher,' 'Ein

unschuldig verurteilter Arbeiter' etc. [...] Bei seinen Lesern erregt der Schauerroman schließlich Unzufriedenheit und Begehrlichkeit und ebnet so den Boden für die sozialdemokratische Agitation." Paul Dehn's assessment is quoted in Kosch and Nagl 43.

40. "[Diese Literatur] sei danach angethan unser Volk von Gott zu entfremden, die Morde und Selbstmorde vermehren zu helfen, die Unsittlichkeit zu fördern, die Sozialdemokratie groß zu ziehen und zum 'Klassenhaß' aufzufordern" (quoted in Kosch and Nagl 43).

41. My profound thanks to Gerhard Lindenstruth for allowing me a preview of his forthcoming Groner-bibliography.

42. Tannert and Kratz, "Introduction" 7.

43. Rahmatian.

44. Ziehensack 82.

45. Colbron 407.

46. Literature on Groner is scant. Introductory work on her has been done by Colbron, Ziehensack, Kirchmeier and Tannert. I have been unable to find any serious assessment of her as an author outside of these sources, and Groner makes no appearance in Sussex's recent *Women Writers and Detectives*. Gerhard Lindenstruth's 1992 bibliography of her work is now out of print, but currently being updated for re-edition.

47. This is Colbron's description of Müller, offered in her introduction to all of her translations of Groner-stories (see bibliography), unpag.

48. This and all following quotations from *The Case of the Golden Bullet* are taken from Colbron's unpaginated translation. *The Golden Bullet* has also been included in the anthology published in 1999 by Tannert and Kratz (190–216), which is, however, already out of print.

49. "So schaute die Mutterliebe—der Wahnsinn der Mutterliebe meinetwegen—und doch die stärkste, die herrlichste Liebe, selbst dann noch unbegreiflich groß, wenn sie vom Verbrechen besudelt wurde." I am using the German edition available at Projekt Gutenberg: Groner, *Nach zwanzig Jahren*, in *Kriminalnovellen*, http://gutenberg.spiegel.de/buch/kriminalnovellen-6383/4. All translations from this text are my own.

50. "Und wenn die jüngere Generation an seinem Haus vorüberging, erinnerte sie sich wohl zuweilen, wenn auch ein bißchen unklar an das, was die ältere sich von diesem Hause und dessen Eigner erzählt hatte, und fragt ein in der Gasse Fremder einmal einen anderen, der in ihr heimisch ist, wie der weißhaarige, stille Mann heiße, der so gern im Sonnenschein am Fenster sitzt, so antwortet dieser andere wohl: 'Man nennt ihn nur den alten Herrn'" (Groner, *Nach zwanzig Jahren*, *Kriminalnovellen*, unpag.).

51. I am using the unpaginated German edition available at Projekt Gutenberg at http://gutenberg. spiegel.de/buch/der-rote-merkur-6223/1 (all translations are my own; here: "der redliche Mensch").

52. "'Joseph,' schrie Fritz, 'ich bin schlecht, und ich bin ehrlos geworden, aber so tief gesunken bin ich nicht! Um Gottes Barmherzigkeit willen, glaube mir—ein Raubmörder bin ich nicht!'" Groner, *Der rote Merkur*, unpag.

53. "Fritz hatte sich erhoben. Sein hübsches Gesicht war sehr blaß und sehr ernst. Er richtete sich stramm auf, schaute seinem Schwager und dann seiner Schwester fest ins Auge und sagte: 'Ich will nach Wien zurück. Joseph, Hanna, verzeiht mir die Schande, die ich euch mache. Ich glaube, daß ich von heute an ein anderer sein werde. So—und jetzt laßt mich allein.' [To his mother:] 'Geh, Mutter, sonst könnte ich im Guten und Wahren wieder schwankend werden.'" Groner, *Der rote Merkur*, unpag.

54. "Ich danke Ihnen. Sie haben mir eine kaum mehr erträgliche Last von der Seele genommen!" Groner, *Der rote Merkur*.

55. "Nicht wahr—es ist Sympathie, eine echte Sympathie zwischen uns. Sie fühlen, daß ich kein Schurke bin, und daß ich den Namen, den ich trage, nicht in einen Kerker schleppen darf." Groner, *Der rote Merkur*.

56. "Ich danke Ihnen, daß Sie mir zu dem einzig Richtigen rieten. Das Grauen, das ich vor mir selber empfand, ist von mir abgefallen. Dank also—innigen Dank!" Groner, *Der rote Merkur*.

57. Eck's final statement of the novel: "Ich habe gebüßt nach außen und nach innen. Ein gut Teil meiner Seele ist leer gewesen—trostlos leer. Ich habe sie jetzt mit Liebe ausgefüllt, mit Liebe zu allen, die der werktätigen Liebe bedürftig" (Groner, *Der rote Merkur*).

58. "'Fritz Stegmann soll sogar wieder seine Kasse haben,' sagte Leibner. 'Ich denke, er wird jetzt für sein Lebenlang gut tun.'" Groner, *Der rote Merkur*.

59. "[...] wie paradox es auch klingen mag, der gefürchtetste Feind und der treueste Freund aller Verbrecher" (Groner, *Der seltsame Schatten*, in *Kriminalnovellen*, http://gutenberg.spiegel.de/buch/kriminalnovellen-6383/2; unpag., all translations mine).

60. "Auch Sträflinge sind Menschen, Menschen, die sich zuweilen mit aller Gewalt bessern wollen, aber man stößt sie mit aller Gewalt zum Verbrechen zurück. [...] In drei Wochen habe ich sieben Herren gehabt. Jeder hat mich fortgeschickt. Nicht, weil ich schlechter oder weniger arbeitete als die anderen. O nein! Es hat mir keiner etwas anderes nachsagen können, als daß ich ein entlassener Sträfling sei. Und der letzte, der hat mich gar mit den Hunden aus dem Hause gehetzt. Das war in *jener* Nacht. Damals hat wohl nicht viel gefehlt, und ich hätte den Nächstbesten getötet—denn alle, alle waren ja meine Feinde. Denn keiner wollte es mir möglich machen, ein ehrlicher Mensch zu bleiben" (Groner, *Der seltsame Schatten*, *Kriminalnovellen*, unpag.; translations mine).

61. "'Warst so brav im Gefängnis,' redete der Oberpolizeikommissar ihn an, 'hast dich dort so gut aufgeführt, daß es uns wohl überraschen kann, wie schnell du wieder gesunken bist.'/'Bin ich's? Herr! Haben Sie Beweise?' fuhr der ehemalige Sträfling auf./'Die, welche wir noch brauchen, die werden sich finden. Einstweilen genügt es uns, daß du das Haus Werners seit der Tat umschlichen hast—daß du heute verkleidet dort festgenommen wurdest.'/'Sonst können sie nichts anführen, Herr Oberpolizeikommissar,' sagte ruhig der Gefangene./Man fing an, ihn für frech zu halten" (Groner, *Der seltsame Schatten*).

62. "Ich heiße Müller, wie so viele" (Groner, *Wer ist es?*, *Kriminalnovellen*, unpag.; my translation).

63. Many of Hyan's works have been assembled in the Hans-Hyan-Archive at Berlin's Akademie der Künste, which contains 612 entries (see https://archiv. adk.de/bigobjekt/9135, accessed September 21, 2017). Beyond brief encyclopedia entries (Brümmer, Geißler), and one source that includes remarks on Hyan (Jazbinsek), I have been unable to locate any critical literature on Hyan.

64. Claßen 325.

65. Hyan, *Schwere Jungen* 7. All translations from this and other Hyan-texts are mine.

66. "Denn es besteht für mich kein Zweifel, daß, je einsichtsvoller der Verbrecher, das heißt, besonders der jugendliche resp. erst einmal strauchelnde, behandelt wird, das Verbrechen an sich immer mehr verschwinden und zum Schluß, besonders wenn die soziale Gesetzgebung ihre Schuldigkeit tut, nur das crimen pathologicum, das Verbrechen aus Leidenschaft, übrigbleiben wird." Hyan, *Schwere Jungen* 8.

67. See, for example, his *Schwere Jungen* 74–6.

68. Hyan, "Wie man Verbrecher züchtet," *Schwere Jungen* 9–14.

69. "Bottenwilhelm" appears in "Baldower und Flatterfahrer," 15–22; the rest of the characters in "Geldschrankknacker," 23–34; both in *Schwere Jungen*.

70. All expressions from *Schwere Jungen*, see glossary on 74–6: "Chochem loschen"; "Chawrusse"; "Bruchkadett"; "Dufte Schale"; "Schwenken"; "Masematten schieben"; "Die Asche vergraben"; "Kesse Penne"; "Platte reißen"; "Kletterhanne"; "Flanellwache halten"; "Pfeifen"; "Greiferei"; "Krachen gehen"; "Kittchen"; "Tauben haben." According to Michael Berkowitz (Email correspondence with the author, January 25, 2018), several of the Yiddish terms can have different meanings in other contexts, such as "Chochem" (which can also mean "wise"; "wise man") and "Chawrusse" (also: study partners in a yeshiva).

71. For example in "Geldschrankknacker," *Schwere Jungen* 23–31.

72. In "Baldower und Flatterfahrer," *Schwere Jungen* 22.

73. "Im Kittchen," *Schwere Jungen* 55–65.

74. "Herr Gott! Er kann ja nicht lesen und schreiben! Das einzige, was er auswendig gelernt hat und weiß, ist das Ave Maria und das Paternoster. Außerdem hat er in ewig dumpfer Mühe das Floß gestoßen und Erde gekarrt! Die Fuselflasche und ein schmutziger Frauenkörper sind seine Freuden gewesen" (Hyan, "Zum Tode," *Schwere Jungen* 66–73, the citation 70–1).

75. "dann glich er so recht einem der starken masurischen Bullen, der einen Menschen auf die Hörner genommen und zu Tode gestoßen hat, und den nun bald der Schlächter holen soll" (Hyan, "Zum Tode," *Schwere Jungen* 66–73, the citation 66).

76. "Aber abends die Bratkartoffeln—Bratkartoffeln!!—und das Beefsteak, der Rotwein und die Cigarren, ah, das ist fein!. .. Da lächelt der Bewer. Und die Nacht schläft er, schläft fest und traumlos, wie einer, der das beste Gewissen von der Welt hat. .. [...] Im Gefängnishof wirft er sich gegen die Aufseher. Die Knechte des Henkers eilen herzu—ein Kampf, sein letzter. Denn der Feind ist stärker.../Ha! ... Da kommt etwas Blitzendes durch die Luft! ... Das Gebrüll hört auf. Plötzlich. Und der Nachrichter, rasch herzutretend: 'Herr Staatsanwalt, die Exekution ist vollzogen!'" Hyan, "Zum Tode," *Schwere Jungen*, the citation 73.

77. "... ein Bengel, den niemand für vierzehn Jahre gehalten hätte. Nur das schon von allen Lastern gestreifte und früh verwelkte Gesicht des Jungen deutete darauf hin, daß er älter sei, als er aussah. Im übrigen hätte man ihm keine zehn Jahre gegeben mit seinem kleinen, engbrüstigen und offenbar rachitischen Körper" (Hyan, "Baldower und Flatterfahrer," *Schwere Jungen* 16).

78. Hyan, "Die Jugendlichen," *Schwere Jungen* 35–44.

79. "Das ganz kleine langt nach dem Mond, wenn es die Mutter auf dem Arme hält, und will den hübschen silbernen Taler herunterholen. Zehn Jahre genügen nicht, um in dem blinkenden Silberstück einen jener Sterne erkennen zu lassen, die man nicht begehrt./Aber wenn schon in völlig ruhiger Gemütsverfassung dem Kinde, dessen Instinkte stark und rege sind, oft die Kraft fehlt, sie durch den Verstand zu meistern, so bedarf es nur eines einzigen Affektzustandes, um dem schwachen Händchen die Zügel des Lebenswagens aus der Hand zu reißen, der dann in toller Fahrt bergab kollert." Hyan, "Die Jugendlichen," *Schwere Jungen* 44.

80. The entire passage is worth considering: "Von einem Kinde, das vom ersten Momente seines Lebens in einer von schmutzigen Menschen überfüllten Stube geatmet hat, dessen Blut vom ersten Tage seines Daseins an ebenso vergiftet wurde, wie seine Seele, die nichts anderes als Eindrücke der Rohheit und sexueller Gemeinheit in sich aufnehmen konnte; dieses arme Kind, das in sechzig Fällen vom Hundert durch den Trunk des Vaters mit einer Reihe von bösen und schädlichen Instinkten, mit der Widerstandslosigkeit des Blutes und ähnlichen schweren Schäden behaftet war, dieses Geschöpf, das im höchsten Grade unverantwortlich ist, bei dem der Verstand nur langsam reifen und das kontrollierende Bewußtsein so gut wie gar nicht gedeihen kann, wird fast immer in einem Alter sich selbst überlassen, wo die Kinder anderer, besser situierter Menschen noch fortwährend beaufsichtigt, von den ängstlichen Augen der Liebe behütet und bei dem kleinsten Fehlschritt durch den Verstand der Erwachsenen zurückgehalten und wieder auf den rechten Weg gebracht werden./Und nun tritt die Not, der Hunger an jenes kleine, armselige Menschenkind heran. Und überall rings um sich her sieht es, wie die andern essen und trinken und voller Freude sind. Und mit dem neidischen Vergleich verbindet sich in dieser armen kleinen Seele der wilde Wunsch, auch so zu leben und zu genießen" (Hyan, "Die Jugendlichen," *Schwere Jungen* 43).

81. "Das Kind ist kein Strafobjekt. [...] Ein Kind kann keine Rechtshandlung vornehmen, es kann sich nirgends selbst vertreten, es ist der Obhut seiner Eltern oder Vormünder unterworfen und darf sich ihr nicht entziehen. Für Beschädigungen an fremdem Gut, die ein Kind begeht, haften seine Eltern. Man verlangt von Kindern keinen Schwur, ihre Zeugen-Aussagen werden, in einer allerdings immer noch nicht genügenden Weise, unberücksichtigt gelassen. Aber mit dem Augenblick, wo es die doch offenbar nur für Erwachsene gemachten Strafgesetze verletzt, wird es als eine selbstständige Person angesehen, die das in Empfang nehmen muß, was unsere heutige Gesellschaft 'Recht' nennt und was besonders in diesem Falle doch das bitterste Unrecht ist." Hyan, "Die Jugendlichen," *Schwere Jungen* 42.

82. The statistics in Hyan, *Sherlock Holmes* 36. For a brief analysis of this treatise, see Galle, *Groschenhefte* 85–6.

83. "... die Lektüre dieser Statistiken wird zu einem Schrecken für jedes mitfühlende Eltern- und Menschenherz, wenn man aus dem Munde des Staatsanwaltes Dr. Wulften-Dresden vernimmt, dass im Jahre 1899–1901 insgesamt 9520 Kinder zwischen 12 und 13 Jahren wegen folgender Delikte verurteilt worden sind:/wegen /gefährlicher Körperverletzung 1495

Knaben 90 Mädchen/Hausfriedensbruch 230 " 9 "/Sachbeschädigung 1969 " 44 "/Unzucht 227 " 15 "/Urkundenfälschung " 190 " 41 "/wegen, jawohl!—, wegen Majestätsbeleidigung! 2 noch nicht dreizehn-jährige Jungens/und wegen/Gotteslästerung sogar 33 Knaben 8 Mädchen" (Hyan, *Sherlock Holmes* 37–8).

84. "Kann man bei solchem mittelalterlichen Wahnsinn der Bestrafung überhaupt von einer Kinderkriminalität reden?!—Abgesehen davon, dass zwölf- und dreizehnjährige Kinder überhaupt nicht vor den Strafrichter gehören—was weiss denn ein Kind von Urkundenfälschung! Es ist ja nach seiner ganzen Denk- und Empfindungsart gar nicht im-stande, das Wesen dieses Delikts überhaupt nur zu begreifen! Und Gotteslästerung! Majestätsbeleidi-gung! Was muss das für ein Gott oder König sein, den ein Kind beleidigen kann! Ebenso Hausfriedensbruch, Sachbeschädigung usw.! Das sind Ungezogenheiten bei einem Kinde, keine Verbrechen!" (Hyan, *Sherlock Holmes* 38)

85. "Tut das Kind reicher Eltern so etwas, so wird's mit Geld wieder gutgemacht, und zwar von Rechtswe-gen!—Der kleine Proletarier wandert dafür ins Gefängnis! Wegen eines Nichts wird ihm von Leuten, die das Leben nicht einmal in ihren eigenen Kindern kennen lernen, das ganze Sein verdorben und ru-iniert!" (Hyan, *Sherlock Holmes* 38)

86. "Denn zweifellos ist das Verbrechertum nur eine letzte und stärkste Aeußerung jener überall gährenden Unzufriedenheit, die den Besitz überhaupt bedroht und die, in der Meinung, eine gerechte Verteilung der Lebensgüter herbeiführen zu können, mit immer verstärkter Kraft an den Grundpfeilern des Kapitalismus rüttelt" (Hyan, "Wie man Ver-brecher züchtet," *Schwere Jungen* 14).

87. Groner, *The Case of the Lamp that Went Out*, trans. Colbron, Chapter 8, unpag.

88. Groner, *The Case of the Lamp that Went Out*, trans. Colbron, Chapter 8, unpag.

89. Groner, *The Case of the Lamp that Went Out*, trans. Colbron, Chapter 9, unpag.

90. Groner, *The Case of the Lamp that Went Out*, trans. Colbron, Chapter 11, unpag.

91. Groner, *The Case of the Lamp that Went Out*, trans. Colbron, Chapter 12, unpag.

92. Groner, *The Case of the Lamp that Went Out*, trans. Colbron, Chapter 12, unpag.

93. Since fraudster literature is primarily con-cerned with social criticism rather than crime, I would not consider it a sub-genre of crime literature. Most contemporary critics didn't either. On *Hochstap-lerliteratur*, see, among others, the works by Neu-mann, Cleric, Frenzel, Claßen, and Sprecher.

94. Sprecher includes in his list of famous fraudster literature of the time and beyond it, often written by the perpetrator, the following: Hans Wachenhusen, *The Fraudster: A Novel* (1887); Georges Manolescu a.k.a. Prince Lahovary, *A Prince Among Thieves: Memoirs* and his *Failed: From the Inner Life of a Crim-inal* (both 1905); Ignatz Strassnoff's *I, the Fraudster Ignatz Strassnoff* (1926); Walter Serner's *The Last Loosening: A Guide for Fraudsters and Those Who As-pire to Be One* (1927); Rafael Schermann's *His Bride, A Fraudster* (1932); and Alfred Müller and Hans Lorenz (i.e., Margarete Paulick)'s *My Friend the Fraudster: Burlesque in Three Acts* (1944). On some of these texts, see also Claßen 19.

95. Sprecher 223–4.

96. Sprecher 465: "soziale Krankengeschichten."

97. On Mühsam's play, see Claßen 93–5.

98. *Denkwürdigkeiten des Hauptmanns von Köpenick* contains a rich collection of such texts, many collected from various newspapers of the time. See the poems on 14, 17, 20, 32, 34, 36–7, 38, 43, 53, 58–9, 61–3, 64, 66, 72, 75–7, 80–1, 85, 88, 90, 91, and 94. Friedländer has famously re-told the story of Köpenick in his collection of *Interesting Crime Trials* (1910–14), but this is a historical recapitulation of the facts, bar of any interpretation or poetic license that could catapult this text into the realm of fiction. On other Köpenick-literature, see Löschburg, *Schuster* 225–8 and Gehrke 17.

99. Leo Leipziger, "Der Grenadier von Köpenick," *Denkwürdigkeiten* 20 (refrain: "Hab' ich zu denken angefangen,/Hat Preußens Größe aufgehört").

100. G.H., "Zu Befehl!," *Denkwürdigkeiten* 80–1.

101. The work is briefly mentioned in Gehrke 17, Löschburg, *Schuster* 107 and Claßen 93.

102. See Claßen's brief interpretation of Hyan's text on 93.

103. Hans Hyan/Paul Haase, "Der Hauptmann von Köpenick," 14 (my translation): "Selbst wenn er ein Mörder wäre,/Mit dem bunten Leutnantsfrack,/Ist er stets der Vorgesetzte/Für das Zivilistenpack!.../Ein'ge wollten's nicht begreifen,/Doch die meisten sahen's ein:/Unser Volk hat die Verpflichtung/Immer nur 'Hurra' zu schrein..."

104. Frieda von Bülow has interested scholars pri-marily as the author of colonial novels. See, among others, the works by Laurien, Renker, Shumannfang, Warmbold, Wildenthal, Eigler, and von Hammerstein. For biographical information on her, see Hoechstet-ter, Bäumer, Brunnemann, Burda and Streiter.

105. On Hermann Bahr, see above all the works by Mayerhofer/Ifkovits, Meridies, Meier, Donald Daviau, Farkas, Karl Johann Müller, and Kupfer.

106. Two revealing contemporary reviews of the novel are Max Foges's review in *Neue Freie Presse* (July 10, 1909): 1–2 and E. Góth's review in *Pester Lloyd* (June 6, 1909): 22. Scholarly assessments of *Drut* are thin on the ground. Donald Daviau offers brief remarks on each of Bahr's novels in Chapters Two and Six of *Hermann Bahr*; *Drut* features briefly in the works by Handl (148–51) and Meridies (14–17).

107. Predictably, Tamara von Hervay was briefly interviewed on Bülow's novel in the year of her great-est notoriety, 1904. She claimed that the novel was a malicious misrepresentation of her character, a low act of revenge born of Bülow's jealousy because she was in love with a man who preferred Hervay to her: "Ich kenne dieses Buch, scheue mich nicht zu sagen, daß es einige Wahrheiten aus meinem Leben enthält, wenn diese auch in der Form zu Gunsten der Schilderung und mit Absicht entstellt sind. Die Ver-fasserin dieses Romans und ich liebten einst densel-ben Mann. Ich blieb Siegerin im Kampfe um das Herz des geliebten Mannes; sie hat sich durch dieses Buch gerächt, indem sie meine Schwächen und Fehler in niedrige Beleuchtung stellte. Sie hat mich damit schwer getroffen" (from an interview in *Grazer Volks-blatt*, September 25, 1904, p. 4).

108. "Solch einen Hexenring hat Susi um Mervis-rode gezogen, [...] alle sind nun durch einen Zauber gebannt der ihren Willen lähmt, sie hilflos von einer Erregung in die andre taumeln läßt und den Wunsch

erstickt, sich aus dieser Giftluft zu befreien." Bülow, *Im Hexenring* 130.

109. "Er fragte lustig: 'Wissen Sie, was bei uns eine Trud heißt? Die Trud kommt in der Nacht und setzt sich einem auf das Herz, bis man nicht mehr atmen kann und elendiglich erstickt. Eine böse Hexe ist sie'" (Bahr, *Die Hexe Drut* 231–2).

110. "sie war ihm unheimlich wie ein alter schwarzer Rabe" (Bahr, *Die Hexe Drut* 317).

111. Bahr, *Die Hexe Drut* 216: "Gar kein Zweifel, dachte er, daß sie eine Hochstaplerin ist!"

112. "Hochstaplerinnen haben immer Heimlichkeiten" (Bahr, *Die Hexe Drut* 223).

113. "Ich bin ja nur ein Abenteuer. Denke bloß: eine Hochstaplerin!" [...] "Wärst du doch eine! Ich will nur dich, so wie du bist! Ob Baronin oder Hochstaplerin, ist mir wirklich gleich. Und schließlich, wer ist heute kein Hochstapler? Den meisten gelingt es nur nicht" (Bahr, *Die Hexe Drut* 284).

114. As a student, Bahr was a member of the German nationalist party, but broke with nationalism over its antisemitic stance in 1887. In 1893, he solicited responses from notable writers on the question of antisemitism and published their accounts in his book *Antisemitism (Der Antisemitismus*, 1894). A year later, in 1895, Bahr married a Jewish woman, Rosalie Jokl, over his parents' strenuous objection, abjuring his Catholicism in order to be able to do so. The marriage ended in divorce in 1909 (coincidentally also the year in which *Drut* was first published). Bahr also occasionally published essays on Jews in Austria, Zionism and antisemitism; see his essays "Die Juden in Österreich" and "Zionismus." On Bahr and issues of Jewishness and antisemitism, see Donald Daviau's article "Hermann Bahr und der Antisemitismus" and his *Understanding Hermann Bahr* 235–55; on Bahr's take on Judaism and antisemitism in his novel *Die Rotte Korahs* (1919), see Meridies 42–56.

115. This is interesting also in view of the fact that Bahr would do precisely this ten years later, in his novel *Korah and All His Band (Die Rotte Korahs,* 1919), whose hero Count Ferdinand, an Austrian nobleman who has never doubted his "Germanic" heritage, finds out to his dismay that he is descended from a Jewish theater director and capitalist. On this novel, see Meridies 42–56.

116. "... obwohl sie Bahr mit seiner ganzen Kraft inszeniert hat. Aber eben nur inszeniert—das Theatralische der Gestalt—diesmal ist Theatralik allerdings Lebenswahrheit—hat sich selbst dem Dichter gegenüber zu spröde erwiesen und erweist sich noch spröder dem Leser gegenüber. Das Exotische, das Rätselhafte, intrigiert eine Weile, dann aber versagt die Wirkung und selbst die Sentimentalität des Abganges in den Tod, den Bahr im Gefühle, daß die Gestalt der Baronin einer stärkeren Retouchierung bedürfe, erfunden hat, vermag über diesen toten Punkt des Romans nicht hinwegzuhelfen./Aber es kommt auch gar nicht auf die Drut an. Sie ist die einzige Person im Roman, die keine Oesterreicherin ist, und der Dichter schreibt eine menschliche Komödie aus Oesterreich und sie ist ihm so lustig und so traurig gelungen, wie das Leben selbst ist und dabei noch ganz genau in jener Art Lustigkeit und jener Art Traurigkeit, die nur in Oesterreich weint und lacht" (Foges 2). Meridies has read the novel in very similar ways (14–17).

117. Katharina Hall, "Crime Fiction in Germany" 23–4.

118. Katharina Hall, "Crime Fiction" 24.

119. Katharina Hall, "Crime Fiction" 24.

120. Hyan, *Schwere Jungen* 45–54.

121. "Mit geschwellten Heldenbrüsten/Ziehn sie zur Verhaftung aus./Baruch Cohn denkt: 'Nu, der Hauptmann/Sieht mer ebbes treife aus!' // Daran sieht man den Hebräer,/Der stets was zu nörgeln find't,/Weshalb unsres Staates Stützen/Meist Antisemiten sind!" (Hyan/Haase, *Der Hauptmann von Köpenick* 8)

122. On Bülow's attitude towards Jews and Jewishness in her colonial novels, see Wildenthal's "'When Men Are Weak,'" Rash's "Living in the Colonies" 121–7, and Shumannfang.

123. Bülow, *Im Hexenring* 11: "Seltsamerweise sah sie jüdisch aus. Ein feingliedriges, schmalschultriges, schmalhüftiges Figürchen war sie, mit flacher Brust und Wespentaille. Das Köpfchen klein, voll von kreppartigem Schwarzhaar, tief in die von Natur ziemlich hohe Stirn frisiert. Unter schön gezeichneten, feinen dunklen Brauen funkelten schmal geschnittene schwarze Augen, eher klein als groß; darunter ein leicht gebogenes, längliches Näschen und über dem kurzen, schwach entwickelten Kinn ein aufwärts gekrümmter, nicht eben kleiner Mund mit schmalen, ein wenig eingekniffenen Lippen."

124. "Wolfine fühlte: sie gehört nicht zu uns. Ihre eigentliche Natur knebelt sie, um sich uns anzupassen. Manchmal gelingt es ihr, öfters nicht. Und manchmal mag ihre geknebelte Natur sich gegen den Zwang auflehnen. Im Grunde haßt und verachtet sie uns dann" (Bülow, *Im Hexenring* 124).

125. From the speech of Wolf von Hohenecke, the novel's noble male, to Susi after her exposure as a Jewish swindler: "Sie sind eine Verkörperung des absolut Schädlichen. Lauter zerbrochene Existenzen bezeichnen Ihren Weg. Sie sind der Reihe nach allen denen, die Sie, um Ihren diversen Gelüsten zu dienen, an sich gefesselt haben, zum finanziellen und geistigen Ruin geworden. Als Schmarotzerpflanze verderblichster Art frönen Sie Ihrer Eitelkeit und amüsieren sich auf Kosten hundertmal wertvollerer Existenzen. Wesen Ihrer Art sollten ohne Skrupel vernichtet werden, wie giftige Reptile" (Bülow, *Im Hexenring,* 138).

126. "... ich bin ein Jude und will ein Jude sein und bin stolz darauf, ein Jude zu sein und dem Volk anzugehören, aus dem der größte aller Menschen hervorgegangen ist. Ich behaupte, daß dies ein Adelsbrief ist, wie niemand sich eines besseren rühmen kann. Aber ich habe mir niemals verhehlt, daß wir Juden ein greisenhaftes Volk sind, trotz aller noch sichtbaren Zähigkeit und Kraft. Und daß unsre Greisenhaftigkeit Erscheinungen von so verderblichem Charakter zeitigt, daß ich sie mit dem Greisenbrand vergleichen möchte. Zu diesen zersetzenden Fäulnissymptomen rechne ich insbesondere diese Leo-Taxil-Naturen, zu denen auch Frau Ilka von Tschirn gehört: die, gänzlich verlassen von der Kraft, wirklich zu leben, sich ein Scheindasein dadurch ermöglichen, daß sie einen Lebensinhalt bewußt vortäuschen. Statt zu leben, taschenspielern sie mit dem Leben, an dessen Ernst sie nicht mehr glauben, und füttern ihre blutlosen Seelen mit Ueberlegenheitswahn ihren viel einfacheren, viel unbewußteren, kindhafteren und darum gläubigen Opfern gegenüber. Diese Spezies meiner Stammesgenossen erachte ich für Leichengift! Sie bringen allem gesunden Leben, mit dem sie in Berührung kommen, Blutvergiftung, die, wenn nicht

rechtzeitig energisch eingegriffen wird, zu Tod und Verwesung führen muß. Ich möchte sie—im Interesse meines Volkes zuallernächst!—mit Feuer und Schwert vom Erdboden getilgt sehen" (Bülow, *Im Hexenring* 147–8).

127. "Als ob eine köstlich herbe, reinigende Luft vom geliebten Meere her das Dorf durchwehe" (Bülow, *Im Hexenring* 140).

128. "Ein wunderbarer Friede war in dem alten Herrenhof eingezogen. [...] Wie wenn in schwülen Sommertagen ein heftiges Gewitter niederrasselt und die stickige Luft reinigt, so war es in Mervisrode: ein unendlich erleichtertes, tiefes Aufatmen!" (Bülow, *Im Hexenring* 154)

129. "Niemand hatte wieder etwas von ihr gehört. Sie schien zerstoben und zu nichts geworden, wie eine schillernde Seifenblase" (Bülow, *Im Hexenring* 159).

130. "Wie schwer sie arbeiten muß! [...] Sie ist doch glücklich" (Bülow, *Im Hexenring* 155).

131. "Mit unheimlicher Voraussicht wird in diesem Roman der damals bevorstehende und seither eingetretene Zusammenbruch in Gestalt einer altösterreichischen Beamtentragödie erlebt und erlitten" (Lyonel Dunin in his introduction to the 1929 edition, 5).

Farcical Criminals or Tragic Victims (1926–1939)

1. "Du warst der größte Schweinhund, den der Teufel in seinem Zorn erschuf. Warum bist, Unglücklicher, du es nicht geblieben?" Walter Serner, "Der gelbe Terror," *Erotische Kriminalgeschichten,* http://gutenberg.spiegel.de/buch/erotische-kriminalgeschichten-6880/1 (unpag).

2. "Nur als Fälschung hat Kunst noch einen Sinn. Meine Bilder und Graphiken liegen in einer Mottenkiste. Aber nach diesen Plattenabzügen werden sich die Menschen reißen, die Sachen ab und die Zungen aus dem Halse! [...] Die Einigung aller Kunststile ist erreicht. Futuristen, Expressionisten, Kubisten, Neusachliche, Neopointellisten, Lichtfarbentonempfindliche: alle werden meine Abzüge schätzen und sie sammeln! Es ist alles Schwindel!" Paul Gurk, *Tresoreinbruch* 48.

3. See Herzog, *Crime Stories* 7–9, and sources cited there.

4. Herzog, *Crime Stories* 6.

5. Baumeister 357–8.

6. On contemporary crime statistics, see Herzog, *Crime Stories* 2, and sources cited there.

7. Herzog, *Crime Stories* 26 and 15 (citation, emphases original); see also Kutch and Herzog, "Introduction" 5: "German-language writers dispensed with the detective altogether and focused instead on criminals."

8. I'm quoting Todd Herzog's paraphrase in *Crime Stories* 21; original in Brecht, "Popularität" 34–5.

9. Statistics in Götz von Olenhusen 108.

10. Götz von Olenhusen 112–3. On the sex killer in the art and film of the Weimar Republic, see Tatar's seminal study.

11. See Lessing, *Haarmann: Geschichte eines Werwolfs*; Hyan, *Massenmörder Haarmann: Eine kriminalistische Studie*; Herbertz, *Verbrecherdämmerung:*

Psychologische Deutung und weltanschauliche Perspektiven der jüngsten Mordfälle Haarmann, Angerstein, Denke u.s.w.; Döblin, *Die beiden Freundinnen und ihr Giftmord*; Weiss, *Der Fall Vukobrankovics.*

12. On this series, see Linder's essay "Außenseiter der Gesellschaft."

13. Siemens has offered a good overview of court reportages of the age.

14. Quoted in Siemens 341: "Der Mensch, der schießt, ist ebenso unschuldig wie der Kessel, der explodiert."

15. Siemens 343.

16. "Vor uns steht eine keineswegs unsympathische Erscheinung. Äußerlich betrachtet: ein schlichter Mann aus dem Volk" (Lessing, *Haarmann* 19).

17. Kracauer, *Caligari* 220; see also Tatar 160 on this passage.

18. Noted, among many others, by Tatar (55).

19. See Tatar 32 and elsewhere.

20. Many documents assembled by Poszár and Farin show this clearly.

21. The article in *Frankfurter Zeitung* (Abendblatt of December 30, 1924) is cited and discussed in Tatar 44.

22. Margaret Seaton Wagner 21; citation and discussion in Tatar 45.

23. "Der Verbrecher als Außenseiter," "als Symbol für die fundamentale verdorbene republikanische Zivilisation," "ambivalente Figur," "als Rebell und als Bürger," "unschuldige Triebtäter," "Gentlemanverbrecher," "Der 'kleine Mann' als Verbrecher," "in psychologischer Sicht," "als Opfer," "zwischen Unschuld und Verantwortung," "in justizkritischer Sicht," "als Bürger." See Kreutzahler's TOC, iv–v.

24. Würmann, "Zum Kriminalroman" 146–7, and "Sternstunden."

25. Würmann, "Deutsche Kommissare" 219.

26. Delabar 167: "Ein wie auch immer aussehendes spezifisch nationalsozialistisches Persönlichkeitsprofil lässt sich aber in diesen Texten kaum finden."

27. Würmann, "Zum Kriminalroman" 172–3.

28. Delabar 174: "Literatur taugt nicht zur Propaganda."

29. Delabar 166.

30. For example Würmann, "Zum Kriminalroman" 172–3.

31. Würmann, "Sternstunden."

32. See Würmann, "Zum Kriminalroman" 176–7.

33. See, among others, Würmann, "Zum Kriminalroman" 145: "Erst zum Ende der dreißiger Jahre, kurz vor Beginn des Zweiten Weltkrieges, und in den ersten Kriegsjahren kam es von staatlicher Seite zu massiven Eingriffen." On the new guidelines for authors from the Propaganda Ministry, see Würmann, "Deutsche Kommissare" 218.

34. Galle, *Groschenhefte* 131.

35. On antisemitism in crime fiction, see Hickethier 20; Würmann, "Zum Kriminalroman" 170–2 and "Deutsche Kommissare" 233–9.

36. See, for instance, the assessment in Maase's *Grenzenloses Vergnügen* 165–75.

37. Erich Thier, cited and discussed in Herzog, *Crime Stories* 143.

38. The quote from Hans Krulick (*"der Jude," "sich dem Ziele der Weltbolschewisierung nahestens während, [...] sein zu Papier gebrachtes Giftdenken ungehindert und maßlos in die seelisch zermürbte Menschheit"*) is taken from Hans Krulick's essay "Für und

gegen den Kriminalroman," cited and discussed in Würmann, "Entspannung" 13 (emphases original).

39. Würmann, "Entspannung" 25–8 ("englisches Wesen"; "*Säuberung der Unterhaltungsliteratur von feindstaatlichen Einflüssen*"; both citations 25). On NS attempts to promote a crime literature satisfying the propagandistic needs of the NS-State, see also Herzog, *Crime Fiction* 144–5.

40. Citation and discussion of Benatzky's report in Würmann, "Entspannung" 23–4.

41. This the conclusion of Würmann: "Es handelt sich bei den deutschsprachigen Kriminalromanen auch nach 1939 mitnichten um eine in Form und Inhalt weitgehend genormte Gattung" ("Deutsche Kommissare 239"; see also his "Zum Kriminalroman" 178.

42. "Es sollen eine Reihe von antisemitischen Romanen geschrieben werden, und zwar von maßgebenden Schriftstellern, wenn sie auch nicht so vorbehaltlos zum Nationalsozialismus stehen, wie etwa unsere Feld-, Wald- und Wiesendichter, die zwar in ihrer Gesinnung sehr tüchtig sind, aber nicht viel können." Goebbels's diary entry dated May 29, 1943 is cited and discussed in von Linthout.

43. "Gerade weil sie nicht auf explizit nationalsozialistische Normen und Werte abhoben, sondern sich auf ein zeittypisches Gemisch bürgerlicher Vorstellungen bezogen, halfen sie mit, die Fiktion einer zwar nicht demokratischen, vielleicht nur bedingt rechtsstaatlichen, aber durchaus rechtschaffenen modernen Gesellschaft aufrechtzuerhalten, die durch jede erfolgreiche Aufklärung eines Verbrechens ihre Bestätigung fand. Solange noch die Möglichkeit bestand, diese Fiktion als vage Entsprechung der persönlichen Gegenwart zu begreifen, mußte dies eine herrschaftstabilisierende Wirkung entwickeln, von der die Nationalsozialisten nur profitieren konnten" (Würmann, "Zum Kriminalroman" 179; see also his identical conclusion in "Deutsche Kommissare" 240).

44. Serner was re-discovered in the 1980s, after the re-edition of his 1927 Collected Works edition in 1984 (on Serner's postwar reception, see Milch). While Serner has attracted more attention as a Dada-theorist (see the works by Backes-Haase; Drews; Puff-Trojan; Peters, and the essays assembled in Puff-Trojan/Schmidt-Dengler); his crime stories have also now been discovered (by Hackenbruch, Bucher, and Puff-Trojan, *Wien/Berlin/Dada* 244–65). Serner's "autobiographical" documents and the posthumous tribute to Serner by Christian Schad (*Relative Realitäten*) are highly illuminating with regard to Serner's creative attitudes, but say little about his biography.

45. Serner's work comprises *The Blue Monkey: 33 Crime Stories (Zum blauen Affen*, 1921); *The Eleventh Finger: 25 Crime Stories (Der elfte Finger*, 1923); *The Whistle Around the Corner: 22 Crime Stories (Der Pfiff um die Ecke*, 1925); *The Treacherous Street: 19 Crime Stories (Die tückische Straße*, 1926), the crime novel *The Tigress (Die Tigerin*, 1925) and the play *Posada or the Great Coup in the Ritz Hotel (Posada, oder der große Coup im Hotel Ritz*, 1926).

46. "Eine Inhaltsangabe der einzelnen Geschichten ist nicht nur schwierig zu geben, weil manche fast unverständlich sind, sondern auch unnötig, weil sie in den verschiedensten Formen und Einkleidungen eigentlich immer nur einen Inhalt haben: das Verbrecher- und Kokottenmilieu [...] und *einen* Grundgedanken variieren, die Schilderung des heroischen Verbrechers, der in seiner Hemmungslosigkeit die

Überlegenheit gegenüber den von Gefühl, Rücksicht oder gar Güte 'verdummten' Mitmenschen herleitet. Vorgetragen werden die oft geradezu widerlichen Geschichten mit einer raffinierten Kühle und Sachlichkeit, die schliesslich ironisch und damit aufreizend wirkt." The passage from the judgment of the Berliner Prüfstelle is cited and discussed in Bucher, "Ereignis" 91–2 (emphasis original).

47. Stories written predominantly in dialect dialogue include "Sprotte schmust" (from *Der Pfiff um die Ecke*); "Im Hotel Fleißig" (*Die tückische Gasse*); "Auf dem Rummelplatz" and "Irma" (all from *Die tückische Straße*).

48. On "Die Bande Kaff" (in *Der Pfiff um die Ecke*), see the brief discussion in Puff-Trojan, *Wien/Berlin/ Dada* 244–5.

49. For example in "Faule Zeiten" and "Eine kuriose Karriere," both in the collection *Erotische Kriminalgeschichten*.

50. For a brief discussion of both and more generally Serner's attitude toward the traditional detective story, see Hackenbruch 51–6.

51. That Serner's stories, unlike Hyan's, offer no such thing has been noted repeatedly; see, among others, Hackenbruch 14.

52. This is Bucher's conclusion in "Ereignis und Wiederholung" 90–1 and "Repetition und Variation" 103–10.

53. "Es war an einem Sonntag unter den Zelten in Berlin, als Fräulein Anna plötzlich die Worte neben sich gelispelt hörte: 'Ik bin wahrhaftig dafür, det man Jurkensalat nich zum Schuhreinigen vawendet.'" "Fräulein Annas folgenschwerstes Abenteuer," *Zum blauen Affen* 194.

54. "Tableau. Das damit endete, dass die beiden sich in die Haare gerieten, Geschirr zerschlugen und kreischend auf den Steinfliesen sich wälzten." "Fräulein Annas folgenschwerstes Abenteuer," *Zum blauen Affen* 200.

55. "Kuhles ganz seltene Stunde"; "Der Lebenskünstler"; "Der Doktor Sahob"; all in *Zum blauen Affen*.

56. "Wenn Madame mit einem andern tanzt, gehen Sie an dem Paar vorbei, natürlich nachlässig rauchend, und rufen möglichst leicht aus: 'Kinder, nehmt Euch senkrechter!' oder: 'Sima, was bist du heute für ne famos festgehaltene Erscheinung!' oder ganz einfach: 'Hört mal, wenn Ihr fertig seid, putzt Euch erst ab!' Und so. Das macht den besten Eindruck." "Der Lebenskünstler" 108–9.

57. "Hör mal! Ich habe gar nichts dagegen, dass du einem reichen Trottel Beträge ablistest. Aber ich muss es wissen. Ich muss alles wissen. Sonst kannst du unter Umständen schwer hineinfallen." "Der Lebenskünstler" 111.

58. "Die für jedes andauernde Lieben unbedingt erforderliche pekuniäre Basis war hergestellt. Und Sima fast verliebter noch als ihr Schüllchen." "Der Lebenskünstler" 111.

59. "Sie sollte es ihm zuliebe tun. Das sei Weibespflicht. Menschenpflicht." "Kuhles ganz seltene Stunde" 64.

60. "Und dann habe ich es, offen gestanden, wirklich bereits satt, mich von dir täglich zwei Stunden unterrichten zu lassen, um diesem alten Esel Bildung vorzumachen. Das ist ja schon fast so, als wenn ich wirklich studieren würde. Eine Schande! Ganz abgesehen von der Zeit, die ich fürs Geschäft verwenden könnte." "Kuhles ganz seltene Stunde" 64.

61. "Doch siehe da: nichts von dem, das sie erwartet hatte, geschah./Kuhle trat lächelnd auf sie zu, umarmte sie väterlich und flüsterte ihr gerührt zu: 'Ich wusste es ja, dass du die Kraft dazu haben würdest. Ich wusste es ja ... Und Sie, Sasso, bitte ich um Verzeihung, daß ich Ihnen misstraut habe. Jawohl, soeben habe ich Ihnen misstraut ...' Er zerriss bei diesen Worten, leidenschaftlich bewegt, den anonymen Brief, den er in der zuckenden Hand hielt. 'O, welch ganz seltene Stunde! Welch erhebende Stunde!' Und er küsste ununterbrochen Marjas Hand und begann zu weinen./Sasso sank verzweifelt auf einen Stuhl./Marja ließ sich angeekelt in die Kissen zurückfallen./Endlich bekam Kuhle Taktgefühl, grüsste menschenfreundlichst und ging, hocherhobenen Hauptes .../Sasso und Marja aber verliessen mit dem Abendschnellzug Lyon, nicht ohne zuvor einen Scheck Kuhles, den Marja für alle Fälle gestohlen hatte, auf eine hohe Summe zu fälschen, um Kuhle jede Möglichkeit zu nehmen, weiterhin Höhenmenschentum zu begehen." "Kuhles ganz seltene Stunde" 65–6.

62. Kyora 64–7.

63. "Als-Ob-Existenz, die von der spielerischen Anwendung des Verhaltenskodexes einer fremden Klasse abhängt" (Bucher, "Ereignis" 91).

64. "Seine Texte stehen den Slapsticks des Stummfilms oder den Grotesken von George Grosz weit näher als den naturalistischen Protokollen von Arno Holz oder Johannes Schlaf" (Bucher, "Ereignis" 92).

65. Definitions of "farce" taken from: Google Dictionary; Dictionary.com; and Merriam Webster.

66. On the ways in which Serner's stories break with the patterns of traditional crime literature, see Hackenbruch 50–1 and Puff-Trojan, *Wien/Berlin/Dada* 246–8.

67. Peters 13.

68. For Serner's biography, see Peters 31–2, Puff-Trojan, *Wien/Berlin/Dada* 12–4, and Christian Schad, *Relative Realitäten*.

69. "Seine Adresse werden Sie nicht in Literaturkalendern, wohl aber bei der Kriminalpolizei erfahren können. Er ist internationaler Hochstapler im allergrößten Stil. In seinen Büchern steht nichts, was nicht gelebt wurde. Sie können dies alles ruhig sagen. Herr Serner pfeift darauf. Er bereist gegenwärtig den Orient als Besitzer großer, öffentlicher Häuser in Argentinien" (Theodor Lessing, "Der Maupassant"). On the Lessing article, see, among others, Puff-Trojan, *Wien/Berlin/Dada* 265.

70. "Bordellnaturen"; "den grauenerregenden Abgrund zwischen dem Menschen und dem Juden" (Rosenberg, "Der internationale Mädchenhandel").

71. "Störend empfinde ich nur, dass man mir kontinuierlich die geschmacklosesten Motive unterschiebt. Ich erkläre deshalb feierlich, dass ich weder Bordellbesitzer bin noch die rechte Hand von Boris Ssawindow, den ich leider nicht persönlich gekannt habe; dass ich den Berlin-N-Jungen liebe, den deutschen Double-Mokka aber als scheussliche Tunke bezeichne; dass ich den Umgang mit Menschen für ein Psycho-Dancing halte und Lichtenbergs Aphorismen sowie Flauberts 'November' für eine gute Vorschule [...], dass mir Politik zum Kotzen ist, der italienische Lazzo aber sympathisch; dass ich zartfühlend bin, faul, neugierig und roh; [...] dass ich weder für Skoda reise noch für den Kaiser der Sahara, sondern zu meinem Vergnügen; und dass ich einen tschechoslowakischen Pass besitze und glücklicher-

weise eine harte Haut." Serner, "Wer ist Walter Serner???" 11612.

72. "Herr Steegemann hat behauptet, in meinen Büchern stünde nichts, das nicht erlebt wäre. Das ist richtig. Hinter jeder Zeile von mir steht Gesehenes oder Gehörtes und gar oft am eigenen Leibe Erfahrenes. Mein Leben aber mit den in meinen Büchern verwendeten Fakten zu identifizieren, ist keineswegs so unabweisbar, wie viele meinen. Es dürfte zwar schwerfallen, einen Autor zu entdecken, der die Verbrecherkreise Europas gründlicher kennt und aufrichtiger geschildert hat als ich, aber ist die Möglichkeit, daß jemand durch diese Kreise hindurchgeht, ohne mehr zu tun als eben hindurchzugehen, denn gar so phantastisch? Es scheint so. Selbst die Kriminalisten, die seit sechs Jahren in allen Ländern Europas mich überwachen lassen, beweisen eben dadurch, daß sie an diese Möglichkeit gleichfalls nicht glauben: wer den Verbrecher und die Arbeit der Polizei so gründlich kennt wie ich, der müßte entweder Verbrecher sein oder ein feindlicher Geheimpolizist. Daß jemand jene Kenntnisse durch bloßes Zuschauen sich aneignen kann, erscheint jedem Kriminalisten indiskutabel. Und dennoch ist es so. Der Umstand, daß ich gänzlich unvorbestraft bin und nichts Handgreifliches gegen mich vorliegt, wäre demnach lediglich der Beweis meiner Verbrecher-Überlegenheit. Das ist schmeichelhaft, aber nicht wahr./Wahr ist vielmehr, daß ich niemals Zuhälter war, niemals internationaler Hochstapler, niemals Mädchenhändler. Es wäre mir ein Leichtes, nachzuweisen, wovon ich bis auf den heutigen Tag gelebt habe. Und es ist geradezu ein tragikomischer Witz, daß die wenigen Irregularitäten meines Lebenslaufes der Zwang verursacht hat, den die Polizei über mich zu verhängen für gut befand." Serner, "Theodor Lessing" 98–9.

73. Letter dated November 18, 1922, printed in Christian Schad, *Relative Realitäten* 87–8, the citation "seul et meilleur ami" 88.

74. "Ich erinnere mich, ihm einmal ohne alle Umschweife die Vertrauensfrage gestellt zu haben. Lächelnd bekam ich eine ausführliche Erklärung, die in den scharf resultierenden Sätzen gipfelte: 'Muß, wer die furchtbarsten Milieus aufsucht und mit den niedrigsten Menschen Umgang hat, dazugehören und mittun? Muß, wer dort das 'offene Tier' findet und die gräßlichste Aufrichtigkeit, darüber empört sein? Muß, wen anderswo die Heuchelei anwidert und die angewachsene Verlogenheit, sich dort nicht wohler fühlen? Muß, wer so ist, sich deshalb dort wohl fühlen?'" Christian Schad, *Relative Realitäten* 7–8.

75. Christian Schad, *Relative Realitäten* 108–9.

76. Bettina Schad 120.

77. Puff-Trojan, "Von Glücksrittern" 75: "Walter Serner, ein luftig-cleverer Hochstapler, der den Holocaust überdauern konnte."

78. First quotation from Noveck, "Hugo Bettauer's assassination" 440; second quotation from Egon Schwarz ("Niemand wird behaupten, das es sich bei diesen und anderen erzählenden Schriften um große künstlerische Leistungen handelt"); third quotation from Hacker 20 ("Aus diesem Grund sind die Bettauer-Romane literarisch betrachtet nicht besonders wertvoll").

79. "Ich muß lange nachdenken, um einen vergleichbaren Autor zu finden: der absichtlich Nichtkunst schreibt, gekonnt, reißerisch, unverschämt aktuell

und zum Drüberstreuen eine Mischung aus progressivem Engagement und zeitloser Geilheit." Günter Nenning is quoted and discussed in Hacker 21 (emphasis added).

80. "Geheimgut des kleinen Intellektuellen-Zirkels"; "wegen des Verrats am Inhalt als an der Form" (133).— "Ja, das war ihres Hasses Grund, deshalb bespieen sie ihn noch nach seinem Tod in Essays und Artikeln! Nichts können die Intellektuellen weniger verzeihen, als zu sehen, daß jemand die Wahrheiten, die sie selbst neben dem Leben und außerhalb der Menge kultivieren, demagogisch unter die Leute bringt! Nichts vergibt der Literat weniger, als seine freieren Gedanken auf der Straße zu sehen. Er spiegelt sich dann vor, nicht die Hinaustragung dieser Gedanken sei es, was ihn erzürnt, sondern der Straßenschmutz, in dem sie kollern—aber er lügt, er meint ja doch immer nur sich./Und das ist dann der Punkt, wo der Halbgeschlechtler dem Nullgeschlechtler, der Literat dem Hakenkreuzler, der Snob dem Mob gefällig die Hand reicht" (Kuh 134).

81. Kuh 134.

82. For a brief assessment of Bettauer's crime novels, see Hacker 18–21.

83. "Vier Mädchen verschwinden, von denen jede einen der banalsten und häufigsten Namen hat, den man sonst nur erfinden könnte. Müller, Möller, Jensen, Pfeiffer! Dergleichen laufen im Deutschen Reiche zu Zehntausenden umher." Bettauer, *Der Frauenmörder*, 15.

84. "Er gehört eben nicht zur Clique und hat nicht das Zeug dazu, sich in Szene zu setzen und Protektoren zu finden." Bettauer, *Frauenmörder* 32.

85. "Krause wurde schwankend, kannte sich nicht aus, Mitleid, Sympathie, Grauen durchströmten ihn. Motiv zur ruchlosen Tat der Auslöschung von fünf Menschenleben? Ehrgeiz, Geltungssucht, Drang zu werden um jeden Preis." Bettauer, *Frauenmörder* 38.

86. "Aber die eigentliche Sensation begann erst. Die wahre Sensation war ja der Roman 'Kämpfende Seelen.' Hatte man denn je erlebt, daß ein waschechter fünffacher Raubmörder einen Roman geschrieben und dieser Roman sogar als Buch erschienen war? Nein, das war noch nie dagewesen" (Bettauer, *Frauenmörder* 41).

87. "Man wird Sie nicht verurteilen, sondern nach Dalldorf bringen und dann nach einem Jahr als geheilt entlassen" (Bettauer, *Frauenmörder* 46).

88. "Man hatte schließlich nicht immer so gute Gelegenheit, genau so zu schreiben, wie man empfand. Bei lebenden Autoren gab es allerlei Rücksichten, Bedenken, persönliche Angelegenheiten, über die man nicht ganz hinwegkam. Aber Hartwig war tot oder d—"h so gut wie tot— — —" Bettauer, *Frauenmörder* 62.

89. "Es ist leicht gesagt: Das Genie bricht sich Bahn! Man kennt eben nur das Genie, das sich Bahn gebrochen hat, nicht aber die vielen, die unterwegs liegen geblieben sind als Opfer oft lächerlicher Widerwärtigkeiten. Hätte ich geduldig weitergearbeitet, so würde mein Roman wahrscheinlich demnächst nur als Käsepapier zur Geltung gekommen sein und mein Drama wäre bei Herrn Direktor Hohlbaum so lange im Schrank liegen geblieben, bis es die Mäuse zernagt hätten. Ich wollte und konnte aber nicht warten und lieber ließ ich ihn durch einen frivolen Schelmenstreich ans Tageslicht zerren, als in aller Bescheidenheit im Dunkel zu verkümmern." Bettauer, *Frauenmörder* 75.

90. "Dröhnendes Gelächter, Schluchzen, Rufe der Entrüstung wurden laut, Leute klatschten Beifall gegen Hartwig zu, andere zischten. Der Staatsanwalt schrie das Wort 'Blasphemie' unaufhörlich vor sich hin, der Präsident brüllte 'Ruhe!,' der Verteidiger stand bleich und fassungslos da und zitterte am ganzen Leib" (Bettauer, *Frauenmörder* 71).

91. The quotation is from the second part of Goethe's drama *Faust*, line numbers 11433–40.

92. Carl Zuckmayer; quotation and discussion in Mews 48.

93. The quotation is taken from the English translation of the tale: Jakob and Wilhelm Grimm, "Rumpelstiltskin," at http://www.eastoftheweb.com/short-stories/UBooks/Rum.shtml (accessed November 22, 2017).

94. Quotation taken from the English translation of the tale: Jakob and Wilhelm Grimm, "The Bremen Town Musicians," at https://germanstories.vcu.edu/grimm/bremer_dual.html (accessed November 22, 2017).

95. "Mensch, hatse jesagt—einmal kneift jeder 'n Arsch zu, du auch, hatse jesagt. Und denn, denn stehste vor Gott dem Vater, stehste, der allens jeweckt hat, vor dem stehste denn, und der fragt dir ins Jesichte: Willem Voigt, wat haste jemacht mit dein Leben? Und da muß ick sagen—Fußmatte, muß ick sagen. Die hab ick jeflochten im Jefängnis, und denn sind se alle druff rumjetrampelt, muß ick sagen. Und zum Schluß haste jeröchelt und jewürcht, um det bißchen Luft, und denn war's aus. Det sagste vor Gott, Mensch. Aber der sagt zu dir: Jeh wech! sagt er! Ausweisung! sagt er! Dafür hab ich dir det Leben nich jeschenkt, sagt er! Det biste mir schuldig! Wo is et? Was haste mit jemacht? *Ganz ruhig* Und denn, Friedrich—und denn is et wieder nischt mit de Aufenthaltserlaubnis." Zuckmayer, *Der Hauptmann von Köpenick* (1997), 101–2. I have not attempted to render Voigt's Berlin accent in my translation.

96. Brief remarks on the film are offered in Kracauer, *From Caligari to Hitler* 229–30.

97. Above all Siegfried Mews, to whose outstanding interpretation of the play my reading is profoundly indebted. For other good interpretations of Zuckmayer's play, see the works by Rosenau, Scheible, and Gehrke.

98. "Na, det weiß doch 'n Kind, daß man bei uns mitn Militär allens machen kann. Det hab ick immer jewußt. [...] Wissense, Herr Direktor, det is weiter nischt, sone Uniform, die macht det meiste janz von alleene" (Zuckmayer, *Hauptmann* [1997], 141).

99. "Meine Herren, das ist die schönste Stunde meiner dreißigjährigen Dienstzeit" (Zuckmayer, *Hauptmann* [1997], 143).

100. "VOIGT *tritt vor den Spiegel, das Portweinglas in der Hand. Er steht mit dem Rücken zum Publikum. Direktor tritt mit den anderen beiseite, beobachtet ihn. Voigt steht zuerst ganz ruhig—dann beginnen seine Schultern zu zucken, ohne daß man einen Laut hört—dann beginnt seine Gestalt zu schüttern und zu wanken, daß der Portwein aus dem Glas schwappt—dann dreht er sich langsam um—lacht—lacht immer mehr, lacht übers ganze Gesicht, mit dem ganzen Körper, aus dem ganzen Wesen—lacht, bis ihm der Atem wegbleibt und die Tränen herunterlaufen. Aus diesem Lachen formt sich ein Wort—erst leise, unverständlich fast—dann immer stärker, deutlicher, endgültiger—schließlich in neuem, großem, befreitem*

und mächtigem Gelächter alles zusammenfassend Unmöglich!!" (Zuckmayer, *Hauptmann* [1997], 143–4, italicization original).

101. This is the interpretation offered by Todd Herzog in *Crime Stories* 101.

102. Mews 51.

103. On *The Muzzle* as a play, see Sabine Brenner, "'Der Maulkorb als Theaterstück"; for other aspects of Spoerl's life and work, see the essays assembled by Joseph A. Kruse.

104. "Das waren keine sehnigen Gestalten mit ehernen Gesichtern und unbestechlicher Sachlichkeit, sondern gutgenährte Leute mit roten Aufschlägen auf blauem Tuch und blitzenden Pickelhauben, Individualitäten, vielleicht auch Originale" (Spoerl 7).

105. "Die Volksseele kochte, hier und allerorten" (Spoerl 6).

106. "Wir sind k-keine Stänker, August, und wir l-lassen uns keinen Maulkorb vorbinden—vorbinden." Spoerl 12.

107. "Oberste Pflicht eines jeden Beamten und einer jeden Behörde ist absolute Sauberkeit. Wird dieser Grundsatz ein einziges Mal, an irgendeiner Stelle durchbrochen, dann wird ein Glaube zerstört, und dann ist es aus mit dem Ansehen und der Autorität der Behörde." (*Der Maulkorb*, dir. Erich Engel, 1938)

108. "Er hauste: schlief, wenn er keine Lust zum Arbeiten hatte, arbeitete, wenn er ausgeschlafen war, und kümmerte sich einen Dreck um die bürgerlichen und astronomischen Tages- und Nachtzeiten; empfing Freunde, wenn es ihm paßte, und schmiß sie wieder hinaus, wenn er sie leid war" (Spoerl 29).

109. "Und von Beruf—das ist ein wenig kompliziert: die Maler halten mich für einen guten Musiker, die Musiker für einen tüchtigen Literaten, und die Literaten für einen ordentlichen Maler. Ich weiß nicht, wer recht hat, ich fürchte, alle drei" (Spoerl 57).

110. "Mit sechs Monaten Haft ist mir nicht gedient. Aber wenn ich aussage, ist der Justiz erst recht nicht gedient" (Spoerl 124).

111. "Jedenfalls habe ich keine Lust, um eines dummen Paragraphen willen einen Menschen unglücklich zu machen und seine Zukunft zu vernichten" (Spoerl 126).

112. "Die Witzblätter. Ich bin eine komische Figur. Der Täter sein eigener Staatsanwalt; der Staatsanwalt sein eigener Täter. So oder so: gehen muß ich, und dann kann ich eine Weinvertretung übernehmen oder Bleistifte verkaufen." The dialogue is taken from Erich Engel's 1938 film, but the scenario is clearly enough implied in Spoerl's novel, where there is talk among Treskow's family members about the possibility that he might have to commit suicide (Spoerl 72).

113. "Vor allen Dingen möchte ich unter allen Umständen vermeiden, daß etwa ein Volksstück daraus gemacht wird. Der Schwerpunkt liegt bei dem Staatsanwalt und dem Konflikt. Wimm und Bätes sind zwei Volkstypen, doch letzten Endes Randfiguren, gewissermaßen zwei Shakespeare-Narren, die quer durch die Handlung laufen und unbewusst ihre vom Schicksal bestimmte Funktion erfüllen." The comment is cited and discussed in Sabine Brenner's "'Der Maulkorb' als Theaterstück" 48.

114. "Notgedrungen wurde mein Vater Rechtsanwalt. Kein guter. Die einen schickte er nach Hause, weil ihre Sache aussichtslos sei. Die anderen, weil er ihre Sache nicht mit Überzeugung vertreten könne. Meine Mutter meinte, er solle auch einmal an die Familie denken und nicht immer an die 'Würde seines Standes.' So wurde mein Vater zwar ehrenwert, aber nicht reich." Alexander Spoerl's comment is cited and discussed in Joseph A. Kruse, *Heinrich Spoerl* 92–3. On Heinrich Spoerl's legal career, see also Wambach.

115. "Spoerl [...] wollte als Rechtsanwalt viel Geld verdienen. Aber das klappte nicht, weil ihm seine spontanen drolligen Einfälle, vor denen er sich nicht retten konnte, das Konzept verdarben. Ich habe seine erste Verteidigungsrede miterlebt. Er wollte einen Spitzbuben freikriegen. Richter, Beisitzer und Publikum bogen sich vor Lachen. Der arme Sünder wurde zwar verknackst, aber zum kleinsten Strafmaß" (cited and discussed in Sabine Brenner, "'Ich bin kein großer Sprecher'" 11).

116. See Alexander Spoerl as cited in Vitz 24 and Wambach 254.

117. Vitz 23–4.

118. "Spoerl war offenbar kein begeisterter Nazi, aber er hat sich im Interesse seines literarischen Erfolgs mehr, als zum Überleben nötig war, mit dem System arrangiert." Vitz 24.

119. See the reviews cited by Sabine Brenner, "'Der Maulkorb' als Theaterstück" 47.

120. "Es geht um menschliche Dinge in diesem Volksstück. Es geht um das tiefe und ursprüngliche Bedürfnis des Volkes, eine Lippe zu riskieren." Review from the *Völkischer Beobachter* cited in Sabine Brenner, "'Der Maulkorb' als Theaterstück" 47.

121. "der humorvolle Menschenkenner Spoerl beschönigt nicht, er rückt nur alles ins rechte Licht und schenkt dem Leser das befreiende Lachen und das nachdenkliche Lächeln über verzeihliche Schwächen" ("Über dieses Buch," dtv-edition, 1st–4th edition, 1965–69).

122. Hunt has compared Gurk to all of these authors as well as some others, including Bertolt Brecht (549–50; 561).

123. Schlösser 5: "schon zu Lebzeiten (1880–1953) zwischen alle Stiltendenzen gefallen, von der schnellfertigen Kritik nicht eingereiht, zum billigen Verbrauch der Nachwelt zur Verfügung gestellt werden konnte." Hunt has come to a similar conclusion (568), adding that Gurk may also have missed out on a major reception because he was too negative (567).

124. There is also not much in the way of a Gurk-reception. For basic biographical information and some scholarly assessments, see Schlösser, Knudsen, Emter, Hunt, and the unpublished doctoral thesis involving Gurk's work by Gleber.

125. "Ich schreibe ausschließlich für mich, unter schauderhaften Umständen, einsam und in einer bis zur Ausschließlichkeit, zum körperlichen Leiden gehenden Menschenscheu. Ich wandere seit Jahren seelisch auf der Landstraße und werde vermutlich auch körperlich auf der Landstraße enden. Das Leben eines wirklichen Schriftstellers mit Sekretärin, Telefon, Landhaus und öffentlicher Menschenliebe liegt mir so außerhalb jeder Vorstellung, daß ich es nicht mehr ertragen könnte. Ich erschrecke vor jedem der sehr seltenen Briefe, die ich noch erhalte, weil ich immer eine Gemeinheit des Lebens wittere... Zuweilen werde ich gefragt, wie meine Arbeiten entstehen. Darauf ist zu sagen: ich habe keine Bücherei und keinen Schreibtisch. Ich schreibe auf den Knien und in großer Schnelligkeit... Aber was ist damit erklärt? Nichts!" Paul Gurk, "Selbstbegegnung," cited in Schlösser 7–8.

126. "Kein Automat gibt etwas heraus, ohne daß vorher ein Groschen eingesteckt wird" (Gurk, *Tresoreinbruch* 75).

127. "Die Brüder arbeiteten nicht mit Messern und Revolvern. Aus Blut entsteht nichts. Viel besser war es, zu gegebener Zeit auszubrechen, wenn es sich nicht vermeiden ließ, die Polizei und das Strafgesetzbuch ein Tor im Fußballspiel ihres Lebens machen zu lassen!" Gurk, *Tresoreinbruch* 77–8.

128. "Keine Förmlichkeiten, lieber Otto! Wir haben uns doch nicht verprügelt oder verpfiffen! Für euch bin ich Schusterkugel und duze mich mit jedem ehrlichen Einbrecher." Gurk, *Tresoreinbruch* 106.

129. "Ihr seid doch eigentlich richtige Bürger und lebt bürgerlich. Ihr hockt zusammen und helft euch. Warum willst du nicht ehrlich sein. Albert, Volk sein, dich in die große Gemeinschaft einreihen?" [...] "Ich *bin* ehrlich! Darum bin ich nicht Volk und nicht Gemeinschaft. Manchmal lese ich Zeitungen. Da steht viel von Gemeinschaft, immer wenn sie sich untereinander prügeln.—Sei du mal ehrlich, Schusterkugel, und denke scharf nach: Hast du schon mal Gemeinschaft gesehen?" Gurk, *Tresoreinbruch* 110.

130. "'Ihr seid aufmontiert wie ein guter, neuer Schrank. Eure Stahlwand ist glatt und fugenlos. Man kann mit Kanteln und mit Knabbern nicht ankommen!'/'Mit Sauerstoffgebläse auch nicht,' lachte Albert Maas auf." Gurk, *Tresoreinbruch* 112.

131. "Ich kenne nicht drei in Deutschland, die diese Arbeit leisten konnten. Den Kopf hat nur Albert Maas!" Gurk, *Tresoreinbruch* 139.

132. "Gesellschaft, Staat und Ordnung schienen ihm ein zertrümmerter Tresor, die Stahlfächer längst beraubt. Er aber stand davor und bewachte mit dem Einsatz seines Lebens zerrissene Sicherungen und leere Fächer!" Gurk, *Tresoreinbruch* 184.

133. "Vielleicht hätte ein Mensch kommen sollen und ihm sagen, daß eine Erneuerung des Mythos geschehen müsse, eine Gemeinschaft aus Verschiedenheit, eine Ordnung aus lebendiger Vornehmlichkeit, und daß er warten und auf die große Wende harren müsse. Aber es war niemand der Art im Präsidium—oder er war gerade beurlaubt.———" Gurk, *Tresoreinbruch* 184–5.

134. The Nazis supposedly outlawed *Tresoreinbruch* because it was too sympathetic to criminals (Hunt 566).

135. Hunt has correctly noted that Gurk's "minor" characters, the other inhabitants of the Maas Brothers' tenement house, are actually central to the novel (558).

136. "Die Aufstellungen der beraubten Bankkunden und ihre Schadenersatzforderungen hatten seltsame Enthüllungen der menschlichen Seele oder des in dieser Zeit üblichen Seelenersatzes zur Folge." Gurk, *Tresoreinbruch* 162.

137. On this figurative terminology in the novel, see also Hunt 564.

138. "Titus Lamm träumte den Traum einer Sehnsucht, einzubrechen in den neunmal verriegelten Tresor der Sprache, sie zu befreien und ein Dichter zu werden..." (Gurk, *Tresoreinbruch* 44).

139. "Sind Sie nicht mehr fähig zum Einbruch in die Frau und spielen darum mit Bällen und Karten?" Gurk, *Tresoreinbruch* 53.

140. "Nun hat die Besessene die Stahltür gespalten und einbrechen können in die verschlossenste Schatzkammer der Welt! Das Atom ist gespalten und hat die Schatzkammer seiner überirdischen Kräfte freigegeben!" Gurk, *Tresoreinbruch* 167.

141. "Einbruch in die Zukunft!" Gurk, *Tresoreinbruch* 156.

142. "Es ist so am besten. Aus Robert wäre doch nichts geworden als ein anständiger Mensch!" Gurk, *Tresoreinbruch* 150.

143. "Ich bin kein Hampelmann, der an der Strippe gezogen wird!" Gurk, *Tresoreinbruch* 111.

144. Hunt has offered a different interpretation of the final passage, particularly its use of the term "myth" (see 565).

145. "warum ist der Mensch hoffnungslos anständig, wenn er doch die Schwindsucht kriegt? [...] Man soll nicht anständig sein. Man soll leben." Gurk, *Tresoreinbruch* 12.

146. Hitler's remark to actor Tony van Eyck is cited and discussed in Hull 20.

147. Hull 7.

148. Citation and discussion in Hull 8; see also the list of non-propaganda films published by Witte 44–8 and the assessment by Leiser 17: "Im Dritten Reich wurden ca. 1150 Spielfilme hergestellt. Davon sind nur rund ein Sechstel direkte politische Propaganda."

149. Culbert 142.

150. Hull 36.

151. Kracauer, *From Caligari to Hitler* 275.

152. See Langenbucher; on this essay, see also Würmann's "Deutsche Kommissare" 228–30 and "Zum Kriminalroman" 170.

153. Among others in Leiser 74 and Hull 157. For interpretations of *Robert und Bertram*, see Schulte-Sasse 235–45, Hollstein, *"Jud Süss"* 48–53, Hull 157–9, O'Brien, *Nazi Cinema* 32–45, Drewniak 308–9, and Courtade and Cadars 181.

154. Schulte-Sasse 242.

155. Schulte-Sasse 237.

156. Hollstein, *"Jud Süss"* 199–203.

157. The applicability of Hitler's statement to the film is discussed in O'Brien, *Nazi Cinema* 41.

158. "Beriehmtes Geschlecht, uralter Adel!" Zerlett, *Robert und Bertram.*

159. Discussed, among others, in Schulte-Sasse 242.

160. "Das Palais muß den Ipelmeyer ein Vermögen gekostet haben."—"Das hat sogar mehrere Vermögen gekostet." Zerlett, *Robert und Bertram.*

161. Robert: "Ja, gibt's denn nun gar keine Ruhe? Wir leben doch schließlich im Jahre 1839." Bertram: "Laß man, mein Junge, in hundert Jahren sieht das alles anders aus." Zerlett, *Robert und Bertram.*

162. On Robert and Bertram's affinity to these characters, see Schulte-Sasse 240 and O'Brien, *Nazi Cinema* 34.

163. See O'Brien, *Nazi Cinema* 35–7.

164. "Du bist nur ein verkommenes Genie und ich bin ein weggelaufener Bourgeois, einer, der lieber ein Strolch sein will als ein Spießer." I am quoting the snippet in O'Brien's translation (*Nazi Cinema* 34).

165. "Siehst Du, Robert, so ist das Leben. Ein Gitter ist überall. Nur, daß die einen durchs Gitter rausschauen und die andern durchs Gitter reinschauen. Ich möchte lieber rausschauen."—Robert: "Na, denn laß Dich doch wieder einsperren" (my translation). The scene is quoted and discussed in O'Brien, *Nazi Cinema* 42.

166. See O'Brien's interpretation of the scene in *Nazi Cinema* 42.

167. On the alternate ending, see O'Brien, *Nazi*

Cinema 43–4 v. Schulte-Sasse 244, Hollstein, *"Jud Süss"* 52–3, and Courtade and Cadars 181.

168. Schulte-Sasse 236.

169. On the parallel portrayals of Jewish criminals and Robert and Bertram in the film, see O'Brien, *Nazi Cinema* 39–42 and Schulte-Sasse 239.

170. Quoted and discussed in O'Brien, *Nazi Cinema* 45; on the studio's advertising strategy, see also 36.

171. For some such reviews, see Hollstein, *"Jud Süss"* 51–2; on the film's supposed "realism," see 48. On reviews of the film, particularly on the film's portrayal of Jewish characters, see also O'Brien, *Nazi Cinema* 44–5 and Drewniak 308–9.

172. Hitler's remark to Goebbels is reported by Alfred Rosenberg: "Im neuen 'Robert und Bertram' sei der Deutsche schlechtgemacht" (cited and discussed in Hollstein, *"Jud Süss"* 52).

173. *"Robert und Bertram* blieb die erste und einzige antisemitische Filmkomödie. Allenfalls bittere Satire war erlaubt, um 'Untermenschen' lächerlich zu machen. Der gefährliche Jude erschien auf der Leinwand, der Unhold, dem erst im letzten Augenblick das Handwerk gelegt wird" (Hollstein, *"Jud Süss"* 53).

174. I have been unable to find any scholarly work on the author, or even his life dates, under either his given name or his pseudonym. Many of his works are still on Germany's register of censored works (see the entries under his name in *Zensierte Schriften in der BRD*).

175. Sebastian Losch's review ("die Vereinigung von politisch-weltanschaulicher Haltung mit spannendem abenteuerlichen Geschehen und der jeweils siegreiche Kampf gegen den jüdischen Weltfeind") is quoted and discussed in Würmann, "Deutsche Kommissare" 233 and Würmann, "Zum Kriminalroman" 170.

176. "Unter einer niedrigen Stirn zwei eng liegende, stechende schwarze Augen, breite Backenknochen" (Coll 8).

177. "Ich hoffe nur, daß die hohen Herren unserer Regierung—nachdem wir ihnen jetzt den Beweis für die verbrecherischen Aktionen der Juden erbringen können—endlich auch ihre Lehren daraus ziehen und mit diesem Gesindel nicht länger paktieren! [...] Unsere Arbeit ist nicht zu Ende, solange von Juda her immer neue verbrecherische Impulse ausgehen" (Coll 178 und 192).

178. "Der Gegner, den er hinter der Mordtat vermutet, ist stark, arbeitet mit den abgefeimtesten Methoden" (Coll 26).

179. "daß der Clown Joco bei seinem Anblick erschrak" (Coll 189).

180. "Er war derartig überrascht und erschrocken, als ich im Lokal auftauchte, daß sein Verhalten ihn verriet" (Coll 187).

181. "Wir haben hier ein Hornissennest ausgenommen, das für unsere Stadt und für unser Land verdammt gefährlich gewesen ist. Aber ich befürchte, daß es nicht viel nützt; denn wenn dieser Hydra ein Kopf abgeschlagen wird, dann werden dafür an anderen Stellen zwei, drei und noch immer neue wachsen" (Coll 177).

Neverending Stories (1950–2001)

1. The sole exceptions I can think of are the occasional Jewish characters in Walter Serner's tales:

Adette in "P.L.M."; Pfeffer in "Pfeffer weiß sich zu helfen" and Stenka in "Der gelbe Terror" (all from *Erotische Kriminalgeschichten*); Brisskij in "Auf schwindelnder Höhe" (from *Der Pfiff um die Ecke*); and Lang in "Im Hotel Fleißig" (from *Die tückische Straße*). Jewish criminals in Serner's tales are in the tiny minority, and yet Serner is the sole crime writer of the time I've been able to identify who seems to make no distinction at all between Jewish and gentile criminals.

2. In this and what follows, I am using the term conceptually, not as denoting a nationality but an (Aryan) self-image that would have applied, to the extent as they self-identified as "Germans" or "Germanic," to Austrians as well.

3. My remarks in this next section pertain exclusively to the Federal Republic of Germany (by which I mean West Germany before unification and unified Germany thereafter) as far as production is concerned, since all films I discuss in this section were made there. I would nevertheless presume an effect of these products beyond the FRG's borders. In other words: the Captain of Köpenick and other lovable heroes of FRG-produced films may well have had their fans in the postwar GDR and Austria as well.

4. The quotation is taken from Joseph von Eichendorff's "Der frohe Wandersmann" (1823), set to music by Robert Schumann: "Wem Gott will rechte Gunst erweisen,/Den schickt er in die weite Welt." I am using the translation by Richard Stokes published at https://www.oxfordlieder.co.uk/song/494 (accessed December 28, 2017).

5. "Ducken! Ducken! So isses in Ordnung!" (Wolffhardt, *Der Hauptmann von Köpenick*, 1960).

6. Original text: "Bis hierher hat mich Gott gebracht/Durch seine große Güte," a hymn in the Lutheran hymnal; text by Ämilie Juliane von Schwarzburg-Rudolfstadt (pre–1685), music by Peter Sohr (1668).

7. "in Deutschland, da ist fester Boden drunter. [...] bei uns ist alles gesund. Von oben und von unten. Und was gesund ist, das ist auch richtig, Wilhelm. Das auf Fels gebaut" (Beyer, *Der Hauptmann von Köpenick*, 1997).

8. "Det is so in janz Deutschland. Weil Ordnung herrscht" (Beyer, *Der Hauptmann von Köpenick*, 1997).

9. Friedrich to Voigt: "Herrgott, Du fährst aufm falschen Gleis, Wilhelm." Voigt: "Du kannst nur so fahren, wie die Gleise liegen" (Beyer, *Der Hauptmann von Köpenick*, 1997).

10. "Was Sie diesmal gemacht haben, ist schlimmer als alles andere. Sie haben sich einen dreisten Eingriff in die militärische Kommandogewalt geleistet. Sie haben die Autorität der Uniform untergraben. Sie haben Schindluder getrieben mit dem Vertrauen in die gottgewollte Rangordnung der Monarchie. Sie haben ewige Werte in den Dreck getreten. Das ist wie Hochverrat, Voigt. Dafür werden Sie wohl streng gerichtet werden" (Beyer, *Der Hauptmann von Köpenick*, 1997).

11. "Was wahr ist, das bestimmen wir! Wenn jeder seinen schmutzigen Schnabel an unserem Allerhöchsten wetzen wollte, das wäre ja Opposition! Undenkbar!" Staudte, *Der Maulkorb* (1958).

12. On the genre of the *Heimatfilm*, see Beindorf, Trimborn, Schacht, Höfig and von Moltke.

13. "Wenn der Bürger nur das Politische liest, bleibt ihm doch die Vierfruchtmarmelade im Halse stecken" (Deppe, *Robert und Bertram*, 1961).

14. "Gesessen. 20 Jahre im Büro. Aber jetzt langt es mir" (Deppe, *Robert und Bertram*, 1961).

15. "Wenn man das sieht, kann man richtig die Wut kriegen. Dafür ist Geld da." Klingler, *Banktresor 713* (1957).

16. "Ich glaube an nichts mehr. Weder an Recht noch an Moral." Klingler, *Banktresor 713* (1957).

17. "Ich kann nicht mehr. Es ist alles aus. [...] Es ist alles verloren."—"Nein, nicht alles. Mich wird er nicht verlieren, egal, was er getan hat." Klingler, *Banktresor 713* (1957).

18. Lars Koch's interpretation of Wolffhardt's film reads the act of breaking into a bank as a metaphor for breaking with Nazi ideology, and the brothers' miserable end as paradigmatic for the fate of those wronged by the Nazi regime (see particularly 154).

19. "Das ist doch das Besondere an den geliebten Brüdern, nicht wahr, daß unsere junge liberale Demokratie heute vor nichts mehr haltmacht! [...] Sondern daß die Gerechtigkeit endlich aus dem dunkeln Hinterzimmer der Justizpaläste an die helle Öffentlichkeit dringt und uns sagt: Ich strafe den Schuldigen, aber ich schütze den Schuldlosen! Und schuldlos ist der, dem man nichts beweisen kann!" Wolffhardt, *Auf Befehl erschossen* (1972).

20. "Schon mal gesehen? [...] Dann werden die Prozesse kürzer."—"Dann ham wer bald gar nischt mehr zu tun." Wolffhardt, *Auf Befehl erschossen* (1972).

21. "Ich will kein Kind von einem, der beim Juden arbeitet." Wolffhardt, *Auf Befehl erschossen* (1972).

22. "Sagen Sie Ihrer Frau, dass sie ein reindeutsches Kind zur Welt bringen wird. Ich habe für mich und meine Familie die Auswanderung beantragt. Ich möchte Ihnen nicht die Hand geben, Bendix. Ihr Kind könnte Ihnen Vorwürfe machen." Wolffhardt, *Auf Befehl erschossen* (1972).

23. "Wer Smutz wegmachen will, muß von Boden anfangen." Wolffhardt, *Auf Befehl erschossen* (1972).

24. "Nur keene Umstände, Herr Kommissar. Machen wir et doch jleich hier."—"Es gibt noch immer Richter in Berlin, Franz." Wolffhardt, *Auf Befehl erschossen* (1972).

25. "Darauf könnense de ganze Verteidijung uffbauen, Herr Bendix. Keen Beweis—Sense! Nich mal Sicherheitsverwahrung springt dabei raus." Wolffhardt, *Auf Befehl erschossen* (1972).

26. "Wir vertrauen dem gesunden deutschen Volksempfinden, seinem Rechtsgewissen, wir wissen, was wir verschuldet haben, aber wir bitten die deutsche Volksgemeinschaft: verstoßt uns nicht auf immer! Nehmt uns eines nicht allzufernen Tages wieder in Eure Reihen auf!" Wolffhardt, *Auf Befehl erschossen* (1972).

27. "Macht doch kurzen Prozeß!" "Hängt ihn doch auf!" "Gleich runter mit der Rübe!" Wolffhardt, *Auf Befehl erschossen* (1972).

28. "Ich hätt sie lieber damals erwischt, 1930. Dann wären sie heut schon wieder draußen." Wolffhardt, *Auf Befehl erschossen* (1972).

29. Lars Koch 166.

30. "Ein Mensch, der keine Hoffnungen mehr hat, hat auch keine Zukunft mehr. Das waren die Aussichten für jeden, der Anfang des 20. Jahrhunderts in Berlin geboren wurde. Ne Kindheit gab's da nicht. Nur Sorgen, Schläge, und Hunger." Rola, *Sass* (2001).

31. "Wir arbeiten wie die Blöden, Tag und Nacht, und was bleibt? Gar nichts. [...] Wir haben keene Chance, egal wieviel wir schuften. [...] Ich hab keene

Lust, 30 Jahre zu warten, um dann mit 55 krank ins Gras zu beißen." Rola, *Sass* (2001).

32. "Wir schieben denen einfach was unter. Wir wissen doch alle, was die aufm Kerbholz haben. Ganz Berlin weiß es!"—"Wenn Sie das machen, zeige ich Sie an." Rola, *Sass* (2001).

33. "Die Geschichte zweier Brüder, die unerbittlich zusammenhalten gegen eine Zeit, gegen Umstände, und die ihr Leben genießen, egal wie. [...] Ich glaub, dass es einfach zwei Proletarier waren [...] das waren die Sass auch. Die hatten auch keine Chance, keine Kohle, wußten nicht, was sie machen können. Und haben sich eben selbst nach vorwärts bewegt, wollten aus ihrem Elend was machen." Carlo Rola in *The Making of Sass*, DVD-supplementary material (DVD version 2002).

34. All interviews with director and cast in *The Making of Sass*, DVD-supplementary material (DVD version 2002).

35. "Die haben gesagt: da haben wir jetzt keine Lust mehr zu, wir lassen uns jetzt nicht mehr verarschen, jetzt müssen wir irgendwie das selber in die Hand nehmen." Ben Becker, interviewed in *The Making of Sass*, DVD-supplementary material (DVD version 2002).

36. All but one under the title *Der Hauptmann von Köpenick*: 1956 (dir. Helmut Käutner); 1960 (dir. Rainer Wolffhardt); 1997 (dir. Frank Beyer); 2001 (dir. Katharina Thalbach); 2005 (Matthias Hartmann), and *The Captain of Nakara*, which sets the Köpenickiade in a fictitious African military dictatorship (dir. Bob Nyanja, 2012).

37. All under the title *Der Maulkorb*: 1958 (Wolfgang Staudte); 1963 (dir. Hans Quest); 1979 (dir. Karl Wesseler); 1997 (dir. Erich Neureuther).

38. Arendt, *Eichmann in Jerusalem* 285. This and all future quotations from the work refer to the English version.

39. Arendt, *Eichmann* 286.

40. Arendt, *Eichmann* 296–7, the quotations 297.

41. See Volkov's remarks on the works of Treitschke and others in *Germans, Jews, and Antisemites* 117–8 and the discussion of her ideas in *Settings*.

42. On the deindividualization of Jews in propaganda, see Katz.

43. Franz Preitler's 2015 novel about Hervay, which offers a positive portrait of her, is, perhaps, the beginning of a new tradition: one in which it is possible to re-individualize the Jewish "criminal" and tell stories about her.

44. Berkowitz, *Crime* 227.

45. "'Place of no meaning,' hat Eisenman den Ort einmal genannt und damit gleich allen Kritikern den Wind aus den Segeln genommen, die befürchtet hatten, hier solle der Holocaust in einem monumentalen symbolischen Grabfeld verbildlicht werden" (Maas).

46. Arendt, *Eichmann* 232.

47. For example in Colette Schmidt's article on an antisemitic political candidate in Austria's Burgenland (September 2017).

48. Arendt, *Eichmann* 233 (emphasis original).

49. Koepnick, *The Dark Mirror* 17.

50. Arendt, *Origins* 35–6, 25, 403 and elsewhere; see the discussion of this idea in "Settings."

51. Volkov, *Germans, Jews, and Antisemites* 110–1; see the discussion of her ideas in *Settings*.

52. At a campaign rally in 1976 (see the article by Black and Sprague).

Filmography

Auf Befehl erschossen—Die Brüder Sass, einst Berlins grosse Ganoven. Dir. Rainer Wolffhardt. TV-film. Ufa Fernsehproduktion GmbH 1972.

Banktresor 713. Dir. Werner Klingler. TV-film. UFA / Berolina 1957.

The Captain of Nakara. Dir. Bob Nyanja. Feature Film. Blue Sky Films 2012.

Der Ewige Jude. Dir. Fritz Hippler. Feature Film. DFG 1940.

Der Hauptmann von Köpenick. Dir. Richard Oswald. Feature Film. Roto Film / G.P. Film 1931.

Der Hauptmann von Köpenick. Dir. Helmut Käutner. Feature Film. Real-Film 1956.

Der Hauptmann von Köpenick. Dir. Rainer Wolffhardt. TV-film. Süddeutscher Rundfunk 1960.

Der Hauptmann von Köpenick. Dir. Frank Beyer. TV-film. Hannover Film 1997.

Der Hauptmann von Köpenick. Dir. Matthias Hartmann. TV-film. Westdeutscher Rundfunk 2005.

Der Hauptmann von Köpenick. Dir. Katharina Thalbach. TV-film. Zweites Deutsches Fernsehen 2001.

Jud Süss. Dir. Veit Harlan. Feature Film. Terra Filmkunst 1940.

M: Eine Stadt sucht einen Mörder. Dir. Fritz Lang. Feature Film. Nero-Film AG 1931.

Der Maulkorb. Dir. Erich Engel. Feature Film. Tobis Filmkunst 1938.

Der Maulkorb. Dir. Wolfgang Staudte. Feature Film. Kurt Ulrich Filmproduktion 1958.

Der Maulkorb. Dir. Hans Quest. TV-film. Westdeutscher Rundfunk 1963.

Der Maulkorb. Dir. Karl Wesseler. TV-film. Westdeutscher Rundfunk 1979.

Der Maulkorb. Dir. Erich Neureuther. TV-film. Bayrischer Rundfunk 1997.

Robert und Bertram. Dir. Hans Heinz Zerlett. Feature Film. Tobis Filmkunst 1939.

Robert und Bertram. Dir. Hans Deppe. Feature Film. Pidax Film 1961.

Sass. Dir. Carlo Rola. Feature Film. Constantin Film 2001.

Bibliography

Archival Sources

Goebbels, Joseph. *Michael Voormann. Ein Menschenschicksal in Tagebuchblättern.* 1923 (typed MS). Bundesarchiv Koblenz, NL 118/127.

Goebbels, Joseph. *Michael Voormann's Jugendjahre. I. Teil.* 1919 (handwritten MS). Bundesarchiv Koblenz, NL 118/126.

Goebbels, Joseph. *Michael Voormann's Jugendjahre. III. Teil.* 1919 (handwritten MS). Bundesarchiv Koblenz, NL 118/116.

Hans-Hyan-Archiv. Akademie der Künste, Berlin. Catalogue at https://archiv.adk.de/bigobjekt/ 9135

Olden, Rudolf. "Abschied von Hugo Bettauer." Typescript from March 31, 1925, 7 pp. In "Konvolut von diversen Zeitungsbeiträgen." 31.3.1925–22.12.1925. Teilnachlass Rudolf Olden. Deutsche Nationalbibliothek Frankfurt: Deutsches Exilarchiv. Document no. EB 79/020-A.02.01.0001.

Olden, Rudolf. "Konvolut von diversen Zeitungsbeiträgen." 31.3.1925–22.12.1925. Teilnachlass Rudolf Olden. Deutsche Nationalbibliothek Frankfurt: Deutsches Exilarchiv. Document no. EB 79/020-A.02.01.0001.

Olden, Rudolf. "Materialien zum 'Fall Bettauer.'" 1924–25. Teilnachlass Rudolf Olden. Deutsche Nationalbibliothek Frankfurt: Deutsches Exilarchiv. Document no. EB 79/020-D.01.0002.

Olden, Rudolf. "Olden Papers." Uncatalogued letters, notes, correspondence, articles, research and typescripts of book drafts, 1927–1940. UCL Special Collections, MS ADD 276/1 and MS ADD 276/2.

"Strafsache gegen Hugo Bettauer und Rudolf Olden." Landesgericht für Strafsachen Wien I: Vr XXXI 1776/24.

"Strafsache gegen Otto Rothstock." Landesgericht für Strafsachen Wien I: Vr XXVII 1748/25.

"Zur Ermittlungssache gegen die Gebrüder Franz und Erich Sass." Berliner Landesarchiv: A Rep. 358–01 Nr. 2746 (Filmnummern B 390–B 392) (18 bound volumes of court files) and F Rep. 290–02-06 Nr. 49 (9 photographs).

Contemporary Newspapers, with Date Ranges Consulted

Arbeiter-Zeitung: Zentralorgan der Sozialdemokratie Deutschösterreichs (Workers' News: Central Organ of the Social Democratic Party in German Austria). November 1904–March 1906; April 1924–October 1933.

Arbeiterwille: Organ des arbeitenden Volkes für Steiermark und Kärnten (Workers' Will: Organ of Working People for Styria and Kärnten); Austria. January 1907; September 1924–January 1928.

Badener Zeitung: Demokratisches Organ für den Bezirk Baden (Baden News: Democratic Organ for the District of Baden); Germany. March-April 1925.

Berliner Börsen-Zeitung (Berlin Stockmarket News): October–December 1906; March 1927–January 1930.

Berliner Tageblatt und Handels-Zeitung (Berlin Daily and Trade News): October-November 1906.

Berliner Tages-Zeitung (Berlin Daily News): December 1927–May 1928.

Berliner Volks-Zeitung (Berlin People's News): October–December 1906; March 1927–September 1930.

Christlich-soziale Arbeiterzeitung: Zentralorgan der christlichsozialen Arbeiterpartei Österreichs (Christian-Social Workers' News: Central Organ of the Christian Social Workers' Party of Austria). March 1924–March 1927.

Cöpenicker Dampfboot (The Cöpenick Steamboat); Germany. November 1906.

Czernowitzer Allgemeine Zeitung (Czernowitz General News); Silesia, East Germany. January 1908.

Deutsche Arbeiter-Presse (German Worker's Press); Austria. October 1924.

Deutsches Nordmährerblatt (German Newspaper for Northern Moravia); Austria. November 1904.

Deutsches Volksblatt: Tageszeitung für christliche deutsche Politik (German People's News: Daily for Christian and German Politics); Austria. October 1904–January 1907.

"Das Eindrucksvolle!" Faschingsblatt des *Grobian* ("Impressive!" Carnival-Paper of *The Brute)* Austria. February 1925.

Fehrbelliner Zeitung (Fehrbellin News); Germany. February 1929.

Feldkircher Zeitung: Stimme der Verfassungsfreunde in Vorarlberg (Feldkirch News: Voice of Friends of the Constitution in Vorarlberg); Austria. June 1904.

Figaro: Humoristisches Wochenblatt (Figaro: Humorous Weekly); Austria. November 1906.

Der Floh (The Flea); Austria. October 1904.

Freiheit! (Freedom!); Austria. August 1928.

Grazer Tagblatt: Organ der Deutschen Volkspartei für die Alpenländer (Graz Daily: Organ of the German People's Party for the Alpine Lands); Austria. September 1906–February 1909.

Grazer Volksblatt (Graz People's News); Austria. June 1904–January 1907.

Hamburger Neueste Zeitung (Hamburg Latest News). January 1940.

Der Hammer: Zeitschrift zur Bekämpfung der Sozialdemokratie (The Hammer: Magazine for the Struggle Against Social Democracy); Austria. April–October 1925.

Illustrierte Kronen-Zeitung (Illustrated Crown News). September 1924.

Illustriertes Wiener Extrablatt (Illustrated Viennese Extra News). March 1925.

Innsbrucker Nachrichten: Unabhängiges Tagblatt für Tirol und Vorarlberg (Innsbruck News: Independent Daily for Tyrol and Vorarlberg); Austria. March 1906–January 1907.

Das interessante Blatt (The Interesting Paper); Austria. June–November 1904; March-April 1925.

Kikeriki: Humoristisches Volksblatt (Cock-a-doodle-doo: Humorous People's Paper); Austria. November 1904–January 1907; July 1924–May 1933.

Das kleine Blatt (The Little Paper); Austria. May 1927–November 1929.

Lähner Anzeiger (Lähn Gazette); Germany. December 1906.

Linzer Tagespost (Linz Daily); Austria. January–March 1906.

Linzer Volksblatt: Für Stadt und Land (Linz People's Paper: For Town and Country); Austria. January 1908; January-February 1933.

Mährisch-Schlesische Presse: Unabhängige politische Zeitung für die gesammten Interessen von Stadt und Land (Moravian-Silesian Press: Independent Political Newspaper for All Interests of Town and Country); Germany. June–November 1904.

Mährisches Tagblatt (Moravian Daily); Austria. June 1904–July 1905.

Marburger Zeitung (Marburg News); Germany. August 1906.

Montags-Revue aus Böhmen: Wochenschrift für Politik, Volkswirtschaft, Kunst und Literatur (Monday's Review from Bohemia: Weekly for Politics, Economy, Art and Literature); Germany. July–October 1904.

Mürzzuschlager Wochenblatt (Mürzzuschlag Weekly). April 1904.

Die Muskete: Humoristische Wochenschrift (The Musket: Humorous Weekly); Austria. April 1929.

Neue Freie Presse (New Free Press); Austria. October 1904–January 1907.

Neue Schlesische Zeitung (New Silesian Newspaper); Germany. October 1906–January 1908.

Neues Wiener Journal: Unparteiisches Tagblatt (New Viennese Journal: A Nonpartisan Daily). March 1906–July 1909.

Neues Wiener Tagblatt: Zeitung für Unterhaltung und Wissen (New Viennese Daily: Newspaper for Entertainment and Knowledge). June 1904–November 1906.

Neuigkeits-Welt-Blatt (News of the World); Austria. March 1906–February 1909; May 1933.

Niederösterreichischer Grenzbote (Border Messenger from Lower Austria). June 1924–November 1925.

Österreichische Buchhändler-Correspondenz (Correspondence of Austrian Booksellers). July 1905–January 1906.

Österreichische Kronen-Zeitung (Austrian Crown News). January 1905–January 1907.

Österreichische Land-Zeitung (Austrian Country News). March–December 1906.

Pester Lloyd (Budapest Lloyd); Austria/Hungary. January 1907–June 1909.

Prager Tagblatt (Prague Daily News); Czechoslovakia/Bohemia. March 1906–January 1907; June 1924–July 1927.

Reichspost: Unabhängiges Tagblatt für das christliche Volk (Reichspost: Independent Daily for the Christian People); Austria. November 1904–January 1907; March 1924–May 1933.

Die Rote Fahne: Zentralorgan der Kommunistischen Partei Österreichs (The Red Flag: Central Organ of the Communist Party of Austria). October 1923–May 1933.

Salzburger Chronik (Salzburg Chronicle); Austria. June 1904.

Salzburger Volksblatt: Unabhängige Tageszeitung für Stadt und Land Salzburg (Salzburg People's Paper: Independent Daily for the Town and County of Salzburg); Austria. January–November 1906; October 1921.

Salzburger Wacht (Salzburg Watch); Austria. September 1924.

Die Stunde (The Hour); Austria. March 1925.

Der Tag (The Day); Austria. September 1924–October 1925.

Tagblatt: Organ für die Interessen des werktätigen Volkes (Daily News: Organ for the Interests of Working People); Austria. September 1924–January 1928.

Tages-Post (Daily Post); Austria. September 1924–May 1933.

Triestingtaler Wochenblatt (Triesting Valley Weekly); Austria. March–October 1925.

Die Unzufriedene: Eine unabhängige Wochenschrift für alle Frauen (The Discontented Woman: An Independent Weekly for All Women); Austria. March 1925–June 1927.

Volksblatt für Stadt und Land (People's News for Town and Country); Austria. March–October 1925.

Volksbote: Sozialdemokratisches Organ für die Interessen des arbeitenden Volkes (People's Messenger: Social Democratic Organ for the Interests of Working People); Austria. June-July 1928.

Volksfreund: Unabhängiges Wochenblatt für alle Stände (People's Friend: Independent Weekly for All Classes); Austria. May 1925.

Volkspost (People's Post); Austria. January 1928.

Vorarlberger Landeszeitung: Organ für amtliche Kundmachungen (Vorarlberg County News: Organ for Official Notices); Austria. March 1925–January 1928.

Vorarlberger Tagblatt (Vorarlberg Daily News); Austria. May 1925–January 1928.

Vorarlberger Volksblatt (Vorarlberg People's News); Austria. April 1925–January 1928.

Vorarlberger Volksfreund (Vorarlberg People's Friend); Austria. July 1904.

Vorarlberger Wacht: Sozialdemokratisches Organ für das arbeitende Volk (Vorarlberg Watch: Social Democratic Organ for Working People); Austria. September 1924–September 1930.

Vossische Zeitung (Voss's Newspaper); Germany. April 1929–December 1931.

Der Welt-Spiegel (World Mirror): Germany. November 1906.

Wiener Montags-Journal: Unparteiische Zeitung (Viennese Monday Journal: A Non-Partisan Paper). January-February 1906.

Wiener Neueste Nachrichten (Viennese Latest News). August 1924–October 1925.

Wiener Sonn- und Montagszeitung (Viennese Sunday and Monday Paper). March–November 1925.

Wiener Zeitung: Österreichisch-kaiserliche Wiener Zeitung (Viennese News: Austrian-Imperial Viennese Newspaper). March 1924–January 1928.

Ybbstal-Zeitung: Wochenblatt for Niederösterreich (Ybbs Valley News: Weekly for Lower Austria). August 1924–May 1934.

Primary and Secondary Literature

Achinger, Christine. "Allegories of Destruction: 'Woman' and 'the Jew' in Otto Weininger's Sex and Character." *The Germanic Review: Literature, Culture, Theory* 88/2 (2013): 121–49.

Achinger, Christine. "Antisemitismus und 'Deutsche Arbeit': Zur Selbstzerstörung des Liberalismus bei Gustav Freytag." *Kapitalismusdebatten um 1900: Über antisemitisierende Semantiken des Jüdischen.* Ed. Nicolas Berg. Leipzig: Leipziger Universitätsverlag, 2011. 361–88.

Achinger, Christine. *Gespaltene Moderne: Gustav Freytags Soll und Haben—Nation, Geschlecht und Judenbild.* Würzburg: Königshausen & Neumann, 2007.

Achinger, Christine. "Threats to Modernity, Threats of Modernity: Racism and antisemitism through the lens of literature." *European Societies* 14/2 (2012): 240–58.

Adorno, Theodor W. *Gesammelte Schriften.* 23 vols. Frankfurt/M: Suhrkamp, 2003.

Adorno, Theodor W. *Prisms.* Cambridge, Mass: MIT Press, 1955.

Alexander-Katz, Richard. "Der falsche Hauptmann." *Berliner Tageblatt und Handels-Zeitung* (October 21, 1906): 2. Beiblatt, 1–2.

Almog, Shmuel. "What's in a Hyphen?" (orig. 1989). http://sicsa.huji.ac.il/hyphen.htm (accessed June 18, 2016).

Alt, Peter-André. *Ästhetik des Bösen.* Munich: Beck, 2010.

Althoff, Martina, Helga Cremer-Schäfer, Gabriele Löschper, Herbert Reinke and Gerlinda Smaus, eds. *Integration und Ausschließung: Kriminalität und Kriminalpolitik in Zeiten gesellschaftlicher Transformation.* Baden-Baden: Nomos, 2001.

Anselm, Sigrun. "Angst und Angstprojektionen in der Phantasie vom jüdischen Ritualmord." *Die Legende vom Ritualmord: Zur Geschichte der Blutbeschuldigung gegen Juden.* Ed. Rainer Erb. Berlin: Metropol, 1993. 253–65.

Antonow, Iwan. *Die Kriminalbiologie im Dienste der Verbrechensbekämpfung und -verhütung in Deutschland.* Sofia: Rosowa Dolina, 1938.

Archetti, Cristina. "(Mis)Communication Wars: Terrorism, Counter-terrorism and the Media." *Propaganda, Power and Persuasion: From World War I to Wikileaks.* Ed. David Welch. London: I.B. Tauris, 2014. 209–24.

Arendt, Hannah. *Eichmann in Jerusalem: A Report on the Banality of Evil.* London: Penguin, 2006.

Arendt, Hannah. *Eichmann in Jerusalem: Ein Bericht von der Banalität des Bösen.* 3rd ed. Munich: Piper, 2012.

Arendt, Hannah. *The Origins of Totalitarianism.* Oxford: Benediction Classics, 2009.

Arkel, Dirk van. *Antisemitism in Austria.* Leiden: n. p., 1966.

Arnold, Dietmar, and Ingmar Arnold. *Dunkle Welten: Bunker, Tunnel und Gewölbe unter Berlin.* 9th ed. Berlin: Ch. Links, 2010.

Aschaffenburg, Gustav. *Das Verbrechen und seine Bekämpfung: Kriminalpsychologie für*

Mediziner, Juristen und Soziologen. Ein Beitrag zur Reform der Strafgesetzgebung. Heidelberg: Carl Winter, 1903.

Aschaffenburg, Gustav. "Zur Psychologie des Hochstaplers." *März: Halbmonatsschrift für deutsche Kultur* 1 (1907): 544–50.

Asmus, Sylvia, and Brita Eckert. "Rudolf Olden— Eine Biografie in Dokumenten und Bildern." *Rudolf Olden: Journalist gegen Hitler—Anwalt der Republik. Eine Ausstellung des Deutschen Exilarchivs 1933–1945 der Deutschen Nationalbibliothek Frankfurt am Main, 26. März–28. Juli 2010.* Ed. Sylvia Asmus and Brita Eckert. Frankfurt/M.: Deutsche Nationalbibliothek, 2010. 11–80.

Asmus, Sylvia, and Brita Eckert, eds. *Rudolf Olden: Journalist gegen Hitler—Anwalt der Republik. Eine Ausstellung des Deutschen Exilarchivs 1933–1945 der Deutschen Nationalbibliothek Frankfurt am Main, 26. März–28. Juli 2010.* Frankfurt/M.: Deutsche Nationalbibliothek, 2010.

Aspetsberger, Friedbert. "'Innere Filme,' Licht- und Schattenspiele angesichts des Berges: Ungefähr ein Vorwort." *Der Bergfilm 1920–1940.* Ed. Friedbert Aspetsberger. Innsbruck: StudienVerlag, 2002. 7–17.

Aspetsberger, Friedbert, ed. *Der Bergfilm 1920–1940.* Innsbruck: StudienVerlag, 2002.

Autry, Curt. "Sniper's ex-wife speaks about motive: Key evidence revealed." *90 WAFB* (aired 2009). http://www.wafb.com/story/11474236/snipers-ex-wife-speaks-about-motive-key-evidence-revealed (accessed June 8, 2016).

Backes-Haase, Alfons. *"Über topographische Anatomie, psychischen Luftwechsel und Verwandtes." Walter Serner—Autor der 'Letzten Lockerung.'* Bielefeld: Aisthesis, 1989.

Bade, Wilfrid. *Joseph Goebbels.* Lübeck: Coleman, 1933.

Baer, Adolf. *Der Verbrecher in anthropologischer Beziehung.* Leipzig: G. Thieme, 1893.

Baeyer, Walter von. *Zur Genealogie psychopathischer Schwindler und Lügner.* Leipzig: Georg Thieme, 1935.

Bahn, Walter. *Wilhelm Voigt, der Hauptmann von Köpenick. Meine Klienten: Beitr. zur modernen Inquisition.* 4th ed. Berlin and Leipzig: n.d.

Bahr, Hermann. *Der Antisemitismus. Ein internationales Interview.* Berlin: S. Fischer, 1894.

Bahr, Hermann. "Das deutsche Wesen ist uns erschienen: Die führenden Männer und Frauen zum Weltkrieg 1914/15." *Das Eiserne Buch.* Ed. Georg Gellert. Hamburg: Gebrüder Enoch, 1915. 73–6.

Bahr, Hermann. *Die Hexe Drut.* Berlin: Sieben Stäbe, 1929.

Bahr, Hermann. "Die Juden in Österreich." *Neues Wiener Journal* (February 21, 1911): 1–3.

Bahr, Hermann. "Zionismus." *Neue Freie Presse* (August 22, 1925): 1–2.

Bald, Detlef. "Zum Kriegsbild der militärischen Führung im Kaiserreich." *Bereit zum Krieg: Kriegsmentalität im wilhelminischen Deutschland, 1890–1914.* Ed. Jost Dülffer and Karl Holl. Göttingen: Vandenhoeck & Ruprecht, 1986. 146–60.

Balke, Florian. "Rudolf Olden: Der Mann, der Hitler früh durchschaute." *Frankfurter Allgemeine Zeitung* (May 4, 2010). http://www.faz.net/aktuell/rhein-main/kultur/rudolf-olden-der-mann-der-hitler-frueh-durchschaute-1984830.html (accessed June 21, 2017).

"Die Balkonreden Wilhelms II." *Frankfurter Rundschau* (July 22, 2004). http://www.fr-online.de/zeitgeschichte/im-wortlaut-die-balkonreden-wilhelms-ii-,1477344,2738694.html (accessed June 16, 2016).

Barbian, Jan-Pieter. *Literaturpolitik im "Dritten Reich." Institutionen, Kompetenzen, Betätigungsfelder.* Munich: Deutscher Taschenbuch Verlag, 1995.

Bärsch, Claus-Ekkehard. *Erlösung und Vernichtung. Dr. phil. Joseph Goebbels. Zur Psyche und Ideologie eines jungen Nationalsozialisten 1923–1927.* Munich: Boer, 1987.

Bärsch, Claus-Ekkehard. "Das Katastrophenbewußtsein eines werdenden Nationalsozialisten: Der Antisemitismus im Tagebuch des Joseph Goebbels vor dem Eintritt in die NSDAP." *Menora: Jahrbuch für deutsch-jüdische Geschichte.* Munich: Piper, 1990. 125–51.

Bateson, Gregory. "An Analysis of the Nazi Film *Hitlerjunge Quex." The Study of Culture at a Distance.* Ed. Margaret Mead and Rhoda Métraux. New York: Berghahn Books, 2000. 331–47.

Bathrick, David. "Introduction: Modernity Writ German: State of the Art as Art of the Nazi State." *Cultural History through a National Socialist Lens: Essays on the Cinema of the Third Reich.* Ed. Robert C. Reimer. Rochester: Camden House, 2000. 1–10.

Baumann, Imanuel. *Dem Verbrechen auf der Spur: Eine Geschichte der Kriminologie und Kriminalpolitik in Deutschland 1880 bis 1980.* Göttingen: Wallstein, 2006.

Baumeister, Martin. "Kampf ohne Front? Theatralische Kriegsdarstellungen in der Weimarer Republik." *Ordnungen in der Krise: Zur politischen Kulturgeschichte Deutschlands 1900–1933.* Ed. Wolfgang Hardtwig. Munich: Oldenbourg, 2007. 357–76.

Bäumer, Gertrud. "Frieda von Bülow." *Die Frau: Monatsschrift für das gesamte Frauenleben unserer Zeit* 16/7 (April 1909): 407–12.

Becker, Frank. *Bilder von Krieg und Nation: Die Einigungskriege in der bürgerlichen Öffentlichkeit Deutschlands, 1864–1913.* Munich: Oldenbourg, 2001.

Becker, Peter. "The Criminologists' Gaze at the Underworld: Toward an Archaeology of Criminological Writing." *Criminals and Their Scientists: The History of Criminology in International Perspective.* Ed. Peter Becker and Richard F. Wetzell. Cambridge: Cambridge University Press, 2006. 105–33.

Becker, Peter. *Verderbnis und Entartung: Eine Geschichte der Kriminologie des 19. Jahrhunderts als Diskurs und Praxis.* Göttingen: Vandenhoeck & Ruprecht, 2002.

Becker, Peter, and Richard Wetzell, eds. *Criminals and Their Scientists: The History of Criminology in International Perspective.* Cambridge: Cambridge University Press, 2006.

Behrenbeck, Sabine. "Heldenkult und Opfermythos: Mechanismen der Kriegsbegeisterung 1918–1945." *Kriegsbegeisterung und mentale Kriegsvorbereitung: Interdisziplinäre Studien.* Ed. Marcel van der Linden and Gottfried Mergner. Berlin: Duncker & Humblot, 1991. 143–59.

Beindorf, Claudia. *Terror des Idylls: Die kulturelle Konstruktion von Gemeinschaften in Heimatfilm und Landsbygdsfilm 1930–1960.* Baden-Baden: Nomos, 2001.

Beller, Steven. *Vienna and the Jews 1867–1938. A Cultural History.* Cambridge: Cambridge University Press, 1989.

"Beltway Sniper Attacks." https://en.wikipedia.org/wiki/Beltway_sniper_attacks (accessed June 8, 2016).

Benjamin, Walter. "Brecht's *Threepenny Novel.*" *Reflections.* Ed. Peter Demetz. New York: Schocken Books, 1986. 193–202.

Berg, Alexander. *Juden-Bordelle: Enthüllungen aus dunklen Häusern.* Berlin: Paul Heichen, 1892.

Berg, Friedrich. "Die Ermordung Hugo Bettauers." *Die weiße Pest.* Vienna: Münster, 1926. 58–69.

Bergen, Peter. "September 11 attacks." *Encyclopaedia Britannica.* http://www.britannica.com/event/September-11-attacks (accessed June 8, 2016).

Bergengruen, Maximilian, Gideon Haut and Stephanie Langer, eds. *Tötungsarten und Ermittlungspraktiken: Zum literarischen und kriminalistischen Wissen von Mord und Detektion.* Freiburg i. Br.: Rombach, 2015.

Berghahn, Volker R. "War Preparations and National Identity in Imperial Germany." *Anticipating Total War: The German and American Experiences, 1871–1914.* Ed. Manfred F. Boemeke, Roger Chickering and Stig Förster. Cambridge: Cambridge University Press, 1999. 307–26.

Bergmann, Siegmund. "Journalisten als Banditen." *Wiener Montags-Journal* (January 29, 1906): 3–4.

Bergmann, Werner. *Geschichte des Antisemitismus.* Munich: C.H. Beck, 2002.

Bergmann, Werner. "Ein 'weltgeschichtliches "Fatum"': Wilhelm Marrs antisemitisches Geschichtsbild in seiner Schrift: 'Der Sieg des Judenthums über das Germanenthum.'" *Antisemitische Geschichtsbilder.* Ed. Werner Bergmann and Ulrich Sieg. Essen: Klartext, 2009. 61–82.

Bergmann, Werner, and Ulrich Sieg. "Geschichte als Akklamationsinstanz und Waffe." *Antisemitische Geschichtsbilder.* Ed. Werner Bergmann and Ulrich Sieg. Essen: Klartext, 2009. 7–22.

Bergmann, Werner, and Ulrich Sieg, eds. *Antisemitische Geschichtsbilder.* Essen: Klartext, 2009.

Berkowitz, Michael. *The Crime of My Very Existence: Nazism and the Myth of Jewish Criminality.* Berkeley: University of California Press, 2007.

Berkowitz, Michael. "Unmasking Counterhistory: An Introductory Exploration of Criminality and the Jewish Question." *Criminals and Their Scientists: The History of Criminology in International Perspective.* Ed. Peter Becker and Richard F. Wetzell. Cambridge: Cambridge University Press, 2006. 61–84.

Berthold, Werner. "Rudolf Oldens Hindenburg- und Hitler-Biografien." *Rudolf Olden: Journalist gegen Hitler—Anwalt der Republik. Eine Ausstellung des Deutschen Exilarchivs 1933–1945 der Deutschen Nationalbibliothek Frankfurt am Main, 26. März–28. Juli 2010.* Ed. Sylvia Asmus and Brita Eckert. Frankfurt/M.: Deutsche Nationalbibliothek, 2010. 127–38.

Bessel, Richard. "Kriegserfahrungen und Kriegserinnerungen: Nachwirkungen des Ersten Weltkrieges auf das politische und soziale Leben der Weimarer Republik." *Kriegsbegeisterung und mentale Kriegsvorbereitung: Interdisziplinäre Studien.* Ed. Marcel van der Linden and Gottfried Mergner. Berlin: Duncker & Humblot, 1991. 125–40.

Bettauer, Hugo. *The Blue Stain: A Novel of a Racial Outcast.* Ed. Peter Höyng, trans. Peter Höyng and Chauncey J. Mellor. Rochester, NY: Camden House, 2017.

Bettauer, Hugo. *The City Without Jews: A Novel of Our Time.* Trans. Salomea Neumark Brainin. New York: Bloch, 1926.

Bettauer, Hugo. *Das entfesselte Wien: Ein Roman von heute.* Vienna: R. Löwit, 1924.

Bettauer, Hugo. "Die erotische Revolution." *Er und Sie: Wochenschrift für Lebenskultur und Erotik* 1 (1924): 1–2.

Bettauer, Hugo. *Faustrecht. Roman.* Vienna: Strache, 1920.

Bettauer, Hugo. *Der Frauenmörder: Ein Kriminalroman aus Berlin.* 2nd ed. Berlin: Hofenberg, 2016.

Bettauer, Hugo. *Die freudlose Gasse: Ein Wiener Roman aus unseren Tagen.* Frankfurt/M.: Ullstein, 1988.

Bettauer, Hugo. *Gesammelte Werke*. 6 vols. Salzburg: Hannibal, 1980.

Bettauer, Hugo. *Hemmungslos. Roman*. Frankfurt/M.: Ullstein, 1988.

Bettauer, Hugo. *Der Herr auf der Galgenleiter: Roman und 7 Geschichten aus dem Alltag*. Vienna: Milena, 2014.

Bettauer, Hugo. "Ich bin freigesprochen." *Bettauers Wochenschrift: Probleme des Lebens* 20 (1924): 1.

Bettauer, Hugo. *Der Kampf um Wien: Ein Roman vom Tage*. Salzburg: Hannibal, 1980.

Bettauer, Hugo. "Ein neuer Anschlag." *Bettauers Wochenschrift: Probleme des Lebens* 33 (1924): 1.

Bettauer, Hugo. *Die Stadt ohne Juden: Ein Roman von Übermorgen*. Frankfurt: Ullstein, 1988 [orig. 1922].

Bettauer, Hugo, and Rudolf Olden, eds. *Er und Sie: Wochenschrift für Lebenskultur und Erotik*. Vienna: 1924 (5 issues).

Beyer, Frank (dir.). *Der Hauptmann von Köpenick*. TV-film. Hannover Film 1997.

Biale, David. *Blood and Belief: The Circulation of a Symbol Between Jews and Christians*. Berkeley: University of California Press, 2007.

Binding, Karl, and Alfred Hoche. *Die Freigabe der Vernichtung lebensunwerten Lebens: Ihr Mass und ihre Form*. Leipzig: Meiner, 1920.

Binkowski, Lorenz. *Betrogene Betrüger*. Limburg: Lahn, 1962.

Birgel, Franz A. "Luis Trenker: A Rebel in the Third Reich? *Der Rebell, Der verlorene Sohn*, and *Der Kaiser von Kalifornien, Condottieri*, and *Der Feuerteufel*." *Cultural History through a National Socialist Lens: Essays on the Cinema of the Third Reich*. Ed. Robert C. Reimer. Rochester: Camden House, 2000. 37–64.

Black, Rachel, and Aleta Sprague. "The 'Welfare Queen' Is a Lie." *The Atlantic* September 28, 2016. https://www.theatlantic.com/business/archive/2016/09/welfare-queen-myth/501470/ (accessed January 7, 2018).

Blair, John G. *The Confidence Man in Modern Fiction: A Rogue's Gallery with Six Portraits*. London: Vision Press, 1979.

Bleuler, Eugen. *Der geborene Verbrecher: Eine kritische Studie*. Munich: J.F. Lehmann, 1896.

Blook, Paul. "Der Hauptmann von Köpenick." *Berliner Tageblatt* (October 17, 1906): Abendausgabe 1.

Bock, Gisela. *Zwangssterilisation im Nationalsozialismus*. Opladen: Westdeutscher Verlag, 1986.

Bockelmann, Paul. *Das Problem der Kriminalstrafe in der deutschen Dichtung*. Karlsruhe: Müller, 1967.

Boemeke, Manfred F., Roger Chickering and Stig Förster, eds. *Anticipating Total War: The German and American Experiences, 1871–1914*. Cambridge: Cambridge University Press, 1999.

Boileau-Narcejac. *Der Detektivroman*. Trans. Wolfgang Promies. Neuwied and Berlin: Luchterhand, 1968.

Boldorf, Marcel. "Die Erfindung des Bankraubs—von den schwierigen Anfängen bis zur Blüte des Delikts." *Vabanque. Bankraub. Theorie. Praxis. Geschichte*. Ed. Klaus Schönberger. Göttingen: Die Libertäre Assoziation, 2001. 14–23, 26–7.

Bondio, Mariacarla Gadebusch. "From the 'Atavistic' to the 'Inferior' Criminal Type: The Impact of the Lombrosian Theory of the Born Criminal on German Psychiatry." *Criminals and Their Scientists: The History of Criminology in International Perspective*. Ed. Peter Becker and Richard F. Wetzell. Cambridge: Cambridge University Press, 2006. 183–205.

Bondio, Mariacarla Gadebusch. *Die Rezeption der kriminalanthropologischen Theorien von Cesare Lombroso in Deutschland von 1880–1914*. Husum: Mattiesen Verlag, 1995.

Bonwit, Marianne. "Michael, ein Roman von Joseph Goebbels, im Licht der deutschen literarischen Tradition." *Deutsche Literaturkritik der Gegenwart*. Ed. Hans Mayer. Stuttgart: Goverts, 1971. Vol. 1, 490–501.

Borresholm, Boris von, and Karena Niehoff, eds. *Dr. Goebbels. Nach Aufzeichnungen aus seiner Umgebung*. Berlin: Verlag des "Journal," 1949.

Borrmann, Norbert. *Das große Lexikon des Verbrechens: Täter, Motive und Hintergründe*. Berlin: Schwarzkopf & Schwarzkopf, 2002.

Botz, Gerhard. *Gewalt in der Politik: Attentate, Zusammenstösse, Putschversuche, Unruhen in Österreich 1918 bis 1938*. 2nd ed. Munich: Wilhelm Fink, 1983.

Botz, Gerhard. "Die 'Hinrichtung' von Hugo Bettauer: Ein Beitrag zur Sozialpathologie der Zwanzigerjahre in Wien." *Aktion für Kultur und Politik* 1 (1967): 8–10.

Boyer, John W. "Karl Lueger and the Viennese Jews." *Leo Baeck Institute Year Book* 26 (1981): 125–41.

Bracher, Karl Dietrich. "Stages of Totalitarian 'Integration' (*Gleichschaltung*): The Consolidation of National Socialist Rule in 1933 and 1934." From *Republic To Reich: The Making of the Nazi Revolution. Ten Essays*. Ed. Hajo Holborn. New York: Pantheon, 1972. 109–28.

Bramstead, Ernest K. *Goebbels und die nationalsozialistische Propaganda 1925–1945*. Frankfurt/M.: Fischer, 1971.

Brecht, Bertolt. *Die Dreigroschenoper*. In *Ausgewählte Werke in sechs Bänden. Erster Band: Stücke 1*. Frankfurt/M.: Suhrkamp, 1997.

Brecht, Bertolt. "Über die Popularität des Kriminalromans." *Der Kriminalroman: Poetik, Theorie, Geschichte*. Ed. Jochen Vogt. Munich: Wilhelm Fink, 1998. 33–37.

Brenner, Michael. *The Renaissance of Jewish Culture in Weimar Germany. New Haven: Yale University Press, 1996.

Brenner, Sabine. "'Ich bin kein großer Sprecher, sondern ein stiller Schreiber': Ein Streifzug durch Heinrich Spoerls literarisches Schaffen." *Heinrich Spoerl: Buch—Bühne—Leinwand.* Ed. Joseph A. Kruse. Düsseldorf: Droste, 2004. 11–16.

Brenner, Sabine. "'Ich habe beim Film meine Erfahrungen gemacht, und gerade diese haben mich zur Bühne getrieben': 'Der Maulkorb' als Theaterstück." *Heinrich Spoerl: Buch—Bühne—Leinwand.* Ed. Joseph A. Kruse. Düsseldorf: Droste, 2004. 45–54.

Brinson, Charmian, and Marian Malet. "Rudolf and Ika Olden in British Exile." *Rudolf Olden: Journalist gegen Hitler—Anwalt der Republik. Eine Ausstellung des Deutschen Exilarchivs 1933–1945 der Deutschen Nationalbibliothek Frankfurt am Main, 26. März–28. Juli 2010.* Ed. Sylvia Asmus and Brita Eckert. Frankfurt/M.: Deutsche Nationalbibliothek, 2010. 117–26.

Bronfen, Elisabeth. *Over Her Dead Body: Death, Femininity and the Aesthetic.* New York: Routledge, 1992.

Broszat, Martin. "Plädoyer für eine Historisierung des Nationalsozialismus." *Merkur* 39 (1985): 373–85.

Broszat, Martin. "Zur Perversion der Strafjustiz im Dritten Reich." *Vierteljahrshefte für Zeitgeschichte* 6 (1958): 390–443.

Bruch, Rüdiger vom. "Krieg und Frieden: Zur Frage der Militarisierung deutscher Hochschullehrer und Universitäten im späten Kaiserreich." *Bereit zum Krieg: Kriegsmentalität im wilhelminischen Deutschland, 1890–1914.* Ed. Jost Dülffer and Karl Holl. Göttingen: Vandenhoeck & Ruprecht, 1986. 74–98.

Brümmer, Franz. "Hans Hyan." *Lexikon der deutschen Dichter.* Leipzig: Reclam, 1913.

Brunnemann, Anna. "Frieda Freiin von Bülow." *Halbmonatsschrift für Literaturfreunde* 5/9 (1902–3): 598–604.

Bucher, André. "Ereignis und Wiederholung: Walter Serners Kriminalgeschichten I." *Repräsentation als Performanz: Studien zur Darstellungspraxis der literarischen Moderne (Walter Serner, Robert Müller, Hermann Ungar, Joseph Roth und Ernst Weiss).* Munich: Wilhelm Fink, 2004. 88–102.

Bucher, André. "Repetition und Variation: Walter Serners Kriminalgeschichten II." *Repräsentation als Performanz: Studien zur Darstellungspraxis der literarischen Moderne (Walter Serner, Robert Müller, Hermann Ungar, Joseph Roth und Ernst Weiss).* Munich: Wilhelm Fink, 2004. 103–24.

Bülow, Frieda von. *Im Hexenring.* Stuttgart: J. Engelhorn, 1901.

Bunzl, John, and Bernd Marin. *Antisemitismus in Österreich: Sozialhistorische und soziologische Studien.* Innsbruck: Innsverlag, 1983.

Burda, Josefine Margarete. "Frieda Freiin von Bülow" [obituary]. *Frauen-Rundschau* 10/7 (1909): 183–4.

Bussemer, Thymian. *Propaganda: Konzepte und Theorien.* Wiesbaden: Verlag für Sozialwissenschaften, 2005.

Bytwerk, Randall L. *Julius Streicher: Nazi Editor of the Notorious Anti-Semitic Newspaper Der Stürmer.* New York: Cooper Square Press, 2001.

Cawthorne, Nigel. *Spree Killers: Devastating Massacres by Unpredictable Gunmen.* Chichester: Summersdale, 2009.

Chickering, Roger. "Die Alldeutschen erwarten den Krieg." *Bereit zum Krieg: Kriegsmentalität im wilhelminischen Deutschland, 1890–1914.* Ed. Jost Dülffer and Karl Holl. Göttingen: Vandenhoeck & Ruprecht, 1986. 20–32.

Christadler, Marieluise. *Kriegserziehung im Jugendbuch. Literarische Mobilmachung in Deutschland und Frankreich vor 1914.* Frankfurt/M: Haag und Herchen, 1978.

Clarissa. Aus dunklen Häusern Belgiens, v. Lord Monroe. Berlin: Hans Lüstenöder, 1892.

Clarke, I.F. *Voices Prophesying War, 1763–1984.* Oxford: Oxford University Press, 1966.

Claßen, Isabella. *Darstellung von Kriminalität in der deutschen Literatur, Presse und Wissenschaft 1900–1930.* Frankfurt /M.: Peter Lang, 1988.

Cleric, Georg Franz von. "Der Hochstapler." *Schweizerische Zeitschrift für Strafrecht* 39 (1926): 16–53.

Colbron, Grace Isabel. "The Detective Story in Germany and Scandinavia." *The Bookman* 30 (Sept. 1909-Feb. 1910): 407–12.

Coll, Pieter. *Der Fall Nagotkin. Kriminalroman.* Berlin: Dr. Friedrich Osmer, 1939.

Comite zur Abwehr antisemitischer Angriffe in Berlin, ed. *Die Kriminalität der Juden in Deutschland.* Berlin: Siegfried Cronbach, 1896.

Connelly, Mark, and David Welch, eds. *War and the Media: Reportage and Propaganda, 1900–2003.* London: I.B. Tauris, 2005.

Courtade, Francis, and Pierre Cadars. *Geschichte des Films im Dritten Reich.* Trans. Florian Hopf. Munich: Wilhelm Heyne, 1975.

Culbert, David. "The Impact of Anti-Semitic Film Propaganda on German Audiences: *Jew Süss* and *The Wandering Jew* (1940)." *Art, Culture and Media under the Third Reich.* Ed. Richard Etlin. Chicago: Chicago University Press, 2002. 139–57.

Czernin, Franz Josef. "Zu Walter Serners *Letzter Lockerung*." *Der Pfiff aufs Ganze: Studien zu Walter Serner.* Ed. Andreas Puff-Trojan and Wendelin Schmidt-Dengler. Vienna: Sonderzahl, 1998. 21–8.

Daluege, Kurt. *Nationalsozialistischer Kampf gegen das Verbrechertum.* Munich: Zentralverlag der NSDAP, 1936.

Dannenbaum, Uwe. "Die Meisterdiebe aus Moabit." *Welt am Sonntag* (January 25, 2004). http://www.welt.de/print-wams/article105556/Die-Meisterdiebe-aus-Moabit.html (accessed March 6, 2016).

Daviau, Donald. *Hermann Bahr.* Boston: Twayne, 1985.

Daviau, Donald. "Hermann Bahr und der Antisemitismus, Zionismus und die Judenfrage." *Literatur und Kritik* 221–2 (February/March 1988): 21–41.

Daviau, Donald. *Understanding Hermann Bahr.* St. Ingbert: Röhrig, 2002.

Daviau, Gertraud Steiner. "Arnold Fanck und Luis Trenker: 'Regisseure für Holywood.'" *Der Bergfilm 1920–1940.* Ed. Friedbert Aspetsberger. Innsbruck: StudienVerlag, 2002. 125–41.

Delabar, Walter. "NS-Literatur ohne Nationalsozialismus? Thesen zu einem Ausstattungsphänomen in der Unterhaltungsliteratur des 'Dritten Reiches.'" *Im Pausenraum des Dritten Reiches: Zur Populärkultur im nationalsozialistischen Deutschland.* Ed. Carsten Würmann and Ansgar Warner. Berne: Peter Lang, 2008. 161–80.

DeLisi, Matt. "Cesare Lombroso." *Oxford Bibliographies.* http://www.oxfordbibliographies.com/view/document/obo-9780195396607/obo-9780195396607-0165.xml (accessed July 14, 2016).

Denkwürdigkeiten des Hauptmanns von Köpenick: Der "Räuberhauptmann" in der internationalen Karikatur und Satire. Berlin: Verlag der "Lustigen Blätter," 1906.

Dennis, David B. *Inhumanities: Nazi Interpretations of Western Culture.* Cambridge: Cambridge University Press, 2012.

Depken, Friedrich. *Sherlock Holmes, Raffles und ihre Vorbilder: Ein Beitrag zur Entwicklungsgeschichte und Technik der Kriminalerzählung.* Heidelberg: Winter, 1914.

Deppe, Hans (dir.). *Robert und Bertram.* Feature Film. Pidax Film 1961.

Deutsch, Helene. "The Impostor: Contributions to Ego Psychology of a Type of Psychopath." *The Psychoanalytic Quarterly* 24/4 (1955): 483–505.

Diesel, Karl. "Gehört der Kriminalroman zur Schundliteratur?" *Der Bibliothekar* 12.1/3 (1920): 1280.

Döblin, Alfred. *Die beiden Freundinnen und ihr Giftmord.* Frankfurt/M.: Fischer, 2013.

Döblin, Alfred. "Das Leben Jacks, des Bauchaufschlitzers." *Autobiographische Schriften und letzte Aufzeichnungen.* Olten: Walter, 1978. 90–2.

Dölling, Dieter. "Kriminologie im 'Dritten Reich.'" *Recht und Justiz im "Dritten Reich."* Ed. Ralf Dreier and Wolfgang Sellert. Frankfurt/M.: Suhrkamp, 1989. 194–225.

Drewniak, Boguslaw. *Der deutsche Film 1938–1945: Ein Gesamtüberblick.* Düsseldorf: Droste, 1987.

Drews, Jörg. "Alles in strahlender—Unordnung. Anlässlich der Mitteilung einiger Briefe und Dokumente zum Leben Walter Serners." *Protokolle* vol. 1 (1980): 154–60.

Drews, Jörg. "'Hinter jedem Satz hat man ein wildes Gelächter unmißverständlich anzudeuten.' Zur geistigen Existenz Walter Serners." *manuskripte* 89/90 (25. Jg., 1985): 149–53.

Drews, Jörg. "'Der Schluck um die Axe: Der Pfiff aufs Ganze.' Fragmente eines Kommentars zu Walter Serners *Letzte Lockerung manifest dada*." *Der Pfiff aufs Ganze: Studien zu Walter Serner.* Ed. Andreas Puff-Trojan and Wendelin Schmidt-Dengler. Vienna: Sonderzahl, 1998. 10–20.

Drexler, Peter. "Der deutsche Gerichtsfilm 1930–1960. Annäherungen an eine problematische Situation." *Verbrechen—Justiz—Medien. Konstellationen in Deutschland von 1900 bis zur Gegenwart.* Ed. Joachim Linder and Claus-Michael Ort. Tübingen: Niemeyer, 1999. 387–401.

Düding, Dieter. "Die Kriegervereine im wilhelminischen Reich und ihr Beitrag zur Militarisierung der deutschen Gesellschaft." *Bereit zum Krieg: Kriegsmentalität im wilhelminischen Deutschland, 1890–1914.* Ed. Jost Dülffer and Karl Holl. Göttingen: Vandenhoeck & Ruprecht, 1986. 99–121.

Duff, Gordon. "Forgotten Terror—The DC Sniper, Another Government False Flag." *Veterans Today* (July 10, 2012). http://www.veteranstoday.com/2012/07/10/forgotten-terror-the-dc-sniper-another-government-false-flag/ (accessed June 8, 2016).

Dülffer, Jost. "Einleitung: Dispositionen zum Krieg im wilhelminischen Deutschland." *Bereit zum Krieg: Kriegsmentalität im wilhelminischen Deutschland, 1890–1914.* Ed. Jost Dülffer and Karl Holl. Göttingen: Vandenhoeck & Ruprecht, 1986. 9–19.

Dülffer, Jost. *Im Zeichen der Gewalt: Frieden und Krieg im 19. und 20. Jahrhundert.* Cologne: Böhlau, 2003.

Dülffer, Jost, and Karl Holl, eds. *Bereit zum Krieg: Kriegsmentalität im wilhelminischen Deutschland, 1890–1914.* Göttingen: Vandenhoeck & Ruprecht, 1986.

Dundes, Alan, ed. *The Blood Libel Legend: A Casebook in Anti-Semitic Folklore.* Madison, WI: University of Wisconsin Press, 1991.

Durchschaudi, I. "Ein uraltes Märchen." *Mürzzuschlager Wochenblatt* (April 30, 1904): 1–2.

Eberle, Henrik, ed. *Briefe an Hitler: Ein Volk schreibt seinem Führer. Unbekannte Dokumente aus Moskauer Archiven—zum ersten Mal veröffentlicht.* Bergisch Gladbach: Gustav Lübbe, 2007.

Eckhardt, Juliane. "Imperialismus und Kaiserreich." *Geschichte der deutschen Kinder- und Jugendliteratur.* Ed. Reiner Wild. Stuttgart: Metzler, 1990. 179–219.

Eder, Jacob S., Philipp Gassert and Alan E. Steinweis, eds. *Holocaust Memory in a Globalizing World.* Göttingen: Wallstein, 2017.

Ehrenfreund, Edmund Otto. *Der Wiener Pitaval: Eine Sammlung der interessantesten Kriminalprozesse aus Alt- und Neu-Wien.* 2nd ed. Vol. 1. Vienna, Leipzig: C. Barth, 1924.

Ehrenfreund, Edmund Otto. *Der Wiener Pitaval, Eine Sammlung der interessantesten Wiener Kriminalfälle des letzten Jahrhunderts von Ubald Tartaruga.* 4 vols. Vienna: C. Barth, 1913.

Eigler, Friederike. "Engendering German Nationalism and Race in Frieda von Bülow's Colonial Writings." *The Imperialist Imagination: German Colonialism and Its Legacy.* Ed. Sara Friedrichsmeyer, Sara Lennox, and Susanne Zantop. Ann Arbor: University of Michigan Press, 1998. 69–86.

Elder, Sace E. "Murder, Denunciation and Criminal Policing in Weimar Berlin." *Journal of Contemporary History* 41/3 (2006): 401–19.

Elon, Amos. "Introduction: The Excommunication of Hannah Arendt." Hannah Arendt, *Eichmann in Jerusalem: A Report on the Banality of Evil.* London: Penguin, 2006. vii–xxiii.

Elster, Hanns Martin. "Der Kriminal- und Detektivroman." *Die Gegenwart* 59 (February 1930): 34–8.

Emter, Elisabeth. *Paul Gurk (1880–1953): Ein vergessener Dichter aus Frankfurt an der Oder.* Frankfurt/Oder: Kleist-Museum, 1995.

Engel, Erich (dir.). *Der Maulkorb.* Feature Film. Tobis Filmkunst 1938.

Erb, Rainer. "Zur Erforschung der europäischen Ritualmordbeschuldigungen." *Die Legende vom Ritualmord: Zur Geschichte der Blutbeschuldigung gegen Juden.* Ed. Rainer Erb. Berlin: Metropol, 1993. 9–16.

Erb, Rainer, ed. *Die Legende vom Ritualmord: Zur Geschichte der Blutbeschuldigung gegen Juden.* Berlin: Metropol, 1993.

Etlin, Richard A. "Introduction: The Perverse Logic of Nazi Thought." *Art, Culture and Media under the Third Reich.* Ed. Richard Etlin. Chicago: Chicago University Press, 2002. 1–39.

Etlin, Richard A., ed. *Art, Culture and Media under the Third Reich.* Chicago: Chicago University Press, 2002.

Evans, Richard J. *Kneipengespräche im Kaiserreich: Die Stimmungberichte der Hamburger politischen Polizei 1892–1914.* Reinbek bei Hamburg: Rowohlt, 1989.

Evans, Richard J. *Rituals of Retribution: Capital Punishment in Germany 1600–1987.* Oxford: Oxford University Press, 1997.

Evans, Richard J., ed. *The German Underworld: Deviants and Outcasts in German History.* London: Routledge, 1988.

Exner, Franz. *Krieg und Kriminalität in Österreich.* Vienna: Hölder-Pichler-Tempsky, 1927.

Exner, Franz. *Kriminalbiologie in ihren Grundzügen.* Hamburg: Hanseatische Verlagsanstalt, 1939.

Ezergailis, Andrew. "Anti-Semitism and the Killing of Latvia's Jews." *Anti-Semitism in Times of Crisis.* Ed. Sander L. Gilman and Steven T. Katz. New York: New York University Press, 1991. 257–90.

Fabich, Max. "Geldschrankeinbrecher." *Kriminalistik: Monatshefte für die gesamte kriminalistische Wissenschaft und Praxis* 17 (1943): 61–3.

Fabich, Max. "Die Straftaten der Gebrüder Saß." *Kriminalistik: Monatshefte für die gesamte kriminalistische Wissenschaft und Praxis* 14 (1940): 85–89; and 15 (1941): 14–17, 64–67, 123–6.

Fabich, Max. "Das Vorleben der Brüder Franz und Erich Sass." *Kriminalistik: Monatshefte für die gesamte kriminalistische Wissenschaft und Praxis* 14 (1940): 37–9.

Faletti, Heidi. "Reflections of Weimar Cinema in the Nazi Propaganda Films *SA-Mann Brand, Hitlerjunge Quex,* and *Hans Westmar.*" *Cultural History through a National Socialist Lens: Essays on the Cinema of the Third Reich.* Ed. Robert C. Reimer. Rochester: Camden House, 2000. 11–36.

Farkas, Reinhard. *Hermann Bahr: Dynamik und Dilemma der Moderne.* Vienna: Böhlau, 1989.

Feraru, Peter. *Muskel-Adolf & Co.: Die "Ringvereine" und das organisierte Verbrechen in Berlin.* Berlin: Argon, 1995.

Fest, Joachim. "Joseph Goebbels oder Canaille Mensch." *Das Gesicht des Dritten Reiches: Profile einer totalitären Herrschaft.* 10th ed. Munich: Piper, 1993. 119–38.

Fiessler, August. "Die menschliche Fortpflanzung und das Strafgesetz: Ein Beitrag zur Frage der Motive zur Bestrafung der Sterilisation und der Fruchtabtreibung." *Archiv für Kriminalanthropologie und Kriminalistik* 56 (1914): 283–326.

Finder, Gabriel N. "Criminals and Their Analysts: Psychoanalytic Criminology in Weimar Germany and the First Austrian Republic." *Criminals and Their Scientists: The History of Criminology in International Perspective.* Ed. Peter Becker and Richard F. Wetzell. Cambridge: Cambridge University Press, 2006. 447–69.

Finetti, Marco. "Rudolf Olden als Journalist—oder: Der vergessene Kern." *Rudolf Olden: Journalist gegen Hitler—Anwalt der Republik. Eine Ausstellung des Deutschen Exilarchivs 1933–1945 der Deutschen Nationalbibliothek Frankfurt am Main, 26. März–28. Juli 2010.* Ed. Sylvia Asmus and Brita Eckert. Frankfurt/M.: Deutsche Nationalbibliothek, 2010. 87–108.

Finkelstein, Lionel. "The Impostor: Aspects of His Development." *Psychoanalytic Quarterly* 43 (1974): 85–114.

Fischer, Lars. "Anti-'Philosemitism' and Anti-Antisemitism in Imperial Germany." *Philosemitism in History*. Ed. Jonathan Karp and Adam Sutcliffe. Cambridge: Cambridge University Press, 2011. 170–89.

Fischer, Lars. "Antisemitism." *The Ashgate Research Companion to Imperial Germany*. Ed. Matthew Jefferies. Farnham: Ashgate, 2015. 143–58.

Fischer, Lars. *"A difference in the texture of prejudice": Historisch-konzeptionelle Überlegungen zum Verhältnis von Antisemitismus, Rassismus und Gemeinschaft*. Graz: Leykam, 2016.

Fischer, Lars. "Public Knowledge of the Shoah in Nazi Germany." *Holocaust Studies: A Journal of Culture and History* (2008): 142–62.

Fischer, Lars. "The Social Democratic response to antisemitism in Imperial Germany: The case of the *Handlungsgehilfen*." *Leo Baeck Institute Year Book* 54 (2009): 151–70.

Fischer, Lars. *The Socialist Response to Antisemitism in Imperial Germany*. Cambridge: Cambridge University Press, 2007.

Fleiter, Andreas. "Punishment on the Path to Socialism: Socialist Perspectives on Crime and Criminal Justice before World War I." *Crime and Criminal Justice in Modern Germany*. Ed. Richard F. Wetzell. New York: Berghahn, 2014. 56–85.

Foges, Max. "'Drut,' Roman von Hermann Bahr" [review]. *Neue Freie Presse* (July 10, 1909): 1–2.

Förster, Stig. "Alter und neuer Militarismus im Kaiserreich: Heeresrüstungspolitik und Dispositionen zum Kriege zwischen Status-quo-Sicherung und imperialistischer Expansion, 1890–1913." *Bereit zum Krieg: Kriegsmentalität im wilhelminischen Deutschland, 1890–1914*. Ed. Jost Dülffer and Karl Holl. Göttingen: Vandenhoeck & Ruprecht, 1986. 122–45.

Förster, Stig. "Dreams and Nightmares: German Military Leadership and the Images of Future Warfare, 1871–1914." *Anticipating Total War: The German and American Experiences, 1871–1914*. Ed. Manfred F. Boemeke, Roger Chickering and Stig Förster. Cambridge: Cambridge University Press, 1999. 343–76.

Förster, Stig. "Militär und Militarismus im Deutschen Kaiserreich—Versuch einer differenzierten Betrachtung." *Militarismus in Deutschland 1871 bis 1945. Zeitgenössische Analysen und Kritik*. Ed. Wolfram Wette. Münster: LIT, 1999. 63–80.

Foucault, Michel. *Discipline and Punish: The Birth of the Prison*. Trans. A. Sheridan. New York: Vintage Books, 1977.

Fox, Jo, and David Welch. "Justifying War: Propaganda, Politics and the Modern Age." *Justifying War: Propaganda, Politics and the Modern Age*. Ed. David Welch and Jo Fox. Basingstoke: Palgrave Macmillan, 2012. 1–20.

Frackman, Kyle. "Vor Ort: The Functions and Early Roots of German Regional Crime Fiction." *Tatort Germany: The Curious Case of German-Language Crime Fiction*. Ed. Lynn M. Kutch and Todd Herzog. Rochester: Camden House, 2014. 23–40.

Fraenkel, Heinrich, and Roger Manvell. *Doctor Goebbels: His Life and Death*. Barnsley: Frontline, 2010.

Fraenkel, Josef, ed. *The Jews of Austria. Essays on Their Life, History and Destruction*. 2nd ed. London: Vallentine-Mitchell, 1970.

Franceschini, Bruno, and Carsten Würmann. *Verbrechen als Passion: Neue Untersuchungen zum Kriminalgenre*. Berlin: Weidler, 2004.

Frank, Reinhard von. *Vergeltungsstrafe und Schutzstrafe: Die Lehre Lombrosos*. Tübingen: J.C.B. Mohr, 1908.

Frank, Richard, G. Roscher and H. Schmidt, eds. *Der Pitaval der Gegenwart. Kriminalfälle der letzten Zeit*. Leipzig: J.C.B. Mohr, 1904–14.

Frenzel, Elisabeth. "Hochstapler." *Motive der Weltliteratur: Ein Lexikon dichtungsgeschichtlicher Längsschnitte*. 6th ed. Stuttgart: Kröner, 2008. 362–72.

Freud, Sigmund. *Der Witz und seine Beziehung zum Unbewußten*. Frankfurt a.M.: Fischer, 1958.

Freund, Winfried. *Die deutsche Kriminalnovelle von Schiller bis Hauptmann*. Paderborn: Ferdinand Schöningh, 1975.

Frey, Erich. "Fritz Haarmann." *Ich beantrage Freispruch: Aus den Erinnerungen des Strafverteidigers Prof. Dr. Dr. Erich Frey*. Hamburg: Blüchert, 1959. 59–82.

Friedländer, Hugo. "Der falsche Hauptmann von Köpenick, Wilhelm Voigt." *Interessante Kriminalprozesse von Kulturhistorischer Bedeutung. Darstellung merkwürdiger Strafrechtsfälle aus Gegenwart und Jüngstvergangenheit nach eigenen Erfahrungen*. 10 vols. Berlin: Hermann Barsdorf / Berliner Buchversand, 1910–1914. Vol. 1, 131–7.

Friedman, Tuviah. *The two Antisemitic Nazi-Leaders Alfred ROSENBERG and Julius STREICHER at the NUREMBERG Trial in 1946*. Haifa: Institute of Documentation in Israel for the Investigation of War Crimes, 1998.

Fritz, G. "Kriminalromane." *Bücherei und Bildungspflege* 11.2 (1931): 81–8.

Fritzsche, Peter. *Germans Into Nazis*. Cambridge, MA: Harvard University Press, 1999.

Fritzsche, Peter. *Life and Death in the Third Reich*. Cambridge, MA: Harvard University Press, 2009.

Fritzsche, Peter. *Rehearsals for Fascism: Populism and Political Mobilization in Weimar Germany*. New York: Oxford University Press, 1990.

Fröhlich, Elke. "Joseph Goebbels—der Propagandist." *Die braune Elite: 22 biographische Skizzen.* Ed. Ronald Smelser and Rainer Zitelmann. Darmstadt: Wissenschaftliche Buchgesellschaft, 1989. 52–68.

Fröhlich, Rudolph Alois. *Die gefährlichsten Klassen Wiens. Darstellung ihres Entstehens, ihrer Verbindungen, ihrer Taktik, ihrer Sitten und Gewohnheiten und ihrer Sprache. Mit belehrenden Winken über Gaunerkniffe und einem Wörterbuch der Gaunersprache.* Vienna: Wenedikt, 1851.

Fuld, Ludwig. *Das jüdische Verbrecherthum: Eine Studie über den Zusammenhang zwischen Religion und Kriminalität.* Leipzig: Theodor Huth, 1885.

Fullerton, Ronald A. "Creating a Mass Book Market in Germany: The Story of the 'Colporteur Novel' 1870–1890." *Journal of Social History* 10/3 (March 1977: 265–83.

Fullerton, Ronald A. "Toward a Commercial Popular Culture in Germany: The Development of Pamphlet Fiction, 1871–1914." *Journal of Social History* 12/4 (1979): 489–511.

Fulwider, Chad R. "Film Propaganda and *Kultur*: The German Dilemma, 1914–1917." *Film & History* 45/2 (Winter 2015): 4–12.

Fürst, Rudolf. "Kriminalromantik." *Das literarische Echo* 10.9 (1908): 607–14.

Gädke, Colonel. "Der militärische Gehorsam im Lichte des Gaunerstreichs von Köpenick." *Berliner Tageblatt und Handels-Zeitung* (October 18, 1906): 1–2.

Galassi, Silviana. *Kriminologie im Deutschen Kaiserreich: Geschichte einer gebrochenen Verwissenschaftlichung.* Stuttgart: Franz Steiner, 2004.

Galle, Heinz J. *Groschenhefte: Die Geschichte der deutschen Trivialliteratur.* Frankfurt/M.: Ullstein, 1988.

Galle, Heinz J. *Populäre Lesestoffe: Groschenhefte, Dime Novels und Penny Dreadfuls aus den Jahren 1850 bis 1950.* Cologne: Universitäts- und Stadtbibliothek, 2002.

Gassert, Philipp. *Coping with the Nazi Past: West German Debates on Nazism and Generational Conflict.* New York: Berghahn Books, 2013.

Gehrke, Hans. *Carl Zuckmayer: Der Hauptmann von Köpenick. Interpretation und Materialien.* Hollfeld: Joachim Beyer, n. d.

Geißler, Max. *Führer durch die deutsche Literatur des 20. Jahrhunderts.* Weimar: n.p., 1913.

Gentges, Ignaz. "Etwas über den Abenteuer-, Zukunfts-, Detektiv- und okkulte Romane." *Bücherwelt* 23.1 (1926): 14–17.

Gerteis, Walter. *Detektive: Ihre Geschichte im Leben und in der Literatur.* Munich: Ernst Heimeran, 1953.

Giles, Geoffrey J. "Drinking and Crime in Modern Germany." *Criminals and Their Scientists: The History of Criminology in International Perspective.* Ed. Peter Becker and Richard F. Wetzell. Cambridge: Cambridge University Press, 2006. 471–85.

Gilgen, Peter. "Lockere Sprüche: Walter Serners *Letzte Lockerung* als Phänomenologie der tabula rasa." *verLockerungen: Österreichische Avantgarde im 20. Jahrhundert.* Ed. Wendelin Schmidt-Dengler. Vienna: Edition Praesens, 1994. 9–49.

Gilman, Sander L. *The Case of Sigmund Freud: Medicine and Identity at the Fin de Siècle.* Baltimore: Johns Hopkins University Press, 1993.

Gilman, Sander L. *Jewish Self-Hatred: Anti-Semitism and the Hidden Language of the Jews.* Baltimore: Johns Hopkins University Press, 1986.

Gilman, Sander L. *The Jew's Body.* New York: Routledge, 1991.

Gilman, Sander L., and Steven T. Katz, eds. *Anti-Semitism in Times of Crisis.* New York: New York University Press, 1991.

Gleber, Anke. "Flanerie oder die Lektüre der Moderne: Franz Hessel und Paul Gurk. Mit einem Exkurs zur neueren deutschen Literatur." Diss. University of California, Irvine (1988).

Gliksman, Shlomo. *Forgeries and Falsifications in the Anti-Semitic Literature and My Lawsuit Against Julius Streicher and Company.* New York: Shulsinger Bros., 2003.

Goebbels, Joseph. *Aus meinem Tagebuch. Aufzeichnungen für Else Janke.* 1923 (handwritten MS). Bundesarchiv Koblenz, NL 118/126.

Goebbels, Joseph. *Aus meinem Tagebuch. Von Paul Joseph Goebbels. Anka Stalherm zugeeignet.* Munich, Christmas 1919 (handwritten MS). Bundesarchiv Koblenz, NL 118/126.

Goebbels, Joseph. *Goebbels Reden 1932–1935.* Ed. Helmut Heiber. Bindlach: Gondrom, 1998.

Goebbels, Joseph. *Judas Iscariot. Eine biblische Tragödie in fünf Akten von P.J. Goebbels.* August 1918 (handwritten MS). Bundesarchiv Koblenz, NL 118/127.

Goebbels, Joseph. *Lyrische Gedichte. Dem Herrn Professor Rentrop, meinem hochverehrten Lehrer, in Dankbarkeit zugeeignet.* n. d. (handwritten MS). Bundesarchiv Koblenz, NL 118/133.

Goebbels, Joseph. *Michael. Ein deutsches Schicksal in Tagebuchblättern.* 17th ed. Munich: Zentralverlag der NSDAP, 1942 (orig. 1929).

Goebbels, Joseph. *Michael Voormann. Ein Menschenschicksal in Tagebuchblättern.* 1923 (typed MS). Bundesarchiv Koblenz, NL 118/127.

Goebbels, Joseph. *Michael Voormann's Jugendjahre. I. Teil.* 1919 (handwritten MS). Bundesarchiv Koblenz, NL 118/126.

Goebbels, Joseph. *Michael Voormann's Jugendjahre. III. Teil.* 1919 (handwritten MS). Bundesarchiv Koblenz, NL 118/116.

Goebbels, Joseph. *Tagebücher 1924–1945.* Ed. Ralf Georg Reuth. Munich: Piper, 1992.

Goebbels, Joseph. *Die Tagebücher von Joseph Goebbels. Sämtliche Fragmente.* Ed. Elke Fröhlich. Munich and New York: Saur, 1987.

Goethe, Johann Wolfgang. *Faust. Part I & II of the Tragedy.* Trans. A.S. Kline. http://goethe.holtof.com/faust/Fausthome.htm (accessed January 25, 2018).

Gold, Hugo, ed. *Geschichte der Juden in Österreich: Ein Gedenkbuch.* Tel Aviv: Olamenu, 1971.

Goldhagen, Daniel Jonah. *Hitler's Willing Executioners: Ordinary Germans and the Holocaust.* London: Little, Brown and Company, 1996.

Göpfert, Peter Hans. "Die Brüder Sass wurden Literatur." *Berliner Morgenpost* (March 28, 1981): 70.

Góth, E. "Drut. Roman von Hermann Bahr" [review]. *Pester Lloyd* (June 6, 1909): 22.

Götz von Olenhusen, Irmtraud. "Mord verjährt nicht: Krimis als historische Quelle (1900–1945)." *Geschichte im Krimi: Beiträge aus den Kulturwissenschaften.* Ed. Barbara Korte and Sylvia Paletschek. Cologne, Weimar, Vienna: Böhlau, 2009. 105–28.

Greenacre, Phyllis. "The Impostor." *Psychoanalytic Quarterly* 28 (1958): 359–82.

Greenacre, Phyllis. "The Relation of the Impostor to the Artist." *Psychoanalytic Study of the Child* 13 (1958): 521–40.

Greive, Hermann. *Geschichte des modernen Antisemitismus in Deutschland.* Darmstadt: Wissenschaftliche Buchgesellschaft, 1983.

Grimm, Jakob, and Wilhelm. "The Bremen Town Musicians." https://germanstories.vcu.edu/grimm/bremer_dual.html (accessed November 22, 2017).

Grimm, Jakob, and Wilhelm. "Rumpelstiltskin." http://www.eastoftheweb.com/short-stories/UBooks/Rum.shtml (accessed November 22, 2017).

Grobian, M. *Der gefangene KÖPENICKER oder der Schuster von Tilsit.* Munich: Dreschflegel, 1906.

Groner, Auguste. *Der alte Herr. Kriminalroman.* Vienna: Hartleben, 1898.

Groner, Auguste. *Die alte Spieluhr.* Vienna, Leipzig: Philipp, 1916.

Groner, Auguste. *Am Verlobungstage. Kriminalroman.* In: *BUW* (vols. 8–13): 1903.

Groner, Auguste. "The Case of the Golden Bullet" [translation of: "Die goldene Kugel," orig. 1892]. Trans. Grace Isabel Colbron. http://www.gutenberg.org/1/8/3/1836/

Groner, Auguste. *The Case of the Lamp That Went Out* [translation of: *Warum sie das Licht verlöschte,* orig. 1899]. Trans. Grace Isabel Colbron. http://www.gutenberg.org/1/8/3/1832/

Groner, Auguste. "The Case of the Pocket Diary Found in the Snow" [translation of: "Ermordet"]. Trans. Grace Isabel Colbron. http://www.gutenberg.org/1/8/3/1834/

Groner, Auguste. "The Case of the Pool of Blood in the Pastor's Study" [translation of: "Der Neunundsiebenzigste," orig. 1891]. Trans. Grace Isabel Colbron. http://www.gutenberg.org/1/8/3/1835/

Groner, Auguste. "The Case of the Registered Letter" [translation of: "Der Brief aus dem Jenseits," orig. 1896]. Trans. Grace Isabel Colbron. http://www.gutenberg.org/1/8/3/1833/

Groner, Auguste. "The Golden Bullet." *Early German and Austrian Detective Fiction: An Anthology.* Ed. Mary W. Tannert and Henry Kratz. Jefferson, N.C.: McFarland, 1999. 190–216.

Groner, Auguste. *Ein Justizirrtum.* Leipzig: Vogel & Vogel, 1910.

Groner, Auguste. *Kriminalnovellen.* http://gutenberg.spiegel.de/buch/kriminalnovellen-6383/1 (accessed February 10, 2016).

Groner, Auguste. *Der Leutverderber. Das Beichtgeheimnis. Die letzte Nacht.* Berlin: Hillger, n. d.

Groner, Auguste. *Der Mann mit den vielen Namen. Kriminalroman.* In: *Das Buch für Alle* (nos. 18–28): 1906.

Groner, Auguste. *Mene tekel… Eine seltsame Geschichte.* Vienna: Ed. Schmid, 1910.

Groner, Auguste. *Neue Kriminalnovellen. An einem Faden. Ermordet?* Leipzig: Reclam, n. d.

Groner, Auguste. *Das Pharaonenarmband. Kriminalnovelle.* Stuttgart and Leipzig: DVA, 1900.

Groner, Auguste. *Der rote Merkur. Kriminalroman.* http://gutenberg.spiegel.de/buch/der-rote-merkur-6223/1 (accessed February 10, 2016).

Groner, Auguste. *Seltsame Geschichten.* [Contains: "Das tote Haus." "Die rätselvolle Statue."] Vienna: Steyrermühl, 1925 [orig. 1917].

Groner, Auguste. *Der seltsame Schatten. Kriminalroman.* Berlin, Leipzig: Hillger, n. d. [1913].

Groner, Auguste. *Das Skelett. Kriminalnovelle.* Berlin, Eisenach, Leipzig: Hillger, n. d. [1900?].

Groner, Auguste. *Warenhaus Groß & Comp. Roman.* http://gutenberg.spiegel.de/buch/warenhaus-gross-comp-6222/1 (accessed February 10, 2016).

Groner, Auguste. *Warum sie das Licht verlöschte?* Berlin: Hillger, n. d.

Groner, Auguste. *Wer ist es? Roman. Der seltsame Schatten. Kriminal-Geschichte.* Berlin, Eisenach, Leipzig: Hillger, n. d. [1898].

Groner, Auguste. *Zwei Kriminalnovellen: Der Neunundsiebzigste. Die goldene Kugel.* Leipzig: Philipp Reclam, 1893.

Groß, Hans. *Criminalpsychologie.* Graz: Leuschner & Lubensky, 1898.

Groß, Hans. "Zur Frage der Kastration und Sterilisation." *Archiv für Kriminalanthropologie und Kriminalistik* 51 (1913): 316–25.

Große, Wilhelm. *Erläuterungen zu Carl Zuckmayer: Der Hauptmann von Köpenick. Text-*

analyse und Interpretation. Hollfeld: C. Bange, 2012.

Grün, Grete. "Attentat!" *Bettauers Wochenschrift: Probleme des Lebens* 12 (1925): 3–5.

Grünes, Willy. "Der Detektive." *Deutsches Volksblatt, Morgenausgabe* (June 29, 1909): 1–2.

Gurk, Paul. *Tresoreinbruch. Roman.* Darmstadt: Agora, 1981 [orig. 1935].

Gütt, Arthur, Ernst Rüdin and Falk Ruttke. *Gesetz zur Verhütung erbkranken Nachwuchses vom 14. Juli 1933 nebst Ausführungsverordnungen.* 2nd ed. Munich: 1935.

Haarer, Johanna. *Mutter, erzähl von Adolf Hitler! Ein Buch zum Vorlesen, Nacherzählen und Selbstlesen für kleinere und größere Kinder.* Munich, Berlin: J.F. Lehmanns Verlag, 1939.

Habbe, Christian. "Gauner-Legenden: Kellerparty der Panzerknacker." *Spiegel online* (January 23, 2009). http://www.spiegel.de/einesta ges/gauner-legenden-a-948136.html (accessed April 11, 2017).

Habicht, Ludwig. *Die Erbschaft. Kriminal-Roman.* Berlin: Gnadenfeld, 1897.

Hackenbruch, Ulrich. *Sachliche Intensitäten: Walter Serners "erotische Kriminalgeschichten" in ihrer Epoche.* Frankfurt/M.: Peter Lang, 1996.

Hacker, Melanie. *Er und Sie: Wochenschrift für Lebenskultur und Erotik. Hugo Bettauers Zeitschrift und die Sexualmoral der 1920er Jahre.* Saarbrücken: VDM Verlag Dr. Müller: 2009.

Hafner, Heinz, and Rolf Winau. "'Die Freigabe der Vernichtung lebensunwerten Lebens': Eine Untersuchung zu der Schrift von Karl Binding und Alfred Hoche." *Medizinhistorisches Journal* 9 (1974): 227–54.

Hahn, Fred. *Lieber Stürmer: Leserbriefe an das NS-Kampfblatt 1924–1945. Eine Dokumentation aus dem Leo-Baeck Institut, New York.* Stuttgart: Seewald Verlag, 1978.

Haibl, Michaela. "'Antisemitische Bilder'—antijüdische Visiotype." *Antisemitische Geschichtsbilder.* Ed. Werner Bergmann und Ulrich Sieg. Essen: Klartext, 2009. 231–56.

Hake, Sabine. *Popular Cinema of the Third Reich.* Austin: University of Texas Press, 2001.

Halbrainer, Heimo, and Heimo Gruber. "Jüdisches Leben und Antisemitismus in Mürzzuschlag im 19./20. Jahrhundert." *Zwei Tage Zeit: Herta Reich und die Spuren jüdischen Lebens in Mürzzuschlag.* Ed. Heimo Halbrainer. Graz: Clio, 1998. 65–77.

Hall, Katharina. "Crime Fiction in Germany: Concepts, Developments and Trends." *Crime Fiction in German: Der Krimi.* Ed. Katharina Hall. Cardiff: University of Wales Press: 2016. 1–32.

Hall, Katharina. "Historical Crime Fiction in German: The Turbulent Twentieth Century." *Crime Fiction in German: Der Krimi.* Ed. Katharina Hall. Cardiff: University of Wales Press: 2016. 115–31.

Hall, Katharina, ed. *Crime Fiction in German: Der Krimi.* Cardiff: University of Wales Press: 2016.

Hall, Murray G. *Der Fall Bettauer.* Vienna: Löcker, 1978.

Hall, Murray G. "'Hinaus mit den Juden!' Von Graffiti und der Zeitung bis zur Leinwand." *Wien und die jüdische Erfahrung 1900–1938.* Ed. Frank Stern and Barbara Eichinger. Vienna: Böhlau, 2009. 59–70.

Hamann, Brigitte. *Hitlers Wien: Lehrjahre eines Diktators.* Munich: Piper, 1998.

Hammerstein, Katharina von. "Einführung zu Frieda von Bülow, 'Eine unblutige Eroberungsfahrt an der ostafrikanischen Küste' und 'Allerhand Alltägliches aus Deutsch-Ostafrika.'" *Kolonialer Alltag in Deutsch-Ostafrika in Dokumenten.* Ed. Ulrich van der Heyden. Berlin: trafo, 2009. 149–57.

Hampel, Ernst Wilhelm. *Schwärmer, Schwindler, Scharlatane.* Berlin: Neues Leben, 1961.

Handl, Willi. *Hermann Bahr.* Berlin: S. Fischer, 1913.

Hannover, H. and E., eds. *Politische Justiz 1918–1933.* Frankfurt/M.: Fischer, 1966.

Harlan, Veit (dir.). *Jud Süss.* Feature Film. Terra Filmkunst 1940.

Harris, Ruth. *Murders and Madness: Medicine, Law and Society in the Fin-de-Siècle.* Oxford: Clarendon, 1989.

Hartmann, Matthias (dir.). *Der Hauptmann von Köpenick.* TV-film. WDR 2005.

Hartner, Herwig. "Erotik und Rasse." *Kikeriki* 1926: March 14 (7); April 4 (7); April 11 (7); April 18 (7); April 25 (7); May 2 (7); May 16 (7); June 9 (7).

Hartner-Hnizdo, Herwig. *Das jüdische Gaunertum.* Munich: Hoheneichen, 1939.

Hartner-Hnizdo, Herwig. *Volk der Gauner: Eine Untersuchung des jüdischen Gaunertums.* Munich: Hoheneichen, 1939.

Hartston, Barnet. *Sensationalizing the Jewish Question: Anti-Semitic Trials and the Press in the Early German Empire.* Leiden: Brill, 2005.

Hehenberger, Susanne. "Sexualstrafrecht und Geschlechterordnung im frühneuzeitlichen Österreich." *Hat Strafrecht ein Geschlecht? Zur Deutung und Bedeutung der Kategorie Geschlecht in strafrechtlichen Diskursen vom 18. Jahrhundert bis heute.* Ed. Gaby Temme and Christine Künzel. Bielefeld: transcript, 2010. 101–18.

Heiber, Helmut. *Joseph Goebbels.* Berlin: Colloquium, 1962.

Heidelmeyer, Wolfgang, ed. *Der Fall Köpenick: Akten und zeitgenössische Dokumente zur Historie einer preußischen Moritat.* Frankfurt/M.: Fischer, 1968.

Heindl, Robert. *Der Berufsverbrecher: Ein Beitrag zur Strafrechtsreform.* Berlin: Rolf Heise, 1926.

Hellering, Kaspar. "Auf zur Selbsthilfe gegen Bettauer." *Deutsche Arbeiter-Presse* (October 18, 1924): 6.

Helpach, Willy. "Berufspsychosen." *Die Zukunft* 14 (1906): 179–88.

Hennig, Jörg. "Gerichtsberichterstattung in deutschen Tageszeitungen 1850–1890." *Erzählte Kriminalität: Zur Typologie und Funktion von narrativen Darstellungen in Strafrechtspflege, Publizistik und Literatur zwischen 1770 und 1920.* Ed. Jörg Schönert in collaboration with Konstantin Imm and Joachim Linder. Tübingen: Max Niemeyer, 1991. 349–67.

Hentig, Hans von. *Strafrecht und Auslese: Eine Anwendung des Kausalgesetzes auf den rechtbrechenden Menschen.* Berlin: Julius Springer, 1914.

Herbertz, Richard. *Verbrecherdämmerung: Psychologische Deutung und weltanschauliche Perspektiven der jüngsten Mordfälle Haarmann, Angerstein, Denke usw.* Munich: Curt Pechstein, 1925.

Hering, Karl-Heinz. *Der Weg der Kriminologie zur selbständigen Wissenschaft: Ein Materialbeitrag zur Geschichte der Kriminologie.* Hamburg: Kriminalistik Verlag, 1966.

Hering, Rainer. "'...ist der Einfluß der Juden auf sittlich-geistigem Gebiete (...) noch viel verderblicher': Antisemitismus in der populären Geschichtsdarstellung von Heinrich Claß." *Antisemitische Geschichtsbilder.* Ed. Werner Bergmann and Ulrich Sieg. Essen: Klartext, 2009. 193–210.

Hervay, Tamara von. *Tamara von Hervay: Ihr Leben und Denken.* Vienna: Szelinski & Co., 1905.

Herz, Hugo. *Verbrechen und Verbrecherthum in Österreich: Kritische Untersuchungen über Zusammenhänge von Wirtschaft und Verbrechen.* Tübingen: Laupp'sche Buchhandlung, 1908.

Herz, Peter. "Leben und Tod von Hugo Bettauer." *Illustrierte Neue Welt* (March 1982): 14.

Herzog, Todd. "Crime and Literature in the Weimar Republic and Beyond: Telling the Tale of the Poisoners Ella Klein and Margarete Nebbe." *Crime and Criminal Justice in Modern Germany.* Ed. Richard F. Wetzell. New York: Berghahn, 2014. 226–46.

Herzog, Todd. "Crime Stories: Criminal, Society, and the Modernist Case Study." *Representations* 80 (2002): 34–61.

Herzog, Todd. *Crime Stories: Criminalistic Fantasy and the Culture of Crisis in Weimar Germany.* Oxford: Berghahn, 2009.

Hesse, Sebastian. "Ernst Reicher alias Stuart Webbs: King of German Film Detectives." *A Second Life: German Cinema's First Decades.* Ed. Thomas Elsaesser with Michael Wedel. Amsterdam: Amsterdam University Press, 1996. 142–50.

Hett, Benjamin Carter. "The 'Captain of Köpenick'

and the Transformation of German Criminal Justice, 1891–1914." *Central European History* 36/1 (2003): 1–43.

Hett, Benjamin Carter. "Justice Is Blind: Crowds, Irrationality, and Criminal Law in the Late Kaiserreich." *Crime and Criminal Justice in Modern Germany.* Ed. Richard F. Wetzell. New York: Berghahn, 2014. 31–55.

Heymann, Robert. *Deutsche Schildbürgerstädte: Ein literarischer Streifzug von Schilda bis nach Köpenick.* Gotha: Bartholomäus, 1908.

Hickethier, Knut. "Der Alte Deutsche Kriminalroman: Von vergessenen Traditionen." *Die Horen* 31.4 (1986): 15–23.

Hickethier, Knut, and Wolf Dieter Lützen. "Der Kriminalroman: Entstehung und Entwicklung eines Genres in den literarischen Medien." *Trivialliteratur.* Ed. Annamaria Rucktäschel and Hans Peter Zimmermann. Munich: Fink, 1976. 267–95.

Hiemer, Ernst. *The Poisonous Mushroom.* With a Foreword by The Bishop of Durham. London: Issued by Friends of Europe, 1938.

Hilberg, Raul. *The Destruction of the European Jews.* London: Holmes and Meier, 1985.

Hippe, Robert. *Kriminalliteratur.* Hollfeld: Bange, 1980.

Hippler, Fritz (dir.). *Der Ewige Jude.* Feature Film. DFG 1940.

Hirschfeld, Magnus. *Sexualpathologie: Ein Lehrbuch für Ärzte und Studierende.* 3 vols. Bonn: A. Marcus & E. Webers Verlag, 1920–22.

Hitler, Adolf. *Mein Kampf. Zwei Bände in einem Band.* 172nd-173rd ed. Munich: Zentralverlag der NSDAP, 1936.

Hitler, Adolf. *Monologe im Führerhauptquartier 1941–1944.* Collected by Heinrich Heim, ed. Werner Jochmann. Munich: Orbis, 2000.

Hödl, Klaus. *Die Pathologisierung des jüdischen Körpers.* Vienna: Picus, 1997.

Hoechstetter, Sophie. *Frieda Freiin v. Bülow: Ein Lebensbild.* Dresden: Carl Reißner, 1910.

Hofer, Walter, ed. *Der Nationalsozialismus: Dokumente, 1933–1945.* Frankfurt/M.: Fischer, 1957.

Hoffmann, Heinrich. *Jugend um Hitler: 120 Bilddokumente aus der Umgebung des Führers.* Introduction by Baldur von Schirach. Berlin: Verlag Wilhelm Andermann, 1935.

Hoffmann, Hilmar. *"Und die Fahne führt uns in die Ewigkeit": Propaganda im NS-Film.* Frankfurt/M.: Fischer, 1988.

Hoffmann, Klaus. *Glitzerndes Geheimnis: Gauner, Gaukler, Gelehrte und Grossmachtpolitiker. Ein Kriminalreport über parawissenschaftliche Hochstapeleien.* Leipzig: Urania, 1988.

Hoffmann, Ludger. "Vom Ereignis zum Fall. Sprachliche Muster zur Darstellung und Überprüfung von Sachverhalten vor Gericht." *Erzählte Kriminalität: Zur Typologie und Funktion von narrativen Darstellungen in Strafrechtspflege, Publizistik und Literatur zwischen 1770 und 1920*. Ed. Jörg Schönert in collaboration with Wolfgang Naucke and Konstantin Imm. Tübingen: Niemeyer, 1991. 87–113.

Höfig, Willi. *Der deutsche Heimatfilm 1947–1960*. Stuttgart: Ferdinand Enke, 1973.

Holl, Karl. "Vorwort." *Bereit zum Krieg: Kriegsmentalität im wilhelminischen Deutschland, 1890–1914*. Ed. Jost Dülffer and Karl Holl. Göttingen: Vandenhoeck & Ruprecht, 1986. 7–8.

Hollstein, Dorothea. *Antisemitische Filmpropaganda: Die Darstellung des Juden im nationalsozialistischen Spielfilm*. Munich: Verlag Dokumentation, 1971.

Hollstein, Dorothea. *"Jud Süss" und die Deutschen: Antisemitische Vorurteile im nationalsozialistischen Spielfilm*. Frankfurt: Ullstein, 1983.

Holzmann, Gabriela. *Schaulust und Verbrechen: Eine Geschichte des Krimis als Mediengeschichte, 1850–1950*. Stuttgart: Metzler, 2001.

Hook, Sidney, William L. O'Neill and Roger O'Toole, eds. *Philosophy, History and Social Action: Essays in Honor of Lewis Feuer*. Dordrecht: Kluwer Academic, 1988.

Hopmann, Stefan. "Über Hochstapler und andere Pädagogen." *Neue Sammlung. Vierteljahres-Zeitschrift für Erziehung und Gesellschaft* 3 (1993): 421–36.

Hopp, Andrea. "Zur Medialisierung des antisemitischen Stereotyps im Kaiserreich." *Antisemitische Geschichtsbilder*. Ed. Werner Bergmann and Ulrich Sieg. Essen: Klartext, 2009. 22–37.

Hoppe, Hugo. "Die Kriminalität der Juden und der Alkohol." *Zeitschrift für Demographie und Statistik der Juden* 2 (1907): 38–41.

Horkheimer, Max, et. al., eds. *Studien über Autorität und Familie: Forschungsberichte aus dem Institut für Sozialforschung*. 2nd ed. Lüneburg: zu Klampen, 1987.

Höver, Ulrich. *Joseph Goebbels—ein nationaler Sozialist*. Bonn and Berlin: Bouvier, 1992.

Höyng, Peter. "A Dream of a White Vienna after World War I: Hugo Bettauer's *The City without Jews* and *The Blue Stain*." *At Home and Abroad: Historicizing Twentieth-Century Whiteness in Literature and Performance*. Ed. La Vinia Delois Jennings. Knoxville: University of Tennessee Press, 2009. 29–60.

Hübinger, Gangolf. "Religion and War in Imperial Germany." *Anticipating Total War: The German and American Experiences, 1871–1914*. Ed. Manfred F. Boemeke, Roger Chickering and Stig Förster. Cambridge: Cambridge University Press, 1999. 125–35.

Huelke, Hans-Heinrich, and Hans Etzler. *Verbrechen, Polizei, Prozesse: Ein Verzeichnis von Büchern und kleineren Schriften in deutscher Sprache*. Wiesbaden: 1959.

Hügel, Hans-Otto. *Die Leiche auf der Eisenbahn: Detektivgeschichten aus deutschen Familienzeitschriften*. Darmstadt: Luchterhand, 1981.

Hügel, Hans-Otto. *Untersuchungsrichter, Diebsfänger, Detektive: Theorie und Geschichte der deutschen Detektiverzählung im 19. Jahrhundert*. Stuttgart: Metzler, 1978.

Hull, David Stewart. *Film in the Third Reich: A Study of the German Cinema, 1933–1945*. Berkeley: University of California Press, 1969.

Hunt, Irmgart Elsner. "Die Berlinromane Paul Gurks: Mythos Stadt, Mythos Mensch." *Autoren damals und heute: Literaturgeschichtliche Beispiele veränderter Wirkungshorizonte*. Ed. Gerhard P. Knapp. Amsterdam: Rodopi, 1991. 547–70.

Hwang, June J. "Alone in the City: Hugo Bettauer's *Er und Sie*." *Seminar: A Journal of Germanic Studies* 47/5 (November 2011): 559–77.

Hyan, Hans. *Der Hauptmann von Köpenick: Eine schaurig-traurige Geschichte vom beschränkten Untertanenverstande*. Illustrations by Paul Haase. Berlin: Hermann Seemann Nachfolger, 1906.

Hyan, Hans. *Massenmörder Haarmann. Eine kriminalistische Studie*. Berlin: Es werde Licht, 1924.

Hyan, Hans. *Schwere Jungen*. 4th ed. Berlin: Verlag von Hermann Seemann Nachfolger, n. d. (first ed. 1907).

Hyan, Hans. *Sherlock Holmes als Erzieher. Mit einem Vorwort von Rechtsanwalt Dr. jur. Halpert*. Selbstverlag 1909. Digitised by Joachim Linder. http://www.joachim-linder.de/data/Hyan.pdf (accessed January 24, 2016).

Ingenlath, Markus. *Mentale Aufrüstung. Militarisierungstendenzen in Frankreich und Deutschland vor dem Ersten Weltkrieg*. Frankfurt, New York: Campus, 1998.

Iwo, Jack. *Göbbels erobert die Welt*. Paris: Éditions du Phénix, 1936.

Jäckel, Eberhard, with Alfred Kuhn, eds. *Hitler: Sämtliche Aufzeichnungen 1905–1925*. Stuttgart: Deutsche Verlags-Anstalt, 1980.

Jaeger, Johannes, ed. *Hinter Kerkermauern: Autobiographien und Selbstbekenntnisse, Aufsätze und Gedichte von Verbrechern. Ein Beitrag zur Kriminalpsychologie. Mit einem Vor- und Nachwort von Univ.-Prof Dr Hans Gross*. Berlin: Konrad W. Mecklenburg, 1906.

Jäger, Georg. "Der Kampf gegen Schmutz und Schund: Die Reaktion der Gebildeten auf die Unterhaltungsindustrie." *Archiv für Geschichte des Buchwesens* 31 (1988): 163–91.

James-Chakraborty, Kathleen. "The Drama of Illumination: Visions of Community from Wilhelmine to Nazi Germany." *Art, Culture and Media under the Third Reich*. Ed. Richard Etlin. Chicago: Chicago University Press, 2002. 181–201.

Jazbinsek, Dietmar. *Kinometerdichter: Karrierepfade im Kaiserreich zwischen Stadtforschung und Stummfilm. Mit Filmessays von Arno Arndt, Alfred Deutsch-German, Edmund Edel,*

Hans Hyan, Felix Salten und Walter Turszin-sky. Berlin: WZB, 2000.

Jefferies, Matthew. *Imperial Culture in Germany, 1871–1918.* Basingstoke: Palgrave Macmillan, 2003.

Jeggle, Utz. "Zur imaginären Topographie von Ritualmordlegenden." *Die Legende vom Ritual-mord: Zur Geschichte der Blutbeschuldigung gegen Juden.* Ed. Rainer Erb. Berlin: Metropol, 1993. 239–52.

Jelavich, Peter. "When are Jewish Jokes No Longer Funny? Ethnic Humour in Imperial and Re-publican Berlin." *The Politics of Humour: Laughter, Inclusion and Exclusion in the Twen-tieth Century.* Ed. Martina Kessel and Patrick Merziger. Toronto: University of Toronto Press, 2012. 22–51.

Jelinek, Elfriede. "Aus dem Weg sein." *Der Pfiff aufs Ganze: Studien zu Walter Serner.* Ed. An-dreas Puff-Trojan and Wendelin Schmidt-Dengler. Vienna: Sonderzahl, 1998. 93–7.

Jochmann, Werner. *Gesellschaftskrise und Juden-feindschaft in Deutschland 1870–1945.* Ham-burg: Christians, 1988.

Jochmann, Werner. "Struktur und Funktion des deutschen Antisemitismus." *Juden im Wil-helminischen Deutschland 1890–1914.* Ed. W.E. Mosse and A. Pauker. Tübingen: Mohr, 1976. 389–477.

Jones, Larry Eugene, ed. *The German Right in the Weimar Republic: Studies in the History of German Conservatism, Nationalism and An-tisemitism.* New York: Berghahn, 2014.

Der Juden Antheil am Verbrechen: Auf Grund der amtlichen Statistik über die Thätigkeit der Schwurgerichte, in vergleichender Darstellung mit den christlichen Konfessionen. Berlin: Otto Henze, 1881.

Jungnickel, Max. *Goebbels.* Leipzig: R. Kittler, 1933.

Kaes, Anton, Martin Jay, and Edward Dimend-berg, eds. *The Weimar Republic Sourcebook.* Berkeley: University of California Press, 1994.

Kaes, Anton, and Bernhard Zimmermann, eds. *Literatur für viele: Studien zur Trivialliteratur und Massenkommunikation im 19. und 20. Jahrhundert.* 2 vols. Göttingen: Vandenhoeck & Ruprecht, 1975 -.

Kaminski, Winfred. "Faschismus." *Geschichte der deutschen Kinder- und Jugendliteratur.* Ed. Reiner Wild. Stuttgart: Metzler, 1990. 266–84.

Kaminski, Winfred. "Weimarer Republik." *Geschichte der deutschen Kinder- und Ju-gendliteratur.* Ed. Reiner Wild. Stuttgart: Metzler, 1990. 251–65.

Kant, Immanuel. *Metaphysik der Sitten.* Ed. Bernd Ludwig. 2 vols. Hamburg: Meiner, 1986–1990.

Kanzog, Klaus. *"Staatspolitisch besonders wert-voll": Ein Handbuch zu 30 deutschen Spielfil-men der Jahre 1934 bis 1945.* Munich: Diskurs Film Verlag, 1994.

Karolle-Berg, Julia. "The Case of the Missing Lit-erary Tradition: Reassessing Four Assump-tions of Crime and Detective Novels in the German-Speaking World (1900–1933)." *Monatshefte* 107/3 (Fall 2015): 431–54.

Katz, Steven T. "1918 and After: The Role of Racial Antisemitism in the Nazi Analysis of the Weimar Republic." *Anti-Semitism in Times of Crisis.* Ed. Sander L. Gilman and Steven T. Katz. New York: New York University Press, 1991. 227–56.

Käutner, Helmut (dir.). *Der Hauptmann von Köpenick.* Feature Film. Real-Film 1956.

Kebbedies, Frank. "Kriminalbiologie und Jugend-kriminalrecht—Verwissenschaftlichung und Moralisierung während der NS-Zeit." *Krimi-nalbiologie.* Ed. Justizministerium des Landes Nordrhein-Westfalen. *Juristische Zeitgeschichte NRW* 6 (1997): 151–67.

Keller, J., and Hanns Andersen. *Der Jude als Ver-brecher. Mit einem Geleitwort des Franken-führers Gauleiter Julius Streicher.* Berlin and Leipzig: Nibelungen, 1937.

Kelly, Alfred. "The Franco-German War and Uni-fication in German Schoolbooks." *1870/71– 1989/90: German Unifications and the Change of Literary Discourse.* Ed. Walter Pape. Berlin, New York: de Gruyter, 1993. 37–60.

Kelly, Alfred. "Whose War? Whose Nation? Ten-sions in the Memory of the Franco-German War of 1870–1871." *Anticipating Total War: The German and American Experiences, 1871– 1914.* Ed. Manfred F. Boemeke, Roger Chick-ering and Stig Förster. Cambridge: Cambridge University Press, 1999. 281–305.

Kessel, Martina. "Introduction. Landscapes of Humour: The History and Politics of the Com-ical in the Twentieth Century." *The Politics of Humour: Laughter, Inclusion and Exclusion in the Twentieth Century.* Ed. Martina Kessel and Patrick Merziger. Toronto: University of Toronto Press, 2012. 3–21.

Kessel, Martina. "Talking War, Debating Unity: Order, Conflict, and Exclusion in 'German Hu-mour' in the First World War." *The Politics of Humour: Laughter, Inclusion and Exclusion in the Twentieth Century.* Ed. Martina Kessel and Patrick Merziger. Toronto: University of Toronto Press, 2012. 82–107.

Kessel, Martina, and Patrick Merziger, eds. *The Politics of Humour: Laughter, Inclusion and Exclusion in the Twentieth Century.* Toronto: University of Toronto Press, 2012.

Kessemeier, Carin. *Der Leitartikler Goebbels in den NS-Organen "Der Angriff" und "Das Reich."* Münster: C.J. Fahle, 1967.

Kiaulehn, Walther. *Berlin: Schicksal einer Welt-stadt.* Munich: C.H. Beck, 1976.

Kiaulehn, Walther. "Der Kürten-Prozeß." *Die Jus-tiz* 6 (1930): 466–74.

Kilpper, K. "Kriminal-Romane und Volksbiblio-thek." *Die Hochwacht* 1.7 (1910/11): 201–3.

Kirchmeier, Christian. "Krise der Kritik: Zur Poetik von Kasus und Rätsel am Beispiel zweier Kriminalerzählungen von Jodokus D.H. Temme und Auguste Groner." *Tötungsarten und Ermittlungspraktiken: Zum literarischen und kriminalistischen Wissen von Mord und Detektion.* Ed. Maximilian Bergengruen, Gideon Haut and Stephanie Langer. Freiburg i. Br.: Rombach, 2015. 19–38.

Klammer, Angelika. "Erfahrung, keine Theorie. Zur Strategie der verstellten Wahrheit bei Walter Serner und Baltasar Gracián." *Der Pfiff aufs Ganze: Studien zu Walter Serner.* Ed. Andreas Puff-Trojan and Wendelin Schmidt-Dengler. Vienna: Sonderzahl, 1998. 29–39.

Klare, Hans. *Das kriminalbiologische Gutachten im Strafprozeß. Eine Untersuchung auf Grund des Materials der bayerischen kriminalbiologischen Sammelstelle in Straubing.* Breslau: Schletter, 1930.

Klaussmann, A. Oskar. *Berliner Gauner: Aus dem Tagebuche eines Berliner Kriminalbeamten.* 2nd ed. Leipzig: List, 1910.

Klaussmann, A. Oskar. *Der falsche Hauptmann von Cöpenick: Ein Gaunerstreich sondergleichen, von der Entstehung im Zuchthause bis zum heutigen Tage ausführlich geschildert und mit zeitgemäßen Betrachtungen versehen.* Berlin: Verlagshaus für Volksliteratur und Kunst, 1906.

Klaussmann, A. Oskar. *Der Hauptmann von Cöpenick vor Gericht: Aktenmäßig dargestellt.* Berlin: Verlagshaus für Volksliteratur und Kunst, 1906.

Kleist, Heinrich von. *Michael Kohlhaas.* Trans. Martin Greenberg. Heinrich von Kleist and Jean Paul, *German Romantic Novellas.* Ed. Frank G. Ryder and Robert M. Browning. New York: Continuum, 2001. 39–121.

Klingler, Werner (dir.). *Banktresor 713.* TV-film. UFA / Berolina 1957.

Klotz, Marcia. "Epistemological Ambiguity and the Fascist Text: *Jew Süss, Carl Peters,* and *Ohm Krüger.*" *New German Critique* 74 (Spring-Summer 1998): 91–124.

Kluger, Ruth. "The Theme of Anti-Semitism in the Work of Austrian Jews." *Anti-Semitism in Times of Crisis.* Ed. Sander L. Gilman and Steven T. Katz. New York: New York University Press, 1991. 173–87.

Knight, Stephen. *Crime Fiction 1800–2000: Detection, Death, Diversity.* New York: Palgrave Macmillan, 2004.

Knops, Tilo. "Cinema from the Writing Desk: Detective Films in Imperial Germany." *A Second Life: German Cinema's First Decades.* Ed. Thomas Elsaesser with Michael Wedel. Amsterdam: Amsterdam University Press, 1996. 132–41.

Knudsen, Hans. *Paul Gurk.* Leipzig: B.G. Teubner, 1925.

Koch, Julius Ludwig August. *Die Frage nach dem geborenen Verbrecher.* Ravensburg: Otto Maier, 1894.

Koch, Julius Ludwig August. *Die psychopathischen Minderwertigkeiten.* Ravensburg: Otto Maier, 1891–3.

Koch, Lars. "Die Volksgemeinschaft als arischer Tresor: Biopolitischer Terror in Rainer Wolffhardts Fernsehfilm *Auf Befehl erschossen—Die Brüder Sass, einst Berlins große Ganoven* (1972)." *Schicht um Schicht behutsam freilegen: Die Regiearbeiten von Rainer Wolffhardt.* Ed. Günter Helmes. Hamburg: Igel, 2012. 153–74.

Koch, Werner. "'Hinaus mit den Juden!' Hugo Bettauer und die unberechenbaren Folgen." *Merkur: Deutsche Zeitschrift für europäisches Denken* 35/3 (March 1981): 254–65.

Koepnick, Lutz. *The Dark Mirror: German Cinema Between Hitler and Hollywood.* Berkeley: University of California Press, 2002.

Komfort-Hein, Susanne. "'Man hat ihn bekanntlich nie entdeckt': Döblins *Das Leben Jacks, des Bauchaufschlitzers* oder Autorschaft und Lustmord im Fokus autobiographischer Erinnerung." *Publications of the Institute of Germanic Studies* 95 (2009): 178–91.

Komfort-Hein, Susanne, and Susanne Scholz, eds. *Lustmord : Medialisierungen eines kulturellen Phantasmas um 1900.* Königstein/Ts.: U. Helmer, 2007.

König, Hans. "Beiträge zur forensisch-psychiatrischen Bedeutung von Menstruation, Gravidität und Geburt." *Archiv für Psychiatrie und Nervenkrankheiten* 53 (1914): 685–737; 777–894. Online version http://link.springer.com/article/10.1007%2FBF01842588#page-1

König, Stefan, and Florian Trenker, in collaboration with Ferdinand Trenker and Hans-Jürgen Panitz. *Bera Luis: Das Phänomen Luis Trenker. Eine Biographie.* Munich: J. Berg, 1992.

Koonz, Claudia. *The Nazi Conscience.* Cambridge, Mass: Belknap Press, 2003.

Koopmann, Helmut. "Hermann Brochs Huguenau: Phänotyp des (modernen) Verbrechers." *Hermann Broch und die Romantik.* Ed. Doren Wohlleben and Paul Michael Lützeler. Berlin: Walter de Gruyter, 2014. 127–40.

Kord, Susanne. *Ein Blick hinter die Kulissen: Deutschsprachige Dramatikerinnen im 18. und 19. Jahrhundert.* Stuttgart: Metzler, 1992.

Kord, Susanne. "Der Fall Wächtler: Die Hamburger Flugblattliteratur zur Folter (1786–88) und die Lust am Lesen." *Zeitschrift für Germanistik* (Februar 2009): 346–60.

Kord, Susanne. *Murderesses in German Writing, 1720–1860: Heroines of Horror.* Cambridge: Cambridge University Press, 2009.

Kord, Susanne. "The Rule of Law and the Role of Literature: German Public Debates on Husband Killers and Human Rights." *Forum for Modern Language Studies* 48 (January 2012): 59–73.

Kord, Susanne. *Sich einen Namen machen: Anonymität und weibliche Autorschaft 1700–1900*. Stuttgart: Metzler, 1996.

Korte, Barbara, and Sylvia Paletschek. "Geschichte und Kriminalgeschichte(n): Texte, Kontexte, Zugänge." *Geschichte im Krimi: Beiträge aus den Kulturwissenschaften*. Ed. Barbara Korte and Sylvia Paletschek. Cologne, Weimar, Vienna: Böhlau, 2009. 7–28.

Kosch, Günter, and Manfred Nagl. *Der Kolportageroman: Bibliographie 1850 bis 1960*. Stuttgart: Metzler, 1993.

Kotzde, Wilhelm. *Und deutsch sei die Erde! Aus der Zeit deutscher Größe*. 4th ed. Leipzig and Berlin: Theodor Weicher, 1921 [orig. 1912].

Kracauer, Siegfried. *Der Detektiv-Roman. Ein philosophischer Traktat*. Frankfurt: Suhrkamp, 1971.

Kracauer, Siegfried. *From Caligari to Hitler: A Psychological History of the German Film*. Princeton: Princeton University Press, 1947.

Kraepelin, Emil. *Die Abschaffung des Strafmaßes: Ein Vorschlag zur Reform der heutigen Strafrechtspflege*. Stuttgart: Ferdinand Enke, 1880.

Kraepelin, Emil. "Das Verbrechen als soziale Krankheit." *Vergeltungsstrafe, Rechtsstrafe, Schutzstrafe: Vier Vorträge*. Ed. Franz von Liszt. Heidelberg: Veröffentlichungen des Akademisch-Juristischen Vereins, 1906. 22–44.

Krafft-Ebing, R[ichard] von. *Psychopathia Sexualis: Mit besonderer Berücksichtigung der Conträren Sexualempfindung. Eine klinisch-forensische Studie*. 2nd ed. Stuttgart: Ferdinand Enke, 1887.

Krajenbrink, Marieke. "Austrian Crime Fiction: Experimentation, Criminal Memory and Humour." *Crime Fiction in German: Der Krimi*. Ed. Katharina Hall. Cardiff: University of Wales Press: 2016. 51–67.

Kratochvil, Antonin. *Abendgespräche mit Luis Trenker*. Munich: Athos, 1980.

Kraus, Karl. "Der Fall Hervay." *Sittlichkeit und Kriminalität*. Frankfurt/M.: Fischer, 1966 (orig. 1908). 75–83.

Kraus, Karl. "Der Hexenprozess von Leoben." *Sittlichkeit und Kriminalität*. Frankfurt/M.: Fischer, 1966 (orig. 1908). 83–97.

Kraus, Karl. "Die Memoiren der Frau v. Hervay." *Sittlichkeit und Kriminalität*. Frankfurt/M.: Fischer, 1966 (orig. 1908). 97–100.

Krause, Willi. *Reichsminister Dr. Goebbels*. Berlin: Deutsche Kultur-Wacht, 1933.

Krebs, Diethart, and Jürgen Reulecke, eds. *Handbuch der deutschen Reformbewegungen 1880–1933*. Wuppertal: Hammer, 1998.

Kreimeier, Klaus. *The Ufa-Story: A History of Germany's Greatest Film Company, 1918–1945*. Trans. Robert and Rita Kimber. Berkeley: University of California Press, 1999.

Kremming, Rolf. "Franz und Erich Sass: Die Meisterdiebe aus Moabit." *Berliner Kurier* (January 8, 2018). https://www.berliner-kurier.de/berlin/polizei-und-justiz/franz-und-erich-sass-die-meisterdiebe-aus-moabit-29441088 (accessed January 26, 2018).

Kreutzahler, Birgit. *Das Bild des Verbrechers in Romanen der Weimarer Republik: Eine Untersuchung vor dem Hintergrund anderer gesellschaftlicher Verbrecherbilder und gesellschaftlicher Grundzüge der Weimarer Republik*. Frankfurt/M.: Peter Lang, 1987.

Kripper, Rainer. "Formen literarischer Erinnerung an den Deutsch-Französischen Krieg von 1870/71." *Krieg und Erinnerung. Fallstudien zum 19. und 20. Jahrhundert*. Ed. Helmut Berding, Klaus Heller and Winfried Speitkamp. Göttingen: Vandenhoeck & Ruprecht, 2000. 17–38.

Krobb, Florian. "'Vienna Goes to Pot without Jews': Hugo Bettauer's *Die Stadt ohne Juden (The City without Jews)*." *Jewish Quarterly* 41/2 (1994): 17–20.

Kruse, Joseph A. "'Waschkörbe' voller begeisterter Briefe: Interview mit Manfred Droste." *Heinrich Spoerl: Buch—Bühne—Leinwand*. Ed. Joseph A. Kruse. Düsseldorf: Droste, 2004. 55–8.

Kruse, Joseph A., ed. *Heinrich Spoerl: Buch—Bühne—Leinwand*. Düsseldorf: Droste, 2004.

Kruse, Wolfgang. "Krieg und nationale Identität: Die Ideologisierung des Krieges." *Eine Welt von Feinden. Der Große Krieg, 1914–1918*. Ed. Wolfgang Kruse. 2nd ed. Frankfurt/M.: Fischer, 2000. 167–76.

Kruse, Wolfgang. "Die Kriegsbegeisterung im Deutschen Reich zu Beginn des Ersten Weltkrieges: Entstehungszusammenhänge, Grenzen und ideologische Strukturen." *Kriegsbegeisterung und mentale Kriegsvorbereitung: Interdisziplinäre Studien*. Ed. Marcel van der Linden and Gottfried Mergner. Berlin: Duncker & Humblot, 1991. 73–87.

Kruse, Wolfgang. "Kriegsbegeisterung? Zur Massenstimmung bei Kriegsbeginn." *Eine Welt von Feinden. Der Große Krieg, 1914–1918*. Ed. Wolfgang Kruse. 2nd ed. Frankfurt/M.: Fischer, 2000. 159–66.

Kruse, Wolfgang, ed. *Eine Welt von Feinden. Der Große Krieg, 1914–1918*. 2nd ed. Frankfurt/M.: Fischer, 2000.

Kuh, Anton. "Bettauer." *Luftlinien: Feuilletons, Essays und Publizistik*. Ed. Ruth Greuner. Vienna: Löcker, 1981. 132–6.

Kuhrt, Aro. "Gebrüder Sass: Meisterdiebe aus der Birkenstraße." *Moabit Online* (May 3, 2007). http://www.moabitonline.de/195 (accessed March 6, 2016).

Kupfer, Peter. *Die Donaumonarchie im Urteil Hermann Bahrs*. Zurich: P. Kupfer, 1983.

Kurella, Hans. *Cesare Lombroso als Mensch und Forscher*. Wiesbaden: J.F. Bergmann, 1910.

Kurella, Hans. *Die Intellektuellen und die Gesell-schaft.* Wiesbaden: J.F. Bergmann, 1913.

Kurella, Hans. *Naturgeschichte des Verbrechers: Grundzüge der criminellen Anthropologie und Criminalpsychologie für Gerichtsärzte, Psychiater, Juristen und Verwaltungsbeamte.* Stuttgart: Ferdinand Enke, 1893.

Kutch, Lynn M., and Todd Herzog. "Introduction." *Tatort Germany: The Curious Case of German-Language Crime Fiction.* Rochester: Camden House, 2014. 1–19.

Kutch, Lynn M., and Todd Herzog, eds. *Tatort Germany: The Curious Case of German-Language Crime Fiction.* Rochester: Camden House, 2014.

Kyora, Sabine. "Liebe machen oder Der Liebhaber als Autor." *Der Pfiff aufs Ganze: Studien zu Walter Serner.* Ed. Andreas Puff-Trojan and Wendelin Schmidt-Dengler. Vienna: Sonderzahl, 1998. 64–74.

Lang, Fritz (dir.). *M: Eine Stadt sucht einen Mörder.* Feature Film. Nero-Film AG 1931.

Lange, Johannes. *Verbrechen als Schicksal: Studien an kriminellen Zwillingen.* Leipzig: Thieme, 1929.

Langenbucher, Erich. "'Der Teufel spielt Verstecken' oder Einiges zur Frage des gegenwärtigen Kriminalromans." *Die Buchbesprechung* 3/2 (1939): 37–41.

Larsen, Egon. *Hochstapler: Die Elite der Gaunerwelt.* Hamburg: Ernst Kabel, 1984.

Laurien, Ingrid. "'A Land of Promise?' Autobiography and Fiction in Frieda von Bülow's East-African Novels." *Africa and Europe: Encountering Myths.* Ed. Carlotta von Maltzan. Frankfurt/M.: Peter Lang, 2003. 203–14.

Lees, Andrew. *Cities, Sin, and Social Reform in Imperial Germany.* Ann Arbor: University of Michigan Press, 2002.

Lees, Andrew. "Moral Discourse and Reform in Urban Germany, 1880s-1914." *Criminals and Their Scientists: The History of Criminology in International Perspective.* Ed. Peter Becker and Richard F. Wetzell. Cambridge: Cambridge University Press, 2006. 85–104.

Leers, Johann von. *Juden sehen Dich an.* Berlin: NS-Druck und Verlag, 1933.

Leers, Johann von. "Die Kriminalität des Judentums." *Das Judentum in der Rechtswissenschaft.* Vol. 3: *Judentum und Verbrechen.* Berlin: Deutscher Rechtsverlag, 1936. 5–60.

Leers, Johann von. *Die Verbrechernatur der Juden.* Berlin: Hochmuth, 1944.

Leimgruber, Florian, ed. *Luis Trenker, Regisseur und Schriftsteller. Die Personalakte Trenker im Berlin Document Center.* Bozen: Frasnelli-Keitsch, 1984.

Leiser, Erwin. *"Deutschland, erwache!" Propaganda im Film des Dritten Reiches.* Reinbek bei Hamburg: Rowohlt, 1968.

Lenk, Elisabeth, and Roswitha Kaever, eds. *Peter*

Kürten, genannt der Vampir von Düsseldorf. Munich: Rogner & Bernd, 1974.

Leonhardt, Ulrike. *Mord ist ihr Beruf: Eine Geschichte des Kriminalromans.* Munich: Beck, 1990.

Lessing, Theodor. *Haarmann: Die Geschichte eines Werwolfs und andere Gerichtsreportagen.* Ed. Rainer Marwedel. Frankfurt/M.: Luchterhand, 1989.

Lessing, Theodor. "Der Maupassant der Kriminalistik." *Prager Tagblatt* No. 109 (May 10, 1925).

Levy, Richard S. *The Downfall of the Anti-Semitic Political Parties in Imperial Germany.* New Haven: Yale University Press, 1975.

Liang, Oliver. "The Biology of Morality: Criminal Biology in Bavaria, 1924–1933." *Criminals and Their Scientists: The History of Criminology in International Perspective.* Ed. Peter Becker and Richard F. Wetzell. Cambridge: Cambridge University Press, 2006. 425–46.

Lichtblau, Albert. "Die Debatten über die Ritualmordbeschuldigungen im österreichischen Abgeordnetenhaus am Ende des 19. Jahrhunderts." *Die Legende vom Ritualmord: Zur Geschichte der Blutbeschuldigung gegen Juden.* Ed. Rainer Erb. Berlin: Metropol, 1993. 267–93.

Lichtblau, Albert, ed. *Als hätten wir dazugehört: Österreichisch-jüdische Lebensgeschichten aus der Habsburgermonarchie.* Vienna: Böhlau, 1999.

Lichtenstein, Alfred. *Der Kriminalroman: Eine literarische und forensische Studie, mit Anhang: Sherlock Holmes zum "Fall Hau."* Munich: Reinhardt, 1908.

Liebe, Georg. *Das Judentum in der deutschen Vergangenheit.* 2nd ed. Leipzig: E. Diederichs, 1923.

Liebermann von Sonnenberg, Erich. "Die Elite des Einbrechertums." *Der Pitaval der Gegenwart: Almanach interessanter Straffälle.* Vol. VIII. Tübingen: J.C.B. Mohr, 1912. 166–92.

Liebermann von Sonnenberg, Erich, and Otto Trettin. *Continental Crimes.* Trans. Winifred Ray. London: Geoffrey Bles, 1935.

Liebermann von Sonnenberg, Max. *Beiträge zur Geschichte der antisemitischen Bewegung vom Jahre 1880–1885, bestehend in Reden, Broschüren, Gedichten.* Berlin: Selbstverlag, 1885.

Liebermann von Sonnenberg, Max. *Der Blutmord in Konitz: mit Streiflichtern auf die strafrechtliche Stellung der Juden im Deutschen Reiche.* 16th ed. Berlin: Deutschnationale Buchhandlung und Verlags-Anstalt, 1901.

Liebermann von Sonnenberg, Max. *Die sociale Frage ist zunächst Judenfrage: Rede.* 3rd ed. Bochum: Selbstverlag des patriotischen Vereins, 1884.

Liebermann von Sonnenberg, Max. *Verträgt sich die Talmud-Moral mit dem deutschen Staatsbürger-Recht? Vortrag.* Leipzig: Fritsch, 1891.

Lindau, Paul. "Der Hauptmann von Köpenick." *Ausflüge ins Kriminalistische*. Munich: Albert Langen, 1909. 241–72.

Lindau, Paul. "Der Schuldige." *Berliner Tageblatt und Handels-Zeitung* (28 October 1906): 2. Beiblatt.

Lindemann, Albert S. *The Jew Accused: Three Antisemitic Affairs (Dreyfus, Beilis, Frank) 1894–1915*. Cambridge: Cambridge University Press, 1991.

Linden, Marcel van der, and Gottfried Mergner. "Kriegsbegeisterung und mentale Kriegsvorbereitung." *Kriegsbegeisterung und mentale Kriegsvorbereitung: Interdisziplinäre Studien*. Ed. Marcel van der Linden and Gottfried Mergner. Berlin: Duncker & Humblot, 1991. 9–23.

Linden, Marcel van der, and Gottfried Mergner, eds. *Kriegsbegeisterung und mentale Kriegsvorbereitung: Interdisziplinäre Studien*. Berlin: Duncker & Humblot 1991.

Lindenstruth, Gerhard. *Auguste Groner (1850–1929): Eine illustrierte Biographie*. Gießen: Selbstverlag, 1992.

Linder, Joachim. "Außenseiter der Gesellschaft: Die Verbrechen der Gegenwart. Straftäter und Strafverfahren in einer literarischen Reihe der Weimarer Republik." *Kriminologisches Journal* 26/4 (1994): 249–72.

Linder, Joachim. "Deutsche Pitavalgeschichten in der Mitte des 19. Jahrhunderts. Konkurrierende Formen der Wissensvermittlung und der Verbrechensdeutung." *Erzählte Kriminalität: Zur Typologie und Funktion von narrativen Darstellungen in Strafrechtspflege, Publizistik und Literatur zwischen 1770 und 1920*. Ed. Jörg Schönert in collaboration with Konstantin Imm and Joachim Linder. Tübingen: Max Niemeyer, 1991. 313–48.

Linder, Joachim, and Michael Ort. "Zur sozialen Konstruktion der Übertretung und zu ihren Repräsentationen im 20. Jahrhundert." *Verbrechen—Justiz—Medien. Konstellationen in Deutschland von 1900 bis zur Gegenwart*. Ed. Joachim Linder and Claus-Michael Ort. Tübingen: Niemeyer, 1999. 3–80.

Linder, Joachim, and Michael Ort, eds. *Verbrechen—Justiz—Medien: Konstellationen in Deutschland von 1900 bis zur Gegenwart*. Tübingen: Niemeyer, 1999.

Lindner, Martin. "Der Mythos 'Lustmord.' Serienmörder in der deutschen Literatur, dem Film und der bildenden Kunst zwischen 1892 und 1932." *Verbrechen—Justiz—Medien. Konstellationen in Deutschland von 1900 bis zur Gegenwart*. Ed. Joachim Linder and Claus-Michael Ort. Tübingen: Niemeyer, 1999. 273–305.

Linthout, Ine van. "'Dichter, schreibt Unterhaltungsromane!' Der Stellenwert der Unterhaltungsliteratur im 'Dritten Reich.'" *Im Pausenraum des Dritten Reiches: Zur Populärkultur im nationalsozialistischen Deutschland*. Ed. Carsten Würmann and Ansgar Warner. Berne: Peter Lang, 2008. 111–24.

Linton, Derek S. "Preparing German Youth for War." *Anticipating Total War: The German and American Experiences, 1871–1914*. Ed. Manfred F. Boemeke, Roger Chickering and Stig Förster. Cambridge: Cambridge University Press, 1999. 167–87.

Lipphardt, Veronika. *Biologie der Juden: Jüdische Wissenschaftler über "Rasse" und Vererbung, 1900–1935*. Göttingen: Vandenhoeck & Ruprecht, 2008.

Liptak, Adam. "Virginia Justices Set Death Sentence in Washington Sniper Case." *New York Times* (April 23, 2005). http://www.nytimes.com/2005/04/23/us/virginia-justices-set-death-sentence-in-washington-sniper-case.html (accessed June 8, 2016).

Liszt, Franz von. "Das Problem der Kriminalität der Juden." *Festschrift für die juristische Fakultät in Giessen zum Universitäts-Jubiläum*. Ed. Reinhard Frank. Giessen: Alfred Töpelmann, 1907. 3–11.

Liszt, Franz von. *Strafrechtliche Aufsätze und Vorträge*. 2 vols. Berlin: J. Guttentag, 1905.

Lombroso, Cesare. *Der Antisemitismus und die Juden im Lichte der modernen Wissenschaft*. Trans. and ed. Hans Kurella. Leipzig: Georg H. Wigand, 1894.

Lombroso, Cesare. *Criminal Man*. Translated and with a new introduction by Mary Gibson and Nicole Hahn Rafter. Durham, NC: Duke University Press, 2006.

Lombroso, Cesare. "Introduction." *Criminal Man According to the Classification of Cesare Lombroso briefly summarised by his daughter Gina Lombroso-Ferrero with an Introduction by Cesare Lombroso*. Montclair: Patterson Smith, 1911. xxi–xxx.

Longerich, Peter. *"Davon haben wir nichts gewusst!" Die Deutschen und die Jugendverfolgung 1933–1945*. Munich: Siedler, 2006.

Lorm, J. "Verbrecherische Liebe." *Czernowitzer Allgemeine Zeitung* (January 11, 1908): 1–3.

Löschburg, Winfried. *Ohne Glanz und Gloria: Die Geschichte des Hauptmanns von Köpenick*. Berlin: Buchverlag Der Morgen, 1978.

Löschburg, Winfried. *Schuster, Hochstapler, Schlitzohr: Die Geschichte des Hauptmanns von Köpenick*. Rostock: BS-Verlag, 2009.

Löschper, Gabi. "Kriminologien und der Komplex 'Verbrechen—Justiz—Medien.'" *Verbrechen—Justiz—Medien. Konstellationen in Deutschland von 1900 bis zur Gegenwart*. Ed. Joachim Linder and Claus-Michael Ort. Tübingen: Niemeyer, 1999. 81–100.

Löwenfeld, Leopold. *Homosexualität und Strafgesetz*. Wiesbaden: J.F. Bergmann, 1908.

Löwenfeld, S. *Die Wahrheit über der Juden Antheil am Verbrechen*. Berlin: Stuhr, 1881.

Lowry, Stephen. *Pathos und Politik: Ideologie in Spielfilmen des Nationalsozialismus.* Tübingen: Niemeyer, 1991.

Ludendorff, Erich. *Meine Kriegserinnerungen 1914–1918.* Berlin: E.S. Mittler und Sohn, 1919.

Ludwig, Albert. "Der Detektiv." *Das literarische Echo* 21.4 (1918): 193–203.

Lüth, Erika. *Meine Liebe zur Literatur: Reminiszenzen an Schuster Wilhelm Voigt, Albatros, Ingwertopf, Poenicher Quintessenzen und an vieles andere mehr.* Cologne: n. p., 1988.

Luxenburger, Hans. "Anlage und Umwelt beim Verbrecher." *Allgemeine Zeitschrift für Psychiatrie und psychisch-gerichtliche Medizin* 92 (1930): 411–38.

Maas, Niklas. "Peter Eisenman im Stelengang." *Frankfurter Allgemeine Zeitung, Feuilleton* (August 15, 2003). http://www.faz.net/aktuell/feuilleton/holocaust-mahnmal-peter-eisenman-im-stelengang-1118767.html (accessed January 5, 2018).

Maase, Kaspar. *Grenzenloses Vergnügen: Der Aufstieg der Massenkultur, 1850–1970.* Frankfurt/M.: Fischer, 1997.

Mahn, Johannes. "Gebrüder Sass: Vorsprung durch Technik." *Vabanque. Bankraub. Theorie. Praxis. Geschichte.* Ed. Klaus Schönberger. Göttingen: Die Libertäre Assoziation, 2001. 24–5.

Maiwald, Manfred. *"Die beiden Freundinnen und ihr Giftmord*: Juristische Betrachtungen zu einem literarischen Prozeßbericht." *Literatur und Recht: Literarische Rechtsfälle von der Antike bis in die Gegenwart.* Ed. Ulrich Mölk. Göttingen: Wallstein, 1996. 370–82.

Majer, Dietmut. "Justiz und Polizei im 'Dritten Reich.'" *Recht und Justiz im "Dritten Reich."* Ed. Ralf Dreier and Wolfgang Sellert. Frankfurt/M.: Suhrkamp, 1989. 136–50.

The Making of Sass. Interviews. DVD supplementary materials to *Sass,* dir. Carlo Rola (orig. release 2001; DVD edition 2002).

Mann, Thomas. *Betrachtungen eines Unpolitischen.* Berlin: S. Fischer, 1918.

Manolescu, Georges, a.k.a. Fürst Lahovary. *Ein Fürst der Diebe: Memoiren.* Berlin: Paul Langenscheidt, 1905.

Manolescu, Georges, a.k.a. Fürst Lahovary. *Gescheitert: Aus dem Seelenleben eines Verbrechers.* Berlin: Paul Langenscheidt, 1905.

Marsch, Edgar. *Die Kriminalerzählung: Theorie—Geschichte—Analyse.* Munich: Winkler, 1972.

Marx, Arndt-H. "Fotosafari: Auf den Spuren der Gebrüder Sass." http://www.blofelds-krimiwelt.de/Wahre-Verbrechen/Gebruder-Sass/gebruder-sass.html (accessed March 6, 2016).

Marxen, Klaus. "Zum Verhältnis von Strafrecht und Gerichtsberichterstattung in der zweiten Hälfte des 19. Jahrhunderts." *Erzählte Kriminalität: Zur Typologie und Funktion von narrativen Darstellungen in Strafrechtspflege, Publizistik und Literatur zwischen 1770 und 1920.* Ed. Jörg Schönert in collaboration with Konstantin Imm and Joachim Linder. Tübingen: Max Niemeyer, 1991. 369–74.

Mayerhofer, Lukas, and Kurt Ifkovits, eds. *Hermann Bahr, Mittler der europäischen Moderne.* Linz: Adalbert-Stifter-Institut, 1998.

McEwen, Britta. *Sexual Knowledge: Feeling, Fact, and Social Reform in Vienna, 1900–1934.* New York: Berghahn, 2012.

Meier, Markus. *Prometheus und Pandora: "persönlicher Mythos" als Schlüssel zum Werk von Hermann Bahr (1863–1934).* Würzburg: Königshausen & Neumann, 1997.

Meinertz, Friedrich. "Der hochstaplerische Betrüger: Infantilismus und Routine." *Schweizer Archiv für Neurologie und Psychiatrie* 75 (1955): 147–72.

Menschik-Bendele, Jutta. "Psychoanalytisches zum Bergfilm: Heldinnen und Helden in den 30er Jahren." *Der Bergfilm 1920–1940.* Ed. Friedbert Aspetsberger. Innsbruck: Studien-Verlag, 2002. 85–99.

Mergel, Thomas. "Propaganda in der Kultur des Schauens: Visuelle Politik in der Weimarer Republik." *Ordnungen in der Krise: Zur politischen Kulturgeschichte Deutschlands 1900–1933.* Ed. Wolfgang Hardtwig. Munich: Oldenbourg, 2007. 531–59.

Meridies, Wilhelm. *Hermann Bahr als epischer Gestalter und Kritiker der Gegenwart.* Hildesheim: Borgmeyer, 1927.

Merziger, Patrick. "Humour in the *Volksgemeinschaft*: The Disappearance of Destructive Satire in National Socialist Germany." *The Politics of Humour: Laughter, Inclusion and Exclusion in the Twentieth Century.* Ed. Martina Kessel and Patrick Merziger. Toronto: University of Toronto Press, 2012. 131–52.

Messerschmidt, Manfred. "Das neue Gesicht des Militarismus in der Zeit des Nationalsozialismus." *Militarismus in Deutschland 1871 bis 1945. Zeitgenössische Analysen und Kritik.* Ed. Wolfram Wette. Münster: LIT, 1999. 81–93.

Mews, Siegfried. *Carl Zuckmayer.* Boston: Twayne Publishers, 1981.

Mezger, Edmund. *Kriminalpolitik auf kriminologischer Grundlage.* Stuttgart: Ferdinand Enke, 1934 (2nd ed. 1942).

Michel, Kai. *Vom Poeten zum Demagogen: Die schriftstellerischen Versuche Joseph Goebbels'.* Cologne, Weimar, Vienna: Böhlau, 1999.

Michels, Helmut. *Ideologie und Propaganda: Die Rolle von Joseph Goebbels in der nationalsozialistischen Außenpolitik bis 1939.* Frankfurt/M.: Peter Lang, 1992.

Mikorey, Max. "Das Judentum in der Kriminalpsychologie." *Das Judentum in der Rechtswissenschaft.* Vol. 3: *Judentum und Verbrechen.* Berlin: Deutscher Rechtsverlag, 1936. 61–82.

Milch, Thomas. "Eine kuriose Karriere. Zur Rezeption Walter Serners nach 1945." *Der Pfiff aufs Ganze: Studien zu Walter Serner*. Ed. Andreas Puff-Trojan and Wendelin Schmidt-Dengler. Vienna: Sonderzahl, 1998. 98–108.

Mitchell, David. *Thinking About It Only Makes It Worse And Other Lessons from Modern Life*. London: Guardian Faber, 2014.

Mittelberg, Ekkehart, Klaus Peter, and Dieter Seiffert. *Texte zur Trivialliteratur: Über Wert und Wirkung von Massenware*. Stuttgart: Klett, 1971.

Möbius, Paul Julius. *Über den physiologischen Schwachsinn des Weibes*. Halle: Carl Marhold, 1903. Online version https://de.wikisource. org/wiki/%C3%9Cber_den_physiologischen_ Schwachsinn_des_Weibes

Modelmog, Ilse. "Kriegsbegeisterung! Kriegsbegeisterung? Zur soziologischen Dimension des Kriegserlebnisses." *Kriegsbegeisterung und mentale Kriegsvorbereitung: Interdisziplinäre Studien*. Ed. Marcel van der Linden and Gottfried Mergner. Berlin: Duncker & Humblot, 1991. 161–78.

Moeller, Felix. *Der Filmminister: Goebbels und der Film in Dritten Reich*. Berlin: Henschel, 1998.

Möller, Eberhard Wolfgang. *Der Führer: Das Weihnachtsbuch der deutschen Jugend*. Ed. Baldur von Schirach. Munich: Zentralverlag der NSDAP, 1938.

Moltke, Johannes von. *No Place Like Home: Locations of Heimat in German Cinema*. Berkeley: University of California Press, 2005.

Mommert, Carl. *Der Ritualmord bei den Talmud-Juden*. Leipzig: E. Haberland, 1905.

Mommsen, Wolfgang J. "Der Topos vom unvermeidlichen Krieg: Außenpolitik und öffentliche Meinung im Deutschen Reich im letzten Jahrzehnt vor 1914." *Bereit zum Krieg: Kriegsmentalität im wilhelminischen Deutschland, 1890–1914*. Ed. Jost Dülffer and Karl Holl. Göttingen: Vandenhoeck & Ruprecht, 1986. 194–224.

Moose, Charles A., and Charles Fleming. *Three Weeks in October: The Manhunt for the Serial Sniper*. New York: Signet, 2004.

Morsch, Günter. *Sachsenhausen: das "Konzentrationslager bei der Reichshauptstadt." Gründung und Ausbau*. Berlin: Metropol, 2014.

Morsch, Günter, and Astrid Ley, eds. *Das Konzentrationslager Sachsenhausen 1936–1945: Ereignisse und Entwicklungen*. Berlin: Metropol, 2008.

Mosse, George L. *Towards the Final Solution: A History of European Racism*. New York: H. Fertig, 1978.

Mosse, George L. "Über Kriegserinnerungen und Kriegsbegeisterung." *Kriegsbegeisterung und mentale Kriegsvorbereitung: Interdisziplinäre Studien*. Ed. Marcel van der Linden and Gott-

fried Mergner. Berlin: Duncker & Humblot, 1991. 27–36.

Mühsam, Erich. *Die Hochstapler: Lustspiel in vier Aufzügen*. Munich: Pieper, 1906.

Müller, Alfred, and Hans Lorenz (i.e. Margarete Paulick). *Mein Freund der Hochstapler: Eine Burleske in drei Akten*. Berlin: Gustav Kiepenheuer, 1944.

Müller, Arnd. *Geschichte der Juden in Nürnberg, 1146–1945*. Nuremberg: Selbstverlag der Stadtbibliothek, 1968.

Müller, Arnd. "Streicher und die Juden." *Der Nationalsozialismus in Franken: Ein Land unter der Last seiner Geschichte*. Ed. Dieter Seifert. Tutzing: Evangelische Akademie, 1979. 30–8.

Müller, Christian. *Verbrechensbekämpfung im Anstaltsstaat: Psychiatrie, Kriminologie und Strafrechtsreform in Deutschland 1871–1933*. Göttingen: Vandenhoeck & Ruprecht, 2004.

Müller, Dorit. "Populärwissenschaftliche Zeitschriften im 'Dritten Reich.'" *Im Pausenraum des Dritten Reiches: Zur Populärkultur im nationalsozialistischen Deutschland*. Ed. Carsten Würmann and Ansgar Warner. Berne: Peter Lang, 2008. 23–44.

Müller, Hans Dieter. "Der junge Goebbels: Zur ideologischen Entwicklung eines politischen Propagandisten." Diss. University of Freiburg (1974).

Müller, Helmut. "Kinder- und Jugendbücher der Kaiserzeit (1871–1918)." *Üb immer Treu und Redlichkeit: Kinder- und Jugendbücher der Kaiserzeit (1871–1918)*. Frankfurt/M.: Stadt- und Universitätsbibliothek Frankfurt am Main, 1988. 9–73.

Müller, Ingo. "Rudolf Olden, Jurist." *Rudolf Olden: Journalist gegen Hitler—Anwalt der Republik. Eine Ausstellung des Deutschen Exilarchivs 1933–1945 der Deutschen Nationalbibliothek Frankfurt am Main, 26. März–28. Juli 2010*. Ed. Sylvia Asmus and Brita Eckert. Frankfurt/M.: Deutsche Nationalbibliothek, 2010. 109–16.

Müller, Karl Johann. *Das Dekadenzproblem in der österreichischen Literatur um die Jahrhundertwende, dargelegt an Texten von Hermann Bahr, Richard von Schaukal, Hugo von Hofmannsthal und Leopold von Andrian*. Stuttgart: Heinz, 1977.

Müller-Dietz, Heinz. "Literatur und Kriminalität." *Juristen-Zeitung* 39 H. 15/16 (1984): 699–708.

Müller-Seidel, Walter. "Alfred Döblin, *Die beiden Freundinnen und ihr Giftmord*: Psychiatrie, Strafrecht und moderne Literatur." *Literatur und Recht: Literarische Rechtsfälle von der Antike bis in die Gegenwart*. Ed. Ulrich Mölk. Göttingen: Wallstein, 1996. 356–69.

Musall, Bettina. "Die Stolzen und die Toten: Militarismus im Kaiserreich." *Spiegel online* (June 14, 2013). http://www.spiegel.de/einestages/

militarismus-im-kaiserreich-a-951161.html (accessed November 28, 2016).

Musil, Robert. "Das verbrecherische Liebespaar: Die Geschichte zweier unglücklicher Ehen." *Gesammelte Werke*. Ed. Adolf Frisé. Reinbeck: Rowohlt, 1978. II: 669–71.

Näcke, Paul. "Rasse und Verbrechen." *Archiv für Criminalanthropologie und Criminalistik* 25 (1906): 64–73.

Nautz, Jürgen. "Der Kampf gegen den Frauenhandel in Österreich vor dem Ersten Weltkrieg." *SIAK-Journal—Zeitschrift für Polizeiwissenschaft und polizeiliche Praxis* 2 (2011): 47–60. Online at http://www.bmi.gv.at/cms/BMI_SIAK/4/2/1/2011/ausgabe_2/files/Nautz_2_2011.pdf (accessed March 23, 2016).

Neff, Bernhard. "'Dekorationsmilitarismus'—Die sozialdemokratische Kritik eines vermeintlich nicht kriegsgemäßen Militärwesens (1890–1911)." *Militarismus in Deutschland 1871 bis 1945. Zeitgenössische Analysen und Kritik*. Ed. Wolfram Wette. Münster: LIT, 1999. 128–45.

Nemes, Robert, and Daniel Unowsky, eds. *Sites of European Antisemitism in the Age of Mass Politics, 1880–1918*. Waltham: Brandeis University Press, 2014.

Neuhaus, Helmut. "Der Germanist Dr. phil. Joseph Goebbels: Bemerkungen zur Sprache des Joseph Goebbels in seiner Dissertation aus dem Jahre 1922." *Zeitschrift für deutsche Philologie* 93 (1974): 398–416.

Neumann, Michael. "Der Reiz des Verwechselbaren: Von der Attraktivität des Hochstaplers im späten 19. Jahrhundert." *Thomas Mann Jahrbuch* 18 (2005): 71–90.

Neureuther, Erich (dir.). *Der Maulkorb*. TV-film. BR 1997.

Nonn, Christoph. *Eine Stadt sucht einen Mörder: Gerücht, Gewalt und Antisemitismus im Kaiserreich*. Göttingen: Vandenhoeck & Ruprecht, 2002.

Noveck, Beth Simone. "1925: Hugo Bettauer's assassination by Otto Rothstock in Vienna marks the first political murder by the Nazis in Austria." *Yale Companion to Jewish Writing and Thought in German Culture 1096–1996*. Ed. Sander L. Gilman & Jack Zipes. New Haven: Yale University Press, 1997. 440–7.

Noveck, Beth Simone. "Maximilian Hugo Bettauer: Sexuality, Politics and the Political Culture of the First Republic in Austria." Diss. University of Innsbruck (1994).

Nusser, Peter. *Der Kriminalroman*. Stuttgart: Metzler, 1980.

Nyanja, Bob (dir.). *The Captain of Nakara*. Feature Film. Blue Sky Films 2012.

O'Brien, Mary-Elizabeth. "The Celluloid War: Packaging War for Sale in Nazi Home-Front Films." *Art, Culture and Media under the Third Reich*. Ed. Richard Etlin. Chicago: Chicago University Press, 2002. 158–80.

O'Brien, Mary-Elizabeth. "Das Feindbild im nationalsozialistischen Film." *Zum Thema Nationalsozialismus im DaF-Lehrwerk und –Unterricht*. Eds. Joachim Warmbold, E.-Anette Koeppel, and Hans Simon-Pelanda. Munich: Iudicium, 1994. 135–41.

O'Brien, Mary-Elizabeth. "Male Conquest of the Female Continent in Veit Harlan's Opfergang (1944)." *Monatshefte* 87:4 (1995): 431–45.

O'Brien, Mary-Elizabeth. "National Socialist Realism and the Problem Film." *The Intersection of Politics and German Literature, 1750–2000: A Festschrift in Honor of Ehrhard Bahr*. Los Angeles: New German Review and the University of California, Los Angeles, 2005.

O'Brien, Mary-Elizabeth. *Nazi Cinema as Enchantment: The Politics of Entertainment in the Third Reich*. Rochester, NY: Camden House, 2004.

Ohmann, Oliver. "Paul Gurk—Ein Genie auf Wartegeld." *Mitteilungen des Vereins für die Geschichte Berlins* 97/1 (2001): 162–9.

Olden, Rudolf. "Abschied von Hugo Bettauer." Typescript from March 31, 1925, 7 pp. In "Konvolut von diversen Zeitungsbeiträgen." 31.3.1925–22.12.1925. Teilnachlass Rudolf Olden. Deutsche Nationalbibliothek Frankfurt: Deutsches Exilarchiv. Document no. EB 79/020-A.02.01.0001.

Olden, Rudolf. *Hitler der Eroberer: Die Entlarvung einer Legende*. Frankfurt/M.: Fischer, 1984.

Olden, Rudolf. "In eigener Sache." *Bettauers Wochenschrift: Probleme des Lebens* 11 (1925): Sonderbeilage 1–2.

Olden, Rudolf. "Konvolut von diversen Zeitungsbeiträgen." 31.3.1925–22.12.1925. Teilnachlass Rudolf Olden. Deutsche Nationalbibliothek Frankfurt: Deutsches Exilarchiv. Document no. EB 79/020-A.02.01.0001.

Olden, Rudolf. "Materialien zum 'Fall Bettauer.'" 1924–25. Teilnachlass Rudolf Olden. Deutsche Nationalbibliothek Frankfurt: Deutsches Exilarchiv. Document no. EB 79/020-D.01.0002.

Olden, Rudolf. "Der Mord und die Apologeten." *Bettauers Wochenschrift: Probleme des Lebens* 44 (1925): 1.

Olden, Rudolf. "Olden Papers." Uncatalogued letters, notes, correspondence, articles, research and typescripts of book drafts, 1927–1940. UCL Special Collections, MS ADD 276/1 and MS ADD 276/2.

Olden, Rudolf. "Prozess Rothstock." *Bettauers Wochenschrift: Probleme des Lebens* 41 (1925): 1–2.

Oppermann, Jürgen. "Das Drama *Der Wanderer* von Joseph Goebbels: Frühformen nationalsozialistischer Literatur." Diss. University of Karlsruhe (March 2005).

Oswald, Richard (dir.). *Der Hauptmann von Köpenick*. Feature Film. Roto Film / G.P. Film 1931.

Oxaal, Ivar, Michael Pollak and Gerhard Botz, eds. *Jews, Antisemitism and Culture in Vienna.* London: Routledge & Kegan Paul, 1987.

Pachler, Barbara. "Der Fall Hervay: Die Rekonstruktion einer der grössten Bigamiefälle des 20. Jahrhunderts." M.A. Thesis University of Graz (2006).

Paret, Peter. *Art as History: Episodes in the Culture and Politics of Nineteenth-Century Germany.* Princeton: Princeton University Press, 1988.

Paret, Peter. *Imagined Battles: Reflections of War in European Art.* Chapel Hill: University of North Carolina Press, 1997.

Pater, Monika. "Producing a Cheerful Public: Light Radio Entertainment during National Socialism." *The Politics of Humour: Laughter, Inclusion and Exclusion in the Twentieth Century.* Ed. Martina Kessel and Patrick Merziger. Toronto: University of Toronto Press, 2012. 108–30.

Pätzold, Kurt. "Julius Streicher: '… he was a very good person.'" *Stufen zum Galgen: Lebenswege vor den Nürnberger Urteilen.* Ed. Kurt Pätzold and Manfred Weißbecker. Leipzig: Militzke, 1999. 264–97.

Paul-Schiff, Maximilian. *Der Prozess Hilsner: Aktenauszug.* Vienna: L. Rosner, 1908.

Pauley, Bruce F. *From Prejudice to Persecution: A History of Austrian Anti-Semitism.* Chapel Hill: University of North Carolina Press, 1992.

Peck, Clemens, and Florian Sedlmeier, eds. *Kriminalliteratur und Wissensgeschichte: Genres—Medien—Techniken.* Bielefeld: Transcript, 2015.

Peters, Jonas. *"Dem Kosmos einen Tritt!" Die Entwicklung des Werks von Walter Serner und die Konzeption seiner dadaistischen Kulturkritik.* Frankfurt/M.: Peter Lang, 1995.

Petersen, Klaus. *Literatur und Justiz in der Weimarer Republik.* Stuttgart: Metzler, 1988.

Petley, Julian. *Capital and Culture: German Cinema 1933–45.* London: BFI, 1979.

Pierucci, Patti. "California Links Beltway Snipers to Jamaat Al Fuqra." *Christian Action Network,* Dec 16, 2013. http://www.christianaction.org/blog/2013/12/16/california-links-beltway-snipers-to-jamaat-al-fuqraadminchristianactionorg (accessed June 8, 2016).

Pipes, Daniel. "The Snipers: Crazy or Jihadists?" *The New York Post* (October 29, 2002). http://www.danielpipes.org/493/the-snipers-crazy-or-jihadis (accessed June 8, 2016).

Pöggeler, Franz. *Der Lehrer Julius Streicher. Zur Personalgeschichte des Nationalsozialismus.* Frankfurt/M., Berne, New York, Paris: Peter Lang, 1991.

Pol, Heinz. "Goebbels als Dichter." *Die Weltbühne* 27/4 (27 January 1931): 129–33.

Possehl, Ulrich. *Moderne Betrüger.* Berlin: Bali-Verlag Berger & Co., 1928.

Postone, Moishe. "Anti-Semitism and National Socialism." *Germans and Jews since the Holocaust: The changing situation in West Germany.* Ed. Anson Rabinbach and Jack Zipes. New York, London: Holmes & Meier, 1986. 302–14.

Poszár, Christine, and Michael Farin, eds. *Die Haarmann-Protokolle.* Hamburg: Rowohlt, 1995.

Preitler, Franz. *Die schwarze Baronin. Roman.* Graz: Leykam, 2015.

Prothero, G.W. *German Policy Before the War.* London: John Murray, 1917.

Puff-Trojan, Andreas. "Von Glücksrittern, Liebeslust und Weinkrämpfen. Serners Konzept einer existentiellen Logik des Scheinens." *Der Pfiff aufs Ganze: Studien zu Walter Serner.* Ed. Andreas Puff-Trojan and Wendelin Schmidt-Dengler. Vienna: Sonderzahl, 1998. 75–92.

Puff-Trojan, Andreas. *Wien/Berlin/Dada: Reisen mit Dr. Serner.* Vienna: Sonderzahl, 1993.

Puff-Trojan, Andreas, and Wendelin Schmidt-Dengler, eds. *Der Pfiff aufs Ganze: Studien zu Walter Serner.* Vienna: Sonderzahl, 1998.

Pulzer, Peter. *The Rise of Political Anti-Semitism in Germany & Austria.* Revised ed. Cambridge, MA: Harvard University Press, 1988.

Quataert, Jean H. "Mobilizing Philanthropy in the Service of War: The Female Rituals of Care in the New Germany, 1871–1914." *Anticipating Total War: The German and American Experiences, 1871–1914.* Ed. Manfred F. Boemeke, Roger Chickering and Stig Förster. Cambridge: Cambridge University Press, 1999. 217–38.

Quest, Hans (dir.). *Der Maulkorb.* TV-film. WDR 1963.

Rahmatian, Ulrike. "Auguste Groner." *Unlearned Lessons.* http://unless-women.eu/biography-details/items/groner.html (accessed September 18, 2017).

Rash, Felicity. "Living in the Colonies: Memoir and Autobiography 1896–1914." *The Discourse Strategies of Imperialist Writing: The German Colonial Idea and Africa, 1848–1945.* New York: Routledge, 2017. 121–39.

Reese, Willy. *Hochstapler.* Munich: B. Funck, 1930.

Reik, Theodor. *Der unbekannte Mörder: Von der Tat zum Täter.* Vienna: Fischer, Internationaler Psychologischer Verlag, 1932 [orig. 1925].

Reimann, Viktor. *Dr. Joseph Goebbels.* Vienna, Munich, Zurich: Molden, 1971.

Reimer, Robert C., ed. *Cultural History through a National Socialist Lens: Essays on the Cinema of the Third Reich.* Rochester: Camden House, 2000.

Reinert, Claus. *Das Unheimliche und die Detektivliteratur: Entwurf einer poetologischen Theorie über Entstehung, Entfaltung und Problematik der Detektivliteratur.* Bonn: Grundmann, 1973.

Renker, Cindy K. "Imperial Motherhood: The German Civilizing Mission in Bülow's *Im Lande der Verheissung.*" Diss. Brigham Young University (2004).

Rentschler, Eric. *The Ministry of Illusion: Nazi Cinema and Its Afterlife*. Cambridge, MA: Harvard University Press, 1996.

Reuband, Karl-Heinz. "Die Leserschaft des 'Stürmer' im Dritten Reich: Soziale Zusammensetzung und antisemitische Orientierungen." *Historical Social Research* 33/4 (2008): 214–54.

Reulecke, Jürgen. "Rassenhygiene, Sozialhygiene, Eugenik." *Handbuch der deutschen Reformbewegungen 1880–1933*. Ed. Diethart Krebs and Jürgen Reulecke. Wuppertal: Hammer, 1998. 197–210.

Reuth, Ralf Georg. *Goebbels: Eine Biographie*. 4th ed. Munich: Piper, 2005.

Reuveni, Gideon. *Reading Germany: Literature and Consumer Culture in Germany before 1933*. Trans. Ruth Morris. Oxford: Berghahn Books, 2006.

Riese, Walther. "Probleme des Kürten-Prozesses." *Die Justiz* 7 (1931/32): 113–16.

Riesenberger, Dieter. "Katholische Militarismuskritik im Kaiserreich." *Militarismus in Deutschland 1871 bis 1945. Zeitgenössische Analysen und Kritik*. Ed. Wolfram Wette. Münster: LIT, 1999. 97–114.

Riess, Curt. *Goebbels: Dämon der Macht*. Munich: Universitas, 1989.

Riha, Ortrun, ed. *"Die Freigabe der Vernichtung lebensunwerten Lebens": Beiträge des Symposiums über Karl Binding und Alfred Hoche am 2. Dezember 2004 in Leipzig*. Aachen: Shaker, 2005.

Ritte, Jürgen. "Schnock, schlass et schlingue! Walter Serners Probleme mit den Apachen und anderen Franzosen." *Der Pfiff aufs Ganze: Studien zu Walter Serner*. Ed. Andreas Puff-Trojan and Wendelin Schmidt-Dengler. Vienna: Sonderzahl, 1998. 49–63.

Robertson, Ritchie. *The Jewish Question in German Literature, 1749–1939: Emancipation and its Discontents*. Oxford: Oxford University Press, 1999.

Rohkrämer, Thomas. "Heroes and Would-Be Heroes: Veterans' and Reservists' Associations in Imperial Germany." *Anticipating Total War: The German and American Experiences, 1871–1914*. Ed. Manfred F. Boemeke, Roger Chickering and Stig Förster. Cambridge: Cambridge University Press, 1999. 189–215.

Rohkrämer, Thomas. *Der Militarismus der 'kleinen Leute': Die Kriegervereine im Deutschen Kaiserreich 1871–1914*. Munich: R. Oldenbourg, 1990.

Rojahn, Jürgen. "Arbeiterbewegung und Kriegsbegeisterung: Die deutsche Sozialdemokratie 1870–1914." *Kriegsbegeisterung und mentale Kriegsvorbereitung: Interdisziplinäre Studien*. Ed. Marcel van der Linden and Gottfried Mergner. Berlin: Duncker & Humblot, 1991. 57–71.

Rola, Carlo (dir.). *Sass*. Feature Film. Constantin Film 2001.

Roos, Daniel. *Julius Streicher und "Der Stürmer" 1923–1945*. Paderborn: Ferdinand Schöningh, 2014.

Rose, Alison. "Bigamy and Bigotry in the Austrian Alps: Antisemitism, Gender, and the 'Hervay Affair' of 1904." *Sites of European Antisemitism in the Age of Mass Politics, 1880–1918*. Ed. Robert Nemes and Daniel Unowsky. Waltham: Brandeis University Press, 2014. 157–77.

Rosenau, Henning. "Der 'Hauptmann von Köpenick' ein Hangtäter?—Studie zu einem Urteil des Königlichen Landgerichts II in Berlin und einem Schauspiel von Carl Zuckmayer." *Zeitschrift für internationale Strafrechtsdogmatik* 3 (2010): 284–98.

Rosenberg, Alfred. *Der Fall Bettauer: Ein Musterbeispiel jüdischer Zersetzungstätigkeit durch entsittlichendes Schrifttum. Flugschrift aus: Der Weltkampf: Halbmonatsschrift für die Judenfrage aller Länder*. Munich: Deutscher Volksverlag Dr. E. Boepple, 1925.

Rosenberg, Alfred. "Der internationale Mädchenhandel." *Völkischer Beobachter* No. 84 (July 8, 1925).

Rosenberg, Alfred. *Der Mythus des 20. Jahrhunderts. Eine Wertung der seelisch-geistigen Gestaltungskämpfe unserer Zeit*. Munich: Hoheneichen, 1930.

Rosenfeld, Gavriel D. *Hi Hitler! How the Nazi Past Is Being Normalized in Contemporary Culture*. Cambridge: Cambridge University Press, 2014.

Rost, Hans. *Gedanken und Wahrheiten zur Judenfrage. Eine soziale und politische Studie*. Trier: Paulinus-Druckerei, 1907.

Roth, Joseph. "Die Frauen Nebbe und Klein." *Werke*. Ed. Klaus Westermann. Cologne: Kiepenhauer & Witsch, 1989. I: 952–4.

Rothbarth, Otto. "Zum Fall Kürten." *Die Justiz* 7 (1931/32): 117–23.

Rothstock, Otto. *Rothstocks Monatsschrift für Politik* 1 (1932). 12 pp.

Rottländer. *Der Hauptmann von Köpenick*. Leipzig-Raschwitz: Volger, 1912.

Rozenblit, Marsha. *The Jews of Vienna, 1867–1914: Assimilation and Identity*. Albany: State University of New York Press, 1983.

Rozenblit, Marsha. *Reconstructing a National Identity: The Jews of Habsburg Austria during World War I*. Oxford: Oxford University Press, 2001.

Rüping, Hinrich. "Zur Praxis der Strafjustiz im 'Dritten Reich.'" *Recht und Justiz im "Dritten Reich."* Ed. Ralf Dreier and Wolfgang Sellert. Frankfurt/M.: Suhrkamp, 1989. 180–93.

Ruppin, Arthur. "Die Kriminalität der Christen und Juden in Deutschland, 1899–1902." *Zeitschrift für Demographie und Statistik der Juden* 1 (1905): 6–9.

Rürup, Reinhard. "Die 'Judenfrage' der bürgerlichen Gesellschaft und die Entstehung des modernen Antisemitismus." *Emanzipation und Antisemitismus: Studien zur 'Judenfrage' der bürgerlichen Gesellschaft*. Göttingen: Vandenhoeck & Ruprecht, 1975. 74–94.

Rzepka, Charles. *Detective Fiction*. Cambridge (UK): Polity Press, 2005.

Saalmann, Dieter. "Fascism and Aesthetics: Joseph Goebbel's [sic!] Novel *Michael: A German Fate Through the Pages of a Diary* (1929)." *Orbis Litterarum* 41 (1986): 213–28.

Sachar, Howard M. *The Course of Modern Jewish History*. London: Weidenfeld and Nicolson, 1958.

"Samuel Bellachini." *Magicpedia*. http://geniimagazine.com/magicpedia/Samuel_Bellachini (accessed February 1, 2017).

Sardar, Ziauddin, and Merryl Wyn Davies. *Why Do People Hate America?* New York: Disinformation, 2002.

Savoy, Bénédicte. *"Vom Faustkeil zur Handgranate": Filmpropaganda für die Berliner Museen 1934–1939*. Cologne, Weimar, Vienna: Böhlau, 2014.

Schacht, Daniel Alexander. *Fluchtpunkt Provinz: Der neue Heimatfilm zwischen 1968 und 1972*. Münster: MAKS, 1991.

Schad, Bettina. "Nachbemerkung." Christian Schad, *Relative Realitäten: Erinnerungen um Walter Serner*. Augsburg: Maroverlag, 1999. 113–22.

Schad, Christian. "Hahnebüchene Geschichten. Eine Kritik" [on Walter Serner's *Zum blauen Affen*]. http://gutenberg.spiegel.de/buch/zum-blauen-affen-6879/35 (accessed October 25, 2017).

Schad, Christian. *Relative Realitäten: Erinnerungen um Walter Serner*. Augsburg: Maroverlag, 1999.

Schädel, Mirko. *Illustrierte Bibliographie der Kriminalliteratur 1796–1945 im deutschen Sprachraum. Unter Mitwirkung von Robert N. Bloch*. 2 vols. Butjadingen: Achilla Presse, 2006.

Scheible, Hartmut. *Erläuterungen und Dokumente. Carl Zuckmayer: Der Hauptmann von Köpenick*. Stuttgart: Reclam, 1977.

Scheicher, Joseph. *Aus dem Jahre 1920: Ein Traum vom Landtags- und Reichratsabgeordneten Dr. Joseph Scheicher*. St. Pölten: Johann Gregora's Buchhandlung, 1900.

Scheit, Gerhard. *Verborgener Staat, lebendiges Geld: Zur Dramaturgie des Antisemitismus*. 2nd ed. Freiburg: Ça ira, 2006.

Schenda, Rudolf. *Volk ohne Buch: Studien zur Sozialgeschichte der populären Lesestoffe 1770–1910*. Frankfurt/M.: Vittorio Klostermann, 1970.

Schermann, Rafael. *Seine Braut der Hochstapler*. Berlin: Schaefer, 1932.

Schiller, Friedrich. *Schiller's William Tell, Translated, with an Introduction and Notes, by Major-General Patrick Maxwell*. London: Walter Scott, n. d.

Schimmelpfennig, Arthur. *Beiträge zur Geschichte des Kriminalromans. Ein Wegweiser durch die Kriminalliteratur der Vergangenheit und Gegenwart*. Dresden: Moewig & Höffner, 1908.

Schirach, Baldur von. *Die Fahne der Verfolgten*. Berlin: Wilhelm Andermann, n. d.

Schirach, Baldur von. *Die Hitler-Jugend: Idee und Gestalt*. Leipzig: Koehler & Amelang, 1936.

Schirach, Baldur von. *Das Lied der Getreuen: Verse ungenannter österreichischer Hitler-Jugend aus den Jahren der Verfolgung 1933–37*. Leipzig: Philipp Reclam jun., 1938.

Schlag, Gabi. "Ehrenwerte Gauner: Die Meisterdiebe Franz und Erich Sass und die Zwanziger Jahre in Berlin." *SWR 2: Feature am Sonntag*. Aired August 22, 2010. Screenplay available at http://www.swr.de/swr2/programm/sendungen/feature/-/id=6632706/property=download/nid=659934/1i0g5mx/swr2-feature-am-sonntag-20100822.pdf (accessed March 6, 2016).

Schlösser, Manfred. "Vorspruch." In: Paul Gurk, *Tresoreinbruch. Roman*. Darmstadt: Agora, 1981. 5–8.

Schmatz, Ferdinand. "Walter Serner und sein Verhältnis zur bildenden Kunst. Ein Hinweis." *Der Pfiff aufs Ganze: Studien zu Walter Serner*. Ed. Andreas Puff-Trojan and Wendelin Schmidt-Dengler. Vienna: Sonderzahl, 1998. 40–8.

Schmid, David. *Natural Born Celebrities: Serial Killers in American Culture*. Chicago: Chicago University Press, 2005.

Schmid, David. "Serial Killing in America After 9/11." *The Journal of American Culture* 28/1 (March 2005): 61–9.

Schmidt, Colette. "FP Burgenland: Kandidat mit antisemitischen Aussagen in Draßburg." *derStandard.at* (September 19, 2017). http://derstandard.at/2000064309750/FPOe-im-Burgenland-Neuer-rechter-Einzelfall (accessed January 7, 2018).

Schmidt, Jochen. *Gangster, Opfer, Detektive: Eine Typengeschichte des Kriminalromans*. Frankfurt: Ullstein, 1989.

Schmidt-Dengler, Wendelin. "Vorwort." *Der Pfiff aufs Ganze: Studien zu Walter Serner*. Ed. Andreas Puff-Trojan and Wendelin Schmidt-Dengler. Vienna: Sonderzahl, 1998. 7–9.

Schönert, Jörg. "Bilder vom 'Verbrechermenschen' in den rechtskulturellen Diskursen um 1900: Zum Erzählen über Kriminalität und zum Status kriminologischen Wissens." *Erzählte Kriminalität: Zur Typologie und Funktion von narrativen Darstellungen in Strafrechtspflege, Publizistik und Literatur zwischen 1770 und 1920*. Ed. Jörg Schönert in collaboration with Konstantin Imm and Joachim Linder. Tübingen: Max Niemeyer, 1991. 497–531.

Schönert, Jörg. "Kriminalgeschichten in der deutschen Literatur zwischen 1770 und 1890: Zur Entwicklung des Genres in sozialgeschichtlicher Perspektive." *Geschichte und Gesellschaft* 9 (1983): 49–68.

Schönert, Jörg. *Kriminalität erzählen: Studien zu Kriminalität in der deutschsprachigen Literatur (1570–1920)*. Berlin: de Gruyter, 2015.

Schönert, Jörg. "Zur Ausdifferenzierung des Genres 'Kriminalgeschichten' in der deutschen Literatur vom Ende des 18. bis zum Beginn des 20. Jahrhunderts." *Literatur und Kriminalität: Die gesellschaftliche Erfahrung von Verbrechen und Strafverfolgung als Gegenstand des Erzählens. Deutschland, England und Frankreich 1850–1880*. Ed. Jörg Schönert. Tübingen: Niemeyer, 1983. 1–13.

Schönert, Jörg, ed. *Literatur und Kriminalität: Die gesellschaftliche Erfahrung von Verbrechen und Strafverfolgung als Gegenstand des Erzählens. Deutschland, England und Frankreich 1850–1880*. Tübingen: Niemeyer, 1983.

Schönert, Jörg, in collaboration with Konstantin Imm and Joachim Linder, eds. *Erzählte Kriminalität: Zur Typologie und Funktion von narrativen Darstellungen in Strafrechtspflege, Publizistik und Literatur zwischen 1770 und 1920*. Tübingen: Niemeyer, 1991.

Schönert, Jörg, in collaboration with Wolfgang Naucke and Konstantin Imm. "Zur Einführung in den Gegenstandsbereich und zum interdisziplinären Vorgehen." *Erzählte Kriminalität: Zur Typologie und Funktion von narrativen Darstellungen in Strafrechtspflege, Publizistik und Literatur zwischen 1770 und 1920*. Ed. Jörg Schönert in collaboration with Konstantin Imm and Joachim Linder. Tübingen: Niemeyer, 1991. 11–55.

Schrafsteller, Susanna, and Alan E. Steinweis, eds. *The Germans and the Holocaust: Popular Responses to the Persecution and Murder of the Jews*. New York: Berghahn Books, 2015.

Schrank, Josef. *Der Mädchenhandel und seine Bekämpfung*. Vienna: Selbstverlag, 1904.

Schreiber, Hans-Ludwig. "Das Strafgesetzbuch im 'Dritten Reich.'" *Recht und Justiz im "Dritten Reich."* Ed. Ralf Dreier and Wolfgang Sellert. Frankfurt/M.: Suhrkamp, 1989. 151–79.

Schröder, Karin. "'Michael. Ein deutsches Schicksal in Tagebuchblättern'—Joseph Goebbels als Romanautor. Beiträge zu einer Interpretation." Diss. Gießen (1993).

Schug, Alexander. "Das Ende der Hochkultur? Ästhetische Strategien der Werbung 1900–1933." *Ordnungen in der Krise: Zur politischen Kulturgeschichte Deutschlands 1900–1933*. Ed. Wolfgang Hardtwig. Munich: Oldenbourg, 2007. 501–30.

Schulte-Sasse, Linda. *Entertaining the Third Reich: Illusions of Wholeness in Nazi Cinema*. Durham, NC: Duke University Press, 1996.

Schultze, Ernst. "Kriminal-Literatur." *Eckart: Ein deutsches Literaturblatt* 5.1 (1910/11): 31–41, 95–115.

Schultze, Ernst. *Die Schundliteratur: Ihr Vordringen, ihre Folgen, ihre Bekämpfung*. 3rd ed. Halle: Buchhandlung des Waisenhauses, 1925.

Schulz-Buschhaus, Ulrich. *Formen und Ideologien des Kriminalromans: Ein gattungsgeschichtlicher Essay*. Frankfurt/Main: Athenaion, 1975.

Schütz, Erhard, ed. *Zur Aktualität des Kriminalromans: Berichte, Analysen, Reflexionen zur neueren Kriminalliteratur*. Munich: Fink, 1978.

Schwab, Lothar. "Deutschland 1932. Die Einheit von genretypischer Ahistorizität und reaktionärer Propaganda in Luis Trenkers *Der Rebell*." *Diskurs* (Cologne) 3.3–4 (1973): 51–64.

Schwanebeck, Wieland, ed. *Über Hochstapelei: Perspektiven auf eine kulturelle Praxis*. Berlin: Neofolis, 2014.

Schwartz, Michael. "Kriminalbiologie und Strafrechtsreform: Die 'erbkranken Gewohnheitsverbrecher' im Visier der Weimarer Sozialdemokratie." *Kriminalbiologie*. Ed. Justizministerium des Landes Nordrhein-Westfalen. *Juristische Zeitgeschichte NRW* 6 (1997): 13–68.

Schwarz, Egon. "Tödlicher Sturm der Entrüstung: 'Der Fall Bettauer' in einer sorgfältigen Dokumentation." *Frankfurter Allgemeine: Zeitung für Deutschland* (June 21, 1979).

Schwarz, Hans. *Ehebruch und Bigamie nach kanonischem Recht bis zum Erlass des Codex*. Zirndorf: L. Behmann, 1927.

Schwarz, Johannes Valentin. "Antisemitische Karikaturen und Cartoons: Fremdbilder—Selbstbilder." www.politik-lernen.at/dl/.../504_karikaturen.pdf (accessed March 22, 2016).

Schwarz, Julia. "Visueller Antisemitismus in den Titelkarikaturen des Stürmer." *Jahrbuch für Antisemitismusforschung* 19 (2010): 197–216.

Schwarz, Mosche Karl. "The Jews of Styria." *The Jews of Austria: Essays on Their Life, History and Destruction*. Ed. Josef Fraenkel. London: Vallentine, 1967. 391–2.

Schwenken, Karl P. *Notizen über die berüchtigsten jüdischen Gauner und Spitzbuben welche sich gegenwärtig in Deutschland und an dessen Grenzen herumtreiben nebst genauer Beschreibung ihrer Person, nach Criminalakten und sonstigen zuverlässigen Quellen bearbeitet und in alphabetischer Ordnung zusammengestellt*. Marburg: Kriegen, 1820.

Schwerk, Ekkehard. "Die Brüder aus der Birkenstraße: Franz und Erich Sass." In: Paul Gurk, *Tresoreinbruch. Roman*. Darmstadt: Agora, 1981. 187–204.

Schwerk, Ekkehard. *Die Meisterdiebe von Berlin: Die 'goldenen Zwanziger' der Gebrüder Sass*. Berlin: Nishen, 1984.

Seibert, Thomas-Michael. "Erzählen als gesellschaftliche Konstruktion von Kriminalität."

Erzählte Kriminalität: Zur Typologie und Funktion von narrativen Darstellungen in Strafrechtspflege, Publizistik und Literatur zwischen 1770 und 1920. Ed. Jörg Schönert in collaboration with Wolfgang Naucke and Konstantin Imm. Tübingen: Niemeyer, 1991. 73–86.

Seidel, Michael. "Balder Olden." *Rudolf Olden: Journalist gegen Hitler—Anwalt der Republik. Eine Ausstellung des Deutschen Exilarchivs 1933–1945 der Deutschen Nationalbibliothek Frankfurt am Main, 26. März–28. Juli 2010*. Ed. Sylvia Asmus and Brita Eckert. Frankfurt/M.: Deutsche Nationalbibliothek, 2010. 153–67.

Seidl, Joseph. *Der Jude des 19. Jahrhunderts, oder warum sind wir Antisemiten?* Munich: Abt, 1900.

Serner, Walter. "Der Doktor Sahob." *Zum blauen Affen. Dreiunddreissig hahnebüchene Geschichten*. Hanover: Paul Steegemann, 1921. 144–9.

Serner, Walter. *Erotische Kriminalgeschichten*. http://gutenberg.spiegel.de/buch/erotische-kriminalgeschichten-6880/1 (accessed January 17, 2018).

Serner, Walter. *Das erzählerische Werk in drei Bänden*. Ed. Thomas Milch. Munich: brb, 2000.

Serner, Walter. "Fräulein Annas folgenschwerstes Abenteuer." *Zum blauen Affen. Dreiunddreissig hahnebüchene Geschichten*. Hanover: Paul Steegemann, 1921. 194–200.

Serner, Walter. "Kuhles ganz seltene Stunde." *Zum blauen Affen. Dreiunddreissig hahnebüchene Geschichten*. Hanover: Paul Steegemann, 1921. 60–6.

Serner, Walter. "Der Lebenskünstler." *Zum blauen Affen. Dreiunddreissig hahnebüchene Geschichten*. Hanover: Paul Steegemann, 1921. 105–11.

Serner, Walter. *Letzte Lockerung: Ein Handbrevier für Hochstapler und solche, die es werden wollen*. Hanover: Paul Steegemann, 1920.

Serner, Walter. "Theodor Lessing und der Mädchenhändler." *Karlsbader Tagblatt* No. 149 (July 4, 1926).

Serner, Walter. *Über Denkmäler, Weiber und Laternen: Frühe Schriften*. Erlangen: Klaus G. Renner, 1981.

Serner, Walter. "Walter Serner über Walter Serner." *Die neue Bücherschau* 4 (June 1925): 23–5.

Serner, Walter. "Wer ist Walter Serner???" *Börsenblatt des deutschen Buchhandels* No. 274 (November 25, 1927): 11609–13.

Serner, Walter. *Zum blauen Affen. Dreiunddreissig hahnebüchene Geschichten*. Hanover: Paul Steegemann, 1921.

Seyrl, Harald. *Tatort Wien: Der neue Wiener Pitaval. Dokumentation der bedeutendsten Kriminalfälle Wiens des 20. Jahrhunderts. 2. Band: Die Zeit von 1925–1944*. Vienna: Edition Seyrl, n. d.

Showalter, Dennis. "Jews, Nazis, and the Law: The Case of Julius Streicher." *Simon Wiesenthal Center Annual* 6 (1989): 143–63.

Showalter, Dennis. *Little Man, What Now? Der Stürmer in the Weimar Republic*. Hamden: Archon Books, 1982.

Shumannfang, Barbara Ann. "Envisioning Empire, Jewishness, blackness and gender in German colonial discourse from Frieda von Bülow to the Nazi 'Kolonie und Heimat.'" Diss. Duke University (1998).

Siebenpfeiffer, Hania. *"Böse Lust": Gewaltverbrechen in Diskursen der Weimarer Republik*. Cologne, Weimar, Vienna: Böhlau, 2005.

Siebenpfeiffer, Hania. "Nachwort." Alfred Döblin, *Die beiden Freundinnen und ihr Giftmord*. Frankfurt/M.: Fischer, 2013. 117–33.

Siemens, Daniel. "'Vom Leben getötet': Die Gerichtsreportage in der liberaldemokratischen Presse im Berlin der 1920er Jahre." *Ordnungen in der Krise: Zur politischen Kulturgeschichte Deutschlands 1900–1933*. Ed. Wolfgang Hardtwig. Munich: Oldenbourg, 2007. 327–54.

Silverman, Lisa. *Becoming Austrians: Jews and Culture between the World Wars*. Oxford: Oxford University Press, 2012.

Simon, Jürgen. "Einleitung." *Kriminalbiologie*. Ed. Justizministerium des Landes Nordrhein-Westfalen. *Juristische Zeitgeschichte NRW* 6 (1997): 9–12.

Simon, Jürgen. "Kriminalbiologie—theoretische Konzepte und praktische Durchführung eines Ansatzes zur Erfassung der Kriminalität." *Kriminalbiologie*. Ed. Justizministerium des Landes Nordrhein-Westfalen. *Juristische Zeitgeschichte NRW* 6 (1997): 69–105.

Sinn, Dieter. "Betrug und Hochstapelei." *Das grosse Verbrecher Lexikon. Mit Abbildungen. Die spektakulärsten Kriminalfälle des 19. und 20. Jahrhunderts*. Herrsching: Pawlak, 1984. 138–48.

Skalnik, Kurt. *Die österreichische Presse: vorgestern, gestern, heute*. Vienna: Bergland, 1964.

Smith, Helmut Walser. *The Butcher's Tale: Murder and Anti-Semitism in a German Town*. New York: W.W. Norton, 2002.

Snyder, Timothy. *Black Earth: The Holocaust as History and Warning*. New York: Tim Duggan, 2015.

Sommer, Robert. *Kriminalpsychologie und strafrechtliche Psychopathologie auf naturwissenschaftlicher Grundlage*. Leipzig: Barth, 1904.

Sparing, Frank. "Zwangskastrationen im Nationalsozialismus: Das Beispiel der Kriminalbiologischen Sammelstelle Köln." *Kriminalbiologie*. Ed. Justizministerium des Landes Nordrhein-Westfalen. *Juristische Zeitgeschichte NRW* 6 (1997): 169–212.

Spark, Clare L. "Klara Hitler's Son: Reading the Langer Report on Hitler's Mind." *Social Thought & Research* XXII 1/2 (1999): 113–38.

Spencer, Elaine Glovka. *Police and the Social Order in German Cities: The Düsseldorf District 1848–1914.* DeKalb: Northern Illinois University Press, 1992.

Sperry, Paul. *Infiltration: How Muslim Spies and Subversives Have Penetrated Washington.* Nashville, TN: Nelson Current, 2005.

"Das Spiel ist aus—Arthur Nebe: Glanz und Elend der deutschen Kriminalpolizei." *Der Spiegel* 43 (October 20, 1949); 44 (October 27, 1949). http://www.spiegel.de/spiegel/print/d-44438652.html and http://www.spiegel.de/spiegel/print/d-44438424.html (accessed March 6, 2016).

Spoerl, Heinrich. *Der Maulkorb.* Munich: dtv, 1965.

Sprecher, Thomas. *Literatur und Verbrechen: Kunst und Kriminalität in der europäischen Erzählprosa um 1900.* 2nd ed. Frankfurt/M.: Vittorio Klostermann, 2015.

Stargardt, Nicholas. *The German Idea of Militarism: Radical and Socialist Critics, 1866–1914.* Cambridge: Cambridge University Press, 1994.

Stark, Adolf. *Im Banne der Leidenschaft. Österr[eichischer] Kriminalroman.* Berlin: Henschel, 1913.

Staudte, Wolfgang (dir.). *Der Maulkorb.* Feature Film. Kurt Ulrich Filmproduktion 1958.

Stazol, Harald Nicolas. "Impostors Revisited—oder warum Hochstapler hochstapeln." *Kultur und Gespenster* 9 (2009): 79–87.

Steinweis, Alan E. *Art, Ideology and Economics in Nazi Germany: The Reich Chambers of Music, Theater and the Visual Arts.* Chapel Hill: University of North Carolina Press, 1993.

Steinweis, Alan E. *Studying the Jew: Scholarly Antisemitism in Nazi Germany.* Cambridge, MA: Harvard University Press, 2006.

Steinweis, Alan E., and Robert D. Rachlin. *The Law in Nazi Germany: Ideology, Opportunism, and the Perversion of Justice.* New York, Oxford: Berghahn Books, 2013.

Stellrecht, Helmut. *Adolf Hitler—Heil und Unheil. Die verlorene Revolution.* Tübingen: Grabert, 1974.

Stellrecht, Helmut. *Die Wehrerziehung der deutschen Jugend.* Berlin: E.S. Mittler & Sohn, 1936.

Stelzner, Helene Friederike. "Zur Psychologie des verbrecherischen Renommisten." *Zeitschrift für die gesamte Neurologie und Psychiatrie* 44/1 (December 1919): 391–435.

Stephan, Werner. *Joseph Goebbels: Dämon einer Diktatur.* Stuttgart: Union Deutsche Verlagsgesellschaft, 1949.

Stern, Jacques. "Über den Wert der dichterischen Behandlung des Verbrechens für die Strafrechtswissenschaft." *Zeitschrift für die gesamte Strafrechtswissenschaft* 26 (1906): 141–71.

Sternberg, Adalbert Graf von. "Bettauer." *Wiener Sonn- und Montagszeitung* (March 16, 1925): 5.

Stevenson, David. *Armaments and the Coming of War: Europe, 1904–1914.* Oxford: Clarendon Press, 1996.

Stewart, Elizabeth A. "Hugo Bettauer and the Culture of Vienna in the 1920s." M.Phil. Thesis, University of Exeter (1995).

Stoetzler, Marcel. *The State, the Nation, and the Jews: Liberalism and the Antisemitism Dispute in Bismarck's Germany.* Lincoln: University of Nebraska Press, 2009.

Stoetzler, Marcel, ed. *Antisemitism and the Constitution of Sociology.* Lincoln: University of Nebraska Press, 2014.

Stoetzler, Marcel, and Christine Achinger. "German modernity, barbarous Slavs and profit-seeking Jews: the cultural racism of nationalist liberals." *Nations and Nationalism* (2013): 1–22.

Stolpe, Elmar. "Wilde Freude, fürchterliche Schönheit: Die romantische Ästhetisierung des Krieges." *Kriegsbegeisterung und mentale Kriegsvorbereitung: Interdisziplinäre Studien.* Ed. Marcel van der Linden and Gottfried Mergner. Berlin: Duncker & Humblot, 1991. 37–53.

Strack, Hermann L. *Der Blutaberglaube in der Menschheit: Blutmorde und Blutritus.* 4th ed. Munich: C.H. Beck, 1892.

Strack, Hermann L. *Die Juden, dürfen sie "Verbrecher von Religions wegen" genannt werden? Aktenstücke, zugleich als ein Beitrag zur Kennzeichnung der Gerechtigkeitspflege in Preußen.* Berlin: Hermann Walther, 1893.

"Strafsache gegen Hugo Bettauer und Rudolf Olden." Landesgericht für Strafsachen Wien I: Vr XXXI 1776/24.

"Strafsache gegen Otto Rothstock." Landesgericht für Strafsachen Wien I: Vr XXVII 1748/25.

Strasser, Peter. *Verbrechermenschen: Zur kriminalwissenschaftlichen Erzeugung des Bösen.* 2nd ed. Frankfurt/M., New York: Campus, 2005.

Strassnoff, Ignatz. *Ich, der Hochstapler Ignatz Strassnoff.* Berlin: Die Schmiede, 1926.

Streckfuß, Carl Adolph. *Das Testament. Kriminal-Roman.* Berlin: Gnadenfeld, 1899.

Streckfuß, Carl Adolph. *Die wilde Toni. Novelle.* Berlin: Goldschmidt, 1899.

Streicher, Julius. *Kampf dem Weltfeind. Reden aus der Kampfzeit.* Ed. Heinz Preiß. Nuremberg: Verlag der Stürmer, 1938.

Streicher, Julius. *Ruf zur Tat. Aufsätze aus den Kampfjahren 1920–1922.* Ed. Heinz Preiß. Nuremberg: Verlag Der Stürmer, 1937.

Streiter, Sabina. "Frieda von Bülow und Ricarda Huch: Briefe aus dem Jahr 1895." *Jahrbuch der Deutschen Schillergesellschaft* 32 (1988): 51–73.

Strem, Nikolaus. "Hakenkreuz und Moral: An-läßlich der Genesung Rothstocks." *Bettauers Wochenschrift: Probleme des Lebens* 2 (1927): 1.

Stumpfl, Friedrich. *Erbanlage und Verbrechen: Charakterologische und psychiatrische Sippen-untersuchungen.* Berlin: Springer, 1935.

Stumpfl, Friedrich. *Die Ursprünge des Verbrechens dargestellt am Lebenslauf von Zwillingen.* Leipzig: Thieme, 1936.

Der Stürmer: Deutsches Wochenblatt zum Kampfe um die Wahrheit. Ed. Julius Streicher. Issues used: 52 (December 1925); 38 (September 1934); 6 and 9 (both February 1937); 14 and 15 (both April 1937); 19 (May 1937); 32 and 35 (both August 1937); 7 (Sept. 1937).

Sufott, Mary Elizabeth (Kutzi). "My Parents—A Personal Note." *Rudolf Olden: Journalist gegen Hitler—Anwalt der Republik. Eine Ausstellung des Deutschen Exilarchivs 1933–1945 der Deutschen Nationalbibliothek Frankfurt am Main, 26. März–28. Juli 2010.* Ed. Sylvia Asmus and Brita Eckert. Frankfurt/M.: Deutsche Na-tionalbibliothek, 2010. 81–6.

Sussex, Lucy. *Women Writers and Detectives in Nineteenth-Century Crime Fiction: The Moth-ers of the Mystery Genre.* Basingstoke: Palgrave Macmillan, 2010.

Szabó, Miloslav. "Rasse, Orientalismus und Re-ligion im antisemitischen Geschichtsbild Al-fred Rosenbergs." *Antisemitische Geschichts-bilder.* Ed. Werner Bergmann and Ulrich Sieg. Essen: Klartext, 2009. 211–30.

Tannert, Mary. "The Emergence of Crime Fiction in German: an Early Maturity." *Crime Fiction in German: Der Krimi.* Ed. Katharina Hall. Cardiff: University of Wales Press: 2016. 33–50.

Tannert, Mary W., and Henry Kratz. "Introduc-tion." *Early German and Austrian Detective Fiction: An Anthology.* Ed. Mary W. Tannert and Henry Kratz. Jefferson, NC: McFarland, 1999.

Tannert, Mary W., and Henry Kratz, eds. *Early German and Austrian Detective Fiction: An Anthology.* Ed. Mary W. Tannert and Henry Kratz. Jefferson, N.C.: McFarland, 1999. 1–8.

Tatar, Maria. *Lustmord: Sexual Murder in Weimar Germany.* Princeton: Princeton University Press, 1995.

Taylor, Philip M. "Losing the (Information) War on Terror." *Justifying War: Propaganda, Poli-tics and the Modern Age.* Ed. David Welch and Jo Fox. Basingstoke: Palgrave Macmillan, 2012. 362–76.

Thalbach, Katharina (dir.). *Der Hauptmann von Köpenick.* TV-film. ZDF 2001.

Thiele, A.F. *Die jüdischen Gauner in Deutsch-land, ihre Taktik, ihre Eigenthümlichkeiten und ihre Sprache nebst ausführlichen Nachrichten über die in Deutschland und an dessen Gren-zen sich aufhaltenden berüchtigten jüdischen Gauner, Nach Kriminalakten und sonstigen zuverlässigen Quellen bearbeitet und zunächst praktischen Criminal- und Polizeibeamten gewidmet.* 2nd ed. Berlin: Reimarus, 1843.

Thompson, Jon. *Fiction, Crime, and Empire: Clues to Modernity and Postmodernism.* Urbana: University of Illinois Press, 1993.

Tietze, Hans. *Die Juden Wiens: Geschichte, Wirt-schaft, Kultur.* Vienna: Wiener Zeitschriften-verlag, 1987 [orig. 1933].

Traudisch, Dora. *Mutterschaft mit Zuckerguß? Frauenfeindliche Propaganda im NS-Spielfilm.* Pfaffenweiler: Centaurus, 1993.

Treitschke, Heinrich von. "Unsere Aussichten." *Preußische Jahrbücher* 44 (1879): 559–79.

Trenker, Luis. *Das große Luis Trenker Buch.* Mu-nich: C. Bertelsmann, 1974.

Trimborn, Jürgen. *Der deutsche Heimatfilm der 50er Jahre.* Cologne: Teiresias, 1998.

Turner, Victor. *The Anthropology of Performance.* New York: PAJ, 1986.

Turner, Victor. *Dramas, Fields, and Metaphors: Symbolic Action and Human Society.* Ithaca, NY: Cornell University Press, 1974.

Uthmann, Jörg von. *Killer—Krimis—Kommis-sare: Kleine Kulturgeschichte des Mords.* Mu-nich: Beck, 2006.

Varga, William P. *The Number One Nazi Jew-Baiter: A Political Biography of Julius Streicher, Hitler's Chief Anti-Semitic Propagandist.* New York: Carlton Press, 1981.

Veelen, Sonja. *Hochstapler: Wie sie uns täuschen. Eine soziologische Analyse.* Marburg: Tectum, 2012.

Veelen, Sonja. "Techniken zur Herstellung gefälschter Identität: Eine soziologische Analyse der Hochstapelei—in Auszügen." *Kultur und Gespenster* 9 (2009): 131–40.

Verhey, Jeffrey. "Krieg und geistige Mobilmachung: Die Kriegspropaganda." *Eine Welt von Feinden. Der Große Krieg, 1914–1918.* Ed. Wolfgang Kruse. 2nd ed. Frankfurt/M.: Fischer, 2000. 176–83.

Verhey, Jeffrey. *The Spirit of 1914: Militarism, Myth, and Mobilization in Germany.* Cam-bridge: Cambridge University Press, 2000.

Vitz, Georg. "Heinrich Spoerl und Düsseldorf—biografische und literarische Spuren." *Heinrich Spoerl: Buch—Bühne—Leinwand.* Ed. Joseph A. Kruse. Düsseldorf: Droste, 2004. 17–26.

Vogel, Jakob. *Nationen im Gleichschritt: Der Kult der "Nation in Waffen" in Deutschland und Frankreich, 1871–1914.* Göttingen: Vanden-hoeck & Ruprecht, 1997.

Vogt, Jochen, ed. *Der Kriminalroman. Zur The-orie und Geschichte einer Gattung.* 2 vols. Mu-nich: Wilhelm Fink, 1971.

Voigt, Wilhelm. *Wie ich Hauptmann von Köpenick wurde.* 3rd ed. Berlin 2014. [Based on the edi-tion *Wie ich Hauptmann von Köpenick wurde. Mein Lebensbild. Von Wilhelm Voigt genannt*

Hauptmann von Köpenick. Leipzig, Berlin: Julius Püttmann, 1909.]

Völklein, Marco. "Schatzsucher: Die Brüder Sass. Flucht nach Dänemark." *Süddeutsche Zeitung* May 17, 2010). http://www.sueddeutsche.de/geld/schatzsucher-die-brueder-sass-verbuddelt-im-grunewald-1.40381-2 (accessed March 6, 2016).

Völklein, Marco. "Schatzsucher: Die Brüder Sass. Verbuddelt im Grunewald." *Süddeutsche Zeitung* May 17, 2010). http://www.sueddeutsche.de/geld/schatzsucher-die-brueder-sass-verbuddelt-im-grunewald-1.40381 (accessed March 6, 2016).

Volkov, Shulamit. *Germans, Jews, and Antisemites: Trials in Emancipation.* Cambridge: Cambridge University Press, 2006.

Volkov, Shulamit. *Jüdisches Leben und Antisemitismus im 19. und 20. Jahrhundert: Zehn Essays.* Munich: Beck, 1990.

Vuorinen, Marja. "Hitler's Enemy Images as Inversions of the 'Good German.'" *Enemy Images in War Propaganda.* Ed. Marja Vuorinen. Newcastle: Cambridge Scholars Publishing, 2012. 35–55.

Vyleta, Daniel M. *Crime, Jews and News: Vienna, 1895–1914.* Oxford: Berghahn, 2007.

Vyleta, Daniel M. "Jewish Crimes and Misdemeanours: In Search of Jewish Criminality." *European History Quarterly* 35/2 (2005): 299–325.

Wachenhusen, Hans. *Der Hochstapler: Roman.* 3 vols. Berlin: Otto Janke, 1887.

Wachsmann, Nikolaus. "'Annihilation Through Labor': The Killing of State Prisoners in the Third Reich." *The Journal of Modern History* 71 (1999): 624–59.

Wachsmann, Nikolaus. "Between Reform and Repression: Imprisonment in Weimar Germany." *Crime and Criminal Justice in Modern Germany.* Ed. Richard F. Wetzell. New York: Berghahn, 2014. 115–36.

Wachsmann, Nikolaus. "From Indefinite Confinement to Extermination: 'Habitual Criminals' in the Third Reich." *Social Outsiders in Nazi Germany.* Ed. Robert Gellately. Princeton: Princeton University Press, 2001. 165–91.

Wachsmann, Nikolaus. *Hitler's Prisons: Legal Terror in Nazi Germany.* New Haven: Yale University Press, 2004.

Wagner, Margaret Seaton. *The Monster of Düsseldorf: The Life and Trial of Peter Kürten.* New York: Dutton, 1933.

Wagner, Patrick. *Hitlers Kriminalisten: Die deutsche Kriminalpolizei und der Nationalsozialismus zwischen 1920 und 1960.* Munich: C.H. Beck, 2002.

Wagner, Patrick. *Volksgemeinschaft ohne Verbrecher: Konzeptionen und Praxis der Kriminalpolizei in der Zeit der Weimarer Republik und des Nationalsozialismus.* Hamburg: Christians, 1996.

Wallace, Ailsa. "Murder in the Weimar Republic: Prejudice, Politics and the Popular in the Socialist Crime Fiction of Hermynia Zur Mühlen." *Detectives, Dystopias and Poplit: Studies in Modern Genre Fiction.* Ed. Bruce B. Campbell, Alison Guenther-Pal and Vibeke Rützou Petersen. New York: Camden House, 2014. 91–116.

Wambach, Lovis. "'Justiz ist Glückssache'—Heinrich Spoerl: Vom Rechtsanwalt zum Erfolgsschriftsteller." *Betrifft: Die Justiz* 93 (March 2008): 253–7.

Ward, Janet. *Weimar Surfaces: Urban Visual Culture in 1920s Germany.* Berkeley: University of California Press, 2001.

Warmbold, Joachim. "Germania in Afrika. Frieda Freiin von Bülow, 'Schöpferin des deutschen Kolonialromans.'" *Jahrbuch des Instituts für Deutsche Geschichte* 15 (1986): 309–36.

Wassermann, Rudolf. *Beruf, Konfession und Verbrechen: Eine Studie über die Kriminalität der Juden in Vergangenheit und Gegenwart.* Munich: Ernst Reinhardt, 1907.

Wassermann, Rudolf. "Die Kriminalität der Juden in Deutschland in den letzten 25 Jahren (1882–1906)." *Monatsschrift* 6 (1909–10): 609–18.

Weiler, Inge. *Giftmordwissen und Giftmörderinnen. Eine diskursgeschichtliche Studie.* Tübingen: Niemeyer, 1998.

Weindling, Paul. *Health, Race and German Politics Between National Unification and Nazism, 1870–1945.* Cambridge: Cambridge University Press, 1989.

Weiss, Ernst. *Der Fall Vukobrankovics.* Berlin: Die Schmiede, 1924.

Welch, David. "Mobilizing the Masses: The Organization of German Propaganda During World War One." *War and the Media: Reportage and Propaganda, 1900–2003.* Ed. Mark Connelly and David Welch. London: I.B. Tauris, 2005. 19–46.

Welch, David. "'Opening Pandora's Box': Propaganda, Power and Persuasion." *Propaganda, Power and Persuasion: From World War I to Wikileaks.* Ed. David Welch. London: I.B. Tauris, 2014. 3–18.

Welch, David. *Propaganda and the German Cinema, 1933–1945.* Oxford: Clarendon Press, 1985.

Welch, David. *The Third Reich: Politics and Propaganda.* 2nd ed. London: Routledge, 2002.

Welch, David. "'Today Germany, Tomorrow the World': Nazi Propaganda and Total War, 1943–45." *Propaganda, Power and Persuasion: From World War I to Wikileaks.* Ed. David Welch. London: I.B. Tauris, 2014. 96–109.

Welch, David. "War Aims and the 'Big Ideas' of 1914." *Justifying War: Propaganda, Politics and the Modern Age.* Ed. David Welch and Jo Fox. Basingstoke: Palgrave Macmillan, 2012. 71–94.

Welch, David. "'Winning Hearts and Minds': The Changing Context of Reportage and Propaganda, 1900–2003." *War and the Media: Reportage and Propaganda, 1900–2003.* Ed. Mark Connelly and David Welch. London: I.B. Tauris, 2005. ix–xxi.

Welch, David, ed. *Propaganda, Power and Persuasion: From World War I to Wikileaks.* London: I.B. Tauris, 2014.

Welch, David, and Jo Fox, eds. *Justifying War: Propaganda, Politics and the Modern Age.* Basingstoke: Palgrave Macmillan, 2012.

Wende, Waltraud "Wara." "'Ich habe Großes vorgehabt.' Der Untergang von Oliver Hirschbiegel." *Der Holocaust im Film: Mediale Inszenierung und kulturelles Gedächtnis.* Ed. Waltraud 'Wara' Wende. Heidelberg: Synchron, 2007. 305–23.

Wende, Waltraud "Wara," ed. *Der Holocaust im Film: Mediale Inszenierung und kulturelles Gedächtnis.* Heidelberg: Synchron, 2007.

Werner, Kurt. *Mit Baldur von Schirach auf Fahrt.* Munich: Verlag der NSDAP. Franz Eher Nachf., 1937.

Werwolf, Der. "Ein Erfolg." *Berliner Volks-Zeitung* (October 21, 1906): 1.

Wesseler, Karl (dir.). *Der Maulkorb.* TV-film. WDR 1979.

Wette, Wolfram, ed. *Militarismus in Deutschland 1871 bis 1945. Zeitgenössische Analysen und Kritik.* Münster: LIT, 1999.

Wetzell, Richard F. "Criminology in Weimar and Nazi Germany." *Criminals and Their Scientists: The History of Criminology in International Perspective.* Ed. Peter Becker and Richard F. Wetzell. Cambridge: Cambridge University Press, 2006. 401–23.

Wetzell, Richard F. *Inventing the Criminal: A History of German Criminology, 1880–1945.* Chapel Hill: University of North Carolina Press, 2000.

Wetzell, Richard F., ed. *Crime and Criminal Justice in Modern Germany.* New York: Berghahn, 2014.

Wild, Reiner, ed. *Geschichte der deutschen Kinder- und Jugendliteratur.* Stuttgart: Metzler, 1990.

Wildenthal, Lora. *German Women for Empire, 1884–1945.* Durham, NC: Duke University Press, 2001. 13–78.

Wildenthal, Lora. "'When men are weak': The Imperial Feminism of Frieda von Bülow." *Gender & History* 10/1 (1998): 53–77.

Wilhelm Voigt der Hauptmann von Köpenick. [Collection of court documents, August–December 1906.] N. p., n. d.

Wilkending, Gisela. "Mädchenliteratur von der Mitte des 19. Jahrhunderts bis zum Ersten Weltkrieg." *Geschichte der deutschen Kinder- und Jugendliteratur.* Ed. Reiner Wild. Stuttgart: Metzler, 1990. 220–50.

Williams, Paul L. "Beltway Snipers Exposed as Muslim Terrorists." *Canada Free Press* (Sept.

17, 2009). http://canadafreepress.com/article/beltway-snipers-exposed-as-muslim-terrorists (accessed June 8, 2016).

Wilson, D. Harlan. *Hitler: The Terminal Biography.* Bowie, MD: RDS Press, 2014.

Wilson, Stephen. *Ideology and Experience: Antisemitism in France at the Time of the Dreyfus Affair.* Rutherford, NJ: Fairleigh Dickinson University Press, 1982.

Winter, Jay M. "From War Talk to Rights Talk: War Aims and Human Rights in the Second World War." *Justifying War: Propaganda, Politics and the Modern Age.* Ed. David Welch and Jo Fox. Basingstoke: Palgrave Macmillan, 2012. 236–48.

Winter, Jay M. "Kriegsbilder: Die Bildende Kunst und der Mythos der Kriegsbegeisterung." *Kriegsbegeisterung und mentale Kriegsvorbereitung: Interdisziplinäre Studien.* Ed. Marcel van der Linden and Gottfried Mergner. Berlin: Duncker & Humblot, 1991. 89–112.

Winzen, Peter. "Der Krieg in Bülows Kalkül: Katastrophe der Diplomatie oder Chance zur Machtexpansion?" *Bereit zum Krieg: Kriegsmentalität im wilhelminischen Deutschland, 1890–1914.* Ed. Jost Dülffer and Karl Holl. Göttingen: Vandenhoeck & Ruprecht, 1986. 161–93.

Wistrich, Robert S. *The Jews of Vienna in the Age of Franz Joseph.* New York: Oxford University Press, 1989.

Wistrich, Robert S., ed. *Austrians and the Jews in the Twentieth Century: From Franz Joseph to Waldheim.* New York: St. Martin's Press, 1992.

Witte, Karsten. *Lachende Erben, Toller Tag: Filmkomödie im Dritten Reich.* Berlin: Vorwerk, 1995.

Wittels, Fritz. "Der Zwerg von Ottakrieg: Ein Vorwort zur heutigen Verhandlung." *Wiener Sonn- und Montagszeitung* (November 9, 1925): 7.

Woeller, Waltraud. *Illustrierte Geschichte der Kriminalliteratur.* Leipzig: Insel, 1984.

Wohlleben, Doren, and Paul Michael Lützeler, eds. *Hermann Broch und die Romantik.* Berlin: Walter de Gruyter, 2014.

Wolffhardt, Rainer (dir.). *Auf Befehl erschossen— Die Brüder Sass, einst Berlins grosse Ganoven.* TV-film. Ufa Fernsehproduktion GmbH 1972.

Wolffhardt, Rainer (dir.). *Der Hauptmann von Köpenick.* TV-film. SDR 1960.

Wulffen, Erich. "Die berühmtesten Sexualprozesse der Nachkriegszeit." *Zwischen zwei Katastrophen.* Ed. Magnus Hirschfeld. Hanau: Karl Schustek, 1966. 469–513.

Wulffen, Erich. *Gauner- und Verbrechertypen.* Berlin: Langenscheidt, 1910.

Wulffen, Erich. *Kriminalpsychologie: Psychologie des Täters. Ein Handbuch für Juristen, Justiz-, Verwaltungs- und Polizeibeamte, Ärzte, Pädagogen und Gebildete aller Stände.* Berlin: Langenscheidt, 1926.

Wulffen, Erich. *Psychologie des Giftmordes.* 2nd ed. Vienna: Urania, 1918.

Wulffen, Erich. *Die Psychologie des Hochstaplers.* Berlin: Elektrischer Verlag, 2013 (orig. 1923).

Wulffen, Erich. *Der Sexualverbrecher: Ein Handbuch für Juristen, Verwaltungsbeamte und Ärzte.* 6th ed. Berlin: Langenscheidt, 1910.

Wulffen, Erich. *Das Weib als Sexualverbrecherin. Ein Handbuch für Juristen, Justiz-, Verwaltungs- und Polizeibeamte, Ärzte, Pädagogen und Gebildete aller Stände.* Berlin: Langenscheidt, 1923.

Wunderlich, Dieter. *Göring und Goebbels: Eine Doppelbiografie.* Regensburg: F. Pustet, 2002.

Würmann, Carsten. "Deutsche Kommissare ermitteln: Der Kriminalroman im 'Dritten Reich.'" *Banalität mit Stil: Zur Widersprüchlichkeit der Literaturproduktion im Nationalsozialismus.* Ed. Walter Delabar, Horst Denkler, and Erhard Schütz. Berne: Peter Lang, 1999. 217–40.

Würmann, Carsten. "Entspannung für die Massen—Die Unterhaltungsliteratur im Dritten Reich." *Zwischen den Zeiten: Junge Literatur in Deutschland von 1933 bis 1945.* Ed. Uta Beiküfner and Hania Siebenpfeiffer. Berlin: Lotos, 2000. 9–35.

Würmann, Carsten. "Sternstunden für Mörder: Zur Auseinandersetzung mit der nationalsozialistischen Vergangenheit im Kriminalroman." *literaturkritik.de* 9 (2005). http://www.literaturkritik.de/public/rezension.php?rez_id=8525&ausgabe=200509 (accessed March 6, 2016).

Würmann, Carsten. "Volksgemeinschaft mit Verbrechen—zum Krimi im Dritten Reich." *Krimijahrbuch 2008.* Wuppertal: Nordpark Verlag, 2008. 162–75.

Würmann, Carsten. "Zum Kriminalroman im Nationalsozialismus." *Verbrechen als Passion: Neue Untersuchungen zum Kriminalgenre.* Ed. Bruno Franceschini and Carsten Würmann. Berlin: Weidler, 2004. 143–86.

Würmann, Carsten, and Ansgar Warner. "Im Pausenraum des 'Dritten Reiches': Zur Populärkultur im nationalsozialistischen Deutschland." *Im Pausenraum des Dritten Reiches: Zur Populärkultur im nationalsozialistischen Deutschland.* Ed. Carsten Würmann and Ansgar Warner. Berne: Peter Lang, 2008. 7–19.

Würmann, Carsten, and Ansgar Warner, eds. *Im Pausenraum des Dritten Reiches: Zur Populärkultur im nationalsozialistischen Deutschland.* Berne: Peter Lang, 2008.

Wyrwa, Ulrich. "Genese und Entfaltung antisemitischer Motive in Heinrich von Treitschkes 'Deutscher Geschichte im 19. Jahrhundert.'" *Antisemitische Geschichtsbilder.* Ed. Werner Bergmann and Ulrich Sieg. Essen: Klartext, 2009. 83–101.

Zeman, Zbynek Anthony Bohaslav. *Nazi Propaganda.* 2nd ed. London: Oxford University Press, 1964.

Zensierte Schriften in der BRD [last updated January 2004]. https://www.scribd.com/doc/15963013/Zensierte-Schriften-in-Der-BRD (accessed December 6, 2017).

Zentner, Christian. *Adolf Hitler's Mein Kampf: Eine kommentierte Auswahl.* 8th ed. Munich: List, 1992.

Zerlett, Hans Heinz (dir.). *Robert und Bertram.* Feature Film. Tobis Filmkunst 1939.

Ziehensack, Ilse. "Auguste Groner." In: "Kinder- und Jugendliteratur der zweiten Hälfte des 19. Jahrhunderts aus historischer Sicht." M.A. Thesis University of Vienna (2008). 82–8.

Ziertmann, Paul. "Die Unfruchtbarmachung sozial Minderwertiger." *Monatsschrift für Kriminalpsychologie und Strafrechtsreform* 5 (1908/09): 734–43.

Zimmermann, Moshe. *Die deutschen Juden 1914–1945.* Munich: R. Oldenbourg, 1997.

Zinke, Peter. *"An allem ist Alljuda schuld": Antisemitismus während der Weimarer Republik in Franken.* Nuremberg: Antogo, 2009.

Žižek, Slavoj. *The Sublime Object of Ideology.* London: Verso, 1999.

Zmegac, Viktor. "Aspekte des Detektivromans." *Sinn und Form* 24 (1972): 376–94.

Zmegac, Viktor. *Der wohltemperierte Mord: Zur Theorie und Geschichte des Detektivromans.* Frankfurt/M.: Athenäum, 1971.

Zuckmayer, Carl. *Als wär's ein Stück von mir: Horen der Freundschaft.* Vienna: Fischer, 1968.

Zuckmayer, Carl. *Der Hauptmann von Köpenick.* Frankfurt/M.: Fischer, 1997.

Zuckmayer, Carl. *Der Hauptmann von Köpenick: Illustrierte und kommentierte Ausgabe.* Bonn: Deutsche Post AG, 2006.

Index

Numbers in **bold italics** indicate pages with illustrations

335